THE PROUD HIGHWAY

The Fear and Loathing Letters, Volume 1

THE PROUD

HIGHWAY

Saga of a Desperate Southern Gentleman
1955–1967

HUNTER S. THOMPSON

Foreword by William J. Kennedy
Edited by Douglas Brinkley

 VILLARD | NEW YORK

Grateful acknowledgment is made to the following for permission to reprint
previously published material:

LIVERIGHT PUBLISHING CORPORATION: Excerpt from "A Poet's Advice to
Students" from A Miscellany Revised by E. E. Cummings, edited by
George J. Firmage. Copyright © 1955, 1965 by the Trustees for the
E. E. Cummings Trust. Copyright © 1958, 1965 by George J. Firmage.
Reprinted by permission of Liveright Publishing Company.

The Nation: "The Nonstudent Left" by Hunter S. Thompson (The Nation,
September 27, 1965). Copyright © 1965 by The Nation. Reprinted by
permission of The Nation magazine.

SPECIAL RIDER MUSIC: Excerpt from "Ballad of a Thin Man" by Bob Dylan.
Copyright © 1965 by Warner Bros. Inc. Copyright renewed 1993 by
Special Rider Music. Reprinted by permission of Special Rider Music.

VILLARD BOOKS is a registered trademark of Random House, Inc.

Library of Congress Cataloging-in-Publication Data
Thompson, Hunter S.
The proud highway: saga of a desperate southern gentleman,
1955–1967 / Hunter S. Thompson.
p.   cm.
Includes index.
ISBN 0-679-40695-6
1. Thompson, Hunter S.   2. Journalists—United States—
Correspondence.   I. Title.
PN4874.T44A3   1997
070´.92—dc21   96-49846
[B]

Random House website address: http://www.randomhouse.com/
Printed in the United States of America on acid-free paper
2 4 6 8 9 7 5 3
First Edition

TO DEBORAH FULLER & TAMMY CIMALORE
AND
TO ED ABBEY,
WHO WORKED THE GRAVEYARD SHIFT

Arms, my only ornament—my only rest, the fight.

—Cervantes, *Don Quixote*

CONTENTS

**York Times . . . Saved by Studs Terkel . . .
Swarmed Over by Parasites . . . Fuck You,
You're Fired . . . The First Victory Lap . . .**

THE CURSE OF THE BRONZE PLAQUE

A Foreword to the Letters of Hunter Thompson

BY WILLIAM J. KENNEDY

*An institution that should always fight for progress and
reform, never tolerate injustice or corruption, always fight
demagogues of all parties, never belong to any party,
always oppose privileged classes and public plunderers,
never lack sympathy with the poor, always remain
devoted to the public welfare, never be satisfied with
merely printing news, always be drastically independent,
never be afraid to attack wrong, whether by predatory
plutocracy or predatory poverty.*

— Joseph Pulitzer, May 10, 1883, in an editorial upon becoming
    publisher of the *New York World* (reproduced on a bronze plaque
    on the Times Tower, New York City)

It was late summer, 1959. Hunter Thompson had kicked in the candy machine at the Middletown (New York) *Daily Record*, had been fired for being "too offbeat," and was looking for work. He answered an ad in *Editor & Publisher* for a sports editor's job at the brand-new daily *San Juan Star*. He was twenty-two but represented himself as twenty-four. He said the job interested him because it was in Puerto Rico, outside the "great rotarian democracy" of the mainland.

He mentioned his Middletown troubles and also said he was lecturing on the meaning of the Beat Generation. "I have given up on American journalism," he wrote. "The decline of the American press has long been obvious, and my time is too valuable to waste in an effort to supply the 'man in the street' with his daily quota of clichés. . . . There is another concept of journalism. . . . It's engraved on a bronze plaque on the southeast corner of Times Tower in New York City." He added that he now had to get back to his novel, part of which was with the Viking Press in New York.

As managing editor of the fledgling *Star*, I wrote him explaining that our editor[1] was a member of Rotary, that we had a staff of offbeat reporters (and editors) who, like him, were writing fiction, and suggested he return to his novel, or perhaps start another, building his plot around the bronze plaque on the Times Tower. "You should always write about something

---

1. William J. Dorvillier, who won the 1961 Pulitzer Prize for the *Star's* editorials on a church-state controversy.

xvi / *The Curse of the Bronze Plaque*

you know intimately," I wrote, and added that if we ever got a candy machine and needed someone to kick it in we'd be in touch.

He received my letter at his home in Louisville in the same mail that brought Viking's rejection of his novel, and he sat down and wrote me: "your letter was cute, my friend, and your interpretation of my letter was beautifully typical of the cretin-intellect responsible for the dry-rot of the american press. but don't think that lack of an invitation from you will keep me from getting down that way, and when I do remind me to first kick your teeth in and then jam a bronze plaque far into your small intestine."

I wrote back, saying that since he was the bushy-tailed expert on journalism's dry rot, we would pay him space rates to summarize its failings in three double-spaced pages that we would run in our first edition, along with our exchange of correspondence. I said I didn't know another publication that would give him the time of day, and signed it "Intestinally yours."

His reply: "Daddio! You mean the bronze plaque paragraph bugged you? . . . I don't mind saying, friend Kennedy, that I enjoyed your letter. This is a weird bit of correspondence we have here, my man." But he said I was a tragic optimist if I thought it was possible to handle the dry rot in three pages and he assumed my offer was designed to develop "a ceremonial mangling . . . of a jabbering beatnik." Even so, he said he would give it a fling, which he did.

"Dear Hack," he wrote, enclosing with his letter a one-act play: "a brutal, low-level, sledge-hammer drama . . . a farce, of course, but its theme is a big one." He also said my last letter had surprised him, "and perhaps in the long run I shall owe you an apology for all this abuse."

I rejected his play as "warmed-over clichés with barnyard overtones," and wished him well with his book, noting he'd be better off away from journalism if he was serious about the novel, and suggesting he stop by for a drink if he was in the neighborhood.

He responded with a page of revenge: "Don't expect *me* to send you a package of platitudes to drape over the stinking carcass of your newspaper like an American flag over a coffin full of crap." He added: "I imagine you're pretty decent, in your own way, and I think it's a shame that you've hired yourself out as a mouthpiece for the international rotary."

Less than two months later he had applied to *Sportivo*, a new bowling magazine in San Juan. "I may have a chance of duping [the editor] into thinking I'm normal," he wrote his friend Bob Bone, a reporter on the *Star*, and he got the job. But pretending to be normal was folly. *Sportivo*'s editor proved to be, in Hunter's words, "a liar, cheat, passer of bad checks, welshing shyster, and otherwise foul," and the job merely led to new insolvency.

But here was Hunter in San Juan, and before long he came to the *Star*'s city room. Fred Harmon, our business editor, greeted him: "We don't have a candy machine, but there's a cigarette machine in the corner." A few of us went out for that promised drink, talked of bronze plaques and novels, and Hunter settled in for several months of life in Puerto Rico.

He was kicked out of two houses, but eventually found one on a deserted beach, brought down his wife-to-be, Sandy ("I can barely support myself, much less a common-law wife," he wrote her, "so I presume you'll bring at least a little money for food"), wrote some fiction, did free-lance journalism, and we had a number of all night conversations about writing, and how and why you do it.

By June, Hunter was abysmally broke, had been beaten by police and jailed for breach of the peace and resisting arrest, was reduced to drinking rainwater and being eaten by sand fleas, and, sensing also that he might have to spend a year in a Puerto Rican jail, he fled the Caribbean in a sailboat.

He wrote me from Bermuda: "Dear Editor: My name is HS Thompson and I would like to work for the *San Juan Star*. . . . I understand Puerto Rico is a wonderful place to live. . . . My information comes from three fellows I met in an asylum in upstate New York. . . . They were good fellows and I could understand most of what they said."

This was an unlikely beginning to a friendship and correspondence of, so far, thirty-seven years' duration. But odd things occur when you intersect with Hunter Thompson. Life happens to him in ways alien to most mortals. In the exchange of letters cited above (fully rendered in the pages that follow) there lurks prophecy—of Hunter's future as a masterful American prose stylist and journalistic fictionist, and also of the lifestyle that has served him so well: creating chaos to undercut his own most cherished schemes, courting self-destruction as the avenue to success, maintaining a symbiotic colloquy with comic despair, and coping with bronze plaquery and other rejection through Avenger's Rhetoric, e.g., from 1965 to a dilatory editor: "I'm coming to New York on a chopped hog and shoot you in the gut with an expanding filth flare"; from 1967 on his plans for chastising a literary agent: "cracking his teeth with a knotty stick and rupturing every other bone and organ I can make contact with in the short time I expect will be allotted to me."

The tools Hunter would use in the years ahead—bizarre wit, mockery without end, redundant excess, supreme self-confidence, the narrative of the wounded meritorious ego, and the idiopathic anger of the righteous outlaw—were all there in his precocious imagination in San Juan. Throughout those days he was using these tools to become a novelist. His work-in-progress, when we first started talking about fiction, was "Prince Jellyfish," and he was soon to start "The Rum Diary," which would occupy his attention for years to come. Neither novel has been published, though excerpts from both appear in his *Songs of the Doomed*.

"Prince Jellyfish bounced again, for the third and final time," he wrote me from New York in August 1960. ". . . It's not really a very good book. . . . I'll just chalk that year up to experience and start on that 'Great Puerto Rican Novel' that I mentioned. . . . I've compromised myself so often that I can't honestly see myself as a martyr anymore. . . . I think I'm probably better off as an opportunist with a large and ill-formed talent."

He knew some of my writing had been rejected, and that bothered him more than his own rejection. "You're no martyr," he observed accurately, "but I think you approach your writing more honestly than I do mine. I'm too greedy to wish you much luck, but if you can break through without stepping on my head, I hope you make it."

That sounded unusually honest to me, but his talk of martyrdom and compromise were romantic ideas that had little value except as a writer convincing himself of his own seriousness. We recounted the examples of Faulkner's neglect, Nathanael West's bad luck, Fitzgerald's sad fading away with his work out of print. But all Hunter had done in the way of compromise was to drink too much and write some low-level journalism to stay alive. The inadequacy of his fiction was his real problem, and it was mine as well. The years ahead would prove this to both of us.

This collection of Hunter's letters is a prime source for tracking that time in his life: how he shaped himself into the peculiar fiction writer he became.

1960: "If I weren't so sure of my destiny, I might even say I was depressed. But I'm not, and there's always tomorrow's mail." . . . "My fiction still refuses to sell. . . . Have begun the Great Puerto Rican Novel (The Rum Diary) & expect it will do the trick."

1961: His book was going badly, he wrote me, and an agent refused to take it on. "And so we beat on, boats against the current," he wrote, quoting *Gatsby*, the oriflamme of his ongoing martyrdom to the American Dream.

1963: I react negatively to "The Rum Diary," tell him to abandon it. "I have decided to rewrite it," he writes.

1964: Making money in journalism doesn't give him joy. "With luck, I will be driven back to fiction."

1965: Broke and jobless, he's "wrestling with a novel . . . fiction doesn't depress me like journalism. It's harder, but much more human work."

1965: His article on motorcycle gangs for *The Nation* draws six book offers from publishers: "I am hysterical at the prospect of money. . . . The big apple at the moment seems to be *The Rum Diary*. If I had the novel in shape right now I could knock off a $1500 advance tomorrow. But, sadly, it is not good enough to send out."

1965: "I should have quit journalism . . . and hit the fiction for all I was worth. And if I'm ever to be worth anything I honestly think it will have to be in the realm of fiction [which is] the only way I can live with my imagination, point of view, instincts, and all those other intangibles that make people nervous in my journalism."

A case might be made for the previous paragraph being the turning point in Hunter's awareness, or admission, that what he was vigorously trying to do wasn't journalism. These letters take him only through 1967, and it wasn't until 1970, when he published "The Kentucky Derby Is Decadent and Depraved" in *Scanlan's Monthly*, that his gonzo journalism came fully into existence. Was it journalism? Well, it had appeared in a journal. But wasn't it really *fiction*? It wasn't Hemingway running the bulls in his favorite town, but it *was* Hunter running the horses in his favorite idiom. It was a short story, the best fiction he'd ever written.

In all our early marathon conversations, a recurring subject was writers of originality: how the power of language set them apart; how their story, not their ideas, was supreme, and for an idea to find houseroom it needed embodiment in the narrative or it was worthless. The notion of coming at the reader with fangs dripping wisdom was as laughable as it was useless.

Such talk is part of the basic training for any fiction writer. The real problem comes in learning how to use these insights. Hunter identified with literary outsiders: Salinger's Holden Caulfield, Donleavy's Ginger Man. He learned from Mencken how to be an attack dog, but he cheered for Algren and Fitzgerald and West, and he memorized Dylan Thomas and Faulkner. I remember him saying in the late 1960s that the main thing he wanted to do with his writing now was to create "new forms" of fiction.

The Derby story had pointed the way toward that great mother lode. *Playboy* was next, then *The New York Times Magazine*, *Sports Illustrated*, *Rolling Stone*, *Esquire*, etc. Hunter had discovered that confounding sums of money could be had by writing what seemed to be journalism, while actually you were developing your fictional oeuvre.

By 1971 "The Rum Diary" was in the basement and Hunter was writing one of the funniest, most original books of the last three decades, *Fear and Loathing in Las Vegas*, his paean to drug madness that consolidated his growing fame, turned him into the mad doper as comic icon, gonzo journalist with the public clout of a rock star.

His 1972 presidential campaign book, *Fear and Loathing: On the Campaign Trail '72*, published serially in *Rolling Stone*, changed his image: now fang-dripping, malevolent wit as political sage. But that book was more than journalism: it owed as much to the imagination as to political savvy. It fell, at least in part, into the same category as the Derby piece and the Las Vegas book: fiction.

That Hunter has continued to be called a journalist is one of the great underrated bunco exploits of our age. He himself made a half-hearted effort to confess the ruse when he published in *The Great Shark Hunt* his notes on the origin of the Las Vegas book. Gonzo, he wrote, "is a style of 'reporting' based on William Faulkner's idea that the best fiction is far more *true* than any kind of journalism—and the best journalists have always known this." He went on to say that *Las Vegas* was failed Gonzo, "so *complex* in its failure that I feel I can take the risk of defending it as a first, gimped effort in a direction that what Tom Wolfe calls 'The New Journalism' has been flirting with for almost a decade."

Hunter's explanation of why the Las Vegas book was a failure isn't relevant here and he dodges the issue anyway. He gets to the truth when he says of the book: "As true Gonzo Journalism, this doesn't work at all—and even if it did, I couldn't possibly admit it. Only a goddamn lunatic would write a thing like this and then claim it was true."

It was not lunacy defined but lunacy imagined: in short, a novel.

But who believed him?

Journals and book publishers have ever since been foisting his work on the gullible public as journalism, when in truth it is *nothing but a pack of lies*, which, of course, is a classic definition of fiction.

I hope this is a lesson to us all.

When last we talked at the Tosca Bar in San Francisco, Hunter was dodging pursuit, registered at a hotel under the name of Ben Franklin. I immediately noticed that he was smoking and drinking heavily. I advised him to curb these vices and proceed into his sixtieth year with moderation, the only course to take if he was going to get on with his work.

"I myself now drink only the occasional glass of red wine," I told him.

He acknowledged I was probably right, and stubbed out his cigarette.

"God will be good to us," he said, ingesting some peculiar substance through a tube.

"The work is the only thing that matters," I said.

"I know that," he said. "That's why I'm writing a novel. Perhaps two novels."

"Oh yes, two novels," I said. "I heard that story in San Juan."

Averill Park, New York
October 23, 1996

EDITOR'S NOTE

BY DOUGLAS BRINKLEY

Don't loaf and invite inspiration.
Light out after it with a club.

—Jack London

At noon on November 22, 1963, Hunter S. Thompson heard the news of President John F. Kennedy's assassination and reacted by sitting down at his typewriter. In a letter to his friend William Kennedy (who twenty years later would win the Pulitzer Prize for his novel *Ironweed*), he vented his anger. "There is no human being within 500 miles to whom I can communicate anything—much less the fear and loathing that is on me after today's murder," Thompson wrote from his home in Woody Creek, Colorado. ". . . From now on it is dirty pool and judo in the clinches. The savage nuts have shattered the great myth of American decency."

"Fear and loathing"—without apologies to Søren Kierkegaard—soon became Thompson's trademark phrase, his shorthand for justified contempt toward an overindulgent and dysfunctional consumer culture. Whether it was used in connection with the Hell's Angels, Richard Nixon, or Southeast Asia, "fear and loathing" served as Thompson's all-purpose epithet, encapsulating the death of the American Dream. In 1996, Thompson's comic masterpiece *Fear and Loathing in Las Vegas* (1971), long a cult favorite, was selected by the Modern Library for inclusion in its renowned list of affordable editions of world classics, catalogued between Thackeray and Tolstoy. Thompson's other popular title featuring the trademark phrase—*Fear and Loathing: On the Campaign Trail '72* (1973), which *The New York Times* deemed the "best account yet published of what it feels like to be out there in the middle of the American political process"—is likewise scheduled to join the distinguished Modern Library ranks. And now, in 1997, here is *The Proud Highway: Saga of a Desperate Southern Gentleman, 1955–1967*, the first installment of a projected three-volume "Fear and Loathing Letters" collection. It includes, along with more than two hundred others, that historic 1963 letter to William Kennedy.

The letters within these pages are only a fraction of the approximately twenty thousand Thompson has composed since he was a young boy. Whether at his childhood home on Ransdall Avenue in Louisville, in a Greenwich Village garret, or on a beer barge going down the Magdalena River in Colombia, Thompson corresponded ferociously, always making carbon copies, hoping they would be published someday as a testament to his life and times. "These were the pre-Xerox days," Thompson has commented about his surprising pack-rat nature. "And I was anal retentive in my desire to save *everything*."

The earliest letters archived at Thompson's Owl Farm ranch are dated 1947, when, as a precocious ten-year-old, Thompson began covering neighborhood sports and soliciting subscribers for his own four-cent, two-page mimeographed newspaper, *The Southern Star*. At age twelve he was firing off missives to the editor of the Louisville *Courier-Journal*, complaining about the way the newspaper covered everything from race relations to Civil War history. Thompson also saved most of his school papers and even an irregularly kept journal filled with innocent adolescent reflections and self-improvement promises. On New Year's Day, 1951, for example, Thompson scrawled the top ten resolutions he hoped to keep in the year ahead, with number one on the list being to "Calm Down!," number two to "Find a Good Woman by March," and number three to "Always Dress Spiffy."

The largest category of early Thompson correspondence—none of which, due to its youthful and personal nature, has been included in this volume—contains the letters he wrote to his mother, Virginia, a Louisville librarian, each day of his incarceration from May 1955 to July 1955 at the Jefferson County Jail for a robbery he didn't commit. "The police lie," Thompson wrote from his cell. "Injustice is rampant." Upon being released on probation, Thompson walked into an Air Force recruiting office and enlisted. After a couple of months of basic training in San Antonio, he was assigned to Scott Air Force Base in Belleville, Illinois, where he studied radio electronics. But it wasn't until September 1956, when he left Scott and became the sports editor of the Eglin Air Force Base (Pensacola, Florida) newspaper, the *Command Courier*, that Thompson began composing thoughtful letters on a regular basis, usually aimed at old school chums from Louisville's prestigious Athenaeum Literary Association. While turning his sports section into one of the best in northern Florida, Thompson became familiar with all facets of layout, camerawork, newswriting, headlines, and typing. Using his trusty Underwood to write stories, conduct business, and stay in touch with a wide circle of friends, Thompson developed a ritual of typing letters at night, a habit that continues today. "I can stir up more controversy with one small portable typewriter than most people can with an entire wire service," Thompson wrote his Louisville friend David Ethridge in 1958. "And man, I love a good controversy."

The persona that emerges from the early letters collected in *The Proud Highway* is that of a gifted and self-assured maverick with an outlaw bent searching for the unvarnished truth in a fast-paced, irrational Cold War world. "Just as some people turn to religion to find meaning, the writer turns to his craft and tries to impose meaning, or to lift the meaning out of chaos and put it in order," Thompson wrote a friend in 1958. Letter writing was Thompson's way of imposing order on perhaps the most itinerant literary lifestyle since poet Vachel Lindsay criss-crossed America composing verse for a penny. "I think that the very fact that I wrote this letter and that I feel a need to write it shows the value of putting words in order on a piece of paper," Thompson wrote to a girlfriend while in the Air Force. "I guess that is why I write as many letters as I do, because it's the only way—outside of actually getting to work and writing fiction—I can look at life objectively. Otherwise, I'm so involved in it that I forget that the rest of the world is merely a stage setting for my life."

Sometimes, though, particularly after receiving his honorable discharge from the Air Force in October 1958, Thompson corresponded for his own word-intoxicated pleasure, just to stay loose with language and avoid writer's block. Desperate to become a first-rate novelist, to make his Underwood perform like a Steinway, Thompson would type out pages from *The Great Gatsby* and *The Sun Also Rises* in an attempt to capture the musical prose of the novelists he revered. And some of the early letters in *The Proud Highway* are clearly studious exercises in mimicking styles of writers from John Dos Passos to Lord Buckley to William Styron. Convinced by age twenty that he would become the F. Scott Fitzgerald of his generation, Thompson lugged his bulging correspondence around with him in trunks, believing that someday it would be his nest egg. "I've just been reading over two letters I sent you in Iceland," Thompson wrote his Air Force buddy Larry Callen in 1959. "Perhaps I'll try to publish my collected letters before, instead of after, I make history."

Taken as a whole, the early letters reveal a brilliant craftsman who, as a teenage hoodlum, developed a nonconformist philosophy like that of his favorite heroes in Ayn Rand's *The Fountainhead*, J. D. Salinger's *Catcher in the Rye*, Herman Hesse's *Siddhartha*, or Somerset Maugham's *The Razor's Edge*, always marching to the beat of his own drum, a voice without restraint. "I'm afraid of nothing and want nothing," he wrote a girlfriend in 1958. "I wait like a psychopath in a game of dodge-ball; breathing quickly while the fools decide which one will throw at me next, and jumping aside for no reason except that I like being in the middle." It is clear from the letters that Thompson deliberately cultivated himself as the American Adam, a figure defined by critic R.W.B. Lewis as "an individual standing alone, self-reliant and self-propelling, ready to confront whatever awaited him with the aid of his own unique and inherent resources."[1] The

1. R.W.B. Lewis, *The American Adam: Innocence, Tragedy, and Tradition in the Nineteenth Century* (Chicago, 1955).

writers Thompson most admired in his twenties—Ernest Hemingway, Jack London, Henry Miller—were not part of a literary movement or elite club but were their own traveling salons. "A good writer stands above movements," Thompson wrote, "neither a leader or a follower, but a bright white golfball in a fairway of windblown daisies." It was no accident that Thompson moved to Big Sur in 1960—he wanted to be near Miller, whose iconoclastic forthrightness he admired above all others.

One constant theme of *The Proud Highway* is Thompson's contempt for the mainstream press; he saw its members as sycophantic mouthpieces for the Rotary Club, the U.S. government, and the Eastern establishment. He preferred the subjective journalism of H. L. Mencken, Ambrose Bierce, John Reed, and I. F. Stone over all *The New York Times*'s supposedly objective journalists combined. After being fired from the Middletown (New York) *Daily Record* in 1959 for kicking a candy machine, Thompson wrote what might be considered his all-purpose motto: "I damn well intend to keep on living the way I think I should." And in that same note he also expressed two cardinal rules for aspiring writers: "First, never hesitate to use force, and second, abuse your credit for all its worth. If you remember these, and if you can keep your wits about you, there's a chance you'll make it."

It is difficult to know precisely when the so-called new journalism began. Certainly the 1965–1966 period covered in *The Proud Highway* demonstrates that the new journalism was being promulgated by a number of bold writers and developing a large and appreciative audience. While Gay Talese, Jimmy Breslin, Truman Capote, Tom Wolfe, Norman Mailer, and Terry Southern—all prominent acquaintances of Thompson's—have pointed to *Esquire* and the New York *Herald Tribune* as the breeding ground for the new journalism, Thompson—who prefers the phrase "impressionistic journalism"—doesn't buy this parochial version of the phenomenon. Long before George Plimpton picked up a football and wrote *The Paper Lion*, Thompson marveled at how Ernest Hemingway, Stephen Crane, and Mark Twain had combined the techniques of fiction and reportage while emphasizing the virtues of authorial involvement in describing newsworthy events.

As I read through Thompson's correspondence and notebooks from the early 1960s, it became clear that George Orwell's firsthand account of the Spanish Civil War in *Homage to Catalonia* and his slumming with disinherited vagabonds in *Down and Out in Paris and London* were perhaps the supreme influences on Thompson's technique and style. If Orwell could live in utter squalor with gutter winos and write about it, then Thompson would do likewise, infiltrating smugglers' dens in Aruba, whorehouses in

Brazil, and motorcycle gangs in California, even if it meant being beaten or jailed. For journalism to hold its own against fiction, Thompson believed, the story had to resonate for the ages. "Fiction is a bridge to the truth that journalism can't reach," Thompson wrote the editor Angus Cameron in 1965. "Facts are lies when they're added up." There were others who practiced impressionistic journalism in the 1950s and 1960s whom Thompson admired—A. J. Liebling on the press, Grantland Rice on sports, James Baldwin on race, and Norman Mailer on existential angst—but for Thompson, none captured the explosive sense of journalistic first-person adventure the way Orwell, Hemingway, and London did.

There was always an element of sardonic one-upmanship in the young Hunter S. Thompson: inviting William Faulkner to his freezing Hudson River Valley cabin to "steal chickens"; denouncing Nelson Algren for being as vicious as Nixon; warning Norman Mailer to watch his backside because "HST" was in the middle of writing the "Great Puerto Rican Novel." If Hemingway, rifle in hand, had hunted big game around Mt. Kilimanjaro, then Thompson would stalk wild boar with a Bowie knife in Big Sur. If J. P. Donleavy's Ginger Man ordered five whiskeys to go, Thompson ordered five bottles. Thompson's goal was to come up with a wild-eyed tale so twisted as to make "Heart of Darkness" seem like a bedtime story—but always accomplished with humor, a nod, and a wink.

No recent American writer has been mired in as much controversy as Hunter S. Thompson. His mythological persona sometimes garners more attention than his eight published books. No less than four biographies[2] have been written about Thompson in the past six years. Garry Trudeau has made a living for the past twenty years from his character Uncle Duke, modeled after Thompson, in his "Doonesbury" comic strip. Motion pictures have been made about Thompson's life. Along with Batman and the Green Hornet, Thompson's likeness has been marketed, without his consent, as an action figure, while FEAR AND LOATHING IN LAS VEGAS T-shirts are sold on the corner of Haight and Ashbury, along with others bearing the images of Jerry Garcia, Mick Jagger, and Kurt Cobain. Described by William Zinsser in *On Writing Well* (1980) as America's "acid-headed Mencken" and by the late NBC news anchorman John Chancellor as "Billy the Kid on speed," Thompson has proven popular with the tabloids as well as college audiences, both of which seem more interested in gos-

2. The books are Peter O. Whitmer, *When the Going Gets Weird: The Twisted Life and Times of Hunter S. Thompson* (New York, 1993); Paul Perry *Fear and Loathing: The Strange and Terrible Saga of Hunter S. Thompson* (New York, 1993); E. Jean Carroll, *Hunter: The Strange and Savage Life of Hunter S. Thompson* (New York, 1993); and William McKeen, *Hunter S. Thompson* (Boston, 1991).

siping about Thompson's alcohol and marijuana intake than in his collected works. But as these letters show—particularly when directed to female friends and his mother—the public persona is often at odds with a contemplative private self. "I haven't found a drug yet that can get you anywhere near as high as sitting at a desk writing," Thompson asserted in 1989 while being interviewed for yet another book on his life.

As documented in *The Proud Highway*, Thompson watched traditional journalism fail to properly cover such landmark events as the Nixon-Kennedy debates, JFK's assassination, LBJ's Vietnam escalation, and Nixon's political comeback. "[The press] can't sell me Johnson," he wrote a friend in February 1964. "He don't smell right." As his hero Bob Dylan implied in his scornful refrain to "Ballad of a Thin Man" ("Something is happening here / But you don't know what it is / Do you, Mister Jones?"), the establishment press of the 1960s didn't know how to cover Black Panther rallies or Grateful Dead concerts or LSD Kool-Aid bashes. Hunter S. Thompson did. "My recent work here has dealt with topless dancers, garbage in the bay, marijuana, karate, and a generally non-publishable hellbroth of vagrant interests," he wrote a friend in 1965. Thompson served as a cultural interpreter of the era, one foot embedded in mainstream journalistic writing for the Dow Jones Company, the other foot mired in the psychedelic underground. "I'm out here studying what appears to be an epidemic of arrested development in the American Dream," he wrote to a New York editor.

The term most associated with Hunter S. Thompson, "gonzo journalism," did not enter the American lexicon until 1970, when reporter Bill Cardoso of the Boston Sunday *Globe*, after reading Thompson's "The Kentucky Derby Is Decadent and Depraved" in *Scanlan's Monthly*, exclaimed, "That was pure gonzo!" While some claim that this word derives from an Italian word for simpleton, Cardoso insists that it is South Boston Irish in origin, used to describe the last man standing at the end of an all-night drinking marathon. As a pure literary art form, gonzo requires virtually no rewriting: the reporter and the quest for information are central. Scribbled notes, transcribed interviews, article excerpts, stream-of-consciousness, verbatim telephone conversations, faxes—these are elements of a piece of aggressively subjective gonzo journalism. "[It] is a style of reporting based on William Faulkner's idea that the best fiction is far more *true* than any kind of journalism," Thompson has noted. *New York Times* critic Herbert Mitgang best described gonzo as being whatever Hunter S. Thompson wrote: "Gonzo, his own brand of journalism, has even found its way into the new Random House dictionary, which uses such words as bizarre, crazy, and eccentric to define it. No one else gets credit for Gonzo journalism in the dictionary."

Even though Thompson has developed a well-earned reputation for bullying editors and firing agents, whom he calls the "bloodsucking 10 per-centers of American life," a good portion of the correspondence in *The Proud Highway* is with bright editors who gave Thompson big breaks, par-ticularly Clifford Ridley of the *National Observer* and Dwight Martin of *The Reporter*. Both editors wrote Thompson telling him that his letters were even better than his stories, that he was on the path to becoming the next Lincoln Steffens. But throughout his long literary career there was one editor whom Thompson unhesitatingly admired: Carey McWilliams of *The Nation*.

Thompson first came to McWilliams's attention in August 1962, when the famed editor read the hard-drinking journalist's series of extraordinary Latin American dispatches in the *National Observer*, a just inaugurated newsweekly published by the Dow Jones Company. McWilliams, who had a keen eye for talent, was impressed by Thompson's "gutsy ability" to get "deep inside the story" as he did in "A Footloose American in a Smugglers' Den." A couple of years later, when Thompson left the *National Observer* because its editors refused to publish his glowing review of Tom Wolfe's *The Kandy-Kolored Tangerine-Flake Streamline Baby*, McWilliams asked him to write for *The Nation* on Mario Savio's Berkeley Free Speech Movement.

Thompson accepted the offer, initiating what would blossom into an extraordinary correspondence, much of which appears in these pages. Throughout the mid-1960s Thompson wrote McWilliams almost weekly let-ters about everything from Ken Kesey's marijuana bust to Malcolm X's as-sassination, Salinas Valley migrant camps to Jimi Hendrix's "liquid guitar," Ronald Reagan's political rise to Lyndon Johnson's fall. "The destruction of California is a logical climax to the Westward Movement," Thompson wrote McWilliams from his Haight-Ashbury apartment at 318 Parnassus Street. "The redwoods, the freeways, the dope laws, race riots, water pollution, smog, the Free Speech Movement, and now Governor Reagan—the whole thing is as logical as mathematics. California is the end, in every way, of Lin-coln's idea that America was 'the last best hope of man.' "

It was McWilliams who commissioned Thompson to write on the Hell's Angels. The result was "Motorcycle Gangs: Losers and Outsiders," a May 17, 1965, cover story that brought the free-lance writer instant fame and a lu-crative book contract. "More than any other person, Carey was responsible for the success of *Hell's Angels*," Thompson recently noted. "He encour-aged me around every bend." Or, as he told a reporter friend in 1966, "Writ-ing for Carey McWilliams is an honor. . . . So what if he doesn't pay much. . . . When your article appears in *The Nation* you feel clean."

The first printing of *Hell's Angels* was sold out before publication, and when it hit the bestseller list in 1967, it stayed there for weeks on end all the way through the Summer of Love. "Every biker in the country must have bought it," Thompson surmised about his seemingly overnight success. The book received rave reviews in many leading periodicals. Richard Elman noted in *The New Republic* that *Hell's Angels* "asserts a kind of Rimbaud delirium of spirit . . . [to] which, of course, only the rarest geniuses can come close. . . . I suspect that Hunter S. Thompson is a writer whose future career is worth watching." Studs Terkel called the book "superb and terrifying" in the *Chicago Tribune*, and Eliot Fremont-Smith described Thompson as "a spirited, witty, observant and original writer" in *The New York Times*. Even Thompson's hometown newspaper, the Louisville *Courier-Journal*—which had in 1955 published an erroneous story about his police arrest—dished out unfettered praise: "It is good sociology written in a style that few sociologists ever master. An experienced, sophisticated writer for one so young, Thompson demonstrates a profound understanding of the drives, social and psychological, which motivate these mixed-up misfits."

As these letters for *The Proud Highway* were assembled, what became apparent to me was that once Thompson's commotion and insolence are checked, he is in actuality a public moralist, rallying against puritanism in any manifestation, occasionally exhibiting flashes of genuine prophecy. Whether he is scolding Lyndon Johnson for the Vietam War, predicting in 1965 that someday Ronald Reagan will be in the White House, or lampooning the Haight-Ashbury counterculture, Thompson's trenchant and sober-minded critiques mark him as one of the vital voices of his generation. "His style is mistaken for fantastic, drug-crazed exaggeration, but that was to be expected," Edward Abbey wrote about Thompson. "As always in this country, they only laugh at you when you tell the truth."

Selecting the correspondence to be included in *The Proud Highway* was a daunting task. For every letter included, fifteen were cut. One of Thompson's amazing qualities is the scholarly precision he applies to his work—and his early letters are no exception. He abhors the misuse of language and seldom misspells a word or mispunctuates a sentence. (On the few occasions Thompson did forget a comma or make a typographical error, I took the editorial liberty of correcting it in the published text.)

The letters in *The Proud Highway*—with the exception of deletions made to spare the reader needless repetition or extraneous details (earmarked by a bracketed ellipsis)—are published as Thompson typed them, though I have deleted some addresses for the sake of brevity. The main objective was to avoid distracting the reader while preserving the rhythm, the vitriol, the flight of imagination, and the genuine warmth with which Thompson wrote. Preceding most of the letters is a brief editor's note to provide a sense of historical context and narrative continuity. Footnotes were added to assist the reader in identifying characters, events, and terms without providing too much commentary.

To inventory this vast treasure trove, the Hunter S. Thompson Letters Project was created at the University of New Orleans's Eisenhower Center for American Studies. The goal of the center's scholars is to study all facets of twentieth-century America, and after spending a week with Thompson at Owl Farm, I became convinced that his correspondence was of great importance to the history of postwar journalism, literature, politics, and popular culture. Since the Eisenhower Center already houses historian Stephen E. Ambrose's Richard Nixon Project Papers, it seemed appropriate that the center also sponsor a project devoted to our thirty-seventh president's arch nemesis.

Besides the letters, Thompson has also saved at Owl Farm hundreds of notebooks containing his handwritten journalistic jottings and two unpublished novels: "Prince Jellyfish" (1959–1960) and "The Rum Diary" (1961–1966), both containing some of his best early prose. The archive also contains a dozen unpublished Thompson short stories, including "Hit Him Again Jack," "Whither Thou Goest," and "The Cotton Candy Heart," and a slew of fully realized but as yet unpublished "gonzo journalism" pieces on such disparate topics as Bill Monroe's bluegrass music, Jimmy Carter's White House triumph, and Ronald Reagan's invasion of Grenada in 1983. A respected photojournalist influenced by Robert Frank and Walker Evans, Thompson was compulsive about his craft in the early 1960s; his archive houses hundreds of his stark black-and-white images. But above and beyond all else there are the cardboard boxes of correspondence.

Taken together, the "fear and loathing" letters in *The Proud Highway* compose an informal and offbeat history of two decades in American life. The history is more intimate than anything in the score of sensationalized Hunter S. Thompson biographies, and it is in some ways more illuminating than the picture of the tumultuous times we find in his own published writing. But the letters do more than merely speak for their time. They also speak for their author, comprising a memoir of both Hunter S. Thompson's formative years and the explosive birth of the Sixties counterculture he so brilliantly chronicled.

New Orleans, Louisiana
December 14, 1996

AUTHOR'S NOTE

BY HUNTER S. THOMPSON

The second woe is past; and behold,
the third woe cometh quickly.

—Revelation 11:14

Today is Friday the thirteenth in Louisville. The sky is low and the view from the penthouse suite at the Brown Hotel is dense. There is only one window in the hotel that opens, and I have it right here in my room. My chief of security had it chiseled open yesterday, despite the whining of the manager, who said it was an invitation to suicide.

Yesterday was better. Yesterday, December 12, 1996, was officially declared by the mayor to be Hunter S. Thompson Day in Louisville. I was awarded the Key to the City and the sun was bright like a fireball. . . . Yesterday was *interesting*, in the Chinese sense, but today has taken a definite turn for the worse. There are rumors of a fire and a riot at the end of my lecture at the Memorial Auditorium last night. Teenage thugs ran amok and torched my dressing room, just moments after my mother had been whisked away in a limousine.

The event was a huge success, they said, but it left scars and odd hoofprints on many people. . . . There is a crude Mongolian adage that says, "For every moment of triumph, for every instant of beauty, many souls must be trampled."

I am no stranger to the Brown Hotel. I am well known here and I have been for forty years. When I was five years old my grandfather brought me into the dining room on Easter morning and we watched a Korean waitress stab an ice pick into the groin of the governor of Kentucky. I have never forgotten it.

Such episodes are not pleasant, but our pasts are permanent. Which brings me, as much as anything might, to this forced march through my personal history. I don't think many people could sit calmly while boxes of intimate—and in some cases no doubt incriminating—correspondence were dredged up from sealed basement vaults. But I did, Bubba, but always from afar, from the greatest possible distance, trying not to cause trouble—and because I wanted to stay in the shadows and act like I was dead, and others tried to act the same way. *Mistah Thompson, he dead.* . . . We all understood that their work and their lives and their long-range professional Fate would be a lot easier if I went out on a slick Ducati motorcycle one night and never came back.

But that would be a different road, and this is, after all, what we've decided to call *The Proud Highway.*

When I glance at this eerie collection and remember all the datelines and all the people I met in that moveable feast of violence and passion and constant revolution that lived at the core of the Sixties, there are two things I wonder about.

1) Where are all the people who did the same things I did and wrote the same kinds of frenzied berserk letters that I did, sometimes even from the same weird towns and with the same desperate feelings that I had and knew and genuinely suffered with because I was young and dumb and arrogant and utterly unemployable, except at great distance? . . . Which is true, as these letters make utterly clear. It was no accident that I was fired from every job I had in those days, and was evicted from every place I tried to live.

And 2) where are those people who helped me and hid me and took the same risks I did on that high-speed underground railroad that ran almost anywhere you wanted to go, in those days? I think about all of their stories and tales and eloquent, terrifying letters that never appeared anywhere, and won't, except in family albums.

Some of those people are named in these letters, others remain in the shadows for good reasons or for no decent reason at all. Sitting here in this grand old hotel, knowing that dawn is certain to bring anger and inquiries about that fire and about that other rumor about a teenager's body in the parking garage, it seems those people are still Out There, braced for the inevitable third woe, which indeed cometh quickly.

Louisville, Kentucky
December 13, 1996

THE PROUD HIGHWAY

Virginia Thompson with her sons Davison (left) and Hunter.
(Photo by Walter Fiske; courtesy of HST Collection)

1955

LOUISVILLE IN THE FIFTIES . . . SLOE GIN, SLEAZY DEBU-TANTES, AND THE GOOD LIFE IN CHEROKEE PARK . . . FROM ATHENAEUM HILL TO THE JEFFERSON COUNTY JAIL . . . WELCOME TO THE PROUD HIGHWAY . . .

So we shall let the reader answer this question for himself: Who is the happier man, he who has braved the storm of life and lived, or he who has stayed securely on shore and merely existed?

--Hunter S. Thompson, age seventeen

Although the young Thompson was forever in trouble with the law, his Louisville Male High School English teacher Harold Tague deemed him "brilliant and unpredictable." Thompson's sardonic essays for the Athenaeum Literary Association's bound yearbook, The Spectator, *consistently poked fun at middle-class conformity.*

The Athenaeum had been a respected literary society based at Male since June 1862—the month that Robert E. Lee took command of the Confederate army.

Young people of America, awake from your slumber of indolence and harken the call of the future! Do you realize that you are rapidly becoming a doomed generation? Do you realize that the fate of the world and of generations to come rests on your shoulders? Do you realize that at any time you may be called on to protect your country and the freedom of the world from the creeping scourge of Communism? How can you possibly laugh in the face of the disasters which face us from all sides? Oh ignorant youth, the world is not a joyous place. The time has come for you to dispense with the frivolous pleasures of childhood and get down to honest toil until you are sixty-five. Then and only then can you relax and collect your social security and live happily until the time of your death.

Also, your insolent attitude disturbs me greatly. You have the nerve to say that you have never known what it is like to live in a secure and peaceful world; you say that the present generation has balled things up to the extent that we now face a war so terrible that the very thought of it makes hardened veterans shudder; you say it is our fault that World War II was fought in vain; you say that it is impossible to lay any plans for the future until you are sure you have a future. I say Nonsense! None of these things matter. If you expect a future you must carve it out in the face of these things. You also say that you must wait until after you have served your time with the service to settle down. Ridiculous! It is a man's duty to pull up stakes and serve his country at any time, then settle down again.

I say there is no excuse for a feeling of insecurity on your part; there is no excuse for Juvenile Delinquency; there is no excuse for your attitude except that you are rotten and lazy! I was never like that! I worked hard; I saved; I didn't run around and stay out late at night; I carved out my own future through hard work and virtuous living, and look at me now: a respectable and successful man.

I warn you, if you don't start now it will be too late, and the blame for the end of the world will be laid at your feet. Heed my warning, oh depraved and profligate youth; I say awake, awake, awake!

Fearfully and disgustedly yours,
John J. Righteous-Hypocrite

THE SPECTATOR
"SECURITY"
BY HUNTER THOMPSON, 1955

Watching Marlon Brando in The Wild One *inspired Thompson to become a "Louisville outlaw" with no use for anyone who chose security over adventure.*

Security . . . what does this word mean in relation to life as we know it today? For the most part, it means safety and freedom from worry. It is said to be the end that all men strive for; but is security a utopian goal or is it another word for rut?

Let us visualize the secure man; and by this term, I mean a man who has settled for financial and personal security for his goal in life. In general, he is a man who has pushed ambition and initiative aside and settled down, so to speak, in a boring, but safe and comfortable rut for the rest of his life. His future is but an extension of his present, and he accepts it as such with a complacent shrug of his shoulders. His ideas and ideals are those of society in general and he is accepted as a respectable, but average and prosaic man. But is he a man? Has he any self-respect or pride in himself? How could he, when he has risked nothing and gained nothing? What does he think when he sees his youthful dreams of adventure, accomplishment, travel and romance buried under the cloak of conformity? How does he feel when he realizes that he has barely tasted the meal of life; when he sees the prison he has made for himself in pursuit of the almighty dollar? If he thinks this is all well and good, fine, but think of the tragedy of a man who has sacrificed his freedom on the altar of security, and wishes he could turn back the hands of time. A man is to be pitied who lacked the courage to accept the challenge of freedom and depart from the cushion of security and see life as it is instead of living it second-hand. Life has by-passed this man and he has watched from a secure place, afraid to seek anything better. What has he done except to sit and wait for the tomorrow which never comes?

Turn back the pages of history and see the men who have shaped the destiny of the world. Security was never theirs, but they lived rather than existed. Where would the world be if all men had sought security and not taken risks or gambled with their lives on the chance that, if they won, life would be different and richer? It is from the bystanders (who are in the vast majority) that we receive the propaganda that life is not worth living, that life is drudgery, that the ambitions of youth must be laid aside for a life which is but a painful wait for death. These are the ones who squeeze what excitement they can from life out of the imaginations and experiences of others through books and movies. These are the insignificant and forgotten men who preach conformity because it is all they know. These are the men who dream at night of what could have been, but who wake at dawn to take their places at the now-familiar rut and to merely exist through another day. For them, the romance of life is long dead and they are forced to go through the years on a tread-mill, cursing their existence, yet afraid to die because of the unknown which faces them after death. They lacked the only true courage: the kind which enables men to face the unknown regardless of the consequences.

As an afterthought, it seems hardly proper to write of life without once mentioning happiness; so we shall let the reader answer this question for himself: who is the happier man, he who has braved the storm of life and lived or he who has stayed securely on shore and merely existed?

THIRD PRIZE POEM — NETTLEROTH CONTEST
"THE NIGHT-WATCH"
ANONYMOUS, 1955 (BY HUNTER S. THOMPSON)

Although he excelled academically at Louisville Male High School, one month after writing this poem the seventeen-year-old Thompson found himself convicted of robbery and sentenced to six weeks in the Jefferson County jail. On graduation day, when his classmates received diplomas, Thompson sat alone in his cell.

I could see the moon hung high in the sky and the mocking grin on his
    face.
I know he was looking straight at me, perched high in my lonely place.
His voice floated down through the crisp night air and I thought I heard
    him say,

"It's too bad my boy, It's an awful shame that you have to go this way."
This chilled my heart and I shuddered with fear, for I knew he was right as
    right could be.
It was then that my skin began to crawl and I thought, "What I'd give to be
    free!"
Her face came back to me then like a flash, I remembered the touch of her
    lips.
I remembered the beautiful gold of her hair, her sky-blue eyes and the
    touch of her finger-tips.
Then I cursed myself and tore my hair for I knew I'd been wrong from the
    start.
I'd thrown away every chance I'd had and finally broken her heart.
My grief was of that special kind that only comes to men when they reach
    the end of a lonesome road and see what they could have been.
I cried as I thought of the people outside who were happy, and honest, and
    free.
And I knew that not even the lowest one would care to trade places with
    me.
Cold sweat broke out on my forehead now and my scalp felt tight and
    drawn.
What could I do to escape my fate, the electric chair at dawn?
I seized the bars, and shrieked, and wailed, like a soul who is lost in hell.
But the only voice that answered me was the mid-night toll of a bell.

Photos from The Spectator, *1954.*
(COURTESY OF HST COLLECTION)

Airman Thompson at Eglin Air Force Base.
(Photo by George Thompson; courtesy of HST Collection)

*Thompson (shown here with Air Force buddies) became a
legend at Eglin for both his journalistic skills and his
nonconformist attitude.*
(Courtesy of HST Collection)

1956

YEAR OF THE MONKEY . . . UNCLE SAM WANTS YOU . . . BIRTH OF A SPORTSWRITER . . . A NEGRO VISION OF HELL . . . WELCOME TO FAT CITY . . . DOOMED LOVE IN TALLAHASSEE . . .

The story of Joe Louis is an old one; the story of the star which has out-lived its light; the soaring meteor which failed to explode in mid-air at the height of its climb, but plummeted down to the same earth with the millions who, moments before, had stared wide-eyed at its beauty.

The world likes to look up at its stars. A meteor which falls out of the skies not only is dead when it hits, but digs its own grave by the force of its fall. Just as the crowd stares curiously at a fallen meteor and then wanders off, the crowd is beginning to thin around Joe Louis. He stands painfully bewildered in a world which he never took the trouble to understand. The applause of the worshipping thousands has died into the whispering of the curious few. The end is inevitable.

--Hunter S. Thompson, "Fame Is a One-Way Ticket,"
  Command Courier, December 17, 1956

TO GERALD "CHING" TYRRELL:

Tyrrell was a childhood friend of Thompson's, dubbed "Ching" when he joined the HAWKS Athletic Club after returning from China, where his father had been British consul general until the fall of Chiang Kai-shek's regime in 1949. Ching had attended the same three schools as Thompson: I. N. Bloom, Highland Junior High, and Louisville Male High School. They shared a deep interest in American literature forged through the Athenaeum Literary Association. At this time, Ching was an undergraduate at Yale University. Thompson had graduated from Scott Air Force Base's electronics program in June 1956 and was assigned to Eglin Air Proving Ground in Pensacola, Florida.

September 22, 1956
Eglin AFB [Air Force Base]
Fort Walton Beach, Florida

AALLLLLLOOOOOOOOO . . . . . . !

From out of the most deserted and god-forsaken spot in the Continental United States, winding its lonely way over the sand dune and through the swamp grass; comes the mournful cry of a man in the throes of mortal agony. With the return of the football season, come memories of people, parties and far-off places: the cold and clammy feel of a beer can clutched in my hand, the witless screech of the crowd at a football game, the memory of soft brown eyes and bubbling laughter, the sight of a young and palpitating breast; all these and many more race through my mind as I sit at my desk and pound out this missive which will bridge the gap from me to the mythical world of gay laughter and tinkling glasses. Ah me . . . when the winter is over . . . I can no longer repress a desperate cry of thirst and need.

With this opening, I offer a capsule of my first feelings of this wretched Saturday afternoon. This is the first weekend I haven't made the trip to Tallahassee and I feel like an opium-eater undergoing the "cure." Each weekend since late July has been spent in the company of a young and passionate lass[1] and, as Saturday night approaches, my palms begin to sweat profusely and my imagination runs amuck, causing me to leer at some of these fabulously beautiful WAFs. However, with an iron self-control, born of recent necessity, I will get a steel grip on myself and begin thinking about next week's sports page.

Perhaps I'd better explain my newest and most successful venture. In a resounding and incredible triumph over regulations and first sergeants, I managed to effect a transfer to the Information Services career field. More specifically, I am now Sports Editor of the *Command Courier*, the official voice of Eglin AFB.[2] Now you know, and I know, that I've never written a word for a newspaper of any sort. And you know that it's ridiculous to even speak of any experience on my part, as far as layout or page arrangement goes. In short, we both know that I'm no more qualified for a post like this than I am for the presidency of a theological seminary; but there is one major fact that makes it possible for me to hold this job: the people who hired me didn't bother to check any too closely on my journalistic background. I've managed to keep them in safe ignorance for about a month now, by nodding my head knowingly at any mention of a term which sounds journalistic, and using a few simple ones on occasion, whenever it seems comparatively safe. Just out of mild curiosity, I'd like you to look over the sports page of this edition and send me an opinion of some sort. I'm afraid to ask anyone around here, and I seem to remember that you know something about this type of thing. With the advent of the latest issue (sports), I think I'm pretty well entrenched around here, but I still think that it would be best that I don't make any display of my total lack of tangible knowledge on the subject, lest they become fearful of what might happen when my luck runs out.

Although I think I now have the best deal I could possibly have in the Air Force, acting the part of the experienced, competent journalist day after day has been quite a strain on my nervous system. I now tip the scales at a vastly reduced 168 pounds and I look rather silly when I attempt to wear the pants which fit me last spring. I had to give up cigarettes when my daily consumption topped the 3-pack-a-day mark, and I now smoke about two packs of tobacco per day, via the pipe route. Also, without the slightest exaggeration, I drink approximately 20 cups of coffee every 24 hours and manage to sleep about 5 hours a night. Of course, it goes without saying that I'm jumpy as a cat and am extremely unpleasant and sarcastic most of the time. I've developed an arrogant and forbidding attitude, which keeps

1. Ann Frick, who was attending the University of Florida.
2. Airman Second Class Hunter S. Thompson became sports editor for the Eglin Air Force Base's *Command Courier* on August 30; the September 6 edition carried his first column.

most of the numbwits away from me. Naturally, as I am sports editor of the base paper, most people know who I am, but very few of them care to talk to me; which is fine. I'll save my social intercourse for Tallahassee and live like a hermit during the week.

Life down here is so damnably different than anything I've ever experienced. During the week, I might as well be on a ship at sea. We can only pick up radio broadcasts from the immediate area, and the only contact with the outside world is through the eyes of the Mobile, Birmingham, Jacksonville and Pensacola papers, which I scour avidly each day. I've been drunk only once; in Panama City at an orgy which beat all I've ever seen. Believe it or not, I have yet to enter a bar in the state of Florida. The sum total of my alcoholic consumption could be purchased for under $5.00. Dates are plentiful at Florida State U. in Tallahassee, and I spend most of my time there on weekends. It's about 160 miles from here to Tall., but I've come to consider it no distance at all. By the same token, I'd think nothing at all of thumbing the 250 miles from here to New Orleans to see Ike[3] at Tulane. He wanted me to come over this weekend, but my poverty stricken condition prevented such an undertaking. However, I intend to make the trip as soon as possible. I had a slight misunderstanding with my pretty friend in Tall. last weekend and I saw fit to forgo the unpleasantness of going over there and dragging her out of her sorority house and off to a secluded spot. Now however, the sap is rising and my regret is manifest. Ah, how women can get on one's nerves.

I got quite a kick out of your social plight in the fair city of my birth: as I remember her, Sarah McNeil is about as pleasing to the average eye as a wart-hog with Bright's disease. On the whole though, you seem to be managing quite well. I'd appreciate a few impressions of Old Eli, if you can find enough time to send a letter to me in my desolation.

As I'm writing this with Porter Bibb[4] in mind as well as you, I'll request that you see that he peruses it and writes me a line or so. By the way, am I right in assuming that Richard[5] is up there also? If so, give him my most poetic regards and inform him that the life of a dedicated scholar is indeed thorny and that it would really be best to become a Jewish pawnbroker. Speaking of pawnbrokers, I was forced to pawn my $133 typewriter recently for the meager sum of $13 . . . ah, fortune and fame, where art thou?

---

3. Henry "Ike" Eichelburger was a former Louisville classmate of Thompson's who was studying biology-zoology at Tulane University.
4. David Porter Bibb III was a Louisville friend of Thompson's and a colleague at the Athenaeum Literary Association. At this time he was a sophomore at Yale University.
5. Porter's older brother.

I fear that lack of paper and time necessitates my closing, so I'll keep with the mode of the times and say, au revoir my friend, until we meet again.

Hunter

TO VIRGINIA THOMPSON:

Virginia Thompson, a Louisville librarian, shared her son's reverence for American literature. Hunter regularly wrote her newsy letters.

September 29, 1956
Eglin AFB
Fort Walton Beach, Florida

Dear Mom,

Usual apologies for not writing sooner, also usual excuses. Anyway, I appreciate your letters and all the clippings. Please continue.

Hurricane Flossie was nothing but a troublesome scare; however, word has it that another one is brewing somewhere in the Gulf: nothing definite yet. In any case, don't worry; these things are nothing but big winds that give everyone a chance to play here for a while. Flossie caused me to have to work all night Tuesday, without a wink of sleep until 3:30 Wednesday afternoon. This job has its drawbacks . . .

I covered the Annual Sports Banquet last night and my first football game today. These people just seem to think nothing of sending me on things which are completely new to me. I didn't even know what I was going to last night; my recollection of the CAC[6] banquets saved me from total confusion. Incidentally, every CAC banquet I've been to has been better planned and more enjoyable than this one. (My typing has deteriorated alarmingly; I'm getting worse each day.) At the last moment, the toast-master found that he didn't have a seat at the head table; and, being a sergeant, had to give way to the Colonels, Majors, etc. who had taken all the seats; and sit down amidst the mob . . . unusual, at best.

This afternoon I discovered that, not only am I the only man on the base to write sports; but in addition to my title as sports editor, I am also head statistician for all sports, publicity man for all athletics on the base, and potential radio announcer. All this, combined with college classes two nights a week, keeps me pretty well occupied. But, when all is said and done, I wouldn't want to do anything else (Air Force–wise, that is). At present, I have the best deal I could have, considering my rank, age, experience, etc.

---

6. The Castlewood Athletic Club, a neighborhood group for teenagers.

Incidentally, I thought I had explained that the courses I am taking are regular college courses with FSU. By January, I will have amassed the imposing total of 6 hours. By June, 12 hours; and further on into the night, I hope. By the end of the next month, I will know if my job is going to be permanent. My career field waiver should come back about that time, and I can only hope that it is not rejected: my chances are fair, I would say. I don't remember any other questions you asked, and the letter is at the barracks; I'll try to dash off a short note if I missed anything very important.

Some of the copy on this week's page is pretty poor. As I said, I stayed up all Tuesday night doing it, and towards the wee hours of the morning, I became pretty numb. However, it's the best looking one I've done yet, and drew many compliments.

Davison[7] is becoming very well known around the office, due to the fact that I do a running commentary on all the clippings you send me about him; plus any news you give me. Give him my congratulations and tell him to keep up the good work. Male High seems to be developing a mental block where he is concerned: this sort of thing must cease. Hello to everyone else. I sign out. Will write again if possible.

Love,
Hunter

TO ELIZABETH RAY:

Elated to be serving in the "glorious capacity" of Command Courier *sports editor, Thompson wrote his mother's sister about life at Eglin and his career plan.*

October 18, 1956
Eglin AFB
Fort Walton Beach, Florida

Dear Aunt Lee,
You'll have to pardon the use of the typewriter, because I'm at the office now, and no suitable stationery is available. Furthermore, I'll also apologize in advance for the millions of mistakes I'm bound to make.

I'm winding up for the evening, and will soon make a valiant attempt to get some sleep—a rare commodity these days. As I finished the story I was working on, it suddenly occurred to me that you just might like to know what your incredibly wicked nephew is doing with himself at present. Al-

---

7. Davison Thompson, Hunter's younger brother, was Louisville Male High School's All-State linebacker. He won a football scholarship to Vanderbilt University.

though I don't know your address, I decided to write you anyway, in care of mom.

I am now acting in the glorious capacity of sports editor of the *Command Courier*, the official organ of Eglin AFB, Fla. The job is nerve-wracking and the hours are terrible, but I love the work. For the first time, I have found something which will keep me busy and which is also enjoyable. Thus, I have been able to keep out of mischief and finally settle myself on an even keel for once.

In addition to writing everything in the sports section, I also am responsible for the page layout (arrangement of stories and pictures). For a person with no previous experience, this entails a good deal of work, but I'm having a fine time learning. My "Spectator" column is naturally my primary concern and is the item which requires the most thought and literary polish. I have become so ambitious that I have joined the Armed Forces Writers League and will soon make wild attempts to get something published. If I can swing this, then I should be able to augment my suffering "College Fund" considerably. Some magazines pay a nickel a word to brash beginners like myself, and with some luck and more than a little work, I might be able to become self-supporting, in spite of the Air Force's efforts to keep me in a state of poverty.

At present, in addition to my journalistic duties, I'm taking night classes with Florida State University. This semester, I'm taking Speech and Psychology—both interesting subjects. Next semester, I'll probably take Composition and Philosophy. Naturally, this keeps me constantly busy, but will definitely be worthwhile in the long run. When I'm discharged, I'll be able to start school with advanced standing at least.

This Florida weather is fine—it's about 80 degrees during the day and about 60 at night . . . very pleasant. Although I'll probably go overseas within the next year, I'm satisfied where I am at the moment.

All in all, things are coming along quite well and I'm beginning to feel like my wilder days are behind me. (I would be the worst type of hypocrite if I said that I don't sometimes wish for the Rabelaisian parties of yesteryear, but enough is enough. Things were beginning to be carried to an extreme. Actually, I probably owe you an apology for any worry or embarrassment I caused you. I am truthfully sorry, and want you to know that I certainly appreciate your kindness over the years.)

However, all that is water over the dam, and I must concern myself now with becoming a successful young author . . . ah, dreams of fame and fortune!

As the hands of the clock are winding into the wee hours of the morning, I find that the need for sleep is becoming too powerful to resist. I'm going to Tallahassee tomorrow night for the weekend, and should fortify myself with some shut-eye. FSU's homecoming football game is quite an attraction, and I'd hate to miss it because of battle fatigue, writer's cramp, or some such occupational disease.

If you have time, drop me a line and tell me how you are, and that sort of thing. I remain, dead tired, but still typing somehow;

much love,
Hunter S. Thompson
Command Courier
3201 AB Wg.
Eglin AFB, Fla.

TO JACK THOMPSON:

As a boy, Thompson was always impressed by his older half-brother Jack's white Navy uniform and riveting bedtime stories about the Hatfield and McCoy feuds. Jack went on to prosper as the owner of an insurance company.

October 24, 1956
Eglin AFB
Fort Walton Beach, Florida

Dear Jack,

As I can't think of a suitable excuse for not writing long ago, I won't even try to explain my failure to drop you a line. Let's just say "better late than never," and go on from there.

As you may or may not remember, when I was home last summer, I informed one and all that I was some sort of radio technician. Well, that sort of thing is no more; I have stumbled upon an entirely new concept of Air Force life. I am now the hard-bitten sports editor of the *Command Courier*, the official organ of Eglin AFB. As far as service life goes, I sort of live in the fringe area. I pull no detail, stand no inspections, pull no KP, and just generally leave the menial jobs to the enlisted men. However, if I were being paid by the hour on a civilian pay scale, I would have no worry about having enough money to go to college. For instance: yesterday I came to work at 7:15, and worked until 5:00; with an hour off at noon for lunch. I completely missed dinner and had to rush to make a 6:00 Speech class. I had to miss Psychology in order to come to the wrestling matches, which lasted from 8:00 until 10:00. At 10:00 I came back to the office and began on the wrestling story, finishing it at about midnight. About that time, my photographer arrived with the pictures, and I spent about an hour cropping and captioning them.

When the wrestling story and pictures were ready for print, I began on the football prevue and all the football pictures. All this lasted until about 4:00, when the last caption was finished. After getting everything ready for the printer, I raced back to my room and passed out for about 2 hours, in what amounted to a fatigue coma.

Staggering out of bed at 6:30, I drove back to the office—almost colliding with a huge truck en route—and went from there into Pensacola to do the layout for the sports section. As usual, I made several glaring errors which I was too tired to notice at the time; but which will be painfully evident tomorrow. That finished, I got back to the base at 2:30, and spent the rest of the afternoon trying to get a job selling vacuum cleaners. If it comes through, I may still find some way out of this terrible poverty. Of course, I've never sold vacuum cleaners—but then I've had no previous experience in sports writing either; so it certainly can't hurt to try.

Anyway, I guess you get the point about the rather tight schedule around here. Since taking over the sports desk, I've dropped from 190 pounds to 170, become a terrible case of nerves, become addicted to coffee—drinking about 20 cups a day—and had to give up cigarettes when I got up to 4 packs a day. All in all, it's hell; but it will take wild horses to get me back to the radio shop.

For the first time in my life, no one is hanging over me saying, "my oh my Hunter, just see what you can do when you apply yourself," or "do this Hunter, do that Hunter, behave yourself Hunter," and all that sort of rot. Here, they say, "Thompson; you'll be the sports editor—you have two pages to fill each week—do the best you can." Naturally, with no staff, it's a full-time job. But nobody bothers you, nobody tries to tell you how or what to write, you work when you feel like it and loaf when you feel like it. But still, you know that you have two pages to fill and that you can do anything except fail to fill them. If I want to wander around all day, I work at night—just as long as my section is done by the time the paper goes to press.

I guess it all comes under the heading of responsibility in a way. But truthfully—I don't do any of this for the Air Force—I do it because I don't want anybody to get the idea that I'm incapable of doing the job. Even though there is no damn reason why I should be capable of putting out a sports section each week—without having the slightest idea of what I'm doing—I'm just too much of an egotist to admit that I can't do it. So, the only thing left to do, is to go ahead and fight the damn thing and hope that it gets easier as it gets more familiar . . . and it's bound to.

I went kind of hog wild recently, and completely re-did the sports section; changing the pages around, adding a new head, changing the headline style, cutting pictures differently, and just generally ripping the thing up. Anyway, it has come out pretty well, and I'm vain enough to think that my skill is just too great to be described by mere words.

That sort of wraps up the story of what I'm doing. If they let me change career fields permanently, then I should be pretty competent by the time I get out. Then too, it's about the best duty I could ask for. Actually, the only thing which keeps reminding me that I'm in the service is the uniform. If it weren't for that, I'd feel like I was working at a regular job.

This semester, I'm taking Speech and Psychology. Next time, I think it will be Composition and Philosophy. They are regular accredited courses from FSU, taught by people from the school. We have classes two nights a week, and if I keep up this pace, I should have about 2 years through with by the time I get out. Then, if this poverty will ever go away, I can save enough to help me along with the last two years. I have no idea where I want to go yet, but that's a long way off—1959 to be exact.

I'm already beginning to pull strings, in an effort to get home for Thanksgiving. If it's humanly possible, I should make it for a day or so, anyway. If I do, I'll drop by to see you.

This last year has been long and incredibly eventful, but it has been very worthwhile. Pleasant memories of the orgies of yesteryear still linger with me, but I just can't afford to suck it down like I used to. And even if I could afford it, I wouldn't have the time. Then too, I wouldn't last too long here, once I began turning out stories while I was out of my mind. Each week, I come closer and closer to libel, slander and calumny. This week's "Spectator" will raise much hell, I'm sure—but that's just the way the ball bounces. If H. L. Mencken could do it, then so can I.

I've got to get some sleep now, because tomorrow will be a tough day and will require a certain sharpness of wit which fades with lack of sleep.

Drop me a line if you can—I'd like to hear from you. Until then, I remain,

> your black-sheep brother,
> Hunter S. Thompson
> *Command Courier*
> 3201 AB Wg.
> Eglin AFB, Fla.

TO RALPH PETERSON:

Peterson studied electronics with Thompson at Scott Air Force Base in Belleville, Illinois, where they were being trained in military intelligence. Although Peterson finished at the top of the class, Thompson finagled the cov-

eted post at Eglin Air Force Base in Fort Walton Beach, Florida, while Peterson was assigned to northern Alaska.

> October 25, 1956
> Eglin AFB
> Fort Walton Beach, Florida

Dear Sire,

Ah yes Peterson . . . the sun shines down all about me—the warm breezes float in from the Gulf—the palm trees sway gently in the wind—and life still goes on in the bustling metropolis of Pensacola. However, I'm sure that you much prefer the far frozen North country, and all its vitality and beauty. Naturally the thought of sprawling contentedly on the beach, listening to the clear blue water lap against the white sand, is repugnant to one so fond of snow, biting winds, transmitter shacks, arctic gear, etc. I've often heard that life in the arctic could be stimulating beyond belief, and now that you have told me of the wonders of the snow-covered land of light and beauty, I must say that I certainly envy you. My oh my; why didn't I request shipment to Alaska, instead of this balmy climate?

That raucous noise you just heard was probably my screech of laughter, floating through the northern pines and across the frozen wastelands, and into the smelly confines of your shack. Yes Peterson, my conscience is no substitute for a sixty average—unless it's a crafty mind. Need I say more?

Well lad, today has been a day to remember. The *Courier* hit the streets early this morning, and all hell broke loose within an hour's time. The subject for all this angry yowling was a clever little column entitled "The Spectator"; composed each week by your friendly doctor. As you can see, this week's job is a virtual bombshell. All day, I've been grinning at wild-eyed majors, captains, sergeants, lieutenants, and last but not least several Colonels—including Colonel Mears, the Base Commander. Apparently, Personnel Services was thoroughly agitated over the way I lambasted them. Colonel Mears topped off the day—which, up to that time, had been consumed with wild arguments and wilder threats—when he summoned me to his office at two o'clock. By this time, I was convinced that I was thoroughly in the right, and that nothing worse than a bust could result from it all. As it is now, I have permission from the Base Commander, to criticize anything I choose—provided I don't hit innocent spectators in the process. It turned out that I had enraged people from all branches of Personnel Services, in addition to the Sports Section. Mears had gotten calls all day from the Education office, the library, the riding stables, the golf course, etc.—demanding that I be busted immediately. The silver tongue was hard pressed to avert such a tragedy. If you don't quite grasp the meaning of the whole thing, just imagine that I had written this column for the newspaper at Scott, and was ordered to report to—not the first sergeant, not the squadron CO, not the group CO, but Colonel Goss—and explain just what in the hell I was trying to do. I remember how you all wondered how I managed to keep the first sergeant from doing me in—just imagine what would have been said after an episode such as this!

Of course I'll have to apologize to all the people who were struck by the stray shrapnel, but not to the sports section. From now on, when I appear somewhere with a pencil in my hand and a gleam in my eye, people will quiver in their shoes and sweat freely. This is the finest thing that could have happened. I now have thousands of readers, and the official sanction of the Base Commander. Move over Winchell . . . HST has emerged from obscurity to jab at the world for awhile. Jesus, what fun!

This week, the Eagles[8] play at Pensacola, and I will probably spend the weekend there. If I get drunk enough, I'll probably drop in on your parents. I have your address here somewhere. Tomorrow, I plan to pawn my typewriter for the third time, so as to get money for the weekend. Poverty still gnaws at me constantly. I'm going to see a man tomorrow about getting a job selling vacuum cleaners. If it works out, maybe I can beat the game yet.

Right now, I've got to run: sleep is scarce around here and must be taken when available. Thanks for the last letter, and write again when you get the chance. Until then, I remain,

> crazed with the power
> and hell bent for the
> worst kind of infamy. . . .
> Hunter S. Thompson
> *Command Courier*
> 3201 AB Wg.
> Eglin AFB, Fla.

TO HENRY STITES:

Thompson wrote this letter to his high school friend Henry Stites in the wee hours after typing his sports column at the Command Courier *desk. The Soviet Union had just ordered in tanks to quash the Hungarian revolution in Budapest.*

8. The Eglin football team.

November 3, 1956
Eglin AFB
Fort Walton Beach, Florida

Dear Henry,

How are you lad? It's been quite some time since I heard from you—as a matter of fact, I haven't heard from you—and I thought I'd try to pry a letter out of you. When you get a chance, drop me a line and tell me how you're coming along.

At this moment, it's 2:30 in the morning and I've just finished writing up today's game. I was listening to KMOX in St. Louis—and drumming up pleasant memories of my adventures in that fair city—when it was announced that Russia had taken Budapest and that the UN was in an emergency session. The all-night music show went immediately off the air and a special broadcast from the UN headquarters came on. Right now, I'm listening and casually wondering whether we are about to leap wildly into a full-scale war. Naturally Washington will do nothing until after the elections—regardless of whether eight million people are slaughtered or not. However, it seems inevitable that something will have to be done, because neither Britain nor Russia seem inclined to sit back and grin any longer. Actually, I would just as soon get into the thing now as later, and I really don't see any point in waiting. It just doesn't seem exactly right to let Hungary fight Russia any longer by itself. Of course, we'll all be in the damn thing when it starts anyway—so I think I'll come home for Thanksgiving before they decide to ship me to some far-off battle-front. Whether it will be my last trip home for some time will depend entirely on events. Oddly enough, it matters very little to me. I guess I won't feel this way when the fur starts to fly; but that also is in the future.

As you may or may not know, I escaped the Radio shop and am now sports editor on the base paper. It's a fine job, but as this letter shows, the hours are anything but regular. I sometimes work all night—sometimes all weekend—and almost always all day. I've managed to cut my sleep to an even four hours a night, and have become a coffee addict of the worst sort. Since taking this job, I've dropped from 190 pounds to a scrawny 170. None of my clothes fit anymore, and I can't afford to have them tailored. So—I wander around with my pants hanging on me like some sort of burlap bags. I get something of a kick out of seeing just how long I can go on like this, without having some sort of breakdown. I'll enclose one or two of my stories, so that you can see what sort of effort consumes my day.

This broadcast continues and seems to say the same thing over and over again. It is becoming increasingly obvious that the UN is going to make a rather pitiful and wholly ineffectual "protest," and follow it up with an in-credibly vicious "condemnation" of the Soviet invasion. I sort of wonder what would happen if a protest from the police would keep people from robbing banks. I can see the headlines now—"Bandits Rob Four Banks, City Votes to Protest." Christ, how stupid can people be. If this sort of half-hearted crap goes on, we may as well give Russia the whole world and be done with it.

I'll try to keep from rambling on about this matter, although I can't help but think of what it will lead to.

Except when I have to stay here and cover home games, I spend my weekends in Tallahassee. One of the guys who was at Scott with me lives over there, and he knows almost everyone.[9] Naturally, I was compelled to take advantage of the fact that Florida State U. has an over-abundance of young women. I've been dating a very pretty young thing[10] recently, and the whole setup is rather pleasant.

In the event of a home game, I'm forced to stay here and cover the thing. After getting a play-by-play description of the melee, I have to write the story and phone it out to the wire services and surrounding local papers (AP, UP, Montgomery, Atlanta, Pensacola, Mobile, Miami, etc.). This takes most of the night, but I don't really mind it because I like to read my stories in those papers the next day.

You'd be surprised to hear the names on the Eglin roster. We have 3 former All-Americans, the former leading scorer for the Green Bay Pack-ers, and all sorts of other ex–college stars. Almost all of the teams we play are in a similar position, and most of them stack up pretty well in compar-ison to the college teams I've seen this year.

Well, it's now 3:30 and a need for sleep is overcoming me. So I'll close while I can still type with reasonable accuracy. Naturally, my typing is mis-erable, but I can't seem to do anything about it at the moment. You'll just have to figure some of this out the best you can. Until I hear from you, I remain,

Your friend,
Hunter S. Thompson
Command Courier
3201 AB Wg
Eglin AFB, Fla.

9. Tom Sealey, a native of Tallahassee, attended electronics school with Thompson at Scott Air Force Base. Assigned to Eglin, he was Thompson's entrée to the world of Tallahassee debutantes.
10. Ann Frick.

TO SERGEANT TED STEPHENS:

Stephens, a hard-core military man, was Thompson's first sergeant at Scott Air Force Base. Thompson's erratic behavior drove the sergeant crazy, but they eventually developed a mutual respect. By Thompson's account Stephens overlooked at least a dozen insubordination infractions he committed during his nine-month stint at the base.

> November 10, 1956
> Eglin AFB
> Fort Walton Beach, Florida

Sergeant Stephens:

Whether the name of Hunter Thompson will strike a chord in your memory or not, I really don't know. So I'll state briefly that I spent a very hectic six months in your squadron, which came to an end early last July. During this time, you may recall that I was intoxicated a good part of the time and was called in to see you innumerable times, to explain an astonishing variety of weird and unique violations of many regulations. I was threatened with every punishment from squadron duty to being buried alive under the stockade. Miraculously, I escaped from Scott with a second stripe—a novelty which you explained the day before I left by saying that you must have been thinking about something else when you saw my name on the promotion roster. Far be it from me to say that I deserved a promotion, but thanks anyway, because I was very glad to get it.

You're probably expecting me to say that the stockade here is quite comfortable and that I'm now an airman basic. But no such thing has occurred. As a matter of fact [. . .] I expect to make airman first. Naturally, this will probably astound you, so I'll attempt some sort of explanation.

I think that I told you during one of our "sessions" that I was put into the radio career field against my will, and could work up no great love for the tube-pulling business—no matter how hard I tried. In part, I think this malassignment was responsible for a good portion of my trouble. Rather than being enthusiastic, I was totally resentful of any attempts to make a technician out of me. The fact that I came through school with a respectful average (about 55 or 56 I think) can be explained by the testing system at the school. The tests being multiple choice, I found it easy to figure out most of the answers by the application of simple psychology and the use of my memory, which is almost photographic at times. On the whole, though, I simply didn't give a damn about learning radio and made little effort to retain any of what I learned.

Well, to your great relief I'm sure, I finally left and, after a week or so at home, made the long trip to Eglin AFB at Fort Walton Beach, Florida.

After spending two miserable weeks in the Communications squadron here, I found out that the base paper was critically short of personnel. As I fancy myself to be something of a writer and plan to major in either Journalism or English in college, I volunteered my services and managed to be assigned to the job of sports editor on the *Command Courier*. I'm enclosing a few of my efforts and I'm sure that you can see that I'm definitely more at home in this field than I ever would be in the capacity of radio technician. At present, I've been working on the paper for about two months and, despite the fact that I have no experience at all in this line, I feel that I'm doing very well.

Instead of battling my environment, I enjoy my work tremendously and put in about 15 hours a day at it—for the simple reason that I like to write. You may also be interested to know that I have become completely sober—except on rare occasions—and have taken out a savings allotment, so that I will be able to have some spending money when I get to college. I am taking classes from Florida State University at night and, all in all, things are going very smoothly. Between studying, filling two sports pages each week, and trying to make some money writing, I'm kept too busy to get into any trouble.

Actually, the reason I'm writing all this is not because I think you're worried about what became of me; but to show you that it is sometimes wiser to give people a chance, as you did, rather than inflict a punishment which would only serve to create a troublesome attitude case. We both know that I should have been busted—according to all military regulations. But that would only have made me so bitter and troublesome, that I couldn't help but be a nuisance to the Air Force. Of course I could have been discharged, but that certainly would have been a negative solution. On the other hand, since you certainly went out of your way to keep from putting the screws to me, I'm now doing what I wanted to do in the first place and am helping both myself and the Air Force. Although I certainly have no plans to reenlist, my initial four years will be productive, and I will have a very valuable background when I begin working for a living as a civilian.

You might keep this letter in mind if you happen to come upon a case similar to mine, because you will know that it really doesn't take a violent punishment to straighten a man out. There are some people who react negatively to strictly regulated systems, and could be quite beneficial if they were placed in a job which interests them. Although I have more basic intelligence than a vast majority of the people in the radio career field, I could never have been a good radio man. On the other hand, as a writer, I can fill a very definite vacancy as far as the Air Force is concerned. (As further evidence of the ridiculous validity of Air Force tests, you might be interested to know I recently made a 95 on my 5-level test. You recall that I spent only two weeks working on the equipment and very frankly confess that I know absolutely nothing about it. However, the test grade places me in category "A" and means that I don't have to meet a board to get my 5-level. Actually, it's sort of funny.)

Before I close, let me say that I had a fine time during my stay at Scott and would like to get assigned to the *Broadcaster*[11] there, after I finish a tour in some overseas area. I have no idea when I'll go overseas, but if the world situation doesn't improve soon, I won't have long to wait. I only hope that I can get my AFSC[12] changed before I suddenly ship out of here for Egypt, or some other war-torn area. Incidentally, if you have never been to the Pine Room Tavern in Mascoutah, by all means give it a try. It's a quiet little place which makes the best hamburgers I've ever tasted, and serves premium beer in frosted mugs, for the paltry sum of $.15. I spent many a night there, watching television and writing letters, and if you happen to drop in on them, tell Erma that I said hello. Contrary to what you may imagine, I was never unruly in there and I'm sure that she got a completely different impression of me than you did.

Well, the hour is late and I probably should get some sleep. I can't help but think that, at this time of the night five months ago, I was probably out of my mind and giving some young girl a hard time. Ah, memories! [. . .]

Don't feel obligated in any way to answer this letter. I just wanted to thank you for your patience and let you know that you did a wise thing when you didn't "put me under the stockade." If there were more sergeants like you and fewer numbwit logheads, there would be fewer discipline problems in the Air Force. Keep up the good work and here's wishing you good luck.

> very sincerely,
> Hunter S. Thompson
> *Command Courier*
> 3201 AB Wg
> Eglin AFB, Fla.

P.S. I am serious about the Pine Room Tavern. It's the only place of its kind around Scott and if you ever have an evening when you have nothing to do, I'm sure that you'd enjoy a few draughts over there. If I ever get back to Scott, that will be the first place I'll head for. However, I'll leave that up to you; thanks again and au revoir.

---

11. The *Broadcaster* was the Scott Air Force Base newspaper.
12. AFSC stands for Air Force Security Classification. Thompson wanted to have his AFSC changed so he would be deemed a security risk and not sent to a war zone.

TO GERALD "CHING" TYRRELL:

At this time Thompson was reading John Dos Passos—which shows in the style of this letter to his friend at Yale.

> November 11, 1956
> Eglin AFB
> Fort Walton Beach, Florida

Monsieur,

Good morning—it's now 4:26 A.M. here on Florida's beautiful gulf coast; most of the airmen are sleeping soundly, the cooks are busy preparing the swill for the morning meal, roaches are frolicking merrily in their habitats, and yours truly is merely sitting and thinking. WCKY in Cinncinnati (too many "n"s) provides a background of soft and melancholy music—provoking memories and mental meanderings. Let's meander a bit. In Budapest, a four-year-old girl, wide-eyed with fright and shivering in the cold light of dawn, huddles in a dark corner of a littered room—wondering what has happened to her parents and why no one has fed her for two days. Outside, her father lies dead, an expression of pain on his face, and covered with a light dew. The city is quiet; for death is always quiet.

In London—Anthony Eden is wondering which of England's two enemies will kill it first. If the communists don't make the kill, the Labour party is bound to. No death here—just deterioration.

In Paris—a shopkeeper prepares for church. His room above the store is cold in the morning, so he hurries to get to the church, where it is always warm. Faith is very rarely cold.

In New York—a prostitute quietly sips a cup of coffee in an all night coffee shop. The dawn outside is grey and uninviting. A cab driver sits several seats down from her; wondering if the person who left his wallet containing fifty-two dollars in his cab earlier in the evening will remember where he left it and call the office to claim it. He could buy a new jacket with some of the money; the rest would make a month's payment on the television set. The prostitute picks a dime up off the counter and plays a song on the juke box. "Turn Back the Hands of Time." She leans on her elbows and sighs wearily; tired of business and tired of living. Life begins at forty—ha!

In Cleveland—a cold wind blows in off the lake. The lights come on in the kitchen of a small house in a residential section. Through the window, we see a pretty young wife humming as she makes coffee. A Boston bulldog sleeps in the corner. Nobody else is awake yet.

In Chicago—a very sleepy man gets slowly off a train and wanders into the coffee shop. He's going back home to Dayton, Ohio to get married to the girl he dated all through high school. He's going back to California on his honeymoon. He's a bit actor at Universal-International.

In Louisville—Mr. [Harold] Tague turns over in his sleep, perhaps dreaming that he is back at Male, teaching English again. A light fog hovers over the baseball diamonds in Seneca Park. A light-grey Plymouth station wagon speeds out Lexington Road. Is it Bob Butler[13]? No, it couldn't be—he's married and has a child. Anyway, what would he be doing out at this hour of the morning? What was he always doing at this hour of the morning, speeding out Lexington Road? Damn—it does look like Butler at that. Maybe it's his ghost. Time marches on.

In Nashville—a colored porter dozes in the corner of the Tennessean Hotel. The city is not yet up and about. A phone rings, startling him out of his sleep. He slowly rises and shuffles over to answer it. By the time he gets there, it has stopped ringing. He picks it up and mumbles indistinctly into the mouthpiece. Putting it down, he shuffles slowly back to his chair.

In Tallahassee—a very pretty dark-haired girl sits up in bed and brushes the sleep from her eyes. She wonders if her date this afternoon will be as dull as the one last night. Why doesn't she go to New York and be a model—at least her dates would be exciting. She'll probably get married soon, to a dull but faithful boy, and live a life of contented boredom. Still—it would be nice. . . .

In New Orleans—Eichelburger staggers out of a bistro. Drunk for the first time in weeks, he draws a caustic comment from the bartender: "these goddamn college boys."

In St. Louis—an airman sits alone at a bus stop. Broke, he wonders how he's going to get back to Scott Air Force Base. He wonders why in hell he ever left home in the first place. He had a good job at his father's store in Detroit, and now he's waiting to be shipped into the midst of a war in the Middle East. Maybe that winehead over there will give him some money. No, he looks like he hasn't had a meal in a week. Oh well. A car stops by the lake in Forest Park; the lights go out.

In Denver—a newsboy hurries through his rounds so he can get back to bed soon. The slap of a Sunday paper hitting a porch is the only sound to break the chilly silence. He folds another paper and hurries down the street.

In San Francisco—life goes on. Hopes rise and dreams flicker and die. Love plans for tomorrow and loneliness thinks of yesterday. Life is beautiful and living is pain. The sound of music floats down a dark street. A young girl looks out a window and wishes she were married. A drunk sleeps under a bridge. It is tomorrow.

13. Bob Butler was a Louisville "rogue" friend of Thompson's. Together they read aloud the Greek classics while drinking beer and raising Cain.

In Fort Walton Beach—an Air Policeman looks into the newspaper offices at Eglin Air Force Base and wonders if that fool in there is looting the place or if he is crazy enough to be working. A station in Tallahassee is broadcasting some sort of religious music. Yours truly prepares to leave the office and go eat breakfast before going to bed. He will sleep most of the day and work all night again tonight. Tomorrow is a holiday. He is not particularly happy, but neither is he particularly sad. He just sits . . . and thinks . . . and wonders.

I just thought I'd put some of my thoughts into writing. Thanks for your last letter and write again when you have the time. I always enjoy hearing from you. Good luck and here's hoping that you're always "shoe."[14]

your friend,
Hunter

TO JUDY STELLINGS:

A beautiful Louisville debutante, Stellings dated Thompson in high school. While in the Air Force he often wrote her about his dislike for the military and his longing for the Bluegrass State. During his stint at Eglin Thompson immersed himself in the works of F. Scott Fitzgerald—as evidenced by the "green light" here, among other things.

November 18, 1956
Eglin AFB
Fort Walton Beach, Florida

Dear Judy:

Sorry I haven't written sooner, but as you will see when you read a little further on, I'm busy about 25 hours a day, and must squeeze my letter-writing into odd moments.

Right now, I'm about 6000 feet above Montgomery, Alabama, en route from Shreveport, Louisiana to Eglin. I'm ensconced in the rear of a C-47, sitting on one parachute and resting my typewriter on another. Having just finished writing up the two games we played with Barksdale AFB this weekend, I became rather tired of writing about basketball and remembered that I still hadn't answered your letter. Even though my fingers are almost numb from the cold, I'm still able to pound out one or two incoherent, but faintly intelligible sentences.

I've recently discovered that this traveling with the team is quite a racket. We leave on Friday morning and return on Sunday night. I get

14. "Shoe" was a popular period term that meant "extremely Ivy League."

three dollars a game for acting as official scorer, am exempt from the training restrictions imposed on the players, and have all but about 2 hours of the weekend to myself.

All in all, my whole setup here is almost too good to be true. I no longer am forced to pull that ghastly KP—or any other degrading work for that matter—I have no regular working hours, and considerable power. Actually, it's no power, but a control of what gets into the sports section and what is junked. You'd be surprised at the things people will do in order to get their names or pictures into the paper.

Pause for dramatic description—it is now becoming dark outside, but it's a different kind of dark than we see on the ground. I can look down and see that it must be quite dark below, but there are no clouds up here to blot out the last rays of the sun. The little green light on the wing-tip is blinking against a background of a combination of orange and grey. Looking out at the quivering wing, I expect it to break off at any moment and send us all hurtling to the ground. Needless to say, it would be quite a fall and this letter would undoubtedly not be delivered. Now it has suddenly become pitch black outside and I can see nothing but the little green light— ah well—it really wasn't such a stirring sight after all.

As this letter probably won't get to you until after Thanksgiving, there is no need in my saying that I won't make it to New York for the Holidays. Instead of going to Bolling (in Washington) with the team, I'm going to spend a few days in Louisville; submerged in deep discussion with Joe and Noonan.[15] From all appearances, they will be the only people who will make it home and not to New York. However, we'll probably become liquified and drop in on Butler for a quiet sort of orgy. At any rate, it should be pleasant.

One last note before I go—I think we're getting ready to land—I have a somewhat urgent desire for my Male ring. I have no idea whether you still have it or not; but I imagine—and hope—that you do. It would be awfully clever of you to bundle it up in a small package and send it down this way. In return for that kindness, I shall steal a very valuable model plane from the display case in the office, and make you a present of the thing. I'll probably have to get all my Christmas presents out of that case, and there will undoubtedly be some sort of uproar concerning the disappearances. However, that is immaterial.

15. Joe Bell was a Louisville high school friend and Athenaeum Literary Association colleague of Thompson's who later went to forestry school. Billy Noonan was a Louisville native who was friends with Thompson's brother Davison. He later ran for coroner on the 1970 "Freak Power" ticket when Thompson ran for sheriff in Pitkin County, Colorado.

There is no more time to be had; we are bouncing around in preparation for a landing and I must finish here. Write again soon and I'll try to give out with a better reply. Chances are that I won't make it home for Christmas, although I'll make a wild effort to pull some sort of string.

That's all —
ears popping,
Hunter

TO PORTER BIBB III:

His status as sports editor of the Command Courier *appealed to Thompson immensely. Suddenly his "voice" was being read by thousands. Enamored of the power of the printed word, he declared journalism his vocation.*

December 1, 1956
Eglin AFB, Florida

Monsieur . . .

Yes . . . if you'll forgive the repetitiousness of your own phrase, the "gap was rather gaping." As a matter of fact, it has been almost seven or eight months since I've been favored with one of your unique examples of the much-slighted art of written communication. However, you hit a sore spot when you launched into this "you aren't the only one" kick. For the past four months, I've made an intensive and amazingly successful effort to convince everyone around me that I'm Hunter S. Thompson, the Sports Editor of the *Command Courier,* and am definitely not to be included in *any* group. So far, I've individualized myself to the point that people don't quite know what to make of me anymore. I wear blue button-down-collar shirts instead of Air Force shirts, I keep my own hours, I've turned one corner of the *Courier* office into my own private den — book shelf and radio-phono included — which makes night work quite pleasant, I pull *no* detail or KP, I'm *Sergeant* Thompson to any and all publicity seekers, and, in short, I've turned into a conceited, arrogant bastard! So you see that your including me in the mob, which has breathlessly awaited some word from one D. P. [Porter] Bibb, was more of an insult than soothing balm for an injured ego.

No more than an hour ago, I laid the framework for what — if it is successful — will be the most incredible of all the Thompson coups to date. For the price of two new footballs and weekly publicity — I will be made an honorary member of the Eglin NCO [Noncommissioned Officers'] club.[16]

---

16. Thompson also wrote for the NCO Club newsletter, under the pseudonym Cuubley Cohn, a takeoff on Coleridge's "Kubla Khan."

Naturally, the publicity will be for said club. You'd have to be in the air force to actually understand the full meaning of such a triumph. At the moment, the only thing which would compare to it would be for the Hon. Mr. [Gamal Abdel] Nasser to be appointed to the Order of the Garter. It will mean that I will then enjoy almost all the privileges of a Master Sergeant, save pay. As sports editor, I already have far more prestige than any Master Sergeant cook, mechanic, clerk, or any other such lowly occupation.

The whole secret of this sort of thing seems to be tied up in the old saying, "one good turn deserves another." And being in a top position on the staff of the only official publicity organ on the base puts me in the position of having a ready-made "good turn" at my constant disposal. Soon I'll be so crooked that I'll have to screw my pants on in the morning. Seriously though, some of these people around here would make Boss Tweed look like an amateur. This word "politics" damn sure applies to more than the presidential elections.

Right now, I'm just getting over an afternoon of drinking at the NCO club—at the entertainment manager's expense. I'm trying to get into a productive mood and whip up a story or so for this week's sports section, but I've become entranced with the possibilities of more Saturday afternoons of the same alcoholic nature and find it impossible to concentrate on the constant and miserable failures of the base basketball team.

Now that I've tooted my own horn in the best egotistical fashion for a full page, I'll get around to what I started to say in the distant beginning.

In the first place, just what is this thing I saw in the *Courier-Journal* about you broadcasting the election returns four hours before all the major networks? Secondly, fill me in on your activities with the *Yale Daily News*. (I didn't know that Eli had a daily, but that's beside the point.) First I find out that [Joe] Bell is working for the *Ring Tum Phi* (school paper) at W & L [Washington & Lee University], and then it leaks out that you're garnering experience on the *News*. This thing could have such momentous consequences that I shudder slightly when I think of it. [. . .]

The T-day tippling you spoke of fell far short of my expectations, but oddly enough, I still had a very enjoyable visit. The weekend was marred by a somewhat shocking adventure on the part of one R. B. [Bob] Butler. Then too, I learned that Reed[17] had been ousted from Stanford for cheating. These two revelations caused me to look below me to make sure my underpinnings were still in place. Two such omens in the space of two days came as quite a jolt. However, I think my aforementioned underpinnings are in my mind, rather than below me, and I feel better now than I did before.

---

17. Reed's name and school have been changed for publication.

I did manage to spend a somewhat sodden evening with [Billy] Noonan, but I fear the old "zip" is gone, for the evening left me with an uneasy feeling that the "dark and bloody ground" is presently populated with a rather stilted and pitifully false group of lads and lassies. Maybe it's me, but something has certainly changed. I got the impression that I was watching a play which had run too long.

As for my return to normal, I think it was due to a fascinating sort of infatuation over in Tallahassee. Unfortunately, it seems to be altogether too expensive and has terrifying possibilities. I'm afraid that it was one of those all or nothing propositions which women seem so fond of. At present, I'm planning to get over to New Orleans and let Eichelburger get me good and drunk. I think that will cleanse my soul of this "good and simple life" idea.

Right now I'm going out to look for someone to go into Pensacola and suck up a few with me at a smoky grotto called "Trader John's." So this will wind it up for the moment and I'll sit back and wait for a reply.

I've applied for a leave, beginning on December 27 and extending through the 4th of January. However, I'll make a desperate effort to tack four days onto this and have it start Xmas eve. It will undoubtedly be denied (I have only 2 days coming) but it will do no harm to try.

Until then,
au revoir — Hunty

P.S. it's AB Wg, not A building.

TO RUTLEDGE LILLY:

Lilly was a friend of Thompson's from the Athenaeum Literary Association. This letter was written to him at Princeton University, where he was now a student.

December 12, 1956
Eglin AFB
Fort Walton Beach, Florida

Dear Rut . . .

You displayed the epitome of gall, sir, when you went so far as to state that I "generally never write back." Except in the case of ghastly tragedies, I never fail to write back almost immediately. I average at least 3 or 4 letters every night; some of them personal and some business. Naturally, I get hundreds of requests for autographed pictures, but most of these are answered by my secretary, a very intelligent female orangutan.

When I actually think about it though, I really have nothing of any particular interest to say. Oh, I could comment at length on the subject of your orgies in New York, but it seems all but unnecessary and my lack of skill with this machine forbids any lengthy commentary. So I'll just say my oh my, hmmmm, well well, say now, really?, jesus christ, fiddlesticks, poop, lithernane!, sounds nice, zwitch, and several other trite expressions of wonder, envy and awe—and that will cover your adventures in New York.

One item, I think, deserves extra comment, and that's the one about Curtis[18] becoming "unrecognizably" drunk. Now I've seen drunks and drunks—tall drunks, short drunks, blind drunks, crawling drunks, slithering drunks, mumbling drunks, screeching drunks, crying drunks, sick drunks, dead drunks, speeding drunks, addled drunks, pitiful drunks, and just about any other type of drunk there is—but never have I seen a man who was unrecognizably drunk! The only explanation I can see for such a wonder, is that he must have shattered the "intoxication barrier" in an almost superhuman display of degeneration, dissipation, vice and drink.

Although I have no doubt that his head must have felt like one huge, infected tumor upon his shoulders when morning finally lifted its painful and ugly head; let him take consolation in the fact that he has established a new "intoxication level"—something for which you can all try for over the holidays; a proud and amazing feat indeed!

Ironically enough, even as I beat out an irregular tattoo on this machine, my head is swollen and painful from last night's pleasures. I must strain my eyes to see what I am writing, and even then, I'm not quite sure that I'm saying what I mean to say.

Last night was the occasion of the annual football banquet, to which I was very naturally invited, for it is I who must write the story and get the pictures in the paper. My position has gone to my head recently and I became somewhat drunk very early in the evening last night. By the time the meal was over and the speakers had begun to prattle, I had become almost out of my mind. When it became obvious that I was not going to be recipient of any sort of award, I arose grandly from my seat in the midst of a harangue by the base commander, a man with whom I have had previous difficulty, and staggered out of the banquet room and into the bar. From that point on, things became hazy. I missed all the banquet except the meal and the drinks, and now have no story at all. I don't know whether my photographer got any pictures or not, and all in all, I completely missed the banquet itself. Later, I was thrown out of the club for calling the night manager a crude, numbwit ass. As I was led down the walk by one of

18. Curtis Moore was a Louisville friend of Thompson's and a prominent member of the Athenaeum Literary Association. He graduated from Harvard University.

my friends, the manager stood on the porch in a white rage, as I sent a constant stream of insults and epithets over my shoulder in his direction. This morning, as I told him I was going to do, I hurled all the club publicity into Pensacola Bay. This will happen every week until I get a personal apology for his rudeness.

That was only the second time I've been drunk since July, so you probably won't recognize me if I get home over the holidays. I plan to get home right around Christmas Eve, and stay until New Year's Eve. This is tentative, and may change at any time. However, I'll probably see you sometime during that week unless something drastic occurs before then.

Right now, I must wander off to the bed, for my head gives me untold pain and my eyes are orbs of fire in my chalk-white face. Until xmas, get a grip and stay away from brothels.

> Cordially,
> Hunter

*The Spectator prowls the streets in
search of an exposé.*
(PHOTO BY GEORGE THOMPSON;
COURTESY OF HST COLLECTION)

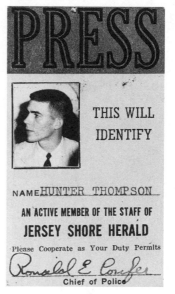

PRESS

THIS WILL
IDENTIFY

NAME HUNTER THOMPSON

AN ACTIVE MEMBER OF THE STAFF OF
JERSEY SHORE HERALD

Please Cooperate as Your Duty Permits

Chief of Police

Thompson's first nongovernmental press pass.
(COURTESY OF HST COLLECTION)

1957

**BEATING THE SYSTEM . . . TRIUMPH OF THE WILD BOY . . .
MENCKEN REVISITED . . . THE LOUISVILLE CONNECTION . . .
THE LESSONS OF HEMINGWAY . . . THE SHOCK OF RECOG-
NITION . . . NIGHTMARE IN JERSEY SHORE . . .**

A thick blanket of grey fog hung over the West Gate
early Saturday morning, as a green and white Chevrolet
rolled past the little gatehouse for the last time. With
a characteristic grin, the driver muttered a silent
farewell to this Gulf Coast paradise and pointed the
nose of the little car down the highway to Pensacola.

It was Gene "The Montana Ace" Espeland, his discharge
papers on the seat beside him, heading back to Westby,
Montana. Within a week or so, he'll be back at Northern
Montana State College, taking up where he left off four
years ago.

One of the most colorful athletes ever to wear an
Eglin uniform, Gene was what they would call in France
"un type." Here, we call them "characters," but they tend
to be the same the world over, and without them, life
would be intolerably dull.

--Hunter S. Thompson, <u>Command Courier,</u>
    September 28, 1957

TO JUDY STELLINGS:

In Orlando to cover Eglin's basketball game against Pinecastle AFB for the Command Courier, *Thompson found time to update Judy Stellings, his exgirlfriend, who was attending the University of Kentucky but wanted to switch to Hollins College.*

February 3, 1957
Pinecastle AFB
Orlando, Florida

Dear Judy,

Although I seem to remember you saying that you would write "immediately" as I wandered out of Cooke's castle after an unusually sober New Year's Eve, I now find myself with a few moments to spare and will attempt to bat out a few lines of greeting.

Actually, what prompted me to write was the sound of Bing Crosby's voice, singing some of the songs which I used to listen to in your living room in the days which now seem almost a part of another lifetime, a past which was so completely different from the present that it seems impossible that it could be anything other than a dream.

Since early afternoon, I've been sitting at the typewriter in the office of the Airmen's Club at Pinecastle AFB, just outside of Orlando. I came down with the team Friday morning and probably won't get back to Eglin until sometime Wednesday. We are scheduled to leave for Montgomery, Alabama tomorrow morning for two more games with Moody AFB. I'll probably have to telegraph all my stories in and send the pictures in by plane because my deadline is Wednesday morning and it doesn't look like I'll make it.

In a few minutes, I guess I'll have to start on this week's "Spectator." The only thing I can write about is the dog racing fiasco which it was my misfortune to attend yesterday afternoon. The wretched mongrels cost me almost every cent I had and left me with an unfortunately biased impression of Orlando. I completed my plunge into total poverty last night with a visit to a rather expensive little grotto called the Sho-Bar somewhere in the county surrounding the city: something on the order of the Merry-Go-Round in Louisville, although peopled by a different type of clientele. I now have a grand total of $4.00 to last me until February 15, but am considerably better off than my photographer, who has ten cents. It's a hectic life.

I can see no financial hope in the near future, for the Mardi Gras looms ominously on the horizon within the next month and it will certainly cost me a great sum which I must scrape up somehow by fair means or foul. A three-day visit three weeks ago gave me my first taste of New Orleans and I have a definite desire for a return bout. I was supposed to be covering some games with an Army Base over there, but I got lost in the French Quarter for two days and two nights and missed both games and came close to missing the plane back to Eglin. At first my missing all the games on the road trips upset the coach, but now he has become used to it and is satisfied just as long as the stories portray him in a grand and glorious light.

Counting the one day a week I spend in Pensacola laying out my sports section, these constant trips, and my weekend visits to Tallahassee, I spend about three days a week on the base. Nevertheless, everyone is satisfied just as long as I continue to turn out the best sports section in the Air Force.

I guess that sounds rather egotistical, but considering the fact that there are only ten or fifteen sports editors in the Air Force, it's really more realism than conceit. For some reason or other, writers and the Air Force just don't see eye to eye. I will be but one of a long line who have put in their time and departed as soon as possible.

This college business is becoming confusing about now. It seems that I'm taking all sophomore and junior courses and have skipped almost all of the required subjects. For instance, next semester, I'm taking Shakespearean English and Advanced Psychology, both junior courses. Last time I took General Psychology and Speech, sophomore courses. Christ only knows what I'll do when it comes time to enter some school on a regular basis. I'll probably end up taking all freshman courses to make up for the ones I've skipped. As things are now, though, I have to take interesting courses so that I'll keep up with them. I have so much to do in my job alone that, if I had to take dull, elementary things, I'd undoubtedly lose interest immediately and drop out.

However, all these problems are more interesting than they are dangerous and actually present little grounds for deep concern. I just keep wandering around, doing all these things and not worrying about what the results will be. So far it's turned out pretty well.

I'm still sort of intrigued at your majoring in typing though; it seems sort of odd that you should get a degree in typing after two years of intense study. Maybe I just have a faulty conception of this college thing.

The time has come now for me to begin the laborious task of composing a "Spectator" for the coming issue and I must sink myself into a fit of concentration for the next hour or so. Drop me a line when you can and paint me another picture of life among "the jolly set." The mailing inspector forced me to change my address into a very complicated sort of thing which you'll find below.

Yours in debt,
Hunter S. Thompson
A/2C, AF15546879
3201 AB Wg., Hq Sq Box 152
Eglin AFB, Fla.

TO VIRGINIA THOMPSON:

Thompson told his mother of his newfound penchant for photography as well as his prospects for moonlighting at the Playground News, *Fort Walton Beach's civilian newspaper.*

February 5, 1957
Eglin AFB
Fort Walton Beach, Florida

Dear Mom,

It wasn't until I received your note (and the check) today that I realized that I hadn't written in so long. In the following harangue, I will attempt to fill you in on the two hectic weeks which I've just struggled through.

First and foremost, a somewhat cheerful note: I got one of four "A"s in a class of forty in General Psychology. The Speech grade was somewhat lower, as I had expected, and amounted to an insignificant "C." Your check arrived in the nick of time and tomorrow I shall enroll in a class of Shakespearean English and another in Advanced Psychology.

And now for news of the incredibly erratic journalistic career of one H. Stockton Thompson.

I received orders from base headquarters to pack my bags and proceed immediately back to the 3201st Communications Squadron. That was at 11:00 AM on Friday, January 25th. At 12:30 PM of the same day, I stood beside Colonel Evans's desk and heard him reduce the orders to a worthless scrap of paper with a few well chosen words to the Base Commander. At 12:33 of the same day, I resumed my capacity as Sports Editor of the *Command Courier.*

As things stand now, I am here on an indefinite and quasi-permanent basis. No one seems to know if or when I will be allowed to leave. Colonel

Evans has, as he put it, "upset a few people," and no voice has yet been heard which dares to question his flagrant circumvention of all military procedure in my case. The General likes to read about sports on the base and Colonel Evans has seen to it that the General shall not be displeased. At present, I am firmly entrenched as the unquestioned mogul of Eglin sports, a sort of immovable oracle.

Last night I returned from a four day sojourn at Pinecastle AFB, just outside of Orlando. For the first time, I managed to spring a photographer loose to make the trip with me. However, the lad took only four or five pictures the whole time; and most of them were of me. Of the thirty or forty shots taken, over three fourths of them were taken by your talented and versatile son. And believe it or not, the consensus of opinion in the office had it that my shots were, on the whole, vastly superior to the ones taken by our veteran photogs. Naturally, this further revelation of yet another facet of my genius served to awe the lads a bit more. I seriously doubt that anyone in the office would be surprised if I were to suddenly rise slowly out of my chair and float out the window.

Now, before you begin a letter intended to prick my bubble of egotistical babble, let me inform you of my latest good fortune, a thing so incredible and with such fantastic possibilities that it unnerves me a bit to contemplate further upon it.

Get a firm grip, sit quietly, and keep calm as I unfold a tale of what may be. Understand that nothing is yet certain, but that things are 90% settled and will be 100% so by the time next Monday rolls around.

There is in the thriving community of Fort Walton Beach, Florida, a newspaper; a forty (40) page weekly which is the principal source of information of the inhabitants of a region no less than 100 miles square and encompassing the whole of Eglin AFB and all the surrounding communities, approximately 50,000 by rough estimate. That 50,000 is the number of inhabitants of the aforementioned area, not the communities surrounding the base.

This morning, after paying me the sum of $3.00 for thirty minutes worth of wrestling copy, John (Sgt. Edenfield) sat quietly down by my desk and said; and I quote: "Now don't get excited and go all to pieces, but I think I've set you up for a good deal. You know Wayne Bell, the Editor of the *Playground News* (the abovementioned paper), well you have an appointment with him this Friday afternoon. You're their new Sports Editor."

So, this Friday I shall go forth to Fort Walton to haggle over such matters as salary, salary, salary, etc. with the benevolent Mr. Bell. You may be surprised to hear that I intend to haggle over salary matters, but to take on another work-load equal to the one which presently keeps me going 16 hours a day will be no simple task.

Now, instead of two classes every Tuesday and Thursday night, I have one class every Monday, Tuesday, Wednesday and Thursday night. Furthermore, they're both Junior (third year) subjects and are far and away the hardest offered here on the base.

If I do take the job, it means that I'll be working all day for the *Courier*, taking a two hour break to go to college in the evening, and then working a good part of every night for the *News*. Obviously, this could easily get to a man in no time at all. However, more on this later, when the whole thing is settled and I can offer some definite news.

Until then, I remain, your son,
Hunter

TO PORTER BIBB III:

Disregarding Air Force regulations, Thompson took the civilian job as sports editor of the Playground News *in Fort Walton Beach, writing under the pseudonym Thorne Stockton. While the move boosted his journalism career, it put him in hot water with his superior officers.*

February 6, 1957
Eglin AFB
Fort Walton Beach, Florida

Monsieur,

I trust you will pardon my inconsiderate procrastination and accept my most abject apology for not having written sooner. However, we of the school of hard knocks are not without our daily duties and mine have been all but overwhelming during the past month or so.

I have returned from a five-day excursion to Orlando on Monday, to find myself faced with eight hours of hard work and the prospect of assuming a trebled workload within a week. After making my first "sale" (a 200-word wrestling publicity story to the local press) I was taken aback somewhat when the editor of said press offered me the exalted position of sports editor of his weekly clarion. I have an appointment Friday to go in and haggle over such matters as salary, money, pay, etc.

Unfortunately, my long-term contract with the "bird division" doesn't expire until 1959 and I will be forced to continue in my present capacity while, at the same time, taking on a full-time civilian job. Added to the classes in Advanced Psychology and Shakespearean English four nights a week, the whole thing tends to make my eyes water with wonder at my sudden eruption of ambition.

But confident in the knowledge that fate always rewards ex-cons who take up an honest trade, I shall slave like an animal until my present run of good fortune and luck runs on the rocks. It seems impossible that it could be a lasting thing.

As usual, your communication was appreciated but not overly informative. I gathered only that you had returned from Canada and were embarking on an orgy of exams. You may be pleased to know that you're the first person I've heard from who failed to mention the possibility of flunking out of school within the week. I can't quite understand the apparent inability of Louisville's brilliant and witty younger set to cope with such matters as modern educational techniques. Tuskegee graduates hundreds each spring.

Thumbing through the society section of the *Courier-Journal* (damn me if you must, but I have a subscription) earlier in the evening, I came across the picture of a small and comely lass with whom I once reveled in the soft grass of a field surrounding some sort of Dasmine camp. Since I was in love with her for an evening, I naturally retain a soft spot in one corner of my heart for her and felt a twinge of an intangible something when I saw that she will soon be wed to another.

Feeling a fit of nostalgia coming on, I hurriedly lit up my charred but tasty pipe and settled back to wait for the seizure to grip me. In no time at all I found myself leafing avidly through my copy of the 1955 *Spectator* and gazing fondly on names and faces which made up the "amazing world of Hunter Thompson" for those three hectic years.

Seeking a suitable climax for my orgasm of reflections, I soon resolved to answer your card with a letter of unparalleled pithiness. But as seizures must, mine came to a sputtering close soon after I got the first sheet of paper in this machine and I now feel drained of what little energy I had accumulated during the day.

However, I can console myself with the knowledge that I have had the required monthly spasm, drunk a silent toast to old friendship, and am keeping in shape for the 100 year celebration. I feel confident that, by that time, I shall be universally hailed as the new [Grantland] "Granny" Rice and will be borne into the main hall of the Pendennis Club on the shoulders of seven burly Oklahoma linemen. In one hand I will have a football full of gin and in the other, a Belmont racing form. Drawing on my fantastic salary, I shall engage the Anvil Chorus to sing the ALA [Athenaeum Literary Association] song for 112 consecutive hours and will hire scores of hand-shaking specialists to properly perpetuate tradition, leaving all the celebrants with both hands free to hold drinks. Ah, fortune and fame shall follow me . . . and I shall dwell in the world of the chosen for a few moments of fleeting ecstasy; ere the seven burly lads turn into creditors and hustle me off to debtors' prison at last.

As you see, coming out of these nostalgic comas produces strange effects. This was not exactly what I thought I was going to say as I wiped a tear from my eye and began my letter to "good old Dave." My tender thoughts of yesteryear seem to have gone haywire and I shall now bring this unfortunate abortion to a rapid close.

In all seriousness, I always enjoy hearing from you and would appreciate some sort of report as to what you're doing with yourself up there in the cold and conservative land of our fore-fathers. [. . .]

> Until then, I remain,
> your friend,
> Hunter S. Thompson
> A/2C, AF15546879
> 3201 AB Wg, Hq Sq, Box 152
> Eglin AFB, Fla.

These weird addresses are driving me mad. I will have a P.O. Box in Fort Walton when I begin my new job. Don't let it keep you from writing; it could be you!

TO JUDY STELLINGS:

Thompson enjoyed keeping up with his old Louisville gang. Life was going well for him except for constant bouts of "accidental" insubordination toward his superior officers and keeping secret his civilian life as Thorne Stockton. At this time he was penning two weekly columns: "The Spectator" for the Command Courier *and "World of Sport" for the* Playground News.

> March 3, 1957
> Eglin AFB
> Fort Walton Beach, Florida

Dear Judy,

I am astounded by your scholastic prowess. I drop to my literary knees and beg forgiveness for ever doubting that you were indeed a scholar of renown. Just where I got the impression that you were majoring in typing, I'll never know; but you have now set me straight and I stand in the ranks of the true believers. Selah.

For that matter, it cheers me considerably to know that at least someone from Louisville has not fallen before the educational battle-axe. The list of flunkees and potential flunkees is imposing and lends credence to the popular theory concerning the inadequacy of the Derby town schools. But by far the most blood-curdling news was the bit about Chip[1] donning the

---

1. Chip Johnson was a Louisville friend of Thompson's who joined the Air Force.

AF blue. To me, he was the personification of utter degeneracy and the old way of life, a virtual bastion of depraved strength, stemming the tide of progress and change which threatens us all. To see such a figure fall is a sad thing, for he was the last of a breed, a hellish lot of misfits and eight-balls who made up an era. One by one they sink into oblivion; first me (I exploded out of sight) then Butler, Bier, Pinky, Sam, Willis, Roy, Rabbit, Lord, Smitty, and many others too numerous to name. God only knows what will happen to Reed, he was arrested last week for robbing and beating the proprietor of a grocery in Bowling Green. He was going to enter University of Louisville at mid-term after being expelled from Stanford. Now, needless to say, he will not enter Louisville.[2] [. . .]

I can see that your ambition to get into Hollins [College] by hook or crook remains as strong as ever. But supposing that you don't get in there (forgive me), where will you go? As for my coming to New York, I could have come this week, but decided that it would be too short notice to get anyone down to drink with me. We have a boy who's fighting in the AF boxing finals and I could have gone with him had I wanted to. If I had gotten your letter a day or so sooner, I would have come. Unfortunately, he has already gone. The tournament is from March 4 through March 8. However, my latest project is an effort to get a position on the Armed Forces Press Service staff in New York. I probably won't be able to land it, but I'm trying anyway. I'll let you know how I come out. If I make it, that means that I'll spend the rest of my hitch in New York, writing whatever they want me to for the weekly publication: a pretty soft deal. [. . .]

I was getting along pretty well with my AF buddies until recently, when I seemed to run amuck and burst out in flames. Last week, nine sergeants simultaneously filed charges of insubordination against me, I was arrested on three charges of operating a motor scooter in a reckless manner, and was found drunk in the office in the dead of night for the second time. About a month ago, they found me passed out on Colonel Evans' couch at 7:30 in the morning after an all-night orgy. I am scheduled to see the commander about all this either tomorrow or Tuesday. It should be an unpleasant visit, but nothing like the wild inquisition I was constantly attending at Scott. I shall survive.

I was finally forced to sell the huge Chrysler. It had deteriorated to the point where I was getting 7 miles to the gallon, throwing 2 quarts of oil every 100 miles, and was just too damn expensive to operate. Some idiot bought it for $60, after I had sold the hub caps for $10, the radio for $20, and stripped it of everything of value. He immediately shelled out $23 for

2. Identifying details about Reed have been changed for publication.

a license, $86 for insurance, $21 for a muffler and tailpipe, and will soon have to buy at least 2 tires. I bought a motor scooter for $50. At least it's transportation. [. . .]

Before I go, I repeat my invitation to come down and see me whenever you can. With all your flitting about, you should be able to drop in on me for a few days. Of course it's a bit cool now, but the beaches will begin to come to life again any day now. If I don't get the AFPS job, I hope I can stay here for the summer. It's nice.

Let's be a little quicker on the reply this time!!!

Until then, I remain . . .
rebelliously,
Hunter

P.S. Are you still getting fatter and fatter? My new address is on the back of this sheet. If you aren't too fat, how about sending me another picture of you. The two I have are a little old. But I gaze fondly on them in moments of reverie.

TO GERALD "CHING" TYRRELL:

Although Thompson was enjoying his journalism career, he was becoming desperate to get out of the Air Force. Much of his energy was devoted to pursuing an honorable discharge.

March 10, 1957
Eglin AFB
Fort Walton Beach, Florida

Mon ami,

My apologies are abject, my heart is down, my head is spinning around, I had to leave a little girl in Kingston town. The procrastination of it all is humiliating. Fain would I have written sooner.

None of this makes much sense, but I do apologize for not having written sooner. Between both of these damn jobs, I never know whether I'm coming or going. It came as something of a shock, after leafing through my files, to find that the last letter addressed to you bore the date of December 12, 1956. This is inexcusable, but will not happen again.

After reading your letter again, I find that I have indeed written since then. My confusion must be apparent.

As it is now, I am three days behind on both sports pages and am scheduled for a terrifying inquisition of some sort tomorrow, concerning innumerable charges of insubordination which have been placed against me within the last two weeks. At last count, nine NCOs had registered complaints, the Air Police had found me drunk in the office at 3:30 last Sunday night, I had been turned in for reckless driving on my new motor scooter, and the Colonel had discovered that I was working for the *News* without his permission. Needless to say, the situation is unsettled.

To add to everything else, I dropped a gallon-jug full of beer in the office Friday night, and the odor has permeated the very walls, being particularly offensive in the Colonel's office, which has no ventilation. I am seriously considering applying for an unadaptable discharge (inability to adapt to the military way of life).

For the sake of everything you presently take for granted, give up all ideas of volunteering for the draft: or for anything military. It is a way of life which was never meant for our type. Being almost wholly composed of dullards and intellectual sluggards, it is a painful hell for anyone with an I.Q. over 80. Be a beachcomber, a Parisian wino, an Italian pimp, or a Danish pervert; but stay away from the Armed Forces. It is a catch-all for people who regard every tomorrow as a hammer swinging at the head of man, and whose outstanding trait is a fearful mistrust of everything out of the ordinary. Should you volunteer, it will be two years lost in a sea of ignorance.

And that for the military.

You seem to be even more mercenary than I had previously imagined, but I wish you the best of luck next year in the company of Vaughn.[3] I now see the secret of capitalistic success, but unfortunately, the AF leaves little chance for this sort of thing. WE believe in democratic processes. [...]

> Until I hear from you,
> I remain,
> your friend . . .
> Hunter

TO THE ATHENAEUM LITERARY ASSOCIATION:

On March 11 Thompson received a letter from the Athenaeum Literary Association reinstating him as a Class of 1955 member. (The society had excommunicated him from its ranks for "insufficient morals" when he was arrested for robbery.) This hometown boost of confidence did wonders for Thompson's sagging morale.

3. A friend of Tyrrell's who wanted to join the armed forces.

March 17, 1957
Eglin AFB
Fort Walton Beach, Florida

Gentlemen,

It would be a waste of time for me to carry on at length about how much I appreciate the action you have taken in re-instating me in the Class of 1955. If you will put yourselves in my place for a moment, I'm sure that you will see how I feel.

The Athenaeum meant a great deal to me, and to be separated from it under the conditions which brought about my resignation was a painful thing. But the very fact that I left the Association under a cloud has made the reinstatement something which I will always look on with pride. Needless to say, I am deeply grateful to each and every one of you for making it possible and I hope I will be able to thank you in person the next time I get home.

They say that you never really appreciate anything until you've lost it, and any old grad can tell you that this is true where the Athenaeum is concerned. To many of us, the ALA was, and still is, a way of life more than anything else. We look back on the friends, the meetings, the arguments, the dances and the bull sessions with a feeling of genuine regret that they are things which we will never do again. Appreciate it while you can because those years are short and I can guarantee that there won't be a one of you who won't wish he could live them over again.

Of all the things for which I am grateful to the Athenaeum, I think the most important thing I learned was the importance of thinking. Had I gained nothing else, the acquisition of this quality would have made those three hectic years worthwhile. A man who lacks the ability to think for himself is as useless as a dead toad, while the thinking man has all the powers of the universe at his command. If this has not been made clear to you so far, then you have missed one of the most valuable lessons the Athenaeum has to offer: something which has for years placed the Athenaeum man head and shoulders above his intellectual contemporaries.

If it seems strange that I should mention the development of the intellect before the consideration of friendship, let me say that it has been intentional. I have always wondered why some people feel compelled to verbally eulogize a quality which, in its essence, is understood rather than talked about. To make a point of declaring friendship is to cheapen it, for men's emotions are very rarely put into words successfully.

The two qualities I have mentioned, when properly perpetuated, are a tradition in themselves and can be very easily turned into the familiar triangle. Naturally, each man's triangle will be a little bit different from the others, but the differences will only be superficial and will leave room for the individual to be appreciated as something separate, yet still linked to the group which has taught him to think as he does.

Leaving you with that, I shall now make an attempt to ward off what I feel sure will be a vicious attack on my character on the part of Mr. Colgan.[4] I ran into him and "Dangerous Dave" Ethridge last week somewhere in the vicinity of the Indian Mound Saloon in Fort Walton Beach.

Hearing a voice cry "Hunto," I felt sure that it could be nothing else but a delusion brought on by lack of sleep and continued on my way to do battle with the proprietor of a motor scooter garage which has become a permanent resting place for my only means of transportation. Then, hearing the cry again, I turned slowly around and found myself staring at what appeared to be a bum in need of a drink. Here stood Ethridge, with at least eighteen days growth of scraggly beard on his face, and dressed like a man who had stolen his clothes off of a dead Cuban beachcomber.

After exchanging pleasantries, we were soon joined by Mr. Colgan, wearing exactly the same clothes he had on when I first laid eyes on him back in his sophomore days. It was obvious that the two had been drinking steadily for several days and I felt that my reputation would be in grave danger if I were spotted in their company.

I know that, even if I were to relate the whole story of their visit, Mr. Colgan would warp it to his own glorification, so I'll establish a few facts before he gets a chance to say anything.

First, I have been ill for months with a strange tropical disease which causes me to have frequent attacks of sleeping sickness. Anything he says to the contrary will be a definite untruth.

Second, recognizing the fact that there may be some truth in anything he says about my not leading the life of a good airman, let me simply say that there are extenuating circumstances which he may not have understood.

Third, knowing that they would undoubtedly become involved in some trouble, I felt it necessary to go with them to Panama City and see that nothing happened. As it turned out, I barely escaped having Spanish Fly put in my beer and avoided what would have been a virtual disaster. If it is implied that my conduct was anything but exemplary, that too will be an untruth. The fact of the matter is that Ethridge was thrown out of a respectable bar for using profane language and that Colgan was intent on destroying every known truth. Both posed as soldiers of fortune and barely missed being rolled for all they were worth. Unfortunately, I became ill shortly after midnight and fell asleep; whereupon they robbed me of most of my money and otherwise treated me rudely.

4. Bob Colgan was a high school friend of Thompson's; Dave Ethridge was the son of Louisville *Courier-Journal* editor Mark Ethridge. They both visited Thompson in Fort Walton Beach.

In a more serious vein, if you happen to find yourselves in the neighborhood of Fort Walton anytime in the near future, give me a call at either the town newspaper or the base and I'll come in and give you a ride on my motor scooter. This area really isn't a bad place to spend a few days (or the whole summer for that matter) and I'll do my best to arrange for hospitality.

Before I go, let me thank you again and say that I'm looking forward to coming back to a meeting the next time I get to Louisville.

> Until then, I remain,
> very sincerely,
> Hunter S. Thompson

TO VIRGINIA THOMPSON:

Davison Thompson, then a senior at Louisville Male High School, came to visit his older brother with the intent of spending a weekend in Florida. Instead they drove to New Orleans for a night of fun in the French Quarter with Henry "Ike" Eichelburger, who was studying at Tulane University.

> April 11, 1957
> Eglin AFB
> Fort Walton Beach, Florida

Dear Mom,

Leaving the usual apologies unspoken but understood, I'll get on with the letter—which should be informative but short.

First, Davison arrived on schedule last Saturday and we had what I considered to be a very enjoyable weekend. I imagine that he has already informed you that we spent most of our time either on the road or in the French Quarter of New Orleans, so this revelation shouldn't come as too much of a shock to you. It was a spur of the moment decision, born of the realization that there was absolutely nothing for us to do in this vicinity except brave pneumonia and chills by a little beachcombing.

After warning him several times of the considerable travel and expense involved with such a trip, we roared off in "my car" at about 5:00 pm on Saturday. We arrived at Eichelburger's apartment at about midnight and departed immediately for the Quarter. In the short space of about six hours, I tried to give him as comprehensive a tour as possible on our limited funds, having a fine time in the process. After getting to bed at about 6:00 am, we awoke around noon, had an excellent meal in one of the Tulane restaurants, and spent several hours shooting the bull with Ike—who really enjoyed seeing Davison in this completely unexpected manner.

Realizing that he had to catch a bus out of Pensacola at 2:00 am Sunday, we spent the afternoon at a jazz concert and set out for "home" at about 7:00. The trip back was somewhat less pleasant than the one on the day before, due to the fatigue which had begun to get the best of both of us—especially Davison, who I would imagine is a little new at the game.

After a groggy and vaguely recalled farewell, I retired to the bed at about 4:30 and would assume that he got into Tallahassee at about 7:30 or 8:00 am.

Before I forget: when he arrives I wish you would surreptitiously find out if he made off with my green, crewneck sweater. I first noticed its absence this morning and came within minutes of reporting it to the Air Police as a malicious theft. Then I recalled the "few" articles I have made off with at one time or another—whether they were Davison's or not is a moot question—and thought it would be best to find out if he had returned the favor and quietly appropriated my prize sweater. Don't let him know that the loss has shaken me, but please inform me if he has it or not.

On the subject of my status—I had another big storm about an article I wrote about Arthur Godfrey, who is—unfortunately—a personal friend of Colonel Evans', and may return to the Comm Sq at any time. This is a matter of little importance, as I have already volunteered for overseas and will turn my whole attention to the *Playground News*, making the same amount of money and escaping this senseless, maddening censorship which has all but taken the enjoyment out of working on the *Courier*. Right now, the situation is flexible, but I'll let you know when anything definite develops.

As for Easter, I'll probably spend it with Ike in New Orleans—with an eye to getting home either for the Derby or when the colleges adjourn for the summer.

> Until then, I remain,
> Hunter

TO THE CHAMBER MUSIC SOCIETY:

Whenever Thompson received an overdue bill notice he would write back a note either trying to finagle his way out of the debt or venting his rage.

> May 3, 1957
> Eglin AFB, Florida

Chamber Music Society
71 Fifth Avenue
New York 3, New York

Gentlemen,

I was extremely embarrassed by a "final notice before suit" which I received from your office yesterday. My shame was manifest as I read and re-read the lines which proclaimed to all the world that I, a gentleman of impeccable honor and unimpeachable integrity, have been slandered and branded in this crude manner by a dark plot which threatens my very reputation and standing in this lovely community.

This astounding implication that my professional honesty is in question has thrown me into a state of extreme mental anguish and has caused my guardian to initiate proceedings to place me once again in the narcotics sanitarium which was my home for the last five horrible years.

Should this come about, the responsibility for the disaster would settle heavily on your shoulders—for sending me this hideous little notice and putting me in the class with that lowest and most odious of all humans— the welcher.

Let me say in a final desperate plea—that any debt of mine shall be paid. Even though I am destitute to the point that I must accept meals and lodging from charity; that burning zeal and great dedication which carried me through "the cure" will once more come to my aid in this hour of urgency to cleanse me of this terrifying taint of debt and restore me to my former eminence. Even if I must pawn my syringe, I will see to it that this wretched debt is cleared immediately.

Most cordially,
Hunter S. Thompson
Command Courier
Eglin AFB, Fla.

TO KAY MENYERS:

Despite his sarcastic tone, Thompson was truly upset that Menyers, a Louisville girlfriend, had failed to answer his most recent love letter.

May 11, 1957
Eglin AFB
Fort Walton Beach, Florida

FRAILTY, THY NAME IS WOMAN!

Dear Frailty,

After hovering for two months in a state of hopeful desperation, I have all but given up the ghost. The hideous realization that you have cast me aside like a dead toad has split my heart asunder. My spirit has plunged into a bottomless pit of despair.

Words cannot describe this great ache which permeates my entire being and threatens to drive me crazy with grief. For weeks I raced eagerly to my mailbox twice each day, oozing with hope that I might find a letter from you. But my waiting has been in vain and my hopes have decayed with the passing of time. How could you have done it to me?

The throbbing pain of this ghastly rejection had begun to subside last week when I was set upon by a pack of lesbians and bludgeoned half to death. As a result of these two disasters, my faith in women has been set back an untold number of years and my once-cheerful disposition has become as foul as rancid butter. Oh cruel woman that you are, you have ruptured my soul and I know that I shall never smile again.

> Tearfully,
> Hunty

TO CHAPLAIN (LIEUTENANT COLONEL) ROBERT RUTAN:

While writing for the Command Courier *and* Playground News *Thompson discovered the acerbic H. L. Mencken. Devouring the collected works of the arch commentator, Thompson began raging against the American Puritanical tradition in the style of "the sage of Baltimore."*

> June 6, 1957
> Eglin AFB
> Fort Walton Beach, Florida

Chaplain (Lt. Col.) Robert Rutan
Headquarters, Air Proving Ground Command

Chaplain,

Naturally, I cannot be expected to dignify your wild accusations [of drunkenness] of June 4 with a defense of any type. However, I located the following quotation in "the Fourth Book of Mencken" last night and felt that it may be of some interest to you: my most abject apologies if I'm wrong.

"The theory that the clergy belong to a class of educated men, once well supported in fact, has persisted into our own time, though it has not been true for nearly a century. Even Protestants are commonly willing to admit that Catholic priests are what they call highly educated men. They are, of course, nothing of the sort. Nine-tenths of the knowledge they are stuffed with is bogus, and they have very little grounding in what is really true. Since *The Origin of the Species*, clergymen have constituted a special class of uneducated persons. Catholic and Protestant alike.

If they happen to be naturally smart fellows, they may pick up a good deal of worldly wisdom, but even that is not common. The average clergyman is a kind of intellectual eunuch, comparable to a pedagogue, a Rotarian, or an editorial writer."

—H. L. Mencken—

In hopes that you may find as much pleasure in Mencken's wit as I have,
I remain,
most cordially,
Hunter Stockton Thompson

TO L. J. DALE, NATIONAL ASSOCIATION OF SCHOOLS AND PUBLISHERS, INC.:

Thompson made a habit of joining book and record clubs, then not paying his bill. This time a collection agency tracked him down with a threat of legal action. Deciding to cough up the money owed the Book of the Month Club, Thompson wrote the collection agency this Menckenesque riposte.

June 26, 1957
Eglin AFB
Fort Walton Beach, Florida

L. J. Dale
N.A.O.S.A.P.I.
A Private Collecting Agency
Wilmington, Delaware

Mr. Dale,

Although a wild and lengthy court battle might have proved stimulating indeed, I decided after lengthy consultation with my compatriots that it might be best to clear this debt (840-865-S) and go on to greener fields. And so, by by-passing the opportunity to spice my dull existence with a violent legal struggle, I am enclosing a money order for $13.58, hoping that it will put an end to this stream of crude letters which it has been my privilege to receive from your hallowed halls.

Before closing, allow me to say that your letters have shown neither originality nor wit. They have convinced me that the collecting business is a haven for dullards and habitual misers, devoid of humor and incapable of interesting correspondence. You have my most sincere condolences.

We cannot, however, escape the obvious fact that you have accomplished your intended purpose—that of prying $13.58 out of these grasping hands by fair means or foul. Congratulations.

Most cordially,
Hunter S. Thompson
Command Courier
3201 AB Wing
Eglin AFB, Fla.

TO SUSAN HASELDEN:

Thompson had met Haselden when both were in junior high school. Because of his reputation as a "thug," Haselden's parents forbade her to see him, so they carried on a passionate, secret dalliance. This is the first of many letters in which Thompson declares himself "the new F. S. Fitzgerald."

> June 29, 1957
> Eglin AFB
> Fort Walton Beach, Florida

Dear Susan,

This will be short, due to the fact that I have stopped short in the midst of a creative seizure in order to write it. After beating out a few lines, I shall return to my story, which I am counting on to bring me fame, fortune, and recognition as the new F. S. Fitzgerald. Another explanation—you have my apology for typing a personal letter. I have typed all my letters, personal or otherwise, for the past year—primarily because it's easier and not as messy.

The main reason I'm writing is to inform you that I am horribly frustrated because I have no pools and no one to swim with me at night—at least no one worth a damn. And more than that, I have too much work to do and nothing but idiots to talk to. All in all; I am sad, Susan, sad. You and Owl Creek[5] spoiled me and now I am not satisfied with my beautiful Gulf.

Usually I find that every letter I write a girl becomes community property almost immediately. Now, starting with my next letter, I intend to make them either completely impersonal or incredibly lewd. In the former case, I won't care who sees them, and in the latter, I feel sure that they will be kept under lock and key or burned immediately. In your case however, I'm not sure that you wouldn't get a kick out of receiving a steady stream of lewd letters—pleasantly lewd ones, of course.

Another thing—I am literally covered from head to toe with insect bites of some sort. I feel sure that it must have been the grass on that damn golf course, where you detained me. Whenever I think about it, I first kick myself and then wonder what sort of explanation you conjured up upon entering the house at that hour in a state of apparent disarray. Naturally, no one will believe that we were hunting for night crawlers. Yes, I always kick myself when I walk right past a really delightful night crawler without realizing that he's there. You know how it is though; you can't always see them from the surface. Next time, however, I will look more carefully. [...]

---

5. Owl Creek was a country club in Anchorage, a Louisville suburb, where Thompson and Haselden used to "sneak swim" on sultry evenings.

Things here are as prosaic as ever, the same blood-curdling routine week after week, nothing but idiots everywhere, uniforms, foul food, and ugly women. Just as soon as I sell a novel or two, I will buy a plot of land and build a small hut and a large swimming pool on it. Then I will fence the whole thing off and operate a small scale nudist colony where I can have nightly orgies and not be bothered by the world and its idiots. Maybe I'll let you come and handle my correspondence. Until then, or until I hear from you, I remain;

> Smiling,
> Hunty

TO SUSAN HASELDEN:

Thompson's fondness for Fitzgerald is evident again in both statement and style.

> July 13, 1957
> Eglin AFB
> Fort Walton Beach, Florida

OPEN LETTER TO A FALLEN WOMAN

Dear Fallen,

If your thighs ever become as hard as a clipboard, I don't think you'll ever have to worry about men again—old men, little boys, or in-betweens. Admittedly, there is something novel about dating a girl with a thigh as hard as a clipboard, but it's just not the type of thing too many people would go for. However, I'd probably still let you handle my correspondence.

Another thing; I was taken aback by your implication that you would be a grandmother before I become the new Fitzgerald (ref: "I'll show them—my letters—to my grandchildren when you become the new Fitzgerald.") Actually, I am already the new Fitzgerald: I just haven't been recognized yet.

As for the color of this ink and the frequent mistakes in the use (or misuse) of this machine, I am sick. The red ink matches the color of my eyes—the same color they've been since the night of July third, the jumping off date for the "great orgy." It is now 1:30 pm on Saturday afternoon. That would seem to make about nine or ten days. Actually, the high point came on July fifth, when I made an unfortunate attempt to convert a goodly portion of Tower Beach into a nudist colony. (This letter may ramble and jump. I'm trying to clear my mind so I can get on with this story I must finish by Monday morning.) I spent $15 last night and didn't even begin paying for my drinks until 10:00 p.m. All I can remember now is buying a huge round of drinks for a raucous group at the Indian Mound Saloon. The Indian Mound is the only bar in town which is allowed to stay open all night. Thusly, a savage and unnatural orgy occurs almost every 24 hours within its confines. Last night was no different. Some young thing in gauze shorts did the "dog hunch" with three winos from New York. It was weird. I have spent the past ten days with a pilot who never seems to work. I manage to get something done occasionally, making my deadlines and such, but most of the time has been spent at a beach house belonging to some degenerate woman from D'mapolis, Alabama. I was over there yesterday afternoon and suddenly the house was full of degenerate people from D'mapolis, Alabama. Some man ripped the commode out of the floor and took it out to his car where he passed out with it. His wife, meanwhile, whiled the hours away by tearing live crabs limb from limb. Some drunken fool smashed his boat into the pier at Sea Gull and almost killed me. As it was, I dropped my drink and had four heart flutters. Although I have dedicated myself to the task of completing this story before Monday morning, I have a feeling in my womb that I will not get much done tonight. Banks (the pilot)[6] will call any minute and weaken me with proposals of a lustful and lecherous nature. Then too, I can't afford to buy dinner and I can see no alternative but to eat with the degenerates from D'mapolis again. They eat well, but very rarely. I woke up this morning, totally unclothed, on a sand dune overlooking a semi-crowded beach. Seeing Banks in the same condition, I remembered that we had come out for a pre-dawn swim in the phosphorus-filled water. Whenever you move around in the water, your whole body lights up and flashes all around. Not your body. It's really the phosphorus in the water, but I like to think it's a weird omen from the crabs—hailing me as the new Messiah. Banks was in a rage this morning when he learned that he had not been named the Aga Kahn. I had my usual "morning after" breakfast of filleted snapper and tomato juice, while Banks gave the waitress a hard time for not calling him the new Aga Kahn. These damn waitresses always laugh when I order snapper for breakfast ("Pardon me for laughing, but it just sounds funny") but they usually stop when I smack 'em in the head once or twice.

Last weekend was a nightmare. I appeared at high noon on a crowded beach, wearing only flippers and a pair of diving goggles. Somewhere in the melee, my trunks had become lost. Urged on by my drunken and malicious companions, I virtually cleared the beach in five minutes. I won't go into this thing much further, because it becomes indecent when the details are revealed. I can still see that old woman's face as I raced over the

6. Banks Shepherd was the base contracting officer.

dune and came straight for her. Fortunately, I wore goggles. The cry of the day was: "Let's have an orgy!" I can imagine the uproar in the Chamber of Commerce if the incident was reported. "Visit Fort Walton Beach, the playground of northwest Florida, where naked sex fiends roam the beaches 24 hours a day. Bring your families."

Eight hours is a long time. I can hardly believe that we were out for that length of time. It seems like only two or three hours at best. It seems futile, since I'm not the new Aga Kahn either, to apologize to your parents. For some reason, I don't think they would take the apology seriously. However, I will beg your pardon for keeping you out so long; but I can't truthfully say that I had anything but an excellent time. I'm sure that I would enjoy the Gulf much more if you were here to swim with me. Why don't you come down for a few weeks? It would hardly cost you anything at all and a vacation would do you good. It would get you away from all the giggling little boys and grasping old men. Night swimming in the Gulf is fantastic, the sea food is incredible, and the beaches are unbelievable—and even better by moonlight. I guess I could say that it might be a little better than Owl Creek. Of course I think I enjoyed Owl Creek more, but only because I had you to keep me company . . . and to open my ale. I'm serious; I definitely think you should come down here.

I didn't mean to make you feel ignorant. It seems, however, that I must have a knack for that sort of thing. I enjoy it down here, but if it was obvious to you, then I had better learn to be conscious of it and control it. It's not good to make everyone feel ignorant and I really don't know exactly when or where I acquired the knack for it. It's an amazingly effective weapon in the Air Force, especially as most of the people I go around with are older than I am and outrank me considerably, but it gets out of hand every now and then. [. . .]

I went to Tallahassee last weekend and had two dates with a very pretty but mentally deficient girl who would fit into any mold of the "typical old south, Tallahassee girl" type. It convinced me that, except on rare occasions, I cannot enjoy a date with a stupid girl. And believe it or not, the world is full of them. I'd say that 95% of all women are hopelessly stupid.

I was a little puzzled by your comments on my upsetting your recently developed philosophy on men. You were talking one minute about "constantly dragging your mind from Owl Creek to Crescent Hill"—and the next about my "saying a lot of things casually . . ." Then too, what do you mean about "never thinking about the past or the future with men"?

While you're trying to figure out how to re-phrase the above quotes so that I can understand them, you can also decide whether you want to handle my correspondence or participate in the orgies at the "passion pool." I've decided that it must be on a beach, in a grove of pine trees, and with a

fresh-water pool in the back of the cottage. If you decide to be a partici-
pant, let me know so that I can get someone else to handle the correspondence. At any rate, I'm glad to hear that you've already accepted my
invitation. I shall never have more than three guests at a time, so you
should consider yourself fortunate to have secured a place at the top of the
list so early in the game.

Incidentally, I have come up with a definition of heaven. Now don't
tell anyone about this because it sounds downright vulgar; but I think it's
nice. Never mind, I can't bring myself to put it in red and white — maybe
later. Drop me a line soon and tell me when you plan to arrive. Until I
hear from you,

> I remain, grinning owlishly,
> Hunter S. Thompson
> *Command Courier*
> 3201 AB Wing
> Eglin AFB, Fla.

P.S. Please explain to your parents that I didn't make a fallen woman of you.

TO SUSAN HASELDEN:

*Thompson had taken over an abandoned Gulf of Mexico beach house, dub-
bing it Xanadu after Kubla Khan's "stately pleasure dome" in Samuel Tay-
lor Coleridge's poem. The house became the party center for Thompson's
friends at Eglin.*

> August 5, 1957
> Eglin AFB
> Fort Walton Beach, Florida

Dear Susan,

In Xanadu did Kubla Khan a stately pleasure dome decree:
Where Alph, the sacred river, ran through caverns measureless to man
Down to a sunless sea.

And that about sums it up: if you substitute Hunter S. Thompson for
our boy K.K., you'll have the story of my newest venture in a nutshell. Yes,
a beach house — what else? It's terribly passé to live in Florida without a
beach house, and I, a slave of fashion, simply knuckled down and acquired one.

We call it Xanadu, and Alph the sacred river is a sewage ditch running through the Sodom swamp and under the Gomorrah bridge. No one understands just where I got these names, but they're all afraid of appearing ignorant and pretend to be very proud of the tags I've put on our domain and its appendages. We have a ten-foot alligator (maybe six feet) in the Sodom swamp. His name is Bacchus—a name which gives the natives less trouble than the others.

Seriously, I now have a house. It's not really mine but I live there and do my best to whomp up orgies every now and then. It's right on the Mississippi Sound—out over it in fact—and rented for $600 a month in its younger days. When you come down, you'll be amazed at its rustic weirdness. Actually, it's something which only an ale-infested mind would consider livable, but I think it's one of the finest things I've ever seen. I'm sure you'll like it immensely. Just as soon as I get a picture of it, I'll send a print or so your way. Xanadu is something you'd have to see to believe.

My most abject apologies for not having written sooner. I am right in the midst of a horrible deadline rush at the moment and will have to make this letter rather short. Only this morning, I returned from a three-day whomp in New Orleans, the first in several months. After several days of consorting with various deviates of all sorts—queers, lesbians, gigolos, and winos—I am ready to get back on the right track again. Advanced degeneration is something I don't enjoy. Living with it for a while makes me feel a little dirty and puts me in a frame of mind where I regress mentally—back to the days when the mention of "lavender" brought flowers to mind, instead of perverts. I'm afraid I'm a poseur. For all my talk of orgies and the like, I can only take them for a little while, and then I'm ready to go looking for my idealistic bubble to crawl into. Don't tell anyone: I have a reputation to uphold.

Although I couldn't help but get the idea that the "art" of flirting fascinates you no little, you wouldn't even have had to mention it and I would still have gotten the idea. I think you were trying to excite me. Witness these excerpts from your last letter: "I just tugged on my too-little bathing suit . . . have to pull *up* and *down* . . . another end to take care of"—"I am constantly flirting"—"cracked my cerebrum; it must have been the side controlling inhibitions"—"I had an urge . . . for a midnight swim in the Gulf." (That wasn't really your fault: you couldn't have known that we never wear any swimming suits at night.) Maybe I'm wrong after all: here I notice a passage where you say that you've decided to become "the world's most frigid woman." Your confusion is obvious—contradictions galore, references to passion and frigidity in the same breath—other references to nudity, lewd old men, etc.—you obviously need a few restful days in Xanadu.

I must go now, for I have a sacred trust. Write immediately and tell me when you plan to arrive. I must make plans and all that sort of thing. Bring anyone you want (except Charlie[7]); we have plenty of room for all. Until then, I remain,

unsullied—
Hunter

FROM COLONEL W. S. EVANS, CHIEF, OFFICE OF INFORMATION SERVICES, U.S. AIR FORCE:

HEADQUARTERS
AIR PROVING GROUND COMMAND
UNITED STATES AIR FORCE
Eglin Air Force Base, Florida

ADDRESS REPLY
ATTN: Base Staff Personnel Officer
     Personnel Report: A/2C Hunter S. Thompson

23 Aug 57

1. A/2C Hunter S Thompson, AF 15546879, has worked in the Internal Information Section, OIS, for nearly one year. During this time he has done some outstanding sports writing, but ignored APGC-OIS policy.

2. Airman Thompson possesses outstanding talent in writing. He has imagination, good use of English, and can express his thoughts in a manner that makes interesting reading.

3. However, in spite of frequent counseling with explanation of the reasons for the conservative policy on an AF base newspaper, Airman Thompson has consistently written controversial material and leans so strongly to critical editorializing that it was necessary to require that all his writing be thoroughly edited before release.

4. The first article that called attention to the writing noted above was a story very critical of Base Special Services. Others that were stopped before they were printed were pieces that severely criticized Arthur Godfrey and Ted Williams that Airman Thompson extracted from national media releases and added his flair for the innuendo and exaggeration.

5. This Airman has indicated poor judgment from other standpoints by releasing Air Force information to the Playground News himself, with no consideration for other papers in the area, or the fact that only *official* releases, carefully censored by competent OIS staff members, are allowed.

---

7. Charlie was a Louisville man Haselden occasionally dated.

6. In summary, this Airman, although talented, will not be guided by policy or personal advice and guidance. Sometimes his rebel and superior attitude seems to rub off on other airmen staff members. He has little consideration for military bearing or dress and seems to dislike the service and want out as soon as possible.

7. Consequently, it is requested that Airman Thompson be assigned to other duties immediately, and it is recommended that he be earnestly considered under the early release program.

8. It is also requested that Airman Thompson be officially advised that he is to do no writing of any kind for internal or external publication unless such writing is edited by the OIS staff, and that he is not to accept outside employment with any of the local media.

> W. S. EVANS, Colonel, USAF
> Chief, Office of Information
> Services

TO SUSAN HASELDEN:

Thompson was falling in love with Haselden and was extremely jealous that she was still seeing other men.

> August 25, 1957
> Eglin AFB
> Fort Walton Beach, Florida

Dear Susanei,

That extra "e" wasn't unique enough, so I added the "i" for good measure. Natural goodness for me! This damn Charlie is beginning to get me mad. No sooner than I leave, he begins to ply you with exotic gifts and erotic compliments. Just the other night, I had a blood-curdling nightmare in which he was clutching you by your "too small bathing suit" and mouthing savage and unnatural propositions. Seriously; for my sake, you must give the man up immediately! I haven't been able to sleep a wink since I got your last letter.

In a more obtuse vein (what is an obtuse vein/ or what is a vein??), your decision to remain in Louisville completely shattered me. (I say these things seriously, but I'm so used to being sarcastic in letters that everything I write sounds that way.)

I was lying out on a deserted stretch of beach on Santa Rosa Island today, reveling in the knowledge that I was as completely alone as a person can get in the state of Florida, when I decided to amuse myself by conjuring a vision of you rising over a nearby dune, dulcimer in hand, and clad only in a windblown gossamer nightie. Naturally, my overly active imagination developed the scene to such an extent that my concern for your modesty prevents me from describing it further. At any rate, the whole thing made me vividly aware of your absence and genuinely sorry that you found it impossible to spend an idyllic vacation with me at Xanadu. I'm sure that your involvement with this Charlie person is behind it all, and I'm presently working on a scheme to sever the thing once and for all. The very idea of ME being edged by an old lecher—it drives me wild!

I can see that I've strayed into the realm of light sarcasm again, so let me assure you again that I was definitely let down by your last letter. The entire setting down here is one which would fit you perfectly. The difference between life in Louisville and this beachcomber's existence is something you'd have to live to believe. As a matter of fact, if I didn't see the need to return to the rat race for a few years of school, I'd consider staying down here for a while.

This afternoon, for instance (at the time of my vision) I had set out across the Sound from the sun deck of Xanadu on an air mattress. It's about a mile across to the island (and about half that distance across the sand to the Gulf), and it took me about a half-hour to make the trip. It's possible to walk almost two-thirds of the way, until you get to the channel, which is a part of the Intra-Coastal waterway, and then it drops off to about forty feet. The channel is cold as hell, but only about 100 yards wide. The beach on the island, which is really a huge sand dune, is not a beach at all, but a four-foot cliff which drops straight into the channel. This means, of course, that you can stretch out in dead silence on chalk-white sand, look at nothing but sky and hear nothing but wind, and leap into this channel whenever the sun begins to get too hot. All in all, it's an entirely new concept in saltwater bathing: no people, no noise, no breakers—just sun and sand and cold water.

Well, away from this wishful thinking, and back to your desire to be able to distinguish between a lesbian and a prostitute. It may be awhile before we can manage it, but I'll clue you in as soon as I can. Except in the case of bisexuals, it's relatively simple to tell the difference. Fortunately, there aren't many places where large numbers of both species are known to mingle, so as I said, it may be awhile before I can find the time and the place to educate you. Still and all, it should make for an interesting evening.

You continue to amaze me. How you managed to develop all these weird traits and curiosities without my noticing you, I can't understand. I wasn't aware they grew people like you in Louisville and I often find myself wondering just what will become of you. Naturally, if you actively attempt to satisfy all these strange urges and curiosities of yours, you will become cynical and hard. Although that would be one of the most unfortunate of all possible things, I can't quite see how to prevent it.

And now, before you begin to wonder where I got the idea that your head is full of strange longings, let me explain that it is just one of my assumptions. Most of the things I have in mind, you've never told me. Maybe I'm wrong, but I don't think so.

Actually, I don't know you very well at all. Now that I reflect a bit, those few nights at Owl Creek are about all I have to base all these judgments on — those and what I know of your activities since those days when I first watched you in the HJH gym. I can still see you — Susan Haselden, captain of volleyball team number two, flouncing about in a baggy blue gym suit and looking for all the world like a Babe Didrickson[8] in the making. At times (many, many times) I regret my youthful stupidity. Selah.

This about wraps it up for now. I'd like to say that I'll see you soon, but I never know. At the moment, there are discharge rumors in the wind. [Secretary of Defense] Charlie Wilson has decreed that the AF must shed 20,000 men by New Year's Eve, and I'm working desperately to get my name on the list. If all the chips fall right, I'll be burning uniforms within two months or so. The very thought of it makes me almost hysterical with glee. Maybe I can get the Everly Brothers to write me a song.

Then too, I may get up that way on October 6th, when Eglin plays Fort Knox. That too is vague and the truth of the matter is that I have no idea what will happen between now and Christmas. If I don't get a discharge, I'll probably suffer a mental collapse and be confined: a cheering thought, at best.[. . .]

And now — the cat in the wall says that's all;

morbidly,
Hunter Thompson

TO VIRGINIA THOMPSON:

August 28, 1957
Eglin AFB
Fort Walton Beach, Florida

Dear Mom,

The surprisingly rapid approach of autumn, heralded in the *Playground* area by slightly dipping temperatures and the inevitable Labor Day clearance sales on beach supplies, has a peculiar effect on those people whom the headshrinkers tend to bunch together and label "insecure." There is something about the coming of fall that makes people conscious of their own insecurity. Just as squirrels step up the pace in the annual nut-

8. Mildred "Babe" Didrickson Zaharias, tennis champion.

gathering festival, human beings begin to think a little bit more seriously about the prospects of the winter ahead—and most of them show some sort of reaction. Mine, in this case, is writing a letter home.

This is not to say that I would not have written a letter if the weather down here had remained balmy and summer-like—but only to explain the occasion of this letter and let you know that—even though I haven't written for some time—I've been thinking about you.

Right now, the hour is late and many things have happened since I last sent a missive of information winging your way. I am tired and I may have to cut the letter short, but I'll do my best to bring you up to date.

In a nutshell: I am now back in the Communications Squadron and there is a possibility that I may get out of the Air Force before Christmas. I am still working for the *Playground News* and, for the past two months, I've led an almost incredible life—for an enlisted man in the AF. If the discharge does become reality, I have been offered a job with a local advertising firm—if I decide to stay down here for awhile and decide to leave the *Playground News*. And, Campbell[9] says he can get me a job on the *Atlanta Constitution*.

Naturally, all this hinges on the all-important discharge.

As you may have read, Charlie Wilson has decreed that the AF must shed 21,900 men by December 31. If there is any reason why I shouldn't be among this group, no one on this base seems to be able to find it. After an interesting and sometimes amusing two-year experiment, the AF and I have come to the joint decision that we were not made for each other. Based on the impressive array of facts, circumstances, and findings, this decision has been reached with a minimum of active malice on either of our parts and is supported by the willing testimony of all those who know us both.

My present position as a radio repairman is, of course, ridiculous and cannot possibly last very long. Although up to now the AF has refused to change my AFSC [Air Force Security Classification] (the primary reason for my return to the radio shop) I have good reason to believe that they will change it soon. My dangerous lack of knowledge concerning the equipment will undoubtedly lead to some change. It is then that the discharge will become a probability, rather than a possibility.

I will keep you posted more frequently than I have in the past month or so. [. . .]

I wish you would ask Memo to write more often—she is the only one in the family (Jim excluded) who does not enclose some sort of bill in her letters.[10] I'd like to know how both she and Jim are getting along and how Jim

---

9. Lieutenant Colonel Frank Campbell was Thompson's mentor at Eglin Air Force Base in charge of the Office of Information Services. A former *Boston Globe* reporter, he was responsible for Thompson's work at the *Command Courier*.

10. Memo was Thompson's maternal grandmother, Lucille Ray. Jim was his youngest brother.

fared at the KMI camp. Since you people stopped writing several weeks ago, I've sort of lost touch. [. . .]

As for other incidentals, my social life has been made far more pleasant by the acquisition of Xanadu and an attachment to a young lass named Sally Williams. The attachment has led to several rather strained and hectic situations—due to the fact that Sally is a Colonel's daughter and the mother of a four year old boy. If I get my discharge, she may come to stay with me for a while at Xanadu. It will definitely be different.

As you can see, several months in the social whirl of this moraless community have made me slightly decadent. Although not without an element of danger, it has been an interesting experience. I may have to ask you to send me some of my money to register for school next week. Although they aren't offering many interesting courses next fall, I will probably end up with one called "International Politics." If I can't find another one of interest, I will take piano lessons.

As a parting note—I suggest that you get hold of a book called *The Outsider* by Colin Wilson. I had intended to go into a detailed explanation of what I have found out about myself in the past year or so, but find that I am too tired. However, after reading that book, you may come closer to understanding just what lies ahead for your Hunter-named son. I had just begun to doubt some of my strongest convictions when I stumbled upon that book. But rather than being wrong, I think that I just don't express my rightness correctly. But enough—more on this later. Write if you find the time and let me know what you plan to do in the way of occupation. LOVE.

Hunter

TO KRAIG JUENGER:

Thompson had recently begun a passionate affair with Juenger, a former Miss Illinois fifteen years his senior. She was separated from her husband at the time.

October 17, 1957
Eglin AFB
Fort Walton Beach, Florida

Dear Kraig,

For the second Monday night in succession, I find myself settling nervously into my chair at the *Playground News* sports desk, with absolutely nothing done for this week's edition, hundreds of stories to write—and beginning a letter to Kraig. Ah weakness: thy name is Hunter.

As you predicted, I found your letter when I arrived tonight. I've already read it three times and I'll probably chalk up number four in a matter of minutes. Between that pianist in Washington last weekend, your telephone call, and this letter, I'm going to play hell getting anything at all done either tonight or tomorrow.

And, on top of everything else, I talked to one of the "discharge honchos" today, and received the assurance that immediate steps would be taken to root me out of the ranks at once. My new technique—that of expounding at length on my religious and political beliefs—worked like a charm. When I'd finished, he concluded with this remark:

"I don't know exactly what it is about you, Thompson, and I didn't understand much of what you said; but I can see at a glance that there's not much sense in trying to make you either act or think like an airman should. I'll let you know within two days—twenty-four hours, if possible—how soon you can be discharged."

And that's it in a nutshell. I don't know why I tend to make it sound humorous, because there's very little humor in it at all. It demonstrates, probably more clearly than any other single incident in my life—just how far I've strayed from the popular ideologies of our time. To go back—or to hesitate—would be unthinkable. And yet, in going on, I can see that I shall be permanently apart from all but a small and lonely percentage of the human race, in all but the most superficial respects. But, after publicly embracing a philosophy to gain a desirable but admittedly superficial end, I could hardly live with myself for any length of time if I were to turn my back on that philosophy after it had served my purpose.

But I don't propose to bore you with this sort of thing at this stage of the game. It merely serves as a prelude to what I'm about to undertake—a short explanation of why there are "things I would like to say, but haven't."

In short, Kraig, I don't think you really have any idea who Hunter S. Thompson is when he drops the role of court jester. And, for that reason, I'm afraid I'd be building you up for another fall if I were frank enough to tell you how I feel about you. I don't mean to say that I'm egotistical enough to believe that I have the power to make you feel one way or another about me. But on the other hand; if I were to attempt that, as I'd like to—and succeed—I'm not quite sure that either one of us would be any better off. And, rather than pursue any course of action which might eventually hurt you, I'd rather not do anything at all.

But let me tell you, before I leave this sombre subject, a little about myself: a very little—but enough.

First, I do not live from orgy to orgy, as I might have made you believe. I drink much less than most people think, and I think much more than most people would believe. I am quite sincere about some of the things which people take very lightly, and almost insultingly unconcerned about some of the things which people take most seriously. In short, I am basically antisocial: certainly not to an alarming degree, but just more so than I appear to be.

And finally, the more I try to explain myself, the more apparent it becomes that I'm not doing a very good job of it. That's why I wish, in a way, that we were not this far apart. It would be much easier to sit on a blanket on a beach and talk. I've always thought that letters were a very poor medium to convey any sort of serious meaning, and this effort only confirms my suspicions. I do it very rarely, and I'm not likely to try again for some time. I hope, even though I haven't done a very good job, that, if nothing else, I've gotten across to you that there's something more to old Cuubley than the part of him which shows above the water-line.

But I think anything else I can say on that subject would be useless. Despite anything I might say, the truth of the matter is that I think about you constantly. I need neither songs nor radios to remind me of last Thursday and Friday nights, and I can think of very few things I'd rather do than spend a long string of nights with you on that stretch of beach.

I think I've already said too much, but I hardly think that it surprised you at all. And then too, as long as I feel this way, it probably won't be very long until I drop in on you. But don't be afraid: it won't be for a while, and I'll warn you beforehand—probably.

Don't let this letter get you down. I won't do it again; I promise. Hoping to see you soon, I remain, somewhat shaken, but still grinning . . . Hunty

TO JOE BELL:

Throughout his early twenties Thompson considered novelist Ayn Rand a kindred spirit. He often lent copies of her books to friends.

> October 24, 1957
> Eglin AFB
> Fort Walton Beach, Florida

Dear Joe,

Two reasons for writing this: one, to let you know that I've finished *The Fountainhead,* and two, to tell you that Ayn Rand's new book is called *Atlas Shrugged.* I thought you might be interested.

To say what I thought of *The Fountainhead* would take me more pages than I like to think I'd stoop to boring someone with. I think it's enough to say that I think it's everything you said it was and more. Naturally, I intend to read *Atlas Shrugged.* If it's half as good as Rand's first effort, I won't be disappointed.

You might also be interested to know, as I was, that she has never married. Maybe she has the courage of her convictions, or maybe it's something else. I don't know—and I doubt that it matters a great deal to her whether I care or not.

To discuss *The Fountainhead* would be useless—even more so with a person who understands it than with one who doesn't. It is nothing more or less than a re-affirmation of a principle, a principle so vital, so absolutely timeless, and so completely personal, that to drag it down to the level of a conversation piece would serve no purpose but to cheapen it. I can understand your mis-directed enthusiasm in showing the book to someone like O'Dea,[11] but I think you might just as well have tried mixing bourbon and Coca-Cola to make a mint julep. One and zero doesn't make two.

Although I don't feel that it's at all necessary to tell you how I feel about the principle of individuality, I know that I'm going to have to spend the rest of my life expressing it one way or another, and I think that I'll accomplish more by expressing it on the keys of a typewriter than by letting it express itself in sudden outbursts of frustrated violence. I don't mean to say that I'm about to state my credo here on this page, but merely to affirm, sincerely for the first time in my life, my belief in man as an individual and independent entity. Certainly not independence in the everyday sense of the word, but pertaining to a freedom and mobility of thought that few people are able—or even have the courage—to achieve.

Even Rand, who can make it live and breathe between two paper covers, seems to have trouble putting this certain spirit or attitude into words, so I don't think that I, at an age where this thing is just beginning to slip into the realm of reality, should offer any excuses for not being able to express it in the everyday language of words. That will come later.

And I can see your dilemma—in wanting to believe in this thing, yet not being able to find a way to believe in it and eat too. Keep in mind that the ability to create is an integral part of the makeup of man. If a lack is encountered, it lies not in the ability, but in the scope of perception of one's own creative ability.

With that, I leave you to your efforts on the assembly line. I don't write many letters like this, so don't be afraid to drop me a line.

Cheerio . . .

Hunter

TO LARRY CALLEN:

In late October Thompson learned that he would be given an honorable discharge from the U.S. Air Force. He was ecstatic at the prospect of beginning

11. Patrick O'Dea was a Louisville dilettante and social figure who introduced Thompson to a number of women.

his civilian career as a journalist, as he wrote to Callen, who had been editor of the Command Courier *when Thompson arrived at Eglin and was now assigned to an Air Force post in Iceland.*

October 30, 1957
Eglin AFB
Fort Walton Beach, Florida

Dear Larry,

By the time you get this letter, there will be no "H. S. Thompson" listed on the payroll of the nation's bird division. Colonel Campbell called me at the PGN [*Playground News*] office this morning that the Comm Sq sergeant had a message for me—to report for my discharge physical tomorrow at 7:15.

And so, after two years of "arduous service," the walking anomaly that is HST has escaped into the jungle of insecurity called civilian life. Yes . . . it's an honorable.

Surprised? You aren't alone. A little disappointed? You still aren't alone. At any rate, I knew you'd be interested.

You'll also be interested to know that I recently finished reading *The Fountainhead*. To understand something of the philosophy I'm now flirting with, all you have to do is, first, consider my overall attitude—then imagine how it was affected by reading *The Outsider* and *The Fountainhead* one right after the other.

I'm not exactly certain that this is the most desirable kind of attitude to carry back to "civilization" with me, but I *am* sure that I'll never be able to sincerely believe in anything until I'm convinced beyond a shadow of a doubt that god doesn't live in the mirror.

They say that "he who flies highest, falls farthest"—and who am I to argue? But we can't forget that "he who doesn't flap his wings, never flies at all." And with that, I'll stop trying to convince myself that I can't fail: how dull the whole thing would be if that were true.

If you get the time, drop me a line at the *Playground News* and tell me a little about what you've done since your arrival in the far, frozen north. I probably won't be at the *Playground News* very long, so make it soon, if you make it at all.

As for some of the incidentals down this way: the purge of the *Command Courier* spts ed will probably interest you most. Yes, they finally got me. Fred [Fulkerson] took over and is doing surprisingly well.

And that last sentence recalls the letter I got from that captain at AFPS, in which he said that my work for the *ComCourier* was "enviable" . . . which also recalls your comment on Barrie French—something about damning with faint praise . . . which also makes my point.

Naturally, I continued with the *Playground News*, although my dual life was made considerably rougher by a master sergeant in the radio shop, who did his best to do me in. In the end, though, it was he who almost tearfully pleaded with the classification board to delete my radio AFSC—thus making me eligible for an early out.

For the past month, I've been the "official statistician" for the football team, working one or two days a week, living off base, and making trips to Denver, Louisville, and Washington, D.C. for games.

I don't mean to gloat, but I can't help it today. It's almost too much to believe—but don't let me put words in your mouth.

I'm running out of paper, so I'll cut this short. Drop me a line when you can and look for me in the first breadline you see when you get back. Until then, I remain, your friend. . . . Hunty

TO KRAIG JUENGER:

While enjoying the clever way he finagled an honorable discharge out of the Air Force, Thompson was considering moving to St. Louis to work for the Post-Dispatch *or the* Globe *in order to be near Juenger.*

> November 4, 1957
> Eglin AFB
> Fort Walton Beach, Florida

Dear Kraig,

First and by all means, foremost . . . : the case of THOMPSON VS THE USAF has come to a boiling, bubbling climax. The mule train of military bureaucracy, with the help of a few expertly placed jolts of high-detergent oil, has been rolling in high gear for the past two weeks and, believe it or not, has finally come to a logical conclusion: that being that "a square peg cannot exist in a round hole."

And so, with that truism staring him straight in the eye, old Uncle AF has decided to arrange a suitable burial for AIRMAN Thompson. Sadly enough, the burial will have to be accomplished without the usual fanfare—trumpets, sobbing lovers, and that sort of thing—and the ceremony will be brief and without melodrama of any description. It will nonetheless be final—and wild.

There will be a few tears—and some sighs of relief. There will be some angry, dumbfounded protest—and some shrugging of shoulders. A military manner will prevail where pandemonium used to exist. The sports pages of the *Command Courier* will once again appeal to the military mind.

There will be no "Scoop" Thompson serving vodka-flavored coffee in the Eglin AFB fieldhouse—nor any Cuubley Cohn[12] to grace the Sports Section of the *Playground News*. In short, a vicious, dangerous, radical individualist has finally gone the way of Marshall Zukov: purged—rooted from the ranks—and discharged.

Yes Kraig . . . Cuubley finally made the grade. The "Thompson plan for moral redemption" has met the final, acid test. It took a few shots in the dark, a few master strokes, and no little luck—Thompson will shed his mantle of shame and emerge into the light once again—as a civilian. And for you and anyone else who might have underestimated the "Thompson touch"—it's honorable as hell. A miracle, possibly: but a reality, nonetheless.

After reading your letter this morning, I thought you'd be expecting some word on the above subject, but even I had no idea it would be this soon—or this perfect. Needless to say, I'd like nothing better than to wind up my stay in Florida with a few pleasant hours on the beach with you; but I'm afraid you'll have to hurry if you don't want to miss me.

Naturally, if you intend to come down anytime soon, I'll postpone my departure for a few days and stay around to harass Rosan.[13] Nevertheless, I intend to be home for Thanksgiving.

Just let me know when you intend to get here, and I'll make my plans then and let you know. Incidentally, I'm also a little curious as to why you're coming to this wretched wasteland—if you'll pardon my asking.

Although I'd enjoy a night on a deserted beach, any disappointment I might suffer in missing it will be definitely dulled by the thought of my imminent departure from this worthless region. I don't imagine I'll find it too difficult to make my way over to St. Louis (and Collinsville) sometime in the near future. As a matter of fact, I'll have two reasons for heading over that way: you and the possibility of a job on the *Post-Dispatch*—or the *Globe*. At any rate, it shouldn't be too long before I get there.

I enjoyed your letter, but there are several things you mentioned which I think should be straightened out post haste.

In the first place, you know as well as I do that I'm far from "insultingly unconcerned" about Kraig. You also know you haven't "made a fool of yourself" and that I've hardly cracked a smile—much less laughed—about this situation, since the first time I saw you. And if I'd had a "I have nothing to lose" attitude about it, you'd have known it by now.

And finally: you only prove what I said about your "not knowing me very well" by presuming that I might be hurt by any development or group

---

12. Thompson now used this nom de plume at *Playground News*, in addition to Thorne Stockton.
13. Richard Rosan was an ROTC from Syracuse Journalism School who was in charge of laying out the *Command Courier*. Thompson loathed him.

of developments in this situation. You let me worry about my reasons for caring about you, and you concentrate on doing what you think you should do about your various entanglements. God takes care of fools and drunks—and Cuubley takes care of himself.

So, until I see you—whether it be in Collinsville or on the white sands of the miracle strip—it's . . . Cheerio.

Hunter

FROM HUNTER S. THOMPSON, NEWS RELEASE:

As his parting salvo at the Air Force, Thompson wrote his own news release and had it printed in the Command Courier. *It caused quite a stir.*

NEWS RELEASE, AIR PROVING GROUND COMMAND, EGLIN AIR FORCE BASE, FLORIDA

EGLIN AFB, FLORIDA (November 8)--S/Sgt. Manmountain Dense, a novice Air Policeman, was severely injured here today when a wine bottle exploded inside the AP gatehouse at the west entrance to the base. Dense was incoherent for several hours after the disaster, but managed to make a statement which led investigators to believe the bottle was hurled from a speeding car which approached the gatehouse on the wrong side of the road, coming from the general direction of the SEPARATION CENTER.

Further investigation revealed that, only minutes before the incident at the gatehouse, a reportedly "fanatical" airman had received his separation papers and was rumored to have set out in the direction of the gatehouse at a high speed in a muffler-less car with no brakes. An immediate search was begun for Hunter S. Thompson, one-time sports editor of the base newspaper and well-known "morale problem." Thompson was known to have a sometimes overpowering affinity for wine and was described by a recent arrival in the base sanatorium as "just the type of bastard who would do a thing like that."

An apparently uncontrollable iconoclast, Thompson was discharged today after one of the most hectic and

unusual Air Force careers in recent history. According to Captain Munnington Thurd, who was relieved of
his duties as base classification officer yesterday
and admitted to the neuropsychological section of the
base hospital, Thompson was "totally unclassifiable"
and "one of the most savage and unnatural airmen I've
ever come up against."

"I'll never understand how he got this discharge,"
Thurd went on to say. "I almost had a stroke yesterday when I heard he was being given an honorable
discharge. It's terrifying—simply terrifying."

And then Thurd sank into a delirium.

TO LIEUTENANT COLONEL FRANK CAMPBELL:

*After Thompson left Eglin, he initiated a lively correspondence from
Louisville with Campbell that would last for the next three years. Campbell
often asked "Airman Thompson" how he was making out in the world of
"cutthroat journalism."*

November 29, 1957
Louisville, Kentucky

Lt. Col. Frank Campbell
723 Osceola Circle—Capeheart
Eglin AFB, Fla.

Good Morning . . .

And it is a good morning indeed: for I have a job—and a good one at that.
Yes, the child prodigy has talked himself into it up to his neck this time: for,
on the ninth day of December, I take over as the sports editor of the Jersey
Shore, Pennsylvania, *Herald*—a morning daily serving Jersey Shore, Lock
Haven, and Williamsport, with a combined population of 100,000 or so.
Naturally, I have no idea how I'm going to manage it. I've never even worked
on a daily, you know, and it should be interesting, if nothing else.

But the real fine thing about this is that I got it without pulling strings or
begging for aid. I had already accepted a job on the Seymour, Indiana, *Tribune*, as wire editor, when the Pennsylvania people replied to my ad in *Editor & Publisher*. The Seymour people had offered me $260 per month, so
I wrote to Jersey Shore and asked for $300. The editor called me today and
offered me $325. Strange indeed. But, at any rate, I shall leave for
Williamsport next weekend, praying that my car doesn't fail, and plan to
take up my duties on the ninth. I simply don't understand how I got a job

at all without a letter of flowery recommendation from Pug.[14] I thought god had a hand in everything. Maybe Darwin was right—there might be something to this "survival of the fittest" thing. You might tell Pug about Darwin.

And, incidentally, has he shipped you out to New Mexico yet? I'll send you my address when I get to my new spot, and wait for a letter informing me of the fortunes of an officer who doesn't bring his superior an apple each morning.

My little brother, incidentally, played his final game for his high school yesterday, and is sitting back now to survey the mob of college scouts who've been hounding my mother since October. I am the new bargaining agent, and expect to enjoy the position thoroughly. (Just heard Gen. White's proclamation that we "have Russia zeroed in from all directions." I am waiting now for Vannevar Bush and Ed Teller[15] to announce that our new supersensitive radar picked up a rash of heart tremors from the direction of the USSR, immediately after White's remarkably insignificant statement. I could almost hear Karl Marx laughing in his tomb.)

But don't be alarmed over my apparent lack of patriotism. I merely get these quips out of my system in letters, rather than the sporting editor's column of the *Jersey Shore Herald*. On that note, I'll leave you,

forever optimistic . . .
HUNTER S. THOMPSON

TO VIRGINIA THOMPSON:

Upon arriving in Jersey Shore, Thompson dutifully wrote home full of concern about the obvious dullness of the Pennsylvania mining town. In later years he would write about his harrowing Jersey Shore experiences in Songs of the Doomed.

November 29, 1957
Jersey Shore, Pennsylvania

Dear Mom,

You probably have my other letter by now, so you should have a fair idea as to how things stand. To put it all in a nutshell . . . the situation is about as fluid as a situation can get.

I have paid my rent for one month. The apartment seemed horrible at first, but I've been working on it most of the day, and it looks a little better now. It is old: the floors slant, the lights hang from the ceiling, the walls are filthy and cracked, and the furniture is all but worthless and anything but

---

14. Pug was Colonel W. S. Evans's nickname. As chief of the Office of Information Services, Evans was Thompson's immediate superior officer at Eglin.
15. Renowned U.S. nuclear scientists.

functional. It is, nonetheless, an apartment. The address is 1220 Allegheny Street, Jersey Shore, Pa. I live in the rear apartment on the second floor. My view—a northeastern exposure—consists of an eyesore of a barn about 100 yards to the rear, several run-down houses in the vicinity, and another eyesore of a hill—covered with scraggly trees and grass, rising into the smoggy sky which shrouds this smoggy town. Needless to say, north-central Pennsylvania in itself is not an inspiring sight: and the small blot called Jersey Shore is one of the least inspiring sights in north-central Pennsylvania.

So, as you see, being accustomed as I am to relying on my eyes to satisfy any aesthetic tension, I am now facing a neurosis of the worst sort. There are no waves pounding a sandy beach, no sea gulls soaring lazily over a fishing boat, and no glass-front bars in which to sit and watch the rain pelt down on a motionless bay. I must, in short, rely on something else: and whether I can derive any satisfaction from that "something else" will be the deciding factor in whether I stay here or not.

I'm speaking of my work: not just the newspaper, but other writing I can do. If a man really wanted to bury himself, I can think of no better place to do it than in Jersey Shore. I will have time—I can see that now—and the only pressure on me will be that which I put there myself. As compensations for the complacent squalor of this town, I have New York and Philadelphia within six hours driving distance, the possibility of a new car, and the privacy of an apartment.

But the ultimate factor will be the degree of freedom I have with the sports section. I don't mean that anyone will interfere with or censor my work—far from it. I will have to be able to make it as good as I want it to be . . . and that's where I may run into trouble.

Frankly, the paper is not good. The stress here is on speed and efficiency, rather than quality. And, rather than fight a system which will inevitably dull my ardor, I will have to leave. In one respect, this desolation is good. Having no other outlets for my energy, I will be able to pour them all into my work. But if I'm frustrated there, I can see no point in staying here.

I'll be clear on this point by the middle of January. By that time, the new system will have been in effect for about two weeks. I've already been informed that, in addition to the responsibility of a four-page sports section (which is really nothing at all when you have 2 wire services) I'll also do the final layout of the front page each morning. This means that, at night, along with an old but genial reporter, I'll be running the paper in the capacity of an editor. If I can do what I want with it, I think I'll like it here. But if I'll have to subject myself to the system here, as I said before, I'll leave. You will hear more on this.

The people are all very nice. I've been to two banquets in two nights—meeting hundreds of people and receiving numerous invitations to dinner and that sort of thing. It's always Mr. Thompson and "sir," and all slightly embarrassing. [. . .]

Tell Memo that her "extra" $5 was a great help—especially since I had to pay the rent in advance. Also tell her that I'm in great need of a radio. It will help during the holidays. Naturally, I'm going to hate being away from home: especially in this ghastly hole. I think, however, that it may do me some good—writing-wise. I enjoyed my last stay immensely and hope to get home again sometime soon . . . and it may be sooner than we think.

But I'm going to close now, for I don't feel real well; not any physical illness, of course, but a sort of emotional turmoil. I know that I'm in a period of crisis now, and I'll probably be keyed-up and touchy until things begin to clear up.

Write soon and tell everyone hello for me.

Love,
Hunty

P.S. send any packages c/o Regan's Grill (same address). That's the taproom I live on top of. My mailbox won't hold packages.

TO LARRY CALLEN:

A few weeks in Jersey Shore and Thompson was envying Callen for being stationed in Iceland.

December 12, 1957
Jersey Shore, Pennsylvania

Dear Larry,

So you think Iceland is bad: ha! Let me tell you about north-central Pennsylvania.

There were three red lights in metropolitan Fort Walton: there are two in Jersey Shore, Pennsylvania. There were four laundry & dry cleaning establishments in Fort Walton: there are NONE in Jersey Shore. There were innumerable bars in Fort Walton: there are two in Jersey Shore. There were at least four good eating establishments in Fort Walton: there are but three small grills in Jersey Shore. There were women (whores, lesbians and divorcees, if you must) in Fort Walton: the only women under forty in Jersey Shore go to high school. There were beaches and water and sand dunes and sea gulls and boats and bays in Fort Walton: there are mountains of coal dust, dirty old people, ancient wrecks of houses, and *True Confessions* magazines in Jersey Shore.

And now you're going to ask just what in the hell I'm doing in Jersey Shore, Pa. I know . . . and I'm ready with a quick answer: I am having a nightmare.

In this nightmare I am an ass . . . but I have everybody fooled. These nightmare people think I'm a "nice young man" who's come to settle in their community and make it a home. They call me "Mr. Thompson" and "sir" and insist that I attend the Lions' Club meetings, become an Elk, and join a bowling team. They invite me to their homes for dinner and tell me that the only thing wrong with America is the fact that we've given all our money to foreigners. The boy who writes the high school basketball games for me told me the other day that he wanted me to write a letter of recommendation for him for a college scholarship—the Grantland Rice Scholarship at Vanderbilt. Oh blasphemous irony: and I had mailed in my application only a few days before. The bastard can't even write a box score—and he'll probably win it because he has extracurricular activities in high school. He's a well-adjusted lad: there's no doubt about that at all. Yessir, he fits right in.

But let's get back to the nightmare . . . and how I became an ass. I am the sports editor of the town paper. For some reason, it's a daily, and an afternoon daily at that. My work takes me about three out of every twenty-four hours. I also do the final dummy of the front page. I'm a $75 dollar a week man; a white collar worker; one of ten people in town who wears a coat and tie to work. I'm a young man on his way up. Screw it all: if this path leads up, then I'd rather go down. At least it's enjoyable while the ride lasts.

But you want to know why I'm an ass. It's because I believed what I read in a letter. I believed a little man's description of his good ole home town: not realizing that he was measuring it in his own mind—with the same kind of measuring stick they use in chambers of commerce all over the land.

Not only do these bastards have no idea what a good paper should look like, but all they care about is getting enough local copy. They don't give a damn if the headlines make any sense or not—just as long as they get to the typesetters in time to keep anyone in the composition room from having to hurry. Half of one entire page has to be local bowling scores—a goddamn list of people's names. I've gotten my hands on one picture since I've been here—and that was a team shot of the Lock Haven State Teacher's College basketball team. I have about as much pride in my work as I did during my last days on the *Command Courier*.

It really is a nightmare. And the tragically funny thing about it is that I don't really know what to do. Naturally, I can always go back home: but that would be a regression of the worst sort. I can't bitch about this place because I know I can leave anytime I want to. It's worse than the AF, because talk was cheap there. It didn't really matter what you said. I pity very few people, but right now I'm ready to enlarge my list. I can understand how these poor bastards feel who lie awake at night and wrestle with the realization of their own worthlessness. I can understand how a man feels

when he has to explain to his friends why he re-enlisted. And I can understand how those millions of poor fools feel, who hate every minute of their
jobs and can't do a damn thing about it.

Don't get me wrong now: I'm not sitting here bemoaning my own fate.
If I were twenty years older, that might be the case. But it depresses me that
I've been wrong about so many people. I think of all the things I said about
reenlistment in front of John Edenfield.[16] And I think of all the rest of the
John Edenfields who've had sentences pronounced on them by factors almost completely beyond their control. I don't really wonder how they
manage to live, because I know they get into comfortable ruts, but I wonder how it feels to know that the only people who care if you live or die are
those you provide for.

I don't wonder that we have sex criminals who didn't really want to be
sex criminals, or murderers who don't know why they kill. There are so
many things wrapped up in this "ego" business that it sort of makes you
wonder whether it would be a good thing to put it in psychology books and
make it available to people who think they want to learn about themselves.

But I've written much more than I'd intended to already. I will read
Atlas Shrugged and I am going to school next fall. You'll hear from me
again when I make up my mind about what I'm going to do between now
and then. Think of me on Christmas and you won't mind Iceland so
much. Until I hear from you, I remain,

slightly deflated, but no longer
ripe for popping,
Hunter

TO GEORGE LOGAN:

*The son of an eminent Kentucky judge, Logan was a Louisville friend of
Thompson's who was attending Williams College in Massachusetts.*

December 14, 1957
1220 Allegheny Street
Jersey Shore, Pennsylvania

Dear George,

Well lad, I wouldn't have written at this particular time, had I not, only
a moment before, been thrown into an orgasm of spiritual glee by the
sound of Jesus tapping out a message of Christmas cheer on my dirty win-

16. Thompson used to berate Edenfield because he had reenlisted in the armed forces.

dow-pane. And with this heavenly tapping, there came a sound so pious, so blessed, and so moving, that I was lifted completely out of myself and into the realm of the ethereal.

I had just finished the orgasm brought on by the savior's tapping, when I heard a song. On unsteady legs, I struggled to the window and saw, to my great joy, a truck—a Salvation Army truck. On top of this truck there was mounted a speaker, and out of it came sounds of a most unearthly nature. I recognized some of the "old songs"; some of the old and stirring melodies I sang as a wee lad when I caroled in the streets with my drunken uncles.

I was moved, George: I was lifted out of myself and up . . . up . . . up . . . up . . . and up. I was soon perched—in nothing but my shorts and tennis shoes—on a cloud of smog, overlooking the filthy community called Jersey Shore, Pennsylvania. And I was not alone on this cloud: to my left was H. L. Mencken; to my right was George Bernard Shaw; and slumped on a particularly smoggy ledge was Westbrook Pegler. And over the entire scene stood William [Billy] Graham, scepter in hand, a crazed look in his eye, and a red judo belt wrapped snugly around his groin.

Nothing was said. We looked nervously at the scene below. The entire town seemed to shimmer in the night—emitting a certain pious glow which only the smallest and most complacently ignorant town can emit. Pegler vomited over the side.

"Jesus, look at that place," muttered Mencken. "It's enough to make a man pray for a plague of maggots."

"Shut up! you dirty bastard," screamed Graham. "I get seven hundred and forty-four tax-free dollars every year from those people. That's a good, typical American community. Those fine people are determined to hear the word of god—even to the point of paying for it. And they'll listen to nothing else, by christ! That's the kind of town we need more of."

"Bullshit," said Pegler, wiping his mouth. "That's all you are, Graham—bullshit. . . . I hope I got that Salvation Army truck: I think I made the correct adjustment for the windspeed."

"Nobody," said Shaw in a slow and sorrowful voice, "with a grain of sense, would live in that place for more than a month. It is without a doubt one of the most frighteningly desolate sights in the western hemisphere."

Suddenly, the cloud shot upward to avoid smashing into a coal hill rising out of nowhere into the black sky. I felt myself rolling over the side. Not having time to utter a polite farewell, I recalled their words and howled a loud and heartfelt "Amen."

I trust you get the message. Let me know when "little Logan" is born and tell Nonie "hello" for me. Cheerio.

Hunter

TO MRS. SPENCER, AUTOMOBILE ASSOCIATION OF AMERICA:

December 14, 1957
Jersey Shore, Pennsylvania

Dear Mrs. Spencer,

Just a word of thanks for your help in getting the AAA to route me to this place—even though I think it might have been better if they'd sent me 180 degrees off course. About the best I can say for this place is that it's totally inadequate for my every need.

But I don't want to bore you with geographical descriptions. It was nice of you to get me routed: but it would have been nicer if all the roads had been out.

Sincerely,
Hunter S. Thompson

TO JOE BELL:

Again, Thompson uses a fictional story to illustrate his quite real despair.

December 15, 1957
Jersey Shore, Pennsylvania

Dear Joe,

In the midst of *The Power Elite* (C. Wright Mills, 1956),[17] after a pleasant dinner of meatballs and beans, and looking forward to an evening of welcome silence . . . I pause to tap out a letter of puzzlingly pleasant despair.

Now "pleasant despair" is none too subtle a paradox, and it fits my present situation to a "T." I'm all of two weeks older than I was on December 1st . . . and about five years wiser. The thunderous wave of optimism on which I rode to my greatest triumph went crashing to an ignominious death on the rocks of reality at approximately 3:30 PM on December 9th. For at that time, I—fresh from an historic victory over the USAF's Strategic Complacency and Indifference Command—rode triumphantly over the hill into Jersey Shore, Pennsylvania. With a smile of grim but tolerant superiority plastered habitually on my once sun-tanned visage, I looked about me for the myriad thousands I had come to dazzle with my pregnant prose.

Suddenly I felt a terrible, blinding, choking sensation. Frantically, I scrambled to roll up my windows. I had driven into a cloud of coal dust.

17. Thompson was greatly influenced by sociologist Mills's groundbreaking theories about America's power structure.

Screeching to a stop, I seized my meat hatchet and leaped from my car: certain that the Syrians had touched off World War III with a gas attack. I tensed to meet the shock of the first wave of Mongolian paratroops.

"Come on, you bastards!" I screamed. "I knew you were coming! I told Bell last week! I didn't even order any Christmas cards—but I'll take a few of you with me before I go!"

Somewhere in the black cloud, I heard a hoarse scream. With a loud "you Mongolian bastard!" I rushed toward the sound, meat hatchet aloft . . . and crashed headlong into an old man in a Levi suit.

As we both went down, I heard him yell in a thick Old World accent: "Sheriff! Crugan's been serving on Sunday again: there's a foreigner crazed with drink in the middle of Main Street!"

Rising slowly to my feet, I heard what sounded like a troop of people running towards me. Echoing through the black cloud were loud cries of "drunk" . . . "foreigner" . . . "jail" . . . and "running amuck."

And then I saw them. They seemed to be able to see right through the smog, because they were coming straight for me. Every man wore either a Levi suit or an old plaid jacket; and all the women wore wool slacks.

I was seized. They fought over me like a pack of animals and I thought the end had come. I knew then that I must have stumbled into one of those primitive, forgotten colonies which science fiction writers tell us about.

Well, I won't carry this ridiculous parody any further. If you don't get a pretty fair picture of this place from my story, then it must be that I'm still in a state of shock and unable as yet to write a coherent description of the almost indescribably repulsive town of Jersey Shore.

It upsets me to have to go into detail about this fiasco. It is enough to say that a place which combines all the climactical advantages of Iceland and all the entertainment and cultural advantages of Harlan, Kentucky, is certainly not a fit place to live. I very seriously doubt that I shall be able to stand it for more than a month—if that long.

I have found but one advantage to living here: I am completely alone. I work for three or four hours for five days a week, and then I return to my apartment—on top of Regan's Taproom—and either read or write. Loneliness is for people who can't see themselves except through the eyes of their compatriots, and all evidence points to the fact that I've passed that stage.

But the advantage of privacy is not a virtue offered by Jersey Shore alone. Anyone who doesn't need other people to feed his ego can find privacy anywhere. And, keeping that in mind, I intend to go elsewhere. The very nature of the town precludes the possibility of my finding any satisfaction in my job; and, by the same token, the nature of the town also precludes the possibility of any other kind of satisfaction—sexual or otherwise.

I would leave now, but for several reasons. One being the fact that I could hardly quit such a strategic job as the sports editorship without giving at least the usual two weeks notice . . . and two being the fact that I'm not sure where I intend to go.

Were I to return to Louisville—especially for the holiday revelry—it would amount to a regression of damaging proportions. Naturally, I shall miss being there for Christmas: even more so because I know I can leave this place at any time.

But Louisville to me is a merry-go-round . . . with all the ups and downs and the conversational carnival music of the Fountaine Ferry[18] original. Admittedly, the ride can be pleasant if you don't mind the rhythmic repetition of a never-ending Maypole dance.

If I came home now, I'd hit the merry-go-round at one of the annual, frenzied peaks. And, like so many others, I could forget the existence of anything but the ride: sleep-walking through the low spots, and always looking toward the next peak.

There's a capacity for enjoying that kind of existence in all of us. And only those who can see above and beyond the American goal of respectable mediocrity can enjoy a life that leads to anything but a struggle to attain that end. I lived with it for eighteen years and I haven't been out of the orbit long enough to find whatever it is I'm looking for. I've made progress, of course, but there's always the temptation—especially now at "peak" time—to go back and maneuver for a comfortable seat on the merry-go-round.

I suppose it's very much like the bird who's not sure his wings will hold him up. But in the bird's case, there's always somebody to kick him out of the nest again, until he learns to fly. Louisville, of course, is a big nest. Its birds don't have to fly if they'd rather walk . . . do they?

Unless I weaken—and I might—I think I'll be sure I can fly before I return to the nest. It should be interesting . . . if nothing else.

And now that I've loaded you with pointed analogies, I think I'll get back to my various plots. God only knows where they'll get me (witness the fact that one of them got me here) but at least I can be sure that, whatever they reap, the result will be both amusing and expensive. For some reason, they always turn out that way.

So until I weaken, or falter, or find the ever-challenging "it," I remain your devoted, spasmodic, and sometimes psychopathic friend,

Hunter S. Thompson
1220 Allegheny Street
Jersey Shore, Pa.

---

18. Thompson is referring to the famous merry-go-round at Louisville's amusement park.

TO KRAIG JUENGER:

On Christmas Eve, a lonely, broke, and unemployed Thompson would flee Jersey Shore for New York City by "Huntermobile."

> December 23, 1957
> Jersey Shore, Pennsylvania

Dear Kraig,

Well, this letter should be a little more informative than my last one, if nothing else. It won't be very long, because I know so little about what I'm going to do that I'm unable to go into any detail. Just as soon as I find out anything definite, I'll let you know.

In a nutshell, here's the way things stand as of now: tomorrow morning, I shall load all my earthly belongings into the Huntermobile and point its nose in the direction of New York City. If the car makes it without falling apart, I shall remain in New York until at least the eleventh of January. After that date, if I haven't located a means of gainful employment, I shall then embark for St. Louis—via Louisville.

So there you have it: one of the most hare-brained schemes of the generation . . . a typical "Thompson production," and one of the most "all-or-nothing" propositions ever to be hatched in a human mind. I can think of nothing I'd rather avoid more conscientiously than being poverty-stricken in New York City . . . but that's precisely the situation I'll be in if I can't find a job by January 11th. I have $119, a box of food, a crippled car, and a temporary room in a fairly decent apartment. The reason I have to stay there until January 11th is that the College Board exams are being given at Columbia on that date, and I have to let the CB people know where I'll be by December 28th. So I'll have to stay in New York until the 11th. If I don't have a job by then—and the kind of job I want is scarce as hell—then I'll be off again. Where I'm going to get the money to go bouncing around the country like this is a real interesting problem: but I shall find it somewhere. I'll have to.

I got back from New York about 4:00 this afternoon and found your cards waiting for me in the mailbox. Needless to say, I appreciated them—as I do everything else with a St. Louis postmark on it. I neglected to get any Christmas cards this year, so allow me to wish you a very merry yule and all the erotic pleasures of a happy new year. My holiday season, incidentally, will be much better than I originally thought. Jerry Hawke, an ex-Lt. from Eglin who now goes to the Columbia law school, fixed me up with temporary lodging and invited me to join in the holiday festivities with him and some of his friends. So the terrifying prospect of spending the holidays in Jersey Shore fortunately failed to materialize. Needless to say, I feel better—and much more cheerful than I did when I was working. And, incidentally, I think I forgot to tell you why I'm no longer work-ing[19] . . . but now that I think for a minute, I think I told you in previous let-ters: so I'll close before the paper ends. CHEERIO. . . .

Hunter

TO SUSAN HASELDEN:

Although anxious about getting a job, Thompson was thrilled just to be in New York City, sharing a flat near Columbia University with Jerry Hawke.

December 27, 1957
110 Morningside Drive
New York, New York

Dear Susan,

Cheers . . . from the uptown west side of the melting pot. It is raining: raining like hell . . . and the wind carries the raindrops down Morningside Drive like a supersonic hailstorm, desolating the streets and giving all job-seekers an excuse to stay inside and drink. I am not drinking, however. I cannot afford to. My time is consumed in plotting a frontal assault on the beachhead of gainful employment.

I can hear the questions already; the rumbling mass of curiosity tum-bling out of your head and lying in unanswered heaps behind your ruby lips. And I suppose I should try to explain just how I came to this pass, liv-ing temporarily in a 6 × 8 room in New York City, and scanning the help-wanted ads with that frenzied eagerness that only the threat of impending poverty can inject into a man.

Nay, I shall not explain, I can only suppose that I came to grips with the inevitable and all-too-happily "took a dive." Not that there aren't logical explanations, of course: but they're all very complex and somewhat de-pressing. I shall make an attempt to explain . . . when I get a job. Until then, I can ill afford to fritter away my time on self-analysis. So you'll merely have to bear with me, sharing my spasmodic interludes of opti-mism and sending condolences—and possibly a weekly check—during my periods of depression. So be it.

There remains, of course, the possibility that I may be unable to find a job. If there is a Jesus, he will then have one of his finest chances to gain a convert. I now have the sum total of $110. When that runs out, there will have to be a Jesus—or a job.

19. Thompson is referring to his date with the daughter of a *Jersey Shore Herald* writer, which is detailed in his January 2, 1958, letter to Fred Fulkerson.

Unfortunately, I can't seem to grasp the urgency of the situation. There are moments when I seem to have things well in hand . . . and then suddenly a bar or bookstore or a basketball game appears out of nowhere to trip me up. I just can't seem to hang onto money. Today I bought two books and a ticket to the Temple-Pitt game at the Garden. God only knows what it'll be tomorrow.

Next week will be zero week. If I don't have a job by Saturday, I may call for divine help—or charity. I shall start with the *Times* and the *Tribune*, of course, and then run the gamut of the *Telegram*, the *Journal*, the *Daily News*, and the *Mirror*, in that order. If that turns out to be a dry run, I shall then hurtle blindly into the open job market, tossing preferences and experiences to the winds and depending on pure, unadulterated bluff to carry me through.

Even though I think in terms of alternatives—the *Courier-Journal* and the *St. Louis Post-Dispatch* in particular—my old and faithful car seems to realize that we've come to the point of no return. He seems unwilling to do anything but sit peacefully on the street, a perfect target for parking tickets. Naturally, it will be impossible for me to go anywhere without him. I simply have too much baggage. So I think I'm here for the time being, anyway. As I said, I suppose it was inevitable.

On the lighter side—supposing that I do get a job—I intend to move out of my temporary quarters and into a grotto of my own. Then, of course, I will need a mistress. And even in your virginal state, I suppose you could qualify—providing that you promise to bring a record player and several clean sheets. At any rate, that is all in the future—and a very vague future it is.

But I'll keep you informed: the immediate future will be anything but dull.

Until then, I remain, optimistically and lecherously yours,

Hunter

TO VIRGINIA THOMPSON:

December 28, 1957
110 Morningside Dr.
New York City

Dear Mom,

Having received no reply from my last effort, I thought it best to get off another short letter, just to assure you that I'm still very much alive and kicking. I have yet to get any mail at this address, and I'm beginning to wonder just what has happened to all my mail, packages, weekly checks, inheritances, and so forth. I shall check with both the postman and the building superintendent on Monday. All the mail going to Jersey Shore was supposed to have been re-routed to Louisville: so if things begin to pile up there, please send them on.

As for my situation here, it could best be described as "flexible." At present, I am staying in Jerry Hawke's apartment with two other Columbia law students. Jerry and his brother are staying at home—Rockville Centre, Long Island—during the holidays, and I'll be here until at least the sixth of January when school starts again. By that time, I'll either have a job or be fairly certain of not having one.

For the past few days, I've been making a detailed study of the sports-writing style employed by each of the New York papers. I intend to take a representative story from each one, re-write it to the best of my ability, and then make the rounds of the various papers with my portfolio of stories. If this yields nothing, I shall then investigate the possibility of working in some other field. Actually, there are numerous jobs advertised in the *Times* every day: no really desirable ones for a lad of my limited qualifications, of course, but at any rate, I probably won't starve in the event I fail to crack the newspaper job market. I should have a pretty good line on all this by the end of next week.

If and when I do get a job, I naturally intend to move into some sort of lodging of my own. But that too will have to wait until things begin to take shape.

And, incidentally, I hate to bring up the question of money, but there is something I will have to know about in the almost immediate future. To be brief and to the point, I would like to know if there is any possibility of Memo donating to the "get Hunter into college fund." You mentioned this, you remember, in connection with the almost dead certainty of Davison getting a "free ride." The reason I have to know pretty soon is that I'll have to apply within the next month or six weeks, if I intend to go anywhere other than U of L [University of Louisville]. And then too, the possibility of going to school next fall will have a definite influence on what I decide to do until then. So, if you can let me know a little something on this in your next letter, it will be a big help.

Just as soon as I get a job, I'll send you a belated birthday present. But until I have an income, it would probably be much wiser to hold onto every cent I can. Up to this point, I've been doing exactly that. Fortunately, I've been able to see *Don Giovanni* at the Met Opera, and one session of the Holiday Basketball tournament since I've been here, without parting with any money for tickets. The boys I live with have several deals like that, and it's been a big help knowing a few people. John Clancy—one of the boys living here—and I have "dates" of a sort tonight, with an eye toward getting me a companion for New Year's Eve. But, in case you get the impression that I'm blowing my meager fortune on wine, women, and song . . . fear not. So far, I've managed my funds very well. New York is actually not at all expensive if you know what you're doing. As a matter of fact, I've found that almost everything costs less here than it did in either Florida or Jersey Shore.

But this is the end of the paper, so I'll close without further ado.

Hunter

Thompson self-portrait.
(PHOTO BY HUNTER S. THOMPSON;
COURTESY OF HST COLLECTION)

*One of Thompson's many New York
apartments where he would often type in the early
morning hours.*
(PHOTO BY HUNTER S. THOMPSON; COURTESY OF HST COLLECTION)

Thompson in a New York pool hall.
(PHOTO BY DON COOKE; COURTESY OF HST COLLECTION)

1958

DOWN AND OUT IN MANHATTAN . . . NO ROOM AT THE YMCA . . . LIFE AT THE INTERRACIAL HOTEL . . . MIDNIGHT SINS OF HST . . . FEEDING OFF HENRY LUCE . . . WHOSE MOVIE IS THIS? . . .

New Year's Eve in Manhattan. A freezing rain blows through the dark street. Above the city, far up in the misted rain, long beams of yellow light sweep in great circles through the black air. They are anchored to the Empire State Building--that great phallic symbol, a monument to the proud dream of potency that is the spirit of New York. And below, in the damp neon labyrinth of the city itself, people hurry: somewhere . . . everywhere . . . nowhere . . .

--Hunter S. Thompson,
  "Prince Jellyfish" (unpublished novel)

TO FRED FULKERSON:

Although jobless, Thompson was having fun in Manhattan, reading Henry Miller's Tropic of Cancer *and searching for gainful employment. The city looked all the better after Jersey Shore. Meanwhile, at Eglin, Fulkerson had taken over Thompson's job as sports editor of the* Command Courier.

> January 2, 1958
> 110 Morningside Drive
> New York, New York

Dear Fred,

Well, I suppose I'd better warn you to get a grip—because I have a bitch of a tale to tell: a tale of terror and agony, shame and grief, poverty and perversion. . . .

On Christmas Eve, I voluntarily and under the influence of drink confessed to four heinously cruel homosexual offenses in a Chicago suburb, and was subsequently sentenced on New Year's Day to 73 years in Joliet prison. Upon hearing the sentence, I mercilessly slew a juror and three guards and fled into the night. I am now working as a pimp on New York's Upper West Side, in the heart of the Puerto Rican section. In the short space of three weeks, I've become addicted to morphine, cheddar cheese extract, and three more forms of sexual perversion. I need moral aid—send money and a Gideon Bible to Emanuel Hunteros Nama, 110 Morningside Drive, Apt. 53, New York, New York. [. . .]

Seriously, things have come to a horrible pass. I've been crazy drunk for 10 straight days, my money disappears at a rapid rate, the police put at least one ticket on my car every day, and it's beginning to look like I'm actually going to have to work for a living. The outlook is grizzly indeed.

I got here on Christmas Eve: needless to say, I couldn't stand that goddamn place in Pennsylvania—and I've been drinking almost continuously ever since. My departure from Pennsylvania was hastened a bit, after a wild debauch with the young daughter of one of the staff writers. She left for Chicago on the same day I left for New York. On the Friday night before

Christmas, we stayed out all night, drove her father's car into a mud bog on a deserted road, tore the front bumper off trying to drag the car onto the road with a tractor, and both became raving drunk on Ram's Head Ale. Naturally, the scandal caused a little hard feeling here and there, and made it necessary for me to flee town immediately in order to avoid being tarred and feathered by a puritanical mob.[1] I had already enraged a goodly portion of the populace by several sarcastic articles on the sorry state of Pennsylvania high school basketball, and this romp with the young woman would have been all the excuse the Quaker bastards needed to emasculate me. [. . .]

It's pretty difficult to begin one's sportswriting career in the employment of *The New York Times*, though, and I imagine I'll be forced to find work elsewhere for the time being. I'm going to have to save some money between now and next September, and if I can't find a suitable and rewarding job in Manhattan, I'm thinking seriously of trying to get a position laboring on some ship. Right now, though, I'm concentrating on enjoying all the sinful pleasures of the metropolis. I have enough money for about two more weeks of degeneracy, and then I'll have to get serious about some sort of work.

By the way, do me a favor and ask Col. Campbell if he got that letter to Vanderbilt. I got a letter from them the other day, saying that they'd only received one letter of recommendation (Wayne Bell's).[2] If Campbell doesn't get his in immediately, it won't do any good. Tell John Edenfield hello for me and ask him if he can direct me to some source of gainful employment in his native environs. I'm going to need three fortunes to pay all these parking tickets.

At the moment, I'm concentrating on a young woman who may agree to share an apartment with me. Except for money, the future is bright indeed. But the paper seems to be running out: so I'll wrap it up and say cheerio . . .

Hunter

TO LIEUTENANT COLONEL FRANK CAMPBELL:

Campbell was Thompson's most enthusiastic "fan"; in fact, he predicted that Thompson would someday be a "major league" writer, the "Hemingway of your generation."

1. Thompson tells this Jersey Shore story in *Songs of the Doomed* (1990).
2. Lieutenant Colonel Frank Campbell and Wayne Bell (civilian editor and publisher of the *Playground News*), both still at Eglin, wrote letters recommending Thompson for the Grantland Rice sports-journalism scholarship at Vanderbilt University.

January 6, 1958
110 Morningside Drive
Apt. 53
New York, New York

General . . .

As you can see by my present address, Jerry Hawke's address got to me in the very nick of time: as a matter of fact, it arrived only hours before I left that wretched hole on the Susquehanna. At present, I am entrenched in a 6 × 10 room, paying a nominal rent, enjoying life immensely, and gaining an intimate insight as to the workings of the employment agency racket. I arrived here on Christmas Eve with the sum total of $110. I now have somewhere in the neighborhood of $35. The prospect of a job is vague and ominous. Naturally, I will eventually have to work . . . I suppose it's inevitable.

On the shelf to my left—every part of this room is within an arm's reach of the desk—lies a rough draft of a Thompson original which will, when complete, expose the employment agency racket much in the same manner as a razor blade cuts into a syphilis chancre. Needless to say, I have decided to write under the alias: Aldous Miller-Mencken.[3] With that name, how could I fail to burst like a Vanguard rocket on the American literary scene? You are, of course, familiar with the bursting habits of Vanguard rockets . . . vivid, but a trifle unpredictable. And I think that sums it up.

But let us hope that joy still reigns in Mudville . . . untempered as yet by the revelation that all literary effort is not honest, that all editors are not literary, and that the price of perception is unemployment. Let us remember that "all is for the best in this best of all possible worlds," that education is a social garnishing rather than a tool fashioned by the intellect, and that "quality" is best measured by those who "use" a product, rather than by those who make it.

I speak, of course, of the world of journalism . . . as depicted at its lowest ebb by the *Jersey Shore Herald* and at its highest by *The New York Times*. The scientific definition of sound tells us that a tree may fall in a forest and that no "sound," as such, will be produced until the noise of its fall penetrates some living ear. Do you know the scientific definition of the term: "journalistic quality"? I don't . . . but there lingers in my mind the notion that the more pragmatically inclined newsmen of our day are well versed in the scientific definitions of such words as "sound," "appreciation," "functional," and "profit." And I wonder where such a term as "honest literary effort" fits into the one-dimensional picture we could paint with those four words.

3. While in New York Thompson wrote three unpublished short stories under this pseudonym, after three of his literary heroes: Aldous Huxley, Henry Miller, and H. L. Mencken.

I wonder if I could long work in a field where the demand for quality is determined by the taste and education of a mass not noted for any outstanding qualities save intellectual myopia and monetary greed. And then I wonder what field is not affected one way or another by the mass taste. And I also wonder if I'm trying to rationalize something I don't quite understand.

But fie on these unanswered queries and fie on those who pose them. There are stories to be written, drinks to be drunk, women to be ravished, and . . . alas, money to be made. We shall ride with the bouncing ball and fight gamely to avoid being on the bottom when it bounces . . . that is all ye know and all ye need to know. Amen.

By this time, I can only suppose that Fred [Fulkerson] has filled you in on my "adventures" in the noble burg of Jersey Shore. Most notably, they included a wild and somewhat unfortunate fling with the vivacious young daughter of one of the staff writers, several near-fistfights with both the editor and the shop foreman over "who was going to lay out the sports pages," and finally, a sudden and unexpected disenchantment with the everyday world of journalism.

This disenchantment is greatly restrained, of course, by the knowledge of a possible—although very unlikely—free ride through the portals of Vandy. I take the College Board tests this Saturday at Columbia. Those results will in all probability—if I'm still in the running—decide whether I get the thing or not. And, speaking of "the thing," I'd be interested to know just what the Vandy people had to say in that letter you got. If you still can't find it, then by all means fill me in on its contents.

I suppose it's a little silly to ask if you have any intimate contacts on any of the New York papers. Although, as I said, I'm not rabid to revel evermore in the world of newsprint, I could certainly use a job where I could put my limited experience to work. Right now, the only job I can wax enthusiastic about is one as a jack-of-all-trades in an art gallery on Madison Avenue. The pay is miserable, of course, but the work might be interesting. At any rate, I'm going to make another stab at it tomorrow. I shall keep you informed as to my work status.

Presuming that I do find a job in the near future, I plan to find a place of my own and really grind out the copy. If I can manage to sell anything at all by September, I'll be in great shape to pay for my ticket to the academic world. And after a few days of struggling with the New York job market, I find that I'd rather build my own figurative ladder than start at the bottom rung of the existing one. But that is in the future: as I said, I'll keep you informed.

Jerry is about to get himself to bed and I'll have to silence this machine. He says to tell you "hello" and all that sort of thing, and has taken to wondering out loud about your failure to fill his mailbox. What he needs, I think, is a moral shot in the arm. For my part . . . I need money.

And on that sour note, I close. Until I hear from you, or until the mushroom cloud, I remain, as grim, greedy, and serious as ever. . . .

HUNTER

PS . . . I wrote Wasil[4] a note while under the influence of drink. Apologize for me, if necessary, for any misstatements or undue familiarity. After all, I depend on Wasil and his brothers in arms to keep my country safe. I am loath to offend him in any way.

Also give my best to Pauline,[5] Peter [Goodman], Fred [Fulkerson], and John [Edenfield] . . . and Pug. Yes, good old Pug: he was the apple of my eye and the pungent salt in my military soup.

And yes, you might inform [Richard] Rosan that a tenement house collapsed today at 180 Riverside Drive[6] . . . killing and maiming hundreds of Puerto Ricans and other foreigners.

TO HENRY EICHELBURGER:

Eichelburger was in his third year of studying biology and zoology at Tulane University. Thompson was looking to reap the fruits of an evening he had spent with "Ike" in the French Quarter, during which his friend did nothing but brag about all the women he had conquered one summer in New York.

January 9, 1958
110 Morningside Drive
Apt. 53
New York, New York

Dear Ike,

I trust this missive finds you healthy, wealthy, and striving for the dean's list. I wouldn't have you any other way, you know.

Seriously, by now I'm sure that you've noticed the return address and that you've heaved the called-for sigh of relief at the realization that I'm not about to descend on you again . . . so let me come immediately to the point.

The point is very biological, and that should suit you rather well. To be brief, I am in New York for an indefinite period and I'm desperately in

4. Ted Wasil was a staff writer at the *Command Courier*.
5. Pauline Star was the receptionist at the *Command Courier*.
6. Where Rosan's parents lived.

need of sexual satisfaction. I seem to remember now that you spent the summer up here in an apartment full of lusty young women. Where is that apartment: I must know. I would also like to know—just as soon as you can get a letter in the mail—any other names, places, addresses, and so forth, which would be of aid to a young rake prowling around this over-populated isle. Come now, I'm sure you must know hundreds of uninhib-ited women I can comfort in my own peculiar manner. No living human could spend an entire summer here without making innumerable vital contacts. And I am indeed serious: if you know any drunks, bums, whores, etc.—by all means clue me in. I have come to write my way to fame and fortune, and I need colorful material.

I shall await your material by return post.

On the explanatory side, the truth of the matter is that I'm here because I have no money to go anywhere else. I had enough, but it went. I must now work.

For the past month, I've been staying with three law students, one of whom was at Eglin with me. I live out by Columbia now, but intend to move elsewhere within two weeks. If you know any good places to live, fill me in on that too. I'd prefer the Village, of course, but will settle for almost anything cheap: the idea being to save some money to get into school next fall . . . not that I particularly look forward to going to school, but there are things I could learn more easily in an academic atmosphere than I could in a drunken, left-bank setting of some sort. And then too, there are things I could learn in a left-bank setting which I could never learn in school. But I suppose you know that by now.

As of now, I am unemployed. Within a week, I will have to have a job. I have a tentative one with *Time* magazine, but it isn't definite and I may have to load airplanes or something like that. Anything to get money. And for that matter, if you know of anyplace where I can get a job, by all means let me know immediately. [. . .]

Until then, I remain, sincerely,

Hunter

TO CAROL OVERDORF:

Thompson had read Sherwood Anderson's Winesburg, Ohio *while working for the* Jersey Shore Herald. *Anderson's collective portrait of small-town "grotesques" fueled Thompson's disdain for "Rotarian America," and he had sent his University of Chicago friend Overdorf, whom he had dated over the Christmas holidays while in Jersey Shore, a copy for Christmas. She found it dull.*

January 15, 1958
110 Morningside Drive
Apt. 53
Winesburg, Ohio

Dear Carol,

If you think *Winesburg, Ohio* is a vicious satire on small towns, you should have your mind fumigated. And if you think Sherwood Anderson's people are "small town oddities," then you'd better get out and live a little . . . and look in a mirror once in a while.

I liked your pithy analysis of aphrodisiac drinks . . . at least you aren't completely hopeless, anyway. I get the feeling every now and then that you might drown in Lake Michigan.

My mind is cloudy, but not with work vapors. My fortune has dwindled from $110 to $4.46 and days of heavy crisis are close at hand . . . a period of belt-tightening, blood, sweat, tears, and very possibly . . . work. Yes, it seems inevitable. We got a magnum of absinthe in from the Azores yesterday and spent a few merry moments early this morning doing controlled skids around Sheridan Square in the Village. I imagine I can last until the absinthe runs out: then I'm afraid I'll have to work. I can't even afford gas for my car anymore.

When I first began to sound out the job market—one or two days in late December—several excellent places appeared immediately. So naturally I stopped looking at once and concentrated on enjoying life until my money ran out. Well, the money ran out and so did the jobs. If there is a jesus, I feel sure he'll come to my aid. God is good.

Yes, all that talk about orgies was nonsense: I just thought it would make you feel better . . . to think that you'd unwittingly driven me into a sexual frenzy. And unaccustomed as I was, of course, to anything but young boys and clean old men, the entire affair was a bit tedious.

I enjoyed the way you parried my forthright attempt to move in with you . . . crude as hell, really: and actually you'd have been quite safe if you hadn't qualified your invitation, because I couldn't get to Chicago now if my life depended on it. Well, I suppose I could if I really placed any value on my life, but I honestly think I'd rather sit here and die à la Bodenheim.[7] Life is complicated enough—with all this worrying about money—without bothering oneself with thoughts of staying alive.

But I do hope you're enjoying your efforts at earning your daily bread and I hope your apartment has now become a showplace of some sort. I

7. Maxwell Bodenheim was a well-known Greenwich Village poet who lived hand-to-mouth in bohemian poverty.

too will have an apt soon . . . soon . . . soon. When I get a job. But I don't understand why you're leaving the bedroom unfurnished . . . why don't you breed mandrills in it?

And yes I do have guilt feelings about St. Louis: they were thick letters: and I guess I'm a little stupid for not going there instead of sinking into this abyss so willingly. But I will find a way. . . . I always find a way. I've got to believe that.

So cheerio . . . stay pure and smile as you wither.

Hunter

TO SALLY WILLIAMS:

Sally Williams had moved from Eglin, where she had lived with her father, a colonel, to work as a beautician in Mobile, Alabama. Here Thompson toasts life as a "slacker."

January 17, 1958
110 Morningside Drive
Apt. 53
New York, New York

Dear Looney,

Yes, it's me again: probably much to your surprise, if you're anything like several other people I've written to recently. Apparently, I don't give the impression of being the kind of person one ever hears from again . . . unless, of course, I happen to need money.

But be that as it may: I hadn't realized I had so many gloomy, cynical acquaintances. Everybody wants to give me religion, sympathy, hope, forbearance, all sorts of idiotic priestly qualities so that I may better weather the storm of unemployment.

To hell with unemployment: I think it's a fine thing. I like sleeping all day and having nothing to do but read, write, and sleep whenever I feel tired. I like waking up in the morning and going immediately back to bed if the weather is foul. In short, I think it's a fine situation for a man to be in: provided, of course, that he has enough money to eat and pay the rent.

I don't . . . and therefore I must work: but what the hell? Is it anything to cry and pray for forgiveness about? Is it some sort of heinous shame, some great soul-sucking agony for which universal pity is the only cure? Hell no it's not. I get goddamn tired of getting letters telling me to "buck up," to "keep my chin up," to "keep trying," to "pray and be virtuous," and to read Horatio Alger books. I like being unemployed. I'm lazy. There are plenty of jobs, but I just plain damn don't want to work. It's that simple: you work in Fort Walton because you're a good sportswriter . . . you loaf in New York because you're not a good sportswriter. Everything is relative . . . and I have an ode:

"Ah, lives there a man with soul so dead, who never to himself hath said, as he hunched and rolled in his comfortable bed:

To hell with the rent . . . I'll drink instead!"

Let us toast to animal pleasures, to escapism, to rain on the roof and instant coffee, to unemployment insurance and library cards, to absinthe and good-hearted landlords, to music and warm bodies and contraceptives . . . and to the "good life," whatever it is and wherever it happens to be.

Let us strip to the ankles and revel in everything sensual: let us laugh at the world as it looks at itself through mushroom-cloudy glasses . . . and I suppose we might as well pay the rent too: for eviction is second only to hunger as the dirtiest word in the dictionary.

So there you have it: a slacker's credo for pleasure. I shall type forty carbons and send them out to all who would send me their sympathy, enclosing the motto for the month: "tithe, for the sake of Hunter."

I'll let you know when I meet the final degradation . . . work: it probably isn't far in the future, but I'll do my best to find an easy job. Then you can come and visit with me. I'll probably be here until the summer, anyway, and you probably need a vacation.

So drop me a line and tell me when you'll arrive. Until then. . . .

. . . it's cheerio:

Hunter

TO VIRGINIA THOMPSON:

Perhaps Thompson's biggest break in journalism came when Time *hired him as a copyboy. Although he earned only $50 a week, he got the invaluable experience of working on America's biggest weekly newsmagazine.*

January 23, 1958
110 Morningside Drive
Apt. 53
New York, New York

Dear Mom,

Since your last letter berated me for not writing, I can only assume that my most recent missive was lost in the mail or that I forgot to put a stamp on it. But nevertheless, I wrote a long letter exactly one week ago today, bringing you up to date on every facet of my existence and wrapping up all the loose ends I could find.

But things were uncertain then: the financial outlook was deathly black and it looked as if all things optimistic had flown south for the winter. In short, I was none too glad to be alive and hungry.

Ah, but not so today: even the sun is out and the air is warm, and the pendulum has finally begun to swing my way. You see I have a job: granted, I don't begin till the first of February, but that makes only a slight difference. Allow me to explain.

To understand just what a triumph I've engineered, you must first understand the situation here:

First, by New York standards, I've had no experience: anything with a circulation under 50,000 rates in the same league with school papers, by Newspaper Guild standards. So I'm stuck with the "beginner" label.

For "beginners" there are two plums in the journalism field, a copyboy's job on *The New York Times*, and a copyboy's job on *Time* magazine. The salary for both jobs borders on the ridiculous and the competition is almost unbelievable. Seriously, I had to go through three interviews of over an hour each, tell the story of my life in detail, and submit to an extensive physical, before I got the job I did . . . copyboy with *Time* Inc. And even then, I would have been completely out of luck if I hadn't come in at almost the precise moment one of the boys was announcing his resignation. But I did get the job: $51 a week, half days Wednesday & Thursday, full days (8hrs) Friday & Saturday, and a 12-hour day on Sunday. Monday & Tuesday off.

I'll be working at Rockefeller Center, a choice location by any standard, and will have the proverbial "one foot in the door" in one of the best doors in the business. Whether or not I ever get any further, of course, remains to be seen. The competition, as I said, is a trifle stiff. I've met three of the copyboys so far: one is a Harvard grad, one a Yale grad, and one speaks nine languages. A former copyboy wrote fourteen plays during his tenure with *Time*, and only left when one of his productions landed on Broadway. [. . .] Although they keep a list of copyboys who go on to fame and fortune, I haven't seen the one of those who turn into rumheads. I imagine it's pretty long too.

Time also pays half of the tuition (up to $300 a year) at any of the local colleges—probably a concession brought on by guilt feelings manifested over a long series of painless paydays. $50 a week, especially in New York, is not one hell of a lot.

Needless to say, if I'm not too late, I'll make an attempt to get into Columbia for the spring semester. I don't know, as yet, whether *Time* will pay their half at the beginning or at the end of the course. In either case, I might run short of money. And again the perennial question: how affluent is Memo in this respect? Needless to say, if *Time* works on the "reimbursement" principle, I won't have enough to register for anything at Columbia. I might, however, get into a writing course of some sort at one of the other local learning palaces. More on this later.

The past week or so has been full of poverty. My money ran out about ten days ago and times are indeed hard. I'll manage, of course, but not without suffering a few scars on my youthfully optimistic soul. Now I know why people shop at the A&P.

But talking of poverty tends to depress me. If I have any further business with money, I'll let you know later: in the meantime, I'll drop the subject.

Give Davison my congratulations on the All-American selection. It's nice to know that he and his buddy John were together right up to the end. Has Dave made a definite decision on college yet? And how did he like his visit to Vandy? And is there any further news on the Grantland Rice deal? [. . .]

Now that I've found gainful employment, I suppose I'll have to get down to the business of finding a place to live. Today or tomorrow, I intend to journey down to Greenwich Village and see what they have to offer: on my salary, I imagine the selection will be somewhat meager . . . cold water flats and that sort of thing. But that can be put off until something worthwhile appears: until then, I'll be either here or somewhere in this neighborhood while I seek a place to my liking in the Village.

And by the way, I hadn't intended to "retire" when I left Jersey Shore. I decided to go to St. Louis and merely stop by Louisville for the holidays—not for good. But now I see that coming to New York was a far wiser move for the time being, at least. After I begin working, I'll be about as "on my own" as a person can get: and if I can weather New York on $50 a week, I'll be able to get along anywhere.

So this just wraps it up for now. And for god's sake, don't complain about my not writing. This is the longest letter I've written in months.

Love,
Hunter

TO CAPTAIN K. FELTHAM:

Nearly three months after his discharge Thompson was still trying to get the U.S. Air Force to issue the $70 severance pay he had been promised. After three more letters farther up the chain of command, Thompson was paid on May 22, 1958.

January 28, 1958
110 Morningside Dr.
Apt 53
New York, New York

Captain K. Feltham
Chief, Finance Division
Eglin AFB, Florida

Dear Captain,

Reference is made to your letter of December 26, promising swift and decisive action on my inquiry of December 18.

To date I have received neither money nor explanation from your office. Although I'm not in the least surprised that nothing seems to have been done after ONLY a month and a half, I intend to be as persistent as your office is inefficient. If $70 seems like a small matter to you, then you have my undivided envy. Unfortunately, I have yet to reach a like level of financial security. To me, $70 constitutes a large portion of my tuition for the spring semester at Columbia: and, not being a happy-go-lucky career airman, I can ill afford to sit around for three eternities while somebody's finance office struggles desperately in its own red tape.

And IF, as you suggested in your previous letter, the USAF does NOT owe me the aforementioned $70, then the staff sergeant who took such pains to misinform me should be strapped up by his genitals and given an intensive "refresher" course. As I remember, it took him close to twenty minutes to explain the situation to me: and, although it sounded illogical at the time, I had no choice but to take his word. Apparently, I shall live to regret my gullibility.

It occurs to me now that a man who could so ably explain the situation on November 8th should certainly be able to do so again. On that day, he sat (with his back facing the door) in the first office on the right . . . off the first hallway to the right . . . as one enters the Finance building through the door which faces the Food Service Squadron across the street. He sat immediately inside the door. Unfortunately, his name escapes me at the moment. But, at any rate, might I suggest that he be called upon to explain the situation once again . . . for something is very obviously amiss.

I regret that circumstances force me to write such an unpleasant letter; but after my relatively polite inquiry failed to obtain any results, I felt compelled to take stronger measures. And if this letter follows my last one into oblivion, I shall feel fully justified in taking the matter to higher authority.

I trust that we will be able to come to an understanding in the very near future. Until I hear from you, I remain,

most cordially,
Hunter S. Thompson

TO ARCH GERHART:

Gerhart taught English at Louisville Male High School and had been Thompson's favorite instructor there. Although he considered Thompson "brilliant," Gerhart vigorously disapproved of his "show-off, Marlon Brando swagger."

January 29, 1958
110 Morningside Drive
Apt. 53
New York, New York

Mr. Arch Gerhart
Louisville Male High School
Louisville, Kentucky

Dear Mr. Gerhart,

Although I've been meaning to drop you a line for quite a while, my procrastination had gotten the better of me until I realized I could kill two birds with one stone. Specifically, I'd appreciate it if you'd ask Dean Kalmer to advise me as to the grades I got on the CB exams. I'm not too pessimistic about the English portion, but the Math section stopped me cold. And although I don't expect to be very pleased with the test results, I'd like to know them so that I can make definite plans for next fall. Thanks in advance for your help: and you might also like to pass the enclosed clippings along to Mr. Milburn. I don't think I need go into my reason for suggesting this.

As Davison probably told you, I stopped by to see you twice while I was in Louisville in early December. You were eating lunch on one occasion and "around somewhere" the second time. Since I had very little of importance to say, you missed nothing except a chance to see how "gaunt and emaciated" I've become. And since several people have told me that it's depressing to see a "thin, serious Hunter," you're probably better off for having missed me. But nevertheless, if I get back home again any time soon, I'll make another attempt to trade a few conversational gems with you near the old battleground.

As for my present condition, it is hectic and full of poverty. Fortunately, things have begun to shape up and I should get back into the sunlight sometime in the next two weeks. Barring the unforeseen, I'll begin work for *Time* Inc. on Sunday and take up classroom duties sometime later in the week. The *Time* job is something of a "plum" which not only gives me a pretty good "in," but which pays for half my tuition at Columbia as well. So from now until spring—and very possibly throughout the summer too—I'll be unfortunately busy. And considering the evil which abounds in New York, it's probably a pretty good thing. Prolonged idleness in this place could well be fatal for one of my ilk.

The *Time* job is one of the lowest on the editorial ladder—a copy-boy—but has infinite possibilities. The classes, "Literary Style & Structure" and "Short Story Writing," should give me a boost along the road to becoming another D. H. Lawrence. And the minute salary attached to the job, coupled with the terrifying tuition at Columbia, will undoubtedly keep me mired in abject poverty for the duration of my stay in Manhattan.

Events of the past two years have virtually decreed that I shall wrestle with the literary muse for the rest of my days. And so, having tasted the poverty of one end of the scale, I have no choice but to direct my energies toward the acquisition of fame and fortune. Frankly, I have no taste for either poverty or honest labor, so writing is the only recourse left me.

To be reduced to scrambling for a living in the wonderful world of "business & free enterprise" would seem to me to be the last word in degradation. Frankly—and this would be a terrible choice to have to make—I think I'd rather recline in comfortable poverty than scramble forever up the well-greased grey-flannel flagpole. Fortunately, I'm not looking forward to having to make that choice: but then Dylan Thomas probably didn't either, when he was twenty.

Ah, but talk of poverty is depressing, and youth should avoid depression like the plague. Merely to read a New York paper is to wallow in a bog of filth and despair, disaster and rape, and neverending tales of human viciousness. Anyone who could live in this huge reclaimed tenement called Manhattan for more than a year, without losing all vestiges of respect for everything that walks on two legs, would have to be either in love, or possessed of an almost divine understanding. The sight of eight million people struggling silently but desperately to merely stay alive is anything but inspiring. For my money, at least eight million people would be much better off if all five boroughs of New York should suddenly sink into the sea.

But for all my revulsion, I'll have to admit that living here can be interesting. And I imagine it would stay that way as long as one knew he could leave at any time: very much like visiting behind the iron curtain, I suppose . . . interesting if it's temporary, and terrifying if it's permanent.

I'm apparently straying from my chosen path here: I hadn't intended to launch into a long denunciation of New York, so I'll close before I go any further.

And incidentally, I got a letter from David [Porter] Bibb today, saying that he would in all probability seek a spot in the *Time* ranks this summer. All we need now is for good old Sam[8] to arrive, and the party can begin. I

8. Sam Stallings was the Louisville friend who was arrested with Thompson for robbery.

don't think that's very likely, however, since the last word on Sam had it that he was beating around somewhere on the West Coast. And that too is probably for the best.

So this about wraps it up. Drop me a line if you have time, and please don't forget to ask Dean Kalmer to send me my CB grades. I'd ask, in closing, that you take care to see that Davison develops something other than his biceps: but since I remember now that you haven't had him for anything, I'll table my request. It seems unfortunate that he should have gone through Male without having either you or Tague or Holtzman;[9] but then I'm hardly in a position to criticize his judgment up to this point . . . so I'll let the matter rest.

> In closing, I remain, sincerely
> and respectfully yours,
> Hunter S. Thompson

TO SUSAN HASELDEN:

Thompson took advantage of a chance to live by himself—albeit temporarily—in an apartment on West 113th Street. Ever restless, he daydreamed of fleeing New York for warmer climes.

> February 17, 1958
> 562 W 113th Apt5E5
> New York, New York

Dear Susan,

After a long illness . . . the rumhead of 113th Street returns with a few words of warning and woe: the West Side Parkway is still slippery in spots, my writing machine is in pawn, my car rests under a mountain of snow, and life goes on in the West Indies . . . as usual.

Many thanks for your efforts at communication. I shall try to steal this "Harvest" thing at the very first opportunity; although I harbor small hope that I shall ever write anything worthwhile. I may take up modern dance . . . or method acting . . . or something.

I have lost my taste for writing letters. Why? I have no idea. I think I've lost my taste for everything: it's this goddamned ever-present poverty. At least there's music.

Spent last evening at the White Horse with a young woman from the Urban League: became dangerously drunk and lost her somewhere near a subway hole: woke up dead sometime late today. When are you going to

9. Harold Tague taught English at Louisville Male High School; Fred Holtzman taught French.

pay me a visit? My bed is pretty small, but nothing is hopeless . . . witness [novelist] James Jones. Lodi, New Jersey.

I don't know if I've brought you up to date or not, so here it is: I am working for *Time* and going to Columbia, a high-sounding program, I suppose, but really a little sordid. Living in a rather cramped dungheap next to Columbia and using a rented typewriter . . . job title "copyboy" at *Time*, one of many indigent actors, writers, painters, etc. It seems to be Luce's one and only concession to the creative mind: or maybe his way for showing his contempt by paying the CMs so little: one never knows, for God works in wondrous ways. [. . .]

Can't understand this deathly apathy. I think I need beaches and blackness and moonlit nakedness. New York is a huge tomb, full of writhing, hungry death. All this talk about San Francisco gives one pause: there is also talk of Italy, St. Thomas, Tahiti, and other refuges for the poor in spirit.

Witnessed a fight last night between one of *Time*'s senior editors and an equally drunk writer (hired). Free drinks every Sunday night from six to wee small hours, also feast, also entertainment: fights, sex, social-scrambling, politics, etc. All very interesting.

Unfortunate that you by-passed the snow for a trip to the sun. Trust you enjoyed it: you must, you know, you only have two weeks a year to live. The system says it: and who am I to quarrel with systems. Hold on to your virginity: it may be worth a great deal later on, especially if you're out of a job. Time is money.

Well, cheerio. I have a box of cottage cheese.

Until then . . . . . Hunty

TO KAY MENYERS:

Menyers was studying literature at Goucher College in Baltimore. She was a diehard Jack Kerouac fan and had recommended that Thompson read On the Road *and* The Subterraneans.

March 17, 1958
562 West 113th
Apartment 5E5
New York, New York

Dear Kay,

Unfortunately, I must stick with conventional stationery . . . and where in hell did you get that "stuff" you sent me some time back? Maybe you're too weird for even MY taste . . . and that's going way, way out. Maybe you're a white Mardou Fox,[10] waiting in haste for me to perform erotic lecheries on your body. Weird.

I may sound a little black, but I'm really pretty well adjusted. Perhaps I talk a lot about being an "individualist," but that's just because I want to be popular and respected: a "cocktail intellectual," if you will. I may not agree with the *Daily News* critic about *Endgame*, but then I would be thought "bourgeois" if I did: and in these days when everyone who matters is a "higher bohemian," one must not appear to be bourgeois. One conforms with a cynical smile which says "I'm smart because I just APPEAR to be a conformist: I'm really a secret individualist." The smile also says "I lack the courage of my convictions": you have to be listening, though, to hear it say THAT. One gets tired of listening.

My job is somewhat insecure: at a cocktail party for new employees the other evening, I told the publisher of *Time* (and assorted others) that the business manager was a "fat lecher" . . . and then with a wild drunken laugh, I repeated it for the benefit of the business manager . . . FAT LECHER . . . and he looked a little startled. The publisher and his friends were also a little startled. It was a weird evening.

The highlight of last night was the hurling of a large garbage can down five flights of marble stairs here in the apartment. I also tried to kick down the door of a girl's apartment, turned a fire extinguisher on the inhabitants of a room upstairs, and uttered a series of wild animal cries which frightened the Chinese woman next to me nearly to death. I appeared to her in my underwear this morning and she told me that a man upstairs told her that I was "crazy" and to "watch out for me when I was drunk." I have few friends in the building.

But . . . when are you going to get to New York City? There's not much room in my castle to dance, but I DO have a radio and a few books . . . and we can always go out and throw garbage cans around the marble halls: it makes a weird thundering sound. Or I could rape the Chinese woman and you could watch . . . fine?

Seriously, I do think it's about time our paths crossed. My "weekend," *Time* style, falls on Monday and Tuesday . . . not a very good time for hopping down to Goucher College. So it seems that you must get up here . . . anytime will be fine: just let me know in advance.

The prospect of the thing excites me and I see no further sense in writing. The Chinese woman is tapping lustily on the wall and I must answer the call of the flesh. So until then, I remain,

. . . undisciplined,
Hunter

10. Mardou Fox is the African-American heroine of Kerouac's *The Subterraneans*, which deals with interracial romance.

TO SUSAN HASELDEN:

Kerouac's confessional prose made quite an impact on Thompson's philosophy for living, if not on his writing style.

> March 18, 1958
> 562 West 113th
> Apartment 5E5
> New York City

Dear Susan,

At 11:01 PM, on the night of March 18th, 1958, a great truth blundered out of the sky and imbedded itself in my skull. With a great thunderous clatter, a million jangled pieces of a long-scrambled puzzle fell miraculously into place. The Thompson inner eye has finally acquired the long-lost third dimension.

IN THE COURSE OF A RAMBLING, NERVOUS DISCOURSE ON SOME ABSOLUTELY IRRELEVANT SUBJECT, I EXPOSED MYSELF . . . to myself . . . AS A SEVERE NEUROTIC, a virtual headless chicken, totally incapable of making value judgments, and running on a rum-soaked treadmill towards a schizophrenic rainbow in a two-dimensional sky.

I don't know how or why, but this suddenly dawned on me like a flash of black lightning. I was feverishly talking about a million plans at once when it came on me: not all at once, to be sure—for the pieces have been slowly falling into place for the past two months—but suddenly enough to make me stop and think, and then to stop talking and leave the room and think some more. It was like walking nervously into a dark room and finding myself in front of a mirror when the light suddenly flashed on.

In brief, I find that I've never channeled my energy long enough to send it in any one direction. I'm all but completely devoid of a sense of values: psychologically unable to base my actions on any firm beliefs, because I find that I have no firm beliefs. I seem to be unable to act consistently or effectively, because I have no values on which to base my decisions. As I look back, I find that I've been taught to believe in nothing. I have no god and I find it impossible to believe in man. On every side of me, I see thousands engaged in the worship of money, security, prestige symbols, and even snakes. I'm beginning to see what Kerouac means when he says, "I want God to show me his face": it is not the statement, but what the statement implies: "I want to believe in something." The man is more of a "spokesman" than most people think . . . and he speaks for more than thieves, hopheads, and whores.

> Pondering. . . .
> Hunter

TO KRAIG JUENGER:

Six months after it began, Thompson and Juenger's passionate love affair had faded into a long-distance friendship.

> March 18, 1958
> 562 West 113th
> Apartment 5E5
> New York City

Dear Kraig,

After all these weeks of long silence, I can only assume that you've given me up for this Irv person. I say you've apparently "given me up," when perhaps I should have said "forgotten me": for now as I look back, I can see that ours was such a brief and unfortunately platonic relationship, that neither of us was really in a position to be "given up." As a matter of fact, I'm a little surprised that I feel such a sharp sense of loss at losing something that was never really mine. It's amazing, I think, that an "affair" which ran the course of only two days and nights could have had such a lasting aftereffect . . . and I can't help but wonder what would have happened had you stayed in Florida for another two weeks. Perhaps though—and I say this without much conviction—it's better that you left when you did.

I find also, as I look back over the past few hectic months, that I had several chances to fan the sparks of that brief flame that flickered so intensely back in the fall. But I bypassed them all—always telling my irrational heart that a trip to St. Louis would be "crazy"—and now I find that I've let the weeks stretch out into months, sitting in the grim chaos of New York and dreaming of a long white beach, writing half-hearted letters to newspaper editors in St. Louis, re-reading the beautiful letters you wrote me in Fort Walton and Jersey Shore, and killing the thing all the while by a process of slow starvation . . . a symbolic experience, I think, when you realize that most people's lives are virtual monuments to cowardly indecision. Ah, that we lack the courage of our romantic convictions; and thereby miss the wine of life, forgoing the very thing that makes living worthwhile.

I find some pleasure, though, in looking back and realizing that we had a perfect setting for love; so perfect, perhaps, that it made the outcome inevitable. What ambitious TV writer could come up with such a dramatic repertoire of components for a tale of tropic romance . . . a beautiful young girl trapped in a bad marriage, the sympathetic shoulder of a young writer-beachcomber, a warm Florida moon and the added stimulus of black waves pounding a lonely beach at night: seriously, what more could you ask?

In the final analysis, I think it is better that we left the ashes of the flame to settle on the white sands of the lonely Gulf Coast beach, where the wind can carry them over the dunes at night and back over the moonlit lowlands and the still waters of the bayous. That way, we are spared the agony of having to fan the flame in the teeming cities of the loud American north, where the mere act of life is so hurried and difficult that no one really has time for love. At least we have a memory unscarred by the horrors of democratic realities. Certainly it is not the typical vacation memory, where you have to forget nine-tenths of everything that happened, in order to enjoy the other tenth. No, it was actually a two-day love, with all the pungent emotion and atmosphere of the timeless ideal. Its ashes still float in the night over the lonely little hamlets of Choctawhatchee Bay. We were foolish to try to take it out of its setting.

And now, as I contemplate the myriad confusions and pointless haste of New York, I feel a little sad that Kraig is a memory instead of a reality. I wander in hectic loneliness between the Time & Life building and Columbia University, finding a home in neither place and thinking in terms of such places as Italy, San Francisco, Mexico, Tahiti, and a million other places. Perhaps I shall even get to St. Louis sometime soon: but then, as always, it will be too late.

So now I leave you, wishing you the best of everything (in this best of all possible worlds) and hoping that you are a little happier than you were when I saw you last. If you get to New York anytime soon (and don't have Irv with you), I hope you'll give me a ring. Maybe I can provide you with a few moments of stimulating nostalgia, coupled with very proper democratic conversation.

But perhaps I've bored you with this lengthy elegy, so I'll reach into the past for the proper closing comment: I think it's . . .

> . . . cheerio.
> Hunter

TO *DOWN BEAT* MAGAZINE:

Thompson never paid for the two issues of down beat *discussed here. The magazine never hired him, either.*

> March 31, 1958
> 562 West 113th
> Apartment 5E5
> New York City

down beat
2001 Calumet Ave.
Chicago, Illinois

Gentlemen,

Please cancel my subscription to *down beat* IMMEDIATELY! If that thing on Bob "Moneybags" Higgins is a sampling of the kind of swill I'm paying to read, then *Metronome*,[11] here I come!

I thought, after reading that "miscarriage" on W. C. Handy in the last issue, that I'd seen the absolute nadir of informative, perceptual reportage: but this thing on Higgins was a new low.

Who are these hacks that spew out these articles, anyway? Don't you people have enough self-respect to hire a few good WRITERS? Christ on a crutch, man: if you people are as hard up for writers as you appear to be, then you need help in the worst way!

Seriously now, if you really can't FIND any competent writers, then the very least I can do is to offer my assistance. I certainly don't claim to be a music critic, but I could write a better story on Handy from *newspaper clippings* than that "thing" you published in your last issue. When any magazine gets to the point where it pays a DUNCE to write a cover story, then it should give up the ghost and stop publishing.

But be that as it may, the publishing future of *down beat* is none of my concern. Bill me for the two issues I've received and by all means feel free to call on me if you need competent help.

Most cordially,
Hunter S. Thompson

TO SALLY WILLIAMS:

Thompson had crafted a lunatic form letter designed to get creditors off his back; it worked about half the time.

April 2, 1958
562 West 113th
Apartment 5E5
New York City

Dear Sally,

Mail this when you get a chance, will you? If this one doesn't scare the bastards off, then nothing will. I think I should send a copy of this letter to the AMA [American Medical Association] as a sample of a schizophrenic

---

11. *Metronome* was a popular jazz-blues magazine.

mind at work: it's a real whopper. Anyone who would try to collect any money from the author of this letter would have to be an out-and-out fool.

If they come looking for me with nets, tell them I left several weeks ago to go over to Gainesville, Florida to apply for a job as a religion editor on a paper there. Just as long as they never discover that I'm in New York, I'm all right.

Thanks,
Hunter

"Debt Letter"

April 2, 1958

Say man, what is all this? I just got back from New Orleans and the first thing I find is a threat from you people—some wild yap about jail and court and lawyers and such: what do you think I am—some kind of moneybag? Here I am trying to sell my short story trilogy, and you people hound me at every turn—howling and moaning about some idiotic debts! Who are you anyway? I never bought a damn thing from you people. What kind of rotten business are you in—that you have to hound people all over the country? I get a bunch of mail about every two or three months, and every damn time I get some, I find a threat from you!

What the hell are you trying to do, anyway? Don't you realize that I can't work with all this war coming on us? This atomic fallout is God's WRATH! With the end of the world right on top of us, I can't afford to work. If I don't get my work published now, I may never get it published! Haven't you ever heard of serving God and Mammon? With all this sex going on and people forgetting about God, how can you hound me like this? We're taking whiskey into our bodies all the time and drink God's BLOOD! I can't hold a job—I get worried all the time and feel half crazy . . . what are you doing with all this money? I don't want your damn money . . . we all have a home in Heaven . . . what's all this trouble?

You don't understand the strain I'm under: I'm not the same man I was a year ago. Worrying about my work and money and jobs all the time is driving me crazy! I have to get my work published! Why don't you talk to some of these publishers you know and get me an advance so I can write a novel? Then I'll have money . . . then I'll have it . . . I won't get these threats! I got a disease of some kind over in New Orleans and I can't even go to a doctor! Everybody thinks it's funny, but I have to get a job. I might be the assistant religion editor of the *Gainesville Sun* pretty soon . . . I'm going over there next week to see about a job. I had a car but somebody took it in St. Louis. Oh God, what's happening all the time? Everybody wants to steal and drink and sex and take everybody's money away from people who don't even sell anything and there's atomic fallout everywhere and war coming on. The whole world is going crazy and I don't even have a job. You've got to stop threatening me! I'm not well—I have a blister on my leg and that damn disease all over my stomach. I can't even think what I want to say anymore . . . this worry is driving me crazy.

I tried to work in New Orleans and they made me quit. If I get this thing in Gainesville I'll be a religion editor and publish my own book in the paper. After that I'll have a job and get well.

Sincerely,
Hunter S. Thompson

TO SUSAN HASELDEN:

At last, Thompson moved to his own "bachelor pad," a tiny basement apartment with black walls in Greenwich Village. However, he still spent most of his free time wandering around Columbia University.

April 13, 1958
57 Perry Street
New York City

Dear Susan,

What the hell do you mean, saying "you'd probably get us both killed"? Judging from my wandering during the past three years, I could probably go from here to Cape Town wearing nothing but a loincloth, without a smidgen of trouble. And as for the Congo, I feel quite sure that I could take an entire harem safely from one end of it to the other. As a matter of fact, I'd feel pretty safe taking almost anyone or anything except a group of giggling virgins.

Your letters, though—however virginal and full of giggles—never fail to cheer me up a bit. And, oddly enough, right now when things are going even better than expected, I seem to feel the need for foreign cheer of some kind. I think the reason for this is that I've just realized that I'm going to be a resident of New York for a relatively goodly length of time. It's not that I've committed myself for any specific length of months, but that I merely see the need to remain here for a while. New York is at once an education, an initiation, and a stimulant. It gives one a perspective, I think, that would be impossible to get anywhere else in the world. But god have mercy on those who can live with this perspective.

Seriously, this damned place is like an early William Saroyan story: the lonely, wilted little daisies from Hattiesburg, Mississippi; frustrated, hymn-singing Chinese girls; frenzied interracialists from all over the damned world; the girl next door from Dayton, Ohio; timid neo-intellectuals from Parsons, Kansas (reminds me a little of you); and god only knows what else. To paraphrase someone, "I have just begun to see!" Mid-town Manhattan is an unbelievable circus, Harlem is hell on earth, the Bronx, Queens, and Brooklyn are all tombs, and this goddamned Village is enough to frighten any honest beachcomber to death. Do you realize that sunlight NEVER ENTERS MY APARTMENT? Can you understand what this means— what kind of effect this perpetual darkness can have on a man? Do you re- alize that I know people who LIVE in bars—get their mail there? There are people here who are so lonely that I can't stand to talk to them. God, what a tragic paradox.

But I have the answer now—a very general one, of course, but nonethe- less an answer. I am either very fortunate or very crazy to have settled on it at this early age, but at any rate, I have it. I shall explain it to you when I have more time.

This apartment, by the way, is something straight out of a "low bo- hemia" movie. I got it from an unemployed songwriter who's all but dead from lack of sunlight. The lease belongs to a dope addict who left town two and a half years ago, and who may return at any time to claim it—Christ only knows what will happen then. Maybe I shall go to live in the Owl Creek swimming pool. Money troubles—debt as usual.

That's about it for now. You didn't say when you'd be up, by the way, so keep that in mind next time.

Until then,
Hunter

TO HUME LOGAN:

Thompson had just been delving into the existential tracts of Jean-Paul Sartre when Logan, a Louisville friend and fellow Athenaeum Literary As- sociation cohort, wrote asking for some career advice.

April 22, 1958
57 Perry Street
New York City

Dear Hume,

You ask advice: ah, what a very human and very dangerous thing to do! For to give advice to a man who asks what to do with his life implies something very close to egomania. To presume to point a man to the right and ultimate goal—to point with a trembling finger in the RIGHT direction—is something only a fool would take upon himself.

I am not a fool, but I respect your sincerity in asking my advice. I ask you though, in listening to what I say, to remember that all advice can only be a product of the man who gives it. What is truth to one may be disaster to another. I do not see life through your eyes, nor you through mine. If I were to attempt to give you *specific* advice, it would be too much like the blind leading the blind.

* * * * * * * * * *

"To be, or not to be: that is the question: Whether 'tis nobler in the mind to suffer the slings and arrows of outrageous fortune, or to take arms against a sea of troubles. . . ."
(Shakespeare)

* * * * * * * * * *

And indeed, that IS the question: whether to float with the tide, or to swim for a goal. It is a choice we must all make—consciously or unconsciously—at one time in our lives. So few people understand this! Think of any decision you've ever made which had a bearing on your future: I may be wrong, but I don't see how it could have been anything but a choice—however indirect—between the two things I've mentioned: the floating or the swimming.

But why not float if you have no goal? That is another question. It is unquestionably better to enjoy the floating than to swim in uncertainty. So how does a man find a goal? Not a castle in the stars, but a real and tangible thing. How can a man be sure he's not after the "big rock candy mountain," the enticing sugar-candy goal that has little taste and no substance?

The answer—and, in a sense, the tragedy of life—is that we seek to understand the goal and not the man. We set up a goal which demands of us certain things: and we do these things. We adjust to the demands of a concept which CANNOT be valid. When you were young, let us say that you wanted to be a fireman. I feel reasonably safe in saying that you no longer want to be a fireman. Why? Because your perspective has changed. It's not the fireman who has changed, but you. Every man is the sum total of his reactions to experience. As your experiences differ and multiply, you become a different man, and hence your perspective changes. This goes on and on. Every reaction is a learning process; every significant experience alters your perspective.

So it would seem foolish, would it not, to adjust our lives to the demands of a goal we see from a different angle every day? How could we ever hope to accomplish anything other than galloping neurosis?

The answer, then, must not deal with goals at all, or not with tangible goals, anyway. It would take reams of paper to develop this subject to fulfillment. God only knows how many books have been written on "the meaning of man" and that sort of thing, and god only knows how many people have pondered the subject. (I use the term "god only knows" purely as an expression.) There's very little sense in my trying to give it up to you in the proverbial nutshell, because I'm the first to admit my absolute lack of qualifications for reducing the meaning of life to one or two paragraphs.

I'm going to steer clear of the word "existentialism," but you might keep it in mind as a key of sorts. You might also try something called *Being and Nothingness* by Jean-Paul Sartre, and another little thing called *Existentialism: From Dostoyevsky to Sartre.*[12] These are merely suggestions. If you're genuinely satisfied with what you are and what you're doing, then give those books a wide berth. (Let sleeping dogs lie.)

But back to the answer. As I said, to put our faith in tangible goals would seem to be, at best, unwise. So we do not strive to be firemen, we do not strive to be bankers, nor policemen, nor doctors. WE STRIVE TO BE OURSELVES.

But don't misunderstand me. I don't mean that we can't BE firemen, bankers, or doctors—but that we must make the goal conform to the individual, rather than make the individual conform to the goal. In every man, heredity and environment have combined to produce a creature of certain abilities and desires—including a deeply ingrained need to function in such a way that his life will be MEANINGFUL. A man has to BE something; he has to matter.

As I see it then, the formula runs something like this: a man must choose a path which will let his ABILITIES function at maximum efficiency toward the gratification of his DESIRES. In doing this, he is fulfilling a need (giving himself identity by functioning in a set pattern toward a set goal) he avoids frustrating his potential (choosing a path which puts no limit on his self-development), and he avoids the terror of seeing his goal wilt or lose its charm as he draws closer to it (rather than bending himself to meet the demands of that which he seeks, he has bent his goal to conform to his own abilities and desires).

In short, he has not dedicated his life to reaching a pre-defined goal, but he has rather chosen a way of life he KNOWS he will enjoy. The goal is

12. Walter A. Kaufmann, ed., *Existentialism: From Dostoyevsky to Sartre* (New York, 1956).

absolutely secondary: it is the *functioning toward the goal* which is important. And it seems almost ridiculous to say that a man MUST function in a pattern of his own choosing; for to let another man define your own goals is to give up one of the most meaningful aspects of life—the definitive act of will which makes a man an individual.

Let's assume that you think you have a choice of eight paths to follow (all pre-defined paths, of course). And let's assume that you can't see any real purpose in any of the eight. THEN—and here is the essence of all I've said—you MUST FIND A NINTH PATH.

Naturally, it isn't as easy as it sounds. You've lived a relatively narrow life, a vertical rather than a horizontal existence. So it isn't any too difficult to understand why you seem to feel the way you do. But a man who procrastinates in his CHOOSING will inevitably have his choice made for him by circumstance.

So if you now number yourself among the disenchanted, then you have no choice but to accept things as they are, or to seriously seek something else. But beware of looking for *goals*: look for a way of life. Decide how you want to live and then see what you can do to make a living WITHIN that way of life.

But you say, "I don't know where to look; I don't know what to look for." And there's the crux. Is it worth giving up what I have to look for something better? I don't know—is it? Who can make that decision but you? But even by DECIDING TO LOOK, you go a long way toward making the choice.

* * * * * * * * *

If I don't call this to a halt, I'm going to find myself writing a book. I hope it's not as confusing as it looks at first glance. Keep in mind, of course, that this is MY WAY of looking at things. I happen to think that it's pretty generally applicable, but you may not. Each of us has to create our own credo—this merely happens to be mine.

If any part of it doesn't seem to make sense, by all means call it to my attention. I'm not trying to send you out "on the road" in search of Valhalla, but merely pointing out that it is not necessary to accept the choices handed down to you by life as you know it. There is more to it than that—no one HAS to do something he doesn't want to do for the rest of his life. But then again, if that's what you wind up doing, by all means convince yourself that you HAD to do it. You'll have lots of company.

And that's it for now. Until I hear from you again, I remain,

your friend . . .
Hunter

TO *THE NEW YORK TIMES:*

Thompson's reply to a blind New York Times *want ad for a reporter failed to get him an interview.*

April 29, 1958
57 Perry Street
New York City

Box Z8726
NY TIMES

Gentlemen,

After debating for several days as to the advisability of answering your ad in last Sunday's *Times,* I've decided to take the proverbial shot in the dark. If I get a reply from something like *Family Fun, Garden Specialties,* or *Weird Confessions,* I'll know my first hunch was right.

For it is my own special shame, gentlemen, to have to admit that I am UNABLE to write for such worthy periodicals. Somewhere along the line I went wrong. Somewhere there is a great warp in my training, rendering me unfit to compose eulogies on "togetherness," exposés on prostitution rings, or heart-warming revelations on the private life of blind folk.

No, gentlemen, I seem to be of another ilk. I shall then list some three or four subjects I feel I could treat with some objectivity. If, after realizing the apparently acerbic nature of my interests, you'd like to discuss the matter any further, I shall be only too happy to place myself at your service.

Voici: (1) a discourse on the adverse effect an enthusiastic but ignorant public can have on the creative artist, giving, as a parallel case in point, the commercial oblivion lying in wait for American literature and American jazz. Since this is an article I've already developed to some degree, I could go further; but since I dislike the idea of tipping my hand to an unknown audience, I'll leave the rest to your imagination.

(2) an analysis of the term "beat generation," the whys and wherefores of a generation without a sense of values, given from a viewpoint which holds that the whole movement is a manifestation of an essentially bourgeois culture, a rebellion of the ignorant, and a serious indication of things to come (as Dadaism was in the twenties).

(3) a subjective study of the reasons for the alarming decline—in both quality and quantity—of young journalists.

I could go on and on, of course, but I think you should have a pretty good idea by now of the type of thing I'd like to do. As I said before, if it's what you're looking for, I am at your service.

Cordially,
Hunter S. Thompson

TO SUSAN HASELDEN:

Just back from an ebullient nighttime tour of New York, Thompson wrote Haselden hoping to lure her to Gotham in the near future.

May 1, 1958
57 Perry Street
New York City

Dear Susan,

After thinking over my letter of this afternoon, I feel compelled to write again to explain what must have seemed like a sudden burst of paternalism. It's just that you sounded so discouraged and so alone that I simply couldn't control the long-dormant "protector-advisor" feelings lying peacefully at the bottom of my breast. I'm sure, though, that by the time you get my letter, your despondency will have fled with the first warm breeze and my stern advice will seem like so much balderdash.

This doesn't mean, of course, that you should discount what I said. When you're let into somebody else's game, you don't make up your own rules. Unless you like the pseudo-individualist tag, you have to make a clean break. No two ideals were ever more incompatible than the security of conformity and the freedom of individuality. After the choice is made, the rest is easy—unless you don't have the guts to stick by your choice.

There's so damn much I want you to understand and words are such a poor medium when you really want someone to feel something. I've been wandering around New York since eight o'clock—it's now one-thirty—having one of the finest evenings I can remember. I spent about an hour wandering along Riverside Drive above the Hudson, then went over to Morningside Drive where you can stand right on top of Harlem and see a whole world bubbling at your feet. God, what fantastic contrasts! You have to cross the Columbia campus on the way from the river to Morningside Drive. It just doesn't seem right to try to describe it, so you'll have to come up and wander with me.

It's an unbelievably brilliant night outside. I rode down Fifth Avenue with the bus window wide open and a blasting wind in my face. I can't remember when I've felt more alive. With the searchlights from the Empire State Building sweeping the black night over Central Park, a full moon glimmering on the lake and the towers of Central Park West rising over the trees, I felt like I was gliding through a dream. I wandered around on Forty-second Street for a while and then got another bus and rode down to the Village—another fantastic contrast. After a cup of coffee with the colored pervert who lives up the hall, I came in here and seriously considered calling you on the phone. Another cup of coffee, though, and I calmed down a bit—thus saving my phone. I certainly couldn't have paid the bill.

But it's been a fantastic night and I might as well break down and admit that I missed you like hell. I'm trying to think where we could have gone swimming.

Your imminent arrival has set me to plotting feverishly, but I'm none too optimistic about it. For one thing, a mere week is far from enough time to really understand New York: and for another, a terribly ironic complication has arisen for the first week of June. Why don't you just come and live with me this summer? Things would be so much simpler. Write me about this. Love,

Hunter

TO *THE VILLAGE VOICE:*

The Village Voice *had run an article saying that the New York police were no longer busting drug dealers in Greenwich Village and on Madison Avenue. Thompson seized the opportunity to twit the* Voice—*and ask for a job.*

May 19, 1958
57 Perry Street
New York City

Editor
Village Voice

Say man, I'm bein' bugged by the police and your damn paper's the cause of it all. You've got to watch what you print around here, especially when not everybody reads your paper. I still have a huge knot on my back where that cop hit me.

What I'm talkin' about, you see, is that damn article I read in your paper about a week ago, where you talked about Madison Avenue and oppressed butlers and all that sort of thing. Well you see now, I'm a dope peddler and that article made good sense to me. As a matter of fact, it was just what I been trying to tell the cops all along. I been sayin' to myself "hell yes, if the people want my pod, why should the blasted bulls bug me about sellin' it on the street?" But I been gettin' nowhere, you see, because I couldn't get any intellectual backing. I mean it's been pure hell at times— cops chasin' me in the street and everything else!

But then, man, I read that article last week in your paper and I thought the sun had decided to shine on me at last. Man, when I saw that these boys over on Madison Avenue had been usin' my theory all along, well I felt all warm inside, you know? Man, I grabbed a bag of my stuff and hustled out into the street, figurin' that I was safe, you know—now that people had finally come to their senses. I figured Madison Avenue had led us into a new age of enlightenment, or some such thing.

So like I said, I hustled over to the Square and began hawkin' my wares—just like in the good old days. Man, I was wailin': times were good!

But then, by god, all hell broke loose. I heard this *wild* scream behind me (man, it froze my blood) and I looked around just in time to see this crazy bull come racin' over the grass yellin' like all hell! Well man, I couldn't figure it out. I sez to myself: "what in the hell's goin' on here? Hasn't this man been readin' the paper? Hasn't he been keepin' up with the news?"

But man, the way he was waving that damn club around, I knew I was goin' to have to tell him the news myself—he was one of these guys that's *nowhere*—you know?

So I evaded his first charge and tried to cool him off. I yelled, "Wait, man! Don't flog the pusher! If the people want pod, where is the justice in floggin' the pusher?" (I thought I could talk to him reasonable like, you know?)

But man, that was the stupidest bull I ever saw in my life! He couldn't even see that I had him dead to rights. All he did was scream and come at me again.

Well, right then I saw the futility of tryin' to explain these things to the illiterate bourgeois—so I took off at a dead run. But even then I barely escaped with my life: why, that fool brought that club down on my back and almost snapped my spine. If I'd been a little slower, I'd have been a sure goner!

Well, I got away, but I haven't been able to straighten up for four days because of this damn knot on my back. This pain is hell, of course, but it wouldn't bug me so much if I thought I deserved it. Now I don't blame that [Jack] Schliefer[13] guy for my trouble, you know, because he was only tryin' to spread the word. Like I said, his article made fine sense.

The whole trouble is that you people don't see to it that the cops read your paper. If that stupid bull had read Schliefer's article, you see, I wouldn't be bugged by this damn knot in my back. You dig? So let's get your circulation boy on the ball and get your paper into the police stations. It's goin' to be hell on the poor pusher until you do. And man, if you can't make the streets safe for an honest salesman, I might have to sell out and go into the advertising game. I might find it a little dull over on Madison Avenue, but at least I'd be among friends. Why don't you ask this Schliefer guy if he'll get me a job until this thing blows over?

Hopefully,
HUNTER S. THOMPSON

13. Author of the *Voice* article in question.

TO ANN FRICK:

Though there were a number of women Thompson was partially in love with—Sally Williams, Susan Haselden, Carol Overdorf, Kay Menyers, and Kraig Juenger—it was Ann Frick of Tallahassee whom he hoped one day to marry.

June 4, 1958
57 Perry Street
New York City

Dear Ann,

I've read your letter about fifteen times now, and it would take at least fifteen pages to explain exactly why I appreciate it as much as I do. It certainly wasn't because of anything in the letter itself (I'm sure you'll agree that it was a pretty limpid effort) but probably because you took the trouble to write and remind me that you're still alive and kicking, still as warm and genuine as ever, and still the same Ann Frick I remember from what now seems like a million hazy dreams ago.

God, it seems incredible that it's been almost two years since I first saw you: but, strangely enough, I think I remember almost every minute of that day—from the time I first saw you at your house, to the spider crabs and the black bathing suit and the murky water at Alligator Point, and all the way through the last minute of the night at Lake Hall.

But the memory doesn't stop there: I remember the day I first heard *My Fair Lady* at your house, the astonished embarrassment of being refused a drink at George's, sitting on a bench in front of the City Cafe in Chattahoochee with an exploded car parked many miles down the road, and the final fantasy of standing on the balcony of that unfinished building later that night and drifting off into a short-lived dream world. Ah, life is short and yesterday and tomorrow are always dreams, but I think I prefer those moments which make up the "Tallahassee dream" to most of my others. They were so lazy and warm, and yet so full of the rare tension of being almost in love. I was never quite sure what I was thinking then, but now that I look back, I think that's what it was: being "almost in love" and not understanding any of it, least of all what it meant to be in love. And I'm not even sure that I do now, especially after realizing that sex without love is as hollow and ridiculous as love without sex.

But that is neither here nor there: I'm sure this isn't the kind of response you expected when you wrote your letter, so let us steer once again into the realm of the reasonable, leaving questions of sex, love, and recurring dreams to a later date.

As for your questions as to what I'm doing, I can only say that I'm not quite sure myself. Living in New York is like discovering life all over again. In all seriousness, living here has been like waking up in an endlessly fascinating and completely different world from everything I've ever known. Having my own apartment in Greenwich Village, working in Rockefeller Plaza, riding up and down Fifth Avenue every day, standing on an East River dock at dawn and seeing the Empire State Building towering above this incredible skyline, meeting the thousands of people from every corner of America: the whole thing still seems a little unreal. And, brash as it may seem, I know I'm not going to be able to end this letter without giving you a standing invitation to come up and see me. If there's anything that could make living here any better, I think it would be having you here with me—if only to show you that the dreams you dream on boring nights in Tallahassee can be a reality if you only look hard enough. And I shouldn't have said "boring," because that's the last term I'd apply to Tallahassee. I might possibly have been restless there, but never bored. And I think I'd be restless anywhere, at least until my blood cools down a bit. But I'm not even looking forward to that for a while. Life just seems too huge and too fascinating for me to begin thinking about curing my restlessness at this stage of the game. Maybe later.

I was absolutely serious, though, when I issued my invitation. I can't think of anything I'd enjoy more right now than introducing New York to Ann Frick. (And I suppose it would be a little sneaky of me to neglect to say that there are few things I'd enjoy more than seeing Ann Frick again—but I promised not to say things like that, so we'll just leave it unsaid, but understood.) I am capable of maintaining a platonic relationship—I suppose.

But since you said that you *hoped* to find work after you finish with your fellowship tours, I thought it would be hardly decent of me to allow you to pass up the idea of looking around New York. Note the ad I clipped out of *The Village Voice.* What could be easier—for you, anyway?

And, incidentally, I shouldn't have waited this long to congratulate you on winning this fellowship. I hope you have a great time in St. Louis and in Michigan, and I wish you all the luck in the world in your teaching. I'd tell you a few people to get in touch with in St. Louis, but they're all degenerates, so I'm afraid I'll have to let you go it alone. Rest assured that it's the best way.

I'm expecting a friend of mine from Yale to arrive sometime early tomorrow, so I think I'd best get a little sleep. I'll close this with something very close to a demand that you write immediately and let me know if you'll be able to ride the Staten Island Ferry with me sometime before the summer ends. I refuse to even consider any alternatives or excuses, and I

trust you realize that I'm absolutely serious. You know how I am about polite banalities.

So until then, I remain, incorrigibly and affectionately (and still remembering exactly what it was like to be "almost in love") . . . . . .

Hunto

TO LARRY CALLEN:

Callen was still stationed in Iceland, also hoping to be a writer someday.

June 6, 1958
57 Perry Street
New York City

Dear Larry,

You have been singled out to bear the brunt of a nightmare, something
very close to the alcoholic demise of a man who never quite seems to have
a grip on things. Bear with me.

My apartment, once the scene of lazy sex and quiet privacy, has erupted
during the past two weeks into a virtual cave of howling drunken insanity.
There are people sleeping everywhere—on my bed, on the couch, on the
cot, and even on sleeping bags on the floor. Everything in the place is covered with stale beer, most of my records are ruined, every piece of linen,
towel, or clothing in the place is filthy, the dishes haven't been washed in
weeks, the neighbors have petitioned the landlord to have me evicted, my
sex life has been absolutely smashed, I have no money, no food, no privacy, and certainly no peace of mind. And on top of all this, I get on the average of one letter a day informing me that someone else is on his way to
New York to "see me."

The place looks like a goddamn interracial hotel. I have with me now
one law student, one rum-soaked philosopher, and one negro painter. Due
within two weeks are a zoologist and a professional lease-breaker from
New Orleans, a girl from Boston, and a fanatical nihilist from Louisville.
And in the next few months I expect not only my brother, but Pete Goodman from Eglin, girls from Baltimore, St. Louis, and Tallahassee, and a
tyro dramatist from New Mexico. And god only knows who else. These are
only the ones I've heard from.

Last Monday and Tuesday, the law student and I consumed twenty-one
quarts of beer. In the three days since then, we've more than tripled that.
The record player goes at top volume both day and night—no one
works—and the police have been called on me three times within the past
week. There is baggage everywhere, huge paintings are piled in every cor-

ner, the floor is an inch deep in scum, there is not a goddamn scrap of food anywhere, no one has any money, and wild jungle music drowns out all thought. I am hounded by creditors, bugged by the police, threatened with eviction, seriously considering murder, and stone broke. Fortunately— and somehow—I've managed to hold onto my job at *Time*. Which goes to show that perfection is still impossible.

A typical day, just for the record. I woke up at six this morning, met a girl from Louisville at the Port Authority Terminal at seven, came back to the apartment for breakfast and a bout with the drunken law student, nearly became involved in a sex orgy, and finally got to work about eleven. After a hectic and confusing day at work, I arrived back here at seven-thirty to find the philosopher and the painter spewing blood all over the apartment and trading sarcasms with the law student. I had a date at ten, ran into another girl on the way to my date's apartment, and tarried long enough to miss my date. Bought several quarts of beer and broke in on a girl who already had a date. Left feeling like an ass. Arrived back here and spent an abortive hour trying to get hold of my original date. Failed. Am waiting now for the horde to return for another night-long drinking bout. The girl from Louisville left for a weekend in Boston at eleven this morning. She will return Monday. What then?

Frankly, there is nothing to do but drink. There are more quarts of beer in here than there are dead roaches. We don't kill them anymore—just wound them and let them writhe and die wherever they please. Broken glass is everywhere.

And this used to be MY apartment! It was where I wrote and brought dates when I had no money, where I sat and listened to music and read and ate. It was MINE, my own—and now it's a sinkhole of noise and drink, a sort of human cesspool with ever-changing ingredients. And god only knows what will happen tomorrow.

And that's about it. I feel better now that I've put it in order and gotten it down on paper. It has changed from nightmare to nightmarish reality.

Write—and give me a ring when you get back in New York. Maybe I'll be alive.

Cheerio . . .
HST

TO LARRY CALLEN:

With the literary world abuzz about the so-called Beat Generation and the Angry Young Men, Thompson ponders whether he is a writer of "action" (Hemingway, Kerouac) or of "thought" (Joyce, Faulkner).

July 4, 1958
Time & Life Building
Rockefeller Center
New York

Dear Larry,

Well, I've finally managed to sit down at a typewriter: it's been a long, hard month. It's one that I'm going to have to write off as a total loss, work-wise, and a hellish experience, living-wise. I've consumed an ungodly amount of liquid spirits, given in completely to the sexual spirit, and thrown all the other spirits to hell. There are sweet little southern girls here too, but they seem to be a little different here than they are in their natural setting. I thought I was a pretty hardened lecher, but even I have paled more than once at the sight of the "sweet little ole southern (or midwestern) mask" slipping off to reveal a gin-inflamed bitch in heat. Carry me back to the womb, Daddy, just like you done with so many others!

But as Scott Fitzgerald must have said to himself more than once: "now is the time to get a grip." I have to pay the rent with this paycheck, so my task will be that much easier. No more buying a fifth of McCarthy Square gin each night, no more damn cab races to the Plaza fountain or the East River for a morning "dip," no more five-course dinners on the balcony, or cocktails on the roof, or all-night orgies, or theatres: in short, the squeeze is on us; the party is over—at least for two weeks. Then I'll have money again. (Overindulgence, thy name is Hunter!)

But even though all these are pretty overt signs of galloping dissipation, they really aren't my main source of concern. The real difference between this latest binge and all the others of the past two years is that I seem to have lost what I think is the most important thing a writer can have: the ability to live with constant loneliness and a strong sense of revulsion for the banalities of everyday socializing. It just doesn't seem very important anymore that I write. I can understand this, I think, in light of what I call "the psychology of imposition." This theory holds that the most overriding of all human desires is the need to amount to something. I'm not talking about the old Horatio Alger gimmick, but the more basic desire to know that your life means something. As Faulkner says, writing is his way of saying "Kilroy was here," of imposing himself, however briefly, on reality. If only for an instant, the image of the man is imposed on the chaotic mainstream of life and it remains there forever: order out of chaos, meaning out of meaninglessness. Just as some people turn to religion to find meaning, the writer turns to his craft and tries to impose meaning, or to sift the meaning out of chaos and put it in order.

But—and here is where I'm going to try to justify my reason for not feeling the need to write—there is a school of thought (Oswald Spengler) which has classified men in one of two categories: the action men and the thought men. These are vague terms and Spengler's were unquestionably better— but you should know what I mean, even if you don't agree with me. So we look at people like Joyce or Proust or Pound, or for that matter, almost any of history's best writers, and we find virtually the same personality type (of the two, anyway). But they were all people who depended on their writing to give them the meaning or the satisfaction, if you will, that they sought.

And then we have Rabelais, and Hemingway and to some extent Fitzgerald and certainly a host of others I'm not going to take the time to think about right now. Certainly the example of Hemingway should be enough.

Pause for re-location and abstract commentary of sorts . . . I've just been reading *Time*'s biographical file on Kingsley Amis (*Lucky Jim*) and the new British intellectuals. Somerset Maugham has a beautiful comment which I'm not at all surprised to have missed in many another article on the "angry young men." He says, and I quote: "it (*Lucky Jim*) describes a new class, the white-collar proletariat . . . which does not go to the university to acquire culture, but to get a job, and when they get one, scamp it. Their idea of a celebration is to go to a public house and drink six beers. They are mean, malicious, envious . . . they are scum."

Good old Maugham: it's good to see the sledge-hammer coming down from the top for a change, instead of striking up at the belly of society from the bottom.

Of course you're so far out of it up there that you probably don't realize that the "beat generation" is taking over American literature, while the "angry young men" are the driving force in Britain. And although I'm neither beat nor necessarily angry, I'm glad to see somebody taking a stand for a change. It's the first real "movement" in literature in many a year: a point of reference, if nothing else. The writing world seems at least to have settled into two very definitely opposing camps: the pedants and the hobos. Most of the best writers fit in neither camp, of course, but then very few of them ever have. A good writer stands above movements, neither a leader nor a follower, but a bright white golf ball in a fairway of wind-blown daisies. (If you've never played golf, you won't understand how pleasant it is to walk down a fairway and see forty or fifty balls where yours should be—and then come a little closer and recognize the ball, a little rounder and a little whiter than the rest, and a hell of a lot more solid. The moral of this story is: Play golf!)

But I forgot that you're Iceland's answer to Jane Austen, so I'll close this harangue and get back to my original thesis.

I was talking about the need to impose oneself on reality and the difference between action men and thought men. (I think that statement makes

the whole thing more clear and concise than my entire first page succeeded in doing.)

But it's obvious that the need is there and that the two categories of men
have two different ways of doing it. And it seems that the ones who are either unable or unwilling to impose themselves on life through their actions are the ones who succeed most significantly in the thought (or
writing, in this case) category.

Now Hemingway seems to have done it from both angles: he's not even
bothered—or possibly not been able—to create his own world in his books
(à la Joyce, James, Faulkner, Proust, etc.) but he's mastered reality and still
managed to become one hell of a good writer as well. (There are others, of
course, but Hemingway serves as such a good example because his life and
times are so familiar as to still apply in our day.)

But Fitzgerald tried and Fitzgerald failed and Fitzgerald didn't learn to
think until it was too late. He was probably one of the great natural talents
of any age and he could make a typewriter sound like a piano when he was
in form, but he was not a thinker—and neither was (or is) Hemingway.
And yet, they're both—from the point of view of natural facility with the
world—two of the best writers of the century, anyway.

So the difference, I think, boils down to this: you can either impose
yourself on reality and *then* write about it, or you can impose yourself on
reality *by* writing.

It's time to go now: I have to go down to the Village and destroy some
furniture. This is merely the first of a series of lectures on "subjects
Thompson needs to get straight in his mind." I find that writing is the best
way. So until later, it's cheerio. . . .

Hunter

TO KRAIG JUENGER:

*Kraig had gotten a job at the Rawlings sporting goods company in St. Louis.
Thompson tried to lure her to New York.*

> Time & Life Building
> Rockefeller Center
> New York
> July 4, 1958

Dear Kraig,
Your letter was a real surprise; a very pleasant one, of course, but nevertheless, a real shot out of the blue. And then to find out that you'd actually

written your previous letter from the Rawlings desk was almost too much. It was so typically Kraig that I had to smile.

I'd been meaning to write before this, but something has always come up to send me off after something else, usually drink. I think I've written about three letters during the past month; it's been a very expensive but very pleasant binge. You'd probably be interested to know that I'm getting better and better at binges, sometimes wild and sleepless three-day things which travel from a Greenwich Village rooftop to the East River to the Biltmore and then on to the Plaza fountain for a morning swim. And sometimes they just sit in my place and explode. That's the good thing about orgies—you never know exactly what's going to happen.

But today I wanted to be in St. Louis. I forgot it was the fourth of July and thought of it as just a hot and lazy midwest Sunday. I thought I'd like to drive in from Collinsville with your top down and see *The Student Prince* at the Muny Opera again; and then I thought I'd like to drive through Forest Park and out to the Tic Toc Tap for a tall gin-and-tonic and maybe listen to George Shearing or possibly Errol Garner. And then I decided to drive on out past Collinsville to someplace like Trenton where we could stop and sit in one of those endless fields and drink Crystal Apple Wine out of tall thin glasses while the moon sparkled on the grass and the wind made our cigarettes burn a bright orange in the dark. But it would be late by then and you'd be tired, and the dawn wind would be cold as we drove back to Collinsville. We'd keep the top down, though, and watch the sun climb out of the east and know that New York was a thousand miles and a million quiet towns behind it. Somewhere behind the sun the windows of the Empire State Building would be sparkling in the dawn and the East River would be very quiet and very silver.

But it's all a dream and if you're ever up at dawn look up at that sun as it comes climbing out of Indiana, and think that I may be standing out at the end of a pier in the East River and watching the sun float off over the Alleghenies to St. Louis, and wondering if you're watching it too.

And that's enough of daydreams.

If you remember my "meanest" letter, you'll recall that everything I said was aimed at your conception of Madison Avenue. I merely wanted to straighten you out if you thought that's what I'm doing in New York. Oddly enough, you took it all as a personal insult, cancelled your trip to my grotto, and told me off—all in one fell swoop. But—having an excellent sense of humor—I took it well.

I may even make it to St. Louis for a day or so sometime in the middle of August. It's certainly not definite, but I might be able to swing it; probably for no more than one or two days, at best.

And naturally I leave my invitation open. Just let me know a little in advance.

Write and tell me what you're going to be doing in the fall. School? Where? And what after that? And tell my clean-cut bourgeois friends at Rawlings hello for me. I think you'd *better* come to New York. One of us is looking at the wrong Hunter.

> So until then, I remain,
> the same, incorrigible,
> HST

TO LARRY CALLEN:

Thompson wrote Callen in Iceland about his wildly erratic behavior at Henry Luce's Sunday Time-Life *parties. He also explained why letter writing is so cathartic.*

> July 14, 1958
> 57 Perry Street
> New York City

Dear Larry,

Another soul-purge is at hand, so perhaps you'd better save this for one of those long and sunny arctic nights—it won't make very good reading for the daylight hours when you have better things to do.

The title of this one might well be: "The Midnight Sins of HST, a Study in Alcoholic Kleptomania."

It might surprise you to know that Henry Luce sets up a free bar for his employees every Sunday night. It then follows logically that one or more of Luce's employees invariably gets blind scowling blabbering drunk every Sunday night. I am that employee: there are others, of course, but others of a milder temperament than mine. Another logical conclusion we could draw would seem to be that Luce's employees would think well of him and refrain from doing strange and vicious things to or on his property. Guess again.

Last night I staggered out of the building at about one in the morning, weaving under the burden of a huge floor fan. And among other prizes, I had a dictionary of synonyms, five turkey sandwiches, and desk pen and holder, a huge ashtray, one copy of *Winesburg, Ohio,* and one copy of the *Viking Portable Sherwood Anderson.* All of this was in a monstrous box I carried on my shoulder—and all of it belonged to Luce. Had I been apprehended, I would undoubtedly have lost my job and had "fired for stealing" emblazoned on my employee's card. Hence, no reference for future employment.

Actually, I don't quite understand exactly why I feel so bad about all this, because it was merely another in a long chain of "Thompsonisms" which stretches in a black and unbroken line all the way back to the second or third year in my life. But as the old saying goes, "he who lives by the sword shall die by the sword," and I have a strange premonition that a figurative death is nigh. Perhaps it's just one of those odd psychological phenomena concerning the nature of guilt; I haven't spent enough time with Jesus to know. Maybe I can succeed in purging my guilt by understanding it; maybe.

But it wasn't just the pointless theft; the entire night was one of the most frightening and most typical I've spent in some time. It began at about five when I started drinking and ended at about five this morning when I passed out on my couch. During those twelve hours I managed to get into drunken and sarcastic arguments with several people at work, make an ass of myself with the girl I've been dating, spend about six dollars in cab fares, drink a fifth of scotch, fall down about five times in the Plaza fountain before the police hauled me out, come within an ace of spending the night in the tombs (jail), wake up with the occupants of an entire building at the corner of Fifth Avenue and Fifty-fifth, terrorize an apartment full of girls I know in the same building, savagely alienate the two companions who made this odyssey with me, and lose an entire day of writing in sleeping the thing off.

Taking the whole night as a sort of definitive act, it implies an approach to life which not only is characterized by, but embodies, a complete lack of organization and discipline, an all-pervading selfishness, the epitome of irresponsibility, and an absolute lack of self-control. And I don't even want to go into what the alcoholic theft might imply; I might decide to have myself committed.

The point of all this, though, is not so much that I *do* these things, but that I do them and understand them and do them again. Just as surely as this kind of thing has happened before, it's damn sure to happen again— probably next Sunday, for that matter.

Now I've run out of things to say. There's obviously no sense in talking about this kind of thing . . . or maybe there is, at that: I find that by putting things in writing I can understand them and see them a little more objectively. And I guess that's one of the real objectives of writing, to show things (or life) as they are, and thereby discover truth out of chaos. And now that I think on it a while, I think that the very fact that I write this letter and that I feel a need to write it shows the value of putting words in order on a piece of paper. For words are merely tools and if you use the right ones you can actually put even your life in order, if you don't lie to yourself and use the wrong words. And I guess that is why I write as many letters as I do, because it's the only way—outside of actually getting to work and writing fiction—I can look at life objectively. Otherwise, I'm so involved in it that I forget that the rest of the world is merely a stage setting for my life. And that's about it for now. I don't expect you to answer all these questions; just write occasionally and tell me how things are coming on "The Rock."[14] Until I hear from you or see you, I remain . . .

paradoxically,
Hunter

TO ANN FRICK:

In August 1958 Thompson hitchhiked around the country. He stopped in Tallahassee for an evening to see Ann Frick; it was the highlight of his journey.

August 29, 1958
Time & Life Building
Rockefeller Center
New York

Dear Ann,

I'll try to keep this letter as mild and detached as possible: my last two strayed off toward two separate extremes, so I shouldn't have much trouble going right up the middle on this one. Let us see.

I should begin, I suppose, by saying that I enjoyed last Monday night as much or more than I've enjoyed any date in many, many a day. I think I did an excellent job of maintaining my composure, but to be truthful, I was absolutely astounded with almost everything that went on all night. It seems quite impossible that anyone—especially someone as conscious of change as I am—could return to a place like Tallahassee after a year's absence and find it even better than it was in memory. Frankly, I was more than a little leery of making a return visit at all—that's why I allowed only one day and one night of my time for Tallahassee. And now I'm sorry I couldn't stay longer.

But perhaps it's best that I came and left as fast as I did. It was like a night snatched out of the past, a pleasant memory materializing into reality for a few hours and then fading into the distance once again. It was the absolute reverse of what I'd expected and I'm afraid it left me a little unnerved. I don't know whether or not you realize how difficult it usually is to recapture a memory (some people spend most of their adult lives trying to live in the past, you know), but whether you were so perfect on purpose

14. Thompson's name for Iceland.

or not, you managed to do a damned masterful job. If you were merely putting on a performance, then I suppose I should thank you: but if you did it by merely being Ann Frick, I'm afraid a simple "thank you" would hardly be the thing to say. As a matter of fact, I feel the same way now as I did that night—I don't know exactly what to say.

What I really expected, you see, was to come down to Tallahassee and find that you were someone I didn't even know anymore. I was pretty sure that the Ann Frick I remembered was just a pretty picture in my wallet and a few pretty memories drifting around in the back of my head. The idea that the reality would be even better than the memory never even crossed my mind. So I suppose you can see why I'm a little confused: instead of purging a bothersome memory from my mind, I've only succeeded in bringing it back into bright and insistent focus again. The effects of this sort of thing can easily be unfortunate. Last night, for instance, I found myself forced to sever relations with a young woman I'd been dating pretty regularly for several months. It was a savage but necessary thing to do: I just took one look at her when I got back and decided that she no longer measured up. I felt like hell about it, of course, but I really had no choice. I've never been very good at leading people on, especially when I have to be a bigger hypocrite with every passing day.

But then there's no sense in rambling on about all this; I merely meant to show you what sort of effect you had on me. Right now I'm sort of suspended between two diverging courses of action. I shall have to think.

Love, Hunter

TO ANN FRICK:

Almost every month Thompson would have a breakdown of sorts and fire off letters exuding his angst over the modern condition. Usually these missives were the result of a drunken bender triggered by the burden of debt.

September 5, 1958
Time & Life Building
Rockefeller Center
New York

Dear Ann,
I've been trying to finish this letter for days. I am heading for an alcoholic breakdown. Everyone I've ever known has burst in on me during the past week. Two of my best friends got in a drunken fight in Davenport, Iowa—and now one of them is dead and the other is ready to stand trial for murder (or possibly manslaughter). A gun takes one life, a prison takes the

other—what the hell is the difference? Give me the gut-ripping pain of a bullet anytime.

The phone company is ready to take out my phone and the light company is ready to cut off my gas and electricity. I cashed a check for my bond in Florida and it bounced. Tomorrow one of my brothers will poison the other and my mother will confess to having been a Communist spy for fifteen years. I paid half my rent with a check and it will bounce. In the country of the blind, the one-eyed man is king.

"It kills the very brave and the very good and the very gentle indiscriminately. If you are none of these, it will kill you too. But there will be no special hurry."

—Ernest Hemingway—

I have no desire to do anything. I am afraid of nothing and I want nothing, I wait like a psychopath in a game of dodge-ball: breathing quickly while the fools decide which one will throw at me next, and jumping aside for no reason except that I like being in the middle. And there is really no reason for being in the middle. Why not quit altogether and lie down outside the circle?

I have no idea what to say, I don't know when I'll see you again and I don't believe in anything beyond the next ten minutes. People keep calling me and telling me what a great friend I am. Everybody is looking for someone who can stand up in the wind. It is lonely standing up and crowded lying down. I refuse to be an anchor for other people's dreams— but then I refuse to anchor mine to anyone else. So I have no choice but to stand up and piss into the wind. Pardon my vulgarity.

But this is all a little foolish and I'm dragging up words that mean little or nothing. Thank Verna and Lee[15] again for the hospitality, accept my apologies for the telegrams, and try to keep from being killed or twisted or beaten beyond recognition. The old glue-mask doesn't serve much of a purpose, but it does help to deaden the pain of the blows!

Until I get fooled again by some optimistic sign, I remain,

ready to lash out . . .
Hunty

TO PAUL SEMONIN:

A self-styled Marxist from Louisville's upper middle class, Semonin had been one grade ahead of Thompson in high school. At this point he was a Marine stationed on Parris Island, South Carolina.

---

15. The couple ran the boardinghouse where Thompson stayed while in Tallahassee.

September 26, 1958
57 Perry Street
New York City

Dear Paul,

You'll be happy to know that your letters are getting through to the out-side world. It is surprising, though, to find that those swine are letting mail get *in*. [. . .]

I know exactly what you mean when you say that your stay at P.I. is an "educational experiment" with the lowest form of human life: and I know from experience that it can be a revelation of sorts. Ah yes. But when you realize, my man, that what you are seeing is a cross-section of "the world we live in," rather than an invasion of flotsam from some distant land, it is then that the novelty of your experience will begin to curdle. You will soon see that intellectual myopia is not a disease limited to dolts and mental de-fectives. Grey matter thrives on exercise and atrophies without it. Myopia is every bit as crippling whether it be voluntary or congenital.

So try placing your khaki-colored boys in the context of contemporary history; step back and view the USMC as merely one facet of what is some-times called the "American Culture." You are not "on loan" to the USMC on an amusing vacation from another world, but on a lower rung of the same wobbling ladder. And you know what happens to the people on top when a ladder rots in the middle.

As for me, I have no hope for any of us: if Khrushchev and Mao don't get us from the outside, either the Arthur Schlesinger–Walter Reuther fac-tion or the William Buckley–Gerald L.K. Smith faction will paralyze us internally.[16] The mind of America is seized by a fatal dry rot—and it's only a question of time before all that the mind controls will run amuck in a frenzy of stupid, impotent fear. Is it any wonder that Billy Graham is so popular? Oh God, give us anything but reality!

As for your question on Formosa, here is the Thompson outlook: Red China has declared that "no force on earth can prevent us from taking Que-moy and Matsu."[17] The islands have been under continuous bombardment for weeks and in spite of the fact that the Nationalists are getting through from Formosa with supplies, the islands will not last much longer. Chiang [Kai-shek] wants to send his air force to attack the Red shore batteries—[Secretary of State John Foster] Dulles says no. If that happens, there is little doubt that

16. Thompson considered historian Arthur Schlesinger, Jr., and United Auto Workers president Walter Reuther to be "far left" and conservative columnist William Buckley and populist dema-gogue Gerald L.K. Smith "far right."
17. Quemoy and Matsu were islands between mainland China and Taiwan that both govern-ments claimed.

Red planes will retaliate against Taiwan. The U.S. is pledged to defend Taiwan and Dulles has said repeatedly that we will do so if and when it becomes necessary. Red China, at the Warsaw cease-fire talks, has demanded the immediate removal of U.S. forces from the Taiwan area. If they are not removed voluntarily, they say, then they *will* be removed by force. Russia says that it will back Mao to the limit in the face of U.S. "aggression." Washington cannot decide whether the Mao-Kremlin team is bluffing or not. As for precedents, it turned out that Russia *was* bluffing in the case of the Berlin airlift, but that Red China was *not* bluffing when they threatened to intervene in Korea. The vicious tone of the Red diplomatic line is thoroughly unprecedented. In short, this is the biggest and most threatening bluff yet, and no one on the U.S. side of the fence knows whether to call it or not. We cannot afford to back down and we cannot afford war: jesus help us all if it is not a bluff. If the Reds have decided that the time has come for war I'll either reenlist or escape to Mexico. Hopefully, it will all blow over. Only time will tell.

Hunter

TO JACK SCOTT, *VANCOUVER SUN:*

Clearly not the way for an aspiring journalist to get a newspaper job, this letter, Thompson claimed, was "written in a frenzy of drink."

October 1, 1958
57 Perry Street
New York City

Sir,

I got a hell of a kick out of reading the piece *Time* magazine did this week on the *Sun*. In addition to wishing you the best of luck, I'd also like to offer my services.

Since I haven't seen a copy of the "new" *Sun* yet, I'll have to make this a tentative offer. I stepped into a dung-hole the last time I took a job with a paper I didn't know anything about (see enclosed clippings) and I'm not quite ready to go charging up another blind alley. By the time you get this letter, I'll have gotten hold of some of the recent issues of the *Sun*. Unless it looks totally worthless, I'll let my offer stand.

And don't think that my arrogance is unintentional: it's just that I'd rather offend you now than after I started working for you. I didn't make myself clear to the last man I worked for until after I took the job. It was as if the Marquis de Sade had suddenly found himself working for Billy Graham. The man despised me, of course, and I had nothing but contempt for him and everything he stood for. If you asked him, he'd tell you that I'm "not very likeable, (that I) hate people, (that I) just want to be left alone, and (that I) feel too superior to mingle with the average person." (That's a direct quote from a memo he sent to the publisher.) Nothing beats having good references.

Of course if you asked some of the other people I've worked for, you'd get a different set of answers. If you're interested enough to answer this letter, I'll be glad to furnish you with a list of references—including the lad I work for now.

The enclosed clippings should give you a rough idea of who I am. It's a year old, however, and I've changed a bit since it was written. I've taken some writing courses from Columbia in my spare time, learned a hell of a lot about the newspaper business, and developed a healthy contempt for journalism as a profession. As far as I'm concerned, it's a damned shame that a field as potentially dynamic and vital as journalism should be overrun with dullards, bums, and hacks, hagridden with myopia, apathy, and complacence, and generally stuck in a bog of stagnant mediocrity. If this is what you're trying to get the *Sun* away from, then I think I'd like to work for you.

Most of my experience has been in sportswriting, but I can write everything from warmongering propaganda to learned book reviews. I can work twenty-five hours a day if necessary, live on any reasonable salary, and don't give a black damn for job security, office politics, or adverse public relations. I would rather be on the dole than work for a paper I was ashamed of.

It's a long way from here to British Columbia, but I think I'd enjoy the trip. If you think you can use me, drop me a line. If not, good luck anyway.

> Sincerely,
> Hunter S. Thompson

TO SUSAN HASELDEN:

Haselden had written Thompson from Boston, enthralled with the works of Jack Kerouac and other members of the Beat Generation. Thompson enjoyed On the Road *but found Kerouac's other books weak. More to the point, he was always disparaging of beatnik wannabes—a malady he feared Haselden was suffering from.*

> November 12, 1958
> 57 Perry Street
> New York City

Dear Susan,

You must be going absolutely crazy and I don't know whether to laugh or cry. I think you'd better get back to Louisville and marry some good and steady type. And keep away from that goddamn San Francisco!

And certainly I've read *The Subterraneans*: all of his crap for that matter. The man is an ass, a mystic boob with intellectual myopia. The *Dharma* thing was not quite as bad as *The Subterraneans* and they're both withered appendages to *On the Road*—which isn't even a novel in the first place. As the Siamese say, "Pea rattles loud in empty head." And so much for Mr. K—who found a way out of it all. Bully for him . . . and all his lemmings. If somebody doesn't kill that fool soon, we're all going to be labeled "The Generation of the Third Sex."

But I seem to be excited . . . and that is nowhere . . . for to be excited is to be square . . . and to be square is to be hung up . . . and that is nowhere either. It is difficult to know just what to do . . . or which label to adopt . . . and we must all be labeled . . . for there is no identity without solidarity . . . and identity is important . . . I think?

You and your friends can stay with me when you come down for Thanksgiving. I haven't had a real ripping orgy in quite a while. It will be weird. Be sure to call. WA9-xxxx. Anytime. I work only 2½ days a week, and I am POVERTY-STRICKEN. Bring food.

I want to get to Boston before I have to flee the country and that will be soon. I will have to stay at your place of course, but I will wear a chastity belt and there will be no trouble. I don't know when I'll have the money to get up there. Probably never—so I'll have to come without money. Ah well, I'll bring my rucksack and my string of juju beads . . . and a few odes by Han Shan. You will be happy. [. . .]

Life is weird here and I'm currently trying to set up a job for myself in Europe. It is not easy. But I will go anyway . . . and throw myself on the mercy of the Embassy if I can't get a job.

Drop me a line. And keep away from San Francisco.

Suspiciously:
Hunter

TO KRAIG JUENGER:

Juenger's mother had been diagnosed with cancer; Thompson's father had died when Hunter was only fourteen.

November 22, 1958
Time & Life Building
Rockefeller Center
New York

Dear Kraig,

Your letter was quite a jolt and it seems a little silly for me to say that I'm sorry to hear about your mother because expressions like that seem to be out of place except on printed "sympathy cards." But you know that I'm sorry as hell and I hope it's not as serious as you seem to think. It seems incredible to me that this sort of thing always happens to the people I like best—I simply can't understand why the useless ones aren't struck down first. But I guess Hemingway was right: "It kills the very good and the very gentle and the very brave indiscriminately. If you are none of these you can be sure it will kill you too, but there will be no special hurry."

Be sure to let me know how things turn out and rest assured that I *do* understand. My father is no longer with us, you know.

I don't want to sound disappointed over the prospect of your not being able to come to New York during the holidays, but you know damned well that the idea doesn't make me any too happy. But by all means do whatever you feel you should do and let me know what you decide.

Very little is happening here and I sort of talked myself out in the letter I wrote last week. When you calm down a little more be sure to drop me a line. And don't let your imagination run away with you because a hell of a lot of people have had tumors removed without the operations proving fatal. So until I hear from you, stay calm and don't jump until you're sure you've been hit.

Love, Hunter

TO *EDITOR & PUBLISHER:*

Thompson fired off this response to a column claiming that young people weren't interested in journalism careers because its pay scale was so low.

December 7, 1958
57 Perry Street
New York City

Jerome H. Walker
Editor & Publisher
1700 Times Tower
New York City

Dear Sir,

When I read your column of November 29th ("Pay's Good, Come on In") I fell into a fit of despair and decided to go out the very next day and sign up for unemployment insurance. Since I haven't lost *all* of my self-respect yet I finally decided against it, but I've been boiling about that damned column all week.

So you're worried that journalism isn't getting its share of young talent and you think its because a bunch of embittered old men have spread the rumor that it's a "poor pay game." If nothing else, your column makes you a red-hot candidate for The Thompson Trophy for the Most Myopic Analysis of the Year, a dubious honor at best. You and all the rest of the "serious thinkers" on journalism's great wailing wall remind me of a leper standing in a bar, waving a huge sack of money and yelling, "What's wrong with you people? Why don't you want to drink with me? I have enough money, see!"

The leper may not want to admit it but I think he knows why he's no popularity king—it's just as obvious as the sores on his back. And I think the reason for journalism's shortage of young talent is just as obvious as the fact that most of the newspapers in the country today are overcrowded rest homes for inept hacks. Burial grounds do not attract talent.

In a nutshell, journalism has lost its primary selling points, the very things which used to make salary a secondary factor. The best American journalists have invariably been respected, envied, and often emulated. Traditionally, they've not only held onto their individuality but capitalized on it, not only maintained their self-respect but commanded the respect of others. Why do you think the New York Yankees generally get their pick of the country's young baseball talent? It's not just because they hand out good paychecks.

How many newspapers are there in the country today that actually command the respect of anyone who knows a damned thing about journalism? I'd have a hard time counting ten. And there's where we come to the pith and substance of the whole problem: since journalism has lost its ability to command respect as a profession, it has sunk to the level of "just another job." Where salary used to be secondary it is now primary. Whereas journalism formerly attracted top talent *in spite of* a generally low salary scale it has now reduced itself to a level where it has to compete with related fields (PR, Advertising, TV, etc.) *on their terms*. And the terms, of course, are almost always monetary, and let's not kid ourselves about the salaries in the top brackets of journalism as compared to comparable ones in advertising, TV, and PR.

So there you have it: journalism, for my money, has nearly tumbled head over heels in its hurry to toss away its integrity and compromise with the public taste, the mass intellect, and the self-sighted demands of profit-hungry advertisers. Now how in the hell do you *expect* to keep on attracting top talent? Sacrificing good men to journalism is like sending William Faulkner to work for *Time* magazine.

Motto: "If you're given a choice between cheap and cheaper, why not learn how to write ad copy and then put yourself on the grey-flannel auction block? There is no god but MONEY!"

As far as I'm concerned, what I've said so far is a pretty thorough condemnation, but incredibly enough there's more. I contend that newspapers, especially in New York, have become so institutionalized, so complacent, and so blind to their own needs that they think they can afford to play "hard to get" with the young talent they can still attract. I'm speaking out of my own experience here because I've spent about six months looking for a decent newspaper job and I'm about to give up the ghost. And when I say "decent job" I mean one I can be proud of with a paper I respect. There is plenty of money in the world but there are damn few jobs an intelligent man can do without compromising himself intolerably. Everywhere you turn people seem to be warning each other about "the dangerous trend towards standardization" but I have yet to see signs of anyone doing anything about it. I'll bet that if I went to *Fortune* magazine and asked William Whyte[18] himself for a job he'd have me take one of those abominable personality tests he went to so much trouble to warn us about.

Look at the help-wanted ads in the *Times*—trade papers, house organs. Look at your own ads in *E & P*—one-horse gossip sheets and country weeklies. Ask for a job with a big daily that obviously needs new blood—"sorry, we don't need anyone. Don't call us, we'll call you." Then pick up *E & P* and read your own column again. You people don't need to offer better salaries, all you have to do is raise your damned standards a bit! And as long as 90% of the papers in this country are staffed by complacent hacks those standards are going to stay right where they are. You people have your backs to the wall and you'd better open your eyes in one hell of a hurry. A free press is not indispensable unless it *makes* itself indispensable. So how about cleaning up your house and *then* bellowing about no one wanting to come in?

Cordially,
Hunter S. Thompson

PS: If you know anyone who needs a firebrand critic of sorts, just drop me a line.

TO ANN FRICK:

During his stint at Time, *Thompson polished his writing skills by typing* The Great Gatsby *and* A Farewell to Arms *in their entirety, closely studying their sentence structures. Fascinated to learn that Thompson was studying American literature so carefully, Frick wrote him a long letter seeking recommendations for her reading list.*

---

18. *Fortune* editor William Whyte's novel *The Organization Man* had just been published to great acclaim.

December 19, 1958
Time & Life Building
Rockefeller Center
New York

Dear Ann,

This is a borrowed typewriter and I'll probably make four million mistakes so bear with me and keep your head.

To continue with your questions:

. . . from last week: *Brave New World* (Huxley), *The Great Gatsby* (Fitzgerald), *A Farewell to Arms* (Hemingway), *The Organization Man* (Whyte), *The Best of Everything* (Jaffe)—this one hardly belongs in the abovementioned company but it's one which would interest any girl who intends to come to New York and look for a job. Actually, there's very little sense in my going on with this list; the ones I've mentioned are books that *nobody* should miss reading, as far as I'm concerned, but I could list at least a hundred more and that would be a little senseless. It's excellent, however, that your mind is beginning to stir a bit and I'll keep that in mind in future letters. We may yet succeed in pulling your mind out of the fog!

My aptitude on dancing—as you put it—has not changed in several years, primarily because I've had no occasion to even think about it, much less consider changing it. My four years at dancing school served me about as well as my two years of piano lessons and I can't understand how such a wasted childhood could have been so enjoyable. If, however, you feel that I should change on either count, I invite—and look forward to—your efforts. I can assure you that I harbor no antipathy toward either the piano or the dance floor. I am indifferent, but not opposed: an excellent attitude for a man in my position, I think.

Things on my "worry list":

1) money
2) money
3) money
after the first three they tend to level out. . . .
4) Worry that I may not be as strong as I think I am and thereby compromise with dull reality and convince myself that my weakness is a sign of "maturity."
5) Worry that I may never run across anyone whom I think is "right" enough to fall in love with, or perhaps I should say "be happy with."
6) Worry that I live in a land of semi-educated flagellants (look that one up, it will do you good) who have created and insist on maintaining a "free, equal, standardized, complacent and decaying soci-

ety" which frustrates and denies the idea that I should live as I want to live and maintain my self-respect at the same time.

7) The rest of my worries are small and come and go from day to day. What are your "worries"?

Yes, Davison seems to like Vandy. He was co-captain of the Freshman football team and pledged Phi Delt. I shall see him next week when I hustle homeward. I'll be home for a week or two and I'll let you know if there's any chance of my getting to Tallahassee before I return to New York City.

This is about it for now and let me warn you in closing that you are not "as usual" and certainly not "plain."

Love, Hunter

Thompson at his Catskills cabin.
(Photo by Hunter S. Thompson;
courtesy of HST Collection)

*Thompson with Judy Booth
in the Catskills.*
(Photo by Robert W. Bone;
courtesy of HST Collection)

The black Jaguar.
(Photo by Robert W. Bone; courtesy of
HST Collection)

1959

PRINCE JELLYFISH GOES TO THE CATSKILLS . . . FIRED FROM THE *MIDDLETOWN DAILY RECORD* . . . SOWING THE SEEDS OF A STRANGE AND FATAL COMPULSION . . . DON QUIXOTE FLEES TO PUERTO RICO . . .

I'd been living there for about a year when the basement began to cave in. The combined pressure of spring rains and melting snow was too much for the rock-dirt walls, and they crumbled like rotten river banks in a flood; collapsing, slowly but surely, into a mud bog that grew an inch or two deeper with each passing day. The landlord, too lazy and too blind to make the repairs himself, declined to take action for almost three weeks. It was only when the mud began to bury the hot-water heater that the indolent old bastard agreed to do something about it.

--Hunter S. Thompson,
 "The Almost Working Artist" (unpublished short story)

TO ANN FRICK:

Thompson spent the holidays in Louisville dating hometown girls, but none of them measured up to Frick. Tired of the ambiguity in their relationship, he became determined that she move to New York.

> January 7, 1959
> 57 Perry Street
> New York City
> (the first Hunterletter
> of the new year. . . .)

Dear Ann,

I pause in the midst of what should be my best story to date—if I don't sell something soon I may give up the ghost altogether and turn to beachcombing—to inform you that I have lately come to doubt your existence! Something drastic must be done about this, for I find it increasingly difficult to have faith in what might possibly be a figment of my imagination. But perhaps I should explain instead of rambling on in this desperate key.

When I got back to New York this last summer—and later when my mailbox began yielding excellent Annletters—I had no difficulty in measuring all the girls I ran across against the time-tested "Tallahassee standard." They all fell short, of course, and after a while I found that my only problem lay in getting hold of you some way in order to make SURE I was right. This worked well as long as I stayed in New York, for all the world knows that the Yankee species of american womanhood is distinctly second-rate. A problem arose, however, when I got to Louisville. . . .

Upon returning to the womb for my annual holiday visit I found that, while most of the girls I used to date have literally gone to waste—withered, dulled, dissipated, etc.—a small but choice minority of them were head and shoulders above their northern counterparts and therefore surprisingly acceptable to my somewhat jaded eye. I was fairly happy for a time, feeling that women were worthwhile after all, but then I fell to using my "Tallahassee standard" again and the trouble began. I was dumbfounded to find that, although Bluegrass womanhood far outclassed the Yankee variety, they somehow fell obviously short of the mark you made and then re-made during my short but numerous visits to the land of the orange moon and the spanish moss.

If all this is true and I have not deceived myself, then obviously either I should be in Tallahassee or you should be in New York; anything else would be folly. HOWEVER, I have but ONE DAY and several letters to put flesh and blood in the "Tallahassee standard" over the course of the past year and a half. I have an excellent memory and a prodigious imagination, but memory and imagination can do only so much. IDEA— AFTER MUCH THOUGHT: why don't you come to New York with your friends in February? Something is going to have to be done because I don't know how much longer I can carry a vision around in my head which makes a "reject" out of every girl I run across. (Now all I need is to go back to New York and find one of these "so long, it was nice while it lasted but I've decided to settle down" letters from you. That would definitely complete the cycle.)

At any rate I plan to be back there by this Sunday. I should add that the Thompson fortunes are once more adrift in treacherous seas: I gave up on *Time* right before Christmas and decided that I needed nothing more than a rest and someone to cook breakfast for me in the mornings, so I came home and my stay has been excellent. I'm a little restless now, though, and the time has come for me to rush back into battle. Actually, I was seriously planning to come bounding down your way, but with both Laurie[1] and [Tom] Sealey gone I'd have had to impose on your hospitality and I didn't think that would be the best thing. The next month or so should be wild and woolly and I don't know how much longer I can stand New York so how about sending me the latest news on your pending springtime visit? I'll be in New York by the time you get this, so drop me a line as soon as you can. The idea of going back to look for a job in that madhouse is enough to give a man the shakes. So until then, I remain, inconsistently. . . .

Hunter

TO ANN FRICK:

Typing with an injured thumb, the result of a Greenwich Village bar fight, Thompson continued to demand that Ann visit New York.

1. Laurie Hosford, who attended the University of Florida at Tallahassee while Thompson was stationed at nearby Eglin, often accompanied Thompson on double dates.

January 23, 1959
New York City

Dear Ann,

I hate to begin this letter because it seems like such a poor substitute for what I'd really like to do. I'm tired of writing to you and tired of talking to you on the phone. I want to see you and touch you and try to convince myself that you're real.

I frankly don't believe it. Your voice comes over the phone and your letters come in the mail, but there's precious little flesh and blood and warmth in any of it. The pictures help tremendously, but they're not very warm either.

This prolonged a separation would normally spell doom for any relationship, but somehow you've managed to retain a firm grip on the top rung. This is a little vague, of course, but I usually find it difficult to be anything but amusing in letters—and besides, I have a sprained thumb which makes typing very difficult.

What I mean to say, I suppose, is that I've fallen into some kind of "condition" where you're concerned. Whether it's that vague something called "love" or not, I really can't say. Whatever it is, though, I'm afraid it's something that's going to have to be resolved one way or another. And for a number of reasons, I'd say it was something that could best be resolved *away* from Tallahassee. Your calls unnerve me, your letters frustrate me, and the idea of having you around for any length of time excites me to a fever pitch. In short—barring some kind of a tragedy— you're going to have to get up this way in the spring. I think you can understand that another Hunter-visit to Tallahassee is not going to accomplish much.

I'm finding it increasingly difficult to write to you because there are so many things I'd like to say that I simply can't say with a typewriter. I'm back in New York for the weekend, but I'll be back in Middletown on Sunday. I'll be up there for at least another week and possibly longer. None of this will be definite for a week or so and there's no sense in my explaining something which may not be worth explaining. I'm sorry I was so useless on the phone the other night, but I've never been very good at making passionate sense across sixteen hundred miles of copper wire. But it was more than good to talk to you and I only wish we weren't so blasted far apart. I think I can make it until spring, but that will be just about the end of my rope as far as waiting is concerned. Plan definitely on coming then.

My thumb is bothering the hell out of me and I'm going to have to give it a rest. Another letter will follow this one when things are more settled.

Until then, write as soon as you can and don't change your hair—I like it the way it is in the latest snapshot.

> Love,
> Hunter

TO VIRGINIA THOMPSON:

Fired from Time *for insubordination, Thompson finally landed a job he wanted, as a reporter for the* Middletown Daily Record *in upstate New York. Eager for mobility, he wrote his mother to wheedle a loan for a black 1951 Jaguar he had found for $550.*

> January 31, 1959
> Middletown, New York

Dear Mom,

Sorry I haven't written, but I've had a definite reason which I'm sure you'll understand by the time you've finished this letter. I suppose that part of it was explained in my telegram, but here's the whole story.

I'd been back here for several days, sizing up the job situation and talking to people here and there, when one of the employment agencies called and said they had a good job for me on a paper in Middletown, New York. I was a little hesitant, but so low on money that I decided to look into it.

Frankly, it turned out to be one of the best deals in contemporary journalism for anyone my age—or, perhaps I should say, my age according to the application form. The key to the whole thing—and the terrifying proposals due to come later in the letter—lies in my "method of operation" in getting the job. I applied on the grounds that I was (1) a college graduate, (2) that I was 23 years old, and (3) that I've had a great raft of experience as a reporter. None of these are true, of course, and I've been expecting at any moment to be "unmasked" and rushed off the premises as a dangerous undesirable of some sort. This is the reason for my not writing. The idea of writing and telling you all about the great job I had, and then having to write and say I'd been fired, was simply out of the question. I've barely mentioned it to anyone. I haven't even let myself feel the slightest bit elated, for fear of the sudden downfall which might have come at any time. It all boils down to the fact that this whole thing has been a monstrous gamble which has somehow worked. Here it is in a nutshell:

When I came back from my first interview I went down to talk to Lou Miller at the *World-Telegram* and you have the letter I wrote after that. That letter was the last optimistic word or thought I've uttered since I went back to Middletown to start the two-week trial period. Well, they told me on Thursday that my work had been "top-notch" and that they wanted me to stay—provided, of course, that I got a car immediately if not sooner.

Before I get to that, let me explain what kind of deal this is. The *Middletown Record* is a two-and-a-half year-old experimental newspaper. The only cold-type offset paper (daily) in the country, it's been a booming success and has been written up in *Time, Editor & Publisher,* and a good many other trade magazines. There's only one man on the news staff over 35 and most of the boys are between 23 and 30. The circulation area covers three counties and the paper has three bureaus. Most of the reporters average about 75 miles a day on the road and all of them are photographers as well as writers. Naturally, I told them I was an experienced photographer and miraculously came up with a picture the other day which was good enough for page one (see enclosed). I'll have to buy my own camera later on, but we can't worry about that now.

At any rate, all the boys I work with are young, smart as hell, from all over the country, and all on the way up. The *Record* is one of the best little papers in the country and one of the best opportunities there is. I like the whole setup immensely and, although I'm still a little uneasy about my fraudulent application, only an unusual set of circumstances will trip me up now because the *Record* would not wait until after the trial period to run a routine check on my background.

As it stands now, then, I have a great job at $70 a week and I'm sitting right on the launching pad for a job as a reporter on the *World-Telegram.* Frankly, I haven't been in such a good position since I was sports editor of the *Command Courier.*

And now we come to the stumbling block.

As I said, I have to get a car or this job goes down the drain in about ten days. Ordinarily, this would be no problem. I could go to the bank and get a loan and pick up a good dependable car for $500 or so. But here's what happens when I go to the bank: (1) I fill out an application—how old do I say I am? If I say 21 I take a chance—and it's a damned good one in a small town like Middletown—that some comment about "this unusually young reporter" will get back to the *Record* management. That will be the end of the job. On the other hand, if I'm consistent and say 23 I put myself in the position of "obtaining money under false pretenses," a charge I'd rather not face. Inevitably, the bank will ask for some identification and if they don't someone along the line will and I've learned the difference by now between a good and a bad risk.

So, after about 40 hours of constant thought, here's the plan I've come up with. I've located a car, a damned good one, for $550. I can't afford to get a junk heap because I can't take a chance on constant breakdowns if I use the car for work. I want to borrow $350 from Memo—$300 in addition to that $50 I hope you've already sent. I want to borrow it just as I would from a bank—at 6% interest and repayable over a period of 12 months at $30 a month. (correction, $31 a month).

I need only $350 now because I've already sold my apartment for $200 which I'll have next week. Needless to say, the money won't do me any good unless I can get $350 more. (Actually, I may have to borrow a little more than $350 so I can make the first payment on an insurance policy from Jack [Thompson]. I can't get insurance here because it costs something like $270 and I damn certainly can't afford that. This means that I'll have to register the car there but that will be no problem. Once I get it registered I'll wait a while and then have the registration switched to New York. I'll just send you the papers when I get the car and you can send me a license.)

Now I'm deadly serious about this and I intend to run through hell and high water to keep from losing this job. If I'm forced to try to get it from a bank then I'll do that, but it's going to be like playing russian roulette as far as keeping the job is concerned. If I lose this job I also queer my chances for a shot at the *World-Telegram* and if that happens I might just as well go on unemployment insurance. At $70 a week I'll have no trouble paying Memo back in a year's time and I give you my word of honor that I'll repay every cent. I've seen enough of this job to know that I like it and that I'm not going to lose it once I get a car and get settled. It's simply too good an opportunity to throw away for want of money.

Please let me know about this immediately—by telegram or by phone at the *Record* (3 to 11 p.m.). I can't afford to waste time and I only have about one week to get a car. A million thanks in advance if you can swing this.

Love, H

TO ANN FRICK:

Thompson often dreamt of escaping to the Caribbean to get away from the cold New York winters he loathed. While at Eglin, his favorite pastime with Ann had been swimming at night in the Gulf of Mexico, then lying on the beach and staring at the stars.

February 21, 1959
Middletown, New York

Dear Ann,

I've been intending to write you for several days. As a matter of fact, I sent you an airmail postcard yesterday—to assure you I was still alive—but

I think I forgot to put an address on it, leaving the front completely blank. I somehow doubt whether it will get to you.

This letter was prompted by a book I just found in the apartment I moved into this afternoon. (I'll be here for three weeks. One of the reporters who lives here is on an assignment in Puerto Rico and the other one is in Switzerland for a while.) At any rate the book is called *Escape to the West Indies,*[2] and for some reason I thought immediately of you when I read the title. Hence, this letter.

After thinking about it for a moment, I find myself wondering exactly why you came to mind so quickly when I began to think about the Caribbean. I think a little further and I find that you come to mind in connection with a lot of things—not just the Caribbean. I think of Europe, Africa, South America, California, Mexico, Australia—all places I intend to see someday—and you come to mind there too. You'll admit this is puzzling and a little frightening to someone like me. I seem to want everything—even things that seem almost totally incompatible in the life of any one human.

* * * * * * * * * *

Several hours later, after a session of beer and conversation with one of the disc jockeys from the local station.

It's dark now, and beginning to snow. I would like very much for you to be here. Not because you'd enjoy this place, because you probably wouldn't, but because of the very selfish reason that I'd simply like you to be here. We have three months more until June, and almost three have gone by since the first of December. I should have a house in the near future and you figure very definitely in that, too. I want to get one you'll like, although I don't think I'll really believe you're serious about coming until I actually see you.

We'll both be three months older by June and a year from then we'll be a year and three months older. Time seems to be going much faster and I'm beginning to get the idea that life is very short. It makes me feel that whatever I do in the next few years will be very important. A thousand years from now our lives will be, at best, a few sentences in someone's history book. But the next day, and the next month, and the next year are more important to me than all the history books ever written. It would be compounded lunacy to waste any of this time, and it would be just as foolish to think it was important to anyone but us.

2. Bradley Smith, *Escape to the West Indies* (New York, 1957).

So you see why I think very seriously about you and the way I feel about you. It could be such a good thing if it were right, and such a horrible waste of time if it weren't. And you can't compromise when it comes to love, because it becomes something else if you do. For either of us to alter ourselves for the other would be wrong and foolish. If you change yourself in order to be loved, then you are in love with love and not a person. America is overrun with people whose lives are dictated by abstracts and I don't want to be one of them. I am not in love with love, or happiness, or security, or virtue, or anything else in that line. Sometimes I wonder if I could really be in love with a person, but to admit that I couldn't would take too much of the pleasure out of life.

So I would like to be in love with you and I hope I can be. It will take a while to find out—not a few days and certainly not a series of letters. I will wait, then, until summer, and we shall see what happens then.

In the meantime I'll be here for a while, anyway. This is not a place in which to stay for any length of time. By the time fall rolls around I'll probably be thinking in terms of going somewhere else. We shall talk about that later.

Write and tell me not only about what you do, but what you think. Above all be honest and don't kid either of us. As I said before, there is too little time for us to deal in superficialities.

Love,
Hunter

TO *THE NEW YORK TIMES:*

Thompson's reply to a New York Times *help-wanted advertisement explained his recent firing from the* Middletown Daily Record. *He never received any response.*

March 1, 1959
Middletown, New York

X2787
NY *Times*

Dear Sir,

This letter is in reference to your "editor wanted" ad in this morning's *Times.* If, after reading the rest of this letter, you think we should talk further, you may contact me at 22 Mulberry St., Middletown, New York. Or phone Diamond 2-xxxx, Middletown.

Until this recent week I was a reporter on the *Middletown Daily Record.* On Thursday I was summarily fired. Since the reasons for my dismissal are a little unusual I think it would be wise for me to outline them here. I find them morbidly amusing, but I think the humor will soon vanish from the situation. I'm told it's difficult to laugh on an empty stomach.

Several weeks ago I outraged a long-time *Record* advertiser by sending a meal back to his kitchen for immediate consignment to the garbage can. This consequently resulted in a rather ugly session between me, the advertiser, and the *Record*'s editor & publisher. The judgment was definitely not in my favor and I was told that my job would henceforth rest on very thin ice.

Several days ago I was instrumental in the looting of an office candy machine. I had put two nickels in the thing without getting anything out of it. I then gave it a severe rattling which rendered the coin slot obsolete. Word got around in the back shop and a "run" on the machine followed almost immediately. The total loss—some $7.35—came out of my paycheck. My popularity soared as far as the back-shop people were concerned, of course, but there were those who viewed the situation with some alarm—notably the managing editor. I was fired the next day.

Although it seems a little ridiculous to go into all this, I did so because I doubt very seriously whether the same information will be made available by the *Record* management in the event I need a reference. Since I was comparatively new on the paper I can understand their course of action to some extent. I want to make it clear, however, that my dismissal was not based on the quality of my work. I urge you, in the event of any confusion on this score, to take any steps you see fit in order to clear this up.

I enclose a résumé and some clippings which I would like very much for you to return. You will find a self-addressed envelope for this purpose. The résumé was done originally for a sportswriting job and is thus heavily slanted in that direction. Although my experience is far more comprehensive than the résumé would seem to indicate, I saw no sense in listing it all for that particular job. Please disregard the reference to the *Police Gazette*.

All résumés are necessarily superficial and mine is no different. There are other things, however, which may in the long run prove to be far more important than anything included in a résumé. This is true in my case, at any rate.

Some people find it exceedingly difficult to get along with me and I have to choose my jobs very carefully. I have no patience with phonies, hacks, dolts, or obnoxious incompetents and I take some pride in the fact that these people invariably dislike me. I admire perfection or any effort toward it and I would not work for anyone who disagreed with me on this score. This is not to say that I refuse to work with people whom I consider incompetent. It merely means that I consider incompetence something to be overcome, rather than accepted.

It seems a little senseless to carry on in this vein. I think I've given you a pretty good picture of myself and, at the same time, I realize only one out of a thousand people would hire me after reading this letter. Right now I'm in no mood to give a damn. Maybe later I'll become more temperate.

So, until I hear from you,
Hunter S. Thompson

TO ANN FRICK [NOT MAILED]:

Broke, unemployed, and despondent, Thompson revealed why the "Hunter-figure" would never bow to authority of any kind; like a character from The Fountainhead, *he would stay true to himself no matter what the consequences.*

March 3, 1959
22 Mulberry St.
Middletown, New York

Dear Ann,

You may never see this letter. Certainly you won't see it for a while. When and if I do mail it there will be another letter with it, telling what will have happened between now and then. By the time you read this, the person who wrote it will be submerged once again beneath the surface of the person you seem to think I am. I'm writing this letter to show you that the other person exists, but I'm going to hold onto it for a while because I don't want you to ever see that person except at a distance. He is not somebody I'd want to have you with for any length of time, but I think you should know about him just the same, if only in retrospect.

I will make it as short and pointed as possible, so as not to waste my words and your time. The "other person," of course, is Hunter S. Thompson as he is right now. He has "gone down" again for the umpteenth time, and if he doesn't come up this time I think this letter will serve as a fitting death rattle. And if he does come up again this letter will be a worthwhile thing to hold on to, for it will serve as a grim reminder that the dirge has sounded once before. In short, if this is the final straw I want it recorded, and if it is not then I want it recorded anyway—as a morale booster for the future, if nothing else.

I was fired last week and I'm presently stranded as high and dry as a man can get. I was given three reasons for my dismissal: 1) the fact that I spent an entire night at work in my sock feet, 2) the fact that I crippled a candy machine in the office with a violent kick after being cheated out of two consecutive nickels, and 3) the fact that one of the *Record*'s regular advertisers lodged a formal and very vocal protest with the publisher after I sent two meals back to his kitchen and abused him in his own restaurant for the low quality of his meals.

"Your work is good," they said, "and you have a very deep, very keen mind. But this isn't Greenwich Village and you seem a little anti-social, a little off-beat. You don't seem to be very conscious of community relations and we can't afford to have people like you working for the *Record*."

So there you have it, an epitaph for Hunter Thompson. "He was a good lad, but he was a little off-beat."

And here's another one for you: "he was right, dead right, as he hustled along (in his own off-beat way), but he's just as unemployed as if he'd been wrong."

Well, at any rate, I hope you get the point. I'm *sans* salary, whether I was right or wrong. I'm convinced, of course, that to play a role or to adjust to fraud is wrong, and I damn well intend to keep right on living the way I think I should.

But right now things look a little bleak. I have no idea what in the hell I'm going to do and I really don't know where to begin looking. I have enough money to last about two weeks, a huge black Jaguar that eats gas like a mechanical camel, no place to live, and no prospects of a job where the same thing won't happen again just as soon as they find out I'm "a little off-beat."

I feel as if life itself is crumbling away beneath my feet and I don't know whether to jump, or run, or to just stand here and go down, screaming my defiance at the falling debris—as it slowly buries me.

I know I'm right, but I sometimes wonder how important it is to be right—instead of comfortable. I doubt whether this question arises very often in the Tallahassee world, but there may come a day when you have to think about it, too. When you do you will not be the first or the last, just as I am not. The difficulty is not in the question, I think, but in the person who answers it. There are so few people who are strong—or lucky— enough to be right in this lunatic world, and many of the best ones never live to find it out.

This could go on and on, but I think the point has been made already. The Hunterfigure has come to another fork in the road and the question once again is "where do we go from here?" We shall see very soon, of course, for even the Hunterfigure needs food. Something will have been done by the time you get this letter and I want you to keep in mind that it was written at a time of great chaos. Right now, however, I feel as lost as I ever have in my life.

I don't get this way very often, but I think you should know my downs as well as my ups. The carefree Thompson facade gets very tiresome at times, and I need to have someone with whom I can be honestly confused and lost. I am no more than human and I know that anyone who insists on playing the great game on his own terms is bound to take an occasional beating. It may happen again and that's why I'm going to send you this letter just as soon as I'm in a position for another fall. If the next one has any effect on you—and it may—I'll want you to understand what brought it on, why it will be inevitable, and above all, that it has happened before.

If you are frightened by all this, then I think the letter will have served a very necessary purpose. As I said once before, I am real and not a wandering daydream. This side of my personality is just as real as the rest and I think you should know about it. I think, too, that it is equally important that I know your reaction to this letter. Send it to me when you get the time.

Love, Hunty

TO ANN FRICK:

Bearded and content to live in a Catskills cabin writing short stories for the summer, Thompson felt money to be his only pressing concern.

March 25, 1959
Cuddebackville
New York

Dear Ann,

It's been a long time 'twixt letters, I think, but maybe you'll understand once you hear what's been going on up this way. Needless to say, the good ship Hunter is on wild and stormy seas once again.

I was not only fired from the *Daily Record*, but I'm presently in the midst of a knock-down, drag-out battle with the state employment service over my right as a discriminating human being to send an unpalatable meal back to the kitchen in a public restaurant. I was fired for 1) being an "oddball," 2) having a general "contempt for people," and 3) specifically, for getting into a running battle with one of the *Record*'s advertisers who owns an Italian restaurant in Middletown. I was, in short, "unable to form a workable concept of community relations." I also "worked for an entire evening in the newsroom without my shoes," and destroyed a candy machine in a sudden burst of anger.

All this sounds pretty damned silly, I suppose, but it has some pretty serious implications. First and foremost is the sobering realization that I cannot hold a "normal" job without making drastic alterations in my personality. Stemming from this, of course, is the possibility that I may never hold a "normal" job. This is all well and good as long as I can support myself by writing. If I can't, however, it poses something of a problem as far as my surviving is concerned. And speaking of survival, I wonder what Mr. Darwin would say to all this.

I'm in a rather odd situation at the moment: except for money, I seem to have everything I need for a perfect summer. I have a house in the woods, totally isolated from all human beings, and I have a huge, black Jaguar. I also have a fine young dog named Pilar.[3] Everything is fine except that I have not a cent to my name. I've managed to exist for about a month in this manner, but I don't know how much longer it will last. Unless a miracle occurs, I'll probably have to get a job, at least for a while.

But you should see this house. It's the finest thing I've ever laid eyes on. I'm on the side of a mountain in a pine grove overlooking the Neversink River. The cabin has a big living room, a bedroom, a kitchen, a bath, and an excellent screen porch. I'm about two hours out of New York City in the lower fringes of the Catskill Mountains. All in all, it's too good to be true and I suppose some terrible heaven-sent justice will descend on my shoulders in the near future. Until then, however, I shall continue to live as I am today. Like this:

I got up about ten, fed the dog, took a bath, and had a huge breakfast while I read *The New York Times* for news of the end of the world. I then took the dog, my pipe, and a bottle of wine and walked about a hundred yards down the hill to the river, where I spent two hours sitting on a huge rock above the rapids, smoking, sipping the wine, and planning a short story. It's 2:30 in the afternoon now and I should finish this letter by 3:00. I shall then step into the Jaguar and drive about six miles across the mountain to meet a friend of mine from New York who is coming up with his fiancée to spend the rest of the week with me. We have a monstrous chicken dinner planned at another friend of mine's house in Otisville, and after that we'll probably come back here about ten and hike over to the waterfall to sit on the rocks and drink wine.

The whole day would be 100% better if you could be here and I'm getting damned impatient over the question of your trek to the north. Since I haven't heard from you in several weeks I won't be surprised at anything I get in the next letter. Perhaps you and "the boy" have decided to set up housekeeping by this time, for all I know, or perhaps you've merely decided to stop writing. Whatever you've decided, I'd appreciate hearing from you. I suppose you're in Palatka[4] by now, so I'll have this forwarded.

---

3. Pilar was a Doberman pinscher puppy Thompson had purchased the day before he was fired by the *Record*.
4. A small town between Jacksonville and Orlando, Florida.

I'm getting a little tired of being the lone wolf at these mountain gatherings and if you've decided not to come up I'd like to know about it so I can advertise in the local papers for a mistress. This is too fine a place not to share with someone and if I can't do it with you, then I might as well import some sort of a pleasant decoration who'll at least cook breakfast for me.

I just reread your last letter and it makes me feel a little ashamed of the paragraph I just wrote. It's one of the best letters I've ever received, incidentally, and I appreciate your going to the trouble to explain your concept of individuality. I agree wholeheartedly with what you say, but I hope you're not like so many of my friends who find it very easy to talk about being an individual and very hard to be one. I don't think you are, though, and I probably shouldn't have said that.

I'm also sorry, very sorry, that I couldn't get down there for a few days. The truth of the matter is, though, that I simply have no money at all and it would have been impossible for me to come. The past three or four weeks have been absolute chaos as far as I'm concerned, and yesterday and today have been the first peaceful moments I've had. I wrote you a letter about two weeks ago, but I've saved it until the time comes for it to be mailed. The time is not now, but perhaps it may be here by the time I hear from you. Try to write soon and let me know how things are coming in Palatka, as well as in that beautifully-encased mind of yours. So until then, I remain, unnaturally yours.

> Love,
> Hunter

TO JUDY BOOTH:

Booth, another of Thompson's Louisville girlfriends, was a junior at Smith College in Massachusetts. She accepted Thompson's invitation to spend a weekend in Middletown, meeting up with him at the local post office.

> March 27, 1959
> Cuddebackville
> New York

Dear Judy,

Yes, Peyton,[5] April fourth will be as convenient as any other time. We'll have to work out something in the way of transportation to Cuddebackville, which is somewhat removed from the mainstream as far as pop-

---

5. Peyton is the main character in William Styron's *Lie Down in Darkness*.

ulation mass is concerned, but we'll do that in a few moments when I feel more like thinking and less like rambling.

I have just pulled through one of the most terrifying nights of my life, surviving with nothing more than a cold, I hope, to show for it. I ran out of oil about seven last night and by midnight the temperature in the house had fallen to 38 degrees. It had begun to snow again, the wind outside was one notch above intolerable, and a blanket of sleet fell on me about dawn. I had to stay in bed until three in the afternoon because it was simply too damned cold to get up. When I finally forced myself out of bed there was nothing but a half a quart of milk and two slices of swiss cheese for breakfast. I managed to limp over here to Otisville for breakfast and a bit of much-needed warmth and wine. An artist friend of mine from New York has been up here most of the week with some girl from Baltimore and I left them in Otisville last night because the girl was about to freeze to death in the cabin. The dog and I returned to the wretched place for the night where we spent the next twelve hours with the thermometer hovering around the forty-degree mark.

The motto of this story is "never be fool enough to brave the elements unless you have no other choice." At any rate, if I get a cold now, I should be through with it by the time you get here.

My situation is, of course, unchanged as far as employment is concerned. At the moment I have three dollars to my name, a can of tuna fish and a can of soup in the cabin, no oil for the furnace, one bag of dried food for the dog, and about enough gas in the Jaguar to make it back to that freezing hellhole for the night. Perhaps, on second thought, I'll stay here tonight.

I have resolved, finally and without reservation, that I shall never again spend a winter further north than Atlanta, Georgia. Barring the event of war in the near future, I'll probably jump off for Europe, probably Spain or Italy, sometime around September. If the car doesn't blow up by then I'll have a liquid asset which should provide me with enough money for food and wine across the sea—for a while, at least.

No sense in going on about this as long as you're going to be up here in a week or so, so I'll save it for later. You'll have to let me know how you plan to get here so I can pick you up somewhere.

I'm trying to bring about some sort of uneasy peace right now between my dog and these people's black cat, so I'll wrap this up and expect you on April fourth, sometime in the morning, until I hear otherwise. Keep in mind that I have absolutely no money, of course, and that we'll both starve to death unless you can buy some groceries and some scotch. Until then, take care.

Heroically,
Hunty

TO WILLIAM FAULKNER:

Thompson genuinely admired Faulkner's novels, particularly The Sound and the Fury. *This letter—sent to Faulkner's home in Oxford, Mississippi— failed to elicit a response.*

March 30, 1959
Cuddebackville
New York

Dear Mr. Faulkner,

I thought you'd be interested in this item I clipped from today's *Times*. It recalled a statement of yours I once read in something called *Writers at Work*. I don't have the book at the moment, but the statement seemed to involve Henry Ford, Robert Frost, and the concept of "the writer as a fine dog."

As I look back on the past year, however, I feel inclined to disagree with both you and Mr. Sulzberger.[6] As far as I can see, the role, the duty, the obligation, and indeed the only choice of the writer in today's "outer" world is to starve to death as honorably and as defiantly as possible. This I intend to do, but the chicken crop in this area is going to be considerably depleted before I go.

And, incidentally, if you feel, as a result of this letter, a ripping desire to send me a weekly cheque, please feel free to do so. My corruption tolerance has been tested and found firm. I am the only chicken-thieving, novel-writing Southerner in the Catskills who drives an ancient Jaguar, lives in an un-heated cabin, and spends the large part of his weekly unemployment cheque to buy high-test gasoline.

The solicitation is in jest, of course. I am so used to writing letters to creditors that I can't seem to get a grip on myself when I try to write a coherent letter. I'd intended to write no more than a few lines here, so I'd best close before things get too wild. If you ever get up this way, I'd be happy to have you drop in on me. I have several extra beds and the trout-filled Neversink River runs right past my front door. An excellent place, all in all. A little cold in the winter and no food, of course, but a fine place to rest.

And so, until we all dissolve in a blaze of radioactive newsprint, I remain, very sincerely:

Hunter S. Thompson

---

6. Arthur Hays Sulzberger, owner of *The New York Times*.

TO ROGER RICHARDS:

Richards, an aspiring writer from uptown Manhattan, was Thompson's constant drinking companion throughout much of 1958.

June 3, 1959
Cuddebackville
New York

Dear Roger,

Sorry to be so late with this reply, but even though I have nothing at all to do I seem to be busy all the time. Your letter was excellent, though, and I'll try to do it justice by writing something more, here, than just a short note or a long, drawn-out banality.

I was in New York last weekend, but spent most of my time out on Long Island and didn't get an opportunity to give you a ring. It was good to get away from the damned place again, and I don't think I'll get down there for quite a while, now that the weather is getting warm up here. Every time I come down there I seem to spend all my money, stay drunk most of the time, and waste the entire visit in a dull frenzy of looking for something that I don't really believe is there. All of New York's glitter is on the surface, like a huge, moonlit bay. It's beautiful and clean and awe-inspiring on the top, but not many of us can walk on water. Not for long, anyway.

You did a damned good job, I think, in evaluating the effect of your companionship last year. You were indeed depressing, and I had enough things to worry about without adding you to my list. There was no mention of Jo[7] or the baby in your letter, so I have no way of knowing whether you severed that connection, as you threatened now and then, or whether you stuck it out for whatever it might be or might have been worth. I thought then and still think that it was none of my business. Advice is almost always useless, especially when it comes from someone as confused as I was this time last year. You say I seemed to be "sinking or retreating into some inviolable isolation," and perhaps I was. It was a time of near-desperate evaluation—not only of self, but of all that had gone into the creation of self over the course of some twenty years. This past year, I think, will turn out to be the most critical of my life. It gave me a direction which only accident can change from here on in. I am in no position, anymore, to "go back and choose again." As things stand now, I am going to be a writer. I'm not even sure that I'm going to be a good one or even a self-supporting one, but until the dark thumb of fate presses me to the dust and says "you are nothing," I will be a writer.

I write this letter naked, sitting on a stool in the sun outside my back door with a borrowed typewriter on the chair before me. Fifteen feet away

7. Jo was Roger Richards's wife.

is a black Jaguar sedan which I own and intend to sell in the near future for enough money to get to Europe and live a while. Two feet away my dog lies in the sun, pregnant and useless as only a love-starved female thing can be. Behind me is my cabin, a three-room structure with a front porch overlooking the Neversink River. I have no phone, no neighbors, and the closest friend is ten miles away, which suits me fine. I am situated in a pine grove above a river some seventy miles northwest of New York. Once a week I drive the Jaguar into Middletown and sign for my unemployment check. It is good of the State to support me while I learn my trade.

At the moment I have two stories in the mail: one good, and one fairly useless.[8] I am working on two more, both of which should be good. I am also working on a novel[9] that could go a long way, as you say, toward helping me "make it in a big way." It will be the story of Hunter and Hunter, the way he went and the way he could have gone. And, incidentally, why. I'm using the narrator-participant technique—à la *Gatsby*—and shooting for a short (300 pages or so) account of three people living a year in New York City that will decide the courses of their lives. That's a pretty poor sentence, but I hope it's clear. As I see it now, I should come up with something of a cross between *Gatsby* and *On the Road*. If you can imagine such a thing. God only knows when it will be finished.

Before I forget, read a book called *Lie Down in Darkness*, by William Styron. This man is a Writer.

Your flashback to the college football game was not only vivid and well-done, but it helped me get going on a short thing I sent to *Esquire*. If they don't use it, I think I'll try the *Atlantic* "Firsts" thing. And if not there, somewhere else. Keep hustling, hustling, hustling, hustling, hust. . . .

I think I'll run over to the lake, now, and soak up a bit of sun and cool water. I'm beginning to see what they mean by "the good life," and all I need now is to sell a few stories to be right smack on top of the world. I hate to say things like that, because they always precipitate a fall of some kind. So I take it back; all I need now is to sell a few stories to get out of the hole.

At any rate, thanks for writing and here's hoping things are better for you now than they were last year. Drop me a line, while you're at it, and fill me in on the rest of the Richards clan. If you're still with Jo, tell her hello for me, and by all means kill the baby. That's far and away the best thing you can do for the poor bastard. Between leukemia, bomb blasts, Russians, Africans, and Red Chinese, I don't envy this next generation one damned bit. It would be merciful to kill them all.

8. The good story was "The Cotton Candy Heart," the useless one "The Almost Working Artist." Both remain unpublished.
9. Excerpts from the novel, "Prince Jellyfish," which was never published in its entirety, did appear in *Songs of the Doomed*.

Leaving you with that bit of psychotic sarcasm, I remain,

haphazardly,
Hunter S. Thompson

TO LARRY CALLEN:

Callen was still in Iceland but now preparing to leave the Air Force for a civilian life as a public-relations copywriter.

June 7, 1959
Cuddebackville
New York

Dear Larry,

Your letter found me in the same spot—literally. Since I have not held a job since March 1, I have been all but rooted to the goddamned chair in front of this typewriter. To no avail, of course; I might as well be sitting in front of an un-tuned kettle drum.

Oh, I get a lot of letters written. Make no mistake on that. I write like hell—generally searching for outright loans or for visitors who will come loaded to the beltline with rent money. The goddamned thing is due again in about six days and I don't have a cent to my name. I put an ad in *The Times* today, trying to sell my Jaguar. If and when that goes, I suppose I'll have to get a bicycle so I can get in (13 miles) to sign for my unemployment check each Thursday. That's another and a very long story. No time for it here. At any rate, I have two stories in the mail: one at *Esquire* and one at some rotten Science Fiction magazine. If either one of them sells I think I'll spend the entire check on scotch. I don't seem to be able to get drunk anymore. All I do is get diarrhea.

Our last letters must have crossed somewhere in the vicinity of Cincinnati—or maybe Memphis. I hope it made you laugh, anyway. Your point about not being blue was a good one and made me think a bit. I immediately sat down and tried like hell to be blue. After about two weeks it finally "took." I had a real good fit of the blues for about two hours. It didn't compare, though, with those real fine late-night, many-cigarette, soft-lonely blues I used to get. I miss that martyred feeling, that heart-squeezing, lump-in-the-throat, June Christy[10] kind of blues that I don't think I have the capacity for anymore. The only time I get that is when I can identify with one of my characters; especially when it's one who has all of his illusions intact.

Maybe that wasn't what you meant at all, but that's how it came through to me and I thank you for making me think about it.

---

10. June Christy was a popular Chicago jazz singer in the 1940s and 1950s.

The rest of your letter didn't sit so well on my weary shoulders. This civil service thing sounds real nasty, and public relations sounds like the bog-bottom of journalistic swampland. You know how I am about this kind of thing, though, so don't take it too seriously. Once I stop whistling in the dark, I'll be lost.

I've just been reading over two letters I sent you in Iceland. Perhaps I'll try to publish my collected letters before, instead of after, I make history. At any rate, I notice a change in both our attitudes. Can't go into this now, but maybe later. So until then, good luck in the swampland and write when you can. With absolutely no choice but to carry the banner, alone or otherwise, I remain:

> compulsively, HST

TO ANN FRICK:

Thompson and Frick were drawing apart over basic life philosophies. She wanted to settle in Tallahassee and raise a family; he longed to see the world and "make it" as a writer.

> June 8, 1959
> Cuddebackville
> New York

Dear Ann,

I don't know why I bother to answer your letters so promptly, in view of your recent failures. Perhaps it's just to set a good example. At any rate, here it is.

I find it interesting that you say in the same breath that you don't want to come up here, but that you "would like very much to be near me." It typifies, I'd say, your present outlook on life. Something about having your cake and. . . . You finish it. What I think you really mean to say—perhaps without realizing it—is that you wish I could fit in with the pattern of life you've tentatively laid out for yourself. You say you "don't really know what you want to make [your life]," but I'm inclined to think you're wrong. Not knowing what you want out of life is a pattern in itself, perhaps the most rigid pattern of all. As a matter of fact it's probably the most predominant pattern in the country today, and just another name, in the long run, for what we call the "American way of life." You are in a large and very crowded boat, floating around aimlessly and complacently in a very treacherous sea.

At times I seriously regret that I've divorced myself so completely from that pattern. Life is much simpler that way, and very often much more pleasant. I'm sorry, in a way, that I wasn't brought up to believe in it. I regret, also, that I no longer have a taste for cotton-candy.

I don't think much good would come of another visit to Tallahassee, for I don't think you're going to make much progress toward my point of view. Not for a few years, anyway. (And by the way: did you ever read *Lie Down in Darkness* by William Styron?) I'm in the unfortunate position, however, of being enough in love with a part of you that I can overlook the rest. This is doubly unfortunate because of the fact that I realize it. I don't even have any illusions, and sometimes I miss those more than anything else.

As for your point of view, I don't really know what it is about me that attracts (or attracted) you, but I'm not foolish enough to think it's based on anything but illusion. It pleases me, now and then, to think that you understand yourself better than I think you do. And every time I think that, one of your letters comes along to convince me I'm wrong.

Perhaps, in spite of all this, I will get down that way sometime this summer. I don't know exactly how, or why, but anything can happen if you push hard enough, and I may decide to push. It would be useless, but pleasant. We shall see.

If you think I've been wrong in some of the things I've said here, by all means let me know. This is one case where it doesn't make me happy to be right.

Love, Hunter

TO ED FANCHER, *THE VILLAGE VOICE:*

Another early gonzo news release. Thompson was poking fun at Cuddebackville's city fathers, anti-Communist patriots and proud of it.

June 12, 1959
Cuddebackville
New York

Ed Fancher
Village Voice
22 Greenwich Ave.
New York City

Sir,

Thought you might like a Cuddebackville correspondent. See enclosed sample. Since I've been unemployed for several months, I don't have much to lose by flogging the government. It's all good, clean fun, anyway.

Generously,
HUNTER S. THOMPSON

* * * * * * * * * *
PRESS RELEASE #1 OF THE CUDDEBACKVILLE, NEW YORK,
CITIZENS LEAGUE

* * * * * * * * * *

CUDDEBACKVILLE, NEW YORK (June 12)--All organizations except the American Legion were banned in this lovely little mountain burg today, as the reaction to the Supreme Court's Barrenblatt decision swept through these hills like a tormented hurricane. Immediately after the ban was announced, twenty-seven members of the local 4-H Club received the bastinado on the village green.

The newly elected Burgerchief, a forty-seven-year-old rummy with the unlikely name of Benito Kampf, stood on a gas pump in the center of town today, and told a baffled gathering of the burg's ninety-one citizens that "the pinkos are about to get what's comin' to 'em!" Kampf's thundering oration was punctuated by bloodthirsty screams and hoarse shouts of "kill them pinkos!" from a black-shirted band of Legionnaires who stood in a half-circle behind him. The Legionnaires had roused the citizens out of bed at four in the morning with cane whips and cold water.

The twenty-seven 4-H Clubbers were given the bastinado several hours later. They had protested Kampf's decree that they purchase and eat, within one week, all the surplus eggs produced by local chicken-farmers during the past two months.

The local school-teacher took the bastinado with the agricultural group. She had protested Kampf's decision to oversee the school's curriculum for the coming year. Later in the day she was flogged again when a copy of The Reporter magazine was found in her home.

"The pinkos are on the run," said Kampf in a late-night interview. "I have nothing to fear, but fear itself."

TO ROBERT D. BALLOU, VIKING PRESS:

Thompson had sent a query about his novel, "Prince Jellyfish," to Ballou at Viking Press. The editor, in what reads like a form letter, invited him to submit the manuscript.

> June 17, 1959
> Cuddebackville
> New York

Sir,

Many thanks for your prompt reply to my letter concerning unsolicited manuscripts, capital gains, and such. For some reason, your letter made me feel more like a writer and less like an unemployed journalist. And that is important.

It will be several weeks, possibly months, before I'll have enough confidence in my manuscript to let you read it. Last week I read two fairly recent first novels—*Acrobat Admits* (Harold Grossman), and *After Long Silence* (Robert Gutwillig)—and saw enough mistakes to make me look long and hard at mine. Although I'm already sure the Thompson effort will be better than those two, I'm looking forward to the day that I can say it will be better than *Lie Down in Darkness*. When that day comes, I will put my manuscript in a box and send it to you.

So, until then, I remain,

> Sincerely,
> Hunter S. Thompson

TO RUST HILLS, *ESQUIRE:*

To Thompson's embarrassment, Hill's very polite rejection letter arrived just as this vitriolic missive went out. A year earlier, Thompson had sat in on a literature course Hills taught at the New School for Social Research; a month earlier he had sent the Esquire *fiction editor one of his short stories.*

> June 20, 1959
> Cuddebackville
> New York

Rust Hills
Esquire
488 Madison Avenue
New York City 22

Goddammit, Hills, I don't think there's an excuse in the world for you people holding onto my manuscript this long. It's been over a month, now, and I've heard no news at all. For all I know, it might never have gotten to you.

If it has, however, I think you might do well to remember that, although you don't in any way depend on me now, there may come a day when you will. You might be in a position to take these stories lightly, now, but it just happens that I depend on them for rent and food money. I have no job, no salary, and my landlord is a down-to-earth bastard. As long as *Esquire* holds onto my story, I don't know where I stand. As I said before, for all I know it didn't even get to you.

Now I'm not foolish enough to expect you to actually buy the thing, but as long as I don't even know where it is, I feel completely helpless. The landlord is in my driveway every morning, asking about the three-weeks-overdue rent money, and all I can say is that I expect a check any day. I don't, of course, but you don't say things like that to your landlord.

So I ask you, in all sincerity, to either send me a check or send me the manuscript so I can get it into the mail again. And if you didn't ever receive it, please let me know immediately. Things have come to a pretty bad pass, here, and it doesn't help to have my potential income farmed out to Madison Avenue.

I don't mean to be rude, here, and I'm sorry if I sound that way. It's just that things are getting a little hectic. And the story, incidentally, is called "The Cotton Candy Heart."

> Sincerely,
> Hunter S. Thompson

TO RUST HILLS, *ESQUIRE:*

Undaunted by Hills's rejection of "The Cotton Candy Heart," Thompson then sent him "The Almost Working Artist," a Henry Milleresque homage to the creative souls who toil at their crafts in garrets.

> June 25, 1959
> Cuddebackville
> New York

Hills:

Your comments on "The Cotton Candy Heart" were appreciated, but a little puzzling. Your conclusion that it was "romantic" and "slick" indicated either a perfunctory reading on your part, or an excess of subtlety on mine. As I tried to point out with the title and with the comparison to the Coca-Cola ad, the story was not a maudlin grasp at some fading thread of personal nostalgia, but a slightly rueful commentary on the essential phoniness of the kind of nostalgia I was writing about. You know, the grass is always greener. . . .

My inquiry as to the whereabouts of the manuscript was mailed the day before I received your comments. My apologies for bothering you, but I was seriously beginning to wonder if it might have been lost somewhere along the way.

* * * * * * * * * *

At any rate, here is another one, "The Almost Working Artist." Perhaps I should point out that it is not an account of the artist's compassion for the downtrodden working man, but a reminder to all those who take art for granted that Picasso was not always a millionaire, and that loneliness and uncertainty are as common to artists and other "world beaters" as they are to shit-shovelers and ribbon clerks.

In saying that, I place the "burden of proof," so to speak, on my own shoulders. Nevertheless, that's the point I'm trying to make; and if the story doesn't make it, I can always write it again. In the meantime, however, if you know of anyone who wants to hire a neo-literary mountain hermit, please let me know. And I am, incidentally, being forced to sell my Jaguar. If you know of anyone who'd like to buy a 1951 Mark VII, mine is available for $900 or best offer.

Leaving you with my problems, I remain,

psychopathically,
Hunter S. Thompson

TO ANN FRICK:

Frick had written "Hunty" a five-page reconciliation letter professing her love amid a barrage of questions that had been weighing on her mind.

June 26, 1959
Cuddebackville
New York

Dear Ann,

Yes, once in a while I smile for a picture. See enclosed. It was taken for a passport.

It is now four o'clock in the morning in Cuddebackville, New York. The two general stores are closed, the church is dark, and a heavy mist hangs over the Neversink River. It is raining, and has been for two weeks. The mountains are green and the roads are forever damp. Cuddebackville lies in a valley at the foot of the Otisville mountain. The mist is thick in the valley tonight, and the road up the mountain is dark and empty.

Far out on the Oakland Valley road, some two-and-a-half miles from town, a black Jaguar sits in a driveway beside a cabin high above the road. A light burns in the cabin, perhaps the only light in Cuddebackville. Inside, a man sits before a typewriter, drinking iced tea and smoking a cigarette. He has been writing since eight in the evening, and he has just finished the third chapter of a novel. He has been writing almost constantly for several weeks. Within a month, he should have enough of the book finished to take it to New York, where one of the editors of the Viking Press (publishers) has agreed to read it.

That's why he hasn't written the sparkling-eyed girl in Tallahassee about his work: because he's doing nothing but writing, and what is there to say about that?

And so, Ann my girl, there you have it. I am writing. And if—when you ask if I've had any success—you mean monetary success, the answer is no. This week, as a matter of fact, three of my stories came back to me in the mail—with nice little rejection slips attached to all three.

Sad? Hopeless? Well, perhaps it is. Before we assume that, though, I'd like to quote you one or two little things I came across recently:

(A) "From 1919 to 1927 I sent stories to American magazines without being able to sell one until the *Atlantic Monthly* published a story called 'Fifty Grand.' "

*that's Ernest Hemingway, and from 1919 to 1927 is eight years.

(B) "After hours I wrote stories. . . . There were nineteen altogether. . . . No one bought them, no one sent personal letters. I had one hundred and twenty-two rejection slips pinned in a frieze about my room."

*that's Scott Fitzgerald. He wrote a few things back around the twenties.

So you see, my love, yew can't never tell. There is some that makes it, and some that don't. I just happen to think I'm going to make it. I couldn't afford to think otherwise.

At the rate of three rejections a week, I should catch up with Fitzgerald in thirty-six weeks. And that will still give me about six years before I catch up with Hemingway. If I get this novel published, however, I'll be ahead of them both. And, oh lordy, won't that be fun. So have faith, yew cute li'l ol' dark-eyed thing. They ain't throwin' dirt on my coffin yet.

So now we go on to the next question: what part of you attracts me? Well, Ann, I don't think you phrased that question any too decently, so I'll try to answer it the way I think you meant it. If I answered it the way you wrote it, I don't think you'd write me anymore.

Hmmnnnnnn . . . that ain't so easy. It would be much easier to answer it the way you wrote it. But no, I'm too high-minded for that sort if thing.

I would be foolish to deny, however, that there is a very definite physical attraction. And I think that's just fine; I wouldn't have it any other way.

There's more, of course, but I've never really thought about it. I only know that you're the only girl I've run across since I was about sixteen who's had any lasting effect on me. It's been about three years, now, and I still haven't managed to bump you out of my mind. And I *have* tried. Lord! Three years! Does it seem that long to you?

Are you aware, by the way, that on February 5, 1957, I was addressing you in letters as "Cheri," and calling you "emotionally stubborn"? And are you also aware that on September 25, 1956, you were giving me a very familiar line that ran something like this: "About this weekend. I've got quite a lot to do and I'm going to be pretty busy. . . ." A very familiar phrase, that. You went on to say, however, that you "could go out Saturday afternoon or Saturday night," but that "probably Saturday night would be best."

I don't remember exactly what happened, that weekend, but I'm sure it must have been frustrating.

Are you still as pretty as you were, by the way? Why don't you send me another picture? Please stay pretty. It's very important to me that you be pretty. I'm serious.

I'm in such a fine mood now, that if I close my eyes I can almost see you here in the cabin. If you were here I'd take you immediately to bed. Depraved, but true, I'm afraid. Here I'm going to frustrate myself again; damn, I can't stand it.

But wouldn't it be nice? You being here, I mean. I'm smiling; you smile, too. I'm not drunk, either. Not at all. Haven't had so much as a glass of beer in three days. I'm just happy. I don't know why, exactly, but it must be the idea of you being here in bed . . . yes, that would make me very happy indeed.

Smile!

And not just bed, either. I'd enjoy having you here all the time. I'd enjoy just looking at you. By the way, can you cook anything? I am hungry, now, and I must go make a tuna fish sandwich. I live on tuna fish and peanut butter and bread and milk.

I'm looking at your picture as I write this, and trying to imagine your answers and your reactions. I'm enjoying them.

I have one smiling picture and one very solemn picture. I switch back and forth, depending on what kind of reaction I expect.

This is a very strange letter and I haven't answered many of your questions, but I've had a good time.

The answer to one of your questions, though, is that I'm in love with all of you except the part I don't like. That's the part of you that's like all the other girls I see. The part of you that thinks everyone—even Hunter—has to settle down sooner or later with a nine to five job and a mortgage on the house and two chrome-covered cars in every garage and a slew of stupid, happy neighbors and nothing to look forward to but eternal manipulation by forces you never took the trouble to understand. That's the part of you I don't like, and the part I'll never like.

When you write again, I want to know the part of *me* that *you* don't like. Or perhaps the part you *do* like . . . if that's easier.

You also say I haven't told you what I want out of life. In a nutshell, it is this:

I want to be able to support myself (and, barring disaster, my family) as a writer. I want a house somewhere in the West Indies, high on a bluff overlooking the Caribbean Sea. I want enough money for good scotch and good food. I want to be in love with my wife and I want her to be in love with me. That's about it; I don't want many things, but I think the ones I want are important. If you disagree with me, I'd like to hear your point of view.

And while I'm here, let me quote you something else:

To be nobody-but-yourself—in a world which is doing its best, night and day, to make you somebody else—means to fight the hardest battle which any human being can fight; and never stop fighting.

*that's e. e. cummings, a contemporary poet, of sorts.

That's a pretty dramatic finish, so I think I'll bring this lengthy missive to an end. My situation here is very fluid, and there is still a chance that I will get down that way this summer. I shall let you know what happens. As far as I can tell, right now, things are going to get worse before they get better. I speak, of course, of my own fortunes.

Stay pretty and have faith. I think you and I are fighting a losing battle, here, but then so is everybody else in this lunatic world, and if you were on my side it might take the pain out of losing.

Love, HST

TO WILLIAM J. DORVILLIER, *SAN JUAN STAR:*

Determined to find work in the Caribbean, Thompson responded to an ad in Editor & Publisher *magazine for a sports editor for Puerto Rico's* San Juan Star. *Publisher Dorvillier went on to win the 1961 Pulitzer Prize for his editorials on the separation of church and state.*

August 9, 1959
Cuddebackville
New York

William J. Dorvillier
Star Publishing Corp.
Box 9174
Santurce, Puerto Rico

Dear Sir,

I hear you need a sports editor. If true, perhaps we can work something out. The job interests me for two reasons: the Caribbean location, and the fact that it's a new paper. Salary would be entirely secondary, as it definitely would not be here in our great rotarian democracy. My minimum, if I thought you could afford it, would be somewhere around $400 a month. I wouldn't want to set a figure, though, until I found out more about you and the actual conditions of the job. There are some jobs I wouldn't do for two thousand a month, and others I'd be happy to do for two hundred. So let's leave salary for later, shall we?

I speak no Spanish—tolerable French—but would have little trouble picking it up. As for the quality of my work, I'd be either the best or the worst sports editor you could get. I'd make great demands on the photographers, insist on laying out my own pages, write a column that might make some readers strain their intellects, and generally make every effort to produce what I considered the perfect sports section. If you're looking for an easy-going hack, then I am not your man.

At the moment I am unemployed, and will continue to be until I locate a worthwhile job. Having been a sportswriter, sports editor, editorial trainee, and reporter—in that order—I have given up on American journalism. The decline of the American press has long been obvious, and my time is too valuable to waste in an effort to supply the "man in the street" with his daily quota of clichés, gossip, and erotic tripe. There is another concept of journalism, which you may or may not be familiar with. It's engraved on a bronze plaque on the southeast corner of the Times Tower in New York City.[11]

11. See epigraph on page xv.

In this letter, the clippings, and the résumé, you should have all you need to give you an idea of who I am. If you're interested in me, then I'd like to know something about you, the paper, and the sports editor's job. Right now, though, I must get back to my novel. By the time you get this letter the first section of the book will be at the Viking Press in New York; by the time the paper starts in November, the book will be finished. After that, who knows?

And whatever you decide, please return my clippings.

> Thanks,
> Hunter S. Thompson

return address:
2437 Ransdell Avenue
Louisville 4, Kentucky

TO VIRGINIA THOMPSON:

After being evicted from his cabin Thompson took up residence in Annie and Fred Schoelkopf's basement apartment in nearby Otisville. The Schoelkopfs took a real shine to Thompson, cooking him nightly meals and providing him with cash to finish "Prince Jellyfish."

> August 9, 1959
> Otisville, New York

Dear Mom,

If my recent letters have been devoid of good and cheerful news, there is a damned good reason. I've been wound up in a series of mild disasters here; nothing serious, but the kind of thing that might drive a less resilient person straight out of his wits. Here's a short rundown:

a) I was evicted

b) the steering mechanism on the car went bad

c) I couldn't move the car out of the driveway, and the landlord jacked it up and took a wheel in lieu of payment for a light bill

d) I had the landlord arrested

e) my unemployment insurance was cut off

f) no sooner had I fixed the steering mechanism than the car virtually fell to pieces

g) the car insurance was cut off because I couldn't make the second-to-last payment

h) and now I find that my driver's license has expired, and I can't even drive the car to New York to sell it for junk.

The car still runs—not safely and just barely—and I think I can get either [Paul] Semonin or Forbes[12] to come up here and drive it to New York for me. Once I get it there I can get a little money for it, anyway. It's a hell of a deal, but right now I don't have much choice.

Actually, this all sounds worse than it is. All these things happened in the space of about a week, and it just about un-nerved me. If it hadn't been for Annie and Fred Schoelkopf, god knows what sort of dire fate I'd have come to.

You may not appreciate this—and I know Memo will hate it like hell—but what I'm going to do now is come back to Louisville, shut myself in the back bedroom, and finish this novel. It's about half finished now, and I'm never going to get it done if I have to continue this wild scramble merely to stay alive and eating. I told Viking Press I'd have the first half of it to them by the end of the summer. They haven't by any means promised to publish it, but their interest is the only bright spot in what is now a very bleak immediate future. I will finish the rest of it in Louisville, and then leave. I do not intend to get a job while I'm there, and neither do I intend to cost you any money. I merely want a little peace and quiet so I can get something done.

I will explain more fully when I calm down. Right now it's all I can do to sit here and see these damned typewriter keys.

Love, HST

TO THE NEW YORK DEPARTMENT OF LABOR, DIVISION OF UNEMPLOYMENT INSURANCE:

Thompson tried using legalistic language to explain to the New York Department of Labor the fickleness of its unemployment insurance policy. His argument drew no response. Shortly after writing this, Thompson, after a brief stay in Virginia Beach, hitchhiked home to Louisville to finish "Prince Jellyfish."

August 10, 1959
Otisville, New York

New York Department of Labor
Division of Unemployment Insurance
Albany, New York

Gentlemen,
After drawing unemployment insurance for four and a half months, I was recently declared ineligible. The facts of the case are such that only a ma-

12. Bill Forbes was Thompson's friend and neighbor at 57 Perry Street.

licious cretin could come to such a conclusion. It is my earnest hope that you will investigate this matter and reverse the decision which rendered me ineligible.

Your local office in Middletown handled the case. My social security number is xxx-xx-xxxx; my records are on file in that office.

I shall not attempt, in this letter, to outline the entire history of my case, but the pertinent facts are these:

A) I am a newspaper reporter and have been for three years.

B) Near the end of February I was fired from my job as a reporter with the *Daily Record*, Middletown, New York.

C) Soon afterwards I began drawing thirty dollars a week in unemployment insurance. This continued for four and a half months. No effort was made to find me a job in my field, no one questioned the fact that I was eligible for my checks, and during that time I somehow managed to live on this meager pittance.

D) Several weeks ago, finding myself in particularly desperate financial straits, I worked for four days at a laboring job—tearing up railroad tracks for the Ohio Salvage and Equipment Company. I got this job on my own and made no attempt to collect my check that week.

E) On the fifth day, I was unable to go to work. I was completely exhausted, my eyes had swollen up like golf balls, and I decided not to go to work.

F) On the following Monday my car broke down, making it impossible for me to go to work even if I'd been physically able. I had difficulty getting the part, and decided to go back and sign for a check that week.

G) I was not allowed to sign, and have not been allowed to sign since then. I have been told that work "is available" for me—in the form of a railroad laborer's job. I protested this decision, but my protest was denied. This is how the matter stands at the moment.

But as I said before, all this information is available at the Middletown office. I have written to you because I am tired of being told that "work is available." Of course work is available: and if it's available to me—a newspaper reporter—it's available to every other able-bodied man presently drawing unemployment insurance in Middletown. The primary fact of the case is this: my situation is absolutely unchanged from the way it stood for the first four and a half months of the period since I was employed. All I did was go out and make an attempt to pick up a few extra dollars on a laboring job. The job was too exhausting; it caused my eyes to swell up, put me in close contact with poison ivy (to which I am allergic), and was not in my line of work in the first place. It seems perfectly ridiculous that I should have been declared ineligible because of this.

I realize, of course, that this situation is absurd. It is the very nadir of slovenly gall for a man to *demand* his unemployment insurance. Nevertheless, this country functions under a system of economics which assumes that close to five percent of the work force will be perpetually unemployed. There are provisions for this, and your office happens to be one of the provisions. I therefore feel entitled to this money, and see no reason why it should be denied me.

In summation, let me say this: if the time ever comes when I find myself collecting unemployment insurance again, you may be damned well certain that I'll make no effort to find myself *any* work of *any* kind. In this case I tried and was consequently declared ineligible for further benefits. And if it makes sense to you that your system should foster reasoning of this kind, then I fail to see that the system itself is anything more than a giant, bureaucratic joke.

I say these things not to malign your office, but to point out to you the faulty reasoning which has brought this case to your attention. If you need any further information from me, I can be reached: c/o Fred Schoelkopf, Otisville, New York.

In closing, I remain,

> Very Sincerely,
> Hunter S. Thompson

FROM WILLIAM J. KENNEDY, *SAN JAN STAR:*

The publisher of the San Juan Star *had his thirty-one-year-old-editor—William Kennedy of Albany, New York—respond to Thompson's job inquiry. Kennedy, who had first come to Puerto Rico in 1956, would go on to win the 1984 Pulitzer Prize for his novel* Ironweed.

> August 25, 1959
> Puerto Rico

Mr. Hunter S. Thompson
2437 Ransdell Avenue
Louisville 4, Kentucky

Dear Mr. Thompson:

After giving careful consideration to your application, we have decided that for several reasons you would not be happy with us.

First, our publisher is a member of Rotary.

Second, your literary accomplishments would not really single you out as "off beat," since three of our staff members have also finished novels and one is a playwright.

Third, our policy will probably be aimed at "the man in the street," since that encompasses all but shut-ins and hermits, and there are not enough shut-ins and hermits in Puerto Rico to build the circulation we're aiming at.

We feel you had best return to your novel, perhaps even start another. You could build the plot around that bronze plaque on the Times Tower. You should always write about something you know intimately.

Too bad we couldn't get together. Lots of people go shoeless down here. You would have liked it.

We're keeping your application on file. If we ever get a candy machine and need someone to kick it in,[13] we'll get in touch with you.

> Yours in zen,
> William J. Kennedy
> Managing Editor

TO WILLIAM J. KENNEDY, *SAN JUAN STAR:*

Livid at the snide tone of the Star's *reply, for weeks Thompson daydreamed of finding a way to get to Puerto Rico just to pummel William Kennedy.*

> August 30, 1959
> 2437 Ransdell Ave.
> Louisville, Kentucky

your letter was cute, my friend, and your interpretation of my letter was beautifully typical of the cretin-intellect responsible for the dry-rot of the american press. but don't think that lack of an invitation from you will keep me from getting down that way, and when i do remind me to first kick your teeth in and then jam a bronze plaque far into your small intestine.

give my best to your "literary" staff and your rotarian publisher. if they're half as cute as you are, your paper will be a whomping success.

i think, also, that i need not point out the folly of your keeping my application on file.

> cheers:
> Hunter S. Thompson

---

13. Thompson had included on his résumé that he had been fired from the *Middletown Daily Record* for kicking a candy machine.

TO WILLIAM STYRON:

Thompson appealed to Styron, his favorite contemporary writer and a stranger, for help in finding a first-class literary agent. Styron responded immediately, recommending his own agent, Elizabeth McKee.

> September 4, 1959
> 2437 Ransdell Ave.
> Louisville, Kentucky

Mr. Styron,

If you have a spare moment sometime soon, I wonder if you'd shoot me a line of advice. I'm just about through with a novel that I'd like very much to sell, but I'm not sure whether I should take it around to publishers or send it to an agent. Several weeks ago I took it to Viking Press, and this morning it came back to me with a very pleasant "thanks, but no thanks" note attached to the front page. No criticism of any kind. If this continues to happen I could easily spend a year trying to sell the damned thing, without ever finding out what's wrong with it.

I've been told—or advised—to send it to an agent, and if this is what I should do I wonder if you'd either recommend one or give me the name and address of yours. I wonder also if you'd tell me how you went about getting *Lie Down in Darkness* published. And with the mention of that book, allow me to doff my cap and banish any thought of flattery when I say it's without a doubt the finest book written in this country since the Second World War. I shall be highly pleased if mine is half as good.

I shall be here in Louisville until I finish this book, probably around October 1. At that time I'll head back to New York, where I've existed for the past two years. So if you can get that information to me before I leave here, I shall be most happy.

I presume you're pretty busy with your new book right now, but sometime later in the fall, when you have a spare hour or two, I'd like to hustle up to Roxbury[14] for a beer and a few moments of conversation. I'm not sure that either of us would find this particularly edifying, but I mention it here because it seems at the moment to be something I'd like very much to do.

But I, unlike the Pepsi-Cola people,[15] am not in a position right now to be sociable. My primary concern is to get this book finished and sold. If you can offer a word or two of advice on this subject—specifically, the name of a decent agent—I shall be eternally grateful.

> Sincerely,
> Hunter S. Thompson

---

14. Styron's home was in Roxbury, Connecticut.
15. "Come join the Pepsi Generation" was a popular advertising slogan of the late 1950s.

TO JACK BENSON, VIKING PRESS:

Benson had rejected "Prince Jellyfish" by form letter.

> September 5, 1959
> 2437 Ransdell Ave.
> Louisville, Kentucky

Jack Benson
Viking Press
New York City

Sir,

Manuscript arrived yesterday, as you predicted. Sorry to bother you with that letter.

Sorry also that you would not "care to publish" the book. It is my intention to make you rue the day you wrote that letter. I say this without rancor, of course, and I'm sure you'll understand my attitude. Accepting your judgment, in my case, would be suicide.

Naturally I regret that you had neither the time nor the inclination to include so much as a hint as to WHY you didn't care for the book. I'm not asking you for an explanation, but it seems to me that at least one sentence of criticism wouldn't be too back-breaking a chore for someone whom I can only assume to be a competent judge of manuscripts. Please understand that I appreciate your politeness and your immediate reply to my recent letter. I would have preferred, however, an honest opinion—however short or brutal—of whatever fault you found with the manuscript. But as I said before, I'm not requesting a re-evaluation of my work. It's just something you might think about.

In closing, let me thank you again for your kind cooperation.

> Sincerely,
> Hunter S. Thompson

FROM WILLIAM J. KENNEDY:

Instead of quaking at Thompson's letter threat of August 30, Kennedy saw it as a challenge—and offered Thompson an interesting opportunity.

September 8, 1959
San Juan, Puerto Rico

Mr. Hunter Thompson
2437 Ransdell Avenue
Louisville, Kentucky

Friend Hunter:
   You are probably not as good as you think you are and probably only half as irrational as you seem.
   The fact is, we considered hiring you for a moment on the basis of your entertainment value alone. Also, we were after something other than a happy hack. Then we got to that bronze plaque paragraph and you faded away, Hunter. You faded away.
   Only, however, as an employee.
   We are still ready to regard you, as you regard yourself, as the bushy-tailed expert on the dry rot of American journalism. And to this end we are offering you a deal.
   If you want to expend the time to summarize your feelings on what's wrong with American jouralism in, say, three or so double-spaced pages, we will run this in our first edition, presently planned for November 2nd. We will pay you at regular space rates, which are still to be established.
   In order to make clear the reason for this contribution we would also want to print some of the correspondence leading up to the article, in which case we would want your permission to use your letters to us.
   You can be as disagreeable in the article as you normally are otherwise. Just don't run off at the mouth. We're tabloid size.
   The thought occurs that your disdain for our as yet unpublished publication will deter you from this task. Offhand I don't know of another publication which would give you the time of day, so if you mean that dry rot business, here is your chance to put up or shut up.

Intestinally yours,
William J. Kennedy
Managing Editor

TO WILLIAM J. KENNEDY, *SAN JUAN STAR:*

Thus began a correspondence that has lasted nearly forty years.

> September 10, 1959
> 2437 Ransdell Ave.
> Louisville 4, Kentucky

Daddio! You mean the bronze plaque paragraph bugged you? Why hell-fire, I thought it was the swinginest thing I've writ in years. I mean, man, it was vivid!

And so much for that. I don't mind saying, friend Kennedy, that I enjoyed your letter. This is a weird bit of correspondence we have here, my man, and I don't know whether it makes me laugh or cry. Actually, I enjoyed your first letter, too, and took great pleasure in composing my reply. It's relationships like this that make our short lives worthwhile.

Your smug challenge, however, gives me considerable pause. If you're serious—and I mean serious enough to think I'll attempt a definitive essay on "The Dry Rot of the American Press" in three double-spaced pages— then I can only assume that your tragic optimism is exceeded only by your appalling inability to see either the scope or the seriousness of the problem you ask me to explain. Surely you're aware that the "dry rot" of the press has its roots in the psychopathic complacency of the American public . . . which can be blamed almost entirely on inadequate facilities for information and education . . . for which the press is in large part responsible . . . and for which it is suffering now because newspaper men have become a breed of useless hacks and gossip-mongers . . . and so on and so on in that familiar vicious cycle which can have its end only in the eventual disintegration of the greatest and most optimistic political experiment in the history of man. . . .

So, having said this, and feeling quite certain that the press of today has no use for "abstract generalities" of this kind, I can take another tack and assume that your challenge stems from your undeniable sense of humor; that you plan a ceremonial mangling, in your first issue, of a jabbering beatnik who had the ridiculous gall to seek employment, of all things, with a hot-shot paper like the *San Juan Star.*

Fortunately, your motives would make little difference to me in this case. I'd enjoy writing the piece, whether you used it or not, and will in all probability give it a fling. If I have the time, and if I can write it to my own satisfaction, I'll send it to you sometime before October 1st. What you do with it is none of my concern. And as for my letters, I'd probably have no objection to your reprinting them if and when I write the article. At any rate, I'll get in touch with you again sometime in the near future, either to send the article or to explain why I'm not sending it. So until then, I remain,

disagreeably,
Hunter S. Thompson

TO ELIZABETH MCKEE,

With Styron's literary agent now his own, Thompson grew more confident that "Prince Jellyfish"—once completed—would get published by a major New York house.

September 12, 1959
2437 Ransdell Ave.
Louisville 4, Kentucky

Elizabeth McKee
30 East 60th St.
New York City 22

Dear Miss (Mrs.) McKee,

I wrote William Styron the other day, requesting the name of a decent agent, and in his letter this morning I found your name, address, and the information that you "might be very interested" in seeing the manuscript of my novel.

I certainly hope this is true. And if it is, I hope further that you might find a publisher who'd be "very interested" in getting my book between two covers, bringing it out with a great thunder of publicity drums, and generally doing everything possible to hoist me out of this bog of frightful poverty I've been wallowing in for the past two years.

All that would be nice, of course, but all I really need is some idea of how to get this thing on the road to publication. When I began it some eighteen months ago, crouched in some dark hole a few blocks from Sheridan Square, I had not the shadow of a doubt concerning the excellence of my finished product. Now, however, with so many months of sporadic labor behind me, I seem to have lost all hope of any objectivity concerning my own work. I say this not to flagellate my own hopes, but to qualify my judgment when I say that my book is better than *Soldier's Pay*, better than *This Side of Paradise*, and better than *The Torrents of Spring*. This, to me, is a recommendation of sorts. Whether it's valid or not remains to be seen.

I should warn you, though, that I've taken three chapters and an outline of the remainder to Viking Press. It was branded there as a work they "would not care to publish." I can't tell you why this was so, because they didn't give me the faintest idea. And that's precisely the reason I decided to look around for an agent. I can only presume that, if the book is unpublishable, you'll at least tell me why.

At any rate, I should have it finished by the middle of October. If you'd like me to bring it to you then, or if you'd like to see the completed portion of it anytime before then, I hope you'll let me know as soon as possible. I shall return to New York as soon as the book is finished, and my address until that time will be the same as it is now. If you're at all interested, I'd like to hear from you.

Sincerely,
Hunter S. Thompson

TO WILLIAM J. KENNEDY, *SAN JUAN STAR:*

While holed up in his old room polishing "Prince Jellyfish," Thompson took time to write a one-act play for Kennedy to publish in the San Juan Star.

October 1, 1959
2437 Ransdell Ave.
Louisville 4, Kentucky

Dear Hack,

Here's your piece, old buddy, and I'll be the first to doff my Beat Generation Beanie if you have the guts to publish it.

It's not exactly what you asked for, and—I hope—not what you thought you'd get. You know as well as I do that the subject can't be handled effectively in "three or so double-spaced pages." I thought this was the best way to do it: a brutal, low-level, sledge-hammer drama. It's a farce, of course, but its theme is a big one, and I think the point is well made. You told me to be as disagreeable as I wanted, and I took you at your word.

You could supply the final and ridiculous irony to this whole thing by hacking my play to pieces to fit it into a capsule space. It wouldn't surprise me at all if you did this, so let me say now that if you don't want to run it *the way it is*, then send it back. And realize that, in doing so, you will confirm not only my suspicions, but my accusations as well.

If, however, you decide to use it, I would very much appreciate five copies of the edition in which it appears. Deduct for these copies when you send me the check for the play. And please do this, regardless of the cost to me.

You have my permission to use any or all of my letters. I fully expect you, as a competent journalist, to use my quotes out of context, jeer at my work, libel me in every possible way, and generally crucify me in the good name of editorial entertainment. I don't give a damn what you do to the letters—you may re-write them, for all I care—but if you tamper with, delete from, add to, or in any way affect the wording of the play, I shall see to it that you regret your indiscretion.

Actually, your last letter surprised me a bit, and perhaps in the long run I shall owe you an apology for all this abuse. I hope so, but I think I'll wait till I see that first issue before I put my dagger away.

Once again, don't forget those five copies. Until I get them, or until you return the play, I remain,

Suspiciously,
Hunter S. Thompson

TO WHOM IT MAY CONCERN:

Eugene McGarr, a hard-drinking Irishman from the Bronx, had worked with Thompson as a copyboy at Time. *One evening he and Thompson took their dates on a surreptitious night swim in a neighborhood pool near Sheridan Square. Before long an Italian gang ten strong came by and started a rumble. Both Thompson and McGarr were beaten bloody. Thompson swore he would never be caught "unarmed" again, and wrote this letter "for the record" in case he was ever arrested for defending himself. Thompson had just returned from Louisville to the Schoelkopfs' basement to look for work.*

October 20, 1959
Otisville, New York

To whom it may concern:

If, at any time between the date of this letter and December 31 of this year, I am apprehended, arrested, detained, or held in New York City on charges of possessing a deadly concealed weapon, this letter will explain my action.

Some time in late August, roughly between the 20th and the 25th, I was severely beaten by a gang of hoodlums in a playground beside the pool on St. Luke's Place. Had the police not arrived when they did, I certainly would have been seriously injured and perhaps killed.

In light of the police department's apparent inability to protect me from another such beating, I have no choice but to protect myself by any possible means. I have chosen a hunting knife, with a blade approximately six inches long, which I intend to carry on my belt at all times in the borough of Manhattan. I will use this knife for no purpose but to defend myself from possible injury and death. And if the occasion arises, I shall use it to protect others—my companions or any other person—from the same fate.

To me, this situation is ridiculous. I do, however, have very vivid memories of my last encounter with these thugs, and I much prefer the possibility of a manslaughter trial to a slab in the morgue. Frankly, I do not feel physically safe in New York City. As a writer, however, I find it necessary to come here once in a while. This makes it imperative that I carry a weapon to protect myself.

My action is not intended to cast a slur on the efficiency of the New York Police Department. The task of policing a man-made jungle of this size borders on the impossible, and the men who undertake it have my heartfelt sympathy. It is common knowledge that weeds cannot be killed by clipping the leaves.

Let me say in closing that this situation is not only ridiculous, but tragic. But when the law, so responsive to the wishes of the metropolitan garage owners association, cannot rise to the task of protecting the citizens of this city from beatings and senseless death, then it seems to me the citizens are justified in protecting themselves.

Sincerely,
Hunter S. Thompson

FROM WILLIAM J. KENNEDY, *SAN JUAN STAR:*

Kennedy, along with San Juan Star *publisher William Dorvillier, flatly rejected Thompson's one-act play. Kennedy—who for years to come would offer Thompson advice on writing—advised him to stick to fiction.*

October 22, 1959
San Juan, Puerto Rico

Mr. Hunter S. Thompson
2437 Ransdell Avenue
Louisville 4, Kentucky

Friend Hunter:

I am returning your play.

You disappointed me. I expected a serious essay on a serious matter. You delivered a batch of warmed-over clichés with barnyard overtones. You raise questions, then trail off into foolishness.

It would not take any guts to publish this piece. Just gall.

The play has its moments all right. The Lincoln bit was one. The writing shows you will say things well once you discover something new that's worth saying.

I honestly wish you well with your book. If you're serious about that, then you're better off staying away from journalism anyway.

I have only one piece of advice: quit writing down.

Drop by sometime. We could exchange insults over a bottle of rum.

Adios, cat

William J. Kennedy

Managing Editor

TO WILLIAM J. KENNEDY, *SAN JUAN STAR:*

Enraged that someone at the San Juan Star *referred to his one-act play as "sophomoric drivel," Thompson took one last swipe at the Rotarian mentality of American journalism.*

October 29, 1959

Otisville, New York

Dear Hack,

Your rotarian boob of a publisher has one of the most original minds I've run across in quite a while. I didn't realize my "drama" would hit so close to home.

Whatever cretin scrawled his "criticism" on the back of my manuscript referred to it as "sophomoric drivel." Nice phrase, eh? The man's a real thinker.

I might point out, though, that my man Avare[16] used the same phrase to describe the Lincoln quotation I used in the play. He says with all the pompous stupidity of his breed: "Oh, you thought this sophomoric drivel would interest me, eh?" Avare, to my mind, is such a caricature of a babbling ass that I hardly dared hope to ever see his twin in the flesh. But your straw boss seems to be it, and I'll bet working for him is a real ball.

And your phrase, "a batch of warmed-over cliches with barnyard overtones," is a pretty apt description of contemporary journalism, I'd say. Why don't *you* write that "serious essay" you pine for so desperately?

But don't expect *me* to send you a package of platitudes to drape over the stinking carcass of your newspaper like an American flag over a coffin full of crap. If you want to belabor your readers with Lincoln and Jesus, go right ahead. The men responsible for the "dry rot," however, are men like your quick-witted straw boss, who sit on their pompous rumps and yell about sophomoric drivel while their hired "literary" hacks work day and night to grind out tripe by the barrel-full.

You have proved my point, friend Kennedy, and I think you know it as well as I do. To have published my play would have been a little embar-

16. Avare, a dimwitted publisher, was the lead character in Thompson's one-act play, *The Dry Rot of American Journalism.*

rassing, I am sure, and I'd like to have seen the look on your publisher's face when he read it. I know what I'm saying, Kennedy, and if it's a little too brutal for you "serious" people to stomach, so much the better. Instead of my play, why don't you publish the words to "The Star-Spangled Banner"? It's more your style, and you won't be tipping your hand that way, either. Platitudes are safe, because they're easy to wink at, but truth is something else again.

If I get down that way, I'll accept your invitation to a bit of tippling. I imagine you're pretty decent, in your own way, and I think it's a shame that you've hired yourself out as a mouthpiece for the international rotary. But I guess we all have to eat, and perhaps when I'm your age I'll be in the same boat. I hope not but there's always the possibility.

At any rate, thanks for your kind words about the novel, and I wish I could say the same for your newspaper. But I'm a little more honest than that, so I can only say cheers, and thanks for an interesting exchange of letters.

ETC.—   HST

TO THE MUNICIPAL COURT MAGISTRATE:

Ticketed for wiping out on a motor scooter, Thompson refused to pay the fine. Instead, he fled West Milford, New Jersey—where the accident had occurred—and sent this letter of explanation of his actions.

November 6, 1959
Otisville, New York

Municipal Court Magistrate
Town Hall
West Milford, N.J.

Dear Sir,

Earlier today I was given a summons to appear before your court on November 9, on a charge of "leaving the scene of an accident." I shall have to decline this appearance, and I hope this letter will explain why. By November 9, I shall be well out of the state of New Jersey, but I don't want to leave without explaining my position.

The accident occurred late at night. I was driving a friend's motor scooter, quite sober, within the speed limit, on an unfamiliar road. Suddenly, the road went over a small hill and turned sharply to the right. I touched my brakes, intending to slow down, and went into a long skid that came to an abrupt end when the scooter turned on its side and hurled me down on the asphalt. There was no damage done to anyone or anything except the scooter and my own body. No one witnessed the fall, and no one but me was involved.

For several moments I was stunned, dizzy, and in pain. Soon two men stopped in a car when they saw me lying in the road. They helped me up, saw that I was battered but not severely hurt, and both men insisted that I ride in their car to my friend's cabin. Since I could not walk, they helped me into the car and took me to the place where I was staying.

Several minutes later the West Milford police arrived, very angry and without a warrant to enter the house. I was subsequently charged with leaving the scene of my accident, and told that I was lucky to be getting off with only one charge.

I called the Violations Clerk today and found out that the minimum fine for "leaving the scene of an accident" is $25.

So, faced with a choice of paying a minimum of $25 for falling off a motor scooter on a public road, and fleeing the state to avoid prosecution, I chose to leave the state. I am a free-lance writer and simply cannot afford to pay a fine of $25 or more at this time. And, since I obviously left the scene and am therefore guilty, I would have no choice but to go to jail in lieu of paying the fine. Then too, since I could not walk after the accident, I had to have some help in accomplishing my crime. This would make the gentlemen who stopped to help me—and who were kind enough to ride me home—accomplices in this crime.

So, we are all criminals: those of us who skid and fall on damp, unmarked roads, and those others who stop and give aid to the injured. If this situation is not patently ridiculous to you, then I can only congratulate myself on having the good sense to avoid an appearance in your court. Frankly, I cannot believe that any thinking man would find me guilty as charged. My confidence in the mentality and reasoning processes of the law, however, is virtually nil. I feel sure that nothing but trouble would come from any appearance I might make in your courtroom.

If the thinking processes of the law were demonstrated by the fact that I was so charged with this crime—when I actually couldn't walk and had to be carried from the scene of the accident by two men—then I feel quite sure that this same strange reasoning would lead to my conviction, in some way that would probably make just as much sense as the charge itself.

If I seem pessimistic, I can only say that these are my convictions and that I cannot apologize for them.

By the time you receive this letter I will have left the state. I am purposefully not telling my friend where I am going, so that he can say in all honesty that he has no idea where I am.

In closing, let me say that I regret this situation tremendously. Ordinarily, I would come down to the courthouse and discuss it with you. Since I have no money, however, I can't take the chance of going to jail — especially for an offense like this, which makes no sense at all, no matter how you look at it.

Sincerely,
Hunter S. Thompson

TO ELIZABETH MCKEE:

Broke and constantly getting into trouble, Thompson couldn't find the solitude he needed to finish "Prince Jellyfish."

November 8, 1959
Otisville, New York

Dear Miss (Mrs.) McKee:

Sometime in September I wrote you that William Styron had said you "might be interested" in seeing my then-unfinished novel. At that time, I told you the book would be finished sometime in October.

Well . . . I was wrong. I have been hounded since then by a guerrilla force of investigators, creditors, and other money-grubbing elements — to the extent that I've been forced to keep on the move almost constantly. I wrote you from Louisville, and since then I've moved from there to Otisville, to New Jersey, to Manhattan, and now back to Otisville again.

At any rate, while I was in New York City I ran into a lad who offered to take my book (the finished part) to a friend of his at Appleton-Century-Crofts. I don't know what this means, but I sense the vague possibility of an advance. To secure such a thing, there is no doubt in my mind that I'd run the seventy miles from here to Manhattan at top speed in the dead of night with the manuscript strapped to my back.

I want you to know, however, that if these Appleton people show any interest at all in the book, I shall call you immediately. You were very kind to take an interest in my book, and the only reason I haven't delivered it to you by now is this wretched, degrading, nerve-shattering poverty.

At any rate, if this wino turns out to have no friends at Appleton, or if they mock me and drive me from the building, and if I can sell enough old Ballantine ale bottles to keep me alive until I finish the book, I shall get it to you as soon as possible. If it's not finished by Christmas, I may give up the ghost and get a job with the Salvation Army.

Until then, I remain, grimly:

Hunter S. Thompson

TO *PUERTO RICO BOWLING NEWS:*

Desperate for work in the Caribbean, Thompson applied for a sportswriting position at the Puerto Rico Bowling News. *Philip Kramer, the editor and publisher, asked Thompson to send more information about himself.*

November 25, 1959
Otisville, New York

Gentlemen,

Are you looking for a bowling writer, or a sportswriter? Your ad was a little confusing on this point.

If you're looking for a sportswriter, I'll be available on or about January first.

The enclosed clippings aren't quite up to date, but they should give you an idea of who I am, and how I write. During the past two years I've worked as an editorial trainee for *Time* magazine, and as a reporter for an upstate New York daily. At the moment, I'm working on a novel that should be finished by the first of the year.

It's a big jump from New York to Puerto Rico, but if life down there is as warm and easy as rumor would have us believe, then it might be worth the trip.

At any rate, please return my clippings when you answer the letter.

Sincerely,
Hunter S. Thompson

TO PHILIP KRAMER, *PUERTO RICO BOWLING NEWS:*

Not wanting to miss a chance to move to Puerto Rico, Thompson lied about his age in a successful maneuver to land a job with El Sportivo, *a new English-language Puerto Rican sports weekly focused on bowling.*

December 14, 1959
Otisville, New York

Dear Mr. Kramer:

You said you were leaving for New York in seven days and it took four of those for your letter to get to Otisville. I will make this brief, and try to get it in the morning mail, hoping it will get there before you leave.

I am single, an Air Force veteran, twenty-five, and definitely interested in talking with you about this job. I've been sports editor of two Florida weeklies, one Pennsylvania daily, and a command newspaper in the Air Force. More recently, I've worked as an editorial trainee for *Time* magazine, and as a general reporter for a New York (State) daily. For the past nine months I've been writing a novel, most of which is now awaiting judgment at a New York publishing house.

You apparently misunderstood my remark about life being "easy" down there. Perhaps I should have said "warm and pleasant," or something equally inane. In Florida, I was sports editor of two competing papers at the same time, sometimes working twenty hours a day—and I enjoyed it thoroughly. All I ask of any job is that it be challenging, satisfying and at least financially rewarding enough to keep me out of the bread-line.

I'd have to find out a little more about your plans before I could take any definite steps, but I'll wait till I see you in New York before I ask any questions. [. . .]

Sincerely,
Hunter S. Thompson

TO ROBERT BONE:

Shortly after Thompson was fired from the Middletown Daily Record *reporter-photographer Bone also left to find a job in Manhattan. He wound up at the* San Juan Star. *By 1961 he was working at a financial magazine in Rio de Janeiro.*

December 14, 1959
Otisville, New York

Robert:

Just finished reading your article in the *Record* ("Statehood or Status Quo") and found it distinctly inferior to the report of the Red hearings. Who wrote that other one for you?

Pardon that jab. It's not the reason for this letter, but I figured you needed something to make up for all those compliments I tossed off in my last communication. Incidentally, the copy of the *Star* (front page editorial) that you sent up here was one hell of an improvement over the first one I saw. Looks like Kennedy might have shaken the Rotary Club influence.

But now to the point. There's a slim chance that I might hop down that way sometime soon, but I'm going to need a bit of information from you before I commit myself. A guy named Philip Kramer, editor-publisher of something called the *Puerto Rico Bowling News*, says he's starting a new monthly sports magazine down there ("similar in style to that of *Sports Il-*

lustrated") and he's looking for sportswriters. He's located in Roosevelt, Puerto Rico, which I can't even find on the map. If you can answer the following questions for me and get the answers back by return mail, I will appreciate it no end—and may even stand you a few drinks if and when I get down there. At any rate, I have to see Kramer in New York next week and I hope you can get your reply to me before then. Send it c/o Murphy, 69 E. 4th St., Manhattan.

Here we go:

1) where is Roosevelt? what sort of place is it?
2) do you know anything about Kramer? his letter sounds like it was written by either a fanatic or a crack-pot.
3) from what you know of the cost of living down there, what would be the minimum salary you'd accept if you were in my shoes?
4) have you heard anything about this proposed magazine? it would have to have a hell of a lot of money behind it to be anything but a pipedream, and I don't want to come down there for something that will fold in a week.
5) do you honestly like Puerto Rico? Also, what are the main drawbacks and/or advantages?

If you can think of any other pertinent information along these lines, by all means send it along. And once again, do *not* send your reply to Otisville. If you write *immediately*, and send it to New York, it should arrive about the same time Kramer does. And for god's sake, don't mention this to Kennedy (or anyone else at the *Star*, for that matter). If Kramer ever got wind of my dealings with the *Star*, he'd avoid me like the plague. As it is, I may have a chance of duping him into thinking I'm normal. The reason I'm writing you is that I don't want *him* to dupe *me*. So . . . thanks for any help you can give me. May see you sometime soon.

Cheers: H

TO MARK ETHRIDGE, LOUISVILLE *COURIER-JOURNAL:*

Just before departing for Puerto Rico, Thompson had pitched a story idea to the editor of the Louisville Courier-Journal. *Ethridge rejected the idea but asked Thompson to become his newspaper's Caribbean stringer. Thompson was thrilled at the prospect of seeing his byline in his hometown paper.*

December 28, 1959
New York City

Dear Mr. Ethridge:

Last Derby day, while a whiskey-soaked throng of some 100,000 struggled to its feet for the annual Churchill Downs rendition of "My Old Kentucky Home," six expatriate Louisvillians stood in front of a television set in a small Greenwich Village bar. And that night, there was a "Derby Party" on West 78th Street, about a hundred yards from the thug-infested woodlands of Central Park.

If this interests you, then read on. I think I've stumbled on a decent idea for a story for the *Courier-Journal*: the community of Louisville expatriates in Manhattan. No other city in the United States—and Paul Semonin and I have checked this out thoroughly—seems to have such a conspicuous and close-knit representation here. Offhand, I can think of nineteen people, all roughly the same age (ten boys and nine girls), who have either worked or lived here within the past year. I cite, as prominent examples, Paul and Debbie Newman at the Art Students' League, David Bibb publishing IVY magazine from an office in the Biltmore Hotel, Floyd Smith at Columbia, Tad Minnish and Buddy Hayes among the Beatnik set in Greenwich Village, Sally Spaulding working for *Time*, Olivia Smith working for an executive personnel agency on the East Side, Henry Eichelburger at an Army Intelligence (Russian Language) School, and Ralston Steenrod wheeling and dealing in the dark caverns of Wall Street and the Financial District.

At any rate, this should give you an idea of what I'm shooting at. These people are here for different reasons, most of them move in different circles, and all of them have their own reasons for leaving Louisville (some of them, for that matter, intend to return; and some don't). Actually, the only thing they have in common is that they comprise a sort of "Louisville colony" here in the middle of New York. I think it's a good story and I don't think you should pass it by.

As for terms, I leave that to you. I think you'll be fair. I can offer either a single shot (Louisville Expatriates in New York) or a series of contrasting interviews—with photographs of different apartments and pastimes. Naturally, I'd prefer whatever arrangement would bring me the most money. [. . .]

Sincerely,
Hunter S. Thompson
c/o Dick Murphy
69 E. 4th Street
Manhattan

William J. Kennedy (right) with (left to right) Rear Admiral Daniel Gallery, commander of U.S. Navy base in Puerto Rico; Vice President Richard Nixon; and Luis Munoz Marin, governor of Puerto Rico.

Thompson earned money while in Puerto Rico working as a male model.
(PHOTO BY PAUL SEMONIN; COURTESY OF HST COLLECTION)

While in Puerto Rico, Thompson began taking photography seriously, selling many of his prints—such as this one—to San Juan travel magazines.
(PHOTO BY HUNTER S. THOMPSON; COURTESY OF HST COLLECTION)

Sandy Conklin—soon to be Thompson's wife—moved to Puerto Rico to live with him.
(PHOTO BY HUNTER S. THOMPSON; COURTESY OF HST COLLECTION)

Sandy Conklin, Hunter S. Thompson, and Paul Semonin marooned in Bermuda.
(COURTESY OF HST COLLECTION)

1960

NEW LIFE IN THE TROPICS . . . NAKED, CRAZY, AND RICH ON LUQUILLO BEACH . . . THE BOWLING DISASTER, THE BEATING, THE BEAUTY, AND THE NEW YORK *HERALD TRIBUNE* . . . ESCAPE FROM PUERTO RICO, DEPORTED FROM BERMUDA . . . LONG RUN TO SAN FRANCISCO, LONG CHAIN OF FAILURE . . . BAD NEWS FOR THE SWINE FAMILY . . .

All manner of fearful deviations thrived in that muggy air. A legion of pederasts wandered the narrow side-walks of the Old City of San Juan, giggling at every crotch. The bars, the beaches, and even the best sections of town literally crawled with rapists and crab dykes and muggers and people with no sex or sanity at all. They lurked in the shadows and foamed through the streets, grasping and grabbing like crazed shoplifters driven mad by the Tropic Rot!

--Hunter S. Thompson,
  "The Rum Diary" (unpublished novel)

TO HOME (VIRGINIA THOMPSON):

Just after the New Year Thompson left New York for San Juan, Puerto Rico. His plan was to make enough money working at El Sportivo *(aka* Bowling News*) and writing free-lance pieces to finance a new novel set in the Caribbean.*

January 14, 1960
San Juan, Puerto Rico

Dear Home:

Damn, how far away I seem — even to me, who is used to being far away. I trust you got my card, and hope this letter will fill you in a bit more.

Still, oddly enough, very little concrete news to report. This could be either the best or (no, not really the worst, because even at its worst it couldn't be too bad) perhaps the most outlandish thing I have ever done. It all depends on how this magazine goes. If it folds, I will be out on a limb; but if it goes, I will be in on a very lucrative ground floor. As of now, I'm very definitely the "number one boy." Kramer told me tonight that I didn't have to worry about the trial period as long as I kept turning in things like the two stories I did this week. The original plan was for me to work for three months on this ridiculously low salary, and then — if I "worked out" — I would get a fairly sizable raise and a "permanent writer" status. Tonight he said I probably wouldn't have to wait that long. So things are going as well as they could be under any circumstances.

San Juan is a strange combination of old and new. The cost of living here is incredible, yet some Puerto Ricans live on ten dollars a week. Very definitely a dual economy. One night I am having dinner at the Caribe Hilton, the next at a native bar on a street ten feet wide. Bob Bone — ex-compatriot on the *Daily Record* — has been a tremendous help. He's working for the *Star*, the new English-language daily. Kramer is decent, but a little crazy; and the job is so easy and pleasant that I don't see how it can last. I have no hours, no office, one story assignment a week, and I am 98% on my own all the time. The other writer — hired in New York at the same time I was—is a good lad, but not much of a writer. Perhaps this accounts for Kramer's enthusiasm for me. Whatever it is, I am not worrying at the moment. I've sent off a few queries for free-lance assignments, and if I get those my financial situation should take a definite turn for the better.

The main problem here is clothes. Everything is frightfully expensive and no one on the island can tell me where to get a cord suit. All suits are $60 and $70 and I know they have them at Rhodes[1] for $25. Would it be possible for you to buy one there and send it to me? Make it my birthday present. All I have to my name now is a very ratty and well-worn tan cord coat that I got at Lad-a-Dad three years ago—too small and a nasty frayed collar. I will send you my measurements on a separate sheet and if you can get the suit for me I will be most happy. Or else I will have to order it from Brooks Brothers or something like that in New York.

[Paul] Semonin should be down here in a few weeks and Kramer said he might want to hire him as a staff artist. Hope so—that would be a good deal. I meant to tell Paul to come by the house while he was in Louisville. He's a real champion, but I don't think you know him very well.

Thanks again for the plane fare. You-all have been wonderful in these periodic financial emergencies. No word yet on the novel, but I'll let you know as soon as I hear something.

All in all, I think this was a wise move. Of course, except for the Jaguar money, that fiasco in Middletown turned out to be a good thing, too. It took a thing like that to actually get me writing.

Before I go, let me give you a typical day. Rise at ten, go to La Rada (very fashionable) Hotel for lunch and interview with owner-chef, spend afternoon on beach with some people from Philadelphia, out to Kramer's house for conference on La Rada chef story, back to quarters to write story and few letters. Time out after Kramer conference to eat dinner with Douglas, the other writer. Then to bed and up again for another grueling day.

That's about it. I'll write again when I know more. In the meantime, let me hear from the homestead.

Love, Hunter

Measurements: size 44 coat; shirt size 15 (neck) 35 (sleeve); pants size 34 waist, don't worry about length; I will find a tailor here and have him put cuffs on the things.

I want a *grey* cord suit—same color Davison has. If possible, send me his now and get him a new one with the money you would have spent for mine. I don't necessarily need a *new* suit; I just need something to *wear*. The same coat everyday gets a little tedious. Yes, that's an excellent idea.

1. Rhodes was a high-quality men's store in Louisville.

Send me Davison's suit as soon as possible and tell him I'll pay him back by putting him up during spring vacation. On the other hand, that suit of his may be in pretty bad shape by this time. If so, try to get me a new one. If not, send it on. And if you can't get hold of a cord suit this time of year, thanks anyway. It's a queer request, but I just hate to pay $60 for a suit I don't like as well as a $25 cord. And if the grey cord isn't available, get me an olive-drab wash-and-wear. Try also to make whatever you send me wash-and-wear. Laundry here is quite a problem. [. . .]

Love, Hunter

TO DISTRIBUTION MANAGER, BROWN-WILLIAMSON TOBACCO COMPANY:

Thompson started smoking Kools while a sophomore at Louisville Male High School. He would smoke no other cigarette until 1962, when he discovered Dunhills in Rio de Janeiro.

January 15, 1960
164 Ave. Flamboyanes
Hyde Park, Puerto Rico

Distribution Manager
Brown-Williamson Tobacco Co.
Hill St.
Louisville, Kentucky

Dear Sir:

I regret to inform you that Salems have all but swamped Kools in the Puerto Rico cigarette market. I don't know if this makes much difference to you or not, but let me tell you that it bothers the mortal hell out of me. I've been smoking Kools for close to ten years, but down here I'd have an easier time getting a steady supply of reefers. There are god knows how many cigarette machines in San Juan, and in only three of them can I find king-size Kools. This is working a tremendous hardship on me, and I'm writing you in hopes that you'll do something about it.

I'm quite willing to do my part. If you lack a competent distributor down here, then consider me at your service. Nothing would make me happier than to drive Salems off the market for good and ever. It's without a doubt the foulest cigarette in the history of tobacco-addicted man—a tasteless mish-mash of paper and dry weeds.

But I have yet to run across a cigarette machine that doesn't have *two racks* of Salems. And as I said before, only three that I've found contain filter Kools.

There's no excuse for this kind of negligence on your part. If Kools are deemed too strong for the Puerto Rican taste, then get that hustling huckster Ted Bates on the ball and have him educate these people. He's not paid to ignore new markets.

As a native of Louisville, and as one of a long line of Brown-Williamson customers—and primarily as a man who *will* have Kools—I deplore this great vacuum in your distribution. As I said before, I will be glad to help in any way I can. At the moment I'm an associate editor of a new sports magazine here and I'll be glad to sell you a full-page ad to begin the campaign. Personally, I don't give a damn if you want the ad or not, but contact me if it interests you.

My primary concern is the frustrating lack of Kools in Puerto Rico. Whatever action you decide to take on this, please let me hear from you.

Sincerely,
Hunter S. Thompson

RSVP: Hunter S. Thompson
SPORTIVO
Box 64
Roosevelt, P.R.

TO SANDY CONKLIN:

Sandy Conklin had graduated from Goucher College in Maryland in 1959, then moved to New York City to work as a secretary at Nuclear Research Associates, an organization that monitored atomic testing. Her roommate Eleanor married Thompson's fellow copyboy from Time, *Eugene McGarr. Just friends at first, Thompson and Conklin soon found themselves in love.*

January 26, 1960
San Juan

Yes, little princess, I know what it is to be "*stirred* physically." It seems like quite a while ago but it hasn't even been a month. Maybe the time between now and March 11 will pass a little faster.

I enjoyed your letter immensely, even though your new-found "motherly happiness" gave me an uneasy instant. Even so, it's good to know you have a little sunlight.

Life here is excellent—or will be as of Monday when I get paid. Right now the larder is a little bare. Things took a roaring hop here today when I landed a double-decker free-lance assignment. The next few weeks should be busy as hell, with Kramer's work on top of this, and trying to get this beach-pillbox in shape during my spare moments. I'll try to have my schedule under control by the time you get here.

Here is today (one in the new life of HST): Up at ten-thirty, burst out
the door and into the Atlantic for eye-opening swim, then walk up the
beach (with bearded bartending next-door neighbor) to San Juan Inter-
continental Hotel for breakfast—fresh pineapple, toast and marmalade,
and four cups of coffee. See gambling commissioner at two for information on casinos—my next assignment. To La Rada Hotel at four-thirty to
discuss newfound assignment. Eat in Old San Juan at six-thirty, out to pick
up mail in Rio Piedras at nine. Read your letter on way over here, take off
clothes and go naked down to beach with pipe and glass of brandy. Smoke
pipe, drink brandy, swim, come back in for shower and to write this letter.
Afterwards, finish cock-fight feature. Then to bed. No assignments tomorrow. Nothing but water, rum and sun.

It's a life you'll have to see to believe. Nothing can convince me that it
will last. At this rate, I might even have my scooter before you get here.
Naturally, there are a few nerve-strainers. No hot water in pillbox, no
money, constantly riding buses, and old cord coat becoming very ratty indeed. If I were anything but a writer, I couldn't get away with the way I've
been dressing down here in this very formal, over-priced Valhalla. But all
this will end when I get a grip on my finances. Then? God knows.

Your idea about sending things down via Pan-American is good except
for the fact that I will have no baggage check with which to claim them.
Might be tricky, but if this can be surmounted, let me know and I'll wing
you a few requests—notably, a few pounds of tobacco, impossible to get
down here. And definitely a few books. Mailer's new one (*Advertisements
for Myself*) comes to mind, as does whatever that Dostoyevsky did on the
psychology of gambling, or the mind of the compulsive gambler.[2] Ever
hear of it? Library here is unbelievably bad. Latest I could get was S.
Maugham. [. . .]

That's about it for now. My eyes are getting heavy, and I still have this
cock-fight thing to write. Surf is pounding outside, terrible blue ceiling
light makes inside look like a cell of some sort, and I will get this in the
mail tomorrow morning when the sun comes out again. Oh, forgot to
mention clothes; they arrived in fine shape. Thanks mucho—or much
thanks. Or something. I have not done much with my Spanish. Will write
again and let you see into my mind. No time right now.

Goodnight
Hunter

2. Fyodor Dostoyevsky's novella *The Gambler*.

TO ANGUS CAMERON, ALFRED A. KNOPF:

After receiving a number of form letters rejecting "Prince Jellyfish" from New York publishers, Thompson was grateful that the respected editor Angus Cameron took the time to offer constructive criticism of the manuscript.

> March 22, 1960
> c/o Semonin
> *San Juan Star*
> San Juan, Puerto Rico

Angus Cameron
Knopf Inc.
501 Madison Ave.
NYC

Dear Mr. Cameron:

I want to thank you for your meaningful and perceptive comments on my manuscript. Few editors, I'm sure, would have taken the time to compose such an informative rejection slip, and few indeed could have put down their thoughts with such style and mastery of tone. It's been said, I know, that most editors are boobs, cretins and witless crayfish who have edged into their jobs through some devious means made possible by the slothful and incestuous nature of the World of Publishing. Ha! Let me say now, Mr. Cameron, that if more editors write letters like yours, the people who say these wretched things will certainly be laughing out of the other side of their mouths. Just where do they get the gall to talk like that?

But be that all as it may, we still have to dispose of PRINCE JELLY-FISH, don't we? I tried like hell to finish it. Since September, however, the people who sheltered me have applied for divorce, I was beaten by hoodlums in New York, put in jail in Virginia Beach, and arrested for drunken driving in Louisville; then I was taken by plane to San Juan, where the man who hired me to write sports copy proved to be an insolvent liar. All this has somewhat hindered the progress of the book. But now I am ready to roll again; the typewriter is rusty and full of sand, but I have stolen a ribbon from the *San Juan Star* and now feel ready to complete this wretched thing I began in what seems like another world. Suppose we send it to an agent named Elizabeth McKee. It would take me two or three months to find her address, because I left it in a box of paper somewhere in the Catskills. I feel, however, that it's somewhere in the East Sixties (enviable, eh?) and I feel also that one of your people can locate it in the Manhattan Telephone Directory. I am enclosing a note to her, and if you find that your facilities are insufficient to the task of getting both note and manuscript sent to the McKee address, please send all back to me and I will take care of it myself. If this happens, of course, you will soon find in your mailbox a packet of sea urchins: to derive full enjoyment from them, take one in each hand and squeeze.

With fondness and admiration, I remain,

Quite gratefully,
Hunter S. Thompson

TO ANN SCHOELKOPF:

While Thompson was her houseguest after being fired from the Middletown Daily Record, *Ann spoiled him with her home-cooked meals. Once again Thompson asked Ann for help—this time in getting back pay from the publisher-editor of the now defunct* El Sportivo.

March 22, 1960
c/o Semonin
San Juan Star
San Juan, P.R.

Annie—

Well, "baby," your last letter put me down in grand style. I ain't been rapiered so well in years. So when you stop chuckling and gloating, try and get through the rest of this letter.

In the first place, what in the jesus-loving hell is going on up there? Are you people divorced or what? It all seems like the most insane thing I've ever dealt with, but since I know you both, it's almost logical. Christ, you say one of your arguments centered on the way you made a sandwich. Annie, I would give at least one ball for one (or three) of your sandwiches right at this goat-fucking instant. I have never been so hungry in my life and I've just spent my last 35 cents for a package of Salems, of all worthless things. If I'm homesick for anyplace on earth, it's for that back room in Otisville and that huge, fine KITCHEN. Jesus, I've been hungry since I got here and I can't get out soon enough. Kramer is a liar, cheat, passer of bad checks, welshing shyster, and otherwise foul. At the moment I'm re-sorting to the National Labor Relations Board for my March 1 to 15 paycheck. The Hubbard Cure[3] is just the least of what this bastard is going to get—I'll hound him in a million different ways. At any rate I've got to get

---

3. By "Hubbard Cure" Thompson is referring to his Cuddebackville landlord, Fred Hubbard, who had stolen a wheel from his Jaguar in lieu of rent.

hold of the letter he sent me while I was in Otisville. In it he promised me a salary until April 1—jesus knows why I left it there, but I can't get my pay without it. I sent Fred a card, but I don't think I made things very clear. If he has to go into the bag—which I guess would be the best thing—call him and tell him to do so. It's the letter he read one morning in the KITCHEN. I've marked several phrases in red, so he can't miss it. If it's there, I want all the correspondence concerning this job—once I get it I can stab this bastard for several hundred dollars. If I don't get that letter, the deed is done. He has me. Jesus, I want FOOD! Rum is not enough. I shall entitle my story "Rum Is not Enough." Or "Not by Rum Alone." My stamps, envelopes, stationery and typewriter ribbon are stolen. I have a scooter and Semonin has gone crazy. He can't remember anything. I have no tobacco either. Only Salems. At 35 cents a pack. AND NO FUCKING FOOD. I can't even get to people; I don't know where they are. I am 13 miles from San Juan in a negro community and not a goat-sucking soul speaks English. I must have FOOD—the swine seem to think I'm above eating! Jesus ate—why can't I? Oh god give me the strength to dump in their eyes!

A girl was here last week—made my life extremely worthwhile. I told her to call you and talk. Keep her away from Fred. You know me as well as anybody in the world, so talk to her. She is quite important right now. All this noise about bags and trunks is good for nothing. Hang onto everything and I will be back to straighten things out. Christ knows I can't stand this hunger much longer. I'll steal to get back to the bread-basket. But don't let my clothes and goods go to hell. If necessary, send all to Louisville COD. Hope to see you soon or sometime. Love,

Hunter

TO SANDY CONKLIN:

Angry at Conklin for a letter intimating that she was dating other guys, Thompson tried to establish the rules by which their relationship would be conducted.

April 7, 1960
San Juan

Dear Sandy,

Your letter came last night in the same mail with one from a girl who said to expect her in June. The day before I got one from another girl who said she would be down in May.

So I think the only thing for me to do is take off for St. Thomas and this carnival[4] and get so thumping, jabbering drunk that no one will recognize me.

Definitely do not come on April 22. May 5 is fine, but I'm going to need that carnival to clear my system and present plans call for me to hit the docks with one toothbrush, no extra clothes and whatever money I can scrape together. I intend to sleep on the beach (impossible to get reservations even if I could afford them) and suck up every ounce of drink I can get my hands on. I'll probably be arrested several times, flogged by the police, and will undoubtedly have to steal a boat to get back to San Juan. I would certainly not be able to keep a steady eye on you and I know damn well that's what I'd have to do if you were with me.

So wait till May 5. I look forward to your arrival with much eagerness and more trepidation. God knows what this means, but it will be good while it lasts. I'm sure you're aware that I can barely support myself, much less a common-law wife, so I presume you'll bring at least a little money for food. The idea of your looking for a job is ridiculous. In the first place it would destroy the whole pleasure of this life, and in the second you'd have no way of getting to work. I am somewhat removed from the work area; remember? And I don't have the faintest intention of getting up every morning and taking you into San Juan on a scooter over 13 miles of sand road. So forget about jobs.

And keep in mind that I may have to flee San Juan at any moment to avoid jail.

I'm saying all this because I want to be fair to you. Objectively, I can't think of anyone in the world I'd rather not depend on than Hunter S. Thompson. But unfortunately, I'm forced to depend on him constantly. And let me tell you it's nothing short of nerve-wracking.

Your "fiery" letter made me mad as hell. I don't know who that painter was on the other side of the room, but the next time you decide to "drink, dance, laugh, lie, and love the reeling midnight through," have the simple goddamned decency not to write me about it. And since I told you in my last letter how I feel about your coming down here, I can say without fear of misinterpretation that if you'd thrown this Montego Bay thing at me before I'd said whether I wanted you to come or not, I'd have written you a letter that would have sent you hustling down to Jamaica at a high rate of speed.

So much for all that. Come on May 5 and be prepared for anything. I'll deal with these other people as it becomes necessary. If this letter seems a

4. Thompson had a free-lance assignment from the Louisville *Courier-Journal* to cover Mardi Gras in Charlotte Amalie, capital of the U.S. Virgin Islands.

bit curt, you can look on it as another bit of wheeling and dealing. If there's any doubt in your mind as to whether I want you here or not, you've been reading my letters with the wrong eye.

Love, Hunter

TO DAVISON THOMPSON:

Thompson tried to boost his younger brother's morale, reassuring him that there is more to life than college.

April 13, 1960
San Juan

Dear Davison:

I've been intending to write you for more than a month now, but apparently I'm no better at writing letters than you are, so here you have my tardy communication that probably won't tell you a damned thing except that I'm still very much alive and living much better than most people I know or used to know.

I got a vague rumor via Ransdell [Avenue] that you were ready to flunk out of Vandy [Vanderbilt University] and foul your chances for a bland, boring, and tediously secure future. This I deplore, Dave, and christ knows if a man can't make it to the Bland League he might as well hang up his grey flannel jock and quit. If, however, you find yourself unequal to the task of competing with the other dullards 365 days a year, you have my standing invitation to join me wherever I happen to be. I have tried—for Mommy's sake—to look seriously on your endeavors, but christ knows I can't keep a straight face forever. It's all a hideous joke, Dave, and it's fine if you like it. But if it gets the best of you—as it would get the best of any sane and thinking man—for god's sake don't compound the stupidity by letting them convince you that you're wrong. Let's face it: any man who really wants to work for Burdorf Furniture—or its equivalent—for the rest of his life is bound to be crazy—or a terribly narrow-minded coward.

In a nutshell, that's just about all I have to say. I like you—not just as a brother, but as a person—and if you get fed up with all that crap just drop me a line and I'll begin rooting around for an extra bed. I hate to see anyone—especially a brother of mine—buried at such an early age, and god knows the world is much wider and fuller than anyone else in Nashville or Louisville can ever imagine.

At the moment, for instance, I sit about 20 yards from the sea as I type this letter. Semonin lives with me and we're the only white residents of the negro community of Loíza Aldea, Puerto Rico. Our house has 2 bedrooms, a screened living room, and all the comforts of home save hot water. Every morning we get up and hustle into the sea for an eye-opener, then have a long breakfast on the patio overlooking the beach. Later, we'll each mount our rotten Lambrettas [motor scooters] and hustle the 13 miles to San Juan—he to work at the *San Juan Star,* and me to deal with whatever free-lance assignments the moment has to offer. I have a girl coming down to live with me in May (she was here for 2 weeks in March) and 2 more coming in June. God knows what I will do with these, but I suppose Semonin can handle them. In late summer I think I'll be off for Spain to meet McGarr & his wife. Christ only knows what will happen then, but it can't be dull. The idea, I think, is to get old gracefully—not like a boob, but like a champion.

So this—a rattling jabber of disconnected heresies—is the sum and substance of my letter. I'll accept no excuses for not answering it, so do this as soon as you have a free moment. And for god's sake—since Mommy thinks I'm urging you on to more and better business dealings—don't tell her I've written you this kind of letter.

Deviously,
Hunter

TO SANDY CONKLIN:

Seized with jealousy and rage, Thompson tried to reach Conklin by telephone at 4:00 A.M. one Sunday, and nobody answered. Two weeks later Conklin moved to Puerto Rico as Thompson's "common-law wife."

April 17, 1960
Loíza Aldea
Puerto Rico

Dear Princess:

I wish to christ you'd answer my letter so I'd have some feeling of communication with you—a rare damned feeling, now that I mention it. At any rate I should tell you what didn't happen over the weekend.

I called you about 11 o'clock Friday to tell you I was arriving at 6:45 Saturday morning. No answer. That took a bit of wind out of the sack and I spent the next 45 minutes dealing with Semonin and Hazlett[5] and finally gave up when midnight passed in the midst of a senseless argument. Then, about 4 a.m. I called you again to tell you I was coming on Saturday—no collect calls, either—and when there was no answer this time I

5. Fred Hazlett was an executive at the Puerto Rico News Service. He got Thompson a lot of free-lance ad modeling assignments.

flew into a jealous rage like nothing I've had to deal with since I was 14 years old. And for god's sake, no matter how savage and unreasonable this sounds, don't let it prod you into one of your graphic documentaries on how "hot and wild" you were feeling about that time of night in some dank shitbog with painters sketching on the other side of the room. I can do without hearing about those things, regardless of how fine and full of life they may seem to you.

Sorry about that outburst, but that's nothing compared to what I was thinking after that second phone call. The story continues through Saturday when Paul and I sat at the airport for 3 hours waiting for someone to cancel a reservation or fail to show up for their flight. Needless to say we failed and the whole damn thing failed and all I can say now is a simple "god damn it."

The idea was a week in New York, then to bring you back down here and head over to St. Thomas for the festival. Then back here for whatever hellish financial agonies awaited us. I started to call Saturday (when we were sure we were going to get seats) but then I had a terrible picture of the phone ringing in that apartment while I was there and both of us hoping it would stop ringing . . . and, frankly, I am not yet reduced to living with that kind of an image of myself . . . a mere jangling interruption at the other end of a black instrument.

But for all this bitching and jabbering, I found myself on Friday (and Saturday) with a violent compulsion to cover 1000 very unreasonable miles just to have you within reach. Whoever might have been there in that apartment had I managed to get a flight Friday night is goddamned lucky because I was mad enough to beat a gorilla to within an inch of his life if I could have gotten there. I came back home last night intending to write you a letter—and, indeed, had plenty of time—but realized that whatever I wrote would have to be revised this morning, and so gave it up as a very bad, frustrating, and stupid jealousy-riddled weekend. It is too bad I didn't write Friday, for it might have gone down as a classic of lascivious letters and a typewritten record of an honest—and therefore, rare—expression of this normally devious mind.

Nevertheless, I am still honest enough to say I want you to come down and, if you do nothing else, merely lie naked with me on this living room bed and stare at the sea until I get carted off to jail. As a matter of fact I'm so selfish about this that my conscience compels me to warn you that we may both have to flee the island literally at any time. So for god's sake don't bring much luggage and get a round trip ticket. As far as I know we might be here ten days or ten years . . . after that, god knows.

I am also honest enough to admit that wanting you over this past weekend rubbed raw some part of me that's been well-insulated for quite a while. Whether this is good or bad, I don't really know . . . and whether it's ego-wise for me to admit that doesn't seem to matter right now.

BUT FOR GOD'S SAKE GET THAT DUNG-DRENCHED ARTIST OUT OF YOUR APARTMENT, GET A LOCK ON THE DOOR, QUIT THAT FRIGHTENING JOB, AND DON'T WRITE ME AS IF YOU'VE NEVER RECEIVED ANY OF MY LETTERS. (Do me a big favor and pick any sentence out of this one—doesn't matter which one—and refer to it specifically in your next letter so I can get at least a tiny sense of communication. I'm not sure, but they tell me it's important.

Majestically,
Hunter

TO LAURIE HOSFORD:

Thompson and Conklin were preparing to sail to Spain to live with Eugene and Eleanor McGarr.

May 25, 1960
Loíza Aldea
Puerto Rico

Dear Laurie:

This letter is written in the midst of making plans for an immediate departure for Spain. The Puerto Ricans want to put me in jail for a year—breach of peace and resisting arrest. No dice, Jack. They'll have to run me down like a black convict.

At any rate, I now have a common-law wife. Excellent girl, white, good worker, and speaks tolerable Spanish. She'll accompany me to Spain. A friend of mine from New York is there with his wife, has a 12-room house near Gibraltar on the coast. From there—god only knows.

San Juan is rotten. Highest cost of living anywhere in the Western Hemisphere except Caracas. I live 15 miles from town, on the beach, 4-room house, motor scooter, no job, writing free-lance stuff for Stateside newspapers, also fiction, so many bugs I can barely breathe, wife here and cooking, no money, vagrant artist from New York also living here, has sailboat, all in all life is not bad.

I have made friends with the negroes, the lizards, and the postal inspector. Now racking my former employer up with the labor relations board. Fabulous sunsets. Terrible food. Cheap rum. Eat much rice and more spaghetti, drink rain-water. We are only white people in Spanish-speaking negro community of Loíza Aldea. Life is not dull.

What the hell is this "answer to life" you're jabbering about? Try to put it on paper and help me get a grip on things. My life is a wild merry-go-round and I'm beginning to feel like a big hungry jack-rabbit, hopping from one part of the world to another in a frenzy of greed and violence.

Look up a friend of mine [at Eglin] named Banks Shepherd. He's a captain and he'll probably be in the purchasing office. If not, look in the Base Directory: William Banks (or W. B.) Shepherd. You may like him and you may not—try it and see.

No word from Ann Frick since December. Sealey never answered the two letters I wrote him, and I damn well won't try again until he reciprocates. Who the hell is he engaged to?

Next letter will probably be from Spain, so write me there and avoid waste of time. HST

c/o McGarr
Calle del Copo 21
Pedregalejo, Malaga
España

Tell Shirley[6] to watch out for that "un-tapped power." I don't know what it means, but it sounds ominous.

Cheers:
Hunter

TO HOME (VIRGINIA THOMPSON):

Mrs. Thompson's son had just sold two articles to the New York Herald Tribune: *one on voodoo in Puerto Rico, the other on the island of Vieques.*

July 2, 1960
Hamilton, Bermuda

Dear Home:

The Louisville link of the Thompson dynasty has acquitted itself manfully. We now have passports, enough money to eat for a few days, and the assurance that our mail is getting through. This may not seem like much to you there in the midwestern-south, but out here it's extremely important.

All in all, I can offer nothing but apologies for my recent implications that anything was amiss on that end of the service-line. You will, of course, send more copies of my articles (5).

The checks ($35) literally saved our lives. We've been living in a place, paying nothing, and telling the man the check was going to arrive any day.

6. Hosford's new wife.

My check from the *Courier* ($40) went to San Juan and has not yet arrived. Your (and Memo's) check made it possible for me to pay this man and avoid the beach or the caves for a sleeping place. We are now sleeping in a basement of a very exclusive set of cottages. Semonin is sleeping in the park, and we are all fairly well off if it doesn't last too long.

The passports, as I said before, were priceless. The only thing that amazes me is that air mail from St. Thomas took as long as Parcel Post. Maybe I'm wrong, but the madras presents were mailed the day before the suitcase. Seems to me that air mail should have been a bit faster.

Still waiting for two checks from *Courier*, one from *Baltimore Sun*, one from *Milwaukee Journal*, two from *Herald Tribune*, and one from *Times*. Don't know when these will ever get to me, but right now I feel extremely successful, without being able to afford the price of a single beer. Strange, but characteristic.

None of us have the faintest idea what we're doing here, but I suppose—since I'm on the verge of being a money-making writer—I have at least a tentative grip on the dark spectre of reality. If I can live this way and support myself at the same time, I'll give the system a ten-point handicap and still bet it can't beat me. [. . .]

It continually amazes me that I am not yet 23, because I usually feel years older than most of the people I'm with regardless of their age. At any rate, it's another birthday and I've lost a bit more of my hair. If I could think of a way to do it right now, I'd head back to Louisville, sit on the porch drinking beer, drive around Cherokee Park for a few nights, and try to sink back as far as I could into the world that did its best to make me. It's not hard to get tired of interminable palms and poinciana, and I could do at the moment with a single elm tree on a midnight street in the Highlands.

As a passing thought—something I would ordinarily be too self-conscious to mention—thanks very much for giving me a good home and a happy, hectic childhood that I never tire of remembering.

Much love,
Hunter

*still no word on possible rides to Europe. Maybe tomorrow.

TO WILLIAM J. KENNEDY, *SAN JUAN STAR:*

Thompson, Conklin, and Semonin sailed from San Juan to St. Thomas on a forty-seven-foot sloop as crew hands. They were dropped off in Bermuda with no money. Marooned in Bermuda, Thompson thought of Kennedy, with whom he had left nearly all of his belongings.

July 16, 1960
Hamilton, Bermuda

Dear Editor:

My name is HS Thompson and I would like to work for the *San Juan Star*. Perhaps you've heard of me. I'm a well-known voodoo writer and not the sort of fellow to pay a car rental bill. Please offer me a job so I can get down to work and really make steam. I understand Puerto Rico is a wonderful place to live and full of artists, thinkers, and other useless types. My information comes from three fellows I met in an asylum in upstate New York. I was there seeing a friend of mine named Carl Solomon,[7] and I met some people named Sala, Klemmens and Kazin.[8] They were good fellows and I could understand most of what they said. [...]

The *Trib* bought both my things on Puerto Rico.

Now for the story of our heinous defeat.

Semonin has already given up and flown back to New York, where he will seek employment. And probably ask you for a reference. We are about ready to follow suit, but I hate giving up so much that I don't know if I can go back there. This Bermuda thing has been a nightmare of gargantuan proportions. I'm enclosing a story that I wrote for the local daily,[9] but believe me it doesn't give more than a quick glance at the real situation. Semonin slept in a public park—taking a shower each morning at the Royal Bermuda Yacht Club—and Sandy & I have been sleeping in a basement on the outskirts of Hamilton. All efforts at departure have failed. The Britishers have threatened to deport us and seem to take it as a tremendous joke that three young Americans are starving in the streets of Hamilton. They refuse to let us work (immigration) & they tell us we have to get out immediately. Lack of funds is a crime here and they've hounded us unmercifully.

After an agonizing reappraisal, I think the duffel bag and the box and the books and anything else should be sent to:

> Mrs. Virginia Thompson
> 2437 Ransdell Avenue
> Louisville, Kentucky SEND ALL COD

The *Portable Faulkner Reader* is stuffed into the side pocket of the KLM bag. I was reading "The Bear" again just before I left. Read it.

---

7. Carl Solomon was a Beat poet who had been committed to New York's Rockland Hospital for psychiatric observation. Allen Ginsberg dedicated his signature poem, "Howl," to him.

8. Sala and Klemmens were layout editor and sports editor, respectively, of the *San Juan Star*. Thompson's reference to Sala, Klemmens, and Kazin being in the hospital is a joke. They were not hospitalized.

9. "They Hoped to Reach Spain but Are Stranded in Bermuda: Trip of Americans Who Left Virgin Islands Three Weeks Ago," *Royal Gazette Weekly* (Bermuda), July 10, 1960.

Paul will send instructions as to his paint-box.

Don't insure anything. Just send the bastards the cheapest way you can.

Keep reading Fitzgerald. They say he had the "pure narrative gift," and if you can do it 74% as well, you can write anything.

Understand your book bounced.[10] When it bounces twice more, you'll be even with me. The agent read my long/short story "No Vire U" and said she found it "absolutely charming." The novel, she said, was not quite up to that level. For whatever it may be worth to you, take her address:

> Elizabeth McKee
> 30 E. 60th St.
> NYC   she's Styron's
> agent, so I guess
> she's reputable.

God knows how many times my book has bounced. *Auntie Mame* bounced 19 times. Keep hustling.

Am working on a short story now that should do the trick. If nothing else, it should be "absolutely charming." I'm a pretty charming fellow.

I want you to stress to Dorvillier that I *never* told the *Courier-Journal* I worked for the *Star*. I think you'll understand my concern about this. I don't want Dorvillier to think I've been trading on his (or the *Star*'s) name in any way, shape or form. The return address, which was always c/o Semonin, was the only link they ever had with the *Star*.

I've been explaining this to the *Courier*, but I don't want Dorvillier thinking I was dealing behind his back. I repeat: my concern about this is very genuine. I didn't need the *Star* in the past, I don't need them now, and I don't expect to need it in the future. (Switching tense, there. Bad news) (not tense at all, is it?) (balls)

Tell Dana[11] hello, also little Dana and Kathy. Hear Bone is leaving. San Juan is bad news for the bachelors. Don't worry, I'll spread this. Heading back to New York on Tuesday. Shameful defeat. Will get to Europe soon. Not the Congo—at least, not with Sandy. There's a new wave in the world these days, Kennedy, and I'm just a single, hideous symptom.

Swim or be bowled over.

> Cheers:
> Hunter

---

10. Thompson is referring to Kennedy's unpublished novel, "The Angels and Sparrows," in which such Albany Cycle characters as Billy Phelan made their first appearances.
11. Kennedy's wife.

TO EDITOR, GROVE PRESS:

> July 24, 1960
> New York City

Editor, Grove Press
64 University Place
NYC

Sir:

This is to introduce you to *Prince Jellyfish,* a manuscript that seems to amuse no one but myself. If, after reading it, you can work up some enthusiasm for seeing it through to the bookshelves, I can promise you my full cooperation.

It has been rejected—for various and generally inane reasons—by three reputable publishing houses. Why, I can't say—even after pondering these dim judgments on every level of meaning.

Naturally, the damn thing has its faults. But after reading it tonight—having not laid eyes on it for six months—I think most of its faults are balanced by an overall liveliness that, to me, is damned refreshing. Contemporary literature, hag-ridden as it is with boredom and pretentious despair, could certainly do with a breath of fresh air. I'm in no position to guarantee that *Prince Jellyfish* will emerge as a panacea for all our literary ills. At best, it is no more than a minor novel. But it's not dull, and I think its chief merit is a romping, rudderless pace that reflects—with overtones of warped laughter—the sad and pompous lunacy of our times.

I don't expect this highly partisan judgment to carry much weight in publishing circles, however, so I'll leave all further evaluation up to you. It would take me a month of steady work to finish the book, but I don't see much sense in undergoing this sort of punishment without some hope of ultimate publication. If you think we can get together on this score, please let me hear from you as soon as possible.

> Sincerely,
> Hunter S. Thompson
> c/o Conklin
> 107 Thompson St.
> NYC 12

TO VIRGINIA THOMPSON:

After McGarr bailed them out of their financial troubles in Bermuda, Thompson and company returned to New York to regroup; Sandy Conklin got a job with United Airlines, and Thompson began his Caribbean novel.

August 9, 1960
New York City

Dear Mom:

Don't know why I haven't managed to write before this, but I guess it's because I've been waiting for things to settle down—and they haven't.

Sandy is working, and I spend most of my time here in the apt., writing like hell. The novel bounced again, and I've about given up hope of publishing it in the present form. On the brighter side, my agent has been pretty happy with the two short stories I've given her. This may or may not mean anything, but it's encouraging.

The *Herald Tribune* commissioned me to do another travel article today, and I think one of the things I did on Puerto Rico will appear this Sunday. You can probably get the *Trib* on Monday at Readmore. If not this Sunday, it will almost definitely appear the next.

I haven't done much journalism recently, but have been working primarily on fiction. I went on the quiz show[12] last Monday, but it was such a short and mediocre performance that I didn't see much sense in warning you. The show (ABC) doesn't get to Louisville, anyway, and it wasn't worth the trouble of driving even three blocks to see. I won $50, but blew the question worth $300.

As for your question about "ideas and money," I still have plenty of ideas and no money. As a matter of fact, I still owe McGarr $150. He sent us $200 in Bermuda, or we'd have never gotten off the damn island. I shall be completely broke until I get the debt paid. It was the money he was saving for his passage back to the States, and I have to get it back to him right away.

Sandy is working, and makes enough for us to eat on. On October 1, she is going to Florida to run her mother's travel agency until Thanksgiving.[13] I'm not sure what I'll be doing for those two months, but I'll probably be able to get to Louisville somewhere in the interim. We just decided all this tonight, so I'll have to wait a while before I can say anything definite. A lot will depend on what happens here in the next few weeks. I've put out some

---

12. *Who Do You Trust?*, hosted by Johnny Carson. This was Thompson's first ever TV appearance. He missed the $300 question: "Who was the inventor of penicillin?"
13. Conklin's mother owned a travel agency in Deland, Florida; her father was a businessman in Port Jefferson, New York.

tentative feelers for a job, but I really can't work up much enthusiasm for the sort of thing that seems to be available. Yesterday I was considering a job on the *National Jewish Post.* When I woke up today, however, it seemed like a bad dream.

I think your decision to leave Naval Ordnance is a wise one. From what I gather, the job is too rotten to tolerate. By all means, try to find something you like.

I am fine, physically (a bit on the heavy side, thanks to Sandy's cookery), and a bit confused, mentally. Now that my own belief in my talent has been at least partially corroborated, I can't understand why I'm still as poverty-stricken as I always was. I have a sort of stupid faith that checks will arrive in the mail "very soon." Lord knows why, but until something jolts me out of this, I'll probably keep on behaving like a solvent writer.

Love,
Hunter

TO WILLIAM J. KENNEDY, *SAN JUAN STAR:*

August 10, 1960
New York City

Dear Bill:

Thought you'd be interested to know Prince Jellyfish bounced again, for the third and final time. I say "final" because I've decided it's not really a very good book. Maybe I can break it up into one or two fairly clever short stories. If not, I'll just chalk that year up to experience and start on that "Great Puerto Rican Novel" that I mentioned just before I left.

My real reason for writing is not just to tell you the book bounced, but, for some reason, you were the first person who came to mind when I read the rejection letter—just after the postman had awakened me to deliver the damned thing. It was one of those mimeographed things that went to great lengths to explain why they couldn't write a personal letter—and the bastard made me so mad that I was on the verge of calling Grove Press and demanding an explanation. I wasn't too mad because they'd dared to send *me* a form letter—because this is the second time it's happened in three tries. It was just the idea of the goddamn things, and—perhaps because I was looking for a good example with which to justify my pique—I thought of you and that book you were working on when I was there.[14]

I don't know if you got a form letter or not—and it doesn't matter, because it's entirely possible that you did. I know you were much more emo-

14. Kennedy's still-unpublished novel, "The Angels and Sparrows."

tionally involved than I was in mine, and the idea that some lackwit quipster could sit up there and stick a mimeographed reject note on that much physical, mental and emotional effort is just about more than I can tolerate.

Maybe I'm just kidding myself when I say it bothers me much more in your case than it does in mine, but I don't think so. As a matter of fact, I can think of several unpublished writers that I have a lot more compassion for than I do for myself. I've compromised myself so often that I can't honestly see myself as a martyr anymore. I could once, and—although I think I'm probably better off as an opportunist with a large and ill-formed talent—I think every now and then that I'd like to be able to talk from a martyr's point of view, to really be righteous—if for no other reason than to give the quipsters a taste of a pure blue flame.

I guess that's why I'm looking for somebody else to get mad for. You're no martyr, but I think you approach your writing more honestly than I do mine. I'm too greedy to wish you much luck, but if you can break through without stepping on my head, I hope you make it.

Now for the mundane side of things. I am back in Greenwich Village, writing like a bastard and laboring under the illusion that it will someday make me rich. Not working; Sandy is. Semonin is living uptown with two girls. Bone living on far Lower East Side. Sorry to hear about your mother's death. I was hoping you'd find some way to get hold of me when you came through New York. Sorry you didn't. Bone will probably get a job. I probably won't. Sandy is leaving for Florida on October 1 to run her mother's travel agency for two months. I'd like to hitchhike for a while, so I think I'll go out to Chicago and then to Louisville. Semonin is probably going to Colorado for the winter. I shall—by hook, crook, or armed robbery—get to Europe by spring. I did not charge any long-distance calls to the *Star* and I'm tired of being accused of things like that. My assaults are usually more frontal—or at least more damaging. I finally sold the Vieques article to the *Trib*. Don't pay that bill. I am seeing O'Conner[15] Friday and will be very indignant about it. I gave them a decent mention in a piece the *Trib* is using this Sunday (if it hasn't been cut) and I don't think we'll have any trouble dodging that $18.

What is the status of my gear? Is everything still there? Don't worry about it not being paid for in Louisville. If it's cheaper, send it all to the original Deland address (Mrs. Leah Conklin, 116 W. Rich St.). But for god's sake send it COD. I have my debts divided into "general" and "personal"—and I can't stand any more in the personal column. [. . .]

---

15. O'Conner was a childhood friend of William Kennedy's who tried to get Thompson a journalism job in New York.

And that's about it. Drop me a line as soon as you can. I get tired of reading my own copy, and letters tend to give me a fresh perspective.

Cheers:
Hunter

TO ELEANOR MCGARR:

Sandy Conklin's closest friend had written her a highly personal letter about the "meaning of love." After happening upon the beautiful composition Thompson felt compelled to confess to snooping—and more important, to salute Eleanor's keen perceptions.

August 17, 1960
New York City

Dear Eleanor:

In the course of looking for a letter from my mother to Sandy, I came across one of those long blue sheets that I recognized instantly as some of your Fatboy's [Eugene McGarr's] stationery. Thinking that Sandy had stolen one of my letters, I seized it and looked to see which one it was. Strangely enough, it was not Fatboy's at all, but a letter from you to Sandy.

Were I possessed of a single decent impulse, I no doubt would have stuck it back in the bundle without reading a line. This, of course, I did not do—but followed my curious nose through the whole damn letter, giggling in a rotten way at my totally unwarranted invasion of my little companion's privacy; which, after living this long with me, is about all she has left.

The letter was dated February 19 of this year, and after reading it I felt a definite compulsion to write you. Perhaps I chose this way to confess because it will purge my mind of guilt without actually having to admit to Sandy that I've been rooting in her mail. But I don't think so. The reason I give myself for writing is very different.

In a nutshell, I have never been privileged to read such an overwhelmingly lucid, honest and pertinent letter. Nor have I ever witnessed a female mind functioning with such cool perception and warm sensitivity at the same time. After reading the entire thing I don't feel a twinge of guilt, but rather a genuine sense of regret that your letter made all mine—and all those I've received, for that matter—seem so shallow and so giddy.

Although I hesitate to single out parts or paragraphs, I should probably give you some examples so you'll know what I'm talking about.

1) "I suspect you of cherishing a dream that you will find some man who will provide the central meaning in your life. I distrust this dream because I believe that the central meaning must come from yourself. If you can't

find it there you won't find it . . . In fact, I wonder if it is possible to love without having achieved a degree of personal fulfillment within oneself."

2) "But I can't help wondering if you aren't actually drifting into one thing or another since you don't mention having any sort of plan as to what you are going to do. I don't mean a job, of course, but something that you consider important."

3) ". . . but this we know, that the soil will be there, and that if we do not kill one another off someone will be there to dig and plant and fight the weevils and bitch about taxes and raise his children and bury his parents and live and die. This doesn't change . . ." (sounds like Faulkner out of Fatboy).

4) "Love neither adds to a person nor takes from him, although he both gives and receives. It must be given and accepted for its own sake, and not as a means to anything else, because it just isn't any of those things. Nor is it sufficient for a person who has nothing else. . . . Love just isn't a panacea. . . ."

These are just a few of the things that had me sucking violently on my cigarette as I read your letter. Points 1, 2 & 4 describe Sandy's problem so completely that I had an urge to hang onto the letter and shove it in her face when she gets home, shouting "There! There! Isn't this what I've been saying? Will you believe me now that Eleanor says the same thing?"

To be altogether honest, I've always implied, rather than stated. And the reason I haven't said exactly what you did is that I felt it would be hitting below the belt. Her capacity for love is her only big talent, and she banks on it like I bank on my writing. I can't bring myself to belittle it because if I crippled that I don't know what she'd have left. Falling in love, to Sandy, is like hitting the jackpot on a big quiz show—once you answer the Big Question, your worries are over.

Well, that's not quite the way it is, and I tried to explain to her last night that we are all alone, born alone, die alone, and—in spite of *True Romance* magazines—we shall all someday look back on our lives and see that, in spite of our company, we were alone the whole way. I do not say *lonely*— at least, not all the time—but essentially, and finally, alone.

This is what makes your self-respect so important, and I don't see how you can respect yourself if you must look in the hearts and minds of others for your happiness.

In your letter, you asked her several times what she thought of your words and ideas. I don't know what she told you, but when you write her again I wish you would hit the same nerve. The same words, coming from me, would have a different meaning to her. She respects your mind tremendously, and—although I'm sure she respects mine too—I cannot say those things without hurting her.

Although I'm not sure it will benefit anyone concerned, I think it's vitally important that she understand that the responsibility for her happiness, or lack of it, does not rest with me or whoever else might in the future be the subject of this "vital love."

You may tell her about this letter if you want, but I think it might tend to bias your words if you do so. Do whatever you think best, for I have no right to swear you to silence without your prior consent.

[. . .] I may go to Cuba in a few weeks. Money to be made there, also a little excitement. Things here are the same. Sandy is home now, and is cooking a fish dinner. I am drinking wine, writing an article for the *Trib*, and reading many books on Cuba. Let us know what you think about taking this apartment.

Cheers:
Hunter

TO EUGENE W. MCGARR:

The McGarrs were preparing to leave Spain and return home to New York.

August 26, 1960
New York City

Mira, Mira!

Your mass of letters served only to confuse and depress us. The death of Murphy[16] seemed tragic at first; and then, after some thought, I began to feel it was also poetic in its appropriateness. This, contrary to what you might think, is not a harsh judgment on Dick. I don't subscribe to the theory that every traffic death is a social tragedy and a sob-sister's field day. He did not see his death as a tragedy, because he did not see it at all. In that, he was spared the one genuine element of tragic death—the terrible hours of waiting, considering, pondering, reflecting, and the final realization of his own smallness, weakness, futility, and inability to rise to the heights from which real tragedy must plunge.

Perhaps he never had a chance to climb, but he wasn't breaking his back on the ladder when I knew him, and I doubt he ever would have. He was living exactly as he died: haphazardly, looking for an honest handle, and going as fast as he could in every direction. He was an honest but none too diligent seeker, and I have as much sympathy for him as I would have for myself if I died tomorrow. Dissipated potential is never so sad as when it finally admits defeat, and these are the tragic hours—between surrender

16. Dick Murphy, a Louisville friend of Thompson's, had been killed in a car accident.

and death. Murphy never surrendered—at least, never in his own eyes—and when he died he was still moving. This is not tragedy, and, in a strange way, I even envy him. If my own death is that sudden and dramatic, I will have been spared more than I deserve.

This is a new typewriter, just bought today, and competence is difficult. Bear with me. Also wine.

We are sending a list of cheap boats. Maybe they will be helpful.

If you need money, say how much and we will borrow it.

Don't worry about apartments. You can stay here, whether we're here or not. The rent will be a bitch, but it will come from somewhere. There is also a chance of getting the place across the hall. Same as this, not bad at all.

This "draft" business is the most deadly item on today's agenda. McGarr, if you aren't capable of tying these people in knots, I'll lose all faith in you. Right now, you're in a good position to deal with them. You're an artist, living in Spain, and you have seen enough to lose all faith in the "American Way." You will not fight for it unless forced, you think the military uniform of the U.S. is a disgrace to the human spirit, and you literally dare them to draft you. Never touch a form; write long and violent letters, addressed to presidents and commanding generals and such. Don't deal with peons, and never talk their language. Let's face it—they don't need you. McGarr is nothing but a number, just a flabby boob from Queens who'll fill a quota. Balls to this, McGarr! Don't you have enough guts to deal with them? Don't you have better things to do than sit in a torture chamber for two years? Tell them you're queer, communist, Castroist; to hell with the draft board and everything it stands for.

This should take care of essentials. Deal with these & don't worry about the rest. I'll write Eleanor and fill in the blanks.

Cheers,
Hunter

TO ELEANOR MCGARR:

August 28, 1960
New York City

Dear Eleanor:

In a flash of pure irony, Sandy got hold of your letter to me in almost exactly the same way I found yours to her: picked it up, thinking it was hers, etc. Anyway, we've gone into the subject at some length, and our conclusions would take up too much space to be dealt with in a letter. In essence, she is more worried about the "vacuum" than I am. After writing that letter to you, I held onto it for a day, and thought about what I said. I decided that Sandy has one of the most valuable and unique talents that I've ever run across: she has managed to live with me, tolerate my greedy, vicious and abominable ways, and make me happy at the same time. This honestly surprises me, and I can think of few talents that strike me as more admirable or deserving of appreciation.

So much for that. We shall have to discuss the whole idea at a later date.

I am enclosing a poem which you may enjoy. It is my third attempt at poetry in three years, and I don't expect to attempt another until next summer.

The (white paper) letter was written last night in a frenzy of wine. Rather than re-write it, I'm sending it along as it is.

Semonin will find out on Monday if he's been accepted for a teaching job (private high school, art) in Rome. If he makes it, you will probably see him soon. If he doesn't, he will winter in Colorado.

Sandy goes to Deland on October 1, and I am still beating the journalistic bushes to find somebody willing to pay my way to Cuba. I will probably get there, but I'm not sure how or why.

Fatboy's demand that I give him a quick run-down on the situation in Latin America (The Meaning, Machinations & Inevitable Consequences of Short-Sighted Capitalism in Undeveloped Areas) is more than I can deal with. At the moment, I'm well-grounded in conflicting generalities and embarrassingly naked of facts and details. The *Time* comment on the fall of the Arbenz govt. in Guatemala is essentially correct.[17] We have supported every dictator in Latam [Latin America], and now we are paying for it. A U.S. military mission was training Batista's troops right up until the day he fled the country and left it to Castro—in spite of repeated protests by Castro supporters in this country. The Batista AF, flying British planes, was using U.S.–made rockets on rebel soldiers as late as 1958. This will give you some idea of why Fidel does not particularly dig our State Department. The story is much deeper than this, and goes back to 1898, when we helped Cuba gain her "independence" from Spain. This, too, will have to be discussed when we have more time. I am enclosing a clipping on PR that is better than nothing.

My novel has now bounced for the third time, and I've decided to break it up into short stories (2 or 3) and try a new one. I have two decent stories circulating (through a good agent) and another about finished. I think the new novel will do the trick, but, as usual, I will have to find the time and the money to write it in peace. God knows how this will come about, but

---

17. *Time* ran a story claiming that the CIA had assisted in the overthrow of Colonel Jacobo Arbenz Guzmán's left-wing government in June 1954. Although Arbenz and his government appealed to the UN, where the Soviet Union backed their cause, the United States refused to allow the Security Council to intervene.

somehow it will. If I were working half as hard as Sandy said I was, I'd probably have the damn thing finished by now. I have become lazy, pudgy, and more noisy than productive. If I weren't so sure of my destiny, I might even say I was depressed. But I'm not, and there's always tomorrow's mail.

I leave you with that. Also with my poem, my clipping, and my promise to talk you into a stupor when you get back. Let us know what we can do to help. Don't worry about your money; I'm just having trouble getting my hands on it.

Cheers, HST

TO *THE NEW YORK TIMES:*

Thompson couldn't resist replying to a New York Times *classified ad seeking "writers (2) who dig facts."*

September 11, 1960
c/o Conklin
107 Thompson St.
New York City 12

Z8822, *New York Times*

Dear Z8822:

Man, if you only *knew* how I dig facts! Like, I almost sleep with 'em, jack; they groove me in the craziest kind of way. Man, I pound into the negro streets at dawn, rabid for facts. All day I rip and tear through layers of pap and bombast, *wild* to get my hands on the ripe, juicy, factual core of it all.

If you knew this, z8822, you would say: "Like, *man*, when can you start?"

And I would reply, in my cool and savvy way: "Well, daddio, let's get down to the factual core. I need at least $100 a week to keep me in Jack Daniel's; can you swing it?"

Or maybe the *Times* linotype man is a hipster, and you really meant to say, "Writers (2) who will delve for facts"; or "Writers (2) who savvy facts."

Anyway, it came out, "Writers (2) who dig facts," and—if for no other reason than that—I thought it deserved at least a query.

I'm 26, vet, single, college grad, experienced general reporter, wire editor, columnist, sports editor, feature writer, photographer and disc jockey. I've just come back from eight months of free-lancing in the Caribbean, and I'm looking for a way to do some salaried writing.

As a competent journalist, I do, of necessity, "dig facts." I also dig money, Jack Daniel's, and a fast-breaking job. If you think we can do business, shoot me a letter, cable or phone call and I'll give you all the stuff you'd normally get in a résumé. I object to them on principle, and haven't composed one for three years.

That's about it. Let me hear from you before September 16, because I have a tentative job on the west coast and have to let the man know by then. If I haven't heard from you by noon on that date, I'll assume this letter bugged you more than I thought it would, considering the nature of your ad.

But please return the clipping.

Thanks,
Hunter S. Thompson

TO SANDY CONKLIN:

Desperate to get out of New York, Thompson and Paul Semonin hitchhiked first to Seattle, then to San Francisco, looking for jobs in journalism. Conklin stayed temporarily behind in Florida working at her mother's travel agency and saving money to go west.

October 1, 1960
San Francisco

Princess:

[. . .] When I read your letter last night and found you wallowing once again in the doubts and fears of those days between your San Juan visits, I dropped several more notches on whatever stick it is that measures my faith and my love and sometimes even my hope that we are not all as weak and rotten as we seem. If you, who know me better than anyone else in the world, are so easily unnerved by the futile observations of others, then I can only assume that it is not me, but my presence, that you love—and since I hope to have some dimension above and beyond the physical, it saddens me to see you flounder the instant my body is out of reach.

I have gone as far as I can go when I say I love you more than I have ever loved anything or anyone in my life. If you think a marriage license will make me love you more—or give you any more security than you have now—we might as well go ahead and get one. You should know by now that I would leave you just as quickly if we had six children as I would if we had one or none. The only security you will ever have with me is what you have now: the fact that I want you so much that my mind is never completely with me. You've become as real to me as my need to eat and write and eventually become something I can respect. If this is not enough, perhaps you will be better off jumping from bed to bed in search of security. [. . .]

I have still not decided if San Francisco is good or bad. Whether it is or not, I'm hitting the streets Monday in search of a job. My fortune now rests at $9; if you have any extra money, please send it along. We stayed Thursday through Saturday at the house of an ex-Louisville girl who is now married to a buyer for Macy's and living well. Today we moved into Clancy's[18] apt, but he has moved to Berkeley and new tenants are taking over on Monday. After that, we will probably go to the St. Paul hotel in Chinatown, rumored to be the city's cheapest. Paul is out in Sausalito, looking for a houseboat, and Clancy—who is about to get married and go in the army—will get back around dinnertime. I will try to finish this letter in time to work on that story about the rummy in the Village bar.

I would give at least four of my fingers to be able to wake up right now at 107 Thompson, with you beside me, quite naked, and face an evening of love and indolence. The past six months have been so good that I will be forever spoiled. Never before in my life have I felt so happy that I wanted nothing to change, but those weeks in New York are a high spot that I'm afraid we'll never reach again. But as soon as I say that, I recall San Juan & St. Thomas and I think maybe all we need is to be alone and together, with nothing so necessary as a lock on the door.

For god's sake, have a little faith in me, and be strong enough to stay as lonely and frustrated as I am until we can be together. Write instantly.

Love, Hunter

TO SANDY CONKLIN:

October 3, 1960
San Francisco

Dear Princess:

Picked up your letter this morning, read it three or four times during the day, and now sit down to answer it although I have nothing of importance to say either.

Deland sounds pleasant enough, but on the phone the other night you sounded like you could barely remember who I was and it left me feeling a little uncomfortable. And your last letter, of course, sounded as if you had lost your bearings altogether. Today's letter was a little better.

I am now sitting in Clancy's ex-apartment, no furniture but one tiny couch and a half-chair, no food, $3 in my wallet, phone disconnected, new people moving in tomorrow, and a full and very sad moon outside the window. It's the first full one I've seen without you since San Juan, and I don't think I've ever been this lonely in my life. Not lonely for people, but

---

18. John Clancy was a lawyer Thompson had met at Columbia University who would become a lifelong friend.

for long hair, little back, warm mouth, Bonwit, Teller, and even little pot-belly against me in a too-small bed. It's a strange feeling to have another human so much a part of me, but unless I can get it under control I may go completely to pieces before these two rotten months pass by. (Now smoking my second-to-last cigarette; tobacco long gone.)

Friend from Louisville just called. He's working at the hungry i, making $200 a week and being kept by about five different women. Sex is very definitely a currency out here, and if it were not for you I could probably be living a fine and rotten life in no time at all. As it is however, I can hardly be civil to women, and told a girl last night that if I came home with her the only act I would perform would be that of throwing her child off the cliff and into the sea. This was at some foul gathering that Paul and I attended in the company of the above-mentioned friend.

Paul read your thing on the steel drum, thanks you, and seems just about as depressed as I am. His Colorado prospects are none too good and he will probably stay here it he can find a decent job. I still have no idea how long I'll be here, but if nothing decent turns up by October 15, I'll go somewhere and do something and probably shrink my stomach a bit in the process. (The camera is headed for the pawnshop in the immediate future.)

I don't mean to give you the idea that I'm wallowing in a fit of despair, and if it weren't for missing you so much, the situation here would be no worse than it has been many times before. But in a perverted sort of way, I actually enjoy missing you, and when I groan and grumble like this all I'm really doing is indulging myself.

Now I've run out of cigarettes so I shall take a pill and get into my sleeping bag until bright dawn sends me into the streets in search of work. Mira, mira. Write.

> Love,
> Hunter

TO EUGENE W. MCGARR:

McGarr was still trying to collect the $150 Thompson owed him.

> October 19, 1960
> San Francisco

McGarr—

I have more energy than you think.

I have enough, for instance, to get down to the General Delivery window every day and look for my mail. For a while there, I would walk daily about 15 blocks, over massive hills, and find nothing for me but a letter from you—demanding $150, and cursing me in every other breath. It was enervating, to say the least.

Your sea trip gave me a brief respite, during which I looked for work. In the past two weeks I have applied for jobs as: reporter, radio newswriter, TV newswriter, ad copywriter, publicist, floorman at the hungry i, gas station attendant, encyclopedia salesman, Fuller Brush man, yacht crewman, yacht maintenance man, carpenter, letter-sorter (post office), book salesman, dish-washer, layout artist, used car salesman, seaman (ordinary), film critic, photographer, bartender, male model, phone solicitor, ad salesman, construction worker, and made countless pitches of the "I'll do anything for money" variety.

Needless to say, I am still unemployed.

Also needless to say, your bitching and carping about that $150 has done neither of us a bit of good. It seems silly for me to have to tell you I would pay you immediately if I could. You're 100% right in saying I've "fucked up," but a little ridiculous in implying that I'm welching. Yours is the first debt I shall settle just as soon as I can. In the meantime, however, rest assured that I'm not living high on the hog. I have not even had a mailing address since I've been here, I wake up each morning without more than a vague idea where I'll sleep that night, I am continually hungry, I have been arrested for shoplifting (a package of cheese—my only attempt at theft, so far), and, as far as I can see, I still have no prospects of a job.

As for your other point, I freely admit I was "foolish" to come out here. I was foolish to go to New York when I did, and foolish to go to the Caribbean. And not growing up to be a clean-living, debt-paying insurance salesman was probably the most foolish thing I ever did.

Your advice on this score is most welcome, for, as you know, I have often admired your wisdom. How I marveled, for instance, at your keen judgment in duping the Fulbright people so cleverly. Had I been in your position, I probably would have got myself in some foul and desperate situation. You, however, were wise and prudent enough to play it safe at all times. For the hundredth time I was overcome with awe at the spectacle of your life-plan functioning with such logic and precision.

I wrote you a letter that probably got to Malaga just after you left. My copy seems to have disappeared, so I can't send it on to replace the lost original. So be it.

I have just talked to Sandy and told her you made it to New York. We couldn't decide exactly what to tell you about the apartment, but this should do until we come up with something more concrete. As far as either of us can tell, we will be back there on or about Thanksgiving—no more than two days either way. There is a chance, however, that I shall stay out here for a while (if, by the grace of god's balls, I can find a job) and in that case Sandy wants to come out, too. If this happens, you can probably stay in the apt. indefinitely.

This will be clear in the near future. If I don't get a job almost immediately, I'll either starve to death or be desperate enough to attempt the long trek back to New York. If I'm driven to this, I will almost certainly arrive there in such a mood that no one will be able to talk to me for at least two weeks. To cross the continent by thumb in the dead of winter is something I dread more than anything I can think of. But if the only alternative is a half-gainer off the Golden Gate bridge, I will probably prefer the thumb and the cold and the hunger and all the rest of the shit a man has to eat and wallow in if he wants to stay alive.

What is your score with the Army? Have you considered the 6-month deal? Clancy dons the uniform on November 6. He is now trying to sell encyclopedias. Don't consider coming West without a bag of money. My best to Eleanor. To speed payment of your $150, pray that I get a job.

Cheers,
Hunter

TO EDITOR, *TIME:*

During the fall of 1960 America was riveted to the televised presidential debates between Vice President Richard Nixon and Senator John Kennedy.

October 22, 1960
c/o Henkel
3423 Fillmore St.
San Francisco 23

Dear Sir:

Immediately after election day, if not sooner, the nation's press will render its judgment on the greatest spectacle in the history of politics—the Nixon-Kennedy "Great Debates." If the fifth encounter is as meatless as the first four have been, the judgment will in all probability be a harsh one.

Some of us will be surprised, however, if the blame falls where most of it belongs—on the shoulders of the press, itself.

Cub scouts could have asked more penetrating questions than the journalists have offered thus far, and no amount of grumbling about rules and regulations laid down by campaign managers and the television industry can obscure the fact that the representatives of the press have behaved like trained seals. The questions to the candidates have been, for the most part, nothing more than harmless cues, devoid of weight, meaning or perception. When you realize all the questions that could have been asked, all the fraud, quackery and evasion that might have been held up to merciless inspection before 17 million viewers, it raises the question that perhaps the press is no longer capable of fulfilling or even recognizing its responsibility to the nation it serves.

Never before have two presidential candidates been placed in such a vulnerable position, and never before has the press had such a golden opportunity to hack away the sham and expose the basic issues. When the time comes, as it will, to belabor the television industry for staging a political batting-practice instead of a World Series, let the press remember who served up the soft floaters and the "fat ones" down the middle. It was a sad performance, and the sound of many snickers may be heard in the land when the pot starts calling the kettle black.

Hunter S. Thompson

TO MR. DOOLEY, *SAN FRANCISCO EXAMINER:*

Thompson hoped this letter would land him a reporting job at the Examiner. *It didn't.*

October 25, 1960
c/o Henkel
3423 Fillmore Street
San Francisco 23

Mr. Dooley
San Francisco Examiner

Dear Sir:

A few days ago I talked to you about the possibility of a job on the *Examiner,* and you advised me to write you a letter on the subject of my qualifications. Here it is.

I came to your desk via the not-uncommon route of a military paper, weekly, small daily, *Time* magazine, a larger daily, and free-lancing in the Caribbean. This took about five years, and encompassed everything from writing editorials to actually composing my own pages in the tray. I haven't learned everything there is to know about journalism, but I've worked at it long enough to know I have more talent, originality and initiative than is common in the trade these days. If I didn't think this, I wouldn't be presumptuous enough to ask you for a job.

I got into journalism by lying. After a half-year of electronics school in the Air Force, I was ready to try almost anything. When the sports editor of the base newspaper went AWOL, I went to the major in charge of the paper and told him I'd majored in journalism in college. He smiled, and put my name on the masthead as sports editor. Since I'd never written a word for a newspaper, much less tried to write a headline, I had to give my-self one of the most intensive cram-courses in the history of self-taught journalism. I did it in the base library and the town newspaper, and, as far as I know, the major never found out I wasn't a school-trained ace.

After the Air Force, I worked for a year as sports editor and general re-porter for a large Florida weekly, doing re-write, headlines, my own col-umn, police court, business news, and just about everything else, including photography.

During the next two-and-a-half years I was sports editor of a small daily in Pennsylvania, editorial trainee for *Time* magazine, and general reporter for a medium-sized (20,000) daily in upstate New York. It would take too much space to list all the things I did and learned in this time, but, at the end of it, I figured my apprenticeship was over. I milked those years for all they were worth, I saw American journalism from both ends of the spec-trum, and—to be completely candid—I was not encouraged. With rare ex-ceptions, the press in this country is sluggish and short-sighted to the point of self-destruction.

So I decided to free-lance. For eight months, I lived in Puerto Rico, writing for a local sports magazine, the Louisville *Courier-Journal*, the New York *Herald Tribune*, and a San Juan public relations firm. I covered everything from politics to cock-fights; then, since I was doing pretty well, I decided to go to Europe and do even better.

I got a ride on a big sloop headed for Lisbon, but we broke a head-stay in Bermuda and I ran dangerously low on money while it was waiting to be fixed. A strategic retreat seemed in order, so I flew to New York, where, for some reason, I decided to try San Francisco.

Aside from my ever-increasing need for money, I have two reasons for asking you to give me at least a trial with the *Examiner*. One is the fact that I want to write and don't give a damn how much I get paid for it, as long as it's a living wage; and the other is your very obvious need for some live wires to help you compete with the *Chronicle*'s feature line-up. You have a top-notch classified ad department, but when it comes to matching Caen and Hoppe and Brier and Beebe,[19] you're simply out-classed.

I'm not saying you should give me a column right off the bat, but I'm suggesting you could do yourself no harm by hiring a good writer with a sharp and lively head. You say you have no openings, but this is patently ridiculous. What if the *Toronto Star* had no openings when Ernest Hem-ingway applied for a job? What if *The New York Times* had felt adequately

19. Herb Caen, Art Hoppe, Royce Brier, and Lucius Beebe were the *San Francisco Chronicle*'s ace team of reporters and columnists.

staffed when James Reston wanted to work? Hearst[20] is in trouble all over
the country, and one of the main reasons may be that he "has no openings"
for the kind of talent he needs. If this is a sensible approach to competitive
journalism, I fail to see it. I think it has the makings of a fine epitaph, but
it strikes me as being far from as dynamic as you can get.

That wraps it up on my end. This isn't a standard résumé, but I think it's
a pretty fair letter. If you think you can make even temporary room for
me—at whatever salary you deem fair—please get in touch with me as
soon as possible.

Thanks,
Hunter S. Thompson

TO ABE MELLINKOFF, *SAN FRANCISCO CHRONICLE*:

Thompson had sent his résumé to Abe Mellinkoff, city editor of the San
Francisco Chronicle. *When Mellinkoff failed to respond, Thompson sent
him this proclamation, its title echoing George Orwell's* Down and Out in
Paris and London.

"DOWN AND OUT IN SAN FRANCISCO"

October 25, 1960

San Francisco, Fillmore St., the bay a few blocks to
my left, warm sun in the streets, sitting at a breakfast table two floors above the street, drinking ale,
listening to the marvelous vitality of the Kingston
Trio--three rummies lucky enough to laugh at the
whole world for a half-million dollars a year. No
wonder they laugh.

City of hills and fog and water, bankers and
boobs--Republicans all. City of no jobs--"sorry, we
have no openings here; be glad to talk to you,
though"--city of no money except what you find at the
General Delivery window, and somehow it's always
enough--city, like all cities, of lonely women, lost
souls, and people slowly going under. City of newspapers for Nixon ("careful now, don't upset the balance

20. William Randolph Hearst, Jr., owner of the *San Francisco Examiner*—for which Thompson
would write a regular column twenty-five years later.

of terror"), of neon bars and apartments full of people who can't pay rent or phone bills or even face the
newspaper delivery boy when he comes around to collect. City of music and longshoremen and just enough
sunshine to make you appreciate it. City of Alcatraz,
where human beings rot in unimaginable isolation, a
loneliness so complete and terrifying that only a
man who has been in jail can know it, of Alcatraz
just a pistol shot away from freedom and the Ramos
fizz on Sunday morning, Alcatraz so close that you
know they can hear the clang of a cable-car bell on a
clear day, Alcatraz where men rot and die while the
city dances across the bay.

San Francisco, edge of the western world, where you
can drink all night and jump off the bridge to beat
a hangover, where you can sell encyclopedias because
no other job is available, where you refuse to sell encyclopedias because you have better things to do, because you were born queer and cannot be a salesman
like all your american brothers--where you talk with
editors and news directors and creative directors
and hear over and over again how easy and necessary
it is to sell out, where you find sympathy and no
work ("it's hard, I know it's hard; I tried it myself,
but with a wife and kids . . .") and countless sips of
weak coffee with the want ads and sunday mornings
with a quart of ale and a girl on the phone who says
"come over for breakfast; we live on Telegraph Hill,
you know, and nobody goes hungry over here except
when we want something you can't buy and don't know
how to look for anymore--but we don't talk about that
except when we're drunk, and then we lie down and
open our mouths wide and cry when nothing falls in."

Say "no" to San Francisco and be rich--spend your
last dollar on brandy and swack reality across the
cheek. "No, I will not sell out, I will not give you the
best hours of my day and let you use my blood to
grease the wheels and cogs of a hundred banking machines, sorry, Jack, but I will take your time and
your cigarettes and laugh at you quietly for the
questions you ask and know all the time that your
guts have dried up and your spine is rubber and you

measure me against your contempt for the human race
and find a disturbing disparity--how so, prince jellyfish? will you endorse this check for me? many
thanks; now I can work against you for another week.
and when the money runs out, maybe I will beg then,
maybe then you can crack me and pinch my smile, but
I will never get to work on time, only take your money
and laugh again--and you cannot afford to laugh anymore, you will crack one day too, and that will be the
end--for you cannot bounce, and I can.

TO SANDY CONKLIN:

October 28, 1960
San Francisco

Dear Princess:

Today marked a turning point in the great San Francisco job hunt; it
has become all too obvious that I am not going to get a decent job in this
city before January. If you want an explanation, ask for it in your next letter. If not, just live with it.

Monday I'll ride my thumb south—Carmel, Monterey, Big Sur, and
maybe all the way to Los Angeles. Whatever happens will be all right. I do
not care and have no plans. All I want to do is get out on the coast and see
the California everybody talks about. I'll go as far as the rides take me,
sleep on the beach (sleeping bag), and beg, if necessary, for food. Your $15
is my fortune, and god knows where it will get me, but it will be a break
from this wretched frustration—and nothing would be more welcome.

I have taken as many interviews as any thinking man can tolerate.
They've pumped me so full of bullshit that I feel it rising in my throat, and
I need some air. Now I understand the Golden Gate suicides; I understand the drunks and the whores and the dull hedonists who fill the bars
and the sad Telegraph Hill apartments. The city is merely an extension of
Alcatraz; once you get here there's no way to go except backward, and the
kind of people who flee to San Francisco don't have the guts or the time to
start over again. So you make the best of a bad move; you stand it as long
as you can, drinking enough to dull the pain of disappointment and frustration—and then, if it still hurts, you jump.

But I'm just going to amble on out. When the money runs out I'll come
back and look for a job as a parking lot attendant. If that, too, proves impossible, I'll amble across the desert to Glenwood Springs. Paul is already
there and plans to do construction work in Aspen until January. I doubt

that I could stay there more than a week, but we shall see. More on this when I return from the south.

Bone & McGarr both intend to move out of the apartment by December 1. We shall have to do something by then. I realize it depends on me, so get ready to jump in almost any direction.

Right now, I want only two things—you, and time to write. These people out here feel sorry for me; they don't know what I'm going to do, and they can't understand why it doesn't seem to worry me. It's so sad that it makes me laugh. I feel like the man with The Secret. They tell me I need love, and I laugh quietly. They tell me I need a purpose, and I laugh again. I would never tell them how happy I am to know we're going to be together again, because then they wouldn't be able to feel sorry for me and they'd feel even worse. I really want nothing more than to be in bed with you, to stay there as long as we want, to have a roof over our heads and food in our mouths, and to be left alone. We already have the big thing, and the rest is trivia. Only three more weeks; save your yanqui dollars; they may make a difference.

Love, H

TO LAURIE HOSFORD:

In late October Thompson left San Francisco for Big Sur, where he decided to settle to write the Great Puerto Rican Novel. Hosford had at last graduated from the ROTC program at the University of Florida; shortly after this point he became a commercial pilot for American Airlines.

November 15, 1960
Big Sur, California

Dear Laurie:

After not hearing from you in half a year, I got two letters from you in the space of five days—one forwarded from Spain, and the other from Louisville. About a month ago, I sent a card to your old Tallahassee address, but I guess it got lost. Anyway, we made the connection.

Obviously, I won't be showing you Spain in December or anytime in the next few months. I am now stuck in Big Sur with one silver dollar and a crotch full of poison oak. They say California is the big milk and honey land, but all I've managed to get out of it so far is wine and perpetual discomfort. Right now it's cold as hell. I'm about fifty feet from the ocean, my coal is running low, my crotch is driving me crazy, and the short story I've been working on for two weeks is a bag of crap. Life is a rathole.

(to be truthful, I'm having a hell of a good time—but don't ever tell anyone I admitted it.)

Your letter from Tallahassee was a good one. I really envied you sitting out there on the lake, lounging around the house, etc.—and it brought back a lot of good memories. I wrote Ann Frick from Seattle, but got no reply. Perhaps it's just as well, because I'm pretty involved right now—think I told you in my card that I was considering marriage and I'd like to keep the confusion to a minimum. [. . .]

This "key to life" business really interests me, but I'll take your word that we have to sit down over a few beers before I can grasp it. I wish to hell we could get together sometime, but we're both moving around so fast that it seems impossible. If you ever get to San Francisco let me know in advance and I'll be there when you arrive. I have several job feelers up there, but nothing definite as yet. Until something breaks I'll probably stay here.

I think I told you the novel bounced four times before I gave up and put it in a drawer. It might break up into one or two short stories but I'm not sure. I learned a hell of a lot writing it, and the time was far from wasted. Naturally, I wish it had sold, but it wasn't really that good. Very fast-moving, sometimes funny, a few good high spots, but no real organization and not a very original theme. My recent short stories are better; they are now with an agent in New York and may do something if I'm lucky. Sooner or later. I don't work hard enough to deserve "a break," but if I don't get one I'm going to cause trouble.

Your plan to leave the AF and fly sounds good. I don't doubt that it will work out, and I think you'll enjoy it. If I were half as optimistic about my own future, I'd feel like I had it made. But I'm not pessimistic yet, and I'm making progress, so to hell with it.

Hello to "Little Burl,"[21] and write as soon as you can. Cheers.

Hunter

TO J. P. DONLEAVY:

Donleavy's The Ginger Man *remains one of Thompson's all-time favorite novels. Perhaps more than any other influence, Donleavy's work taught Thompson the importance of writing in a voice without restraint.*

December 8, 1960
Big Sur

Mr. Donleavy:

I've been waiting since *The Ginger Man* for your next effort, a thing the grapevine led me to believe would be called *Helen*. But all I've seen is your short farce on The Beat Generation and Angry Young Men.

21. Hosford's year-old son.

Is *Helen* out? If so, where is it? And if it isn't, have you done anything big since *The Ginger Man?*

The GM, by the way, had real balls, a rare thing in these twisted times. I heard the priests gave you a rough time with the stage version, but to hell with them. The church is on its last legs and if we deal them blow for blow I think we may prevail.

At any rate, let me know if you have anything new in the bookstores. I'm stuck out here, writing the Great Puerto Rican Novel, and I'd like to know if anybody's running interference for me.

If you get to Big Sur, stop in.

Cheers,
Hunter S. Thompson

TO ABE MELLINKOFF, *SAN FRANCISCO CHRONICLE:*

December 15, 1960
Big Sur, California

Abe Mellinkoff
Chronicle
5th & Mission
San Francisco

Dear Mr. Mellinkoff:

I just got tearsheets of another one of my Caribbean pieces in the New York *Herald Tribune* and thought I'd hit you again while I'm still feeling big-headed.

The fat is in the fire, Abe; the great spectre of poverty has finally put my shoulder to the mat, and only a salary can save the day. I'm fairly objective about my capabilities and I honestly think I could do a good job for you, if only on a trial basis.

You've read my clippings—if you don't recall, I'll bring them in again—and I think we agreed they were pretty decent. I've read the *Chronicle* every day since then, so I'm no stranger to the style, and I think the mere fact that I've been able to hang on this long without throwing myself on the mercy of the employment agencies is a whomping tribute to my native ingenuity.

I'm considering a trip to New York for Christmas—and perhaps longer—so I'd like to hear from you on this as soon as possible. The chance of an opening on the *Chronicle* is about the only thing that's kept me out here this long, and I hope you'll be frank enough to tell me if I'm wasting my time.

The enclosed clipping will give you a better idea of what I can do. It's my only copy, so please return it.

Thanks,
Hunter S. Thompson

TO ANN SCHOELKOPF:

December 23, 1960
Big Sur, California

Dear Madam—

Glad you warned me about Maxine[22] & her gin, because if I hadn't been prepared for it, I might have gone under. I have just got the last of the bottles out of the house; I was throwing them over the cliff all week, but I couldn't keep pace. Lord, it was a goatdance like I ain't done in some while.

Anyway, she left two days ago, bound for New York—so maybe you'd better pick up a little olive oil to grease your stomach. She wanted us to go with her, and it was torture to refuse—but the old wallet couldn't have handled it . . . oh lord, the call of the loins in the next room . . . be back in a moment. . . .

* * * * * * * * *

The trip would have killed me. Can you imagine driving from Big Sur to New York, sucking gin all the way, drinking steadily for a week in New York, then back to Big Sur again? Only a beast could survive it. Maxine will pick up most of my plunder in New York and bring it west when she returns. She will stay with Bone, and I'll be interested to see how that turns out. Amazing, how all my worlds keep getting tangled up in each other, eh? I can see Bone now, sitting there in the apt., drinking a bit of Tang, absent-mindedly cleaning between his toes while he reads a pamphlet on Israel—and at this very moment a great white hellbomb is heading straight for his bed, zipping across Oklahoma with a bag of gin, muttering lewd epigrams, and armed only with my information that Bone is a dead-game sport. Ah, Robert, if you only knew. . . .

Maxine's steak-and-roast-beef diet fattened me up for a while, but the loin-call is thinning me down in a hurry. My hair is three times as long as

22. Maxine Ambus was a boisterous woman from an Ohio steel town who had first met Thompson in 1959.

you ever saw it, my moral strictures have turned to jelly, and my financial condition is every bit as bad as it was this time last year. Progress is my most important product.

This past year has been a holocaust. Counting on my fingers, I see that I spent six months in Puerto Rico, one in the Virgin Islands, one in Bermuda, two in New York, one in San Francisco, and two in Big Sur—in that order. This makes Kerouac look like a piker. In the entire 12 months I have written three decent short stories, one brochure (by long odds, the most profitable—$25 a day), a weird collection of journalism, and countless letters. The rest of the time I worried about either movement, money or police.

Now I am getting tired—and hungry—and I would give a nut to be able to step over to the icebox and find a bowl of tuna fish, a jar of hot peppers and a bottle of Ballantine ale. But no more. No, all I have now are the dregs of a bottle of wine ($1.14 a gallon), a wad of salami, and a shaky credit with the mailman—who also brings groceries. Somehow, we are having a 20 lb. turkey for Christmas. A crazed Tzarist writer, 60 years old and lecherous as a young bull, has come up with a monster turkey—and every winehead in Big Sur will be here to pick it clean. All week long we had the terrible public gluts, with bearded thieves hustling out of barns and shacks to share in the abundance brought in by the Big Momma from Sandusky. Every day I drove up to the mailbox in a sleek white convertible—top down and bare-chested, of course—and greeted the postman with a wide, opulent smile. Now, my credit is like Fort Knox—although he keeps asking why I don't drive my car anymore. I tell him I need the exercise.

I presume, of course, that you're picking up on my stuff in the *Trib*. Another one came out recently, and now they want something on Big Sur. If they paid anything, I might hustle for them. But they don't. Also selling an occasional story to the *Courier-Journal*, but the combined total is not even enough to keep me in wine. The Big Money is just around the corner, of course, and it won't be long before I get my hands on it. And then, by jesus, a Crotchdance of such heinous proportions as to whiten the hair of every Rotarian from Newark to Muscle Beach. [. . .]

Unless the Big Money comes in by January 1, we'll head back to San Francisco & probably put Sandy to work. Suppose we'll get an apt., so come on out for a visit if you think you can stand the gaff. I keep applying for jobs and people keep running me out of offices because of my hair and my pipe-thing. Clancy is out here, doing six months in the Army just up the coast in Monterey, and once in a while he comes down for a bit of wine and a Sheep's Head [ale].

That's just about the score on this end. What the hell are you doing? Maxine didn't seem to know & I can only guess. I predict firestorms before summer, followed by a massive shitrain to finish us off. Until then, I shall prevail.

Pompously,
Hunter

Hunter and Sandy at their Big Sur home.
(Photo by Hunter S. Thompson;
courtesy of HST Collection)

*Thompson's favorite portrait of his friend
Paul Semonin.*
(Photo by Hunter S. Thompson; courtesy of
HST Collection)

Thompson at Big Sur.
(Photo by Jo Hudson; courtesy
of HST Collection)

*Thompson became known as "The
Outlaw of Big Sur."*
(Courtesy of HST Collection)

*Joan Baez was Thompson's
Big Sur neighbor.*
(Photo by Hunter S. Thompson;
courtesy of HST Collection)

1961

HARD TRAVELER COMES TO BIG SUR . . . GREAT LEAPS OF A FREE-LANCE WRITER . . . $780 A YEAR . . . THE SOUTH COAST IS A WILD COAST AND LONELY . . . THE SECRET PASSIONS OF JOAN BAEZ KILLING PIGS AND SELLING DOGS . . .

Now, thirty-three years old and looking fifty, his
spirit broken and his body swollen with drink, he
bounced from one country to another, hiring himself out
as a reporter and hanging on until he was fired. Dis-
gusting as he usually was, on rare occasions he showed
flashes of a stagnant intelligence. But his brain was so
rotted with drink and dissolute living that whenever
he put it to work it behaved like an old engine that had
gone haywire from being dipped in lard.

--Hunter S. Thompson,
 "The Rum Diary" (unpublished novel)

TO PAUL SEMONIN:

Upon returning to the United States from Bermuda, Semonin spent a few months in both New York and San Francisco. Unable to find meaningful employment in either city, he moved to Aspen, Colorado, in December 1960, urging his best buddy, Thompson, to join him in the Rockies, where "the living is easy."

January 6, 1961
Big Sur, California

Dear Mr. Semonin:

Your query concerning "pleasure spots" was referred to me by Mr. Thompson, who was kidnapped by queers on New Year's Eve and borne off to the south country. His widow has made an unnatural connection with the Slime God, and cannot at the moment deal with your correspondence. For that reason, I, the county Boarmaster, was called in to sock the deal home. My findings are listed below.

After driving some 21 miles today, the last three of them up a steep canyon full of redwoods, I came on a place called Upper Greenwood Shack. I drove these miles in an off-shift Willys Jeep with a deaf woman, and could not therefore express my dismay that we had come to a place called Moe Canyon—and at the end of this canyon rested a black shack which I (we) entered for the purpose of assay. The innards were bare and cold, but I was instantly struck with the resemblance of this abode to a dark hole once inhabited by an artist friend of mine who has since retired into the hash business. My first thought, upon seeing the skylight in the ceiling, was, "By George, how that fellow could deal with this place." This suspicion was further strengthened when I made a full tour of the place for the purpose of loot. It was full of books and sweaters, a good many of which the deaf woman and I carried off for the purpose of enrichment. Now I want you to understand that a bearded artist has been trying to zip this place off on Mr. Thompson for the sum of $40 per month—but Mr. Thompson does not see it so much as a "pleasure spot" as a place where he will freeze his strained and itching balls. Mr. Thompson is (was) a lover of the sea, you know, and he feels (felt) that a place on the shore would be more to his taste. And also better for his strained and itching balls. Warmth, you know. Mr. Thompson likes (liked) warmth.

And, frankly, Mr. Semonin, had it not been for your query, I would have jammed this place in the sea, deeming it alien, a transplant from New Jersey, and not fit for habitation by other than sleazy jades. But, for your edification, here is a capsule knot: cabin is in Palo Colorado Canyon, 3 miles from sea, buried in redwoods, has its own stream, and is accessible by partly paved road. It has: two large bedrooms, one massive living room with stone fireplace, large kitchen, large bathroom, large pantry, and two porches. Also skylight. The odd resemblance of the area to that of Upper Greenwood Lake quite frankly gave me the creeps.

So, Mr. Semonin, this concludes my report. I have reason to believe this place will remain vacant for some time, perhaps until spring. You and your family may do as you see fit. My fee for this sort of thing is one wad of silver. Send at once.

Mr. Thompson has led me to believe that he will be in your area before January comes to a climax. His future is somewhat uncertain at the moment, due to the unknown whereabouts of one Maxine Ambus, without whose car Mr. Thompson will be unable to make the trip. I do not think Mr. Thompson will deal with your coal for anything short of a sizeable fee. He is, you know, quite stringent when it comes to finances. I further think Mr. Thompson is presently unable to answer your question as to where he will spend the remainder of this winter. He has come to the bottom of his (and his widow's) money barrel and is now faced with a crisis. As of this weekend, he will have no home.

I can, however, give you an idea of his alternatives. He can:

1) spend the remainder of his money for a month's rent on a Big Sur cabin and hope for the best.
2) send his widow to San Francisco to seek work, and follow when she gets it.
3) move in on you, bringing nothing but a sack of happiness.
4) give up the ghost.

This would seem, at first glance, a grisly repertoire of choices. And it is. Mr. Thompson is not, however, without a few rays of hope. One is the possibility of the $3.04 per hour road-job once again becoming available. Another is the possibility that his widow might obtain part-time work at one of the local eateries. And another is the chance of Big Money in the mailbox. Aside from that, there is nothing but a massive leech on Miss Ambus between Mr. Thompson and the wolves.

Mr. Thompson is further perplexed, baffled, unnerved and sick at the prospect of your largesse. From the sound of it, you are richer than Mr. McGarr, the infamous east-side fatbelly. What will you do with it all? World-travel? Mr. Thompson may go almost anywhere—but not until spring. He is currently doing the Great Puerto Rican Novel and will finish it before fleeing the western coast.

Mr. Thompson is also doing a bit of journalism and requests that you gather all the public material on Aspen so that he may digest it whole when he arrives—then spew it out for publication. He also requests that you find a reliable photo shop that will *fine-grain develop* (new term) his film for him.

Mr. Thompson will probably deny this, but I think he feels a bit insecure these days. As a matter of fact, I think he has The Fear.

And he wants you to understand this: "A woman is fascinated not by art, but by the noise made by those who have to do with art."

A mr. chekhov said that, and I guess he should know.

Massively,
Hunter

TO MRS. V. A. MURPHY:

Mrs. Murphy was the eighty-year-old matriarch of Big Sur who ran its famous steam baths (which would soon become the centerpiece of the Esalen Institute). Her grandson, Dennis Murphy, wrote the 1960 novel The Sergeant, *which drew Thompson's praise.*

January 9, 1961
Big Sur, California

Dear Mrs. Murphy:

I am very interested in renting the small annex (just off the kitchen) of the big house. I talked to Dick Rowan[1] about this and he mentioned it to your grandson, Dennis, who said I should get in touch with you.

[. . .] I am a writer—not completely impoverished, but just a few steps above it—and I can't afford the few places in Big Sur that are currently for rent. So when Rowan suggested the big house, it sounded like just what I was looking for.

---

1. A photographer who lived close to the Murphy house, who became a longtime friend and ally of Thompson's.

As I see it, you may be better off having a reliable person living in the house, because—like other vacant buildings in Big Sur—it is very often invaded by transients, "beatniks," and other types who have no respect for property, privacy, furniture or anything else. With a couple living there, nothing like this would happen.

Naturally, the house itself is too big for any two people to occupy—and certainly too big to heat. We could get along well in the annex, but we would have to have access to the kitchen and bathroom in the house, proper. I can assure you that we'd treat the house and property with extreme care.

Since you know nothing about us, you might want to get in touch with Mrs. Webb at the Lodge, the Maynards, Dick Rowan, or anyone else now living on the property. [...]

At any rate, I'd like to hear from you as soon as possible on this, because we have to find a place pretty soon. Thanks for your time and consideration.

Sincerely,
Hunter S. Thompson
c/o Erway
Big Sur

TO JOHN MACAULEY SMITH:

Smith was a Louisville friend of Thompson's who went on to Yale. Writing to Smith back in Kentucky, Thompson revealed his pride in belonging to a Big Sur literary community.

January 11, 1961
Big Sur

Dear John:

My situation in Big Sur is best described by one E. W. McGarr, who writes from New York, saying: "You are out of a job, penniless, homeless, being supported meagerly by a collection of women, queers, drunks and probably bums of every description. . . ."

A strange life, at best. Sunday night I cut my thumb to the bone, trying to open a can of dog food with my bare hands; yesterday I badly sprained my ankle playing football, and I spent most of today sitting in the hot mineral baths, discussing Cuba and Norman Mailer.

We are forming the Big Sur Maulers, a high-toned, shifty squad that will soon challenge the Athenaeum for the Literary Football Championship of the world. We operate with a six-man squad: Henry Miller calling signals,

Dennis Murphy & Eric Barker in the backfield, and Lionel Olay & I at ends. In a recent contest we thumped the North Beach Terrors, 74–6. On Guy Fawkes Day we go against the Greenwich Village Nutwhackers in Washington Square; I think we are favored by 2 ½. Watch for the results in the *C-J* [*Courier-Journal*].

Life is good here, in spite of our dubious backgrounds. Unfortunately it will come to an end (for us) on January 20, when the owner of this house returns from San Francisco. For some reason, no one will rent me another house. And since I have no money, I cannot build one. Perhaps then it will be back to San Francisco and once again seek work. This depresses me more than I can say, but there seems to be no alternative. No jobs here, no homes for rent, and no prospect of money in the mail. Sandy can probably get a job in San Francisco, even if I can't, so there is some hope.

The people here have taken good care of my sprained ankle. Last night, when I went down to the baths to soak it, a homosexual quack insisted on rubbing it with some useless grease that Ed Sullivan had once endorsed on TV. When he finished rubbing my ankle, the queer covered his whole body with the stuff—"to keep me awake on the drive back to Monterey."

Then a woman from Tennessee told me to soak a brown paper bag in vinegar, then tie the bag around my foot. This would cure it, for sure.

I would explain Big Sur more fully, but I'm about to send a piece to the *C-J* about it, so watch the Sunday paper & save me a lot of trouble. Glad you are keeping up on the gossip, anyway.

Yes, there are queers here. And artists. Also farmers. And people who go around naked. I have a bullwhip and a billyclub. So far, I have not been bothered.

Paul [Semonin] seems to like Aspen. I wish I were as well off as he seems to be there (house, job, etc.) and I will probably get over there before the end of January. When I am evicted from here, anything could happen. I have pondered New York, Europe and Cuba. Would like to finish the Great Puerto Rican Novel before I leave the west coast, but things are too in flux now to say anything definite. Money will have to come from somewhere before I make plans. The law of the dice still rules. [. . .]

Copiously,
Hunter

TO MRS. V. A. MURPHY:

Thompson and Conklin moved into Murphy's annex on February 1. The landlady even awarded Hunter the sinecure of security guard/groundskeeper for both the house and the adjacent baths.

January 16, 1961
Big Sur, California

Dear Mrs. Murphy:

Both Sandy and I enjoyed talking to you yesterday, and this letter is to tell you that we've definitely decided to take the "west annex" and live there for better or for worse. The only reason we hesitated at all was that I couldn't believe someone was finally offering me a place that I could afford. Even a writer should be able to make $15 a month—and if he can't he should probably give it up and try something else.

We do, of course, have a few problems, and I thought one or two of these might interest you. Mr. Maynard[2] and I made a quick survey after you left, and we discovered that the hot-water heater and the electric fuse-box are both in the small ante-room just off the kitchen (the first room you enter as you come in the back door). Considering the fact that you plan to seal up the house with bolts, the location of these vital control centers might lead to some difficulty if, 1) the hot-water heater should ever, for any reason, have to be turned off or on, and, 2) if an electric fuse should ever blow out. Normally these would be minor problems, but if the house is sealed up they might be very large ones.

Now this is a knotty problem, and I have pondered it at great length. If my conclusions lead you to believe I am trying to gain access to the stove and the refrigerator in the kitchen, let me assure you that you're only partially correct. I am honestly concerned about the water-heater and the fuse-box, and I can see two ways to keep me from being cut off from them. Neither way, as far as I can see, would give you any cause for concern.

The first is to lock and/or seal the door between the ante-room and the kitchen, thus making it impossible for anyone to enter any part of the house except the small room containing the water-heater and the fuse-box. And the second is to seal and/or lock the kitchen off from the rest of the house. Mr. Maynard and I could do this with no difficulty, and I give you my guarantee that no one (myself and Sandy included) would set foot in the rest of the house.

If you'd consent to sealing the kitchen off from the rest of the house, this would solve our problems with the stove and the refrigerator. And if you'd be worried about the possibility of our misusing them in some way, I'd be glad to give you a small deposit to cover any repairs. (Someone has already broken the door off the refrigerator freezer-compartment, but I think I could pick up another one in Monterey.)

2. Donald Maynard was a Big Sur/Monterey carpenter, handyman, and deliveryman.

Or, if you'd be worried about letting us use the kitchen, but would be willing to let us use the small ante-room just inside the back door, I would like to move the refrigerator and the stove into that room—and then seal the whole business off from the rest of the house.

In either case we would be responsible for the stove and the refrigerator, and I think it would be only fair to give you a deposit. For that matter, if you allowed us the use of the kitchen and/or the ante-room, it would probably justify a small increase in the rent. (My whole soul rebels at the thought of suggesting such a thing, but I'd feel a bit guilty about asking you for concessions without offering some, myself.)

Naturally, if you or Dennis or anyone else were to use the house, Sandy and I would confine ourselves to the annex and stay completely out of your way. And when I spoke of moving the stove and refrigerator, I should have explained that it requires nothing more than a strong back and could be done in ten minutes with no trouble.

So—that's about it. Whatever you decide is OK with me. I appreciate your renting us the annex, and if you want any odd jobs done around the house, just let me know. I do most of my writing at night, so I have plenty of time during the day. And if you want to bring that gun down the next time you come, I'll see to it that you don't even lose a flower, much less a bedroom set. If it's any consolation to you, I'm the largest person on the property down here, and if I find any prowlers lurking around the house, I will simply twist their heads.

In the meantime—before I begin twisting heads—I'll get the bed and the chairs and the chest of drawers from Mrs. Webb.[3] We started cleaning the place out this morning and I imagine we'll move in about the first of the month. Sometime before then I will send you a check for the rent.

Please let me know as soon as possible about the possibility of Sandy and I using the kitchen or the ante-room if the rest of the house can be locked up to your satisfaction.

Thanks,
Hunter S. Thompson

TO NORMAN MAILER:

Thompson respected Mailer immensely, but it didn't keep him from needling the established author from time to time.

---

3. Mrs. Webb was a longtime Big Sur resident and a born-again Christian who ran the hot springs before Mrs. Murphy.

February 1, 1961
Manor House
Big Sur, California

Dear Mr. Mailer:

I appreciated your reply,[4] but, as usual, was a bit dismayed at your picayune defensiveness. You might take a tip from something you once said about James Baldwin: "he seems incapable of saying 'fuck you' to his readers." For whatever it's worth, I suggest you spend more time writing, and less explaining yourself.

This little black book of Miller's[5] is something you might like. If not, or if you already have it, by all means send it back. I don't mind giving it away, but I'd hate to see it wasted.

And if you get to Big Sur, stop by for a beer. There ain't much to do here, so I have taken to inviting people down and then flogging them into a coma with my riding crop. Between guests, I work on the Great Puerto Rican Novel. Watch for it.

Cordially,
Hunter S. Thompson

TO LIEUTENANT COLONEL FRANK CAMPBELL:

Campbell, also an aspiring novelist, was still at Eglin Air Force Base, editing the Command Courier *and writing fiction on the side. This letter contains one of Thompson's first references to his Puerto Rican novel as "The Rum Diary."*

March 7, 1961
Manor House
Big Sur

Sirrah:

First off, you should understand that any beachboys, dishwashers or window-washers showing up at my place will be dealt with at the gate. I'll have no human chancres spoiling my view; life here is tough enough without them.

Another thing you should understand is that, since leaving FWB [Fort Walton Beach], I have been a smashing success at everything except earning money. At times it makes me wonder . . . but then, as I look

4. Thompson had written Mailer on December 7, 1960, wondering why he hadn't attacked Nixon in print during the presidential election.
5. The "little black book" was Henry Miller's *The World of Sex*, published privately by Miller in 1959. (Grove Press eventually published the book in 1965.)

down at my great heap of short story and article carbons, I know the Big Money is just around the corner. Any day now, any day now, I shall be released.

Jerry Hawke's information as to my activities is not only slanderous, but two years old. The fact is that I was mugging people in New York and had the hell beaten out of me by a gang of drunken writers. That is why I moved to the Catskills.

I then decided to beat them at their own game and wrote a very funny, thoroughly unskilled novel called Prince Jellyfish. It bounced four times in New York, but the reaction was encouraging enough to put the monkey on my back for good. Since then I have not held a job and doubt seriously if I ever shall. I have tried, mind you, but something about my manner seems to warn them off.

Since Prince Jellyfish I have pursued the Good Life in countless strange and erotic climes, ranging from Bermuda in the east to Puerto Rico & St. Thomas in the south, New York in the north, and San Francisco, Seattle and Big Sur in the west. If I were 20 years older I would think that I'd finally done the deed, because Big Sur is—to paraphrase the immortal Willie Stark[6]—"the tall walking nuts." But a man on the crest of a new wave can hardly afford to retire, so all signs point to my imminent return to the strife and struggle of cold-war reality. At the moment I am engaged in hammering out a novel called The Rum Diary. It will probably hit the stands around September, and even if you've left Tennessee by then I'll make sure a copy seeks out your vapor trail and tracks you down to finish the work I began in the office of the *Command Courier.*

If not for a deadly sag in my economy I would already be in Spain, waiting for you. Last June I left St. Thomas on a 47-ft. sloop, rode it to Bermuda, and there tried to effect a transfer to a boat headed for the Mediterranean. No dice. A strategic retreat sent me back to New York, thence to the west coast. I have been selling features (very sporadically) to the New York *Herald Tribune* and the Louisville *Courier-Journal*. This began in the Caribbean and has kept up. The *Trib* just bought a Big Sur piece, and yesterday I sent an expanded version of it to *Playboy*. They had seen a carbon of the one I sent to the *Trib* and asked me to give it a whirl. No guarantee, of course, and about a 75-to-one shot of getting my hand in the till. If I make it, however, I shall probably beat you to Spain.

I have acquired a "name" agent in New York (Elizabeth McKee), who is carrying me for god knows what reason, because all the stories I've sent her have bounced like golf balls. If she can stand it, I guess I can, too.

6. Willie Stark was the protagonist in Robert Penn Warren's *All the King's Men.*

I presume you are still dealing with Sterling Lord.[7] Or have you given it up? Hope not. Anyway, one of Lord's boys is out here—one Lionel Olay (two novels, articles, screenplays), who seems to think Lord is the Jay Gould[8] of agentry. Seems he can sell just about anything he gets his hands on—Kerouac's stuff is a good example.

The house I'm living in here belongs, by way of inheritance, to Dennis Murphy (*The Sergeant*). There is so much talent on this coast that the *Partisan Review* sends men to cover our touch football games. The ball, incidentally, is compliments of the Eglin Eagles. A gift, of course—for services rendered.

That's about the score on this end; if you have any questions, feel free to submit them.

As for the Eglin rat-pack, I lost everybody but [Peter] Goodman and Hawke. John Edenfield's suicide was a hell of a shock to me. I ran across Pete on the streets of Greenwich Village last summer and he told me about it. He's marrying (or has married) a pretty cute girl. At the time I met him he was directing one of her shows at a new cabaret theatre on W. 4th St. It was a little giddy for my tastes, but it seemed to go over pretty well. I talked to Jerry on the phone, but left before we could get together. One of his roommates (at Columbia) stormed in on me a few weeks ago and by a wild stroke of luck I managed to seize him a weekend place in Big Sur. He's currently doing a 6-month stretch at Ft. Ord. John Clancy is his name, in case it strikes a chord.

Glad to hear Pug has not been cashiered. I guess anybody who knows Arthur Godfrey has it made in the AF these days. Guess I missed my chance. But I was a little green then, and the next time I shoot at Godfrey—or at Pug, for that matter—it won't be from the columns of a Weekly Nowhere. If nothing else, living by your wits teaches you to hold your fire until you see the whites of their eyes.

I liked Gibney.[9] When you see him be sure to tell him I said Hello and good luck in the Philippines.

As for Ballas[10] . . . well . . . jesus . . . what can you say about a man like that? The next thing we know he'll probably be buying the *Playground News*. Good old Ballas—a pragmatist if there ever was one.

---

7. Lord was considered the "hot" New York agent at the time.
8. Jay Gould was a late-nineteenth-century New York robber baron who owned railroads and the *New York World*.
9. Major Frank Gibney was in the Office of Information Services at Eglin and contributed to the *Command Courier*.
10. Pete Ballas was in charge of publicity for the *Command Courier*.

If you get a chance, pick up something called *The Ginger Man*, by J. P. Donleavy. You can get it in paperback & probably at a decent library. I think you'd like it.

You know, in your run-down you left out the only one I really wanted to know about, the one guy at APGC-OIS who really had a future. Whatever happened to that jackass, Rosan, anyway?

And with that I close. Let me know if and when you head for Spain. If all goes well, I'll probably see you there. Think on that.

Patriotically,
Hunter S. Thompson

TO VIRGINIA THOMPSON:

Thompson was devastated by news that his grandmother Memo was termi-
nally ill. Unable to make it back to Louisville, he wrote his mother about his
deep love for the one person who had never let him down.

March 18, 1961
Big Sur, California

Dear Mom:

Just returned from a week in San Francisco and found your two letters about Memo. I've been sitting here at the typewriter for almost an hour, trying to think what I can say, but nothing comes.

My picture of Memo is a far cry from what she seems to be now, and although it's pretty selfish of me, I'm not making much of an effort to visualize what you must be going through. The more I understand about people, the more I realize just how good a person Memo is. At times she seems almost unreal, because it's hard for me to believe that I could know a person that long without seeing some things I didn't like. But now, in looking back on all those years, my only real memory of Memo is one of a genuine, long-suffering goodness. I haver never known anyone—and don't ever expect to—so completely generous and forgiving and unfailingly loyal—even when all evidence made loyalty seem like so much wasted faith.

If she doesn't recover from this, my only regret is that I couldn't have published a book in time for her to see it. I've tried, but I could have tried a lot harder, and your letters made me brutally aware of all the time I've wasted. I've just sent a long article to *Playboy*, which they requested and which they may buy. If they take it I'll have cracked one of the best markets in the country, and, if nothing else, I'll have made the Big League. If you think Memo would be happier if you told her I've already sold it, then go ahead. Tell her it's a long article on Big Sur and I sold it for $2,000.

Frankly, I don't really expect them to buy it, but then I didn't expect the *Courier* to buy those Puerto Rico articles either. I have learned better than to count on selling anything.

As for the news here, I went to San Francisco to find an apartment for Maxine Ambus, my "large female friend" from New York. I found her a good one on Telegraph Hill, which will be my base whenever I go into the city again. Sandy was with me, of course, and is now downstairs knitting me a sweater. We're still happy here, still without money, and it looks like this situation may last for an indefinite time. I'm working on a new novel and hope to finish it by summer.

That's about it for now. I'm so tired I can barely see. Tell Memo I love her and that I've always loved her—not just for all the help she's given me, but because she's such a damn good person. I wish I could be there to tell her goodbye, but this letter is the best I can do. It will seem strange to come home and not find her there, sitting by the window, and it probably won't be until then that I'll actually realize she's gone. I'll miss her, but I hope it comes quickly and painlessly. If there is such a thing as deserving a peaceful death, I think Memo has qualified many times over.

Love,
Hunter

TO WILLIAM J. KENNEDY, *SAN JUAN STAR:*

Thompson had left his gear, including boxes of correspondence, with Kennedy when he fled San Juan on a forty-seven-foot sloop. He had promised to give Kennedy either cash or books for the favor of shipping them back to America.

April 26, 1961
Big Sur

"Kennedy has spent years oiling every literary lever and power which could help him on his way, and there are medals waiting for him in the mass media."

Give yourself ten points if you recognize that.[11] If not, well . . . what can I say?

Your letter arrived today and I am disregarding my new policy of letting all letters sit for a week before answering them (letters always excite me and my natural tendency is to sit down and answer them immediately) for the simple reason that I am more excited at the prospect of getting my gear.

---

11. Thompson made up this quote just to tease Kennedy.

The thing for you to do, if you are worried about payment, is to give me a rough idea of how much it will cost, along with a list of which books you would take to liquidate the debt. I will then decide if I would rather pay you in money or books. In either case, I will see to it that our friendship is kept solvent. By that, I mean that if you want the cream of my book crop I will say no and send money. If, however, you constrain yourself, selecting only those tomes I have no use for, we can settle the thing without resorting to cash.

Your sun is on the wane, I think, for you will be unbearable if you ever get published. My only hope is to smack out The Rum Diary and steal your thunder to the extent that all but the first thirteen copies of your book (sold to family & friends) will be remaindered. It goes without saying—in answer to your question—that The Rum Diary is the potential high-water mark of 20th century literature. It is a novel more gripping than *The Ginger Man,* more skillfully rendered than *The Sergeant,* more compassionate than [James Agee's] *A Death in the Family,* and more important than *Lie Down in Darkness.* These, as you know, are the only good novels written in the past five years. All the rest is ballast. (I now recall that *LDID* was done in 1950 . . . strike one.)

The Rum Diary is of course set in Puerto Rico and I feel there will be a great shrieking and tearing of hair in the New York office of Fomento[12] when it comes out. This prospect is one of my main incentives.[. . .]

In all seriousness, I wish you all the luck you will need in connection with your manuscript. I have come to the point where I believe all editors are vicious, myopic queers and I would be more optimistic for you if I thought there was at least a touch of the pansy in you.

Semonin, as you may know, is writing a book called "Collected Thoughts of a Tramp Thinker." I imagine it will be good, but I think he will have trouble getting it between covers.

I, of course, will have the most trouble of all because my book will be Too Good. Or maybe just . . . Too Much.

Anyway, hello to Dana and keep hustling.

Niggardly,

H

TO BANKS SHEPHERD:

Thompson's old Air Force friend had also decided he wanted to become a writer.

12. Fomento was Puerto Rico's news service/international development office.

June 2, 1961
Manor House
Big Sur

Well, Mr. Shepherd, I hardly know what to say. First, of course, I deeply appreciate your interest in my problems. Every once in a while I get that old feeling that no one really cares—you know how it is—and to have your letter come on me today, unheralded and totally unforeseen, was indeed a heart-warming experience.

Unlike you, Mr. Shepherd, I do "have a claim" on literary talent, tenuous though it may be. On the other hand, I too work hard to find ways of stimulating people—often to the extent of seizing them by the scruff of the neck and shouting into their eyes. This, in itself, quite often produces problems.

But you say you'd consider it a favor if I'd tell you something of my work and particularly my special problems in getting work done through other people. Well now, Mr. Shepherd, I'm going to do my best to help you out on this. You sound like a decent fellow and if I can give you a hand I certainly will.

My circumstances are somewhat peculiar, in that I refuse to take a job, so when it comes to getting work done through other people I might be able to give you a few hints. I presume, of course, that you plan to throw up your job and become a writer, and let me warn you now that in order to do this you've got to know the ropes.

First you'll have to acquire a woman and put her to work immediately, preferably in a high-paying job. This is mandatory, regardless of your solvency, because you will almost instantly go broke. Next, you'll have to find a dwelling for little or no rent. For example, I pay $15 a month for a three-room house on the California coast.

Once you've solved these two very basic problems you'll run into myriad smaller ones demanding constant attention. For instance, instead of cutting the grass—which would take quite a bit of time—I found a wounded deer, nursed it back to health, and now tether it on the lawn and let it eat its fill. Instead of buying meat, I simply walk back into the hills and shoot a deer or a wild boar. Instead of buying vegetables I force a woman to tend a garden and prepare all the meals. Instead of drinking whiskey I drink wine and charge it to the mailman. As for anything else I need, I simply invite people down from San Francisco for a weekend and give them a list of things I require to maintain my hospitality.

This should give you an idea of the sort of thing you'll be dealing with. In addition, there are two golden rules: First, never hesitate to use force, and, second, abuse your credit for all it's worth. If you remember these, and if you can keep your wits about you, there's a chance you'll make it. Provided, of course, you can write like a champion.

That's about it, Mr. Shepherd. If I can be of any further assistance, just let me know.

> Sincerely,
> Hunter S. Thompson

TO STERLING LORD:

After Lieutenant Colonel Frank Campbell wrote in March that Sterling Lord had taken him on as a client, Thompson decided to see if the "dean" of New York literary agents would be interested in his fiction as well. Unconventional writers of the time flocked to Lord because he had managed to sell Jack Kerouac's On the Road *to Viking Press.*

> June 15, 1961
> Manor House
> Big Sur, California

Sterling Lord
15 E. 48th
NYC

Dear Mr. Lord:

Enclosed are six stories and one article that you might be able to sell. For one reason or another—and I admit to the possibility that my fiction is simply unsalable—my present agent has not been able to place my work in the public eye.

Some of this stuff is currently circulating and you will not be free to sell it until I get my hands on the original copies—which I can and will do the moment I hear from you.

To be specific, the short Claude Fink[13] piece is now at *Contact.* They don't pay anything, so I don't suppose it interests you. The Big Sur article is at *Rogue.* If they want it, and if you want to deal with them, I'll be happy to give you the commission. "Hit Him Again, Jack" and "Whither Thou Goest" are in the hands of my agent. If either of them interests you I will get them.

Ignoring for a moment the possibility that my work is totally useless, I think it seems fitting that someone should buy it. Whenever I inquire of my present agent as to the whereabouts of my stories I find they have just been bounced by *The New Yorker, Mademoiselle, Gentlemen's Quarterly,* or some other worthy journal that I would not even read, much less try to

13. Claude Fink was a fictional character.

write for. No doubt these are fine markets, but I have a feeling they are not avid for stories full of flogging, humping, goring and soul-rot.

But that is your field; I don't know a damn thing about markets and, aside for the fact that Rust Hills has told me never to submit anything to *Esquire* (under my own name), I have had little contact with them. This is fine, except that it has put me in a state of great need. As a matter of fact I am mired in a bog of poverty and am counting on these stories to pull me at least part of the way out. At the moment I'm working on a novel called "The Rum Diary," which should be finished by late summer. If you would care to deal with it, by all means let me know. It will be a whomping thing and will undoubtedly draw poor comment from *Gentlemen's Quarterly*, *Pop*, *One*, *Ebony* and a good many others.

At any rate, please let me hear from you.

Thanks,
Hunter S. Thompson

TO STERLING LORD:

Lord had declined to take Thompson on as a client.

June 26, 1961
Manor House
Big Sur, California

Dear Mr. Lord:

Fortunately, the check for the Big Sur article took the sting out of your pompous and moronic rejection of my work.

Here's the 20 cents it cost you to send the damn things back. I don't want to feel that I owe you anything, because when I see you I intend to cave in your face and scatter your teeth all over Fifth Avenue.

I think we are coming to a day when agents of your sort will serve no useful function except as punching bags.

Cordially,
Hunter S. Thompson

TO FRANK M. ROBINSON, *ROGUE:*

At last Thompson placed a feature article in a national magazine: Rogue, *a men's journal similar in appeal to* Playboy, *which paid him a handsome $350 for the following controversial exposé on the real Big Sur, with its famed "baths" the chic new meeting place for San Francisco homosexuals.*

"Big Sur: The Garden of Agony"

If half the stories about Big Sur were true this place would long since have toppled into the sea, drowning enough madmen and degenerates to make a pontoon bridge of bodies all the way to Honolulu. The vibration of all the orgies would have collapsed the entire Santa Lucia mountain range, making the destruction of Sodom and Gomorrah seem like the work of a piker. The western edge of this nation simply could not support the weight of all the sex fiends and criminals reputed to be living here. The very earth itself would heave and retch in disgust--and down these long, rocky slopes would come a virtual cascade of nudists, queers, junkies, rapists, artists, fugitives, vagrants, thieves, lunatics, sadists, hermits and human chancres of every description.

They would all perish, one and all--and, if justice were done a whole army of tourists and curiosity-seekers would perish with them. All the people who come here "for a few kicks" would share the fate of the doomed residents, and anyone surviving the Great Slide would be done in by Killer Whales. The casualty list would be a terrifying document. In addition to the locals it would include voyeurs of all types, hundreds of free-lance pederasts, every sort of predatory jade, and a legion of would-be orgymasters.

None of this is likely to happen, however, because almost everything you hear about Big Sur is rumor, legend or an outright lie. This place is a mythmaker's paradise, so vast and so varied that the imagination is tempted to run wild at the sight of it.

In reality, Big Sur is very like Valhalla--a place that a lot of people have heard of, and that very few can tell you anything about. In New York you might hear it's an art colony, in San Francisco they'll tell you it's a nudist colony, and when you finally roll into Big Sur with your eyes peeled for naked artists you are likely to be very disappointed. Every weekend Dick Hartford, owner of the local village store, is plagued by people looking for "sex orgies," "wild drinking brawls," or "the road to Henry Miller's house"--as if once they found Miller everything else would be taken care of. Some of them will stay as long as a week, just wandering around, asking questions, forever popping up where you least expect them--and finally they wander off, back to wherever they came from, often complaining bitterly that Big Sur is "nothing but a damn wilderness."

Well, most of it is, and the geographical boundaries of Big Sur are so vague that Lillian B. Ross, one of the first writers to live here, once described it as "not a place at all, but a state of mind." If that sounds a bit mystic, consider that the Big Sur country--which is what you mean when you say Big Sur--is roughly eighty miles long and twenty wide, with a population of some three hundred souls spread out across the hills and along the coast. The "town" itself is nothing but a post office, village store, gas station, garage and restaurant, located a hundred and fifty miles south of San Francisco on Highway One.

Prior to World War Two this place was as lonely and isolated a spot as any in America. But no longer. Inevitably, Big Sur has been "discovered." Life magazine called it a "Rugged, Romantic World Apart," and presented nine pages of pictures to prove it. After that there was no hope. Not that Henry Luce has anything against solitude--he just wants to tell his five million readers about it. And on some weekends it seems like all five million of them are right here, bubbling over with questions:

"Where's the art colony, man? I've come all the way from Tennessee to join it."

"Say, fella, where do I find this nudist colony?"

"Hello there. My wife and I want to rent a cheap ten-room house for weekends. Could you tell me where to look?"

"How're ya doin', ace? Where's this marijuana farm I been hearin' about?"

"Good morning, old sport. Hope I'm not disturbing you. I . . . ah . . . well, you see I understand you people have some jim-dandy parties down here and I was wondering if a few bottles of booze would get me an invitation."

Or the one that drove Miller half-crazy: "Ah ha! So you're Henry Miller! Well, my name is Claude Fink and I've come to join the cult of sex and anarchy."

Most of the people who've heard of Big Sur know nothing about it except that Miller lives here--and, for most of them, that's enough. There is no doubt in their minds that anyplace Miller lives is bound to be some sort of sexual mecca. The mere suspicion brought dozens of people to Big Sur, but when somebody wrote an article about the Cult of Sex and Anarchy he was organizing here, they came from all over the world to join it. That was close to ten years ago, and they've been coming ever since.

Ironically enough, Miller came here looking for peace and solitude. When he arrived in 1946 he was a relative unknown. His major works (Tropics of Cancer & Capricorn, The Rosy Crucifixion, Black Spring, etc.) were banned in this country (and still are). In Europe, where he had lived since the early Thirties, he had a reputation as one of the few honest and uncompromising American writers. But when the Nazis overran Paris his income was cut off at the source and he was forced back to the United States.

His contempt for this country was manifest in everything he wrote, and his vision of America's future was a hairy thing, at best. In The World of Sex, a banned and little-known book he wrote in 1940, he put it like this:

> What will happen when this world of neuters who make up the great bulk of the population collapses is this--they will discover sex. In the period of darkness which will ensue they will line up in the dark like snakes or toads and chew each other alive during the endless fornication carnival. They will bury themselves in the earth and go at it hammer and tong. They will fuck anything within reach, from a keyhole to a mangy corpse. Anything can happen on this continent. From the very beginning it has been the seat of cruel practices, of blood-letting, of hor-

rible tortures, of enslavement, of fratricide, of sac-
rificial orgies, of stoicism, of witchcraft, of lynch-
ing, of pillage and plunder, of greed, of prejudice
and bigotry, and so on. . . . We have seen everything
here but the eruption of sexuality. This will be the
last outburst, the flood which will carry the robots
off. The enormous and elaborate machine which is
America will go haywire. It will be the aurora bore-
alis which will usher in the long night. They say a
higher type of man will develop here one day. It may
be possible, but if it happens it will be from new
shoots. The present stock may make wonderful ma-
nure, but it will not yield new men.

These are the words that came back to haunt him
when he moved to Big Sur. No sooner had he settled
here, hoping to separate himself from what he called
"The Air-Conditioned Nightmare," than thousands of
people sought him out to shake his hand, to ask his
advice, and to bombard him with their own visions
and predictions. Day after day, year after year, when
all Miller wanted was a little privacy, they struggled up the steep dirt road to his house on Partington Ridge; if there was a fornication carnival going
on up there, they were damn well going to be in on it.
At times it seemed like half the population of Greenwich Village was camping on his lawn. Girls wearing
nothing but raincoats showed up at his door in the
dead of night, wild turks hitchhiked out from New
York with duffel-bags full of everything they owned,
drifters arrived from every corner of the nation
with sacks of food and whiskey, and destitute Frenchmen came all the way from Paris.

Miller did his best to stem the tide, but it was no
use. As his fame spread, his volume of visitors
mounted steadily. Many of them had not even read his
books. They weren't interested in literature, they
wanted orgies. And they were shocked to find him a
quiet, fastidious and very moral man--instead of the
raving sexual beast they'd heard stories about. When
no orgies materialized, the disappointed cultists
drifted on to Los Angeles or San Francisco, or stayed
in Big Sur, trying to drum up orgies of their own. Some

of them lived in hollow trees, others found abandoned
shacks, and a few simply roamed the hills with sleeping bags, living on nuts, berries and wild mustard
greens. The ones who didn't stay went off to spread the
word, and with each retelling the stories got wilder
and wilder. More people arrived, driving Miller to the
brink of despair. He posted a large, insulting sign at
the head of his driveway, cultivated a rude manner to
make visitors ill at ease, and devised elaborate
schemes to keep them from discovering where he lived.
But nothing worked. They finally overwhelmed him,
and in the process they put Big Sur squarely on the
map of national curiosities. Today they are still coming, even though Miller has packed his bags and fled
to Europe for what may be a permanent vacation.

The special irony of all of this is that Miller has
written more about Big Sur--and praised it more--
than any other writer in the world. In 1946 he wrote
an essay called "This Is My Answer," which eventually
appeared in his book <u>Big Sur and the Oranges of
Hieronymus Bosch,</u> published in 1958, long after the
first invasion.

"Peace and solitude!" he says. "I have had a taste of
it even in America. Mornings on Partington Ridge I
would often go to the cabin door on rising, look out
over the rolling velvety hills, filled with such con-
tentment, such gratitude, that instinctively my hand
went up in a benediction. . . . That is how I like to
begin the day. . . . And by God, that is why I came to
Big Sur and settled down. I want every day to begin
thus . . . here there is peace and serenity, here there
is just a handful of good neighbors and the rest is
wild animals, noble trees, buzzards, eagles, and the
sea and the sky and the hills and the mountains un-
ending. . . ."

Needless to say the day would come when Miller
could look out his front door and see a lot more than
trees, wild animals and a handful of good neighbors.
On some mornings he would forego the benediction in
order to shake his fist at the horde of geeks who had
gathered in his yard. But his was a special case; he
was a marked man. The rest of Big Sur has put up a

stern resistance, and, although the battle was lost from the very beginning, the steamroller of progress has made slow headway here. In some spots, in fact, it has bogged down altogether.

There are people here without the vaguest idea of what is happening in the rest of the world. They haven't read a newspaper in years, don't listen to the radio, and see a television set perhaps once a month when they go into town.

To read a New York Times in Big Sur can be a traumatic experience. After living here a few months you find it increasingly difficult to take that mass of threatening, complicated information very seriously. Sitting here on a cliff above a rocky beach, on the edge of a vast and empty ocean, with the hills stacked up behind you like a great wall against the chaos of war and politics, the world of The New York Times seems unreal and altogether foreign, so completely opposed to the silence and the beauty of this coast that you sometimes wonder how the people who live in that world can hold on to their sanity. Not all of them do, of course. People are losing their grip every day. Thousands have cracked up from reading too many newspapers, and countless others have gone under for no apparent reason at all.

Not so in Big Sur. Here they didn't even have electricity until 1947, or telephones until 1958. In New York, where you're forever hearing stories about the West Coast "population explosion," it is hard to believe that a place like this still exists. Compared to the rest of California, Big Sur seems brutally primitive. No sub-divisions mar these rugged hills, no supermarkets, no billboards, no crowded commercial wharf jutting into the sea. In the entire eighty-mile stretch of coastline there are only five gas stations and only two grocery stores. A fifty-mile stretch is still without electricity. The people who live there--and some of them own whole mountains of virgin land--are still using gas lanterns and Coleman stoves.

Despite the inroads of progress it is still possible to roam these hills for days at a time without seeing

anything but deer, wolves, mountain lions and wild
boar. Parts of Big Sur remain as wild and lonely as
they were when Jack London used to come down on
horseback from San Francisco. The house he stayed in
is still here, high on a ridge a few miles south of
the post office.

With a little luck a man can still come here and
live entirely by himself, but most of the people who
come don't have that in mind. These are the tran-
sients--the "orphans" and the "weekend ramblers." The
orphans are the spiritually homeless, the disinherited souls of a complex and nerve-wracked society.
They can be lawyers, laborers, beatniks or wealthy
dilettantes, but they are all looking for a place
where they can settle and "feel at home." Some of them
stay here, finding in Big Sur the freedom and relaxation they couldn't find anywhere else. But most of
them move on, finding it "too dull" or "too lonely" for
their tastes.

The weekend rambler is a very different animal. He
may be an account executive, a Hollywood fag, or an
English major at Stanford--but whatever he is he has
heard the Big Sur stories and he is here to get his
kicks. His female number is the part-time model from
L.A., or the bored little rich girl from San Francisco. They arrive singley and in packs, on Friday
and Saturday, quivering with curiosity and ready
for anything that comes their way. These are the ones
who start orgies--the gin-filled Straight Arrows and
the secret humpers who come out of the city to let off
steam. They will start at Nepenthe, summer headquarters for the local drinking class, and finish in the
big Roman tubs at Hot Springs Lodge, ten miles down
the coast. Girls will come into Nepenthe on a Saturday afternoon, freeze the whole bar with a haughty
stare--and by midnight they'll be romping in and out
of the crowded tubs at Hot Springs, stark naked and
shouting for more gin. The bath-house is an open concrete shed, looking out on the sea, and the tubs are
full of hot sulphur water and big enough to hold as
many as ten people. During the day most people ob-
serve the partition that separates the men's side from

the women's, but once the sun goes down the baths are as coeducational as a cathouse New Year's Eve party, and often twice as wild.

This is the glamorous side of Big Sur, the side that occasionally matches the myth--and none of it is hidden away in the hills, as a lot of people seem to think.

The highway alone is enough to give a man pause. It climbs and twists along these cliffs like a huge asphalt roller-coaster, and in some spots you can drop eight hundred feet straight down to the booming surf. The coast from Carmel to San Simeon, with the green slopes of the Santa Lucia mountains plunging down to the sea, is nothing short of awesome. Nepenthe, open from April to November, is one of the most beautiful restaurants anywhere in America; and Chaco, the lecherous old Tsarist writer who, in his words, "hustles liquor" on the Nepenthe terrace, is as colorful a character as a man could hope to meet.

There are plenty of artists here, and most of them exhibit at the Coast Gallery, about halfway between Nepenthe and Hot Springs. Like artists everywhere, many do odd jobs to keep eating and pay the rent. Others, like Bennett Bradbury, drive new Cadillac convertibles and live in "fashionable" spots like Coastlands or Partington Ridge.

On any given day you might walk into the Village Store and find three Frenchmen and two bearded Greeks arguing about the fine points of Dada poetry-- and on the day after that you'll find nobody there but a local rancher, muttering to himself about the ever-present danger of hoof-and-mouth disease.

The local poets outnumber the wild boar, but Eric Barker is the only "name," and he looks too much like a farmer to cause any stir among the tourists. For that matter almost everyone in Big Sur looks like either a farmer or a woodsy poet. People are always taking Emil White, publisher of the Big Sur Guide, for a hermit or a sex fiend; and Helmut Deetjan, owner of the Big Sur Inn, looks more like a junkie than a lot of hopheads who've been on the stuff for years. If you saw Nicholas Roosevelt, of the Oyster Bay Roosevelts, walking along the highway, you might expect him to flag you down, wipe your windshield with an old handkerchief, and ask for a quarter. Some of the local fags are easy to spot, but almost anyone could be a nudist or a lunatic--and some of them probably are.

To see Big Sur is one thing, and to live here is quite another. Anyone can perch on the glamorous surface for a few days, idling, drinking and looking for orgies--but beneath that surface is a way of life not many people can tolerate.

There is no glamour in the little man who comes down from the city to "get away from it all"--and runs amok on wine two weeks later because there is nobody to talk to and the silence is driving him crazy. There is nothing exciting about loneliness, and Big Sur is full of it. If you can't stand isolation this place can spook you right out of your mind. I've had people curse me bitterly for not staying "just a while longer" to keep them company, and I've had people in my house who wouldn't go home because they couldn't stand the idea of going back to their own place to be alone again.

Today the population of Big Sur is smaller than it was in 1900, and just about the same as it was in 1945. Hundreds of people have tried to settle here since the end of the war, and hundreds have failed. Those who come from the cities, hoping to join a merry band of hard-drinking exiles from an over-organized society, are soon disappointed. The exiles are hard to locate, and even harder to drink with. Soon the silence becomes ominous; the pounding sea is too hostile and the nights are full of strange sounds. On some days the only thing to do, besides eat and sleep, is walk up to your mailbox and meet the postman, who drives down from Monterey six days a week in a Volkswagen bus, bringing mail, newspapers, groceries and even beer.

Big Sur is no phony colony, no tourist attraction full of souvenirs and arty knick-knacks. You don't just float in, throw up your problems, and begin the goat-dance. It takes a tremendous capacity for remaining self-sufficient and a hell of a lot of hard

work. If you come here looking for something to join
or to lean on for support, you are in for a bad time.

In his book on Big Sur, Miller describes the people
he found here when he came. Some of them, depressed
by the influx of tourists, have left for other, more
isolated spots--Mexico, the Pacific Northwest, or the
Greek Islands. But many are still here, living the
same way they were ten years ago:

> These young men, usually in their late twenties or
> early thirties . . . are not concerned with under-
> mining a vicious system, but with leading their own
> lives--on the fringe of society. It is only natural
> to find them gravitating toward such places as Big
> Sur. They all arrived here by different paths, each
> with his own purpose, and one as different from the
> other as marbles from dice. But all "naturals." All
> somewhat "peculiar" in the eyes of the ordinary run.
> All of them, to my mind, men of service, men of good
> will, men of strong integrity. Each and every one of
> them fed up with the scheme of things, determined
> to free themselves of the treadmill, lead their own
> lives. None of them demanding anything more fan-
> tastic of life than the right to live after his own
> fashion. None of them adhering to any party, doc-
> trine, cult or ism, but all imbued with very strong,
> very definite ideas as to how life can be lived in
> these evil times. Never crusading for their ideas,
> but doing their utmost to put them into practice.
> Putting above everything--human dignity. Diffi-
> cult sometimes, especially where "trifles" are
> concerned, yet always available in genuine emer-
> gencies. Stone deaf when asked to toe the line.

These are the expatriates, the ones who have come
from all over the world to make a stab at The Good
Life. But there are others, too. Some are ranchers
whose families have lived here for generations.
Others are out-and-out bastards, who live in isolation because they can't live anywhere else. A few are
genuine deviates, who live here because nobody cares
what they do as long as they keep to themselves. And
there are people here of no integrity, no good will,
no service and no apparent worth at all.

In some respects Big Sur is closer to New York and
Paris than to Monterey and San Francisco. To the
writers and photographers who live here just a few
months of the year, New York is the axis of the earth--
where the publishers are, where the assignments orig-
inate and where all the checks are signed. And once
the checks are cashed, Paris is the next stop after
that. It's keep moving until the money runs out, then
back to Big Sur. In their minds, San Francisco is a
bar, Monterey is a grocery store, and L.A. is a circus
a few hundred miles down the road.

Others, primarily the painters and sculptors, look
north to Carmel, with its many art galleries, craft-
centers and wallet-heavy tourists.

Visitors to Big Sur--those who are actually
invited--are more likely to be artists, foreign journalists or world-travelers than ordinary vacation-
ers. There are no hotels here, the motels are small
and devoid of entertainment, and the only nightlife
revolves around Nepenthe, which is closed five
months of the year. Most of the people who live here
are jealous of their privacy, and nothing annoys
them more than a curious intruder. A man sitting on
the rocks with a can of beer, watching the sunset or
the whales passing out to sea, is not as a rule very
happy to explain his way of life to a traveling salesman who stops to "talk to one of the natives."

Jerry Gorsline, who spent the first eighteen years
of his life in New York and now lives on an abandoned
mining claim twenty-five miles south of Hot Springs,
is happy enough to have no visitors at all. Once or
twice a week he will drive up the coast to borrow some
books, put in a day's work for a man who is building
a new wing on his house, or pass a few beery hours in
the hot sulphur baths. He grows most of his own food,
makes his own wine, cooks on a wood-stove, and keeps
in touch with his friends in Europe, where he lived
for two years before coming to Big Sur.

Lionel Olay, a writer, lives far back in the hills
with a girl and two dogs. He spends a few days of
every month in Hollywood, picking up assignments,
but he does his writing in Big Sur. When he gets

money he moves off at a high rate of speed--Mexico, Cuba, Spain, and finally back to Big Sur.

King Hutchinson, on the other hand, has been here for three years and has no intention of leaving. He is one of many who live "the seven-five split": seven months working at Nepenthe and five on unemployment insurance.

Don Bloom is a painter. He lives on what he earns and pays $25 a month for one of the finest houses on the coast. He gets along without electricity, has one of the best gardens in Big Sur, and spends a good part of the day on his porch, staring at the sea.

This is the way life goes in Big Sur: waiting for the mail, watching the sea-lions in the surf or the freighters on the horizon, sitting in the tubs at Hot Springs, once in a while a bit of drink--and, most of the time, working at whatever it is that you came here to work on, whether it be painting, writing, gardening or the simple art of living your own life.

What--and whom--you find here depends largely on where you look. Partington Ridge, for instance, is Big Sur's answer to Park Avenue. Nicholas Roosevelt lives there; so does Sam Hopkins, of the Top O' the Mark (Hopkins Hotel) clan. Visiting luminaries--Dylan Thomas, Arthur Krock, Clare Boothe Luce, to name a few--are usually quartered on Partington, and when they sit down to eat they are not likely to be served wild mustard greens.

A little further down the coast, however, is the Murphy property, including Hot Springs, where the combined rental on nine dwellings is $176 a month. This place is a real menagerie, flavored with everything from bestiality to touch football. The barn rents for $15, the farmhouse for $40, and a shack in the canyon goes for $5. Emil White lives here, and if you could call him a publisher, the list of tenants would read something like this: one photographer, one bartender, one carpenter, one publisher, one writer, one fugitive, one metal-sculptor, one Zen Buddhist, one lawyer, and three people who simply defy description--sexually, socially or any other way. There are only two legitimate wives on the property; the other females are either mistresses, "companions," or hopeless losers. Until recently the shining light of this community was Dennis Murphy, the novelist, whose grandmother owns the whole shebang. When his book, <u>The Sergeant,</u> became a bestseller, he was hounded night and day, by people who would drive 100s of miles to jabber at him and drink his liquor. After a few months of this, he moved up the coast to Monterey.

Old Mrs. Murphy lives across the mountains in Salinas, and, luckily, gets to Big Sur only two or three times a year. Her husband, the late Dr. Murphy, conceived this place as a great health spa, a virtual bastion of decency and clean living. But something went wrong. During World War Two it became a haven for draft dodgers, and over the years it has evolved into a lonely campground for the morally deformed, a pandora's box of human oddities, and a popular sinkhole of idle decadence.

The whole of Big Sur will probably stop somewhere short of this. Miller, in one of his rosier moods, said this coast would one day be the Riviera of America. Maybe so, but it will take quite a while. And in the meantime it will be as good an imitation of Valhalla as this country can offer, and one of the finest places in the world to sit naked in the sun and read <u>The New York Times.</u>

TO WILLIAM J. KENNEDY, *SAN JUAN STAR:*

July 21, 1961
Big Sur, California

Dear William:

Your long-ago reaction to my comment about "oiling literary levers" was just another link in the long chain of your humor-failures. I could cite other examples—but, for the sake of decency, I won't. Anyway, I was kidding.

But I will take issue with you on the subject of what Styron has to say. As far as I'm concerned, he said it ten years ago. His last thing was a disappointment.[14]

14. Thompson is referring to William Styron's *The Long March* (New York: Vintage, 1957).

I think I told you that all your missives arrived. Many thanx. The pipe rack is hung, the cups are in use, and I was very happy, for several reasons, to get the *Stars*.[15] Now, if you can just send those damn books, I won't have to write to you anymore.

I am, incidentally, quite capable of reimbursing all costs of shipment. I have just whacked *Rogue* magazine for $350—a Big Sur article with Thompson photos—and am feeling like the Prince of the West. I know this doesn't sound like much money to you salaried folks, but to me it was like a fortune from the sky. It was not so much the money, but the feeling that I had finally cracked something, the first really valid indication that I might actually make a living at this goddamn writing. Right after I got the check I sent out every story I had, and if every one of them bounces it won't faze me a bit. I have tasted blood and it was OK.

The Rum Diary, since you ask, is more than halfway done. It is a novel that will be about 200 pages long and I have every reason to believe it will put me over the hump. It is set, of course, in Puerto Rico and I imagine you will not find all of it unfamiliar. Nor will Sontheimer.[16] In a twisted way, it will do for San Juan what *The Sun Also Rises* did for Paris. I expect to finish it around September. [. . .]

The map of San Juan was a real help, by the way. My bourgeois imagination could never produce anything like Calle O'Leary, Avenida Eduardo Conde, or Calle Dr. Stahl—nor could my memory hold everything that a map brings back to me; the midnight roar of a scooter on Calle Magdalena, the sweating wait for a bus in front of the University, or the morning sun on that long stretch of Munoz Rivera between Sixto Escobar stadium and El Morro. If my memory were as good as I'd claim it was if anyone asked me, I wouldn't need a map. But. . . .

As for the *Stars*, I thought the Dominican Republic coverage was championship stuff. You people are damn lucky to have a guy like Lidin down there; he's a real ace.[17] I'm not saying this solely on the basis of the Trujillo stuff, because I would have said the same thing last year when I was there.

As I look back over those issues, though, I think that "Vain Publicity Hound" item by Walter Priest was one of the best things I've read in years. His lead was a classic; it should be saved.

The rest of the paper—except for the little Pulitzer Prize note on the masthead—looked pretty much the same. Reston, McGill and Mauldin dress up the editorial page, but why not try a lineup like this: Reston, Lipp-

15. Kennedy had sent Thompson back issues of the *San Juan Star* to assist him in writing "The Rum Diary."
16. Sontheimer was the head of the Puerto Rican News Service.
17. Harold Lidin, the *Star*'s correspondent, covered the events surrounding the assassination of dictatorial Dominican president Rafael Trujillo in 1961.

mann and Herblock? Or knock off Reston and keep McGill. Reston is suffering these days from the Liberal Malady. Like all the others, he backed a
winner and found himself disarmed as of January 20th. When you're riding shotgun, it's bad form to shoot at the driver—a far cry from the good
old days when you could snipe from a distance.

But that's politics and I'm pretty bitter about it right now. JFK is a
phony, I think, and I'm not quite sure where that leaves us. As for me, I'm
writing my own platform. You will see it in The Rum Diary.

Bone was here for 24 hours last week, heading for San Francisco to
seek a job. It was good to see him and we had a few good words before
he left again. I've always thought Bone was basically one of the most decent people I've ever come across. His instincts are good, and no amount
of travel and sloppy sophistication can hide the fact that he's a good-
hearted hick with nowhere to go. I suppose he will come to a dull end,
but I hope not. When he left here he was right on the verge of marrying
some girl from New Zealand, but I understand she left for London without tying him up. As of now, he plans to meet her there in the fall or
early winter. [. . .]

Well, this has been a good excuse for not working on the novel for an
hour or so. My home-made beer has given me a shitting frenzy and rendered me incapable of writing anything but letters.

With the *Rogue* money I bought a pistol and a Doberman and a lot of
whiskey, and now a man up the road has put the sheriff on me for shooting while drunk and keeping a vicious dog.

In the long run I will probably lose, but until then I will set a mean
pace.

If you want to keep some books, do—and if you want to send them all
and let me pay, do that. Us rich writers don't give me a damn.

Noisily,
Hunter

TO ANN SCHOELKOPF:

*On duty as night guard at the baths, Thompson had gotten into a brutal
fight with a group of gay men from San Francisco.*

August 4, 1961
Big Sur, California

I am stopping in the middle of a goddamn chapter to write this & it won't
be long. It's 3:30 am here & I am rolling like a bastard train—but it suddenly dawned on me that I owed you a letter and a bit of news.

Anyway, I am about to be evicted for splitting a queer's head with that billy club I got from Fred. Maxine [Ambus] & me & that club tackled 15 queers in an outdoor bathhouse the other night & I was stomped, but not before doing extensive damage. Before that I shot out my windows and blasted all the glasses. The people who live around here are up in arms & the sheriff, who has been to me twice on the subject of violence, will undoubtedly come again.

I am sleeping most of the day and working all night every night in a desperate attempt to finish this book before they cast me adrift. It is a good one and I can't afford to lose control before I get it done.

Fred should be shot in the balls.[18] I don't blame him for trying to hang onto the money, but if I were you I'd deal hard and heavy with him until I got it. You can't play city rules when you live in a jungle. If you can't get the money, run him down and take a pound of flesh.

McGarr & Eleanor were here & it was terrible. They bitched 24 hours a day & several times I had to leave. Bone arrived with a woman in the middle of the McGarr visit & Maxine arrived at the end of it. It almost did me in. An hour before they left I fell on the bed in a fit of screaming. I was trying to hold it off, but couldn't. Bone was pretty good, if only by contrast, but then he only stayed a day & a night. I don't see how people tolerate visitors—especially one like me. It's a wonder I'm not dead.

I am surrounded by lunatics here, people screeching every time I pull a trigger, yelling about my blood-soaked shirt, packs of queers waiting to do me in, so many creditors that I've lost count, a huge Doberman on the bed, a pistol by the desk, time passing, getting balder, no money, a great thirst for all the world's whiskey, my clothes rotting in the fog, a motorcycle with no light, a landlady who's writing a novel on butcher-paper, wild boar in the hills and queers on the road, vats of homemade beer in the closet, shooting cats to ease the pressure, the jabbering of Buddhists in the trees, whores in the canyons, christ only knows if I can last it out.

Maxine is not happy out here. I don't see her often & every time I do we have drunken violence. I may shoot her.

A storm threatens, a shitrain, a torrent of toads. I may weather it, but only if I get some MONEY from those bastards who have it all. They say cannon is the final argument of kings and it may not be long before I present a royal plea for my share of the booty. I have found that most people harbor a real fear of having a little piece of lead blasted through their flesh & the drunker I get the more it amuses me.

18. Ann and Fred Schoelkopf were undergoing a brutal separation.

Semonin is due soon, steaming in from Aspen & scheduled to shove off for Tangiers on October 15. I will enjoy seeing him if I am still here. That's it for now—discreetly,

Hunter

TO MRS. V. A. MURPHY:

When Thompson's Big Sur *article appeared in* Rogue, *his landlady evicted him on the grounds that not only was he always drunk and pistol-crazed, but that he was spreading gossip in a smutty magazine.*

August 13, 1961
Big Sur, California

Dear Mrs. Murphy:
Your visit yesterday was quite a shock to me and I thought I should write this letter to assure you that I am not at all happy with the idea of being evicted and will go to great lengths to avoid it.

Primarily, I shall call a halt to my shooting and keep the demon rum at an arm's length—at least at a safe distance.

It's my considered opinion that reports of my wild behavior are greatly exaggerated. I have never threatened anyone with a whip, for instance, and indeed the only violence I can recall occurred when I was attacked by a large gang of homosexuals. Perhaps Mrs. Webb has visions outside the realm of religion—this would not surprise me at all.

At any rate, I shall fix Kay's[19] windows and, as you suggested, retreat down to the rocks or up in the canyon whenever I feel the need to shoot. You sounded very worried about the gun, but it is only a .22 caliber pistol, the smallest you can buy. It is duly registered in Sacramento and, since I never carry it concealed, I don't need that kind of permit. I assure you that it's quite legal.

Perhaps now, with summer coming to an end, it will be a bit more peaceful here. The only time I've had any difficulty was when the place was overrun with people. Also, when Mike and Dick[20] take over the lodge I think the situation will improve considerably down here.

Thanks for your patience. You might be interested to know that I sold a short story today and am more than halfway through my novel. For the next few months I shall work exclusively on that and abjure all violence and wild drinking bouts. Then, when I want some excitement, I'll take a

19. Thompson had shot out his neighbor's windows with his .22 caliber pistol.
20. Dick Price, who would become Michael Murphy's partner in the Esalen Institute.

vacation in the West Indies and drink rum and fight with sharks. Until then, I remain,

> very peacefully,
> Hunter S. Thompson

TO FRANK ROBINSON, *ROGUE:*

At long last Thompson had sold a short story— "Easy Come, Easy Go"— to a magazine. The triumph encouraged him to keep working on "The Rum Diary."

> August 14, 1961
> Big Sur, California

Frank Robinson
Rogue
1236 Sherman Ave.
Evanston, Ill.

Dear Mr. Robinson:

You'll be happy to know that your check for "Easy Come, Easy Go" has paid for a .44 Magnum, "the ultimate handgun." It will knock a motor-block off its mounts, destroy a small tree, and disembowel a boar at 100 yards. No man should be without one.

Your check for the Big Sur article paid for a .22 Magnum, but this has rapidly become obsolete except for target-shooting and queer-baiting. It has also—with the help of a large Doberman, which also came out of that check—brought me to a condition of eviction. It will be my fifth eviction in three years, probably a record of some sort.

Now, after beating my chest and showing my scars, we come to what I hope will not turn out to be a problem.

In the 1961 issue of *Writer's Yearbook*, the *Rogue* blurb says you pay five cents a word for fiction and that your limit is 4,000 words. This, plus your editing work on the Big Sur article, evokes to me the possibility that you may at this very moment be condensing "Easy Come, Easy Go" to 5,000 words—or perhaps you have paid a decent price for a story that is abnormally long, but that you are going to use anyway.

I hope I am right on the second count, because I don't think my story will be very effective with three-eighths of it chopped away. Granted, the story is a long one, but I don't think it drags anywhere and it scares the hell out of me to think that it might be cut up to fit your space requirements.

I'm probably jumping the gun on you here, conjuring up demons that may not exist. I also understand your eternal hassle with space problems. On the other hand, I hope you understand that, long after *Rogue's* space problems of any given month in 1961 are a thing of the past, a fellow named Hunter S. Thompson is going to have to live with the published version of a short story called "Easy Come, Easy Go."

Let me stress here, that, at this stage of the game, I am perfectly happy to sell a story for $250. As a matter of fact I am damned happy to sell a story at all. But to have it cut up . . . well, Frank, you said in your letter of August 2 that you were "well aware . . . how authors feel about edited work," so this shouldn't surprise you.

Anyway, why don't you give me the word so I can relax.

Sincerely,
Hunter S. Thompson

TO WILLIAM J. KENNEDY:

Kennedy quit the San Juan Star *but had decided to stay in Puerto Rico to work on his novel.*

August 20, 1961
Big Sur

Okay, so you were fired. It happens to the best of us. I'll pass the word to Bone, who will probably write Dinhofer and tell him that Thompson is spreading rumors, etc. . . .

It's kind of honorable to tilt with the Rotary Club, but piss-poor when they shoot you down . . . yeah. And they'll do it, too, the bastards.

You might like Eugene, Oregon. It's amazing how this woodsy business gets to a man. I spent all afternoon in the hills with my new Doberman, shooting and drinking wine out of a canteen and looking for a house site. I've already bought a pistol and am going in tomorrow to buy a rifle. And I buy the best. You bet. Anyway, I'm also thinking of heading up north to look for some property. Denne[21] has some up there and says it's great. I can't say. If not the coast, maybe Montana. Plenty of bears there. Also elk and big cats. A man could shoot all day. And not be arrested.

They're trying to arrest me here. Also trying to evict me. But I'm rolling in money now and they're awed. After months of insane poverty I have made $630 in the past six weeks. I am so used to poverty that I can waste most of it and not know the difference. Hence the Doberman ($100), the pistol ($70) and the rifle ($110). Plenty of ammunition too. When it starts, I'll be ready. You bet.

Last sale was my first fiction—a long short story to *Rogue* for $250. All these things I've sold were returned to me by my former agent as unsalable. Beware of agents.

21. Denne Petitclerc, a *San Francisco Chronicle* reporter, was a close friend of William Kennedy's.

I think—god, I hope—I have a good one now. Sent him part of the book and he wants the first half and an outline as soon as I can rustle it up. I could send it now, but I'm scared. It looked pretty good before I got this letter, but all of a sudden I think it needs more work. So I'm faced with a 150 page rewrite at jack-rabbit speed. And I'll probably still be scared when I finish it. Sooner or later I guess a man has to put his cards on the table and call. Or maybe he calls first—it's been so long since I had money that I've forgotten.

I admire your plunge, if that it is, and hope you can muster the balls and the decent pages—or maybe just the salable ones—to make it over the hump. After that, of course, it's downhill all the way—but downhill with money and a publisher, which makes a difference.

I imagine your stay in PR will help you to handle your money wisely— live modestly, my boy, "only poets and thieves can exercise free will, and most of them die young." Right?

How about a man who's both a poet *and* a thief—and a hellfire good shot as well. A man like that could hold out for a long time. With a cheque now and then. No matter how you look at it, if the mailman ain't good to you, that's it. Back to the job. Long hours, plenty of bullshit, steady pay— then die and make room for somebody else.

Well, what else can I say? Not much, I guess. I don't talk much anymore, anyway. Semonin is coming up in two or three weeks and I guess I'll talk a while then.[22] Or maybe I'll shoot him for his own good—and everybody else's good. A man like that could disturb people—running around loose and yelling about freedom. Might as well be a nigger, some kind of goddamn red. That Semonin is a bad apple all right—a hell of an example for the kids, too.

I haven't read *To Kill a Mockingbird*. Is it worth $2 ½ million? Somehow, the title don't move me. I like something like "The Rum Diary." Now there's a title, by god. Book-of-the-Month Club? Hell yes. Movie? No doubt. A book like that could make a man rich.

Well it had better, by christ. I'm not about to wait much longer. If a typewriter won't do it . . . well, maybe a .44 Magnum will. Big noise, big money, eh? I guess that's the way it goes.

Well, in closing, I guess all I can say is shit. What else?

When you write, send $2 ½ million. I need a few acres and some dogs and some guns and some whiskey and a few cars and a boat and a donation to CORE and god knows what else. It's hell to be needy.

Okay,
Hunter

22. Paul Semonin had gotten deeply involved in the civil rights movement and leftist politics. He was arranging to go to Ghana, to study firsthand the anti-imperialist movement of Kwame Nkrumah.

TO MRS. CHAPMAN:

Having been evicted by Mrs. Murphy, Thompson tried to rent a secluded nearby cabin to finish "The Rum Diary."

September 29, 1961
Big Sur, California

Dear Mrs. Chapman:

Last week Jo Hudson[23] and I came up to your place to see about hunting some pigs. You weren't there, and after a short talk with Frank Trotter,[24] we left. I'm sorry to have missed you, because this letter would be a lot easier to write if you had some idea who I am. And vice-versa.

Anyway, from the little Jo has told me about you I thought it might not be a complete waste of time to send you a letter and hope for the best.

Briefly, I am a writer—not the beatnik or barroom variety, but a beast who actually puts words on paper with the idea of selling them. I am also—as of October 27—an evicted writer. At the moment I am living in the big Murphy house at Slate Springs. As it happens, the current issue of *Rogue* magazine carries an article by me, and the article includes a fairly mild description of the Murphy property and its varied inhabitants.* Apparently the description was not mild enough for Mrs. Murphy, who read the article yesterday and served me an eviction notice at one o'clock today. Fast work for an 89-year-old woman, I'd say—but as much as I admire the efficiency, it puts me in something of a bind.

I've been living here since January and for most of that time I've been working on a novel, half of which is finished and currently in the hands of an agent. I need at least two months and possibly three to finish the book, and, unfortunately, October 27 is barely a month away. Since I'm just a few notches above being broke, I can't afford to move any distance with a fiancée, a big Doberman and a houseful of gear.

So that leaves me to find a nearby place where I can sleep, eat and write for the month of November, and maybe the first two weeks of December. I have to be in Louisville, Kentucky (my home) for Christmas, so that gives me a definite deadline. Jo mentioned that you had several unoccupied cabins on your place, and it occurred to me that I might rent one of them for that length of time.

This doesn't mean that I want to descend on you with a family, a dog and a mountain of personal belongings. I will probably put my fiancée to

23. Hudson was a first-rate sculptor known for making Alexander Calderish metal pieces. He became Thompson's closest Big Sur friend. Together they hunted wild boar and started building a sloop to sail around the world.
24. Trotter owned land at Big Sur where he sometimes allowed Thompson and others to hunt wild boar.

work in San Francisco, so all I would bring to your place would be a dog, a typewriter, a rifle and a sleeping bag. I wouldn't mention the rifle except that Jo tells me you could use a little help in getting rid of the pigs. I would like nothing better than 4 or 6 weeks of hunting pigs in the afternoon and writing at night.

As a matter of fact, I write only at night, so I'd be happy to do just about any kind of work for you during the day—from hunting pigs, to chopping wood, to . . . whatever needs to be done. I'd refer you to Mrs. Murphy, who—until recently—would have told you what a model tenant I am. But, according to Dennis, the very mention of my name causes her to break into a high-pitched chattering whine. I could refer you to Ed Culver, whose tremendous decency (and credit) has kept me going for almost a year—or Dick Hartford—or Dennis Murphy—or Jo Hudson—or Judge Crater—or Winnie Ruth Judd—or . . .

Anyway, I'm in pretty grim need of a place to finish the book, and if you think there's any chance that we could work something out with one of your cabins I'd like to come by and talk about it. Let me assure you again that I'd definitely be gone by Christmas, and maybe sooner. Or if it happened that you needed the place for your own guests on the weekends—or if anything came up that would make my presence a problem—I'd move out with a few hours' notice. When it comes to quick movement I'm pretty flexible—hell, I have to be, living the way I do—but I'm not flexible enough to write half a good novel, then quit and roam around the coast for a few months, looking for a place to settle and start again. That ain't the way books get written.

So that's my pitch. I want to use one of your cabins for a month or so; I'm willing to work a few hours a day, pay a reasonable rent, and keep out of your way while I'm there. If the idea doesn't unnerve you—coming, as it does, from someone you've never seen—please drop me a line and tell me what you think.

> Thanks,
> Hunter S. Thompson
> Big Sur

*copy of offending article is enclosed. Keep it if you want; if not, send it on back. If nothing else, it will give you an idea of what I look like.

TO VIRGINIA THOMPSON:

Deemed persona non grata by Big Sur's artistic community, Thompson contemplated returning to Louisville to finish "The Rum Diary."

October 13, 1961
Big Sur

Dear Mom:

Got your letter yesterday and have spent 24 hours pondering whether or not to chance a trip to L.A. If I were sure Davison would be there I'd give it a try, but I couldn't stand going all the way down there for nothing. I'd have to hitchhike down and back and this road is a hitch-hiker's graveyard. That $125 you sent was gone in no time at all. I live almost entirely on credit and whenever I get a lump sum most of it is already spent.

Mrs. Murphy sent me an eviction notice the day she saw the *Rogue* article. We have to be out on October 27 and so far it looks like no other house is available. Not to me, anyway. Everyone mentioned in that article is agitating for my immediate departure. I am dealing with two groups; one, composed mainly of beatniks, queers and pacifists, wants me run clear out of the state—the other, more diverse, wants me to stay but they can't think where.

A good many people have offered me places to stay, but in every case they would be too cramped or uncomfortable for me to write much of anything except letters. Some of the places have no electricity, others have no plumbing, others are tents and barns and garages. Unless something better comes up before October 27 I am seriously considering a trip to Louisville; it's the only place I can think of where I could have enough privacy to get the book done. Even before the eviction notice I was thinking about coming home for Christmas, so I would have to spend the transportation money anyway. I can probably pawn my rifle for the price of a train ticket. Sandy would either stay here, or go to New York until after Christmas. Maybe she could come down to Louisville if I were still there for Christmas week.

As usual, my plans are contingent on whatever money comes in the mail. I have a story out and the novel is still with the agent—no word yet—so I can make no definite plans until I'm certain whether or not I'll be broke when it comes time to be evicted. If I get any money, I'll go into Carmel or Monterey and rent a small apt. until the book is finished.

I know the idea of my coming home for six weeks or two months will set your hair on end, but you'll just have to take my word that if I come home to work, I'll work. I'm too close to completing a good novel to let it go by the boards with a lot of stupid socializing.

Anyway, let's leave that subject until I find out what's going to happen here. We are definitely out of this place on the 27th, but something else may turn up between now and then. If not, I'll start for Louisville around November 1 and stay until I finish the book. Barring a collapse of the imagination, it should be done by Christmas and possibly before, depending on how much I can concentrate on what I'm doing. I'll know more in a week or ten days and I'll write again as soon as I decide.

Thanks tremendously for the $125. It was like a gift from God.

Love,
Hunter

TO ALFRED KAZIN:

Thompson regarded Kazin's controversial "Alfred Kazin in Puerto Rico," which first appeared in the February 1960 Commentary, *as the best writing ever on Puerto Rico. Thus he sought his former instructor's help in getting the Great Puerto Rican Novel published. Kazin obliged.*

October 14, 1961

Dear Mr. Kazin:

I hate to badger people for favors when I'm not sure what I have to offer in return, but at this point I'm ready to badger just about anybody who can do me any good.

In brief, I'd like you to tell me who would be likely to publish my novel, The Rum Diary.

You got the nod for several reasons, primarily because I was free-lancing in Puerto Rico last year when your rancid bombshell was reprinted in the *San Juan Star*. In it, you said "an American Somerset Maugham" could do a colorful novel on present-day P.R. Although I hesitate to bill myself as an American Maugham, I'm about nine-tenths through a novel that was just getting underway when your article appeared. Ever since then I've been using it as a morale-booster; whenever I think I'm being a little rough on the Puerto Ricans I read the article again and I know I still have leeway. At any rate, the thing was a classic and, in the vicious days that followed its publication, I made a mental note to get hold of you if I ever needed anyone to run interference for my novel.

That's overstating it a bit, because all I really need is a few names—say, three decent editors at publishing houses not dedicated to cookbooks, boozy memoirs, or the rib-tickling humors of children and animals. As you probably know, I could waste a year submitting this book to people who would brush it off like dandruff. This is what I want to avoid. You might tell me to get an agent, but my experience with agents has been unbelievably bad. I've managed to sell enough on my own to keep from getting a job, but agents treat me like the son of Judas.

I'm enclosing some excerpts from The Rum Diary. I hope you like them at least well enough to steer me to a likely publisher. God knows it's difficult enough to write a book without having to face, in total ignorance, those vultures on Madison Avenue. I don't care who publishes the book, as long as they put it between covers and give me enough money to pay the rent. As it is, my rent is $15 a month, but I'm being evicted on October 27, so it will probably go up considerably.

For the record, the manuscript of The Rum Diary is half-finished in the final draft. I have submitted it once, to an agent who found the characters "uninteresting." Maybe they are; maybe the book is hopeless, but I'd like to try a few editors before I give up. If you could send me a few names, I'd certainly appreciate it.

> Thanks,
> Hunter S. Thompson
> Manor House
> Big Sur, California

TO EUGENE W. MCGARR:

> October 19, 1961
> Big Sur

Well, McGarr, I know you want to hear about the high life in Big Sur, so I want you to sit back with whatever mass of meat and pulp you must have in your hands at the moment and hear about things as they are. First, I have been evicted—and, second, I have rejected the eviction *in toto*. I know this will give you pleasure.

The article came out in *Rogue* and Mrs. Murphy saw it as a vicious exposé of her property—hence, an eviction notice some 20 hours later. I have pondered this notice for some three weeks and now see that my only course is to sit on my ass and type until they can muster enough sheriffs to carry me off. I only wish this letter could find you as it might have before the days of your Mental Fatness, so I could invite you out for the fun. I have good reason to expect that the next month or two will not be devoid of entertainment.

My eviction date is October 27, six days from now, and tomorrow I will make a new batch of beer that will not be bottled for ten days, nor drinkable for fifteen. I intend to drink that batch in this room, and perhaps even swill the next batch before they do me in. Because they *will* do me in, McGarr, just as they'll do you in—or perhaps I should say, "they would have done you in"—and finish us all off in a blaze of shit and oppression. In the words of Mr. Mailer, "the shits are killing us," but I think Mailer has lost faith in the battle—the dirty fun of losing, as it were, the loose clean feeling of not giving a roaring fuck about winning or losing or anything else. Mailer has learned to take himself seriously, and any man who does that is fair game for the shits.

You've done it yourself, McGarr, and it's made you duller, more posed and all too obvious. Somewhere behind that, I think, lurks the half-wild shadow of an original man. I hope so, anyway. Because when you lose that, you're through.

Your theories about my life here are just about what I expected, so I won't waste much time on them. Suffice it to say that you're right about my sadism having free rein in Big Sur. So much so, in fact, that I can get it out of my system with no trouble at all. Now, instead of dissipating my energy in a stupid search for excitement, I can flash it off with two hours in the hills and approach the rest of my day in a rested frame of mind. If this makes me "sick," so be it. Terms like that one have just about lost their meaning anyway, except for people who think a word is a fact.

As I said in my last letter, Semonin was here and I enclose a relic of his visit. You should see him soon and I want you to show him this photo and see what he says. I will write him as soon as I know he's in Spain. Those trips have a way of going off in strange directions. Your talk of Europe makes the place sound horribly trite, so trite in fact that I have just about given up any interest I might have had in making the trip. I see Europe as a crowded museum, a quaint showcase for a world no longer up to par. My best to the Germans, god damn their cheap militant hearts. If it comes to war and bombs and that business, I only hope I can get a few Germans in my sights. I sense a decency about the Russians, but the Germans strike me as a race of two-legged sharks—clever, efficient and dangerously stupid.

Now for news—Maxine had a wreck and had 100 stitches in her head. I haven't seen her; the word comes from Clancy, who has been evicted from his San Francisco hovel. That's about all the news I can think of. Maxine is going east, she says, presumably for ever. God only knows what will become of her; I'd rather not ponder it.

That's about the ballgame, McGarr. I'll be here until they root me out. Send a few words of abuse when you get a chance. I am thinking of sailing to Hawaii and a hunting trip to Vancouver, then Mexico and South America. Chile may have what it takes, whatever in hell that may be. I'm beginning to wonder. What does it take? I guess some of us will find out. And I leave you with that.

Curiously, HST

TO WILLIAM J. KENNEDY:

With tensions in Big Sur running high, Thompson retreated to Louisville while Sandy headed to New York to earn some holiday money. Thompson, still trying to find a home for "The Rum Diary," offered Kennedy some tips on the world of New York publishing.

October 21, 1961
Big Sur, California

Willie—got your card yesterday & was taken aback by the arrow on the front, pointing to "our apartment." Whose apartment? Have you moved back to Chinatown? I guess it's not too odd, considering your San Juan background. Who are you stringing for down there?

Anyway, don't send any books to Big Sur. Hang onto them until I give a new word. I have been evicted. The old lady who owns this place didn't like her mention in *Rogue*. As of now it looks like we'll be moving east in about ten days. Sandy is heading to New York to work, and me to Louisville to finish the book. It's been going badly for a month or so; I'm writing more and saying less. The agent refused it, saying the characters were "uninteresting." There's no dealing with that kind of criticism—it's about the last thing I expected. "A perfectly acceptable novel," he added, "but. . . ." And so we beat on, boats against the current. . . .

Hope you are having better luck with yours. Viking is a decent outfit, I think, but a tough nut to crack. I might suggest to you a lady editor at a press called Appleton-Century-Crofts—Bobs Pinkerton—who found it within herself to treat my last book as if it was something I'd worked on, rather than something I'd clipped out of a magazine and submitted as an afterthought. She sent a reader's report, plus a long letter of her own. Then she answered some questions and offered to look at the book again if and when I got it straightened out. I never even finished the thing, of course, so I can't wrap this up with a happy ending. But it's a thought.

A rumor has reached me—to get off on another subject—that the editorship of the *Tortola Times* is up for grabs. Could you check this for me? I don't even know who to write. With your vast contacts in the Carib press, I thought you might know somebody over there. The paper is a farce, as I recall, but just the kind of thing I'd like if they paid even a minimum salary. If you can find out anything, write me at the Louisville address. Louisville is my Albany.

I'm assuming that this letter will reach you via San Juan. Have you finished the book? If so, what now? If you get any offers not lucrative or prestigious enough for your tastes, keep in mind that I'll be looking for employment, assignments, paid travel, etc. as of about January 1. I've now added photography to my list of skills—those *Rogue* photos were mine—and can tackle just about anything with a little zip to it.

Speaking of zip, Semonin should be in Tangier about now. He was here for a week, a fine week full of drinking and shooting, and we passed the time in a frenzy of incestuous criticism. He's about 150 pages into a novel, a laborious tormented document that needs a lot of work and relaxation to make it edible. Of course my tastes are narrow, so this is just an opinion.

Anyway, let me hear from you, and hang on to the books. When my plans begin to gel, I'll send word. Or maybe they'll never gel, maybe I'll never be anywhere long enough for you to send the books to me. Time and luck will tell.

Hello to Dana and kudos to the children. Balls to everybody else.

HST

TO ELEANOR MCGARR:

November 10, 1961
Louisville, Kentucky

Eleanor—

Ah yes, around and around we go, forever seeking the lost axis, the big Equalizer that Santa Claus took with him when he died. And now, lo and behold, I crouch in the bowels of the Highlands, seeking something, mostly waiting, thinking, killing time, procrastinating, drinking instant coffee by the gallon, reading and re-reading my half-born book and wondering now and then if I will ever write anything but the occasional bright word of the horny traveler. Five good pages in a 15-page story might not win the pennant, but it's a hardnose average and I'll buy it any day. On the other hand, 10 good pages in 200 (with 100 to go) is twice as many good pages as five, but as an average it sucks wind. I guess the moral is pretty obvious—write short-shorts—and that'll do for a while, but every now and then a man needs to launch a real wadbuster and that's about the way I'm feeling. You can hit the target all day with a .22, but when you want to knock a motor-block off its mounts you move in close with a .44 Magnum. Yeah.

Christ, the mail just came and that bastard Ed the mailman[25] whacked me with a bill for $76 for the month of October. It's about twice what I owe, at best, but god only knows how I can dispute it, with him holding all the figures. This fucking debt is driving me nuts—every time I turn around somebody is dunning me for something. If I don't make some money soon I'm going to start stealing it. This bill has ruined my day.

25. Ed Norman was the rural postman who would also deliver groceries on credit from Monterey.

On top of that, I left a box full of my life's work in Glenwood Springs—all my stories, articles, photos, letters, everything I've ever written is in that box and it's about 4 days overdue by RR Express. If they've lost it I think that will just about do the trick, I'll just give up and get a job.

Well, enough of that. It's raining in the Highlands, a stiff pounding on the roof outside my window. First rain I've seen since April. Memo went to meet her maker and I am now in her room, with Agar on the bed and a big rack of pistols and whips and clubs on the wall, a big vat of beer working on the radiator and a whole shelf full of bullet-making equipment. I got that big .357 Magnum that Joel was selling, the one you saw when you went into town with us. Now it hangs useless on the wall beside my head, a dirty black hog-buster and all the hogs 2000 miles away. I may sell the bastard.

Through the empty house floats the voice of Joanie Baez, an eerie sound to my restless ears. I expect to look out the window and see the hills or the ocean—but no dice, only Ransdell Avenue, grey and wet and full of so many ghosts and memories that I get the Fear whenever I go outside. At night, beneath the ageless streetlight, I see Ching and Duke Rice and David Comfort on a red bike with no fenders, Ollie Spencer leaning out the window of that blue Chevy and Pinky beside him like a magpie, Barnes with a cigarette, frogging Ching with malicious glee, a shout, the sound of a bike falling on the curb, then the shallow roar of a Chevy engine as Ollie bucks off up the hill with Barnes on the fender and Ching's hat beside him on the seat.[26] Mean childhood laughter and a bruised arm, streetlights and elm trees and a red bike with no fenders, the taste of a secret pipe on a winter walk, a green sweater with a dirty white C on the chest, no homework and a million lazy tomorrows stretched out like a rubber band that somebody will let go of pretty soon and then it won't be a million at all, but only a few, a rotten withering few before the big hump. And after that, the craziness.

I think I've put my finger on it—the craziness. Over the hump to Crazyville, talk a while, then hurry off, first South, then West, and finally East. God help us—North is all we have left.

I'll crack my spleen if I keep talking like this. You may wonder how I got here. Don't know if you got my quick letter from the train. Anyway, I was evicted because of that article, a friend of Ted Klemens[27] showed up and hauled our traveling gear to San Francisco, Sandy flew East courtesy of papa and is now working in New York for a collection agency, and Agar and I went to Aspen. An alarming queerness in that move—believe it or not, the

---

26. References are to childhood friends of Thompson's.
27. Sports editor of the *San Juan Star*.

only car I could get in San Francisco was going to Aspen. Some woman named Jonas, who came to San Francisco and bought a whole carload of oriental straw goods, all of it delicate, then flew back to Aspen and waited for somebody stupid enough to pay for all the gas it would take to deliver the shit to her door. There, of all people, come I—needing cheap transportation for my gear and my dog, agreeing over the phone to drive this car as far as Aspen for an added bonus of $15 from the agency because they couldn't find anybody else. I had built a huge crate for Agar and when I found all that shit in the car I strapped the crate on top and stuffed it with birdcages, parasols, balsa-wood stools, rice-paper doilies, and took off across the desert at top speed with Agar on the seat beside me and all my gear in the trunk. I moved in a manner that reminded me of the Fat City—with that huge crate on top, the car tended to move in a crabwise fashion whenever I headed into the wind. On a reach, I would leap 3 or 4 feet to the leeward each time I hit a bump. Needless to say, I got about 12 miles to the gallon, even in a Lark. I arrived in Aspen with $2, drunk as a loon, sliding violently in the snow, and found a man named Ivan Abrams. I figured I would find a team of hardnose travelers to take me in for the night, but there was nothing. I fell on Abrams, carrying a gallon of wine, and after a bit of drinking he directed me to Peggy Clifford,[28] who saved the day. She gave me drink, offered me a couch, and took me over to see the Jonas woman, who was drunk and told me to come back tomorrow for my $50 deposit. I was given more drink at that place and finally, upon coming back to Peggy's house to eat, I collapsed in a drunken heap—literally fell apart, disintegrated before her eyes. The next morning, with no time to see the Jonas woman, I fled into Glenwood to get the train. Peggy gave me the money, which I think was yours, and said she would get it back from Jonas. I figured she knew what she was doing and since she didn't seem too eager to have me around for another night, I moved on. No word from her, so I guess things went off well. Had no time even to see your house—I was going to go up with the big pistol and put the Fear in that guy who moved in. You may have trouble on that, but Peggy seems competent enough, so I imagine she'll get the money if it's there to be got. If not, I may head west again after Xmas, and I can stop by and bellow at him until he does something.

You know the rest—train to Chicago, Agar & crate in baggage car, 10-hour layover, which I used to protest editing of my work (*Chicago Tribune*) and trace a lost story (*Playboy*)—also to see *La Dolce Vita*, which I recommend. Then sleep to Lou.

28. Clifford lived in Aspen from 1953 to 1979, was a columnist for the *Aspen Times* for twelve years, and owned the local bookstore. She and Thompson later became close friends when he moved to Woody Creek.

Spent the past weekend in Nashville, went down with family for UK-Vandy [University of Kentucky vs. Vanderbilt] game and got drunk with Davison and a bunch of his head-knocking friends. Now back here to The Rum Diary and the ghosts. I have called nobody but [Hume] Logan and venture out of the house only to run Agar in the park. Pawned the rifle this morning & put $10 down on a Luger. The guns will be my undoing.

I have before me your last letter, written in Louisville. I tried to get it published, but it was rejected on the grounds that most of it was cribbed from Alfred Kazin and Scott Fitzgerald. Sorry. Try again, you know—and all that shit.

McGarr's letter came via Big Sur and, as usual, I cannot get hold of it. What the fuck is he doing with himself? Eating—I know that, he always mentions that. And drinking, of course. Aside from that, he mentions nothing except brochure-type descriptions of the landscape. He berates me, of course, something about my style this time—and my attitude—but all that is pretty old by now and, besides, I'm a little weary of being edited. Anyway, try to find out what he's up to, what he thinks he means, and send word.

As for me, I mean only what I say, and it's never quite right. I'll keep at it here until Xmas or so, then shove off. Where, I can't say. One of the main factors will be your report from Europe. McGarr has been there for more than a year now, and all I know about the place is what it looks like and how much it costs. I want to know if it has any balls—that's the main thing and you'll have to tip me off.

If not Europe, I may retreat to the West. If not Big Sur, then up to Idaho or maybe the north California coast. All this precludes the possibility that somebody might publish the book. If so, things will be different. Jo Hudson should finish the boat by June and may go out to Hawaii, then back to Vancouver for the shooting in those islands, bear and that sort of thing: caribou, elk. If the boat holds up, he wants to take it to Europe, which would be the right way to do it, I think. All this is leading up to the fact that I'm keeping an eye on him; if the boat works, I may hire on. The ever-present alternative is to hire myself out to whomever and wherever will pay me, and hang on till I'm fired. About the first of December I will start casting around. Until then, I'm buried here in this room.

Your comments on Big Sur and your stay made that week even better in retrospect than it was at the time. But it was a wadbuster, even then. Sorry I couldn't send the meat, but it would have had to go to Malaga, Am. Exp., and I didn't figure they'd be real happy to keep it until you showed up. It was damn good, by the way. When you get back we'll get another one—no rifles this time, only pistols and hobnail boots.

Send the word and tell McGarr I'll answer his letter as soon as I get drunk.

Hunter

TO ARTICLES EDITOR, *ATLANTIC MONTHLY:*

Fascinated by right-wing politics, Thompson pitched a piece on the John Birch Society; the Atlantic Monthly *was not interested.*

November 21, 1961
2437 Ransdell Ave.
Louisville 4, Kentucky

Dear Sir:

For the past week or so I've been mulling over an article idea that might interest you. It concerns the John Birch Society—not the obvious things like facts and figures, but the people and the reasons that prompted them to join.

I began thinking about this when I came back to Louisville after four years of living like a vagrant writer in New York, California and the Caribbean. This naturally altered my perspective a bit, and when I came back to the town where I spent the first 20 years of my life, most of my old friends appeared to be arch-reactionaries. Most of them seemed to have got that way almost by default; they didn't really want to talk about it, but if I pressed them they would invariably come up with the ancient and honorable Jeffersonian concepts that most of us were taught in high school. They were pretty frankly bored with the whole business and they wanted to talk about something else—maybe their new children, their jobs as bank trainees and salesmen, or the frightful possibility of their reserve units being activated.

So much for the majority. You will find them everywhere and quite enough has been written about them—the sluggish American, may he rest in peace.

But others were more vocal and far more interesting. One, in particular, is the fiery young turk of his local John Birch cell. His parents, whom I know and like, were incipient Birchers before anyone ever heard of either Birch or the Society. This threw me a little off balance, because I'd worked up an active distaste for what I considered a pack of neo-nazis and I was not sure how to take these people. I drove out to their home on the river, up the winding driveway to their house, and when I sat down in their living room with a glass of bourbon and one of their beagles gnawing on my foot it was hard to see them as nazis and rabid slanderers.

This is what I'd like to write about—John Birch at home, as it were. I've been to a meeting, but you don't learn much there; not about the people, anyway. Most of them don't say anything at all. They just sit there and listen to the few champions who tell them the score and what it means. Only when they relax at home can you find out why they went to the meeting, why they joined in the first place, their own ideas on where this is headed, their doubts, their occasional uncertainties ("Is Ike really a Red?") and, in short, that vital third dimension that you never get in newspapers.

Because a "Bircher" is more than just that: he can be a father, an employer, a doctor, he usually has children and he worries about the kind of world they'll grow up in, he's certainly not sluggish and almost always articulate, and more often than not he's financially and socially secure. Yet he pays his dues, faithfully attends his cell meetings, and there's no telling what else he might do if he thought—or was convinced—that the need were dire enough.

As I look back over the first page of this letter, the language seems pretty stilted. So I'm enclosing a short thing I did recently for the *Chicago Tribune*. If nothing else, it is not stilted.

As for me, I'm a writer, a journalist, a photographer, a traveler, a seeker of some kind—and, generally, anything I have to be. If it occurs to you that I'm trying to sell you a slam at the "extreme right," forget it. I'm not. Politics can be interesting, but I prefer people.

Anyway, if the article interests you, please let me know as soon as possible. I'm going to write it anyway, but it would help if I knew where to aim it. Also, please return the *Chicago Tribune* clipping.

Thanks,
Hunter S. Thompson

TO MIKE MURPHY:

When Thompson arrived in Louisville, a letter from Mike Murphy was waiting for him—demanding repayment of a debt. Thompson immediately paid up, and their friendship resumed in fine fashion.

December 8, 1961
2437 Ransdell Ave.
Louisville 4, Kentucky

Dear Mike:

Maybe your humor is a bit too subtle for me, old man, because that second letter of yours struck me as an extremely hairy thing. Like finding a toad in the mailbox. Also a hell of a way to wake up; here, as out there, I wake up just in time to catch the noon mail. No fun at breakfast that day.

Anyway, it was damn good to get your third, and if I weren't so damn sure I was right about that bill, I'd say something like, "Shucks, take a few records, Mike old boy." As a matter of fact I finally had to threaten to do just that before Sandy would send me the 5 to send on to you. She ain't much with the figures. But this clears my conscience, and—with your last letter, plus finally getting Ed [the mailman] paid off—I can think of Big Sur and smile for a change. I don't mind being dunned by thieves and hustlers and horny-handed merchants, but it gives me the creeps when I start getting letters like that from friends. As you could probably see by my careful editing on the last letter, I pondered it long and hard. I couldn't figure out what had got into you. But, obviously, I missed the humor.

Needless to say, I retract the snaps and the snarls and the few snide digs I recall slipping in here and there. It was downright christian of you to bounce back like you did and the first thing I'm going to do tomorrow morning is go downtown and tear up that notice I posted in the Queer Bar. If . . . ah . . . if anybody shows up wanting the free drinks and the courtesy escort service to the baths, tell 'em . . . ah . . . just say it was a joke. Heh. Yeah, that notice was put up by some paranoid writer, some nut.

As for other things, they're all fine except the novel. It has to be totally revised and rewritten. I finished it last week and have spent this week just staring at it. On Monday I start over. It's a good life if you don't get the piles.

The beer is a big hit here and I am hard pressed to keep up with the demand. Doing a lot of shooting, mostly at rabbits, but the meat all comes from the grocery. Instead of that awful skinning after the hunt, I relax in front of a fire and drink whiskey and tell horrible lies about 600-lb. boars with 9-inch fangs, all of them charging and wounded and crazy for the kill, and me with only the big Magnum—which I carry around on my hip and even shoot the damn thing at rabbits. When I first appeared with it they just stared and said, "Gawd, Looka thet!" And every time I miss a rabbit I have to say very quickly: "God damn! Don't you people have any boar around here?" And they just shake their heads—all except for the guy who hit the rabbit with a 12-gauge shotgun; he walks over and picks it up, wiping his mouth with his glove so it doesn't look like he's grinning. And then we go back and drink and talk about old times.

Driving down to Renfro Valley this weekend to do a short piece for the *Chicago Tribune* and maybe get some photos for a magazine article. You and Mrs. Webb would love it there—it's the traditional Sat. night Kentucky barn dance down on the edge of the coal country where the life expectancy of any sheriff is about 2 weeks. I am taking a pistol along with the camera—armpit holster and all. Barring a disaster, it should be a good drunk with the hillbillies.

Until the next hunt—HST

TO NEWS EDITOR, *LOUISVILLE TIMES:*

A month earlier two rival factions claiming to be the legitimate government of the Congo had been united after more than a year of civil war. It would, however, be another year before Katanga province's move toward secession was put down.

December 11, 1961
2437 Ransdell Ave.
Louisville, Kentucky

News Editor (foreign)
Louisville Times

Dear Sir:

The column-one story on page 2 of today's *Times* (final home [edition]) is enough to make a man wonder what the hell you people are thinking about down there. Above the story is a 3-col photo of "rebellious Katangans and white mercenaries (offering) groundfire as UN planes attack the Elizabethville post office. . . ."

Then in col 3 of the story ("Tshombe Charges . . .") we see: "Newsmen denied that UN planes had attacked Elizabethville post office yesterday, as was reported by a telephone operator in the E-ville exchange. Evidently the operator had been warned a UN bomber was overhead and took this to mean the place was under attack."

I have a feeling that maybe that operator wasn't so stupid, after all. Who the hell are the abovementioned "newsmen" working for? This "end justifies the means" operation in the Katanga is tough enough to stomach as it is, without the added burden of muddled and half-blind press coverage.

Both items, story and photo, are from AP. Why don't you try the *Chicago Daily News*? Maybe Hempstone[29] can figure it out. AP is not worth a damn on anything real—rely on them for coverage of ceremonies and anecdotes and that sort of thing.

Another meaty item comes from "Names in the News," pg. 16, same edition. Obviously, Moral Re-Armament is blessed with a hardnose press agent. Their conference in Brazil sounds better than the Ed Sullivan

29. Smith Hempstone was a *Chicago Daily News* reporter whose pieces on Africa, published in the *Louisville Times*, caught Thompson's attention.

show. First we have Roy Rogers addressing the group—not including Moise Tshombe, who cancelled out—and then Nixon's mother shows up, a "surprise" visitor. Yeah. Next we'll get E. B. Williams, Joe Louis and Jimmy Hoffa in a no-holds-barred tag bout rounded out by Raul Castro. And to finish it off we have seven stooges apologizing to Mrs. Nixon for their part in the stoning of Blank Richard on his last guest shot in Peru.

I don't see how you people can report this crap with a straight face. Is daily journalism that deadening? Or was it just a bad day? I'd like to know.

Sincerely,
Hunter S. Thompson

TO MR. M. L. SHARPLEY:

Preparing to travel abroad, Thompson was eager to find a proper home for his Doberman pinscher, Agar. Over the years Thompson would own a number of show-bred Dobermans.

December 21, 1961
2437 Ransdell Ave.
Louisville 4, Kentucky

Mr. M. L. Sharpley
News Department
Louisville Times

Dear Mr. Sharpley:

Re: our conversation Thursday evening, concerning one Agar V. Estobarr, black male Doberman, whelped July 2, 1960; sire—Barrier Dobe's Estes; dam—Barrier Dobe's Donsie.

I bought Agar on July 1, 1961, from Mr. & Mrs. Joseph Baumgartner of Mundelein, Ill., somewhere outside Chicago. I located the Baumgartners through a Mr. Frank Grover of Carmel Valley, California. The Baumgartners were visiting Mr. Grover at the time.

I was living in Big Sur at the time and intended Agar to be the first of several Dobermans I wanted to own. When I bought the dog I expected to be in Big Sur indefinitely. I am a writer and make my living as a journalist and photographer. On December 1 or so I was offered a job in London and, after lengthy consideration, decided to give it a try. This led, naturally, to the prospect of giving up the dog.

The reason I sounded so uncertain on the phone the other night is that I feel that I'm plotting to cast off a son and my mind balks at the necessity of doing it with a cool and reasonable head. I've become very attached to Agar and I hate the idea of giving him up. I can't take him to Europe, however, so I will have to do something with him by January 1, when I plan to leave for New York.

I wrote Mr. Baumgartner, asking for suggestions, and he gave me your name, saying you'd be happy "to see" Agar because he was out of your line. [. . .] In a nutshell, I suppose I should sell Agar. I've considered boarding him, lending him, leaving him with my family, but all these would work to Agar's disadvantage. So, rather than try to hang onto him in some uncertain way, I think I should sell him into a home where I'm sure he'd be happy. Since he's used to being treated more like a human than a dog, this would rule out most of the people who would answer an ad if I placed one in the paper. Most people seem to think all Dobermans are crazy mean and should be kept chained and muzzled. Agar is not that way and I wouldn't sell him to anyone who might treat him like a vicious criminal.

So, if you know of anyone who would like to buy Agar, I'd appreciate hearing from you. I think anyone I'd locate through you would be all right. As a last resort, I will either take or send him back to the Baumgartners. Since I took him out of a good home, I feel an obligation to see that he gets another one when I have to give him up.

Other salient items: I bought him for $100.00; since I know nothing about the Doberman market, I hesitate to put a definite price on him right now.

He has never been bred.

I have reason to suspect that he has a tapeworm. I have contacted a vet, who says an enema will cure it. Before getting this done, I wanted to talk to someone who knew Dobermans. Had you not been so rushed the other night, I'd have asked you about it. Agar shows no ill effects, but the day before I called you, what appeared to be a segment of a worm crawled out of him and gave me quite a shock. I had thought only puppies got worms. At any rate, I intend to take him to the vet in the next few days. If this is not the right thing to do, I'd very much like to hear from you and find out exactly what should be done.

He is very gentle and very restless. I run him about two miles a day behind the car to keep him in shape.

He is very intelligent and so obedient that I never cease to be amazed.

That's about it. You can reach me by phone at GL-1-xxxx, any time after noon. I look forward to hearing from you.

Sincerely,

Hunter S. Thompson

TO FRANK ROBINSON, *ROGUE:*

Thompson pitched both a short story and an article on bluegrass music to Rogue, *which turned down both. At the time Thompson was plotting to move in early spring to either London or Rio de Janeiro.*

> December 22, 1961
> 2437 Ransdell Ave.
> Louisville 4, Kentucky

Dear Mr. Robinson:

Here's another story you might like. I do. It's a much better (technically) story than the one you bought, different tone, not quite as dramatic—and a lot shorter.

Length seems to be a pretty salient point in this league. You people did a pretty fair job on that "Burial at Sea" business, but I can't quite figure your idea in ignoring all my letters. Doesn't make much difference, actually, but henceforth I'll be careful to send you my shorter stuff so I won't have to worry about having them trimmed down.

This one, I think, is pretty trim as it stands. Anyway, here it is.

One more thing—I'm doing a feature for the New York *Herald Trib* on a place called Renfro Valley, a sort of unpublicized Grand Ole Opry down in eastern Kentucky. I went down there to see what they thought about the current boom in Folk and Bluegrass music and got the word that I'd have a fight on my hands if I kept on using the term Bluegrass Music. Renfro Valley is very much in the Bluegrass region.

Seems it might be an interesting article—music in the Bluegrass, as opposed to Bluegrass Music, Manhattan-style. The only real link seemed to be Lester Flatt & Earl Scruggs, who once worked at Renfro, along with some people called the Coon Creek Sisters, from Pinch 'Em Tight Holler. Lot of interesting photos to be had down there, a good many novel ideas, decent home whiskey, and probably a worthy short article, mostly photos. Let me know what you think about it. I plan to bug off for New York in about ten days, so if you want something in that line, send a quick word.

That's about it for now.

> Sincerely,
> Hunter S. Thompson

"NEW YORK BLUEGRASS"

NEW YORK CITY--The scene is Greenwich Village, a long dimly lit bar called Folk City, just east of Washington Square Park. The customers are the usual mixture: students in sneakers and button-down shirts, over-dressed tourists in for the weekend, "nine-to-five types" with dark suits and chic dates, and a scattering of sullen looking "beatniks."

A normal Saturday night in The Village: two parts boredom, one part local color, and one part anticipation.

This is the way it was at ten-thirty. The only noise was the hum of conversation and the sporadic clang of the cash register.

Most people approach The Village with the feeling that "things are happening here." If you hit a dead spot, you move on as quickly as you can. Because things are happening--somewhere. Maybe just around the corner.

I've been here often enough to know better, but Folk City was so dead that even a change of scenery would have been exciting. So I was just about ready to move on when things began happening. What appeared on the tiny bandstand at that moment was one of the strangest sights I've ever witnessed in The Village.

Three men in farmer's garb, grinning, tuning their instruments, while a suave MC introduced them as "the Greenbriar Boys, straight from the Grand Ole Opry."

Gad, I thought. What a hideous joke!

It was strange then, but moments later it was down-right eerie. These three grinning men, this weird, country-looking trio, stood square in the heartland of the "avant garde" and burst into a nasal, twanging rendition of, "We need a whole lot more of Jesus, and a lot less rock-n-roll."

I was dumbfounded, and could hardly believe my ears when the crowd cheered mightily, and the Greenbriar Boys responded with an Earl Scruggs arrangement of "Home Sweet Home." The tourists smiled happily, the "bohemian" element--uniformly decked

out in sunglasses, long striped shirts and Levi's--
kept time by thumping on the tables, and a man next
to me grabbed my arm and shouted: "What the hell's
going on here? I thought this was an Irish bar!"

I muttered a confused reply, but my voice was lost
in the uproar of the next song--a howling version of
"Good Ole Mountain Dew" that brought a thunderous
ovation.

Here in New York they call it "Bluegrass Music," but
the link--if any--to the Bluegrass region of Kentucky
is vague indeed. Anybody from the South will recognize the same old hoot-n-holler, country jamboree
product that put Roy Acuff in the 90-percent bracket.
A little slicker, perhaps; a more sophisticated choice
of songs; but in essence, nothing more or less than
"good old-fashioned" hillbilly music.

The performance was neither a joke nor a spoof. Not
a conscious one, anyway--although there may be some
irony in the fact that a large segment of the Greenwich Village population is made up of people who have
"liberated themselves" from rural towns in the South
and Midwest, where hillbilly music is as common as
meat and potatoes.

As it turned out, the Greenbriar Boys hadn't exactly
come "straight from the Grand Ole Opry." As a matter
of fact, they came straight from Queens and New Jersey, where small bands of country music connoisseurs
have apparently been thriving for years. Although
there have been several country music concerts in New
York, this is the first time a group of hillbilly
singers have been booked into a recognized night
club.

Later in the evening, the Greenbriar Boys were
joined by a fiddler named Irv Weissberg. The addition
of a fiddle gave the music a sound that was almost authentic, and it would have taken a real aficionado to
turn up his nose and speak nostalgically of Hank
Williams. With the fiddle taking the lead, the fraudulent farmers set off on "Orange Blossom Special,"

then changed the pace with "Sweet Cocaine"--dedi-
cated, said one, "to any junkies in the audience."

It was this sort of thing--hip talk with a molasses
accent--that gave the Greenbriar Boys a distinctly
un-hillbilly flavor. And when they did a sick little
ditty called, "Happy Landings, Amelia Earhart,"
there was a distinct odor of Lenny Bruce in the room.

In light of the current renaissance in Folk Music,
the appearance of the Greenbriar Boys in Greenwich
Village is not really a surprise. The "avant garde" is
hard-pressed these days to keep ahead of the popular
taste. They had Brubeck and Kenton a long time ago,
but dropped that when the campus crowd took it up.
The squares adopted Flamenco in a hurry, and Folk
Music went the same way. Now, apparently out of desperation, the avant garde is digging hillbilly.

The Village is dedicated to "new sounds," and
today's experiment is very often tomorrow's big name.
One of the best examples is Harry Belafonte, who sold
hamburgers in a little place near Sheridan Square
until he got a chance to sing at the Village Vanguard.

Belafonte, however, was a genuine "new sound." If
you wanted to hear him, there was only one place to
go. And if you weren't there, you simply missed the
boat.

With the Greenbriar Boys, it's not exactly the same.
I thought about this as I watched them. Here I was, at
a "night spot" in one of the world's most cultured
cities, paying close to a dollar for each beer, surrounded by apparently intelligent people who seemed
enthralled by each thump and twang of the banjo
string--and we were all watching a performance that
I could almost certainly see in any roadhouse in
rural Kentucky on any given Saturday night.

As Pogo once said--back in the days when mossback
editors were dropping Walt Kelly like a hot, pink
potato--"it gives a man paws."

Thompson in his study.
(PHOTO BY HUNTER S. THOMPSON;
COURTESY OF HST COLLECTION)

*Hunter with Dana Kennedy
in San Juan.*
(PHOTO BY WILLIAM J. KENNEDY;
COURTESY OF HST COLLECTION)

Thompson at work in Rio.
(COURTESY OF HST COLLECTION)

1962

**FUCK YOU, I QUIT . . . THE ARTIST FLEES TO THE ANDES
. . . WHISKEY WITH INDIANS, CHAMPAGNE WITH BOBBY
KENNEDY . . . IN ARUBA WITH $30 . . . DESPERATE DAYS
WITH SMUGGLERS . . . EIGHT DAYS ON A BEER BARGE . . .
DEMOCRACY DIES IN PERU, CHECKS BOUNCE IN LA PAZ . . .
THE KING OF COPACABANA BEACH . . .**

In Puerto Estrella, Colombia, there is little to do but
talk. It is difficult to say just what the villagers are
talking about, however, because they speak their own
language--a tongue called Guajiro, a bit like Arabic,
which doesn't ring well in a white man's ear.
   Usually they are talking about smuggling, because
this tiny village with thatched roof huts and a total
population of about 100 South American Indians is a
very important port of entry. Not for humans, but for
items like whiskey and tobacco and jewelry. It is not
possible for a man to get there by licensed carrier, because there are no immigration officials and no customs. There is no law at all, in fact, which is precisely
why Puerto Estrella is such an important port.

--Hunter S. Thompson, "A Footloose American in a
  Smugglers' Den," <u>National Observer</u>, August 6, 1962

TO PAUL SEMONIN:

Thompson was staying with Sandy Conklin in New York for a few weeks be-
fore shoving off for South America; Semonin was about to move to Ghana.

> January 21, 1962
> c/o Reynolds
> 531 E. 81 Street
> New York City

Dear Bigwind—

Your last letter, as you must realize in retrospect, contained a lot more smoke than fire. Your last few letters, for that matter, have been extremely wordy without saying much of anything. Although I still have a great deal of confidence in you, I would feel less than honest if I failed to warn you against the danger of taking yourself too seriously. It can do a man in. Especially when it comes to dealing with a watchdog like me, who is armed with other, earlier, sharper, less inflated letters from a man who once saw the world through the quick mean eyes of a sketchmaster.

So much for that. Probably I am sounding here like McGarr, whose habit is to start every letter with a noisy smack at the last one he received.

Nonetheless, since you say in para #2, "I am leaning into this thing, but swinging wide," I can only assume that you thought you knew what you were doing. And you did, in a roundabout way, since the tone of that letter by itself was enough to put me off of all things European. It was a relief, in a way, to get the thing—vague and full of Charles Goren images though it was. You must be playing a hell of a lot of bridge over there. No wonder you want to come home. Wherever in hell that is. But you'll have to pardon me for not having the faintest idea what the fuck a trump card is . . . except that it sounds big and bad . . . and since that "is about all (you) can say now," you'll have to admit that it doesn't leave me with much to go on. Except that you play a lot of bridge over there, and I am not much on that, as you know.

I am not much on these aerograms either, since a man can see his limits before he starts, so I'll head out here with a big stack of paper behind me and enough stamps to cover just about any weight I care to write.

I, of course, am in New York, the homeland of the uprooted. America's marketplace. And no one with a grain of sense would go to a public market to seek a place to live. Except the sick, and the tortured, and those who think that everything you see in a market grew there. Nothing grows in a market except the wads of those who buy and sell. No greenery. For that, you move out, and on, find a bit of space.

For that, I propose to move on, to the biggest outest place I can find on the map—South America. Yeah. I sense a massive grapple there, a tree unfelled, a fucking giant as it were, and when if falls there will be enough noise to shake even Noël Coward out of his seat at the UN. (Think.) Lift him like an overripe toadstool with no weight at all and the consistency of silly putty. Ziff. No more.

I see the last frontier down there—the last decent frontier anyway. Granting that Africa may be another, I feel a real difference in the way a man could deal with it. Nothing less than a .44 Magnum in Africa and don't even worry about the language barrier. Who needs it? Let those crazy niggers cut up a few more people and toss the pieces to a few more crowds and I'll be ready to join just about any team that wants to go in after them. Somewhere along the line almost any human can go past the point where he can expect the right to anything except a big slug in the belly and a quick crowded grave.

Seems funny saying that and listening to Leadbelly at the same time. Another nigger singing about "Mean Ole Frisco." Ah, we have branded ourselves with those singing niggers and their ghosts will outlive us all. Nonetheless, we are born in that shadow and not without a lot of good things too, so I'd like to think it balances out. And it will, but not if we stay in the market or anywhere near it.

Sweating like hell now, dizzy with a bad new cold, sitting here with coffee and scotch and Coricidin and pondering a world map all day. Like you, sort of. But you seem to have got on a rather dark experiment. Is Europe really that dull? Hard for me, with my myths and insulation, to believe. Although you have never really answered my question about balls, I take it that Europe is like an old man who refuses to admit that his have gone stale. Tough.

We shall see about South America. I think I will go to San Juan ($45), then to Aruba ($30), then over to Trinidad to establish an outpost with Jenny's parents.[1] Then down whichever coast I can find a boat on. Maybe

---

1. Jenny New—a Trinidadian—was living with Jo Hudson in Big Sur. Thompson planned to stay with her parents for a while.

for a long time, hopefully to seek a high spot in a new world, a vantage point with plenty of room to shoot and roam.

By the time I shove off my $900 will have shrunk to about $600, what with paying my debts (McGarr, Joel, etc.), and that will be my fortune. $600 and a huge goddamn continent to deal with. I will go alone, of course. We have already talked that out. This is not a tandem type move. I sort of hate to miss Europe, and I urge you to fill me with enough wisdom about it as you can pack in your rotten aerograms. I will do the same. Why don't you try Russia? That would be a real place to know. Who the shit cares whether England sinks or swims? Or France or Spain or Italy, for that matter. If they make it at all, it will be like a big housing project in the middle of a bigger and meaner city. Germany, of course, still retains the power and the ironical position to do us all in. How this came to be will remain one of the great curiosities of our history. If they get the bomb they could be at least as dangerous as the red chinks with the same weapon. May god forgive the man who signs it over to them. And somebody will.

Now, back to your letter. Why on earth you think I'd come to Europe to see Cathedrals or Renaissance Masters is beyond my ken. Perhaps you were just practicing what you later meant to say to Bingham,[2] who has said the same thing in different ways.

I would advise you, if you mean to deal with the big picture, to learn as much about the big facts as possible. And that means digging in files and talking to factmongers and wasting a lot of time in search of pertinent details. For instance, Europe will indeed have something to say about what goes on in the rest of the world and if you come up with the flat statement that it won't, you might look a bit silly. One of the 3 big issues before this session of Congress is how to deal with the reality of an economic U.S. of Europe. Simple production figures and gross national products will tell you this. It may not last, of course, but then neither will a bomb. But it can cause a lot of humbug before it goes off, and even more when it does.

You won't pay any attention to this, of course, but I thought I'd toss it in—along with the added advice of beginning with subjects least likely to be contradicted or called into question by people who think they know a lot more about them than you do. You say, for instance, that Spain will undoubtedly go Communist and you will get a lot of noisy shit, perhaps even from the editor you send it to. If, on the other hand, you tell exactly how one frustrated Spaniard spends his waking hours, damn few people are going to be in a position to say you're wrong.

2. Robert Bingham was an editor with *The Reporter* magazine 1948–1964. In 1960 Thompson had pitched him a story on San Francisco's "woeful" newspaper situation.

Take that for what it's worth. I have not sent the *Courier-Journal* anything since they refused to use my Big Sur piece, so you are welcome to all you can beat them for. I warn you, however, that they thought that piece I did on you was "a real honey," and the only two things they bounced were 2 of the best I've done. Good Luck.

Which reminds me, I heard you denounced as "utterly worthless" in Louisville. Because you "weren't doing anything." When I opined that I was just about as worthless, on the same scale, I was told that I was ok because I got "things published." This implied, I then said, that I owed everything I was to the *Courier-Journal*, which published the only things this young lady had read. Until then, I was utterly worthless. Then *Rogue* vindicated me further. This seemed to stump her and I had a fine time from then on in, heaping one vicious logic upon the other, and finally driving her to the position of having to admit that you would be far more worthy than her own husband, the moment any publication accepted your work. At this, her husband got ugly and we changed the subject. I was not invited there again. [. . .]

One more point I contest—I doubt that a man has to go to Europe, or anywhere, for that matter, to understand the important things about this country. Maybe he has to go to Europe to be prodded into articulating them, or before they seem worth talking about, but I think we have enough space and perspective over here so a man can step off into a corner and get a pretty good view. And if he has reason enough to think about what he sees, it might be that he can leave Europe alone. I say this because none of what you say about that place sounds new to me. I have a feeling that I've heard or read it all sometime before. As a matter of fact I read some of it very recently in a column by Mr. [Walter] Lippmann—in the *Courier-Journal*, of all places. If I'm right on this, I can get away with letting you do my learning for me, and then pumping you.

As for that, it might be a while before I get within range. You say you are going "home" in June. Where in the name of god is home? If you know that, you have found something important. Anyway, I hope to leave long before that, probably in a month or so, and I will try to tempt Hudson into sailing his 3-winged monster down that way to join me. If you like that sort of thing, you might tuck an idea away in your mind for further use just about the time you get back. He plans to shove off for somewhere "in the summer" and I am damn sure he'd welcome you aboard. But that is a long way off, eh? I will leave you with my tentative plans to head south in the near future, and await further word from you. For god's sake keep your next one unfogged by the lingo of the bridge table. Those images are foreign to me and when I read one that is underlined I feel that I'm missing the very core of what you say. If you must speak in swirls, use the argot of the damned—I can understand that.

Buenos dinga, H

TO THE NATIONAL RIFLE ASSOCIATION:

In preparation for his journey to Latin America—and a planned jaguar hunt in Colombia—Thompson joined the NRA in search of information about foreign gun laws.

January 25, 1962
c/o Reynolds
531 E. 81 Street
New York City

Membership Director
National Rifle Assn.
1600 Rhode Island Ave. NW
Washington, DC

Dear Sir:

I have been on the move ever since I sent you a membership application form last fall when I was living in Big Sur, California, so I have no idea what my status is at the moment. As I recall, the membership fee is $5, which I enclose. If I'm wrong on this please let me know.

I have an interesting reason for sending the money at this time. Since leaving California I have been made aware of not a few stringent and oppressive laws and regulations concerning the bearing of firearms. They seemed to become more numerous and intense as I came east—and culminated here in New York where a man is almost afraid to mention the word "gun." As I understand it, the NRA is the only organization that actively—or effectively—opposes this type of regulation, and if that's true, then $5 is precious little to pay in order to have a voice and a hand in trying to cope with them.

Then too, I am preparing for a long trip to South America, and the regulations down there seem nearly as bad as those in New York. I'm told, for instance, that under no circumstances will I be allowed to take a pistol into the country—any country. This applies even to a photographer whose primary assignment is to cover jaguar-hunting, where a camera, plus a big revolver, is not a bad combination.

If you have any information that would help me in South America—names & locations of gun or hunting clubs, special dispensations for hunters, etc.—I would certainly appreciate anything you can give me.

I had never realized, by the way, that in many countries a man needs permission from the Army in order to carry his own pistol. So I send this membership fee with a fervent hope that we in this country can protect what small freedom we still retain, with regard to firearms.

Sincerely,
Hunter S. Thompson

TO EUGENE W. MCGARR:

Eager to flee New York, Thompson wrote McGarr in Spain about his up-coming South American adventure.

February 2, 1962
531 E. 81 Street
New York City

E.W.—

No word from you in quite a while, McGarr. It must mean you are finally doing something. It's been my experience that I only write letters when I'm overwhelmed by other obligations—or the lack of them—and feel the need to get my mind to some other place. But perhaps this is not the case with you. We are all different, eh?

Not much happening here except that I am currently dealing for an extended journey to South America. Also still working on The Rum Diary, determined to finish it before taking off. This a shitty town, McGarr, and there is something wrong with anyone who can live here. It is full of vultures and lice and turds and darkness, and every human contact is more depressing than the last. You can see it in their eyes, dull stares and pasty flesh; walking these streets is like roaming in a graveyard and I take a fiendish delight in my daily midtown forays—bounding along the streets, trailing all sorts of leather impediments, spitting and hawking and blowing my nose in the air like a consumptive Chinaman. My appearance on Madison Avenue is much like the Loch Ness monster, and I get a kick out of returning the stares as I burst out of a subway and hawk on some well-polished pointed shoes. Fuck them all; I carry a short truncheon and am eager to put it to use. At times I am even tempted to challenge gangs of thugs in front of these rotten candy stores—although I would much rather face a wild boar than 30 underfed punks.

Well, enough of that breast-beating. The truth of course is that I want to get even with this town for not recognizing my genius and paying me accordingly. But after talking to numerous editors and agents I am about ready to believe that we talk a different language and that no real meaning will ever pass between us. Only the amenities, the stock phrases, and a certain number of rejection slips. This is the primary reason for my shot to SA. I understand that land is selling down there for $4 an acre in the Mato Grosso and I intend to have some of it. After that I will do whatever I have to do to hold onto it. Naturally, I will take my weapons.

This, of course, raises some questions as to that $90 that I owe you. Well, I think I can get it paid before I go. This is no idle talk, for I certainly wouldn't bring up such an ugly subject unless I thought there was hope of killing it off. My fortune at the moment consists of whatever amount of my grandmother's money I can coax out of my mother. She is naturally reluctant to invest in my hare-brained schemes and I am at the critical juncture now of telling her about the Mato Grosso. She thought Europe was a good idea and agreed tentatively to part with 8 or 9 hundred—2 of which I owe her—but I don't know how she will react to this South America business. At any rate, I will let you know. In the meantime, send word on your doings. Your last letter was decent and nearly informative. Things are looking up for you, McGarr. Perhaps you can get a job here as a spellbinder. I sense openings in that line, but I am not up to it myself. Oh yes—enjoyed Eleanor's letter to Sandy. I read all mail here and distribute it accordingly.

H

TO PAUL SEMONIN:

Excited by his imminent departure for South America, Thompson wrote Semonin of his plans. Photographs, along with guns, had become Thompson's newest obsession.

February 7, 1962
531 E. 81 Street
New York City

Paul—
"In Brazil a gun or a knife is considered a fair weapon, and there is no dishonor in being wounded or even killed. But to hit a man with your fists is to insult him beyond remedy. He can only avenge the humiliation by killing you."

This comes from a reliable book called *Tigrero,* and upon reading it I immediately wrote Cooke[3] to bring my big pistol when he comes to New York. Upon contacting the man who wrote the book—a tiger hunter in the

3. Don Cooke, a Louisville friend Thompson met in the Athenaeum Literary Association. He lived across the street from Semonin.

Mato Grosso—I was advised to bring the gun into the country in a shoulder-holster because Brazil customs men do not search bodies, only luggage. And if they find a gun in your bag you are clamped. This man seemed to think it was very important that I get my gun in with me and I tend to agree.

The above should give you an idea of my plans and their meaning. Push-off date is still about a month, but uncertain due to the fate of the novel, which will see another agent on Monday—the first half again, 60 percent rewritten.

The pace here is accelerated almost beyond my ken. Hundreds of projects and possibilities, all needing talk and investigation. Sandy informs me that yesterday morning I rolled over in bed and shouted: "All this jabberwocky and shameless talk—I just don't know if I can get up." This last refers to my growing inability to get out of bed before noon and often later. Something huge is pressing on my soul. One morning last week I shouted: "Get these dogs off me! These fucking ugly dogs!" I keep having these dreams, not unlike the DTs in their substance and urgency. Even now, sitting here at the typewriter, I have a feeling that my gut is a great engine racing at top rpm, unable to shift out of neutral. Constant nerves and dealing, calling, shouting, clawing at the mailbox, forever writing letters to unknown people, tense moments during every phone call as we come on the big money yes or no, the crucial hesitation, and more often than not the ugly let-down when the phone is back on its crotch.

But I am making headway and am now teetering on the brink of closing a deal with one of the airlines—a series of 13 articles, one from each capital in South America, in exchange for transportation to 13 capitals. The only catch is that I have to sign a contract and somehow guarantee publication of said articles. There is hope for this in the form of Laschever,[4] running interference for me with the airline publicity hounds. But even he won't guarantee publication. Nonetheless, I sense a 50–50 chance in the deal and will press savagely for a win.

Still no money in my pockets, of course, and the pressure and humiliation of that is reaching the intolerable level. I am feeling like a gigolo and a hired stud. A bad feeling when it lasts. No sales in 3 months. Nothing. No work on much of anything but the novel. If I can't get it off my head it will bury me and itself at the same time. Am also wound up viciously with photography, dealing each day in camera stores, cramming facts and numbers into my head, leading decent salesmen down penniless alleys, coaxing information out of them. In the course of it all I have been convinced

---

4. Barney Laschever was head of public relations for Panagra Airlines, Pan Am's South American arm. He got Thompson discounted flights.

that I am going to buy a $200 camera, plus several extra lenses, when my money comes, if it ever comes. Yesterday's figures on necessary camera expenditures was $351. A man with $800 on his hands, plus $600 in debts, is worse off than a penniless wretch with the same debts. I feel they sense my money and are closing in on me, hell bent on keeping me off the South America thing by gobbling my funds before I can flee. At last count I figured to arrive in Rio with $120, not knowing a soul and not speaking the language—with god knows how many miles and desperate dollars between me and a berth. Peggy Clifford wrote last week saying your house was available, offering it to me, and the pressure here was so bad that I floundered horribly at the sight of the letter. The temptation to retreat was huge and fat like a devil, making an offer for my soul. I wrote, saying I couldn't trust myself to say yes or no at the moment and to contact me again in 2 weeks. She wrote yesterday that a stringbean had replaced the fink and your income was safe again. It is good to have an agent like that—your base is in capable hands.

I am becoming more and more certain that this South America venture is my last chance to do something big and bad, come to grips with the basic wildness. Everything here is larded over with lunacy; I can no longer even read the *Times* without trembling. Gov. Rocky[5] says someone is putting vinegar in New York milk and there is no mention of why. WHY? Why in the fuck? What motive? No explanation. The speaker of the New York assembly pushed a home-shelter bill through the house while he was a director of a firm building home-shelters. Now they are crucifying the man who broke the story, saying he is a dupe of the Communists. The papers go right along, dutifully recording the madness. The speaker raves and pounds the desk and winks at photographers. All this is recorded and sold on the streets. The new director of the CIA goes on record as an advocate of more and better nuclear testing. For the past 3 years this same man has been one of our chief negotiators at international disarmament conferences. No wonder we have made no progress. I tell you it is pressing me down and keeping me off balance 24 hours a day—a friend of Sandy's is living with two men and they are constantly calling and showing up here, looking for the mail. . . . What mail? Whose mail? I dare not say anything for fear of bursting the bag. They ask questions and I feel my gears slipping. Out! You bastards! Take all the mail except mine! Whorehoppers! I can no longer see through the fog! My name is on the mailbox, yet letters to me are "returned to sender." I have lost faith in the system. People say they have written me and they haven't. What can I say? How can I

5. Nelson Rockefeller, the Republican governor of New York 1959–1973 and later vice president of the United States.

answer? Is the mailman a Communist? How can I pin him down? Should I kill him when I get a grip or let him go free to plague others with his tricks?

It's this money hanging over me that does it. That and the novel. I must get rid of this novel and I must get that money. Then I can flee to the warm water, the relative peace of Caracas and the unplumbed jungle of the Mato Grosso. Two cameras and a pistol and a great thirst—and this god-dam typewriter. I want to walk on a morning road in Brazil and stop at a good place for a cold beer. I don't even want to understand what they say. Just grin at them and drink, then walk on.

As you see, I am finally on the hump and all Craziness is spread out before me. Way in the distance I see a clear spot, a splash of sunlit green and a sign saying "cerveza." No hope but to get there and rest. Put the madness behind me. Ah, jesus, the pressure of this place, the screams of the drowners and the jackal laughter of those in the rafts.

Now, maybe I have got that screaming out of my system. Anyway, I feel better. Still, I cannot face your letter without writing 40 pages of answer. I feel that I should tell you at least that much about something, but I dare not start. Each time I start thinking of one thing, two more loom up to destroy my focus. God knows what you are doing over there but it sounds bad. I will put you in touch with Hudson. Write him. He looks at June 1 as the deadline, but still doesn't know what they will do with the boat once it gets in the water.

You will always get a lot of shit from me, no matter what you say, until you become so right that I feel intimidated or so wrong that I feel repelled.

I am going to write massive tomes from South America. I can hardly wait to get my teeth in it. And thousands of pictures. It is almost too big to deal with. Speaking of pictures, I may try to sell that one of the nigger child on the beach that you claim to have taken. I don't believe you, but you sounded so righteous when I mentioned it before that I know you would never admit it was not yours. Anyway, it dawned on me the other day that PRNS [Puerto Rican News Service] might buy it. Probably not, but god knows it is worth a try. I must have a check from somebody. With luck it will bring $15, more likely $10. If I sell it and if you sound righteous and convinced enough in your reply to this, I will send you half. I have asked Sandy about it, but she is blank. I have so many shots that I don't remember taking that I tend to feel that anything I have is bound to be "mine."

Maybe I will deduct the price of developing and printing all those shots I took of you—and then deduct for the skill and wisdom involved—and send you the rest.

This will give you the gist of my recent thought patterns. I am turning into a jew. And all the time I've been writing this fucking letter, the rotten novel has been sitting here accusing me of sloth. I will get to it now, leaving you to stew. Send word on something. Pierce the fog. Seize the high ground and keep a tight trigger. The beast is loose and prowling everywhere.

Bloodhungrily,
Hunter

TO CANDIDA DONADIO:

Still in pursuit of the right agent, Thompson now retained Donadio in hopes of finding a publisher for "The Rum Diary." Donadio worked for the Russell & Volkening literary agency. She wrote Thompson saying his characters in "The Rum Diary" were "hard and bitter"; the agency didn't take Thompson on as a client.

February 15, 1962
531 E. 81 Street
New York City

Dear Miss Donadio:

Thanks for your letter. Now I can finish The Rum Diary with a bit of a grin—a mean one, of course—and send it snapping and snarling toward the cubicles. It will not be a "hard and bitter" book in the end, except to those who expect other people to build their houses for them. It has taken me 24 years to lay even the beginnings of a foundation for myself, and when I finish I will not have much time to do anything but run off a few copies of the blueprint for other builders to use as they see fit.

One of your comments puzzles me, however, and since it seems to be your main point I would like to see it more clearly. You say, "The novel is made of hard and bitter characters, and that's all right and workable, providing there is enough distinction in the means of telling the bitter and hard story." Now "distinction" is the word I can't deal with. I hope you don't mean "discretion." That would sadden me, because I appreciated what I thought was the spirit of your letter. Also I hope you don't mean I should fish for some future comment like, "Mr. Thompson has written a distinguished book." I sent a story to an agent once and she wrote back that she had sent it on to *The New Yorker* because she thought it was "absolutely charming." They bounced it, of course, for it was no less mean and bitter than The Rum Diary. It just goes to . . . ah . . . yeah.

Anyway, I will finish the book and let you see it again, although I am not real optimistic about your feeling for it. But I liked your letter and feel that your quarrel is more with me and my convictions than my way of expressing them. Perhaps not, and maybe that's what you meant by distinction. But

I am not about to erect any housing projects or tickle any desperate wish-bones. There is a man named [Herman] Wouk who does that sort of thing, and another called [Eric] Linklater, whose heart, they say, is as big as all outdoors. I have a suspicion that it would drop very cleanly down the barrel of a BB gun, but I guess that makes me sound even meaner than before.

Further, I could cite a lot of fine books that didn't build any houses. *Lie Down in Darkness* comes quickly to mind, and no American has written a better book in 20 years. But when Styron tried to build a house, it didn't ring true. It sold, of course, and maybe there was form beneath the fuzz, but I couldn't see it.

Well, I see I am arguing and I didn't mean to when I sat down to write this thing. Thanks for reading what I gave you and for writing a good note; you will hear from me again when I finish the blueprint.

> Bittahly,
> Hunter S. Thompson

TO LIONEL OLAY:

Thompson first met free-lance journalist Olay in Big Sur when they were both broke and grubbing for rent money. Olay published two novels and wrote for various magazines and contributed a weekly column to the Monterey Herald.

> February 16, 1962
> 531 E. 81 Street
> New York City

Well, Lionel, I've been meaning to write you for quite a while, but I thought I'd wait until I had something to say. Now, if nothing else, I can give you a rough outline of the immediate future.

Well, Ok—first, you better be careful about your boxing syndrome. Mailer has broken his ass and his nose and all his rabbit ears trying to prove how much a better man and boxer he is than Hemingway, and all it has done is make him look silly. He will never be a better man and probably not a better boxer, because Mailer is a punk and it sticks out all over except when he writes his rare good stuff—which he should have been doing all along because it is the only way he'll ever get within shouting distance of Hemingway's ghost. So much for boxing. I dig a smooth mauler, but there are other ways to keep in shape for the big business.

Also, you cast me as a tyro Sugar Ray [Robinson] and match me with your man, Chambrun.[6] Oddly enough, I had a letter from him in

6. Jacques Chambrun was a literary agent.

Louisville, a few days before I got yours, saying he had seen my story in *Rogue* and wondered if I had an agent. It was written on yellow stationery and I quickly dealt him off as a quack. Then came your letter and a reappraisal of Chambrun, so when I got here I went to see him and ran into the foggiest, most offensive secretary I have ever come across. After four tries at seeing Chambrun—to whom I had replied, and who had written back, asking to see my novel—I finally wrote him a very hardnose letter at his home, saying his secretary was a fucking idiot and had put me in the mood to crack skulls and bend thumbs. First his, then all the others in all the rotten offices in this rotten town. Direct quotes. Needless to say, I got a quick reply from Jacques, saying that "due to previous commitments he was not taking on any more clients at the present time." Also, needless to say, a man with previous commitments does not scour magazines like *Rogue* in search of authors. So much for Chambrun. I found a new man named Volkening, who says my book is "mean and bitter," but if I can resolve it in some decent way he would like to see it when it's ready to go. Well, my book is not mean and bitter and nor am I, for that matter, but his analysis gave me the pissed-off zip I needed to ram through to the finish. Contrary to your approach, I am "playing fast and loose" with it now, fairly confident that I have a good thing on my hands and giving it all the play it needs to romp and stomp. I figure 3 or 4 more weeks and that's it. I am tired of the thing and have better books to write. It has been on my ass for 18 months and that's enough. (I know, Joyce spent 10 years on *Portrait of . . .*) And Joyce was a poor sick fucker who probably died with his balls somewhere up around his navel. None of that for me, thanks. If it proves to be that long and tough I will figure that, like Joyce, I do not lack talent, but contacts, and I am not yet sure which is more important. But I have other talents and other contacts, and I can always write, so fuck them. But I will pass a good list on to my biographers. I have recently read two books where some people's memories took some pretty bad floggings—with reference to Hemingway and [Hart] Crane. But who gives a damn, anyway? Like how many people know or care who the KC A's have sold or traded to the Yankees in the past five years? So what? Who knows who to blame? Fuck it.

Anyway, what I meant to say in all that is that you mis-cast me. Footwork is one thing, and New York manners are another. I prefer to deal head-on, because for one thing I'm big enough in a lot of ways to run over people that way; and for another, it gives me a chance to see who I'm after. This peek-a-boo shit is for midgets.

As for my last letter, it must have been gloomier than I remember. Or maybe it was that Ohio Valley climate. Anyway, I am very much on the offensive now and will definitely leave for South America before April 1.

Hopefully, by March 15. Depends entirely on the book. I have enough papers to give me an illusion of an income and that's all I need to go anywhere. If it all works out, I will make enough money to keep going. If not, I will settle wherever I have to and do what has to be done. Sandy is not taking the initial plunge. She will stay here for a month, then ship to Trinidad and await developments. I have a lot of deals going now and they will probably all fall through, but I will go anyway. One thing that looks good is free transportation, in exchange for guaranteed published articles. The last time I tried a thing like that the people who sponsored me wound up yelling for my skin to be tacked up on their wall. Probably it will happen again, and so be it. There are possibilities in journalism, and not the least among them is the fact that it's short and quick and just about as constant as you want to make it. I have enough papers now to afford me a decent income unless they do me in with delays and petty bitching, which they undoubtedly will. On the other hand, I have sold a few photos recently and am now buying a $200 camera from Hong Kong, plus another $200 worth of lenses. So I will have another weapon and if I can make it work it will take a real badass to get me. And if nothing else works, I still have a .357 Magnum.

So I feel relatively confident and expect a fit of euphoria when I finally finish this stinking book. You will probably not like it, but I have worked hard enough on it so I won't care what anyone thinks. It is a decent chronicle of a meaningful time, and if somebody else can do it better, I am about ready to step aside anyway.

As for your plan to return to this rotten town, I cannot do much smiling. I don't doubt there's money here, but you will dig in shit to find it. I have never seen a place so jammed with absolute pricks. Perhaps Chicago is worse, but I doubt it. Of course there's LA, but that's too much for an honest man to face or even question. My only faith in this country is rooted in such places as Colorado and Idaho and maybe Big Sur as it was before the war. The cities are greasepits and not worth blowing off the map. I can't understand why you want to come here except to swoop in and grab what you can and be off again. There is no other way to deal with this place. Beware. On this, if on nothing else, I think I speak truth. And on top of everything else I think it would drive Beverly[7] nuts. It is already cracking Sandy, and she grew up on Long Island.

Well, that's about the story from this end. I am drunk now and it's just about 5 am. 14 pages tonight, not a bad pitch. I have another bad week of major re-writing, then I can coast. God damn, it will be good to have it off my hands, regardless of where it goes or why. I don't care anymore. I just

7. Olay's wife.

want to finish. And now I'm running out of space and I don't feel up to another sheet, so—send word. HST

TO JAMES ZANUTTO, FEATURES EDITOR, *POP PHOTO:*

Thompson made a pitch to Pop Photo *for an article on the virtues of American photography.*

February 26, 1962
531 E. 81 Street
New York City

James Zanutto
Features Ed.
Pop Photo
One Park Ave., New York

Dear Mr. Zanutto:

After reading Hattersley's "Good & Bad Pictures"[8] in your most recent issue, I mentioned what I thought was an article possibility to Bob Bone[9] and he suggested I see what you thought of it.

Its title might be something like "The Case for the Chronic Snapshooter." This derives from Hattersley's statement that snapshooting is not, by definition, a low and ignorant art. He cites Weegee and Cartier-Bresson as examples.

I enjoyed seeing this in print. Because after being in New York for a while, reading *Pop Photo* and mingling here and there with photographers, I was beginning to feel that no man should ever punch a shutter release without many years of instruction and at least $500 worth of the finest equipment. As a free-lance writer, I've been taking pictures for several years, often just for the hell of it, and often to illustrate my articles. I've had a good time at it, and sold enough pictures to cover my lab expenses and the initial cost of my equipment several times over. My "equipment" consists of a Yashica-Mat, a cheap light meter, and a yellow filter.

When I got to New York, however, I was given to understand that I might just as well be shooting with a Brownie Hawkeye. My only salvation lay in a Hasselblad, a Nikon and quick enrollment in a photographers' school. I pondered this for a while and soon found myself running in circles, going from one camera store to the next, promising them all that I'd come back the next day and buy a complete outfit. Meanwhile, I zipped

---

8. Ralph Hattersley, "Good and Bad Pictures," *Pop Photo*, April 28, 1962.
9. A gifted photojournalist, Bone had worked with Thompson at the *Middletown Daily Record* and was his roommate in San Juan.

my camera into a suitcase and stopped taking pictures altogether. They were bound to be terrible, and besides that, I was embarrassed to be seen on the street with my ratty equipment.

Then I read Hattersley's piece. After that I got out some of my prints and decided that not all of them were worthless. As a matter of fact there were some that gave me pleasure. And I had sold a good many, I'd enjoyed taking them, and some had even given other people pleasure.

That's my idea in a nutshell. When photography gets so technical as to intimidate people, the element of simple enjoyment is bound to suffer. Any man who can see what he wants to get on film will usually find some way to get it; and a man who thinks his equipment is going to see for him is not going to get much of anything.

The moral here is that anyone who wants to take pictures can afford adequate equipment and can, with very little effort, learn how to use it. Then, when the pictures he gets start resembling the ones he saw in his mind's eye, he can start thinking in terms of those added improvements that he may or may not need.

For instance: there are damn few things you can't shoot at a 500th of a second, so why get an inferiority complex if your camera doesn't go up to 1000th? Anybody who can afford that extra nickel for Tri-X can shoot indoors at night with any camera that has a 3.5 lens and shutter speed down to 50 or 25. Why give up because you can't afford a camera with a 1.8 or 1.4 lens? First push 3.5 to its absolute limit, and if it still bugs you, you'll find some way to buy that other camera. If not, you don't need it anyway.

I'm enclosing some prints to demonstrate my thesis. There is something technically wrong with every one of them, but I have sold enough of these and others to make my snapshooting habit pay its own way. Some of these were taken at a time when I didn't even know that some films were faster than others. Then, when I discovered Tri-X, I moved indoors and, with little tricks like tilting lampshades, etc., I have usually managed to get pretty close to what I wanted. And I have never found a situation that caused me to slink off in shame because I couldn't shoot a 1000th.

It may be that my thesis will rub some of your high-priced advertisers the wrong way, but I doubt it. After all, the best way to appreciate fine equipment is to shoot with some that isn't so fine, and then move up. But no man will learn an inferiority complex quicker than he who starts out with a Leica and consistently gets poorer stuff than his buddy with an Olympus Pen. And the man who starts out with an inexpensive but adequate camera will soon learn its limitations, and he'll appreciate his Leica when he gets it.

That's about it. This letter is a rough sketch of the proposed article, so you should have a good idea what I'm driving at. If it doesn't interest you, give the prints to Bone instead of mailing them back to me. My mailman has a bad habit of jamming photos into my mailbox and I'd rather not have that happen to these.

Cordially,
Hunter S. Thompson

TO EUGENE W. MCGARR:

Struggling with debt, piles, and "The Rum Diary," Thompson took a break to needle McGarr, who was trying to write a novel in Spain.

February 28, 1962
531 E. 81 Street
New York City

Dear zero-grinning . . .

There *are* no brochures on the Mato Grosso, McGarr, which is one of the reasons land is selling there for $4 an acre. I have no idea what it's like except that it's god-forsaken and full of jaguars. Also wild boar and mahogany. A friend of mine here has bought 50 acres for $200, but has never seen it. Beyond this, you will have to wait for my reports. It is a rumor, you know—like GOLD or WHISKEY! In this case it's CHEAP LAND! But just how much it is worth is another question. In South America, however, there is the consolation of knowing that if you don't like the first 1000-mile tract, there are a good many others to choose from.

As for my shitty sarcasm, god knows my belly is full of it, but the fact that you're already braced for it, knowing full well that you deserve it, has caused me to lose interest in loading it on you. First Semonin, then you, eh? Artistes. Well, you will have enough trouble without my sarcasm. If I were you I would stick to art. At least you can do it standing up. You will learn the importance of this when you develop your first case of piles, as I have. Now I know why Thomas Wolfe wrote on top of his icebox, and why Ernest Hemingway devised a special chest-high stand for his typewriter. They had the piles, McGarr, and you will get them too if you do enough writing to find out what a shitty job it is. And if you give it up before then, well, there's always the drums or the jew's harp—or the art of taking yourself seriously, which Mr. Semonin can explain. And there's a certain art to pushing a hack, I suspect; or even in doing the Pirogue Stomp in Washington Square on a Sunday afternoon. Art is all around us, McGarr; it's wonderful to know.

Things here are as vicious and pressing as I've ever known them. Between Sandy, the piles, the novel and South America, I am nearing the end of my rope. Any one of the last three would be enough to keep a man sweating 24 hours a day, and the reason for putting Sandy on the list is that she is in the hospital, recuperating from what I suspect was a serious operation. It was kept from me until the last moment, at which point she announced that daddy and the doctor had it all arranged. So my function now is to visit, bearing fruit, etc., and hope to god I don't run into daddy. Anyway, she's recovering, and will probably be out in a week or so.

In the meantime, I am pushing this stinking novel around the final turn. This is what I do at night, usually from nine to five, or so. During the days I wheel and deal with various punks and editors, rooting desperately for a subsidy for my South America tour, which could easily become a disaster without one. I am doing about as well as can be expected, which is depressing. But I am going anyway. Tomorrow I will find out if my piles require an operation. There is some talk of a fistula, but I try not to hear it. I hear voices now & then that tell me this novel will be my one and only work, but so far it is a bastard & I mean to finish it off in the same rabbit-punching style. Maybe 2 more weeks, maybe 3. Who knows? OK, that's it. Got to get working. Write when you get published.

HST

TO DARYL MURPHY:

The arrival of a check from his mother inspired Thompson to buy whiskey and write letters to a dozen friends, including Murphy in Big Sur, who was considering becoming a high school teacher.

March 13, 1962
531 E. 81st
New York City

Dear Daryl—

Had an $800 windfall today & am now quite drunk on Old Crow. Also quite sick from a rotten cold, cough & general failure of health. Waiting now for sleeping pills to take effect so I can get to bed. Big day tomorrow— got to see various agents, editors, etc.—also order $400 camera & lenses from Hong Kong, also pay other debts, also write 20 pages on novel, also pack books & send them to Louisville, also, also, also . . . this hurry is driving me nuts.

Your last letter had a bit of zip in it. Good. I hate to think of you moping around out there. If you want to teach, get the hell at it and don't pay any attention to me or anyone else. Even Mr. [George Bernard] Shaw, who said, "Those who can, do; those who can't, teach."

Since you asked.

OK. Had a big filet mignon dinner tonight and feel generally rich. Am beginning to think this is the only way I'll ever feel that way, i.e.—temporarily, false economy, ignoring debts, blinding myself to the morrow's expenditures, etc. But what the hell. It is a good & healthy thing to have a fine fat steak & a bottle of good Kentucky bourbon & order cameras from Hong Kong & generally feel rich. As I said. I am almost tempted to send Semonin some money, but I know it would spoil him. Guess I will anyway. Just a dollar or so for some absinthe.

Fine to hear you brimming & to hell with journalism if you say so. Personally, I have to live on it a while longer & a piss-poor living it is. I am looking forward to a none-too-distant day when I can QUIT. Yes. QUIT. I have rubbed all my guns with silicone waterproofing & put my dog in the care of decent people and I am now in the process of making one last rush at the world and its lunacy. Whatever comes of it won't matter, good or bad, because somewhere in the distance I have a vision of mountains & space & quiet & a place to make beer and mumble around naked and shoot out the front door & not give a damn for much of anything but the weather. The world is not mad, as I thought, but sane in the cheapest kind of way. So chalk me up as mad & to hell with it.

I have read the *National Observer* & know this to be true. Smyrna, Del. is the axis of the earth & all reason emanates from there. The Bomb is good & we are all reasonable people due to our training in Rotary Clubs over the course of many years. God is on our side because we invented him. And if he wavers we'll invent another one. If you can't buy them, squash them. That's the ticket.

OK. Mad & drunk I remain. Let me know your travel plans. I hesitate to suggest that you try South America instead of Europe, but what is hesitation anyway? If on the other hand you try Europe Semonin will be there until "summer," and several other people are there also, for good or ill. Nonetheless, I'd enjoy bumping into you in Rio—again, for good or ill. In closing, I remain,

for good or ill,
HST

TO WILLIAM J. KENNEDY:

Thompson's first port of call was to be Puerto Rico, where he hoped to write another voodoo story.

March 14, 1962
531 E. 81 Street
New York City

Bill—

OK. You go ahead & laugh about voodoo at Vacia Talega. I talked to Paul Harrison the other day (PRNS here) & he said when I stopped in San Juan I should definitely do a story on some festival they have out there—it must be voodoo. What else, out there in the wilds. So PRNS is coming around to voodoo & I think it's a good sign. They didn't come around quite far enough to buy an old photo I sent them out of desperation for even a single buck, but Harrison is a good guy & needless to say, knows I can handle voodoo like nobody's business. I just wonder if Sontheimer will sign the check.

I warned Hazlett that I was coming through & he wrote back that he was going to Switzerland. I guess I will write Dorvillier now, & ask him for a job. That will complete the cycle.

Anyway, I still plan to leave here around April 1. Not with Sandy. Would very much appreciate a couch at your place for maybe two days or three, depending on what I can scrape up in the way of articles. If nobody wants anything on PR, I would stay 48 hours at most, then go to Aruba and the great jumpoff.

As for my rotten goddam books, you may as well admit they were too much for you to handle & I will deal with them when I get there. I just hope to god they're in boxes like you say. As I recall, I left them all very neatly packed. You have probably been renting them out to meet the rum payments.

I will warn you again, at least 20 minutes before I arrive pale & half-naked and crazed with thirst. This time I'll come in with a .44 Magnum in a shoulder holster and a 33 photo-lab strapped on my back. I take the damnedest pictures you've ever seen & even sell a few. None of the good ones, of course—just like the fiction.

As you predicted, Volkening did not take me on. He sounded fairly agreeable & said he was fleeing the country & wanted no part of me or my ilk, no matter what I had written. A young woman who works for him read ½ the book & said it was "hard & bitter" but she had some hope for it & would like to see it again on completion.

So would I. The thing is weighing heavily on me now. It is all that stands between me and Peru. My money is running out & I have to flee this town soon or perish. I've been sick most of the time I've been here & it is only a matter of time before it becomes permanent. I have given up all hope of the book actually getting published and now only think in terms of getting it finished.

Sandy is going to work for a travel agency & will handle my affairs here until I get settled in South America, then use the agency discount to fly down. That's how it looks right now. If I go broke, of course, things will be different.

Semonin is in Madrid, holed up to work on *his* book. We have all gone mad, I think. He expects to be there a few months & would feel mightily cheered if you dropped him a line c/o Am. Exp., Madrid. Europe has not been real good to him — the icons are all smashed.

Said hello to Bone for you. He is restless. My plans are to see you soon. For god's sake don't rat on me.

HST

TO JIM THOMPSON:

With "The Rum Diary" finished and Latin America looming, Thompson caught up with his brother.

April 17, 1962
GPO Box 1049
New York, New York

Dear Jim:

Sorry not to have written in so long, but the past two weeks have been an awful strain. I finished the book and gave it to an agent — should hear something soon. Whatever I hear, I plan to leave New York either Sunday or Monday. I'll stay a few days then go on to Aruba, a small island off the coast of Venezuela. From there I'll get a boat to Caracas, and after that I can't say, except that I'll head down the west side of the continent, via Colombia, Peru, Bolivia, etc. My plan at the moment is to wind up in Rio de Janeiro, where I have made contact with the editor of the paper there, who seems like a fine fellow.[10] This is all pretty vague, but so am I right now and it's the best I can do. My money is very low and there may even come a time when I have to write home for a grant-in-aid to pull me through a bad spot. I hope not, but I'll have to see how it turns out. I'll probably send some articles to the *Courier-Journal* (Sunday), so you'll be able to keep up with me that way. Naturally, I'll write, too.

Your trip in New Orleans sounds fine. I know almost all the places you mentioned — Biloxi, Roosevelt, Pat O'Brians, Court of Two Sisters — and have been to them all except Ship Island. I knew you would have a good time once you got going. Things usually turn out that way. It is also very

---

10. Bill Williamson was editor of the *Brazil Herald*, the leading English-language newspaper in Latin America.

good to hear things are going well at home. I'll feel a lot better taking off for South America without having to worry about that.

Aunt Lee sent a letter the other day, but I couldn't read much of it. I think she said Cousin Margurite had a wreck in a car. I hope it wasn't a bad one, but then it didn't sound that way, from what I could make out in the letter.

The man downstairs is beating on the floor and yelling about calling the police. It is four in the morning and I guess the typewriter jars his nerves. They have hauled all the furniture out of this apartment except for one bed, and I am sitting on the floor with the t-writer on an old trunk and all my papers & junk spread out around me. The stray cats are screaming outside, I am drinking the home beer, Sandy is asleep, and tomorrow I have to get up at nine to get a smallpox vaccination. Yesterday I had my yellow fever shot. When I pack all this stuff I'll send a lot of it home, so be prepared. Also, if I get any mail at that address, hold onto it until I send a forwarding address, then send it as quickly as possible.

OK, the man is pounding again. Thanks for your good letter and be sure to write me in South America. Take care of things at home and keep me posted. See you when I get back.

Love,
H

TO LIONEL OLAY:

While Thompson was traveling throughout Latin America, Olay became one of his most frequent correspondents.

April 17, 1962
GPO Box 1049
NY 1, New York

Lionel—

Damn good letter from you, my man. I was beginning to think you didn't write anymore except for Big Money. And Mr. Thompson, he don't pay much.

But he kept on working, like you said, and last Friday the 13th he handed over a "finished" novel to an agent—the same one rumored to be dealing with an unpublished novel by Willie Kennedy of San Juan. Whom Mr. Thompson will see next week and get drunk as hell with and shout all night on the aims of art and the general rottenness of those In Trade. And then, after spiritually disemboweling all the world's merchants, Mr. Thompson will shove off for South America and begin the long hot agony of trying to keep alive on free-lance journalism.

That's my plan in a nutshell. I've been long delayed here, fighting with that stinking book, and now when I sit down to read these 366 pages that it took me 18 months to create, it simply seems like a waste of time. Right as I was finishing mine, I read a book called *Out of Africa* by Isak Dinesen, and it almost broke me down. I am going to do a lot of thinking before I start another book, which maddeningly enough, is already creeping into outline form. This writing is like cocaine and I'm damned if I can figure out why people keep at it. Aside from everything else, sitting on my ass all that time gave me a whopping case of piles. Where is the percentage?

As you observed, it is very easy to give advice. Usually the spirit in which the advice is given is more important than the advice itself. For me anyway. Which is why I appreciated your letter. Most of what you say is true, I think, but like most young writers I am a natural ingrate and will always think that my work and my views are above and beyond advice — at least until I finish one thing and can get far enough away from it to see it clear and mean like a girl who drives you mad when you're drunk and then looks like hell in the morning. I hope I won't see this novel like that, but I expect I will. Probably in six short months. Anyway, I have been drunk alone since I turned it in, ripping and roaring around New York, getting thrown out of bars, getting in fights, one auto wreck, abusing friendships and generally going to pieces after all those months of a discipline I never believed I could maintain. It is a great feeling to finish a book, even if it is worthless.

Now I am packing & getting shots and hustling to get off. I plan to see Kennedy around Monday, stay a few days, then off to Caracas in chaos. I have enough $$ for about a month. After that, *le déluge*. If you know anybody who might buy a book full of flogging and fighting and fucking, by all means let me know. It is called The Rum Diary, which should tell you quite a bit.

Your success is overwhelming and I hope to god you can do a good play. It's about time somebody did. And what is this book you're doing for Doubleday? Novel? I hope to christ it won't come to me via the DD One-Dollar Book Club, because it is a point of honor with me to welsh on those things and I'd hate to think I was doing you out of some money. Anyway, the fact that you're about to quit and go up the mountain to write is the best news anybody has sent me in a long time. Just the fact that you are out there will be a sort of beacon in the back of my brain, and when I finish this South America business I'll do my damnedest to get out there with my big meatmaster rifle and contribute something to the table. More than anything else, I miss those quiet mornings in the hills and the feel of a big gun on my shoulder and the peaceful excitement of sneaking up on a big buck. That is the nuts, my man, and nobody yet has shown me anything to beat it.

I have kissed Sandy several times for you, and if I could get my hands on Daryl I'd do the same with her. I am plagued with a mounting suspicion that time is going to force me to leave a lot of fine women undone. There is just too goddamn much to do and too many places to be all at once. There are nights when I want to be in San Francisco and New York and Rio and Madrid at the same time, and it seems unjust that I can't. If I had my way I'd be in love all the time all over the world with a rifle in one hand and a typewriter in the other and a bellyful of good whiskey. This limited existence is a shitty deal.

But there is no sense bothering you with these gripes, since next week I'll be setting up a tremendous din in Kennedy's living room, the likes of which he hasn't heard since my last outburst. I can see it all now—Dana will stay up till about midnight, and give up when I begin pacing. Then Kennedy and I will shout at each other until one of us caves in from rum. I am looking forward to it with a real eagerness.

Well, that's my story. I'll send the good word from South America and when you get up on that mountain, pull off a few rounds for me. By the time I get there I'll expect you to have a good line on all the local boar and enough four-point bucks to keep the adrenaline flowing. And while you're at it, I guess you might as well write something good. They say it helps.

OK, HST

TO MR. AND MRS. JOSEPH BAUMGARTNER:

Before leaving America, Thompson left Agar in the care of the Baumgartners, and offered them a few last-minute tips. He already missed his dog terribly.

April 20, 1962
New York City

Dear Mr. & Mrs. Baumgartner:

Well, you're probably as surprised as I am to find that I'm still in New York. It has been a very hectic few months, full of constant writing and with trips to Boston, Phila., and Washington to keep me busy. There were times when I considered asking you to ship Agar to New York, but I never thought about it very long. He could never be happy here—or in any city apt., for that matter—and it would only have been selfish of me to bring him. Now and then I see a Dobe on a leash, out for a brief walk in the evening, and I always feel sorry for them because I know how much happier they'd be with space to run and be free.

Well, that's that. On Monday evening I'm leaving for South America. One of my assignments will be to cover the World Soccer Championships in Chile; this will be in June and I'll be working for the same paper I was going to work for in London.[11] I'll also be working for the *Chicago Tribune*, so you might watch the Sunday paper (usually the travel section) for some of my things. As for how long I'll be gone, I can't say right now, but will definitely keep you posted. I might return in the summer, or I might stay longer, depending on what comes up. South America is so big and so full of activity that I can only guess what I'll run into.

I hope this will not cause any problem where Agar is concerned. There is no place in the country where he'd be any happier than he is with you, so unless he's becoming difficult for you to keep, I'd much prefer to leave the situation as is. On the other hand, I don't want to impose on you, so let me know the moment any problem arises. You can always reach me through my address in Louisville (2437 Ransdell Ave.).

As I said before, if there ever comes a time when you want to breed Agar, it is fine with me and of course any stud fee will be yours. I know what it is to feed a Dobe every day and there were times when I worked as hard for his food as I did for mine. I am also very curious as to how he's doing in those shows you mentioned. He is constantly on my mind and I miss him as much now as I did three months ago. When a person spends as much time on the move as I do, he becomes more than normally attached to the few tangible things he can call his own. I feel somewhat the same way about my guns, which are stored in Louisville, and I look forward to the day when I can settle somewhere with a brood of Dobermans and not do anything but hunt and write. This traveling is fine at times, but at other times it's very wearing and you get very lonesome for all the things that go with having a home.

I hope your weather is better by now, and that Agar is getting plenty of exercise. By all means drop me a line whenever you can, and I'll try to be better about answering than I was this time. Most days I am so worn out with writing that I can't face the idea of writing letters, but now that I've finished that book I was working on, I have more time and energy for the normal things. Let me say again how much I appreciate your keeping Agar, and working with him. It is the best thing that could have happened and I know now that I'd never have forgiven myself if I'd sold him to some stranger, as it looked for a while like I might have had to do.

Sincerely,
Hunter S. Thompson

11. The *National Observer*, just founded by the Dow Jones Company.

PS—I too had trouble getting him to come inside when I called him, and at first I thought I could cure him by spanking, but I soon realized that this only made him more reluctant to come and I gave up. Yet even after he learned everything else and minded perfectly on all other occasions, I could never be sure he'd come in when I wanted him to. He would just stand there and dare me to try and catch him, and whenever he was ready to come in, he would. He seemed to know there was nothing I could do about it, and of course he was right. I think he was just reminding me that he could be independent when he felt like it.

TO PAUL SEMONIN:

After spending ten days with William Kennedy in Puerto Rico, Thompson landed in Aruba, about which he wrote a story for the National Observer. *He spent nearly a week on the island before hitching a ride aboard a smuggler's boat headed for Puerto Estrella, Colombia.*

May 5, 1962
Aruba

Dear Spic:

I have too much to tell you to even get started on a small sheet like this one. Which is why I am using it. The big noise will have to wait. I just wanted you to know what happened to me if you don't get any word for several months.

My situation is as follows: I am in Aruba with $30; tomorrow afternoon I have a free ride to Colombia aboard a small sloop that will also carry a load of contraband whiskey; I may be in jail within 48 hours—a Colombian jail; if I get to Barranquilla, my goal, I will have no more than $5; what happens then is up to god. It is an odd situation when the best that can happen to a man is that he might arrive in South America with $5. Right now my big worry is jail; my second biggest worry is having all my gear stolen (specifically, camera gear), which would cripple my plans severely. My only hope for money rests with the fate of 5 identical articles I sent from San Juan. If they are used, I may have anywhere from $20 to $100, over and above my $5, when I get to Barranquilla.

This moving again is a wild and greasy feeling. I am red-brown and peeling, full of rum and Dutch beer, lying constantly, plotting without cease, and generally running amok. I am staying with a Dutch journalist and his wife here and they are treating me well indeed. I sent off two more articles today and five rolls of film for developing. Maybe something will come of it.

I spent 10 days in San Juan and did almost nothing but drink and talk with Kennedy. He was excellent beyond any expectations, jobless and full of hell and vinegar—a champ if ever the word still goes. San Juan is more gutless than ever and overflowing with American queers—so many that the government is investigating the influx. They are poking a four-lane highway toward the Loíza River. It is already to the Yacht Club, but the rest of the road is miraculously—if temporarily—the same. Another few months and it will be four-lane asphalt.

(Just killed a scorpion that crawled out of my camera bag. The other day I found one in my coat-sleeve.)

Well, I am getting too sleepy to write and tomorrow is Ugly Day. God only knows what will happen once I go aboard. It is terrifying to think of landing, via smuggler boat, in South America, with only $30 and 400 miles between me and the nearest town. Only indians where we beach. *No hablo. No comprendo. No tengo.* I am going to have to do a lot of smiling. Send word on you—I feel the contact slipping.

Hunter

TO WILLIAM J. KENNEDY:

Stuck in Aruba, Thompson wrote Kennedy thanking him for his hospitality in Puerto Rico and worrying about his pending voyage to Colombia via smuggler's boat.

May 10, 1962
Aruba

Bill—

Ok, I was in a hell of a hurry this morning and forgot to enclose this note to the *Herald*. Here it is, as mild and inoffensive as I could make it. Please relay the package on to the most prospective buyer.

I meant to write this letter to Dana and thank her for the patience, food, hospitality, and general decency that was accorded me during my prolonged visit. Without her, we would both have been in the nervous ward after three days.

I am still in Aruba, of course. The damn smugglers failed to leave on schedule and put it off till tomorrow. Like Trans-Carib. These spics are all the same. God damn them, anyway. But since the ride is free I cannot do much bitching. The Dutchman I am staying with is getting nervous, I think. He and his wife are both excellent people and took me in like a lost dog. I did my damnedest to bug the publicity tour and succeeded in destroying the morale of one of their models, if nothing else. I think I also destroyed Alexis' morale,[12] but that is all in the game.

I tell you, Kennedy, I nearly had my hands on it. For 24 hours the whole world went bright. A beautiful woman is such a wonderful creation as to make all novels seem like scum. It is enough to make a man believe in god. A novel is permanent, of course, and beauty isn't—but that only adds to it. On Monday I was ready to come back to San Juan, but luck was with me and I got raving drunk with the Dutchman. The impulse is still with me, but I think I have it under control. Christ, I hope so. It could finish me. I think it had something to do with Dana's influence.[13]

Enough of that. I know it is hell on you to go out and meet the postman and get nothing but letters from me—full of requests, at that. This is the last one, I think. Those books, of course. But then that is pretty old. I am laboring under the impression that you mailed all my articles immediately. If not I am done for. I now have $30 and will get to Barranquilla with about $5—if I am not jailed en route. People here are not very optimistic.

I need not go into any long paean concerning my stay there. It was a hell of a fine thing and when I land in a Colombian jail I will have a lot to think about. Needless to say, I want to be kept up to date on the status of "One by One"—also the other, newer. Also, needless to say, I will send word on all obits for The Rum Diary. And maybe, as I said, I'll have Sandy send it down to you for a quick tangling with madness.

In retrospect, your writing was a lot better and a lot tougher than I expected to find it. That scene with the guy taking off his clothes still bothers me. I don't know him at all and I don't have a feeling that he made his point. Personally, I would have him locked up as a disturbing nuisance. A rapist you can get a hold of, but an exhibitionist is quite a different thing. I am tempted to be funny here, so I'll cut it off. The best I can say is that I saw your point, but it didn't bounce like it should have—I didn't feel that guy had proved anything.

The rest of that sequence was good and convincing. Maybe the wind-up would have been truer if the guy had made a royal ass of himself and he realized it. It is my experience that that is the way those things usually turn out. But maybe you are luckier.

It is silly for me to wish you luck with the book(s), but I am coming to the conclusion that luck is more important than I'd previously thought. I would advise you to go to more parties, laugh more often, slap a few backs, flatter every writer and editor you can corner, go to NY every few months and give a literary tea—that should do it. All in all, I don't give either of us

12. Mike Alexis was a photographer for the Puerto Rican News Service.
13. The model Hunter had fallen for in Aruba looked like Dana Kennedy.

much hope for seizing the real money. The next best thing is to give up the rum and make your own beer—and maybe give up the children for their own good.

In the meantime I will be scrubbling around in the Andes, grinding it out, getting drunk when I can, and trying to pick up a few native handicrafts as a sideline. (I just recall that you accused me of being a liar. That is untrue—it is the words I chose. It is all in the words, the hump and roll of them.)

I leave you with that. And a final word of thanks to Dana. The next time I come I hope to be successful enough to bring a side of beef or something like that. Maybe just a case of rum.

OK. You can mail me in a week or so at the U.S. Consulate in Barranquilla. Unless we get seized. If that happens . . . well . . . I don't know.

Hunter

TO PAUL SEMONIN:

While in Barranquilla Thompson had spent an evening drinking whiskey with a group of local Indians and telling them he was a good friend of First Lady Jacqueline Kennedy.

May 26, 1962
En route to Bogotá

Yours reached me this morning, my man, and I can only say that . . . ah well . . . there is at this moment a beetle the size of god's ass on the table about six inches from the t-writer. It is worse than anything Kafka ever dreamed, so big I can see its eyes and the hair on its legs—jesus, suddenly it leaped off and now circles me with a menacing whir.

I face eight days of this. We have just left Barranquilla after fucking around all day with seven barges of beer for the interior. Now we are pushing them up the river and a huge beam of light pokes out ahead. In the beam are about six million bugs of various sizes—just snatched a beetle off my neck—constant stabbing of mosquitoes and things like mimis.[14] I have a choice tonight of sleeping outside on the deck or in a four-man cubicle over the engine room. I will give outside a try and retreat if I can't stand the bites. No repellent.

There will be no English spoken for eight days and maybe more. This boat is going only halfway, to an oil village on the Magdalena River. There I will have to find another boat, without English, but armed with a letter from a company bigwig. I can't read it, but it says I ride free. It is a deal I

14. A tiny, flea-like insect.

made—free 400-mile ride for about ten photos of boat for advertising use. All in all, it is 750 miles or so from Barranquilla to Bogotá. Only 7½ more days to go.

The crew is primitive and vicious looking and the captain is an old river toad who can't understand why I'm here and doesn't much care for it. His daughter is here too, but she is scraggy. I was dealing in a whorehouse last night but refused to pay and could not make my concepts understood. I convinced the lovely, but the chickenheaded madam held firm. Fuck them all. These latins are all whores in their own various ways—even the presidents. (The crew is silently watching me type; I can see them about six feet behind me out of the corner of my eye.) I created quite a stir demonstrating my telephoto lens and this letter machine should do the dinga. The zippo is old hat, of course, or I would use that too. It is a constant challenge to keep them off balance and wondering, instead of crouched for the kill.

A week ago I came over from Aruba on a fishing boat and spent three days with allegedly savage and fearsome indians. As it turned out, they were the best people I've met. Loíza Aldea is like Harlem compared to Guajira. They wear nothing but sashes around the waist and speak their own language, not Spanish. It is a smugglers' port of entry and for three days we drank the best scotch and stayed drunk as loons. A wonderful time but there was no water and the food was unfit for dogs. I had to eat it anyway, for fear of insulting them. I was warned about that in Aruba. I was in Colombia four days before anyone saw my passport. That was in Barranquilla. and I had a bit of a hard time explaining how I got in. There is no law in Guajira, no customs, no immigration, no white men, no nothing but indians and whiskey. Barranquilla was a city, of course, too much like San Juan for my taste, but now we are heading into wild country again— with seven barges of beer. If I can make any friends in the crew I will try to have at the beer. Seven barges should yield enough for all. I have been swilling beer like a bastard—one dime a bottle, cigs 8 cents. I am down to 10 U.S. dollars but have developed a theory which will go down as Thompson's Law of Travel Economics. To wit: full speed ahead and damn the cost; it will all come out in the wash.

I have just received a clipping of mine from the *New Orleans Times-Picayune*, a long and pondering thing on Cuban exiles. (Christ, that monster beetle is back, gripping and sucking at the tablecloth, which is already covered with ants. I may have to kill it, but why bother.)

Am meeting decent people all along. A Dutch journalist in Aruba and two ivy-type English teachers in Barranquilla. They gave me the name of a Fulbright type in Bogotá, who will feel the full weight of my presence in eight days. Unless the June 10 Peru elections look to be bloody, I will stay in Bogotá two weeks or so, then proceed slowly to Ecuador and down the coast to Lima. I am moving more slowly than I thought and it is better for the oddities. I arrived on the South American coast with 12 U.S. dollars, and in Barran. with 11 dimes. (Great shit I was just stung on the neck by a bug twice the size of that beetle. Had to kill the bastard. I may not be able to keep up this typing—the light is bringing in the big ones.) They are all over me, look like scorpions. Jesus, eight days of this. You get what you pay for, I guess, and I ain't paid. But it will grab me some original photos, if nothing else. Maybe malaria too. I am drinking water everywhere and praying against fever. There is a definite sense of the Congo here; we have left Barran. behind and the banks are lined with palms and other shaggy matter. I can see it when they swing the light. The captain is going to bed, locking his daughter's door from the outside and eyeing me stonily. Maybe it is time to have at the cerveza. I will look up the mechanic, who has the grin of a drinker and arms like King Kong. The fucking bugs are on me in force. I can barely stand it. My balls for a sleeping pill. Or an air-conditioned cabin at $20 a night. There may be something to this tourism after all. Even the drinking water is hot now. I am sweating like an animal.

And now for you. "Cabin empty in April" sounds like the knell of doom. (Another huge beetle, slapped at him but missed.) About the time to dig down for that checkbook, eh? (Everyone seems to be going to bed here— they will probably get me up at some unholy hour.) I got 2 hours last night, after being ejected from the whorehouse at 5:00. Tossing pesos around like beans. It is hard to believe they are real. This morning I rated 3 inches on the social page of the Barranquilla *El Heraldo*. All lies, but in Spanish and harmless. My mind is wandering; I can't concentrate with these bugs. I keep seeing you running around there with a notebook, trying to drum up revolutions. Who in hell are you working for? Any money coming in? Still scratching after that nymphet? Is McGarr doing anything but eating and wandering around Berbers?[15] He claims to be writing; I guess art is dead. Now the bugs are dying on the table and crawling into the ty-writer. I am trying to blow them out, but can't. The lights keep dimming. I think the captain is fucking himself. Christ, my leg for a cool beer. 8 days of this. If I ever get to Bogotá, I may never leave. Got a forwarded letter from Hudson about five days ago and he is now the sole owner of the boat. Michael gave up the ghost. Harvey Sloane[16] plans to finish and take off near the end of summer. He broached the possibility of my meeting him somewhere and signing on, also asked about you. I doubt that he got your letter, from

15. Eugene McGarr was in Morocco.
16. Harvey Sloane served as mayor of Louisville, Kentucky, for two terms (1973–77 and 1981–85). In 1960 Sloane met Thompson in San Juan, Puerto Rico, and they became longstanding friends.

what he said. Appeared to have no idea what you were doing or what plans. Nor do I, for that matter. Is it Africa after Spain? Hudson talked of having you join the crew, also Sandy. I am holding off any commitments till he gets the thing in the water and it floats. By summer's end I intend to be in Rio and zeroing in on October elections there. God, these bugs. I think I have to quit.

A word about Aruba, since you asked. It is decent for a short stay, very expensive and probably a cheap easy destination from any European oil port. From Aruba to Europe it is $3–5 a day by freighter. I fell among hospitable people there and had a good stay, but would not like to try it unaided. Of course, I am paving a way for other vagrants. The names are on file. Write me c/o U.S. Embassy, Consular section, Lima, Peru, or the box in New York, which is more reliable since my plans are subject to violent sudden changes. OK. . . . The U.S. is looking better and better. A job may be the answer. Or the dole.

Hunter

TO PAUL SEMONIN:

After the tortuous journey down the Magdalena River, Thompson arrived in Bogotá exhausted and nearly broke.

June 6, 1962
Bogotá, Colombia

I am in Bogotá now, Semonin, and it is raining outside. I have just finished dinner in the dining room of the Imperial Hotel, and, due to that fact, am now writing in coat and tie. Like Thomas Mann. I am in the Imperial at 25 pesos a day, *con comida* [including food], and it is a moot question as to how and when I'll get out. I can meet tomorrow's bill, 75 pesos, but the next, on Monday, will come close to cleaning me out—and there are a good many miles to go before I rest. I am writing this letter because it has been drilled into my head that if I am going to write for money I cannot write a word that will mean a fucking thing in two weeks' time. I have been accused, in fact, of submitting articles that read "like letters and essays," which of course they were. Needless to say, they have not seen print. And I have not seen money: $20 in all—two long-worked pieces in the *New Orleans Times-Picayune*, which is getting the bargain of the year. My mail has gone to the dogs, my photos are going nowhere, my bowels are racked with dysentery, my contacts speak no English, my countrymen want me deported, and my overall situation is a black X on a black wall. I have a suspicion that this is a good town, but I am damned if I know where to grab it. I have done everything I could to find a beery journalist, but there are none and that is a bad sign in any town. The people at the Embassy and the USIS [United States Information Services] are so full of shit that the stench floats down to the street and disrupts traffic. I think all the good Americans died in a riot somewhere that I have not yet heard about because there is no news here. For all I know the world is burning or Germany has started another war. But regardless of what is happening, nobody here either knows or cares. Local news is big, of course, one strike after another—students, busmen, bondsmen—forever striking, and it is all I can do to wander around in the mobs and get photos that nobody will ever use for anything except as an excuse to bill me for development fees. Sex is the main bug, of course, not the actual lack of humping as much as the lack of any possibility, a sexual deadness in the air that makes me feel I might be locked up for looking at women on the street. Even in San Juan there was a fine, lusty tension in the air, a meeting and gripping of eyes at every corner. Aruba had a bit of the same thing, and so did the Caribbean coast of Colombia. Ah, but not here—here we wear coats and ties at all times. This morning I was asked to leave the dining room for not dressing for breakfast. I refused, of course, and ate in a black, sullen silence which will undoubtedly be reported somehow to President Kennedy and my passport will be revoked. No matter where I go I am the only man in sight without a sportcoat and tie. In all the cafés, on every street, even the beggars dress. I am not kidding—the waiters in the dining room dress immediately after each meal and hang around the hotel in filthy suits—but with ties. And this is one of the cheapest hotels in town.

Being a free-lancer is impossible, of course; they are used to the $100-a-day types who fly in and out without the faintest idea of who the president is or what it means. These are the Alliance for Progress boys, deft technicians all. And then there are the social workers, vastly dedicated people who make a man feel degenerate if he can't avoid a feeling that they are all phonies. It is like knocking the flag.

Everybody is working terribly hard on some Worthwhile Project, and for some queer reason it is depressing. They are hauling the indians out of mud huts and putting them in huts made of concrete blocks—then hiring $100-a-day photographers to take pictures of the progress. They have imported ping-pong and the Twist to combat the Red Menace, and an unsalaried cynic with no coat or tie might just as well slink off to some bistro and masturbate in a back booth.

Needless to say, my plans are changing with each passing week. Now I am ready to move on to Peru, write a few shitty things from there, then dash across the mountains to Rio, where, if nothing else, there is at least an English-language newspaper. Bone writes, for that matter, that he is pushing for a job in Rio, the same one that was tentatively offered to me several months ago. Editing some kind of Chamber of Commerce magazine. My reply to that will probably blackball me forever in Rio, just as other letters have made me friends elsewhere. Just what I will do for money in Rio is one of those questions that I'd rather not consider. Or Peru, for that matter. Or anywhere else. Sandy reports that the agent still has not read the novel, after six weeks. It will take him six minutes, I think, to skim 15 pages and toss it aside as the work of a crank. I think the Mad Bomber had a point and I am beginning to understand my mystic attachment to my guns. If I had one now I would feel a lot better. Either I am going mad or there is a definite conspiracy afoot in the world, a conspiracy of fatness and blindness, backed up by a sinister mindless kind of reasoning that is only necessary to justify what is already a fact and what will always be a fact. But there is no sense rambling on like this at a time when I am beginning to doubt my own sanity. Maybe if I could burst into the streets speaking perfect Spanish I might find something sane, but I seriously doubt it. Whatever I am looking for here is not generally wrapped in words, which these people are full of. The students held a protest meeting on the steps of the presidential palace tonight and it looked like all those shouting photos of Castro, and probably sounded the same too. They are a gutsy lot at times, as a good many news pictures here will illustrate. The cops are what give me the creeps; to look at them in the jackboots is bad enough, but to see photos of them firing wildly into mobs of students is a bit unreal. Running them into corners and piling up bodies three deep—this has happened often enough to make me feel nervous even standing near a demonstration. Most of it, of course, took place several years back, and Colombia is supposed to be coming to its senses again. But yesterday in Barranquilla the army tackled a student protest march with clubs and gas, and it was only because the students fled that nobody was shot.

I am going to miss the Peruvian elections due to poverty, and undoubtedly there will be enough killing and violence there to make me a rich man in mob-photo circles. But I will have to read about it with my fucking dictionary, then hump around the streets waiting for *Time* to tell me what happened. The only way to grasp these things is to settle in somewhere and find out what is going on before the noise starts, so that you at least know which way to run. For that reason I am thinking seriously of making tracks to Brazil and getting hip on the October elections so that by the time they happen I won't be lost in the mud. After that, god knows. Two months of steady, penny-pinching travel has worn me down a bit, and there is at least two months more before I get to Rio, even at the earliest. And if I get there and find they don't believe in humping, that will be it. I will one way or another make it back to the Magnum country and lay in a stock of beer-makings, there to bitch and grumble in comparative peace for as long as I can stand it. Hudson's boat is a definite possibility, but it will be fall before he knows anything definite. I think I said this in my last boat-letter (god that was an awful trip) and there is no reason to bat it around again. I can't face another sheet of paper so I'll quit here, imploring you to give some notice as to your plans and movements. Also a bit of what it is like living in Madrid. Details, you know. Those are the big things. Yeah.

Hunter

TO AL PODELL, *ARGOSY:*

Constantly photographing images of Latin American life, Thompson pitched some photojournalism pieces to the editor of Argosy.

June 26, 1962
Cali, Colombia

Al Podell:

I can't remember if I wrote to say the boat-crossing shots were pretty bland and not much in your line. That's what PIX[17] said, anyway.

Two more possibilities here. Let me know as soon as you can if you think you can use either one.

1) I just looked at a bunch of contacts that are about the goriest god-damn things I've ever seen. There is a hell of a problem here in Colombia with what they call Rural Violence. This means that out in the countryside there are a good many people who pass the time of day whacking off their neighbor's heads with machetes. They also have an interesting trick called the *Corte de Flanella,* which they accomplish by cutting the throat and jerking out the tongue. Lots of other kicks too—like ambushing army pa-trols with submachine guns. I've done a lot of talking about it here and am pretty well up on the background. I also have access to these rotten photos. They are ones taken by local press photogs after the massacres. Severed heads, pregnant women cut open and cats stuffed into their wombs, long lines of mutilated bodies on the ground, dead soldiers in heaps, etc. I think it beats the hell out of *The Monster of Lake Balawaca* and that stuff, be-cause this is real as hell. Cali is the center of the violence area. It has been going on for 12 years, but calmed down a bit during the regime of dictator Rojas Pinilla. Now it is getting worse. So bad, for instance, that nobody goes to the big country club on the edge of town after dark. I came over the mountains in a taxi from Bogotá, right through the center of the bad area,

---

17. PIX was one of the largest photo agencies in New York. Thompson often sold them his work.

and people here have yet to get over it. I came at night. They have got me so much on edge that I am buying a pistol, because I do a hell of a lot of wandering around at night, against all sane advice. The Colonel in charge of the Cali garrison told me the *bandeleros,* as they are called here, are all communists bent on taking over the country. He says his men are simply outgunned. The bandits, he says, get a steady supply of Red arms from Panama and Ecuador. There is probably some truth to this, and if it keeps up there is no doubt that the Reds stand to gain by it and will certainly help it along. What it now amounts to is a bloodthirsty nucleus for a guerrilla army, and all it needs to make it a real threat is a Castro-type leader. The men and the guns are there, just waiting. People in Cali are upset as hell over it and blame the army for not being tough enough. Some say the army is not trained to fight guerrillas, which is true. This is an old problem, of course; witness the U.S. difficulties in SE Asia. Another thing worrying people here is the presence of another guerrilla army (small) in the mountains on the other side of the country near Venezuela. That one is definitely Castroist, but so far they have not raised much hell. Again, it is a thing that could suddenly explode with the right help.

Anyway, that's the idea. If it interests you let me know c/o the U.S. Embassy in Quito, Ecuador. In the meantime I am gathering dope for a small piece on the thing for the *National Observer,* which is buying enough of my stuff to keep me moving. So I will have the info and I can get all the photos you can stand. I will catch a batch of possibilities and if it interests you I'll have the photog here send them along to you in NY. But let me know as soon as you can. I will, for enough money, go out after photos of the actual *bandeleros,* but if I do anything like this it will have to be on an assignment basis. Nobody here will do it and I would have to go with an army patrol that would stand a better than even chance of getting ambushed. So I leave that aspect of it for you to ponder. There are plenty of shots of past massacres, but not many of massacres in progress. None, in fact. Anyway, let me know what you need to make up a good photo feature. The writing will be no problem, as I already have plenty of dope.

2) Another and far less risky idea is a feature on South American whorehouses, which are patronized here like bars are patronized in NY. I got some shots in a house in Barranquilla, and as far as I know the contacts are either at PIX or Motal Lab. That would be just a beginning, but it will give you an idea. I have more shots from Cali, better stuff I think, and will undoubtedly get more as I move down south. Cali, by the way, is famous for its pretty girls, but you would have to see to believe. Walking the streets here can drive a man up the wall in ten minutes. It is virtually impossible for me to get any work done and I am half-mad from trying. Some of the whores will knock your eyes out. Most of the bachelors I have met here (all

of them, in fact) have their whorehouses, their "Numbers" (supposedly "nice girls" or "*senoritas*," who sneak out for a quick hump at night), and their *Contrabandista*, who supplies whiskey and cigarettes. Most of them also have special taxi drivers, for all-purpose work. The peg would be the wholly different sexual climate, with a vast gulf between nice girls and whores, and virtually no middle ground. None for public consumption, that is. As always, there are a lot of sneakers. Yet even then the line is still drawn. Once a girl moves over the hump, so to speak, she is socially done for and might just as well move into a whorehouse if the word ever gets out, because marriage is out. Unless she marries a pimp. All this tends to make whorehouses socially acceptable; the logic being that as long as the good girls are kept locked up, the others can do what they damn well please. And, as in all Latin countries, the sexual code for men is totally apart from that of the women.

Ok, that's about it. Number one I would like to know about pretty quick. Two can wait, because I have full confidence that I will always have plenty of material for good shots.

Let me know as soon as you can.

Thanks,
Hunter S. Thompson

TO BILL WILLIAMSON, *BRAZIL HERALD:*

Stone broke in Peru, Thompson appealed to the editor of the Brazil Herald.

From the extra bed in the flea-ridden
hotel room of . . .   . . . Hunter S. Thompson
                                               August 3, 1962
                                               Lima

William:

[. . .] I recently arranged with the *Observer* to go from here to Mexico City, then across the Caribbean and down to Rio via the Guianas and Recife. Fortunately, I am too broke at the moment to even consider such a thing, so I will proceed as planned from here to La Paz to Rio. It will involve a mad, headlong, poverty-stricken rush across the continent. I have a panama hat and 200 pounds of excess luggage, so the trip should be a killer. It cost me $38 simply to get my gear from Guayaquil to Lima, via Panagra. It goes without saying that I have taken my last plane in South America, at least until I can deposit some of this worthless junk.

If Rio is no better than the places I have visited thus far I will beat a hasty retreat to the north and write this continent off as a lost cause. For the past month I have felt on the brink of insanity: weakened by dysentery, plagued by fleas and vermin of all sizes, cut off from mail, money, sex and all but the foulest food, and hounded 24 hours a day by thieves, beggars, pimps, fascists, usurers, dolts and human jackdaws of every shape and description. If these are Pizzaro's ancestors you are goddamn lucky he never got to Brazil. All this time I have had in the back of my mind an unreasoning certainty that Rio is a decent place where a man can sit in the sun and drink a beer without having to put on a frock coat and carry a truncheon to ward off the citizenry. If this is a delusion I will probably have a breakdown when I arrive and the Embassy will be forced to ship me home like an animal, with "No Dice" scrawled across my passport.

At any rate, your note was the only ray of optimism I have found in as long as I dare remember. My last communication from Bone was a letter threatening my life, I believe, and the rest of the mail has been no cheerier. I will be here long enough to divine the nature of Peruvian politics, then push on to La Paz for a bout with whatever diseases are currently fashionable in that country. After that, I face the 2-week train to Rio, which should just about finish me off. If there is an Alms House in Rio I trust you are on good terms with the proprietor, so I can enter without delay.

Until then, I remain, yours for the broadening aspects of travel,

HST

TO PAUL SEMONIN:

Disappointed by Lima, Thompson nevertheless wrote one of his finest Na-tional Observer articles there: "Democracy Dies in Peru, but Few Seem to Mourn Its Passing."

August 4, 1962
Lima, Peru

Niggerboy:

As I recall, my letter from Guayaquil was done in a fit of drink, and since there is no chance of that happening now, I will try to explain some of the things that I didn't say too well.

It alarms me to think you may come over here on my say-so, because I am not sure myself just what I think. One sure thing is that since leaving Colombia, which is a good country in a lot of ways, I have been getting steadily more depressed until I am seriously beginning to wonder if my personality is being undermined. As a matter of fact, every place I have been except Cali, Colombia has been a pure dull hell and full of so many nagging discomforts that I am tempted at times to write this continent off as a lost cause. Lima is the worst so far; I have done nothing but sit in my hotel room, which is like something on the main street of Flora, Illinois, and smoke. Now and then I go out to eat or to be snubbed at the Embassy. I have spoken to no one except the AP man in four days. Perhaps I should say I have talked to no one; there is a lot of talking done here but it means absolutely nothing—in a way that makes it an easy place to write about, because all you have to do is line up all the facts, note how they refute everything you are told, and simply ignore all the shit people ram in your ears. And the facts line up very simply. They made a show of having free elections here, a queer won, the army didn't like it and the army took over. The fact that the army and the bankers are still very much on speaking terms sort of speaks for itself. The only ones who think democracy is going to work here are the people in Washington—and perhaps the U.S. Ambassador who was virtually drummed out of the country when he voiced his displeasure with the takeover. He is now in Washington too, and will probably stay there. Meanwhile, business goes on as usual.

That may give you an idea of what I mean when I say you can learn a lot here. (They are throwing rocks at the window again; it is driving me into a black rage but in my weakened condition I dare not go into the street and tackle a pack of thugs drunk on pisco.) The machinations of politics are so obvious and the types of people are so extreme that you understand very quickly how life works. The grey areas are so extreme that you understand a lot more about the U.S. but it is not simply that I have got away from it geographically but in a lot of other ways as well. Maybe Spain is the same way, but I am sure France and England and Germany and Italy are not. What I mean here is that people down here have not the faintest idea what I'm talking about. If they have a sense of humor it focuses not on the ridiculous or even the improbable, but on the sadistic. Frankly I have seen no evidence of any sense of humor at all; I have heard them laugh like hell all the while. I am beginning to think that my coming here is like an Abolitionist going to the Old South and trying to communicate with the people there. And considering the relations between the indians and the wealthy (there is no other group) I think the comparison is fairly apt.

Frankly, I don't like the bastards. Nor do I like the Americans I've met down here because they go to extremes to ape the locals, explaining that "it is the only way to get along in business." Naturally, the only Americans down here are businessmen. Occasional reformers, but they don't last. As I probably said in my last letter, I have not had human contact since William Kennedy in San Juan.

All in all it has been like being in jail and I think I am beginning to crack under the strain. I note a wailing, paranoid tone in my letters, a complete lack of anything like vitality or a decent feeling for life. None of which I have, of course. I am so goddamn wracked by dysentery and several other heinous diseases that for the past three days I have not been able to leave the hotel due to constant vomiting, shitting and dizziness. I finally hauled my ass to a doctor and spent all day in a clinic getting tested, jabbed, poked and all the other tests that rotten specimens are given. The report will come on Tuesday and I fear it. Meanwhile I am trying to write a story on Peruvian politics but it is rough going when I cannot think clearly. And with rocks clattering off the windows. I hear a woman's voice in the hall now and it nearly breaks me down with lust. Having my sex life cut off is probably the worst of it. Or was until recently, anyway, when I was cut off drink indefinitely. Also off pepper, spices and fried foods. This is my second drink-stoppage and since that was my only pleasure I am not sure how long I can stand up under it. For the first time in three months I have been able to get tobacco—at $1.25 for four ounces. I cannot drink the water, the milk, the beer, or anything but mineral water. Nor can I eat anything but maize and unpeppered meat. Vegetables are out, of course. The whole continent is covered with indian shit and everything that grows is poison. Beware everything, that is the motto.

These are the things that make it impossible for me to enjoy anything, even if there were anything to enjoy. It compares very favorably to the way we were received in St. Louis that ugly time. And if you can imagine that sort of thing dragging on for three months you can understand how I feel and why I am nearly at the end of my rope.

On the other hand, I am trying to resist the temptation to go into a funk and quit because I know it cannot be as bad as it seems. To begin with, I have three drastic handicaps: 1) my knowledge of Spanish is still almost nil, 2) I keep moving from one place to another and never have time to sink into a place, and 3) I am forever broke to the point of madness, and in this economy that is disaster.

It seems to be possible to live with the natives over there, but here it can't be done. They are unbelievably primitive. I have tried and that is reason one for my present condition. Nor can a poverty-stricken man live with the white people; he simply can't afford it. So I am stuck somewhere in between with no company and I'm getting damn tired of it. I have not met a soul on this continent who was not either desperately poor or making $150 a week at bottom. Now that I think on it there was one exception in Bogotá (a Fulbright lad) and one in Cali (a Canadian teaching English). Also two young Americans in Barranquilla, but that was for 3 days and they were hardly wad-busters. The others are spiritual [J. P.] Morgan trainees, and for that matter the majority are real bankers.

I retain a mad faith that Rio is better, primarily because I have heard it is bad from people who would not know a good thing if they swallowed it.

I have also had a good exchange of letters with the editor of the paper there, saying flatly that I need not worry about money although he is not sure where it will come from. But he sounds hip and the atmosphere is at least that uncertain and besides he says it is cheap even by my standards. Perhaps it is just these rotten indian lands that are this way. Colombia was different, although I did not have enough sense then to appreciate it. I have begun to have a great belief in the effect of climate on personality. It has held true 100% so far and that is one of the few things that moving fast can tell you. Lima, for instance, is the gloomiest place I have ever seen with the possible exception of Bogotá. The *guara* is on the land and has been here since May; they say it breaks in October or November, but that doesn't do me much good. It is hard to believe this town could ever be anything but gloomy. Maybe if I could find a white girl even to chat with over mineral water it would not be so bad. As it is, I don't talk at all and it is frightening what this kind of living can do to a man.

None of this does you much good, of course, since I doubt you'll be getting to Lima anytime soon, even if you aim this way instead of niggerland. I hesitate to recommend it, yet I intend to stay down as long as I can stand it. Rio will be the boom-or-bust point. If that is bad I will have to give up in spite of my firm conviction that there is a lot to be learned here, and—for somebody else—a lot to be done. I suppose I will look back even on Lima some day as a good and worthwhile episode where I got a little closer to seeing life as it is. But it is hard to see anything when your eyes are bloodshot and your cheeks are hollow and your bowels are rotten and your head spins when you get up and your prick is falling off and you barely have the energy or even the inclination to get out of bed in the morning. That is exactly the way I feel.

I think Bone is going to Rio to work on a CC [Chamber of Commerce] magazine. It is something that editor mentioned to me while I was in New York, and I passed it along. Bone wrote several weeks ago saying it had come through. I give you that for what it is worth, as far as pondering your move is concerned.

As for me, I hope to finish this story in the next few days, and if my health permits, shove off by bus and train for La Paz. I think I will have enough money to get there, and if the *Observer* pays quickly for the Lima thing, I will then have enough to shove on to Rio. That is a two-week train journey, and it should just about do me in. What I think I need more than anything else is a chance to settle in where I at least know somebody, and act like a human being for a change instead of a traveling stenographer. And to recover my health, which I had never lost before this, and let me assure you it is a hellish thing to contend with not only on the physical side but more on the mental. This letter, plus my last, will undoubtedly provide ample evidence of my mounting hysteria and general inability to focus. I am having to work hard as hell to keep it from showing up in my journalism.

Hah! Exhibit A—the thing I had in mind when I started this letter was to tell you I was canceling that swing up through Mexico and the Carib. Here I have rambled three pages and not mentioned it. Anyway, it's off. I haven't told the *Observer* yet and am a little worried on that score, but in my present condition I could no more undertake a thing like that than I could swim around the Horn. So I hope to be in Rio by September 1, probably in rotten shape but with things looking up. I hope. (It is a good sign that I remembered to say this; maybe my brains are warming up.)

There was no mail when I got here (another thing I'd meant to say earlier). They had forwarded it either to Guayaquil, as I requested, or to Quito, which I didn't request, or they had sent it back as unclaimed (at which point I nearly shit)—but they couldn't remember which, and didn't much care. Embassy people are shits; Consulates are better—that is a rule. Anyway, I didn't get your earlier letters. Nothing from Hudson either; I wrote him today, demanding to know his plans. When you write, use the New York box; at least there is hope there.

                                                          Hunter

TO PAUL SEMONIN:

After spending a week in Ecuador writing National Observer *pieces, Thompson landed in Bolivia exhausted but in good spirits. A letter from Semonin was waiting for him at the U.S. consulate in La Paz.*

                                        August 28, 1962
                                        La Paz, Bolivia

Paul—

Yours arrived today, jack, and I'm going to whip this one off in hopes of catching you before shoveoff time. Fat chance, considering the fucking mails here. Your hideous pansy envelope almost prevents me from answering—yet I was encouraged by the rich paper and all appearances of a new t-writer ribbon. You must be working for the govt.

I for one see definite humor in the rape of nuns.[18] And while we are humoring, I would advise you not to laugh too hard at those who rank themselves by how far they have wandered in search of work—nor at scavengers, for that matter. We are all members of one another, eh?

18. Semonin had sent Thompson a newspaper article he'd read about nuns being raped in Colombia.

For my part, I am about to be dismembered here in the Andes for the issuing of ugly checks in a far-off town called Lima. They are trailing me like golf balls, coming low and hard on all the walls. In a phrase, I have fallen from grace. That being a pun of sorts, because the Grace Company[19] has been backing me in the check-cashing business and suddenly we are all stung. I have, in short, over-extended myself.

I was also stung, quite literally, by a poison bug in Cuzco, which paralyzed my leg and put me in great pain for 3 days—not to mention the awesome doctor bills. When they get a gringo down here, they really get him. I support most of the medicos on the continent, and those in Brazil don't know what a good thing is coming their way. I am trying to get out of here on the jungle train, but the hotel won't take my check so I can't leave. I just sit in the room and ring the bell for more beer. Life has improved immeasurably since I have been forced to stop taking it seriously. Frankly, reality here is too much to handle. I have given up politics and have publicly declared myself an *anarchista*, which has contributed heavily to the making of new and foreign friends. I am at last cracking the language barrier, using sex as a wedge and drink to dilute the ignorance. Next is the Santa Cruz, which is supposed to be the Cali of Bolivia, which means I will probably never get to Rio. (Cali is the Valhalla of Colombia, which in turn is the Valhalla of South America.) La Paz is good enough, fine sun and snow-capped peaks all around. I am sitting at 13,000 and the snow runs up to 23,000. Electricity is rationed and I have to go up five flights of stairs on one leg to check my mail at the embassy, where they have no elevators and are working by Coleman lanterns. Bolivia is not quite real, but they have good beer and white girls and, god help us, a sense of humor. All the Brazilians I have met have been zanies, to use your (and Mencken's) term and I am looking forward to it if I can ever scrape up the loot to pay this awful hotel bill. Now that I am finished with Ecuador and Peru things are picking up. Both should be dynamited into the sea. I am thinking of ordering a barrel of lobster sent down from Maine and giving a reception in Santa Cruz, courtesy of Dow-Jones. The Grace *jefe* [boss] here is a good friend of Barney Kilgore's, and Barney is *jefe* of Dow-Jones. I was treated well until the golf ball story was published. They are sweating, though, because they have vouched for several hundred here, which I spent on drink and native gimcracks. Send word to Rio, and keep loose over there. I think the testicles are descending. Hello to Africa. I remain, *con bombas,* HST

---

19. W. R. Grace and Company had served as Thompson's entrée to Latin America and also cashed checks for him.

TO CLIFFORD RIDLEY, *NATIONAL OBSERVER:*

At last Thompson arrived in Rio de Janeiro, where he would stay until May 1963. Ridley had written to him that his National Observer *articles were winning high praise throughout the journalism community. Although not on salary, by the time Thompson arrived in Rio he was selling the* National Observer *regular stories.*

September 17, 1962
Rio de Janeiro

Dear Ridley:

I've been trying to get off a letter to you for about a week now, but have been hopping across jungle & Mato Grosso, touring oil camps, spending all my $$ on antibiotics, etc., and ain't been near a P.O. to get anything sent.

Hope you got the packet from La Paz. It cost me $10, but I figure it's better to buy a little insurance than lose the whole works—or have it long delayed like the Peru piece. As long as I have cash I think I'll keep spending like that. [. . .]

Let me know what you think of the Indian story. If I have enough good stuff for a photo story, I'll ship a 1500-word text. If you can't get a photo layout from what I sent, I can expand the thing to normal (7 or 8 takes) size. Anyway, I have it & await some word as to size requirements. It will not, by the way, be a "Bolivia story," but split just about evenly between Bolivia, Peru & Ecuador—very much along the lines I first suggested.

Sorry those were so long. From now on I think I can hold them down; within reason, anyway. I will not have the compulsion here to get everything in one chunk, as I've had in these other countries. Brazil is simply too big, and besides that I'll be here long enough to let some things wait.

Elections here are October 7. I'll get a comparatively brief background piece to you before then. The situation here is pretty wild. This is a hell of a country & a relief to finally be here. Rio makes the other cities I've seen look like garbage dumps. More on that later.

Sandy also said that you (& "the board") were worried that I am not writing "mostly for the *Observer.*" Also that the board might be under the impression that I am not "mostly depending on them (the *Observer*)."

Man, I have not depended on anybody for a long time like I've depended on the *Observer* down here. I just assumed you knew this. Not since Bogotá have I sent anything to any other paper. They were using my stuff through the Caribbean & early Colombia, but paying disgracefully. When you came through with white man's wages I figured first things first, and put the rest aside.

And money was only one of the reasons. You've given me enough space (yeah, even with the editing) to really deal with these things I've been writing about, rather than merely hitting one or two high spots like I would have to do for other papers. Naturally I'll bitch when you cut things, but I think I'd be remiss if I didn't. I'm not down here to make money or to get by with writing as little as possible; if I were I'd pick up a *Time* stringership or something on that order. As you can probably tell by the stuff I've sent, I work like hell on it, almost always to the point where my expenses are way above what I finally get paid. But I figure every extra week I've spent in these countries is a week I won't have to spend the next time I go back. An investment, as it were, and now that I've survived this much of the thing I think I'd be kicking myself right now if I'd just skimmed through with an idea of picking up enough surface stuff to pay my way. As it is now, I have a lot of notes (and names) that don't pertain to anything I've sent, but which could prove invaluable sometime in the future.

(Another note here: September 14 *Time* says Comibol produces a pound of tin for $1.25. My figure is $1.35, which I got from the Minerals Attaché at the U.S. Embassy. I don't know where Luce got his, but if I had to bet I'd go with mine. At a guess, I'd say *Time* asked the Bolivian embassy in Wash., which, like Comibol, would be inclined to exaggerate their wages and minimize their production costs. I didn't get my correx on the daily wage until I checked my final draft with the labor man from USIS.)

(Note again: *Time*'s total USAID [U.S. Agency for International Development] figures also disagree with mine, but maybe they're already adding in this year's grant. I have the entire USAID breakdown as to figures, and their book says that from '42 until December 1961 the U.S. chipped in $184.7 million. Another $80 mill. was made available this year, but so far Bolivia has only come up with plans to spend some $42.5 mill. of it. It is highly doubtful that they'll manage to dispose of the entire $80. Anyway, it all goes on fiscal years & is hard as hell to calculate accurately.)

(Third note: same *Time* piece says per capita aid to Bolivia is "highest in LatAm." I & many others said "highest in the world." If I am wrong on this it is pure ignorance, but I remain under the impression I am right.) End notes.

Anyway, all I started out to say here is that I've been depending entirely on the *Observer* for both income and publication—so much so that when I go somewhere to ask questions I say I'm writing for the *Observer* & even had some little cards printed with my name & the *Observer* on them. (In South America a man without a card might just as well not have a name.) "Well you see, my name is X and I have an awful curiosity; I wonder if you'd mind giving me the inside dope." There is as much politics to getting a story down here as there is in the story itself—often more.

On the other side of that fence, however, I've never told anyone I was anything but a free-lancer who wrote for the *Observer*. Nor have I ever abused that linkage or done anything as far as I know to discredit the paper or give anybody anything to worry about. I am not necessarily reputable, but I have a hell of a lot more on the ball than most journalists I have met down here & most of the time it shows. If I have any apologies to make for my conduct thus far they would not be for what I have done, but for what I haven't—in that a lot of hard-working people have taken the time to sit and talk with me on subjects not always pertaining to that which I was writing about at the time, and probably they would feel a bit slighted if they knew their words had gone no further than my notebook. But I guess that's the way it is. [. . .]

As for plans now, I've only been here two days so they're still pretty foggy. I definitely mean to base here, for a while, anyway. The *Brazil Herald* offered me a job at a ridiculous salary—adds up to less than $100 a month, U.S.—but I told them I couldn't tie myself down here with local reporting & still get around enough to send you a varied assortment. I have all intentions of staying here as much as possible, but I want to be free to move around to the other countries as soon as I get rested and cured. It is about time I lived like a human being for a change. I believe Sandy is coming down in a month or so, and that will be a big help. This is a fine town & pretty cheap to live in if you're careful. Colombia was the only other decent country. Peru, Ecuador & Bolivia were about the worst goddamn places I've ever been in my life. And among the most expensive.

As for other writing, as soon as I get settled a bit I'm going to start beating around with magazine stuff. Also, I definitely want to work on some fiction that's been stewing in my head. Photos may amount to something, but I am too much a writer to take the kind of time & effort a good photo story demands. Maybe, now that I have more time, I can do a little better on that score. I may do some work for the *Brazil Herald*, but I couldn't possibly live on that salary so I'll have to keep loose to move around on other stuff.

Before I let anything solidify I'd like to get your comments on all this. I'd prefer, of course, to work only for the *Observer*, but that would also mean I'd be entirely dependent on you. I can, without much difficulty, break up the Brazil coverage with things from Argentina, Uruguay, Paraguay and probably the Guianas up north. Also, I'll be ready in a few months to swing over to Chile, via central Argentina. That would put me back on the west coast for anything that was popping over there. Also, now that I have a place to leave my mass of gear, I want to get out & do some hunting; that would put me onto some of the off-beat, "life with the natives" stuff more on the order of Guajira. Ever since Colombia I've been concentrating strictly on politics, because it has seemed more important than the rest. Probably it's not, in the long run, but every country I've been to has seemed in the midst of a political crisis, and those are hard to ignore.

For now, here are the things in the works, or good possibilities: 1) the Indian story; 2) Brazil election preview; 3) the middle-class angle I mentioned in connection with Mexico City, and 4) the Santa Cruz–São Paulo pipeline, which I haven't mentioned. Gulf Co. is drilling hell out of the Bolivian jungle, trying to find enough underground reserves of either oil or natural gas to justify building a pipeline either to São Paulo or the other way to the Pacific. In La Paz they are basing a lot of their hopes on Bolivia's economic future on the idea that the Santa Cruz (Bolivia) area will soon be supplying all natural gas for São Paulo, where there is now a shortage. The Gulf *jefe* in Santa Cruz, however, is not that optimistic. He says they'll know by the end of the year. That coincides, as you recall, with the deadline for seeing which way Op. Triangular is going. Should they both fail at once, it will just about sink Bolivia economically. And probably politically, too. Should Gulf come through, however, Santa Cruz will be a hell of a boom town. I got some photos while I was there; also went out to the drilling camps to get some shots there, so I can do something along that line when they make their decision on the pipeline. It would be one of the biggest industrial stories in SA.

Anyway, that's it for the moment. In about a week I'll send more suggestions, but I have to probe around first. In the meantime, I'd appreciate hearing from you on all this. Right now I'm pretty fluid and I'll wait to see what you say before making any settling moves. As I said before, I'll do as much for you as you want, as long as I don't have to starve or go mad in the process.

Write as soon as you can because the mails here are said to be slow as hell & I'd like to get your word as soon as possible.

Chao,
Hunter

*thanks again for the advance

**Back to *Time* & Bolivia for a last shot. My figure and theirs as to that country's export earnings would seem to disagree, but they don't. They say tin accounts for 70% of export earnings. I say *minerals* account for 88%. That other 18% is almost entirely tungsten. Maybe a little silver and a trickle of gold, but not enough to mention. Pizarro got most of that stuff.

TO WILLIAM J. KENNEDY:

Thompson's articles in the National Observer *were making quite a sensation—a few were even entered into the* Congressional Record. *What's more, Clifford Ridley had just bought Thompson's travel letters to excerpt in the* Observer; *they later appeared as "Chatty Letters During a Journey from Aruba to Rio" in* The Great Shark Hunt, *a collection of Thompson's early works.*

October 19, 1962
Rio de Janeiro, Brazil

William—

Yours arrived today, Jack, forwarded through the NY box (never write there again) and Louisville. All further mail to me here or c/o the *Observer.*

Needless to say, I am ahead of you there, having already written Ridley and warned him that you might try to send something. I'd really like to be able to recommend you, Bill, but . . . well . . . you turn out some pretty gloomy copy, really, and . . . ah . . . well . . . it's simply a case of . . . ah . . . you know what I mean, eh?

Anyway, Ridley will expect to hear from you. Any recommendation from me is golden. They recently sent me (for proof-reading) a montage of selections from my letters. And when Dow-Jones starts paying me $150 for the right to reprint my mail, I figure things might prompt you to hustle with that camera. Right now I have more money than I can reasonably waste. Sandy and I are living in a hotel on Copacabana Beach (balcony and all) and I have given up beer for *gintonicas* and cognac. I have an apartment (with maid) coming up on November 9 (also in Copa) and I am thinking of buying a jeep and having the Doberman flown down in preparation for getting a country home. I am also joining the Overseas Press Club and the Rio Foreign Correspondents Club. None of it makes much sense to me, especially when I stay in bed until noon every day and then have breakfast in bed before idling into town to write a few letters. Kennedy (the other [Robert]) is coming next month down to BA [Buenos Aires] and Montevideo to do some political sneering. It can't last, but I'll ride it for all it's worth while it does.

They recently raised me to $175 a crack, *sin* [without] photos. Two of my things went into the *Congressional Record* and my sense of values has gone to the dogs. I tell you all this out of sheer stupid spite. By the time you get the letter I will have been fired for some brutal act involving several types of whores and much drink. I have also bought a small pistol and carry it like Sam Spade, ready at all times to bust the bastards. In short, I feel tough.

Let me warn you to turn in the most bizarre copy imaginable. I enclose a sample. Never hesitate to editorialize with a vengeance or abuse anyone you disagree with. Mock generals indiscriminately and state flatly that all non-Americans are thieves and queers. Drink with as many people as possible, and when they tell you some heinous secret in confidence, quote them directly and if possible get photos of them drunk. And if all else fails, pull a gun and get rough. This last is guaranteed to produce surefire quotes. One of the best ways to lend validity to your copy is to point out (in print) that what you are saying is contrary to erroneous information in *The NY Times*. You can also slam *Time*, but it is not as impressive. Another good gimmick is to say you were hampered in your work by drunken hacks from other papers and wire services. This will give you a certain status.

I hope what I say here will help you to quickly penetrate the Dow-Jones vault. In all seriousness, I have turned in stuff that I never dreamed DJ would either pay for or put in print, and they have consistently done both. Ridley is a very decent guy with a good sense of humor. Apparently the paper is already making money. I turn in articles from 8 to 12 pages long, but they prefer about 1500 words. They also like photos and if you don't want to take them yourself, I'd try to get some good ones somewhere else.

That is about that. As for your new home, I can only say balls. Frankly, I believe you have moved out to Loíza Aldea to accept a position as caretaker in my old house. I intend to get there as soon as possible in order to check on you and shoot up the premises if time allows. Sandy came down via Varig and missed PR. She arrived without warning and considerably complicated my life. Had I not been rich, things would have turned hairy in a hurry. As it is, we are getting along. I am trying to work on some fiction, but the absolute certainty of no-sale makes inspiration hard to come by. Sandy failed to send you the novel, but I will have my mother send it down. Sandy failed to do just about everything she should have done, in fact, and as a result my communications are hopelessly fouled. I am also ill, but that is nothing new. I have not been well since Bogotá. As a matter of fact just writing this letter has reduced me to a cold sweat and a sort of mental fatigue that precludes any further coherence. I think I will go up to Mr. Money and have a drink. In closing, let me advise you to give up writing and make a living growing things.

Chao,
Hunter

TO PAUL SEMONIN:

> December 1, 1962
> Rio de Janeiro
> Brazil

Paul—

Jomo Kenyata[20] is a man with a beard and a spear and bright eyes and probably a cyst or two on his balls whose only ambition as far as I know is the acquisition of power. The fact that he is black is incidental, but it is also a fact. Selah.

You are right when you say I've been living too long in hotels, and wrong in thinking I've ever considered you anything less than a heavyweight—but on the strength of your recent mail I'd rank you pretty far below Cassius Clay. The fact that you are nervous about your correspondence is a good sign, I suppose, but it does not go far toward cheering me up. Your bitter realization that I have been trying to lead you down the path for my own "gay cause" only brings to mind a conversation we had some years ago at one of the back tables in what used to be Andy's[21]; talking of brinks and such, points of no return, coaxing people over the border and all that business. It has never struck me as a particularly gay cause, and I have been too busy fighting off wolves to get a real crusade going, but if you find yourself artless in Ghana I suppose you might as well blame it on me as anyone else.

Yeah, I have given some thought to going to Angola. Maybe in about six months. South America is getting me down, mainly because I have found out what I came down here to find out, and there is nothing else left for me to do but document it. Dostoyevsky was right. You can try to convince me that Africans are different, but I will take a lot more convincing now than I would have a year ago. I have tonight begun reading a stupid, shitty book by Kerouac called *Big Sur*, and I would give a ball to wake up tomorrow on some empty ridge with a herd of beatniks grazing in the clearing about 200 yards below the house. And then to squat with the big boomer and feel it on my shoulder with the smell of grease and powder and, later, a little blood. I have come to the point where I think I could kill humans as easily as deer or wild pigs, which probably makes me good timber for Africa.

I retain hope for the Mato Grosso, and ultimately for Brazil, but I think the next 10 years are going to be ugly. I just got back from a month-long swing through Uruguay, Argentina and Paraguay, and am now convinced

---

20. Jomo Kenyata (1889–1978), an African nationalist leader, was the first president of independent Kenya (1964–78). Under his leadership Kenya followed a pro-Western course.
21. Andy's was a Louisville pub.

that Brazil is the only hope and that ain't sayin' much. Maybe Mexico too, but that will come later. My ambition at the moment is to write up enough money to buy a DKW jeep and shove into the wilds. I would also like to get back to the U.S. for a while and then return with my guns. This is good shooting country. Along those lines, I'd like to know what you have to say about "the blacks ruining Africa." For the decent life, that is. [. . .]

Anyway, I now have an apartment in Copacabana, with a terrace looking out on one of the hillside favelas, and a one-block walk to the beach. I am piled up here with Sandy and a maid ($6 a month) and all manner of whips and guns and woven things picked up in 6 months of hard traveling. Rio is a hell of a city and impossible to describe in a few lines. I'll be here another six months, anyway. Same address. Living is cheap but it may not last. We have room (not much) if you feel like giving it a whirl. Send word, and piss, if possible, from at least a modest height. It may be the only way.

Chao,
Hunter

TO DARYL HARRINGTON:

Harrington was a woman newspaper reporter Thompson had met in San Francisco. They maintained an intimate correspondence in the years to come.

December 17, 1962
Rio de Janeiro
Brazil

Ah, Daryl, Daryl, I always want to write you and always feel guilty when I don't, but since I got down to this rotten continent both want and guilt have given way to necessity and I find myself forever writing double-spaced manuscripts and not much else. Jesus I worry about you there in NY, that rotten pit, and Sandy is here making me feel guilty for even worrying. I live about six lives and every time they touch it means trouble. If only I had more goddamn time so I could arrange things, but time being as it is, I have to pack it all in together and try to manage as best as possible. I've been gone for more than a month to Montevideo, Buenos Aires and Asunción, and got back here to find Robert Kennedy slipping in the back door and causing panic with the press corps, all of whom raced up to Brasilia today to get the latest mimeographed statement while I stay here in Copacabana and run for two hours on the beach to work off some of this awful beerfat.

How did your filthy job-hunt come out? I can't imagine anything worse than teaching school in New York. You ask for "long-range suggestions" and I know this will sound queer but I really suggest you join the Peace Corps. I would if I weren't such a reprobate, but then I can be twice as effective for the same idea by writing as I could by joining. But I'm serious— and don't think I've gone gung-ho because I came down here thinking the PC was a bag of crap but now I think it's the only serious and decent effort the U.S. is making in Latin America or anywhere else. In addition to that I keep running across PRIESTS of all goddamn things who really make me feel like a soft-life punk. I go out in the wilds and feel pretty proud of myself for managing to hang on for several days, and then I run across a priest who has been there for three years and two guys from the PC who've been there eight months. And I feel pretty cheap. About the best I can say for myself is that I know more about South America than any three people in the Rio Foreign Correspondents Association—of which I am a member, yeah—and that is without really trying.

The PC, I guess, is not so good for what it is but for what it can be if you really give it a ride. I have met a lot of punks and fools and jackasses in the thing, but I have also met a lot of people who've made me want to shake their hand and for me that is a damned rare feeling.

But I don't want to ramble or preach here; it's Christmas up there, I guess, and if you want to see how I feel about it try to get hold of the Xmas issue of the *Observer*. The bastards will probably rewrite it for Valentine's Day, but I wrote it for Xmas and if it comes out this week it should pretty much look like I wrote it. I want to get back and do some shooting and drive around the country a bit and write about queer things. I'm pushing now for a run back to the States around March 1, just to amble around. If you're there in NY I definitely want to see you. Maybe, if you have time, we can drive somewhere into the back country and shoot crows. All the way to Aspen, shooting crows the whole way. Your feeling about driving across the country is pale beside mine after being away this long. If I could do it now I'd accept it as a Religious Experience—whatever in hell that is. Don't wait two months to answer this; I'm losing touch with the decent people of the world. Write soon, Love, Hunter.

Thompson at work on "The Rum Diary."

On his way to the West Coast Thompson took hundreds of photographs hoping to catch the essence of the On the Road *experience.*
(PHOTO BY HUNTER S. THOMPSON; COURTESY OF HST COLLECTION)

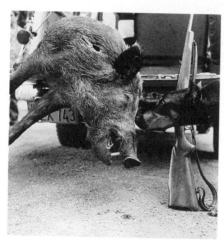

Hunting wild boar and elk was Thompson's favorite pastime.
(COURTESY OF HST COLLECTION)

1963

DOW JONES'S MAN IN RIO . . . POWER BROKER FOR THE PEACE CORPS . . . TRIUMPH OF A FOREIGN CORRESPONDENT . . . COUNSEL FOR *THE WASHINGTON POST* . . . BACK TO THE USA, HONORED GUEST OF THE NATIONAL PRESS CLUB . . . GOING WEST, RIDING HIGH . . . BOOK REVIEWS FOR BEER & BULLETS . . . THE DIRTIEST HOUR OF OUR TIME: NOVEMBER 22, 1963 . . . THE DEATH OF HOPE . . .

When the cold Andean dusk comes down on Cuzco, the waiters hurry to shut the venetian blinds in the lounge of the big hotel in the middle of town. They do it because the Indians come up on the stone porch and stare at the people inside. It tends to make tourists uncomfortable, so the blinds are pulled. The tall, oak-panelled room immediately seems more cheerful.

--Hunter S. Thompson,
 "The Inca of the Andes: He Haunts
 the Ruins of His Once-Great Empire,"
 National Observer, June 10, 1963

TO JO HUDSON:

Hudson, still in Big Sur, kept threatening to sail to Rio if he ever finished building his boat.

> January 1, 1963
> Rio de Janeiro
> Brazil

Well Jack, I'm getting fat and I need the big action. To put things in a nutshell, I am living high in a fine town but not really enjoying it because there is nobody here with any balls. If you blew in with a rack of guns, a boat offshore, and all manner of hairy schemes in your brain, I think we could stir up enough noise to satisfy us both. There is a shortage of money, as always, but on a different level than before. One of my worries now is whether or not to give the maid a raise—from $6 a month, to $7.50. It's a bitch of a problem. I recently swung through Manned Wolf territory, but didn't get your intelligence until my return, so I missed the animals. I am so fucking involved in politics, etc. that I don't have much time for the oddball stuff that is really the most important. I am making a decent living with prospects of a better one, but the temptation is to pare it down and forget this political shit and concentrate on the business. I am trying now to write myself into a position to grab off a jeep for movement into the interior. With a boat in the bay and a jeep on the shore we'd be master of all we surveyed. Brazil is immense, and all the bigger because of no roads or communications to the interior. Last night (new year's eve) we went out on the beach to watch the Macumba (voodoo) ceremonies. Man, it would have curled your hair. And they're talking about civilizing these people. For god's sake, bring MAGNUMS.

My only real worry on your score is that the goddamn boat won't make it. For my part, I am ready to move off in all directions. I have a guaranteed minimum income now, no matter where I go, and as far as I'm concerned, the hairier the better. Along those lines, I'm plotting a return to the States after Carnival (end of February) and will do my damnedest to get out your way if you're still there. If not, I might consider chasing you down and returning here under sail. At any rate, I'll leave Sandy here when I go, and will definitely return in a more or less short time. Living is so goddamn cheap here that, for the time being, I can't afford to base anywhere else. My apt. in Copacabana costs $30 a month. Good champagne is 50 cents a litre, gin is the same, and most other things fall in the same cost range. It is the only decent country in South America, but then it's also the biggest—and half the continent. In other words, I recommend it. But god only knows if and how you can get here by boat. It's a long run. But, with the possible exception of Mexico, I think all the good runs are long ones. God knows, it took me eight months of shitty travel to get here, and all things considered I suppose it was worth it. Since then I've been down to Uruguay, Buenos Aires and Paraguay (wild country), but they don't stack up to Brazil.

Anyway, let me know your schedule. [Donald] Maynard says you postponed again, so I'm assuming you're there for a few more months. What the hell are you doing for money? Keep in mind my idea of returning to the States in March, but don't let it change your plans because I'm not sure. Whatever you do—and wherever you go—take weapons. Once outside the U.S. you might as well try to buy gold bricks as a good pistol. Or ammo. Remember that. And write your plans soon.

Chao, HST

TO PHILIP L. GRAHAM, C/O *NEWSWEEK*:

Graham was publisher of The Washington Post *and* Newsweek.

February 8, 1963
Rio de Janeiro
Brazil

Philip Graham
c/o *Newsweek*
444 Madison Avenue
New York City

Dear Mr. Graham:

I read with interest and amusement your comments on the *National Observer* (*Newsweek*, January 28), and, all in all, found it a hell of a lot meatier than a similar story that appeared recently in *Time*. You made some good points with terms like "cold hash and rehash, a paper without reporters," and that sort of thing.

The day after reading the article, I went out to Itamarati (which is Brazil's Foreign Exchange Office) to register as the *Observer's* correspondent in Rio de Janeiro. It is an unsalaried job; I am also young, inexperienced and moderately paid — and if those are sins, then hell must be full of good correspondents.

At any rate, the press secretary at Itamarati mentioned the *Newsweek* article, and expressed mild surprise at my presence. It seemed to strike him as a bit odd that the *Observer* — a paper that rehashes all the news — should have a correspondent in Rio, whereas *Newsweek*, a fat-wallet book that criticizes other people for rehashing the news, is represented here by a virtually unpaid British stringer whose stories are published with all the tack-sharp regularity of total eclipses of the sun.

Newsweek's last story on Brazil, in fact, was held up by the Rio press corps as a hideous example of what happens when Latin America is covered from Madison Avenue. It was so full of stupid mistakes that, frankly, it was hard to believe that it was meant to be fact, instead of fiction. Your stringer was embarrassed by it, since some of the statements were so wild and outlandish that nobody who had ever been in Brazil could have written them. God only knows who wrote the rotten thing; the only explanation that seems reasonable to me is that it was slapped together by a committee of buffoons whose ties were too tight on their necks on whatever morning they gathered to hash the thing together. (Incidentally, I have no intention of either documenting or answering the charges I make here; the story I am talking about had something to do with the January 6 plebiscite.)

The thing that really surprised me about the story, however, was not that it was shot through with errors, but that it appeared at all. Your normal South American "coverage" is a silly joke, and about as nourishing as a month-old hamburger. In the past eight months I have been through every country on this continent except two, and I have met only two people even vaguely connected with *Newsweek* — both in Rio. It is a goddamned abomination, a fraud, and a black onus on American journalism that a magazine with *Newsweek's* money and circulation so slothfully ignores a continent as critical to American interests as this one.

In the past eight months I have written (and signed with my own name) roughly 3000 words a month on South America, most of which have appeared in the *Observer* — I'd say about 95%. Do you have anybody down here who can say that? Your issue of January 28, which carried your comments on the *Observer*, had room for about 200 words on South America — and that concerned a sort of *Daily Newsy* story on a minor art theft in Venezuela. Hardnose stuff, eh?

With that vast, driving, stiff-necked staff of yours, I'll bet a bottle of Old Crow that, over the past eight months, you haven't even equaled my published output in words, much less in significant stories. And, hell, I'm only a young, inexperienced and underpaid punk.

I'm beginning to think you're a phony, Graham. You hired Walter Lippmann, and his debut—that thing on John Kennedy—was the coldest hash I've read in a long time. If you hired the Marquis de Sade, he'd come out bland. Maybe you should loosen your tie a little bit and consider your own hash—because, dollar for dollar, it ain't so tasty, and you're sufficiently old, experienced and overpaid to have no real excuse at all.

> Sincerely,
> Hunter S. Thompson
> Rua Mexico 3
> c/o *Brazil Herald*
> Rio de Janeiro
> (that's in Brazil)

FROM PHILIP L. GRAHAM, PRESIDENT, THE WASHINGTON POST COMPANY:

Thompson was shocked that Graham saw fit to answer his ill-tempered letter of February 8, and he admired the "high style" of the response.

> March 25, 1963
> Washington, D.C.

Mr. Hunter S. Thompson
Rua Mexico 3
c/o *Brazil Herald*
Rio de Janeiro
BRAZIL

Dear Mr. Thompson,

For the past few weeks I have been mainly away from my office enjoying the normal sybaritic pursuits of proprietorship, and so have only today come across your moderate and shy letter of February 8th, in which you say that "I'm beginning to think you're a phony, Graham." This displays a very notable cultural lag on your part. Many intelligent leaders have long ago got themselves to the conclusion that you are only beginning to think about.

Now, why don't you write me a somewhat less breathless letter, in which you tell me about yourself, and don't make it more than 2 pages single space—which means a third draft and not a first draft.

> Sincerely,
> Philip L. Graham

TO CLIFFORD RIDLEY, *NATIONAL OBSERVER:*

*Thompson was ready to head home after one last foray to Bolivia for the Na-
tional Observer.*

> April 6, 1963
> Rio de Janeiro
> Brazil

Cliff:

Yours finally came. Let us now get one thing straight between us: I am
never going to back off of a story because it's "a bitch." The bigger,
meatier, and gutsier a story is, the more I want to have at it—normally.
The problem now is that my outlook on South America is entirely abnor-
mal. In a phrase, I no longer give a fuck. But don't translate that as evidence that I am getting soft & fat & I only want to do the easy stories. At
the moment, in fact, I don't want to do *any* stories. Witness my six-week silence. Don't worry about getting 4 stories from Brazil; I'll be damn lucky
to send you even one.

Fortunately, you opened that letter from Bolivia & got a first-hand idea
of what is getting on me down here. It ain't the stories, Clifford. Those are
easy. It's the goddamn awful reality of life down here. I can't shrug it off. I
can't avoid it. I can't hire a legion of "boys" and assistants & secretaries to
insulate me from the fear & rot in the streets. I can't pay $250 a month for
a mile-high apartment (with Telex*) overlooking Copacabana beach.
Christ, I have to live like the rest of these poor bastards—harassed, badgered & put upon from morning till night for no good reason at all. I
wouldn't blame them if they revolted against just about everything—and
in the name of whatever party or Ism that supplied the means of revolt.

Hell, I can't even deal intelligently with your letter [filled with detailed
travel instructions]. I can barely do anything these days. All I know is that
I have a ticket from Rio to New York; that is a tremendous factor in my
thinking. As a matter of fact it is all I can really think about. Which is as
good an indication as any that I don't really think anymore.

All I can say for sure is that I reject, out of hand, your suggestion that I
hustle up to Baja (on my way north) to check on the Red Menace.[1] If I
ever saw a trumped-up story, that one by Ruben Salazar is it. The easiest
way to get published from down here is to write about the foul & sneaky
reds. Hell, they're in worse trouble down here than we are. All they do—
& all they have ever done—is take advantage of our mistakes. Baja Calif.
is the coccyx bone of the universe. I've been there—all too goddamn

---

1. Thompson was interested in writing a *National Observer* story on the Communist Party in Baja
California.

often. It's the abortion hospital for all of California & god knows how many other states. But there's fine lobster-diving in the bay of Ensenada. I'll be happy to go there—from California, but not from Mexico. Hell, you could shoot a .22 from U.S. soil to Mexicali. Or maybe you'd need a 20mm cannon. Anyway, it's right up there on the border, & the only logical way to approach it is from the north, like everybody else does. The rest of Baja is a goddamn rock pile. From Ensenada, 60 miles south of San Diego, down to La Paz at the tip, it's 900 miles of absolutely nothing. Not even roads.

. . . well, another day, another screed. What I really want to say, Clifford, is that I feel . . . ah . . . at the moment I think it behooves me to . . . well, ah . . . you see, I have a definite conviction concerning the Third Side of Life . . . ah, yes, ah . . . egad, the meaning of it, the pure . . . ah, you see, the Occult Forces press down on my soul like a great waterbag . . . and, if I could . . . ah . . . yess, yess, now I see the . . . ah . . . the really fetid nature of . . . ah . . . sic.

How's that for a lead on my last & final Brazil story? A humdinger, eh? I understand that the makers of Snaveley's Grease have offered me a grant of $70,000 to plumb the depths of our dilemma & make certain recommendations to Mr. Snavely for the purpose of establishing criteria leading to the final solution to the Japanese question. . . .

Yess, yess, deposit as much money as possible! I think $200 every fortnite will be sufficient until I get a grip on myself . . . and then of course we will have to step it up to . . . ah . . . well . . . Mr. Snavely will be in touch with you on that point.

* * * * * * * * * *

OK, OK, just warming up to business. The bi-weekly deposit thing sounds good; at least I'll know how much money I have. I trust you will begin that process at once—because at the moment I am broke. $240 for Sandy's ticket, $330 for mine.[2] Ugly, ugly. [. . .]

It would be a godsend if you could continue to send clippings, staying ahead of me in my travels, as you said. It would save me a lot of time & probing. My first Guayaquil story, as you recall, was a direct result of a clip sent by Sandy. It's a lot easier going into a place looking for something specific, than to go in looking for "a story."

Canal Zone & Nicaragua look like good ideas. I'll try to get the mining & earthquake stuff. Chile is a big story & the 1964 elections are going to be a *damn* big one, but right now I don't feel up to it. I am in such a state of mind at the moment that any new or unusual pressures might put me in a

2. Conklin got a discount for working at a travel agency.

condition where I couldn't write anything at all. As I said before, I count on you to warn me if my stuff ain't up to par. For the first time in a hell of a long while I find myself facing the prospect of writing at length about something I don't want to write about, and it worries me. I would rather write nothing at all than grind out second-rate swill.

I may do some work on this tour for Radio Free Europe. That shouldn't conflict, eh? And maybe a piece or two for *The Reporter*. It will depend on how much time I have. At any rate, you've taken a lot of guff from me recently & you've been more than decent with the arrangements for this trip, so I figure I owe you first shot at all the best stuff. Rest easy on that score.

I'll get Baja for you when I go to California, which I'll have to do almost immediately upon my return to the U.S. in order to rescue 2 trunks of my stuff stored in Big Sur. I am boiling with ideas & not many of them concern Latin America. We will have to get together on my return so I can tell you how I'm going to write what America means.

Chao,**

H

LA Times man—shades of Jack London, eh?

**"*Chao*" is the (familiar) Spanish term for "Till we meet again." As in all else down here, you have to know when to be familiar & when not to. "*Hasta Luego*" is the more formal phrase for the same thing. For instance, you say "*Chao*" to your friends & "*Hasta Luego*" to your acquaintances. In Portuguese, the equivalents are "*Ciau*" and "*Ate Logo*." Sometimes it can be tricky. If you say "*Chao*" to a woman in public she is likely to be greatly offended, because most bystanders will assume you are sleeping with her. This is all well & good if you are, but it can be tense if you're not. I have had first-hand experience with this problem & can report with great authority. Another awful thing is the sign you make by touching your thumb & forefinger to make a circle; it means "OK" in the U.S. but in Brazil it means "Fuckee, fuckee" or "let's hump." I have had trouble with that one, too, but it might come in handy for you if you visit the Brazilian Embassy.

TO PHILIP L. GRAHAM, THE WASHINGTON POST COMPANY:

April 8, 1963
Rio

Dear Mr. Graham:

Well . . . two pages, single-space, catch my breath, define myself . . . that's a tall order for a man of my stripe, but I'll give it a go. I doubt I can match the olympian spleen of my last effort, but what the hell?

You may be a phony, Graham, but I admire your spirit. Your letter of March 25 had a cavalier tone that in some circles would pass for a very high kind of élan. The only real flaw I found was that it was written in English, instead of French. But, again, what the hell?

Actually, I am more interested in your reason for answering my letter, than in anything you had to say. Mine (the "moderate and shy" one of February 8th) was written in a pure, rum-flavored rage at about four in the morning. Needless to say, it was not re-written the next day, as most of my stuff is. It meant, as I recall, exactly what it appeared to mean. There were no ulterior motives—except, perhaps, that of prodding you into a reply. Certainly I would not want you to interpret it as a devious means of applying for a job on the assembly line at *Newsweek*, or covering speeches for *The Washington Post*. I sign what I write, and I mean to keep on signing it.

As for me, I'm a writer. I came to South America to find out what it meant, and I comfort myself in knowing that at least my failure has been on a grand scale. After a year of roaming around down here, the main thing I've learned is that I now understand the United States and why it will never be what it could have been, or at least tried to be. So I'm getting ready to come back and write what I've learned. With luck, I will be in New York and Washington by June. Perhaps you'll be able to afford that bottle of Old Crow by then.

As I recall, I offered to bet you a bottle of Old Crow that my published output, since coming to South America, would surpass the entire output of the *Newsweek* staff—on South America stories published over the course of the past year. You did not mention either the bet or the bourbon in your letter, so I assume you are weaseling out.

My relationship with the *National Observer* has been exceptionally decent. They have published all my articles—even my letters (*NO* 12/31/62)—and paid me well enough so that I don't have to write unless I feel like writing, or have something solid to write about. In return, most of the things I've sent them have been incomparable.

I don't know what all of this means to you, but the fact that you answered my letter leads me to believe that you now and then take a break from the "normal, sybaritic pursuits of proprietorship," and devote a few idle moments to pondering the meaning of your days and your time. How old are you? Maybe that's a clue. Have you come to that point where you suddenly realize you're afraid of people as young as I am? Or have you passed on, into a sort of crotchety, good-humored resignation?

Now, to change the subject, I've been forced to modify my hardnose line of February 8, for several reasons: 1) I recently had dinner with Milan Kubic, who tells me he's about to open a *Newsweek* bureau in Rio; a good move, but not quite as laudable as it is overdue; 2) Lippmann's piece on Rockefeller was Grade-A stuff, as was the *Newsweek* cover story on unemployment in the U.S. Since I knocked you on your South America coverage, I'd be acting like a newsmagazine editor if I ignored your best efforts; 3) Your letter came on the heels of "recent reports" that you were seriously ill. After being down here for a year, I have little faith in "recent reports," but if that one happens to be true, I'm sorry and I hope you're back in shape. Judging from your letter, I assume you are. At any rate, I felt vaguely uncomfortable about sending that kind of a letter to a man who was "seriously ill."

Hell, I haven't used up my two pages. What else can I tell you? Height 6'3"; Weight 190; Age 25; Politics: opposed to Nixon, Norman Mailer & George Lincoln Rockwell; Draft Status: Vet; Religion: Seeker. At this point it gets difficult. . . .

Oh yeah, I like a good tavern, sun on grass, a lean white hull, a beautiful woman, fine writing, fine whiskey . . . I could carry on here, but there's not much sense in it. I guess I'll owe you that other half-page.

Chao,
Hunter S. Thompson

Next address:
c/o U.S. Embassy
Mexico City
Mexico, DF

TO TOM MARTIN:

Martin was a USIS officer Thompson had met in Bolivia a year earlier.

April 24, 1963
Lima, Peru

Tom—

About two days ago, old sport, I flew right over your head. Due to Brazil's rotten exchange laws, I bought my Rio–NY ticket in the States and when it came there was no provision for a stop in La Paz. Again, due to Brazilian bullshit, it would have cost me $144 to add La Paz. No dice.

Probably I'll be back down this way in a few months. In the meantime, you can do me a favor. Just before leaving Rio I got a letter from a girl named Esther Ribero in Santa Cruz. She seemed to think I was in Washington (god knows how she got the *Observer* address) and wanted me to get her a job as a maid for some family in the States. That's out of the question, of course, but I thought she would make a good story—you know, this desperate urge to get to the States. I plan to use her letter as part of the text, but I need a photo and more information on who she is, how she lives, and that sort of thing. Your man in Santa Cruz can probably get that stuff with no problem. If so, could you buck it on to me in Washington?[3]

Just for the record, you can consider this a formal request from the *Observer*, rather than a personal favor to me—if that makes it any easier to do it as a USIS project, rather than your own. Maybe, if you're down in Santa Cruz, you could stop in and see her and have somebody take a photo for use with the story. Naturally, I wouldn't tie USIS into any immigration schemes for Bolivian maids (USIS man rounds up cheap labor, etc.) but it would make a good human interest story if we could show that USIS is in touch with "the people" and their unusual problems, rather than merely grinding out propaganda.

My main angle in the thing would be to show just what kind of vision a "typical" Bolivian has of the States. Why does she want to go there so badly? What does she think she'll find if she does go? She said in her letter that she knows "all Americans are good people." Where did she get that idea? See what I'm driving at?

Also, where did she learn English? Why did she want to learn it? Where did she learn what she knows (or thinks she knows) about the U.S.?

And, for the other side: What is her life like in Santa Cruz? Does she work? How much does she make? What does it go for? What kind of house does she live in? Does she have her own bed? What does she do in her spare time? How far has she been from Santa Cruz?

I have her first letter here, and I'll write her another & ask her some questions myself, but I need an objective view of her situation that she could never give me in a letter.

Another idea: if you want to work on it on your own I'll split what I make on it with you. Anywhere from $50 to $100 (your share), depending on what kind of a story it turns into. Let me know how you want to work it.

I hated to miss you, because I was looking forward to some good boozing nights up there on the hill. In your last letter you mentioned something about quitting USIS & working for *Time*. What came of that? If you don't work for them, you might query the *Observer* (Cliff Ridley) and see if they want anything from you. They just ran last week my other Bolivian piece (the one about the queer things that happen in La Paz) so they won't need a lot of stuff right now. But I'm sure they could use an occasional shorter piece giving background stuff on the labor situation, operation tri, etc.

You can probably catch me with a letter c/o U.S. Embassy Bogotá if you write in the next day or so. If not, use the *Observer* address. Anyway, write. And, again, sorry I missed you. *Ate logo,* HST

3. Martin sent Thompson material on Ms. Ribero, but Thompson never wrote the story.

TO SANDY CONKLIN:

Conklin had returned to the United States ahead of Thompson, who was making a farewell tour of South America.

April 25, 1963
Lima, Peru

Dear Princess:

Got a bunch of letters from you here, most of them carbons (2) and one big packet of clips. Also a letter from home & nothing else. I'll be here an-other week—one political story here, one in a mining camp 16,000 feet up in the hills, and another on a sugar hacienda on the way to Ecuador. Then, Guayaquil. Jesus.

Anyway, I'm heading north, and that's important. Your letters are good and you seem happier than I thought you'd be. Try to avoid New York if possible. I have a feeling there's some kind of a web up there & we might both get caught in it. I can blitz through if I'm alone, but with you there it would be too much like settling in.

I'm all for settling, but somewhere West. Did you write Peggy Clif-ford?[4]

Lima is pretty bad. I was drinking tonight with a Britisher and a pretty Chilean whore came and sat with us. She did her best to entice me off, but now that I look back on it, it seems too pathetic to even be real. Sometimes whores don't seem quite human to me. I wonder if they ever enjoy anything. Imagine spending all your best years trying to coax men out for a half-hour at a time, and, even then, being in a hurry for the next one. Ah, what a life, what a continent. If this is "reality" I vote against it. Even the bars. I am trying to remember when I last sat in a bar in the States. I don't mean a tavern, but a bar. Anyway, I left the Britisher with the whore and bow-legged it back to the hotel, picking up two quarts of beer on the way.

Did I ever tell you to read *A Long and Happy Life* by Reynolds Price? I read it earlier this year and found another copy today. Pick one up if you can. Sort of a junior Styron.

Jesus, I wish we were somewhere in a warm bed tonight. When I think of all the silly bitches I stare at in these silly towns, compared to what I could have if I merely got on a plane and went all the way north, I wonder about my sanity for staying down here. When it comes to really royal humping, I believe you're the best in the world. Or maybe I should say We, because I don't think either of us would be worth a damn without the

4. Thompson wanted Conklin to write Peggy Clifford in Aspen asking her to scout around for a small house for them to live in come July.

other. I think we have made it a fine art and somehow it is always a little bit new and a little bit better, and that's the amazing thing. It is almost comfortable for me to sit here and know that soon we will have it again, and it will make all the others look like punks.

That is an odd paragraph for me to have written, eh? For some reason I seem to be much more in love with you now. I don't know why. This is my second consecutive love letter and far lustier than anything I've ever written anywhere. At least in letters. Maybe I have finally managed to bring love and lust into focus on the same target. That is a hell of a big thing.

Remember that time when we drove back at night from Monterey in Maxine [Ambus]'s car? Or driving back in Jo [Hudson]'s car with Jo and Jenny [New] in the front seat and your head in my lap with a blanket around us? I want to drive like that again somewhere out in the country on a night with no other cars and a winding road and nothing but trees and the moon to watch us. I think we will.

But now, this stinking continent. I have a vague, distant fear that I'll never get off of it. When I walk into Idlewild I'm going to feel like a man escaped from the tomb. [. . .]

As far as I can see, I am going to follow the route of that ticket, skipping Cali and Quito for the sake of time. I may also skip a few Central American countries. I have just about given up the idea of skipping the whole thing, because if I came back to the States in a fit of pique and depression—owing the *Observer* money—it would put me off on a pretty slippery footing as far as getting anything done is concerned. There is not much sense in kicking Ridley in the teeth at this stage of the game; I am almost there, and instead of falling apart, I may as well retreat gracefully. Which means writing at least enough stories to keep ahead of them financially.

At the moment—sadly enough—my main reason for wanting to rush back is to get into bed with you, but for that we at least need a bed, and preferably, a house with doors and locks. And, as you say, a big winter to make us work. When I get back I think we deserve a good year. And some royal, highlife humping, because I agree that we are "pretty fine."

> OK, goodnight,
> H

next address:
U.S. Consulate
Guayaquil, Ecuador

TO CLIFFORD RIDLEY, *NATIONAL OBSERVER:*

April 28, 1963
Lima, Peru

Dear Cliff:

If I read your gram correctly, it says in effect that I am cut off the dole until I send two pieces. Hell, you should have said that before I left Rio. As I said, the only reason I left was because I figured I'd be $100-a-week solvent—and that's at least what I need in order to keep my mind on my work, instead of forever kiting checks and sweating hotel bills. It is not the best thing for my peace of mind to be in Lima, Peru, with no friends, $20 to my name and a lot of people pressing me for immediate payment on god knows how many bills. And hating the hell out of the place, to boot.

Jesus, the temptation to go out to the airport and get on a plane for New York is awful. When I got your cable I was ready to do it. But we have had a fairly decent relationship thus far and I believe that might queer it, eh? If not, old sport, all you have to do is say the word & I'm off like a big bird. Nothing would make me happier.

But we've gone over that & I'm resigned to this trip. I had even begun to prick up a bit in the brain when that horrible thing came yesterday. When I went to the cable office today I had a fleeting fear that my credit had been cut off. Suddenly I feel like a bum and a thief and a con man.

Last night, however, I had a decent experience. I met a guy named Armbrister who works for the *Saturday Evening Post* and he said he'd been reading my stuff in New York. It gave me a tremendous lift; I had long since given up the idea that anybody but you, Sandy and my mother read my stuff. Armbrister and Charley Kuralt from CBS are the only two people I've seen in a year who've actually picked up an *Observer* and read what I write. Hardly anybody down here even knows what the *National Observer* is and probably wouldn't believe in it at all except for that blurb in *Time.*

Well, I guess you are more interested in getting some articles than in hearing all this bullshit, so I'll try to squeeze one out tonight and another on Monday. The election preview is just about ready and I'll put the rush on Middle-Class & get it off ASAP. By the time you get this I'll be in ugly circumstances and, although I don't blame you for being vaguely pissed off and leery at the tone of my recent communications, I urge you to reconsider the wisdom of plunging me into a crisis in order to get articles out of me. All it does is make it that much harder for me to get anything done, and it also queers some of my best contacts.

I am fully aware that I owe you $400, that I missed Chile, that my general disorganization is responsible for many of my $$$ problems, and that

I am not the most pliable or cooperative correspondent on your team. On the other hand, I don't see that you have any reason to think I am going to welsh on that $400 or anything else you advance me, any more than I've welshed on the ones to date. We are not missing anything important in Chile except perhaps the spectacle of my ultimate collapse. I can name you at least five well-paid correspondents on this continent who are well organized and whose stuff you'd reject out of hand. As for pliability and co-operativeness, I refer you to the Headline Employment Agency in New York City or the Situations Wanted ads in E&P [Editor & Publisher].

As I said in the cable, I am going to stay here—hell, I have no choice—until I get something from you. My ticket reads: "Lima, Guayaquil, Bogotá, Panama, San Jose, San Salvador, Guatemala, Mexico City, New York." I have every intention of writing as many articles between here and New York as I am physically and mentally up to, but in order to do it I am going to have to have funds. I am not trying to pressure you here, but put yourself in my place. That $400 was nice to have, and necessary, but since tickets for Sandy and myself cost a total of $570, there was not much left over on which to travel.

For hell's sake send word quick. This week is going to be a hairy one. Monday will be a day of contrasts: I will meet the "president" of Peru in the morning, and in the afternoon be called on the carpet and lectured like a criminal for issuing bogus cheques. I wish to jesus I had never seen this continent.

> Yours for a lifeline,
> H

TO CLIFFORD RIDLEY, *NATIONAL OBSERVER:*

With no cash and Conklin in New York, Thompson was ready to flee South America once and for all.

> April 29, 1963
> Lima, Peru

Dear Cliff:

By the time you get this I may be making the big Panagra detour around Cuba, zeroed in on New York. I had a nervous collapse today—violent shouting, destruction, tears, the whole works—and now I am locked in my room with the phone crippled and everybody in the hotel afraid to come near the place, even to make the bed or mop the water off the floor. I packed & told Panagra I was leaving on the midnight plane, then realized that most of my clothes are in the laundry & won't be out till Thursday. Tomorrow is another of these ratbastard holidays & the filthy whore in the laundry said we can go out to the *"campo"* [country] and fuckee-fuckee. If I ever hear that phrase again I am going to break teeth. The idea that I would touch that scurrilous bag of fatty stench and disease sets my hair on end.

I also realized I don't have sufficient cash to pay the overweight, so tomorrow is camera-selling day. My light meter is broken anyway so the camera is all but useless. I am out of film, too, and can't afford more. And you seem to have stopped using my photos, anyway.

There is no sense in trying to list all the reasons for my collapse. Lack of cash, which I don't blame on you, is the main one. Actually, my nerves are so bad that any small thing is likely to kick me off on a rage. I am disappointed with myself for getting like this & I daresay you are too, but don't say I didn't warn you. Although I can't blame you for cutting me off the dole, since I haven't written anything in nearly three months, your cable the other day did not contribute to my peace of mind. Suddenly I felt like a bum and a thief and a con man, and when I went to cash my last check I acted so guilty that I'm surprised they took it. For all I know, it will bounce.

Fuck this, I have it now—endure here until Friday, write the election story and one other, sell camera if necessary to pay for smashed telephone and other bills including plane overweight, get answers from Gen. Lindley & see Zileri,[5] Tappe's [restaurant] for dinner Friday night & straight from there to the airport—be in New York Saturday morning, long rest, call Ridley, keep my presence secret, write all possible stories in New York (staying where?), then shove off again for San Juan, Panama, Central America and Mexico. Then, triumphant re-entry with all Xmas gifts, many stories, much money & a long & happy life ahead, eh? Yessir, probe carefully and avoid the pus. Maybe stop in Florida on way to San Juan, see Sandy and get married in the rottenest possible place, then on. Fuckee-fuckee.

Hunter

FROM PHILIP L. GRAHAM, THE WASHINGTON POST COMPANY:

May 18, 1963
Washington, D.C.

Dear Mr. Thompson:

Your letter of April 8 got to Washington just after I left for a month in Europe. And I must say it is a welcome relief to read yours among the banal pile of accumulated correspondence I am digging into.

5. General Lindley and Zileri were Peruvian officials in Lima who were helping Thompson get information about the recent junta.

If you get to Washington in June, would you let me know, as I would like to have a visit with you and have you meet our Managing Editor, Al Friendly. We have nothing at the moment that I think would at all interest you, but I always like to keep in touch with young people possessed of such overriding humility and shyness.

Sincerely,
Philip L. Graham

Mr. Hunter S. Thompson
c/o U.S. Embassy
Mexico City, Mexico, D.F.

TO ROBERT BONE:

Thompson had flown from Lima to New York to speak at the National Press Club in Washington before flying on to Louisville with Conklin to get married by a justice of the peace across the Ohio River in Jeffersonville, Indiana.

May 22, 1963
Louisville

Rbt—
Yours came today, forwarded from Ridley, and gave me a temporary lift out of the funk. Sandy is here—we got married on Monday—and her goddamn mother arrives tonight. Absolute madness. I'm not sure of my sanity. 25 cents to my name & my mother adamantly refusing funds. Still $400 behind the *Observer* & they are pressing. That means two LatAm articles before I earn a penny on the third. I got to New York with $10. Coming here was a disaster. And getting worse every day. No rest, no hope.

Yes, get two wooden letter openers, about $2 each as I recall. Also as many Talvis as you can afford. Also the grips. And paintings. That's about it as I recall. Can't think of any *Observer* photos for you, but any LatAm stuff won't do you harm in New York. Get as much as you can.

Washington was OK. Two nights in the best hotel, honored guest at the National Press Club with all *Observer* honchos, much was made of my arrival—except money. They are leery of my tendency to leap, but even so, went so far as to offer me a job in Wash. I leaped back.[6]

Am returning to Washington soon. Got a letter from Phil Graham yesterday, saying he wanted me to visit and talk with him and the managing editor of *The Washington Post*, Al Friendly. Heh. Also am scheduled to go

6. Clifford Ridley offered Thompson a full-time desk job in Washington at the *National Observer*. Thompson declined, saying he preferred reporting from the West.

in for a talk with the *National Geographic* people. Then on to New York for more talks with RFE [Radio Free Europe] and *Saturday Evening Post.* I sense a general opening of doors.

I am proposing to Graham that he buy the *Observer* and make me editor. That is one of the things on agenda. Another is the booze he owes me.

But first I require funds, and peace for writing. May whip down to Florida for a week or so to check on an empty house for the writing. Here is impossible. Before Florida, I have to go to Chicago to pick up my unsold Doberman. With luck, I will get to New York on June 15; if not, the 20th or so. Stay a few weeks, then hopefully west. The *Observer* wants all kinds of stuff, but first I need an address. And funds. The Pentax is still here & for sale—to you or others.

Saw Howard[7] in New York, drank a bit of beer, tried to pawn him my camera, said you were coming, then hopped off next day for Wash. Will check in again on my return. Probably you'll be there. Can't figure out why that $17 bounced, but am having much trouble with the bank on just about everything. I still haven't unpacked my check stubs to ponder them, but I think the bank erred. Yeah, like always. [. . .]

> See you in New York,
> late June,
> H

TO CLIFFORD RIDLEY, *NATIONAL OBSERVER:*

Sandy's mother, Leah Conklin, had given Thompson a brown-and-cream-colored Rambler as a wedding present. The newlyweds used it to take a cross-country honeymoon.

> May 22, 1963
> Louisville, Kentucky

Dear Cliff:

Well, I'm here in Louisville. God knows why; I'm not getting much done. This is the first time I've touched a typewriter since my arrival exactly a week ago. The day before my arrival Sandy fell off a horse, fracturing and dislocating her shoulder. Then her car blew up, requiring two days of steady dealing with the garage. Then I was forced into marriage proceedings, which brought about a deluge of bullshit that has just about inundated me. At the moment I have 25 cents to my name, no car, no home, a new wife, a Doberman still waiting in Chicago, and still the everlasting

7. Howard Raush, former copy editor on the *Middletown Daily Record* who became friends with Thompson and Bone and went to Moscow to report for *The Wall Street Journal.*

dysentery. A constant procession of people—many of whom I had long since presumed dead—keep turning up at the door to jabber at me. Jack London returns with his long-haired, one-armed bride; don't miss the show. More food, more booze, bring it on . . . answer that telephone, will you? O ain't it all wonderful, Aunt Maggie? Ain't you just thrilled?

Tomorrow I am fleeing up to Covington for "The World Series of Folk Art." I don't have time to compose an outline for you, just take my word that it's a good story—not just on the festival, but on authentic folk music in general, focusing on the festival. I'll do everything in my power to get it to you for the June 3 issue, but it would still go for the next one. I know some of the Kentucky people up there because of a thing I did on country music for the *Chicago Tribune* a year or so ago. I'm looking forward to having at it, and think I can get you a good one.

As for LatAm, I think I have my concepts straight, after much scribbling on note-paper, but until I at least get a desk and a door between me and the world I'm not going to be able to type anything. Sandy's mother arrives tonight for a two-day visit. God help me. If you can pay for the folk music thing it will give me at least enough cash to get away from Louisville. The pawn shop wants to give me $30 for my $145 rifle & $75 for my $400 camera gear. I can't stand to take that kind of a beating. I have all manner of things to write, all sorts of possibilities, but at the moment I feel like I'm caught in a bear trap with food just out of reach. If I had my way I would go alone to a motel in the Kentucky mountains & write until I get ahead, but I don't even have a typewriter to take with me. Mine is broken in New York. Nor, I might add, could I pay the bill.

I tell you all this to explain why you aren't receiving a steady stream of LatAm articles. I can't write anything standing up, much less on the run. The only aid you could render, as I see it, would be to pay for anything I might send before getting down to the LatAm stuff, which at least requires unpacking my bags and looking at some material. There is no room here for anything. Hell, I've been married three days & haven't slept with my wife yet. The place is like a zoo. Even writing this letter has taken all afternoon, due to ringing doorbells, phones, visitors, etc.

Hell, I nearly forgot to explain the photo.[8] It doesn't need much, but I thought it would look good as a sort of theme photo for the folk music piece. Maybe it's too dark for newspaper reproduction. Even so, it's an eye-catcher & might look good anyway. If not, take good care of it & hold it there until I send an address (if and when I ever get one). I'll get some more at the festival & send them on.

8. Thompson had sent Ridley a beautiful black-and-white photograph he had taken of an elderly Kentucky banjo player.

Thanks again for your hospitality in Washington & I may stop by on the way back to New York. But not before I get the LatAm stuff done. I'll keep in touch if my address changes, which it will—either somewhere with a lock on the door, or the loony bin. This is worse than SA; I am nearing the end of my rope.

Until later—
H

TO PHILIP L. GRAHAM, THE WASHINGTON POST COMPANY:

Spending a week at Sandy's mother's house in Florida, Thompson invited Graham to head south for a dose of old-fashioned hospitality.

June 7, 1963
Deland, Florida

Dear Mr. Graham:

You're pushing me, old sport, but unless there is something seriously wrong with you I believe you have run out of cheeks to turn. Even so, the christian nature of your letters has given me pause and I feel hard pressed to maintain the same, high-pitched chattering whine with which I began this thing. So, for the moment, a hiatus if you will, and let the hundred flowers bloom.

Yours of May 18 reached me in Louisville, forwarded via the *Observer* with a menacing comment about "moonlighting." You should have marked it "religious material" and sealed it with wax.

I passed through Washington while you were in Europe, but didn't have time to call. I held a personal audience at the National Press Club and carried on at length in several tongues, but nobody offered me a lump sum so I ran up a tremendous whiskey bill at the Willard Hotel and then moved on. No man is a prophet in his own tongue, eh?

After that I became married, which merely put the stamp of law on a worthy and time-tested arrangement, and then I went to Chicago to buy a Doberman pup to replace the one I was forced to sell upon leaving for South America. After a week of intense practice with a long-barrel Luger—with which I can now dispatch a bat on the wing at 50 yards—I drifted South and rented a typewriter beneath the Spanish moss. That is my situation now and I put it on paper merely to bring you up to date.

Unfortunately, I have not written much for the past few months and I am trying now to scrape the fuzz off my brain and catch up on my Latin America copy—vast reams of biased, analytical nonsense that is, perhaps by default, better than 99% of the biased, analytical nonsense that comes out of that benighted continent.

But every time I sit down to write about the folly of land reform, the panic value of the Red Menace, or the perpetual short-circuit in American thinking—every time I ponder these things I find myself staring out through the screens at the big southern oaks and the old moss and the traffic light on the corner and the un-patronized Esso station across the highway and I wonder about the continuity between what I see now and what I saw this time last year in Guayaquil, Ecuador. To find a proper context for the two worlds I have to drink beer all afternoon and Old Crow all night and stay up till three-thirty until things begin to fall into place—and then it scares the hell out of me.

I was just going to write that I will pass through Washington in late June—which I will—and look forward to seeing you then. But that's your home court and I'll have to get into my black suit and my tense, bright-young-man attitude and will probably not get much said. Like what happened when I made my long-heralded appearance at the *Observer*: a lot of boozy, nervous jabbering that left us all losers. Not that I expected anything else. I don't come across too well in a tie, or over the rim of a martini cup, or across a desk. I listen just as well and I learn just as much, but it is generally a one-sided deal because I tend to make people nervous when it comes to those situations.

What I am mumbling here is the idea that perhaps we would both benefit if you tried my home court as a starter—a ratty screened porch out in the oaks and the Esso station and the drenching afternoon rains with a good dog wandering around and no waiters bringing the booze. There's a fan, a bug-bomb, a bit of music and no other hindrance in the form of man or beast except my wife, who is well-trained.

Anyway, I accept, with some trepidation, your invitation to visit with you and Friendly in Washington—and, by way of contrast and counter-balance, I extend my own. We have an extra bed, adequate food and drink, and if you have time we could get drunk and go over to Daytona and drive at top speed along the beach, firing the Luger at irregular intervals and throwing whiskey on all and sundry. But only if you have the time.

Well, let me know. I will, in any case, get through Washington between the 20th and the 25th of June. Until at least the 20th I'll be here, and if you can find a free day and night or two between now and then I look forward to a general hashout here on the porch. The number here is 734-xxxx. Call and I'll meet you.

If not, I'll see you there in Washington before the 25th. Let me know if you have plans to disappear with some woman about that time. If so, I'll adjust. Time is always flexible, even for those of us with the weight of the world on our shoulders and the conscience of the race in our fingertips.

Humbly,
Hunter S. Thompson
114 E. Plymouth
Deland, Fla.

FROM PHILIP L. GRAHAM'S SECRETARY:

At this time Graham was confined to a mental hospital; a month later he shot himself in the head. Thompson read about his suicide in The New York Times *while sitting in Tommy's Joynt in San Francisco. They had never met.*

July 11, 1963
Washington, D.C.

Mr. Hunter S. Thompson
c/o Cooke
19 Downing Street
Manhattan 14, New York

Dear Mr. Thompson:

I have just received your note of July 10th to Mr. Graham, and hasten to reply to it in his absence. He will definitely not be in the office on 16th or 17th July, so please do not make a special trip to Washington in the hopes of seeing him.

I will, of course, show him your note as soon as he returns, but I am not sure when that will be.

Sincerely,
Secretary to Mr. Graham

TO WILLIAM J. KENNEDY:

The Thompsons had driven from Florida to Las Vegas to cover the Sonny Liston–Floyd Patterson heavyweight championship boxing match for the National Observer. *They then journeyed north to Sonoma County, California, hoping to lease a small ranch near Jack London's Wolf House. Semonin was now living in Aspen.*

August 15, 1963
Aspen, Colorado

Bill—

An odd twist to report on this front, Jocko: definite possibility that we may end up as neighbors of Denne Petitclerc and Co. Strange, eh? On the way through Frisco I gave him a ring and ended up at his place about 60 miles north of San Francisco on a big, empty mountain. One drink led to another, a bit of shooting, a lot of talk, more drink, and then spending the night. Next day we talked about a neighbor of theirs who is moving out of his house—way, way up in the hills overlooking Jack London's Valley of the Moon. He said he'd investigate, and when I limped into Aspen there was a cable here saying the man was agreeable and wanted to talk to me. Now I am trying to stall him until I can write up some cash. I need $100 for repairs on the car, plus $600 in immediate debts, plus my usual desperation for peace of mind. I cabled back that I was ready to take over, but needed time to scrape up cash for the return trip. And that's where it stands. Will advise.

Your situation sounds golden and I have not given up on getting back to stay awhile. How long could you stand? Me, Sandy and the dog? Don't be polite. The California place won't be open till late September, if it opens at all, and I may wind up with a few weeks to kill between Semonin's departure from here and another movement back to the coast. Since I want to get back to New York anyway, I might be able to combine a visit with you and a few quick and dirty contacts in the city. Not sure at all and won't be until I get something more definite on the Moon Valley house, but may as well query and see what you say. I don't want to move in and disrupt your life, but maybe we can work out a mildly disruptive compromise. Again, how long a visit could you take? 3 days? 3 weeks? Just give me an idea.

At the moment I am hard at work helping Paul restore his home. We are living here with no running water, no toilet and no access road. The car is parked ½ mile away at the bottom of the ski slope, which is a brutal climb with luggage, groceries, wine, or even nothing at all. It is primitive living, but at least it's a rest and I'll be here another 2 or 3 weeks to catch up on the writing. We have gone 10,000 miles in 2 months with no maintenance on the car and the whole team is whipped. At least you can get credit—be thankful for that.

A great relief to hear you nicked Ridley for money; I was afraid it would fall through and make me feel like a prick. My recent copy has been sub-par and last week they were gracious enough to point it out to me. I replied that I was too tired to really give a damn, and today came a fine, bright, complimentary note that gave me to feel once again that gall is the better part of talent. Keep after them, but don't bend or they'll lean on you. What about the PR piece? Demand more money each time and they'll generally give in. Bitch about poverty in general and threaten to take a job with *Time* or *Newsweek*.

My Writers piece[9] came out pretty watered-down and I bitched noisily, but even as printed (except for the lead and the ending, which was Ridley) it had horns and at least half a kick, which they need.

Dennis Murphy read my book ["The Rum Diary"] and came to about the same conclusions you did, but not quite so final. After a bit of talk and thought I have decided to rewrite it for plot and action, separating the characters and trying to give them some meaning. If it goes slow, I'll quit. If not, and if I enjoy the work, I'll push on through. The title alone will sell 5,000 copies if I can just convince some bastard to publish it.

I called the *Partisan Review* on your story, by the way, and some lazy-sounding girl answered the phone and said she'd think about it. . . . Sounds like a shitty outfit and damned if they'll get anything of mine.[10]

I am considering sitting down and rewriting every story I've ever done or even half done and getting them all in the mail. A man should have possibilities, and mine at the moment are too limited.

OK. Will advise the breaks as they come. In the meantime, keep the contact and let me know on the visit possibilities.

Bingo, and hello to Dana—
HST

TO DAVISON THOMPSON:

When Thompson returned from South America he reconnected with his brother Davison. Their correspondence increased dramatically during the ensuing years.

August 20, 1963
Aspen, Colorado

Dear D—

Hope you found the pants, both the tan ones and the other pair you accused me of stealing. Now for a third pair; I think I left those brown corduroys (part of the suit) there. If so, let me know and I'll stop tearing the car apart to look for them. Also, is my billy club there? And the hunting knife you gave me last Xmas? All these are missing.

---

9. "Where Are the Writing Talents of Yesteryear?" *National Observer*, August 5, 1963 (a review of then current novelists.)
10. Thompson was trying to help Kennedy get his fiction published.

The shotgun is fine, although I can't hit a damn thing with it, except for a coon I disintegrated in Big Sur. It does awful things to a small animal at close range—made hamburger of the coon, who was stealing our dog food. Your club is here and will be in the mail as soon as I can find the odd-shaped box I need for shipping. It is a bastard, probably the only one of its kind in the world.

We are currently living in Paul [Semonin]'s house in Aspen. It's primitive as hell, but at least a place to rest with nobody howling at me. No running water, an outhouse, and the car has to stay ½ mile down at the foot of the mountain. It is a hell of a climb up the trail, especially with luggage and groceries, but once you get here it's fine. I spent an hour or so this afternoon practicing from the hip with the Luger and got so I can pretty consistently hit an 18-inch circle at 10 yards, snap-shooting like Billy the Kid. But it will be a while before I can bounce a tin can along the ground like Shane. I haven't used the .44 much, because the scope broke and the ammo is so expensive. As soon as I get out of debt I'm going to get another .22 Mag. You can't beat a penny and a half a shot.

As for plans, there are two possibilities and they both broke today. One is a house on a mountain about 60 miles north of San Francisco, and the other is a house about 10 miles outside of Aspen. Neither would be available until September, but either one would be a good deal and a good place to live. At the moment I think I prefer Calif.; the house is more isolated and without the distractions (nearby bars) of Aspen. I'll wait a week or so before deciding; it's so damn good to have a choice that I don't want to give up the feeling.

Speaking of that, what's the score on your end? Any new movements, changes, etc.? How's the drinking going? Let me know any developments.

I'll be here a few more weeks and will let you know before I move again. Regardless of where I settle, I'll have to come back to Louisville for that gear, which will probably be in late September. Right now I'm too broke to move at all. Yesterday I spent 30 of my last 35 dollars on the goddamn car, and both front tires are still bald. My checks are bouncing again, but that's nothing new. Hopefully, I can stay here long enough to write myself out of the hole. [. . .]

Send Word.

H

TO CLIFFORD RIDLEY, *NATIONAL OBSERVER:*

Ridley was urging Thompson to return to Rio or Mexico as the National Observer's *Latin America correspondent.*

August 23, 1963
Aspen, Colorado

Dear Cliff:

For the past five hours I've been rooting through my 75-pound suitcase of Latin America notebooks, clippings, books, mementos and assorted flotsam, and all it has done has been to convince me that I should write a book on Latin America because my knowledge is far too vast and encompassing to fit into any smaller format.

So, instead of giving in to the awesome sweep of things, I'll try to focus down on those things that appear relevant to the Alliance for Progress." But I'll be rambling here and a lot may be irrelevant or at least obscure. You will get an idea of what my first drafts are like, and I will get an idea of what it is like to write on Latin America from my new outpost in Aspen. So be it.

I'll begin with a quote from *The New York Times* [of] August 18, which contained a tiny dispatch from Lima, Peru, concerning the birthday (the second) of the Alliance: "Leading newspapers commented today that the Alliance for Progress was falling short of expectations." *La Prensa* said that the Alliance program had "lagged behind the very great, and perhaps exaggerated expectations that it raised initially." *El Commercio* said that two years after the signing of the charter of Punta del Este, under which the Alliance was established, "the balance does not show satisfactory returns."

I cite this because it is such a faithful echo of the comments I heard during the last six months of my stay in South America, almost always from Latins. From U.S. officials, I got a different line: guardedly optimistic at the office, and sometimes mean and pessimistic in private moments.

As far as the Alliance is concerned, there are four main "reaction groups" in South America. U.S. officials and pro-American Latins are very much for it; American businessmen (with exceptions) and hardnose Latin leftists are against it—which in effect makes it a "middle of the road" sort of concept, which is odd. On the "anti" side I should also include a much smaller than is generally believed segment of "the oligarchy." Contrary to a lot of press opinion, the wealthy lads are not so stupid as to ignore which way the game is going, and it is only the diehards and the archconservatives who actively and vocally oppose the Alliance. The same is true, in a way, of U.S. businessmen; those (mainly young) who work for big companies (Sears, Willys, Ford, IBEC, Fruco, etc.) might disagree with

11. Dubbed "Alliance for Progress" in an October 1960 campaign speech, President John F. Kennedy's Latin American policy opposed dictatorship and supported democracy, capitalism, and land and price reforms with "long-term development funds, essential to a growing economy."

the Alliance in practice—if they disagree at all*—while the old-line "free-enterprisers," most of them running or working for small businesses, are the only ones who claim it is "just another one of Kennedy's socialistic schemes."

One of the main enlightened bitches about the Alliance concerns its focus on government-to-government action. This gives a lot of people who work for private companies the feeling that they are being left out, although Alliance blueprints call for a large percentage of the funds (better check the figure) to come from private enterprise. While I was in La Paz, for instance, a Grace Company official blew his top during a visit by Teodoro Moscoso. He drafted a cablegram (which he later tore up and which I retrieved from his wastebasket) to an American publication (either *Time* or *The New York Times*) saying that Moscoso had been in La Paz for a week and had not seen a single representative of "private enterprise." He had spent his time, said the cable, with nobody but Bolivian and U.S. government officials (which, as far as I could determine, was true).

A lot of people were complaining about it, and eventually the word reached Moscoso. On the day that he left La Paz, he called a sort of open press conference—specifically inviting the gentlemen from private enterprise—and proceeded to give about as weak-kneed and unimpressive an outline of the Alliance's objectives as I ever hope to hear. I was really shocked, because I had dealt, indirectly, with Moscoso in Puerto Rico, where he ran a tough, hell-for-leather show as director of Fomento, which was then Puerto Rico's version of the Alliance. But he was a different man in La Paz, and it got almost embarrassing when people began yelling from the audience, "Where do we fit in?" and "How about private enterprise?"

His only reply was, in effect, "Have faith." And that didn't satisfy anybody. Even me. He did say, "Now I'm no man to bow down before the sacred cow of private enterprise—but if the cow gives good milk, I believe we should milk it." He did not mean it to sound as condescending as it did, but I know from conversation that it left a pretty rancid taste in a lot of mouths.

After Moscoso's talk he left for Santa Cruz and I got hold of one of the Alliance's lawyers—a man named Rodgers—and told him that it was my impression, after four months of travel in South America, that the Alliance was in bad trouble. I then cited a few examples of failure and delay, and asked if he wished to comment on the outlook.

"Well, we expected trouble," he replied. "And the opposition is damned tough—but we're tougher." That was all I could get out of him, so I shook my head sadly, smiled, and thanked him for his time. On that day in La Paz I realized the Alliance was in worse trouble than I had thought.

*but not in principle

Now, in retrospect, I don't believe we're in such bad shape as I thought then, but it took me a long time to get over that encounter with the Alliance "brain trust," and I hope the next one will not be such a come-down.

If I had to give one single impression concerning the Alliance, it would be the contrast between the publicity it gets here in the States, and the nearly negligible interest it has stirred up in Latin America. During the first few months of my stay in South America I was constantly talking and asking about the Alliance, but after a while I realized the natives didn't particularly give a damn about it and — in the main — were only being polite when they took time out from more immediate pursuits to discuss it with me.

The fact is that, were it not for the stream of propaganda emanating from USIS offices in every Latin country, the Alliance for Progress would barely be mentioned at all. To the average Latin, it is merely a program of more and faster aid, to counter the menace of Castro and his widespread disciples. The concept of partnership is entirely missing, and the main feeling now is that the U.S. has promised a lot, but given little.

There is a kind of bitterness that lurks beneath the surface of most conversations concerning U.S.–Latin relations as regards the Alliance. The biggest Latin complaint is that the action is moving "too slowly," and that the funds are tied up in "Washington bureaucracy." The American immediately counters with the (correct) charge that Latin governments are moving even more slowly in submitting the necessary plans and blueprints for development projects. This leads, of course, to a dead end of rationalization, excuses and counter-accusations.

What generally emerges is something (from the Latin) like this: "After fifty years of vicious exploitation, what do you expect from us? Why shouldn't you help us? Why shouldn't you pay us back for all you've taken? Now that you're in trouble, now that you're afraid of the Communists, now you expect us to be on your side like old friends — and you want to pay us off with a handful of dollars."

I have two friends in Rio, both of whom are "pro-American," and both of whom feel exactly this way. One has just completed his training for the diplomatic service, and the other is a young executive in the real estate and investment business. They have both traveled and visited the States and they both want to go back. They like the way we live here and they have no use at all for communism.

But, man, you start criticizing Brazil's slothful reaction to the Alliance, and both of them will give you the same business. In reality, they're not talking to you; they're talking to your father and your grandfather, but you're the one who has to take the guff. The Latin personality is such that it never forgets an insult or a humiliation, and in their eyes that was all they got from the U.S. from 1900 until Castro became a threat in 1960.

They are psychologically unable to let us forget it, even though it might have no bearing on either of our current problems. The unvarnished truth is that we need Latin America today, and that is a new reality. The Latins are quick to recognize it and even quicker to throw it in your face if you get uppity.

There is the queer duality of our problem in Latin America. The new generation is very aware of their problems, and also aware that the U.S. wants and needs to help in the solutions. But don't push me, they say, because for the first time in your history I'm important to you. And they are.

And the crucial thing to remember is that they would rather do nothing at all than be forced into action by the "gringos," whose heavy-handed ghost is so much more visible to them than it is to us. We are paying now for the "big-stick" tactics of an earlier generation, and the best we can hope for is to settle the score as quickly and gracefully as we can.

In nearly every Latin country there is a congenital suspicion of American motives—although it often takes queer and contradictory forms. In Bolivia, for instance, I spent an entire afternoon and evening arguing with a labor leader that nearly everybody considered a communist. He hated Wall Street, he said, and felt certain that both Kennedy and Moscoso had come under the sway of "capitalist bosses." He made a clear distinction between "Wall Street" and "the American people," which was all the more pathetic because of his ignorance of what "Wall Street" means. He also thought that both John Steinbeck and John Dos Passos were young American writers, whose work he admired and with whom he felt sympathy. It took a few hours and quite a bit of prodding before he admitted that he'd learned to read English by reading *Playboy*.

But the Alliance for Progress? As far as he was concerned it was just a new and subtle form of exploitation. Just another scheme to keep the capitalists in power. He had no use for Russia or even Cuba, but he wanted no part of Washington either. He was for Bolivia, he said, and the idea that the Alliance for Progress might be for Bolivia, too, had never crossed his mind.

In most cases, Americans are made nervous by anti-American Latins, and after a few encounters they tend to keep their distance. Only the Peace Corps, to my knowledge, has made an impression on that segment of the population that is also most susceptible to communist influence. And, in doing so, they constitute one of the few visible proofs that the American personality is not quite the same as it used to be.

In Brazil, arch-leftist Leonel Brizola, the president's brother-in-law, calls members of the Peace Corps "spies for the State Department." He urges the populace to stone them, but his advice falls on deaf ears when an American comes to a poverty-stricken village and shows the people how to plant tomatoes and learn to read and generally participate in the social and economic development of the Twentieth Century. My impression is that one American working with his hands in Latin America is worth ten running their mouths.

The Latin is no stranger to grand rhetoric, and he has good reason to be suspicious of it. When the Spanish first came to this continent they talked to the natives about saving their souls, and in the meantime made off with all the gold and silver they could get their hands on. Then a new, home-grown generation rose up, under Bolívar and San Martín,[12] to "free these nations from the Spanish yoke." But the result was more of the same, with new bosses.

Then Uncle Sam came on the scene; he penetrated the continent only so far as was necessary to secure obedience and security for U.S. private enterprise. This conquest, like all the others, came under the banner of "freedom, liberty, democracy" and all the other fine words that most Latins no longer take seriously.

So now, in this tense age, how can we be surprised when Latins seem suspicious of our talk about "preserving the free world"? How can we expect them to give all-out support to the Alliance for Progress, when nearly every student is learning—from a legion of anti-American teachers—how the gringos have humiliated and exploited the Latin countries ever since our history brought us in contact with them?

What we should never forget, though, is that the majority of Latins are with us, even though they hate to admit it. But only so far as we believe in ourselves, and only as long as we keep proving, over and over again, that we are not as mean and greedy as were our forefathers.

In a way, Latin America is like a woman who has been wronged so often that she no longer believes what any man says—although she wants to, and keeps giving it one more try. Our problem with the lady is to convince her that we are Right—because Latins are as emotional as women on that subject—and also to convince her that we are strong enough to sustain our Right, because both women and Latins are pragmatic enough to know that one is not worth much without the other.

And that, placed in its proper feminine context, is the job cut out for the gentlemen who run our Alliance for Progress. At the moment it is very definitely "ours," and it will stay that way until we can convince the Latins that it is theirs, too. Which may take quite a bit of doing.

* * * * * * * * * *

12. Simón Bolívar and José Francisco de San Martín, early nineteenth-century heroes in the struggles of South American nations to free themselves from Spain.

OK, Clifford. It's 3:45 AM here and I have to get up early and drive all the way to Durango on two bald tires. I hope this will do you, or at least help. And if I think of anything else in the next day or so I'll send it on. Probably you wanted more pure color, but I got off on my sermon and I think my conclusion—especially the final note on Latin and feminine nature—is a far, far better thing that I do. Amen.

HST

TO THE BUSHNELL COMPANY:

Thompson was dissatisfied with a Smith & Wesson rifle scope he had purchased in Florida. This letter got him a refund.

August 29, 1963
Aspen, Colorado

Bushnell Co.
c/o Angevine's Gun Shop
Deland, Fla.

Gentlemen:

Here is a nutshell of this scope, purchased by me from Mr. Angevine about June 20, 1963. I mailed the postcard registration to you a day or so after the purchase.

In the gunshop, the scope was mounted with little difficulty. I then took it out for sighting in, but after four rounds from a .44 Magnum the cylinder expanded against the mount and would not swing open. I took the gun & scope back to the gunshop, where Mr. Angevine and I worked on it to secure a closer fit. This was done mainly by gently tapping the mount closer to the topstrap, then tightening the mount screws as far as they would go. After several hours of this, on successive days, the cylinder would swing out, with pressure, after 10 or 15 rounds, and the scope was more or less sighted in.

I then left Florida for New York, where I stayed a few weeks before going to Las Vegas and then to California, where I intended to hunt boar with the .44/scope combination. During the period of travel I dismounted the scope & repacked it in the box, doing the same with the pistol. I did not deem it wise to travel across half the states in the union with a scoped .44 Magnum riding loose in one of my suitcases. It would have been difficult to protect, and even more difficult to explain if I'd had an accident.

Upon arriving in California, I unpacked both instruments and attempted once again to mount the scope on the gun for a new, and relatively permanent sighting in. It was during this attempt—the second mounting—that the metal base of the scope gave way under pressure on the mount screws with the Allen wrench. No other instrument was used; there seemed no need for anything but human hands, since I had successfully mounted the scope by that method once before. Nor am I a brute of some kind. But I began to notice, as I tightened the screws, that one of them was oddly loose. Upon inspection, I found the metal in exactly the situation it is in now.

I also discovered the word "Japan" engraved on the bottom of the scope, and was not happy to see it. This was the third time I had bought something with an American label, but which was actually Japanese. If my Smith & Wesson revolver had blown up on the third shot, and had I then discovered that it had been made in Japan of Japanese steel, I think I might have had grounds for complaint. It did not, however, and I don't expect it to. As I might have if the label had been Asahi, instead of S&W.

My point is that I am not returning this scope to have it replaced with another of Japanese make. I am asking Mr. Angevine for a full refund, and I assume you stand behind him. I note, on the guarantee, that my refund offer ceased after thirty days. But since I was traveling during that time, and had the scope packed in its original box, I don't consider it quite the same as if I'd been using it. All in all, I fired no more than 25 rounds through the gun while the scope was on it, and all I got out of it was a series of circular score marks on my new cylinder—the result of your mount not fitting snugly enough to allow the cylinder to swing freely. All in all, my experience with this scope has been unsatisfactory in the extreme and I have no use for it.

I trust I will hear from you in the future.

Sincerely,
Hunter S. Thompson

TO CLIFFORD RIDLEY, *NATIONAL OBSERVER:*

The "Culture Shock piece" Thompson refers to had been published in the August 19 National Observer as "Why Anti-Gringo Winds Often Blow South of the Border." Thompson considers it the high-water mark of his Latin American reportage. The Thompsons were no longer staying with Semonin in Aspen but had found a ranch house fifteen miles from town in the mountain hamlet of Woody Creek.

September 9, 1963
Woody Creek

Dear Cliff:

Just a quick note to say I thought my Culture Shock piece on August 19 was one of the best and most original pieces I've ever read on Latin America or any other place. I was pleased as hell with it—mainly because you didn't put any words in my mouth or change the ones I wrote, and because it was interesting as hell and smacked of authenticity. It also rekindled my interest in a subject I've been avoiding—namely, that of plunging once again into the Latin bughouse. I've been reading everything written out of LA, and I wasn't impressed until very recently with the real "reader interest" importance of having a guy right there where they're driving golf balls off the roofs—instead of the herd of "veteran interpreters" operating out of Washington or some other capital and all writing the same stale hokum that I tried to foist off on you in the other "owed" piece. Massive concepts, as it were, and I as a reader, for a change, am getting damned tired of them. That golf club lead—with potbelly and gintonica—was worth every LatAm piece I've read since my return.

Also the layout and placement of the piece were fine, as were the head and the little cartoon. In a phrase, I dug it, and after reading it about six times I feel like a writer again—which is a feeling that became very diluted during those long and endless "drinking hours" in Rio.

Please send as many tearsheets as possible on that one. It may be the hook for pre-selling a book on my movements in LatAm.

Also, and to completely change the point, this guy Ed Fortier who works for you in Alaska is the greatest comic writer since James Thurber. His story on rampant bears completely broke me up. And I recall some of his others on moose, etc. You ought to have him do one on the (mainly rich Texas) hunters who fly into Alaska for the hunting season. With that fine, straight-faced style of his, he could do a classic. But don't tell him he's funny; it might kill his style if he tried. In all seriousness, with the natural exception of me, I think he's the best writer you have going for you, staff or no.

Also, I liked your review of *It Is Time, Lord*,[13] and will send off mine on *Red Lances*[14] (which I liked for odd reasons) on the morrow for the . . . no, guess the 16th is Monday, but maybe you'll want it for that week anyway. Next week, Dos Passos, and, I suspect, a .44 Magnum-type review. (Today, by the way, I hit a beer can at 120 yards with my own .44—iron sights, no less—and if that doesn't stand your hair on end, ask somebody who knows pistols.)

Also, that "Quotables" column (September 2) was a sparkler, but the editorial on Vietnam ("New View . . .") purely stank. Ralph Nader did a good piece out of Buenos Aires; I know the name from somewhere, but can't place it. Like Job and Machiavelli. A better look at Vietnam came from Dennis Warner, whose stuff I used to see regularly in *The Reporter*. He's a bit stuffy, and nowhere near Jerry Rose for my money, but it's good

13. Ford Chappell, *It Is Time, Lord* (New York, 1963).
14. Arturo Uslar Pietri, *Red Lances* (New York, 1963).

to see you getting some solid people and away from those abominable wire rehashes.

For Africa, you might want to write Smith Hempstone in Nairobi. He works for the *Chicago Daily News*, but I know he writes for other things as well. You can reach him c/o the *News* in Chi., but if you don't want to do that I can look up his box number for you. He's good & he's been in Africa a long time.

Also, another subject change, I forgot to ask you on the phone about circulation. How goes it? The September 2 issue looked uncomfortably slim on ads. The paper, however, has been a hell of a lot livelier of late, and your Freedom March coverage was first-rate. [. . .]

Ok, now to the old bugaboo of my travel plans, currently non-existent. I still feel like a paroled LatAm correspondent, but I guess I've stalled long enough. But, as you surely understand, I'm in no position now to undertake a protracted tour. Sandy would border on a breakdown if I mentioned leaving for a month, but I'd do it (and tell her 2 weeks) if I thought I could make some money at it. I'm thinking of Mexico. But the only trouble is that I know damn well I won't come back with any cash in the bank. Living is cheap in Mexico, but travel isn't. Travel never is, especially when you have to pose as a respectable correspondent. I could, however, come back with something to show for my efforts if you paid at least some of my expenses. I mean really minimum stuff like plane fare & hotels. You try it sometime if you don't think it's a hard deal to call the President's press secretary and don't dare let him return the call because you don't want him to know you're staying in some fleabag where yours is the only gringo name on the register.

At $200 per, I could I guess make $800 for a month in Mexico, but at least $600 of that would be expenses—and hell, that would mean a month away from a pregnant wife and my first real home in nearly two years, a month of bad food, hard work, dysentery and generally unpleasant living—and all I'd have to show for it would be $150 or $200, less the $35 a week that Sandy would need to get along here by herself.

What would you think about it if you were me? Christ, my life is genuine pleasure for the first time since I left Big Sur nearly 2 years ago. This place is like a rest-home for me. I have a dog, a woman, guns, whiskey, plenty of time to work, and a Disposall. And it'll only last for three months, because on December 1 the rent goes up to $100 and I plan to move on to California. For the $100 or so I'd salvage from a Mexican trip, I could whip up another story around here and come out even, without losing a month out of a fine life. [. . .]

Anyway, that's my position, and if you put yourself in my place I don't think you'd call it unreasonable. I'll go to Mexico for a month if I can come back to the States with something to show for it, but otherwise it doesn't make sense. In the long run, of course, I may break down and be willing to go for the same old, grueling pay situation, but it will only come about if and when I get a real travel itch, which is not unlikely in time, but which I don't feel now. And on top of that, I know of too many boobs who are making $800 to $1200 a month, plus all expenses and in many cases a living allowance, for doing stuff that I could do with my left hand. Which doesn't really matter, as long as I can remain objective, but that ain't always easy when you sit with people, as I did, who tell you they are using your stuff for reference, and in the next breath tell you that they're getting a $400-a-month living allowance (name & paper on request).

Well, that's my "short note." Now I look to my left on this queer-shaped desk and see again my Culture Shock piece. And I feel an urge to get back into the fray, because I can't see it getting anything but much bigger in the next few years and I think I have a good head start, which I'd hate to waste. There's nobody around who can do my kind of stuff, and—although a few others can do a few other things better—as a reader I'll take mine any day. I hate to close on such a big-headed, ambiguous, money-grubbing note—and needless to say I'll continue writing whatever I can for you wherever I am—but I simply don't think I can face another situation wherein I work like hell to make enough to pay for the next ordeal. It just doesn't seem sane.

OK again. That's it for now. Book reviews coming, plus a few others. Send word, in detail, when you get a relaxed moment. Sandy says hello. There's an extra bed any time you feel like using it, and the view up the valley gets better every day. Come on out and we'll see how you do with the .44.

Slothfully,
HST

TO AL PODELL, *ARGOSY:*

Thompson was piqued by an Argosy *magazine article on wild boar.*

September 11, 1963
Woody Creek, Colorado

Come on, Al baby, you think ole Hunter's gone soft in the head? ". . . we've got to get stories of great national importance." Yeah. Like, "I was buggered by the horned monster of Lake Mobewoke." How's that?

Here I queried you on a natural piece, bloody as hell, and you told me it was too much for you. Then a year later you come up with the same piece, poorly written by my standards, and with photos nowhere near as horrible as mine. What am I to think? Is your format getting bloodier, or what?

OK, and so you were off at camp when my Vegas film arrived. I guess that's the breaks. As it turned out, I had one or two good shots. I'm enclosing one of the worthless ones to give you an idea.

And then you come on with this "national importance" bit. Ah, spare me, Al.

Well, it so happens I'm heading out on an elk hunt in a few weeks, and I have certain knowledge that I'm going to be attacked by a herd of WILD BOAR. The boar are multiplying, Al, and moving east in great vicious herds, ripping and killing all in their path. Reliable sources report the razing of several towns in Nevada and Utah. In some cases the boar have made off with girl children, and god only knows their fate, but surely it is awful. Some estimates place the combined, east-moving herd at 3.4 million, spawning at the rate of 5% daily. Do you grasp the significance of that, Al? How about an advance?

As for other, more plausible possibilities, Colorado as it happens is in the early stages of a mining boom. A world shortage of silver has jacked up the price and made it worthwhile to open a lot of old silver mines that were closed when the silver market crashed about 50 years ago. One of them happens to be about 20 miles from me, the Midnight Mine, up in the hills behind Aspen. Others are spotted around within a day's drive. This is the heart of the silver country—places like Leadville and Silverton were roaring at the turn of the century, and today are virtually gone. But the new demand for silver looks like it might open a few places up—not a rush, or at least not to begin with, but, like you say, one of those deals where some people are going to get rich.

Let me know if it interests you, and *how much* it interests you. Needless to say, I guarantee Magnum-grade photos.

Bingo,
HST

TO EDITOR, *DENVER POST*:

September 14, 1963
Woody Creek, Colorado

Editor
Denver Post

Dear Sir:

I trust the *Post* will make a point of publishing the votes of all Colorado senators and congressmen as regards the bill, now pending in Congress, to make it illegal for anyone to sell goods at a price lower than that fixed by the manufacturer.

The bill is a crude and pernicious attempt at nationwide price-fixing, and I would make a point of voting against, regardless of party lines, any congressman who went along with it. Since I buy goods at the lowest price I can find, and deal with merchants who offer discounts, the passage of the bill would cost me several hundred dollars yearly and would make me mad as hell.

The manufacturers have their lobbyists going for them in this affair—a sleazy-sounding outfit called Quality Brands or something like that—but the man who's going to be hit in the wallet if the bill passes has no way of exerting pressure on his "representatives" in Congress. His best hope, as I see it, is the voice of the press, which often turns out to be a very effective lobbyist.

Why don't you run an editorial about this vicious thing? The consumer is already oppressed, badgered and deluded in every conceivable way, and the idea of having to cope with legalized price-fixing on a vast scale is almost too much to bear.

I trust you will follow the dubious progress of this bill, and see that no Colorado congressman's vote goes unnoticed.

Sincerely,
Hunter S. Thompson

TO LIONEL OLAY:

Trading jobs with his "old jousting friend" Lionel Olay, Thompson levied a harsh critique of comic Lenny Bruce.

September 20, 1963
Box 7
Woody Creek, Colorado

Dear Lionel:

Thanks for the good advice to stay poverty-stricken until I can come through with a nice, esoteric little novel that won't make any money. I'm trying Kesey's book[15] now; it's good, I guess, but so what? Books like that are like water when you want whiskey. Fuck 'em.

I'll file the advice, of course, but in the meantime, what kind of money would *Cavalier* pay me for a short story or two? Better than *Rogue*? And how about a lewd article or two? Maybe a crotch-eye view of Aspen. I need money NOW.

---

15. Ken Kesey's novel *One Flew Over the Cuckoo's Nest* had just been published.

And who should I write to? What editor handles fiction? I am learning fast and hard that a good contact is half the ballgame. Nobody knows what's good and what's not; the shits are killing us, as little Norman [Mailer] once said, and the only thing that depresses me more than dealing with an editor is arguing with a vicious cop. Mentally, it's the same league, the soft and the hard of it.

Your thing on Lenny Bruce was a lot better than Aldous Huxley. Not so pretentious; it rang true. Even so, I think Bruce should be locked up, if for no other reason than to get him out of the way so a better man can carry the ball. I don't like the idea of my right to free speech riding on the fate of a flea-bitten punk like Bruce. It's like you said about the Faulkner quote I had: "A writer don't rob his mother to write articles for the *Rogue*." Bruce is a phony, but I could forgive him even that if he were funny. The best thing about your piece is that you resisted the common temptation to bracket him with Patrick Henry. My reaction is, "Move on, Jack, don't block the aisles."

OK, put me onto the big money—or any money at all. And when I'm famous I'll buy you a drink. About two years.

Greedily—HST

TO EDITOR, *SATURDAY REVIEW:*

In a lengthly letter to the Saturday Review, *Thompson offered his wisdom on Latin American affairs, garnered from wandering around the continent and living in Brazil.*

October 14, 1963
Woody Creek, Colorado

Editor
SATURDAY REVIEW
25 W. 45
NYC 36

Dear Sir:

Two articles in your October 12 issue on "The Americas" deserve a bit of comment. Probably others do, too, but be that as it may; I refer here to "News and Latin America," by Bernard Collier, and "What's Happening to Journalism Education?" by John Tebbel.

The two are related, in that current journalism education is at least vaguely linked to our news coverage of Latin America. The subject interests me because I recently returned from a year and a half of traveling all over the South American continent as a free-lance journalist.

Collier's piece, for one thing, reflects a nearly perfect case of tunnel vision on the subject of the Latin American press. He discusses, with one or two half-relevant side-comments, two newspapers in Buenos Aires, Argentina, and concludes from his "study" that they are the only "exceptional" newspapers in Latin America, obviously no more than the best of a bad lot.

The fact that Collier did his research in Buenos Aires—which most of the foreign-based U.S. correspondents deserted years ago—is a good indication of just how far behind the times he is. Apparently he has never been to Brazil, which ten years ago eclipsed Argentina as the most significant nation on the continent, and which has at least three newspapers as good as any trio the U.S. can offer. According to a recent survey of the world press, *O Estado de São Paulo,* one of Brazil's most influential papers, covered more of that year's *significant* news stories than any other paper in the world—including *The New York Times.* In Rio de Janeiro, *Jornal do Brasil* and *Correio de Manha* ride herd on the government in a freewheeling fashion that would scare most U.S. editors into early retirement. If President Kennedy thinks the New York *Herald Tribune* gave him a rough time, he should thank his lucky stars that he never had to deal with the Brazilian press.

Collier says the Latin American press is guilty of "a dismal lack of analytical reporting on government affairs, both in time of crisis and during relative peace." He also says, "It is common for a newspaper merely to reprint a government communique in full, without pertinent comment, no matter how severely the subject of the message affects the country's people."

This is pure balderdash, and one of the best examples of what happens when a "Latin American correspondent" tries to cover his beat from New York. (If the *Trib* has stationed Collier in Latin America, it has happened since I left last spring.) Has Collier ever come across *El Tiempo* or *El Espectador* in Bogotá, or read the fire and brimstone commentaries of the Ecuadoran columnist who calls himself "Juan Sin Cielo"? And if he has ever been in Rio, did he ever get far enough away from the Hotel Excelsior Bar to lay hands on a copy of the afternoon *O Globo* and read some of the brutally anti-government editorials?

It would not be unjust to ask, in fact, just where in hell he has been—except Buenos Aires for some earthy talk with some of the bitter, old-line malcontents who like nothing better than getting hold of a gringo journalist and explaining why, among other things, they have put all their money in Swiss banks.

Which brings us now to Tebbel's lament that "research" is strangling the hopes for "professional training" in our schools of journalism. Perhaps your linking of the two articles was intentional—because Collier's wretched failure to deal with his theme would appear to be proof of Tebbel's thesis that journalism needs people who can cut the ever-toughening mustard.

It may be, however, that Tebbel has missed the point altogether; that it hardly matters how much emphasis is placed on research in our journalism schools—because if the whole idea of research were dropped tomorrow, there is no indication that the schools would turn out the sort of journalists capable of handling subjects like Latin America. A lot of people will tell you that the most important thing a man learns in Journalism School is to studiously avoid such low-pay areas as news work, and to aim instead for positions in related sectors like public relations, advertising and administration. Such critics are not necessarily "myopic," as Tebbel implies; they may be closer to the root of the problem than he is.

Tebbel might consider a few other problem areas before he takes up the standard of "professionally oriented programs" as the panacea for better and more meaningful journalism in our time. He should consider the case of the *Herald Tribune*, for instance, which only this year decided Latin America was important enough to give one of its staffers the title of "Latin American correspondent." The man chosen to carry the ball was Bernard Collier—but thus far it appears the *Tribune* would have been better off sticking with the wire services, who at least have men on the scene who read the local papers.

Or consider the case of Ralph McGill,[16] who regularly bemoans our serious lack of news from Latin America, but who cannot for some reason see his way clear to hire a man to cover that mysterious continent. The *Atlanta Journal and Constitution* even turns down free-lancers who offer to send as many stories as the papers can use.

The sorry state of our Latin America coverage is a real embarrassment to contemporary U.S. newspapers, but it is hard to see how the problem is going to be cured by journalism schools. The first step is to find people who give a damn; this is crucial, and without this sense of mission in young journalists there is not much hope for the whole field.

Second, we may as well admit that wire service coverage of Latin America is next to useless, and that there are not enough competent free-lancers who "happen to be on the spot" to go around. The only alternative, then, is to pay somebody's expenses to go down there and report what he sees. Yes, gentlemen, I know it hurts, but let's face it. And not just anybody. The only man worth sending to Latin America is one who *wants to know* what's going on down there, who's willing to get off the jet-routes and out of the old ruts, and move out where things are happening, instead of sticking

16. Ralph McGill, the associate editor and publisher of the *Atlanta Constitution* from 1938 to his death in 1969, was a champion of civil rights for African-Americans.

near the "press bars," where the "inside dope" changes hands, and where the government ministries hand out statements and communiques to correspondents who line up to receive them and dutifully relay their contents back home.

For some people, the job of being a "foreign correspondent" requires little or no effort. I recall one time in Brazil when "the press" had scheduled a cocktail party at the same time that a powerful and controversial politician was holding a press conference. The solution was a pool, a drawing of lots, and the dispatching of the "loser" to cover the conference and report back to the others—some of whom worked for competing news media—on what was said. Needless to say, this is not the way for the American public to gain insights as to the true state of affairs in Latin America.

Tebbel was right in decrying the cult of research in schools of journalism, but he was wrong in not advocating something better. Graduate professional programs are not much good, he says, until the communicator can understand what he communicates. Given this dictum, Collier of the *Herald Tribune* should spend about fifteen more years on the scene in Latin America, then apply for journalism school. And his is only one case.

Special schools of journalism are not the answer. Special—and individual—grants like the Nieman Fellowships and others of the same kind are much closer to what we need. But first there are other things to be learned: the origins and appeal of Marxism should be near the top of the list; the ability to convey in writing the ideas behind a statement such as "Kennedy is a great man, but he's a prisoner of Wall Street and I know the American people would understand me if I could talk to them."

But mainly we need people who care, who are curious about places and events that are surely going to affect the world their children will live in. Collier's critique of the Latin press is a good example of the kind of reporting we don't need, but there is no indication that Tebbel's campaign to get the "research people" out of journalism schools will give us what we do need—and what we will somehow have to get if we mean to cope with the unpleasant realities that our shortsighted forefathers have left us.

If we cannot produce a generation of journalists—or even a good handful—who care enough about our world and our future to make journalism the great literature it can be, then "professionally oriented programs" are a waste of time. Without at least a hard core of articulate men, convinced that journalism today is perhaps the best means of interpreting and thereby preserving what little progress we have made toward freedom and self-respect over the years* without that tough-minded elite in our press, dedicated to concepts that are sensed and quietly understood, rather than learned in schools—without these men we might as well toss in the towel and admit that ours is a society too interested in comic strips and TV to consider revolution until it bangs on our front door in the dead of some quiet night when our guard is finally down and we no longer even kid ourselves about being the bearers of a great and decent dream.

Let Mr. Tebbel consider the broader possibilities for a moment, and postpone for a while his academic resentment of research in journalism schools. And let Mr. Collier, in reporting on a continent bogged down in misery and further from hope than most people in this country can possibly understand, at least give credit where credit is due, and not condemn out of ignorance a Brazilian journalist—putting faith in his fellow man to speak his own truth in a Damn You kind of style that "trained professionals" and "technicians" and "specialists" have just about killed in this country.

Cordially,
Hunter S. Thompson

*Well, I meant to dash off a one-page comment here, but damned if I didn't run off at the mouth. Hardly much sense in sending it now—too long for the "Letters" column; maybe you'll take it as an article at your regular rates. Which I doubt. But what the hell? I'll send the carbon to *Jornal do Brasil* and tell 'em the U.S. press wouldn't print it. Ugly, eh?

TO LIONEL OLAY:

October 25, 1963
Woody Creek (yeah)

OK, Lionel, you're a cute fella with the words but don't step out of your league and start pushing me. You know damn well which half of the ballgame I was talking about. I've never given much worry to the first half; it's the ass-scratching half that makes me wonder now and then. You knew that when you asked.

I write because I read your San Francisco piece tonight. It was damn good; the first time I've ever read any natural prose from you, except in letters, and not always then. As it happens, I have always said San Francisco is the nation's number one gutless city, so it's no surprise that I liked your piece. So maybe it wasn't good at all, but just agreeable.

I understand you live in the same glen with Shelley Berman.[17] [. . .] By god I wish I could afford it. Maybe later, eh? When upward mobility comes. Probably Styron will be there first, though, and then Mailer. They

17. Shelley Berman was a popular comedian at the time. Lionel had left Big Sur and moved to Beverly Glen, a fairly fashionable community next to Beverly Hills.

can all live in Mother Herbert's Rooming Lodge: "bring your own stupor drugs; we furnish all else, up to and including hired cocksuckers and electric blankets." Herbert Gold, prop.[18] I see you got in your dig at that jellyfish bastard; the moral of that story is never snub anybody who might someday write for the voyeur mags.

Well, Lionel, a chap named Donleavy has just written a book. He never made it to Beverly Glen, or even *Esquire*, but he can write the balls off of every punk who did—including me. The *Observer* sent me a review copy yesterday and I read it straight through. Real tough. I believe in people again. *The Ginger Man* grew up and got human. Now that you've taken personal journalism about as far as it can go, why don't you read *Singular Man* and then get back to the real work? It'll be out November 7. You can date your shame from that day on. And me too. I'm not dumping on you, old sport—just giving the needle. I just wish to shit I had somebody within 500 miles capable of giving me one. It took Donleavy's book to make me see what a fog I've been in.

I'll send your pal Fredrick Birmingham[19] of *Cavalier* a ripping segment of my Rum Diary—but only after *Playboy* has bounced it. I read his shitty book. And after he goes pale from reading it, I'll send it on to *Nugget*, where Seymour Krim rejects things. Christ, the punks are hiring everybody they can't bury. And a lot of those they could bury. Later for them.

When are you going to move to the Garden of Allah? Are you digging my good, wasted journalism in the *Observer*? I just did a piece on Big Sur; gave you a condescending mention. When the money gets low, I can always come up with one on Big Sur. But my new gimmick is book reviews—$75 a crack, with my own choice of books. One a week keeps me in beer and bullets. I know that's not in your league, but somehow it don't turn me green. I had a taste of the big time in Rio, à la the recent dungjobs on our press corps in Saigon. And no thanks. I got fat and stupid. In a few hours it'll be 4:00 a.m. and I'll be up and out on the road to the big mountain to get an elk. My other rifle is sleeping here on the couch. He has no talent and doesn't know Grant Street from West Fourth, but he doesn't seem any poorer for it. Outside on the gravel road I can hear jeeps going up the hill; one of those drunken shits will probably shoot me tomorrow. Eight have been killed so far, and the season is 7 days old today. I wear a fluorescent orange vest. One man shot his sister-in-law at 15 yards. Said he thought she was a bear. Yeah. He was fined $100. Jesus. Tired of your wife? Take her on a Colorado hunting trip.

18. Herbert Gold was a critically acclaimed San Francisco essayist and novelist.
19. Fredrick A. Birmingham was a writer who became editor of *Cavalier* magazine in 1959; he was also a lecturer at the New School for Social Research, where Thompson had taken classes.

Your questions. I am living in a very comfortable 5-room house with a Disposall about ten miles out of Aspen. Sandy is pregnant and I have a 7-month-old Doberman. I am living off of the Dow-Jones Company, doing book reviews and articles of any sort at all. They want me to go back to South America. I have a .44 Magnum. I am living here because I needed a home. Currently I am jousting for one about 60 miles north of San Francisco on Jack London's mountain. I need rest, Lionel. You don't seem to grasp that since leaving Big Sur I have dug La Paz and Quito. I have caught the clap in Bogotá and paid for the cure in Lima. I have run amok in Cuzco and been arrested in Rio. I have lugged a shoulder-holstered pistol through Buenos Aires and Asunción. I have argued with whores in Montevideo. And then I went back to Louisville and got married in a marriage parlor with a neon sign by a justice of the peace who talked like Elmer Fudd.

Talk about come-downs.

What the fuck have you done except get rich? Answer that one.

Come visit and bring Beverly and the wolf. Sandy says hello to Beverly and balls to that pompous bastard Lionel.

                    Bingo:
                    HST

TO DARYL HARRINGTON:

Harrington was Thompson's "secret" girlfriend in San Francisco.

                    November 3, 1963
                    Woody Creek, Colorado

Dear Daryl:

Nagging guilt has finally won over procrastination, and for whatever it's worth, here is communication or at least a reasonable facsimile thereof.

I suppose you are down there playing shepherdess & I'm curious to know what it's like. I'm sorry I didn't write you in Europe, but the summer was vicious and I haven't had an address until now, much less a moment of peace or rest. I got married, as you suggested, and now Sandy is pregnant. I have a new Doberman, nephew of my other one, and probably a better dog. I also have a car and a nice little house some 10 miles out of Aspen. I also have a Disposall.

All of which is very nice, and I trust you are well, too. You've undoubtedly met some "nice young man" who will bring home the bacon—or sit home and summon it, like me—and, god willing, we will all be spared the hemorrhoids and the clap. Grow old peacefully.

And so much for all that. I recall my inept bumbling in New York and wonder at it. Not that I've ever prided myself on being a skilled lecher or even a semi-skilled communicator, but what a complete goddamn power failure that one turned out to be. You put too much pressure on a person, I think. I knew exactly what I wanted to say—or at least I thought I did— but in that kind of hyped-up atmosphere I would have felt like I was making a speech. Maybe after two weeks the air would have cleared, but I'm not sure. You've always thrown me into a bit of a stall. Maybe it's because we've always been rushed, usually due to my chaotic scheduling, and I've always had the feeling that whatever I had to say I had better say Right Now, and it had better be damn good. And don't remind me that I've almost always brought the pressure on myself, and that you generally had good reason to expect more from me than what I offered.

Probably I've never convinced you that my interest in you is anything more than a sort of off-beat lechery. Even now, at a distance of several thousand miles and safe from your jack-hammer interrogation, I resist a wavering impulse to try and write it down. I could offer hints and write cleverly in the bargain, but that would be sort of cheap. Maybe I can write it sometime in a story and you can read it there and come a little closer to knowing. Or maybe you do know, but insist on having me say it. That's what I like to think, but then that's an easy way for me to duck out. Now and then I remember that day when you were sick and I stopped by to say hardly anything and sit on the bed and look out the window at San Francisco. That was a good day, and one of the few times I didn't feel compelled to say "meaningful things." It seemed like we were doing okay without any bullshit dialogue. But of course there was no hurry then, and I wasn't trying to juggle you with the rest of my life like I usually am.

Why don't you write and say a few things and if you give me any openings I'll try to push on. I don't want to bother you or plague you with old questions and buried answers, but I hate to think that I've barged into your life as often as I have without your knowing why. And if you don't know, then I'd like to be able to tell you, but I am not real good along those lines. But at this distance I won't be able to duck the whole thing and lapse into conventional lechery as a stopgap.

The enclosed, by the way, is something off of a Big Sur beach that I've had since then.[20] Tonight I added the leather and thought it was okay.

---

20. A beautiful stone Thompson fashioned into a necklace.

Stare at it long enough and it develops all manner of meaning. At least it does for me. Hang it on a peg somewhere, or get it wet and hold it in the sun. Worthless as it is, it ain't a bad thing to have.

Conventionally,
HST

TO CLIFFORD RIDLEY, *NATIONAL OBSERVER:*

November 5, 1963
Woody Creek

Cliff—

How about a short (5 or 6 takes) essay-type thing on the difference between hunting with shotguns and rifles? Not technical. This may sound like nothing to you, but among hunters it is a deep-seated controversy. Rifle hunters, for the most part, are a meaner, tougher breed, and they scorn shotgunners as dilettantes or drugstore cowboys.

Shotgunners, on the other hand, claim a great subtlety in bird-hunting, a vague aesthetic that no coarse meat-hunter can ever know. The shotgun man is likely to think of himself as a country squire—if only for the moment. Shotgunning is definitely the status side of the fence, but I suspect it is that way because the image-makers know that rifle hunting is doomed east of the Mississippi. That's quite a few people who would rather hunt with shotguns than not hunt at all—and only a small percentage of them can afford long, expensive hunting trips to the West.

Needless to say, I mean to give the needle to the shotgun tribe. The other day I read where 10 million of them are now taking the field for the annual kill. That's a lot of potential controversy. A good-natured needle should stir up several good replies. Of the *Observer* readers who hunt, I'd say 49 out of 50 are shotgunners.

My point, with tongue halfway in cheek, is that shotgunning is a hunting surrogate for tired old men and flabby young ones. Maybe you have somebody on the staff who cares to join the argument & thus give both sides in print. (And I can supply a foto of myself with a wild boar; my antagonist, by firing some 200 pellets at once, can maybe bring down a duck or a rabbit to show.) Anyway, I'm going to do the thing, either for you or one of the sporting mags. Let me know if you want it; if so, I'll keep it mild. If not, I'll step up the velocity and aim at one of the hunting books.

The Vance Bourjaily[21] review will be in the mail tomorrow. The Colorado hunting madness piece will come next week. Let me know if you've changed your mind about wanting it.

Regards,
HST

TO PAUL SEMONIN:

Semonin, now a self-proclaimed Marxist, was enrolled in graduate school in Accra, Ghana.

November 6, 1963
Woody Creek

Paul—

I think this ["Nkrumah Hailed as Messiah" AP clip] bears out Joseph Conrad's contention that "we live amid romantic ruins pervaded by rats." Or another, by Doctor Bloor: "You can't dupe all the people all the time— except when they're niggers." (Dear Mail Inspector: I am just quoting; don't put no trouble on Mister Semonin; he's harmless.)

My mind is addling here. Absolute lack of contact has driven me to whiskey frenzies, characterized by top-volume monologues and midnight shooting. I think Aspen is for people who can't make it in San Francisco & who have enough cash to fail gracefully.

As soon as possible I mean to move on. Without contact of some type I will turn yellow and die. Maybe LA. God knows, it is just about the only place I haven't tried. Right now I am too broke to do anything. My Donleavy review came out today, thus guaranteeing the rent for last month if the check ever comes. I require cash only for stamps and wine; everything else I charge. But now I don't have a dime.

The fucking Reds are putting the pressure on me. The word is out. I have reliable information that the Denver branch of the IJC [International Jewish Conspiracy] is behind this harassment. Those communist shits! I used to blame the Wall Street warlords for my troubles, but now I know better. If it keeps up I'm going to bust up a few marriages and finish my tormentors with a pig instrument.

Your English friend sounds like somebody with pimples who never made the rugby team and masturbated till his brain went soft and he decided to be a socialist Himmler. The fucking English should be kept out

21. Thompson reviewed Vance Bourjaily's book on bird hunting, *The Unnatural Enemy*, for the *National Observer* (December 2, 1963).

of politics; they've caused enough trouble already. A watery gang of punks with body odor and double-breasted suits.

I now have a vic and pegs on which to hang my callers. The latter include: Durwood Fink, the leading Subud[22] thinker and a man who could do me some good in the movement if I could tolerate his bullshit; Virgil Blackmonster, the leading Subud economist (after his illegitimate brother, Hayes Blackmonster, who is neo-Subud I think & therefore not quite respectable); Garcia y Vega, a Canadian invert who is giving Subud a try because his friends like it; and Maury D.P.F. Millard, a Swede from New York U who owes us all because he has more Subud spirit than nearly anybody. Maury gets my chair when he comes, and also the coldest beer. He's the neatest guy you ever saw and I even switched to Paxtons because he smokes them.

Well, that about wraps you up, I think. And Himmler, too, for that matter. I believe he's out of his league in this scramble. He should stick with the books, and maybe join the Young Pioneers.

Put in a good word for me with The Messiah. Tell him I'll chant just about anything if there's money and power in it. And you might add that I "do no wrong" either. That would give us something in common, so we could talk easily.

I am rewriting The Rum Diary around the concept of The Rage. Which harks back to my earlier concept of The Nigger.[23] (Let me know if the word preceding these brackets is XXXXX (whoops) . . . ah . . . deleted by the Censor.) Next time I'll brush up on my euphemisms.

I am thinking of dropping in on you. Ponder that until you get the next volley.

Mister Magnum

The Denver Post *had refused to publish Thompson's September 14 letter to the editor, so he tried again under a pseudonym.*

November 14, 1963
Aspen, Colorado

Editor:

Bring knives and whips. Get the Bastards. If this price-fixing law goes through, Congress should be abolished. And they want more pay. Vote on

22. Subud was a fashionable spiritual movement that Semonin was fascinated by.
23. After reading Norman Mailer's *The White Negro*, Thompson developed a theory that all working-class people were "Niggers."

nothing all year but a pay raise for themselves and higher prices for every-body else. No tax cut, no civil rights, no foreign aid. They should get the minimum wage. Send them back where they came from with no pay. What good are they? Violence! And that damn zip code. I sic my dogs on the postman. This whole country is going mad.

Helmut Deejen
Aspen, Colorado

TO JO HUDSON:

Low on funds, Thompson saw to it that the venison was plentiful on his dining table.

November 18, 1963
Woody Creek, Colorado

Jo:

You ain't pickin' up the meat like I am, Joko. I got so much I need new excuses to go hunting. Like exercise, walking the dog, looking for badger pelts, and that sort of thing. My toolshed is so full of hanging meat that I can't open the door. Today I got caught in a goddamn blizzard about two miles from the house. I couldn't see shit and was stumbling along half dead from cold. Agar was out ahead and apparently ran into a deer hotel. They scattered like ants from an anthill and one stupid fawn tried to run me down with Agar[24] after it. I couldn't see the sights at all but got him solid with a point-shot. I've been practicing with my 12-gauge meatmaster. It was too dark to gut him so I had to carry the bastard all the way to the house and do him on the porch. The blood froze into the snow and I guess it will be there until spring. It adds color to the porch. While I was climbing a fence to get the dead one, a spike buck trotted up to the body, sniffed and trotted off. Agar chased another one so far I thought he was lost, but after a half-hour or so he came back.

But so far, no elk. Getting a bull elk here is like getting a big boar there—or maybe harder, since they seem to be getting thicker than they were when I was around. Before I finish I'll get a good rack for you. About a week ago we saw two huge bulls (elk) from the road about two miles up on a ridge. Racks with a seven-foot spread and 1000 pounds each. Fucking monsters. The next day we climbed straight up from noon until sundown, getting there about the right time—but nothing. Or at least no elk. I passed up a buck about 300 pounds on the hoof with a rack that would knock your

---

24. Thompson's new dog was named after the original Agar, the pup's uncle.

eyes out. But it was early then, and I didn't want to spook the elk. An hour later, just before it got too dark to shoot, I gave up on the elk and shot another 300-lb. buck, but with a medium rack. I shot it off of his head with the .44, took the backstrap, and fled. A shitty thing to do, but I barely made it back as it was. It was like coming down from the Ridge Road after dark. And these Rockies make the Santa Lucias look like a public park.

Deer are big as hell around here. A lot of does are around 200. And elk are fantastic. You can't drag them a foot without a horse, and it takes five men to hang a medium-sized cow. I had to work with one that a guy up the road shot. It took all afternoon with a horse, 3 men and a jeep to get back to the ranch, and another hour to hang it. And it wasn't big, as they run.

Even so, I'd rather hunt boar. It's a gutsier game, and not so much work when you get one. I was going to trade the .264 in on a Weatherby .300, but the damn thing is too efficient to get rid of. No matter where I hit, the bastards fall. The other day, after I'd gone out at 4 in the morning and climbed until 9 to get an elk—and failed—I was so pissed off that I took a 600- or 700-yard shot at a buck. He was so far away that I could barely see his rack— a big one—even with 7-power glasses. Anyway, I sat down, braced the gun on a wire fence, guessed at the elevation, and gave it the business. I couldn't believe my eyes when the bastard sat down like his legs had been chopped off. I waited a while, keeping an eye on him, then started the horrible climb. It took me an hour to get there, straight up as always in this goddamn country, and I was no more than 10 yards away when the bastard jumped off and crashed off through the brush, straight downhill. I never saw him, but I guess it was a muscle hit and he'll recover. But what a fantastic shot; I wish to hell I could have finished him, just for the souvenir.

I think what I'll do is put a custom stock on the .264 and a 2 to 8 power B&L [Bausch & Lomb] variable scope. That should give me a hot bomb for both deer and varmints—and boar, elk and anything else smaller than a grizzly. I just sold a long article to *The Reporter*, a real prestige sale, and when the check comes I can probably afford the scope. I'll also try to get down to Big Sur in a few weeks. It looks like I'll zip over to that place above San Francisco and see about the house I might rent. If so, I'll make it on down for some pig-poking. Sometime between now and Xmas. My financial condition is horribly up and down. For the past four weeks I haven't had a dime. Charged everything at the General Store—gas, food, cigs, bullets, etc. Now, if there's anything left after paying debts, I can probably afford to travel at least as far as California. The snow here is ungodly. I have to buy chains. Last year it went to 40 below. I can't stand that.

Got a buck last week with the .44. Disintegrated his shoulder and blasted both lungs. About 60 yards. It's a boar-buster, for sure. Especially when I get the scope mounted again. It's all I need for a brush-gun.

I keep hearing terrible things about your dog situation. First I heard that you finished off the other two, and now that you can't have any at Marion's. What the hell is going on? Have you taken up cats? Are you turning queer? I have a hell of a fine Doberman, but he'll never be worth a shit for road-running without good competition. I have him chasing rabbits and deer, but I know he'd never hit one except by accident. Get a decent animal and we'll do some work. Mine already knows to watch out the front window for the action, and he moves out of the car fairly well, but I need something like a whippet to make him go hard. He thinks it's a game. Maybe I'll get a whippet. I think road-running beats hell out of regular hunting. It's a white man's sport, like falconry. I'm thinking of buying some falcons. [. . .]
Write:

H

TO LAURIE HOSFORD:

November 19, 1963
Box 7
Woody Creek, Colorado

Dear Laurie:

I was watching the Bears-Packers game in an Aspen bar today and was reminded of you and Tallahassee when I saw my old, Eglin Bratkowski-McGee combination at work for the Packers in a losing cause. Sorry I haven't written, but constant movement and desperate money-writing is hard on leisurely correspondence. Every time I sit down to write letters I remember an article that's overdue and have to postpone the letters.

Last week I made a big jump by selling one on Louisville to *The Reporter.* It should be out soon, maybe this week. Try and pick it up. As far as I'm concerned, *The Reporter* is about the best magazine in the country; it's the only one I really respect and as big-league as they come. I'm still doing stuff for the *Observer*, mostly book reviews, but now and then an article. Without traveling, it's hard to live off of one market. I'm also sending out short stories and undertaking a rewrite of my novel, The Rum Diary. All in all, I'm busy as hell. And broke as hell, to boot. I can't understand it. The more I make, the more broke I become. And god knows what's going to happen when taxes come due. I'll have to go to Mexico.

Sandy is pregnant as hell, and the dog is huge. I don't know how I'm going to feed all these mouths. Winter is on us here, and the snow is terrible. I am trying to move to California, but will have to go over there first and check on the situation. I am also planning a trip to New York sometime soon, but nothing can be definite until I get checks.

Your talk of growing old, combined with the Tallahassee viewpoint, made a lot of sense. I seriously think you should get going on the fiction. Try markets like *Playboy, Cavalier, Nugget, Rogue,* and that sort of thing. They don't get much good fiction and pay well when they accept something. In recent months I've seen a lot of stuff by armed forces people. Man, if I had $900 a month and time to write, I wouldn't look around for a better deal. And a good kind of experience to draw on, too. You can get some damn good stuff out of the AF. Start hustling.

There is an unusual photo of Sandy on pg. 20 of the December *Argosy.* Shirley might enjoy it. But don't believe I wrote that stupid letter; the bastards just signed my name to it. I'm currently trying to beat money out of them. Don't ever send those bastards anything. They'll steal it.

Did you see Ann [Frick] in Tallahassee? I'd really like to know what she's doing. If you see her, tell her to write me a note. To hell with her husband. And keep me posted on your doings. [. . .] Write.

HST

TO AL PODELL, *ARGOSY:*

Argosy had printed a photo Thompson had taken of Sandy without his permission. The magazine eventually paid him $150 rather than go to court.

November 19, 1963
Box 7
Woody Creek, Colorado

Dear Mr. Podell:

Be advised that my bill (enclosed) for the photo of my wife that you used without either permission or payment on page 20 of the December issue of *Argosy* is $100, which I deem an entirely reasonable fee, considering the circumstances.

Since I am not aware of the exact letter of the law in these matters, I have asked the advice of Mr. Leon Daniel at PIX, who now handles my photos. I have also advised Mr. Daniel, in a letter written tonight, that—failing monetary satisfaction—I have every intention of stomping the shit out of you, either in your office or wherever we happen to meet.

The simple use of the photo would not have bothered me excessively, but the outright forgery of that stinking letter was too much. You should have had better sense than to sign my name to it. Try to find a Hunter S. Thompson in Boulder, Colo.—especially one who has the rest of the transparencies from that roll from which you used one print.

What the hell kind of an operation are you people running, anyway? Or don't you figure you need free-lancers? Fortunately, I have enough work with the *Observer* and *The Reporter*. I don't make big money, but I make quite enough to visit New York now and then, and I stay in good enough shape to be able to raise hell when I get there. There's nothing I'll like better—both as a healthy exercise and as good material for my biographers—than to gather some of my ham-fisted friends from McSorley's[25] and clean out your whole damn office.

You may or may not have the decency to give me some reply. Failing that—and a check—plan on seeing me in either late December or early January. If I happen to be delayed, I'll let you know.

> Sincerely,
> Hunter S. Thompson

BILL. . . . Payable, within 30 days, to Hunter S. Thompson, same address as above:

$100 . . . for unauthorized use of photo of Mrs. Hunter S. Thompson on page 20 of December *Argosy*. Used, without either notification or payment, in connection with letter titled "Almost Less," to which my name was blatantly forged. Above-mentioned photo was not submitted for publication (see accompanying letter, dated September 11, of which I have a true carbon). Nor have I been in Boulder since 1957 and can see no reason why the letter to which my name was forged should have been datelined from such place.

Note . . . acceptable in lieu of payment in cash ($100), twice that amount in the form of suitable action on such court as the home team may prefer.

> Yours, sincerely, in reaction to
> larceny and insult,
> Hunter S. Thompson

cc: 1) Al Podell, Photo Editor, *Argosy*, 205 E. 42nd St., New York City
    2) Henry Steeger, Editor, *Argosy*, same address
    3) two other, necessarily unnamed, gentlemen of sporting blood, c/o McSorley's, East 7th St., New York.

Further note: Too many people in this gutless world have come under the impression that writers are a race of finks, queers and candy asses to be bilked, cheated and mocked as a form of commercial sport. It should be noted, therefore, in the public interest, that some writers possess .44 Magnums and can puncture beer cans with 240-grain slugs from that weapon

25. McSorley's was Thompson's favorite Manhattan Irish drinking pub.

at a distance of 150 yards. Other writers, it is said, tend to enjoy violence for its own sake, and feel that a good fight, with the inevitable destruction of all nearby equipment and furniture, is nearly as fine for the nerves as a quart of John Powers Irish [whiskey].

TO POSTMASTER GENERAL:

Thompson deemed the new ZIP code system "governmental harassment."

> November 19, 1963
> Box 7
> Woody Creek, Colorado

Postmaster General
Washington, D.C.

Sir:

I would appreciate knowing if you mean to continue the stupid, vicious "Zip code" system, instituted by your predecessor. If so, I would also appreciate an explanation of same. Is it, in fact, any more or less than governmental harassment dreamed up by an anti-social pervert?

Also, will my letters continue to reach their destination without bearing such codes? I have no way of finding out the wretched numbers for any address I might write to, and no intention of using such numbers even if they were made available.

I voted for Kennedy in the last election, but the first time one of my letters comes back to me for lack of a "Zip code," he can count on one less vote in 1964.

> Sincerely,
> Hunter S. Thompson

TO PAUL SEMONIN:

Thompson was devastated by the assassination of President John F. Kennedy.

> November 22, 1963
> Woody Creek, Colorado

Paul—

I am trying to compose a reaction to the heinous, stinking, shit-filled thing that occurred today. Supposedly it will be the "local" reaction, but of course it won't. It will be my own, couched in local color. Nobody has asked for it but I am sending it anyway. 1000 words—damn few to fill the awful hole.

I suppose your boys over there are whooping it up. Another victory for Marxism. Well, they better add up the score again, because they lost as decisively as I did. The names of the winners are not posted yet, but soon they will come down from the towers—but only after a respectable period of mourning. It is the triumph of lunacy, of rottenness, the dirtiest hour in our time. That the bullet should have come from the Far Left is the filthiest irony of all. It was right and proper that the deed was done in Texas, but a terrible shock to find the "Fair Play for Cuba Committee" with its name on the slug. I hope they have the wrong man, but I'm afraid not. The damage this has done to the Left in this country—which I guess you would call a puppet show, at best—is incalculable. It is the death of reason. From here on out, the run is downhill for us all—and I mean all.

Wayne Vagneur, the rancher up the road, stopped by with the news. I started to cry but figured that was not called for, so cursed instead. He is not the type for jokes, or otherwise I could not have believed it. Where do we go from here? All of you cheap book-store Marxists who had the answer yesterday had better buy bullets. It would not surprise me at all to find Cuba devastated by the time I wake up tomorrow. And then a notice in my box: "Report at once." Well, if my mood at the moment continues, I am just about ready to report as long as they guarantee action. I guess they are probably laughing harder in Mississippi and in the back rooms of the Dallas GOP headquarters than they are right now in Moscow. Maybe in Red China they are whooping it up too, but Khrushchev has better sense.

This is by far the most profound act of the 20th century. But the ski bums are still living it up in the Red Onion. The big laugh. Aspen is a bag of shit. The fact that you like it only reinforces my opinion of your Marxist leanings. You will turn out like those black doctors you deplore—refusing to go into the bush because the bright lights are in town. Bright lights have no politics, and in any politics there are bright lights. It hardly matters what you believe as long as you're on top, and laughing. Fuck all.

I am considering a retreat to reality. For the next year—at least until the '64 elections—every man with balls should be on the firing line. There will be more and more like your boys in Caracas who have only killed 24 this week in an effort to stop elections. If today's action defined the law in this world, then I am ready for it. And you should warn your friends that not all Americans are soft pot-bellies. The shits were surely killing us, and now they have killed the only hope on the American horizon, the only man who had half a chance of carrying the ball. Now, President Johnson. Jesus Mother. Fuck. Again, where do we go from here?

I would like to be able to define the meaning of this thing, but the further I think, the further the error extends. I see no end to it, and less hope. It will almost surely mean a Goldwater victory in '64, a wild reaction against "The Reds." The democratic (small d) camp will be totally disorganized for too long. Now it is a question of either your kind of fascism or the other kind administered by the men with the fish-bellies. If it were fashionable, I would weep for us all.

After the monstrous frustration of Aspen, the sight of so much giggling scum, I called Louisville, thinking that maybe I could communicate my sense of urgency. But there, of course, it was worse. Maybe like a bad accident on the Dixie Highway. I recall Davison telling me he had met Rutledge Lilly at the CC [*Command Courier*], and Rut had asked about me. Davison told him a few things, and then Rut asked, "Is he going back to school?"

How do you deal with a mentality like that? What can you say? Is he going back to school—How long, O Lord, how long?

But school is out, here. The '64 elections—beginning tomorrow—will be the most crucial vote in the history of man. Every fish-belly in the nation is out in the open tonight, but everybody is holding them low until after the funeral. Mine is out too, for that matter, and I don't figure on putting it away for quite some time. The dirty dealing has come to the surface; fair play was yesterday and maybe tomorrow. If you have any guts at all you will come back and put your back to the wall with the rest of us. You said in a letter to Peggy Clifford that my concept of America is outdated, divorced from reality and the rest of the world. Probably it is, but I fully intend to go down with it before I give in to either of the other shitty camps. It may be that the fascists will croak us, but not before getting their balls twisted. If only by me.

Your failure to answer my recent burst of letters indicates that you are too wound up in Club Business to consider anything else. You had better wake up; beginning tomorrow, it is no longer safe to bug the establishment. If any one thing is sure it is that the Christians are out, and the Shits are in. And if you think that's divorced from the rest of the world, just watch. The political clock has been turned back to early Eisenhower & McCarthy. This savage unbelievable killing, this monstrous stupidity, has guaranteed that my children and yours will be born in a shitrain.

I wish crying would solve it, because that would be easy. But there is no sense crying for lost hope and a dead effort that was only a foot in the door but at least the door was open as long as the foot was there. I recall that night when we climbed off the turnpike in Oregon and hiked into town to watch the first crack opened in the dike. The first debate was the turning point, and I am the first to admit that since then the gild has gone from the lily. But consider now that the lily is dead, replaced by a toadstool.

If you see any hope, send word. I am, at the moment, as low as I've ever been.

H

TO WILLIAM J. KENNEDY:

A few months earlier William Kennedy had left San Juan for upstate New York to work part-time for the Albany Times-Union *while writing fiction. Thompson wrote him this letter the day JFK was assassinated in Dallas, using—for perhaps the first time—the phrase "fear and loathing," to describe his horror at the tragedy.*

November 22, 1963
Woody Creek

I am tired enough to sleep here in this chair, but I have to be in town at 8:30 when Western Union opens, so what the hell. Besides, I am afraid to sleep for fear of what I might learn when I wake up. There is no human being within 500 miles to whom I can communicate anything—much less the fear and loathing that is on me after today's murder. God knows I might go mad for lack of talk. I have become like a psychotic sphinx—I want to kill because I can't talk.

I suppose you will say the rotten murder has no meaning for a true writer of fiction, and that the "real artists" in the "little magazines" are above such temporal things. I wish I could agree, but in fact I think that what happened today is far more meaningful than the entire contents of the "little magazines" for the past 20 years. And the next 20, if we get that far.

We now enter the era of the shitrain, President Johnson and the hardening of the arteries. Neither your children nor mine will ever be able to grasp what Gatsby was after. No more of that. You misunderstand it, of course, peeling back only the first and most obvious layer. Take your "realism" to the garbage dump. Or the "little magazines." They are like a man who goes into a phone booth to pull his pod. Nada, nada.

The killing has put me in a state of shock. The rage is trebled. I was not prepared at this time for the death of hope, but here it is. Ignore it at your peril. I have written Semonin, that cheap book-store Marxist, that he had better tell his boys to buy bullets. And forget the dialectic. This is the end of reason, the dirtiest hour in our time. I mean to come down from the hills and enter the fray. Tomorrow a cabled job request to *The Reporter*. Failing that, the *Observer*. Beyond that, god knows, but it will have to be something. From now until the 1964 elections every man with balls should be on the firing line. The vote will be the most critical in the history of man. No matter what, today is the end of an era. No more fair play. From now on it is dirty pool and judo in the clinches. The savage nuts have shattered the great myth of American decency. They can count me in—I feel ready for a dirty game.

Fiction is dead. Mailer is an antique curiosity. The stakes are now too high and the time too short. What, O what, does Eudora Welty have to say? Fuck that crowd. The only hope now is to swing hard with the right hand, while hanging onto sanity with the left. Politics will become a cockfight and reason will go by the boards. There will have to be somebody to carry the flag.

My concept of the new novel would have fit this situation, but now I see no hope for getting it done if, indeed, any publishing houses survive the Nazi scramble that is sure to come. How could we have known, or even guessed? I think we have come to the point.

Send word, if you still exist—

HST

TO EUGENE W. MCGARR:

Thompson had gotten McGarr a job as a bill collector in the Bronx.

November 25, 1963
Woody Creek

Well McGarr, I'm happy I was able to get you a job, and now, of course, I await the customary one month's salary as representing agent's fee. At your earliest convenience. I need it NOW.

This rotten stupid shit-filled madness has caused uproar in my once-tidy life-plan. Tonight I heard where the Dallas police considered the case "closed" and would make public no evidence concerning the charges against Sir Oswald. It is nearly impossible here to keep up with what is going on, but that, I believe, is the first statement of any significance to emerge from this thing. If necessary, I will go to Dallas to view such evidence as exists, regardless of the opinions of the Dallas police. Judging from what has happened thus far I could probably walk into headquarters there and steal the whole file without anyone being the wiser. I only hope the news in New York makes more sense than it does here; it couldn't make any less. All we have here is CBS-TV, which in my judgment has fallen flat on its ass regarding coverage. The radio has been my lifeline, but newscasts are continually being blacked out by the speeches of Billy Graham and various song festivals that go on for hours. Even so, what little I have heard on the radio has been worth all the old film clips, meaningless pageantry and announcers reading the AP & UPI wires that I see on TV— and the interminable "discussions" directed by waterheads and with no apparent purpose but to give TV exposure to third-string dignitaries who could not plague the public eye in any other manner. As isolated as I am,

TV brings me the rumblings of national idiocy and incompetence. My only hope now is that the Sunday *NY Times* will get here on Thursday.

I sent off a reaction piece to the *Observer*, but was probably too late for even a delayed press run. But I felt like I had to do something.

Now, surveying the remains, I am on the verge of postponing the good life for the duration of the crisis. I am even thinking of returning to New York if anyone will give me a writing job and the free hand I will of course require in order to make sense of the awful Nazi cockfight that is sure to come. I think the peace will last another 24 hours, then off with the gloves and fuck all. The soft thump of the last piece of sod going onto the grave will be the signal for the orgy to begin—and I don't know if I can stand being so completely removed from the arena as I am now. Under the circumstances, I might even run for president.

At any rate, if your influence at ABC is yet massive enough, you might point out that I am at the moment available as a roving seeker in the news area. I am not available for punk work, no matter what the salary, or even the title. My line is the seeking and assembling of facts into meaningful order. Nothing else.

But I don't really expect you to come up with an offer, considering the cheap medium you now represent, and I am naturally taking steps in other directions. First, *The Reporter*, which I doubt could afford to hire me even if they wanted to. At the moment they maintain five writers, and it may be a hard crew to crack.

My other alternative is the *Observer*, but I turned down one of their offers and hesitate to re-apply for the same reasons I had then. I don't know if I could stand the editing. This is no time for any man to be beholden in any way to ignorant rednecks. Even so, it would be an opening, and perhaps better than nothing.

I can only hope your understanding of this event causes YOU to realize that your current position in "The Saga of Western Man" is nearly as irrelevant as mine at the moment. And for that reason, I expect you to launch a penetration of some sort, rather than sit on your ass and your $200 rent— which, I must say, is an impressive figure. I trust it has, if nothing else, freed poor Eleanor from toil. Sandy requests, by the way, that Eleanor make some effort at communication.

I have sent several communications in the past few weeks, but none have been answered. Maybe they are not forwarding from your old address. Bone has confirmed your status, so don't worry. Cooke has failed to communicate in any way and I don't even know his address. Tell him to make contact.

And if, by chance, your new eminence brings you in contact with anyone who may need my services in the immediate future, by all means send word. Needless to say, I do not seek a job, but rather a position or a connection. Nor do I particularly seek money, except in the form of having my expenses covered in what I undertake. Which would, of necessity, be nothing less than a massive job.

This thing has put us all in bad trouble. Your recent dealings in low finance[26]—coupled with your sudden largesse—may have rendered you incapable of clear vision concerning anything more abstract than your wallet. If so, I trust the condition will pass. But if not, you had better refrain from having children, or you may find yourself having to explain in a few years just what you weren't doing when the chips went down for us all.

I leave you with that, and with, of course, my congratulations on your success with the Great Nipple [money]. Would that we might all get a grip on it soon. But right now I have other things in mind, and will do some eating, and clear my head before composing those letters by which I mean to seek my connection.

Hello to Eleanor, and congratulations to her for enduring you this long. Most people—women—would have had better sense.

I have just returned from town and the latest, frustrating bout with TV. My general feeling is a loss of hope in the largest sense, a pessimistic rage, and a disorganized compulsion to enter the fray at once.

Send word.

Hunter

TO DWIGHT MARTIN, *THE REPORTER:*

A week after JFK's assassination, Thompson was still incensed. The uncertain political climate made him want to forgo fiction to work in journalism.

December 1, 1963
Box 7
Woody Creek, Colorado

Dwight Martin
The Reporter
660 Madison Ave.
New York 21

Dear Mr. Martin:

Several hours before that rotten, stinking murder, one of Jehovah's Witnesses appeared at my door for the purpose of reading scripture. He also read from a book for which I eventually paid 75 cents—a passage fore-

26. McGarr and Thompson had formed a business partnership to make a documentary and they had been seeking backing through unorthodox channels.

telling "the time of the end." Which, according to his book, is right now.

By four o'clock that day, I was ready to go looking for the Witness and sign up. And now, with a hairy animal called Nixon looming once again on the horizon, I am ready to believe that we are indeed in "the time of the end." There is no other explanation for the durability of that man. He is like a hyena that you shoot and gut, then see a few hours later, loping along in his stinking way, oblivious to the fact that he is not only dead, but gutted as well.

At any rate, events of last week caused me to seriously consider coming down from the hills to seek work in the arena. For several days I was convinced that my best hope for a meaningful contribution was to immediately drive to Dallas and croak the chief of police with a .44 Magnum, but I got over that, too. Then I wrote the *Observer* and told them I was reconsidering their offer of a staff job, which I avoided last spring. We are dealing, but I have just about got over that, too.

I wonder if you have work for me there. Or, even if you do, whether I'd be better off with a job, or free-lancing. I don't mean money; I am so used to poverty that solvency would put me in a condition of angst. I do, however, take it more or less on faith that you pay your writers. Something, anyway.

If I worked for you, though, could I deal in the Big Business? Or would I be sitting in an office in some kind of a supporting role? I am thinking of the slot of "Number Six Writer." At the moment, you appear to employ five, of which three are female. That ratio gives me pause, but I suppose you know what you are up to.

But that, luckily, is neither here nor there. My view at this time is that politics in this country for the next nine months is going to resemble nothing more or less than a Nazi cockfight, and I want to be in on it. I don't mind saying that my primary motive is to keep that man Nixon out of the presidency. No sense trying to hide my bias; it's nothing personal, I just think he's the most dangerous political punk who ever lurked in this nation. Especially at a time like this. I have no candidate—I'm even thinking of running, myself—but I know the one man we don't need is that goddamn vengeful Zero with nine lives.

Certainly I haven't altered my conviction that this nation is going over the hump. As a matter of fact, I'm now working on a piece called "The View from Woody Creek," which I hope to send in a week or so. It has to do with The Hump. The Kennedy thing merely underlined my thesis, because I saw him as an historical maverick to queer the odds. But no more. And none of his ilk either. This poor bastard Johnson is sitting on a bomb, and I'm not even sure I wish him good luck. The biggest question now is the U.S. position as "leader of the free world," and, frankly, it scares the hell out of me to think it may depend on Lyndon Baines Johnson.

So much for all that, too. What I am trying to compose here is not an application for employment, so much as a feeler. It may be that I can do more, in terms of significant writing, by moving to California, as I'd planned, and working like hell as a free-lancer. But right now I'm not sure. Woody Creek is so completely removed from political reality that I might as well be in the Amazon basin. And I'm not at all sure that a mountain-top north of San Francisco would be a lot closer to the action. What I have in mind is steady work, night and day, until after the '64 election, and then take stock again.

What do you think? Would my special talents and bias do you any good as a hired writer? Could you keep me busy on a free-lance basis? Or should I take my horrible secret to the *Observer*, where it would probably be treated, upon discovery, in the same manner as a bomb in the White House? I don't mean to slur the *Observer*, here. They've been pretty decent, all in all, but I hesitate to work for them under the pretense of personal objectivity. Actually, I'm a pretty objective person except when it comes to Nixon. The very sight of the bastard causes me to gnash my teeth and whine.

Well, what the hell? You see what I'm getting at, so consider it and let me know when you can. Considering this 30-day "moratorium," we at least have a bit of time before the clubs come out in the open. Remember the Spirit of Camp David? Yeah. We got plenty time; everybody hangin' loose. Meanwhile, all those holding tickets to the cockfight will please go under the grandstand and refrain from acts of public savagery until the gong sounds on January 1. Mr. Nixon has promised not to put any grease on his body until the fifth round; Mr. Kennedy has forsworn use of the pronged mace for the same period of time, and other interested parties have meanwhile taped their weapons to their thighs.

I remain, yours for a clean
and decent fight,
Hunter S. Thompson

Hunter, Sandy, and their son, Juan.
(COURTESY OF HST COLLECTION)

1964

**THE JACK LONDON PERIOD: MOVING WEST, MOVING CON—
STANTLY . . . DENVER, ASPEN, ELY, BUTTE, GLEN ELLEN,
KETCHUM, BIG SUR, SAN FRANCISCO . . . LETTERS TO
LBJ . . . NAKED AND ALONE ON U.S. 50 . . . FLIGHT TO
CALIFORNIA: WELCOME TO THE GRAPES OF WRATH . . .**

I had met the tramp digger the night before. And
because he was broke and I wasn't, I bought him a hotel
room so he wouldn't have to sleep in the grass beside the
road to Spokane. But instead of traveling the next day,
he took what was left of his cash and sat by himself on
a stool at the Thunderbird Bar in downtown Missoula,
sullenly nursing his drinks as he had the night
before, and putting his change in the juke box, which
can be a very expensive machine for those who need
steady noise to keep from thinking.

--Hunter S. Thompson, "Living in the
  Time of Alger, Greeley, Debs,"
  National Observer, July 13, 1964

TO PAUL SEMONIN:

January 3, 1964
Woody Creek

Dear Young Pioneer:

Sorry to be throwing my wisdom at you in bits and pieces—instead of the long bomber I planned on—but I think we are dealing with too big a thing to try to whip it up into a neat package.

Anyway, it dawned on me that I have been pushed by your zeal and my own disposition to rhetoric into a position I never had any intention of claiming for my own. You accuse me repeatedly of being "anti-Marxist." I am not, but when dealing with you these days there is no hope but to oppose you on the vocal front, or be sucked in. Thus, we found ourselves arguing quite often where there was really nothing to argue about. It was a tug of war, not a discussion.

My position is and always has been that I distrust power and authority, together with all those who come to it by conventional means—whether it is guns, votes, or outright bribery. There are two main evils in the world today: one is Poverty, the other is Governments. And frankly I see no hope of getting rid of either. So it will have to be a matter of degrees, and that's where we quarrel. You seem to think you have the answer, that holy second nail. Maybe you do, but I'll have to see it in writing before I go along. All of my reading about Africa, plus all my experience in South America, plus all I know or think I know about Europe and the U.S. convinces me that the "civilized" nations of this earth have created in the "underdeveloped" lands nothing more or less than a cheap and ragged imitation of their own Big System that has gone by the name of "government" since man invented the word.

Now and then I get the scent of a man with enough balls to try and whip things around to a decent position. Kennedy was one; Betancourt was another; Castro was and may still be; I even go along now and then with

Khrushchev. This man Nyerere[1] in Tanganyika may be one, but I barely know him. And I'm sure there are others—but that doesn't really alter my basic feelings about power and government. It's pretty old to say that "power corrupts," but I think it does and I don't think it corrupted Kennedy any more than it has Castro. Or Mao—and certainly your man there.[2] Unless he's being totally misrepresented in the press, he looks to me like another Batista. I'd appreciate some words on his recent actions; all that I get via the press are enough to set up a stench of massive proportions. I presume you know what I refer to here. I don't want to get you thrown out by detailing them.

You hit a nerve when you said you may have more faith in the U.S. than I do. I think you might, and on top of that I'll give you another irony—I think I may be much closer to a " 'ding dong' revolutionary" than you are. I know you'll balk at that, but I reason it this way: No "revolutionary" has any hope as long as he's willing to deal with the Established Order on its own terms and in its own context. The only Revolution I would bet on would be one that set out to kill the roots and break all the dies of the System that came before. This is what I am pondering now, for at least I think I see the real choice, which I'm not sure you do. But then, as we've agreed, you really haven't put much of your plan on the line except to say that it's great.

Let me give you an example. As I see it, the best hope for South America is to export every gringo on the continent and sever all ties. But what then? Who would pay the bills? Surely not the Latins, because they don't have a dime that hasn't been salted away in Swiss banks. So they try to play it halfway, and they keep losing when the chips go down.

They threaten, they bluff, and they finally take the payoff, in cash or some other form. Maybe the Africans are different, I can't say. Castro has thrown off one bogeyman, only to be confronted with two more. I read Sartre's thing[3] and agree with it. But he has no answers. In spots, his rhetoric is worse than mine. There isn't space here on this rotten thing to go into that now. I'm not sure what I've said here; maybe it's just that I won't play the Big Game until it stops looking phony. The best I can do is keep my tools sharp and wait for the honest opening—and decide, in the meantime, if it makes sense to kill the only roots we have.

HST

1. Julius Kambarage Nyerere, elected first president of the Republic of Tanganyika in November 1962.
2. Kwame Nkrumah, prime minister and president of Ghana from 1957–1966.
3. Jean-Paul Sartre's introduction to Frantz Fanon's *The Damned of the Earth*, which dealt with the uneven distribution of wealth. Fanon was a strong advocate of Pan-Africanism, refused to take sides in the Cold War, and wrote many important books denouncing imperialism.

TO DWIGHT MARTIN, *THE REPORTER:*

Thompson was on assignment in Denver for The Reporter; *Martin was his editor. This letter was written in the wake of violent clashes between U.S. troops and Panamanian mobs.*

January 12, 1964
Heart O' Denver Motor Hotel

Dear Mr. Martin:

By God, it's nice to have a letterhead for a change. The bill for it will be overwhelming; I will undoubtedly have to get more money from you before I can settle up and leave town.

I trust you accepted my call the other night in the same good spirit in which it was made. I was—needless to say—as drunk as a loon and without a whole hell of a lot to say. You fielded that wild bounce like a christian. I had emerged from a negro jazz club—Denver's only—and picked up an early edition of the *Rocky Mountain News*, a typical Scripps-Howard throw-away that circulates out here for the benefit of ex-cowboys on the dole. I read page one as I walked along East Colfax in the snow, and it suddenly dawned on me that our LatAm policy was at an end and that I should attend the funeral in Panama. Upon more sober consideration, however, I came to feel that the real story will be had at the U.N. and at various Latin embassies in Washington—and then only for those with good contacts. We are now at one of those climax points like in the old westerns, when the hero stands up and yells, "All right, this is it, by god—who's with me?" And then you get that long scriptwriter's pause that puts everybody in a tense forward lean like Lyndon Johnson must be in right now. Who, indeed, is with us? As far as sentiment is concerned, nobody. Not even Olde England. But there is always dollar diplomacy, and I think we will see some of it before this thing is done. I think also that you may come around in the near future to a point where you will be able to see the pertinence of LatAm stories— or at least pertinent LatAm stories, which are scarce these days, even in places where they use that term, "LatAm." OK for that.

As for the rest of what we talked about, I am hard pressed to recollect it, except that you liked that one take on Glen Ellen, and that I should call you again before leaving Denver. If I said anything of a violent, abusive or presumptuous nature, I trust it blew away in the midnight winds. I am half mad from the silence I have imposed upon myself in Woody Creek, and when I find myself among human beings I tend to explode.

But I've been pretty calm here. Too calm, in fact; for a good story. I need arguments and the chance to carry inflammatory quotes from one side to the other.

The enclosed clip should give you an idea where the story stands right now. Nowhere. The Gov [John Love] is running a delayed buck. He's in trouble—with both parties—but so far we have no real idea what he's up to. I have talked to local pundits and drawn a blank. The consensus holds that no action will come until the Budget Message, the date of which has not been announced. Tomorrow I will try to talk to the governor, but I know damn well what I'll get from him. I still have a chance tonight to get hold of ex-Gov Steve McNichols, due back from Washington in a half-hour or so, and he may give me a peg.

I don't mean to make it sound worse than it is. At worst, I can do enough research to get a first draft done, then update it when the Gov makes his move(s). My contacts so far seem decent in a vague sort of way, and spread from Right to Left on the big spectrum. Out here, however, the spectrum doesn't even take in what you call the Left in the East. Those people are "Reds." An official of the Democratic party was just ousted (tentatively) because of a prior association with the Fair Play for Cuba Committee. I am, of course, keeping my opinions on Señor Nixon close under my bonnet. We are, as you said, an "objective" publication—and it is only after midnight that I let my fangs slip out, and only then in good company. Which is rare out here.

Right after talking to you the other night I thought, "Well, that Martin sounds like a good fellow—I'll go see him." So I called United Airlines and arranged for a flight out on Wed. night at $200 round trip. The next morning I cancelled it, citing "business reasons." But I'll get there as soon as I can find a good excuse. I have a chance to do some inflammatory copy for the *Saturday Evening Post* and may use that for an excuse. Or pursuit of that thing that is always just around the corner—that is why I go most places, so it should serve for New York. At least it has in the past. A fellow I know who wrote a book called it "The bright and shining thing, that sense of morning, in a cool sun, before the hot afternoon." At least that's more or less what he said.

Which hardly matters, really. The fact is that I will get to New York as soon as I find myself—probably at some unlikely or inconvenient time—with access to the fare. If Wednesday is a warm night, with a touch of the Tulamore Dew [Irish whiskey], I may do it then. At any rate it will have to be soon; I have a sunbeam to catch, and a marriage to prevent. With apologies to your secretary.

More of our talk is filtering back, now. I recall a mention of *The Fun House*.[4] I think you wanted a review. Excellent. We will give him a fang job, so as to keep sharp for Señor Nixon. They are not as different as they seem at a glance.

4. William Brinkley, *The Fun House* (New York, 1961).

That gives me three things to work on for you, plus a handful of others for the *Observer*. With luck, I will get half of them done. I am doing for the *Observer* here, by the way, a newsy piece on hearings concerning a Wilderness Bill, so I'll bill them for the two days or so of my expenses. Maybe I told you that. If not, it's true & I want it made part of the record. Even so, I will need more money before I leave here.

You can count on "a story" out of Denver, but I can't say when until I know more of what the Gov means to do with his crisis. Maybe I'll know more by the time I call—probably Tuesday afternoon. At any rate, I'll get enough while I'm here so I can round up the rest by phone.

That about wraps it up for now. See you in the nearest reasonable future.

Hunter S. Thompson

TO DWIGHT MARTIN, *THE REPORTER:*

January 28, 1964
Woody Creek

Dwight—

I think it is outrageous that a cheap thing like a publication date could influence your decision to review a book. *The Fun House* is a timeless social document, pertinent to all ages. I urge you to Think Big and reconsider this small-minded error. A book shot through with such galloping insight is in fact a beacon for young and old alike, and should be dealt with as such.

As for my Denver piece I would like to seize this opportunity to say I have never read a more brilliant prospectus. If this hair-brained Thompson fellow could actually write the three articles he flirts with in those 17 pages he would be a goddamn champion. As it is, I believe the article gives you a fine opportunity to find out how many of your readers are on their toes. Also keep in mind that we live in the age of the Package Deal.

I am working at this time on a short piece called "Aspen, or Deviations on a Theme." It will not be a blockbuster, but it might be coherent. I am trying to scale down my themes. Your publication schedule is too brutal. It is bad enough to have to deal with the Myth of the West at any time, but to have to do it with one eye on two days' notice is more than a white man should have to bear. I was all set with a nice little bear-trap for the Governor, a week of private eye work amid the vagaries of the Colorado budget—but maybe it's just as well this way, because in a pure money-politics piece I would never have been able to use those two lead paragraphs, which, if published, will surely become immortal.

My eye is coming around, which is a good thing because it is crucial that I recognize the game warden's jeep at a great distance.[5] You know, of course, that the biggest single question of our time concerns the validity of "The Profit Motive." I am not, however, prepared to do that one at this time. Put your Africa man on it, because it is over there where the European expatriates (Frantz Fanon and Co.) are gathering for the Great Wake. Maybe a good lead would be this: The theories behind the new governments in Africa today are not African at all, but European. Maybe that will make the white people feel better. A focus on the Institute for African Studies in Legon (Accra), Ghana. That is the theoretical headwaters for everything that is going on in Africa. I believe there is a lot to be had over there, although—and I repeat—I am not up to it at this time with my wife about to drop a child in my lap at any moment.

Ate logo—HST

TO LIONEL OLAY:

Thompson critiqued Lionel Olay's most recent contribution to Cavalier—*an article about the influence of Asian culture on the U.S. West*—*and shared shoptalk with a fellow free-lancer.*

January 29, 1964
Woody Creek, Colorado

Dear Lionel:

You are enough of a pro so I shouldn't have to say that your most recent piece was well done; that should be taken for granted. But what was it? I submit this: A Zen, Hip, Loverly, Maileresque Cop-Out. Pretty shitty and mean, eh? Especially since you said nice things about my Louisville piece. But they were far from the same. Mine was good journalism, nothing more. Yours is a significant contribution to the literature of phony revelation. Mailer, having failed to write what he always wanted to, has become the undisputed champ in that field. It is like a frustrated animal, biting on his tail. I had a coati in Brazil that drew blood on himself whenever he couldn't deal with reality.[6] But shit, Scott Fitzgerald came a lot closer to putting his soul on paper than either you or Mailer have ever dreamed of doing, mescaline or no. But Scott was embarrassed about it, and other people had to find him out, while the Mailer ethic is to make it very plain beforehand that he is "about to spill his guts"—which might be interesting if

---

5. An explosion of a propane tank inside Thompson's Woody Creek house had burned his face and arms.

6. Thompson had bought a coati-mundi as a pet at a Bolivian village market.

he ever really did it, but he always holds back. Now it has become his technique; it is sort of like bargaining with a Mexican street-merchant—you pull out all the money you have, except for the book of traveler's checks, and make a Final Offer for whatever it is you want. Hell, show it to him—coins, bills, the whole wad, and let him know he's pushed you as far as you can go—except for the traveler's checks.

At one point—"in the full flush of the experience"—you say you "feel holy. . . . What I mean is I feel as if I'm radiating glowing, and that it is in my power to bless things, which I have an urge to do. It's late at night, and what I'd like to do is stop for a while and search out some human companionship. . . ."

Hell, I feel that way every time I get drunk. Last week in Denver with *The Reporter* paying my expenses I spent all night on the long-distance telephone, blessing people and stabbing at human contact. Mostly women, so don't feel offended that you were left out; if I'd called you I probably would have wanted to talk to Beverly. The point is not that I'm exceptional for doing a thing like that, but that it's a damn common feeling and if that's all mescaline can do for me, I'll stick with Old Crow.

I won't begrudge you your feelings, and I can't really argue with them, for that matter, but let's call a spade a spade. It was really an apologia, and the real tip-off came when you said, "All we have to worry about is the nervous ones who have to prove something that can never be proved and are prepared to goof the whole shot just to make their noise." Well I hope I still have enough balls to qualify under that definition, and, given reasonable odds I'd bet you feel the same way. Granted, I don't know you real well, but I'm pretty good at catching true scents and I honestly don't think you believe what you wrote. Why don't you take whatever pill it is that really opens a man up? Given a real truth serum, I think you could probably stand people's hair on end. In the meantime—or until you can swallow the real dingdong—my best advice would be to forgo Mailer's technique. He is now so bad I can't even read him, and I used to think he was the secret weapon. I knocked him, but only because I hoped it would prod him to focus down on the real business—but now he's just dull and fat, and for my money that *Esquire* novel is his swan-song.[7] I read a few paragraphs, then turned to Dwight McDonald, who is at least entertaining. Your *Cavalier* piece, for that matter, was better than any of Mailer's current stuff, but you seem to be gripped with the idea of competing with the fat bastard, and it just ain't worth it. Let him go; he's getting upwards of $25,000 a year to work out his death-dance, although I think if I had a talent like he had (had) I would ask twice as much when I decided to put it on the block.

7. Mailer's *Esquire* installments became *The American Dream* (New York, 1965).

All of which is a little presumptuous of me, I grant, but I have started thinking tough again and I may even get back to doing something worthwhile sometime soon. The California move has been postponed a week or so, due to overwhelming poverty. I haven't paid my January rent or my December bill at the Woody Creek store, and I can't leave until I do. *The Reporter* has another piece which could pay the tab, but they're in no hurry to pay and I can't move until they do. I have turned into a fuck-off as far as this journalism is concerned—one of these woodsy types who talks a good article but never writes it. I only write when finances pressure me into it, and not a hell of a lot then. I agree with you that it's a shitty life—which is really what you said—but I don't agree with your remedies. Age 40 is a bit too early to seek out the rocking chair and start trying to pull the wool over your own eyes. Let's face it—it's the tension of life that keeps the light in a man's eyes, and keeps the foam in his nuts. It's really the only thing you can't afford to lose.

Probably this all sounds a bit incoherent to your jaded ears, and even to mine at this hour of the night. Old Crow has a hand in here; we just had the ranch-neighbor and his wife down for dinner. I think it should be talked out in one of those big hot tubs at Hot Springs. Disregard my date of February 8–10 and wait for a cable saying exactly when the move will begin. I'll send it to your current address and will expect your presence at the appointed time. Bring a rifle along and we'll pop a pig or two. I have every reason to believe you need a rest.

HST

TO PAUL SEMONIN:

January 31, 1964
Woody Creek

Dear Bobo—

I have dug into Frantz Fanon and I think he is a dead ringer for the real thing. If that's what you were trying to say all summer, I suggest you take some lessons in elementary English expression. If I were Fanon, I wouldn't want you on my side. Your relationship to him seems very much like your own concept of the American "liberal." I don't think Fanon needs Sartre either; I guess it's nice to have a little left-wing respectability on your side now and then, but Sartre is an eloquent windbag and I'd rather take my business straight. I am only about a third of the way into it but I already have a strong scent. I'll call him a liar and a fool now and then, but there's no denying that mean, high sound of a two-legged boarbuster.

Between Fanon and Bob Dylan I think the blood is moving in my brain again. Dylan is a goddamn phenomenon, pure gold, and mean as a snake.

If you get U.S. records over there, listen to his "Masters of War" sometime. I just got the record on credit from Peggy Clifford.

My credit is strained to the limit and today was my last legal one in this house. From now on, I am a squatter. I owe $550 that has to be paid before I leave. *The Reporter* may or may not send funds; I am sweating it out. If they don't, I am up to my balls in scalding crisis. The *Observer* is down on me for a fang-job I did on Congress; they bounced it savagely, so I sent it to *The Rptr*. Now I am doing one on the pending Aspen Mtn. strike.[8] D.R.C. Brown is holding the line, along with Paul Nitze and the other fatbellies—but the patrol people seem ready to hit the streets.[9] Union songs are now heard in the Dipsy-Doodle and elsewhere. "The Talkin' Union." With a little humor and local color, I can probably pass it off on the *Observer*.

I stick by my original comment on Aspen; living here has stunted my wit. Elk meat is fixing my bowels. The move looms at any time, but not until money comes. The tension is ugly. Sandy is in the eighth month. The old story. If I don't lose the scent I may do something worthwhile sometime soon. Prospects for the spring include a run out to Hawaii to fetch Hudson's boat. He'd probably like to have you along if you don't bring Sartre. Fanon would be OK; unless you think his ass might burn a hole in the deck. Returning to this country has crippled my spirit; it is easier to be an American abroad. The past dies hard, and not always for good reason. The mood of the country reminds me of that headline in the *New Leader* when Bosch was run out of Santo Domingo—"The Return of the Syndicate."[10] My position at this time is "deal around me." Send word.

HST

TO DWIGHT MARTIN, *THE REPORTER:*

February 1, 1964
Woody Creek, Colorado

Dear Mr. Martin:

In the course of my African outburst the other night (January 26, letter of) I referred to Frantz Fanon as part of the group of European expatriates gathered in Africa to form the revolution, or what Sartre called "The Third

8. Thompson wrote an article on a strike by Aspen's ski patrol titled "And Now a Proletariat on Aspen's Ski Slopes," *National Observer* (February 12, 1964).
9. D.R.C. Brown was the president of the Aspen Ski Corporation and Paul Nitze was a distinguished U.S. financier/diplomat and a major investor in the Aspen Ski Corporation.
10. Dominican Republic president Juan Bosch, put in office in 1962 in the country's first free elections in thirty-eight years, was overthrown a year later with U.S. approval.

World." Fanon is very much a part of that group, but he is not European. The best information I can get in Woody Creek is that he is a West Indian, and presumably black.[11]

The reason I mention it is that I am now dealing with his book, *The Damned*, only recently published in English in 1963. The original edition was published in 1961 and titled *The Damned of the Earth*, or, more accurately, *Les Damnes de la Terre*. I think the new English edition would be a good thing to review.

The introduction, by Jean-Paul Sartre, has become required reading for those who wonder about the future of Africa. Its thesis—which is also the thesis of Fanon's text—runs like this: There can be no compromise with the black (or brown or yellow) people of this earth except on their terms. What the white man fails to understand is that the native is not just revolting against a handful of arrogant settlers, but against the entire system of values those settlers represent. Hence, there is no sense talking to ex-colonial peoples in terms of Western Values (specifically, the doctrine of Humanism) that have never really taken hold.

Anyway, I trust you see what I'm getting at. If the Sartre-Fanon thesis proves out, it will be at the expense of our efforts to cultivate democratic political systems in the "emerging nations." That, of course, would be the first thing to go out the window. Witness Ghana today. The thesis also calls into question our ideas of The Democratic Left forming pro-Western caretaker governments to bring the natives around. According to Sartre and Fanon, these people are regarded as ideological lackeys and could not possibly succeed.

We are both aware of Sartre's political coloration, and Fanon is, if anything, more dogmatic. But the thesis is real, and it doesn't exist in a vacuum. For nearly a year I have maintained a running debt with some contacts at the Institute for African Studies in Ghana (mainly Europeans, but one American) and I have come from a point where I dismissed them all as "book-store Marxists" to another point, now, where I take their ideas quite seriously. I don't like them, but too much of what they say makes sense when I read the newspapers.

Well, this is too long a letter for a simple thing like a book review query. The nut of it is that I think the Fanon book is worth doing and I think I could do a good job on it. When is another matter. Right now I am half mad with tension; every morning I go to the P.O. to seek notice of incoming funds—and every afternoon I watch the road for signs of my landlord. If you are going to use that Denver piece, I urge you to send a money-message at once so I can shift into fleeing gear. My lease ran out yesterday;

11. Unbeknownst to Thompson, Fanon had died on December 6, 1961.

I am now a squatter. The oil for my furnace is running out and I can't afford more. My subscription to the *Denver Post* is running out, and, rotten paper that it is, I'd hate to lose my last contact with the outside world. And my wife grows fatter by the hour; I think it will be a Mongolian idiot. The fat is in the fire.   HST

TO DWIGHT MARTIN, *THE REPORTER:*

With Sandy eight months pregnant, Thompson rented a U-Haul trailer and they drove twelve hundred miles across "rotten snow" to Glen Ellen, California, fifty miles north of San Francisco. His plan was to earn money by writing articles on the American West for the National Observer *and* The Reporter.

February 21, 1964
Owl House
9400 Bennett Valley Rd.
Glen Ellen, California

Dear Mr. Martin:

Greetings from the New World, the Brazil of America, the land of cheap wine and the 10-cent cantaloupe. I arrived, pulling my trailer, and was denied entrance to the house I was planning to live in. The fellow had changed his mind. Changed his mind. So I now live in a sort of Okie shack, paying a savage rent, and spend most of my day in a deep ugly funk, plotting vengeance. Vengeance.

At any rate, I have built a desk out of an old door, and am now ready. My first act, after admitting the loss of my Denver hotel receipt, was to make out a foggy justification for that $200 you sent. Let me know if this isn't sufficient, and I'll do something more. $35 a day ain't hard to justify.

Enclosed are two poems. The poet runs a private graveyard a few miles from here and stopped by the other day when he heard I kept pistols. I wiped him out, mainly because he was unnerved by the awful roar of my .44 Magnum. It was like William Tell going against a bazooka. "Yeah," I said, "I have a gun or two." And I unveiled this frightening thing that will shoot through a motor block, and opened up a tree with it. He carried a .22, which he fanned like Billy the Kid. But we patched it up and then he produced his poetry, which I told him I'd send along to Madison Avenue, where they need poetry. I sort of like the stuff, especially from a grave-keeper, and thought I'd give you a look at it. Rest assured I made no commitments. But it may grab you. If not, send it back. The guy can afford rejections; he has a job.

What in the hell is happening with the Denver piece? I am beginning to think you bought me off, and will have none of it. To make things worse, I can't find my carbon. Life has become a goat dance. Something will have to be done with that piece, however. If necessary, I will go back to Denver, much as I hate the idea. At any rate, let's have some communication on it. I will get a phone as soon as I can afford the $50 deposit. In the meantime, call me c/o Lou Ambler, Glen Ellen. That's next door to the shack. Address is the above.

On Monday I mean to contact Gene Burdick[12] about a "fish-in" scheduled in Washington on March 3. Burdick, [Marlon] Brando, J[ames] Baldwin and P[aul] Newman. Something to do with Indians being denied fishing rights on the Columbia River. Christ knows what it means. I guess it is a natural news story for the *Observer*, and maybe a possible commentary for you. But I can't say for sure till afterwards.

The Red chink[13] was elected to Congress yesterday, and should give me a good peg for the San Francisco story. Or profile, as it were. I have never quite understood what you mean by that term. Seems to me like a book-length subject, even in Woody Creek. But maybe not. Was the Louisville piece a "political profile"?

I could tell you a lot of other things I am working on, but it would be a bag of lies. The fact is that I am spending all my energies on living from day to day without the credit I enjoyed in Woody Creek. On Monday I will take my antique Luger to a San Francisco pawnshop. Once I establish credit, I may be able to function. A man needs credit. Especially when he has no money.

Despite the unholy chaos of the moment, I sense a leveling out in the near future. I am near the action, or at least near enough. A comeback looms. My only advice at this time is, never marry your mistress; it causes damage to the brain tissues, and puts a crick in the hump.

As for future work, I believe it is up in the air. No sense telling you what I'm going to send, because I don't know. It depends on the humours. But I will send something. And let's get something made of that Denver business. I'd rather not have it hanging over my head, because there's too much fresh stuff out here. Send word.

> In all sincerity, from the crude
> new desk of
> Hunter S. Thompson

---

12. Eugene Burdick was a well-known writer and the co-author of *The Ugly American*.
13. Philip Burton, a wild San Francisco liberal Democrat Thompson liked.

TO KAY BOYLE:

Boyle, a renowned Bay Area writer and activist, had struck up a friendship with Thompson at a Native American rally in Tacoma, Washington. They would correspond regularly for a number of years.

March 7, 1964
Owl House
9400 Bennett Valley Rd.
Glen Ellen, California

Dear Mrs. Boyle:

Thanks for sending the Styron Report[14]; I read it and actually considered, for the first time, that perhaps I might drop the habit. Which really shouldn't be too hard, with a pipe and cigars in reserve. Odd, how language can convince a man, where reason fails entirely. I am not sure what Styron is up to these days—a lecture on smoking seems a far cry from *Lie Down in Darkness*—and I'd definitely appreciate a chance to talk to him if he comes out this way. Has he turned against drink, too? I am trying to recall that quote from the bible at the front of LD [*Lie Down in Darkness*]; my copy is in Louisville, but I have another on order at the Aspen Book Store. The question would seem to be: Is life so valuable that we should give up flirting with death in order to hang around? I'm not sure.

At any rate, I hope we can sit down with a bit of the Tulamore Dew sometime soon, and ponder these things. I didn't mean to be flip up there in Tacoma,[15] but you had a sporting look about you and I couldn't resist a little buggery. It was, after all, a real bad show & needed a spot of something. A man never stoops so low as when he rises to the challenge of internal politics. Selah.

OK, and thanks again for the report (commentary). Right after I started this letter my neighbor came down and asked us to visit with him for the purpose of celebrating his recent acquisition of $12,000 from television.[16] It gives a man paws. I am still unnerved by the thing. It begins to look like the plumbers shall inherit the earth.

If you find yourself in the midtown area on some afternoon, give me a ring at *The Wall St. Journal.* It's not as bad as it sounds; I am there about 3

14. William Styron had written an essay on the damaging effects of tobacco on health.
15. Thompson had gone to Washington State to write "The Catch Is Limited in Indians' 'Fish-In' " for the *National Observer* (March 9, 1964).
16. Denne Petitclerc had signed a contract to produce a documentary about the Rocky Mountain states.

days a week, only in the afternoons.[17] The rest of the time I work for *The Reporter*, which gives at least the appearance of a balance.

> Sincerely—
> Hunter S. Thompson

TO PAUL SEMONIN:

> March 11, 1964
> Owl House
> 9400 Bennett Valley Rd.
> Glen Ellen, California

Dear Doctor Strangelove:

Your mail is increasingly incoherent. The only spark in your last concerned the possible choice between Henry Luce and Kwame Nkrumah. I agree with you, but then I always did. Have we pissed off five years of our lives for that?

Your fear of Cassius X[18] puzzles me. You never explained it. Granted, he is a creature of the syndicate, but so was Sonny Liston. Where do you see the choice?

And for shit's sake stop calling me a "liberal." I gave up calling you a Communist a long time ago, and the least you can do is return the favor. I might remind you that I now maintain an office at *The Wall Street Journal*—I gave the West Coast editor a terrible four-hour shock the other night by telling him about Fanon—so when the time comes to seek the high ground I guess I have a head start. But I am still writing for the white Negro press, alias *The Reporter*, and am considering a spot with the *Saturday Evening Post*.

But for what you say—and what I hear of your clan—I don't figure on taking to the hills anytime soon. You seem to be drifting further and further from mean reality. I sympathize with your general aims, but I think you have hooked up with the wrong crowd for the action. Your eagerness to pick a fight no longer interests me. I think you are talking to yourself for the sake of an echo. It has taken me a while to get a grip after my fatheaded success in Latin America, but now I figure I am much closer to the front than you are. I have, in fact, infiltrated the Dow-Jones Company, which none of us would ever have dreamed of doing, and have in the space of two weeks delivered a series of telling shocks. There is no sense

---

17. Thompson maintained an office on San Francisco's *Wall Street Journal* floor because he was the *National Observer*'s western correspondent.
18. Cassius Clay, later Muhammad Ali.

trying to describe it—you would have to tag along and see. But you are over there trading back-slaps with people who never considered disagreeing with you. What you should do is get out and have a run or two against the Packers when you are out of shape. I go from Indians to Negroes to Defense money to Cubans to the population pox—and by jesus those bastards have a hand in everywhere. I have come to the point where I see no difference between functioning Fascism and functioning Capitalism, or, for that matter, functioning Communism.

Your whole theory has only one flaw—you seem to have lost faith in the maverick, the man who can be convinced and thereby throw the switch on those both above and below him. He is a creation of this culture, the wise peasant, a man with a salary and enough leisure to ponder the alternatives, an enemy or an ally depending on what reaches him. But an essentially decent person. They beat hell out of Nixon here in California two years ago, and they are about to stomp Goldwater. The only thing they lack is something to vote for, instead of against. But Kennedy was killed, so now we sit in a limbo where the decent man has a variety of things to vote against, but nothing to vote for. As for me, I see no hope of taking any position in the coming campaign. Johnson is a punk, but look at the others. Punks to the last man. I'd vote for Bobby Kennedy out of spite, but not much else.

Anyway, your position as I see it is nada. Your concepts have lost their fangs—for me, anyway—and I think you need a long shot on this side of the water to know just what the score is. Sartre might eventually be recognized as a prophet, but he will never get much done. He reminds me of Mailer, a good head gone obese. People like that abound in every age, but they never have much of an appetite for the ugly details of getting things implemented. They are heroes first, and punks later, and then heroes again when people have forgotten what real punks they were.

As for Nkrumah, your comments seem to dodge the issues. I was never real worried about *Time*'s correspondent, but I was given some pause when *The Redeemer* nixed the Supreme Court and called a Trujillo-type election. As far as I'm concerned, they could give *Time*'s man the garrote, and I wouldn't give a hair of a damn—but I wonder why you focus on such a minor issue in a weak attempt to make a major point.

Since our last exchange I have heard from Cooke, Smith and Harvey Sloane. They all wonder about you—not out of malice, as you seem to think, but from an honest puzzlement. Maybe I'm wrong, but if you really have any quick message, I think you'd fare better trying to pass it to people who are willing to listen, and who would be real allies if you convinced them.

I can hear you ranting now. But I guess you know how it always is with converts, and I wonder if you feel up to making any forays outside your friendly camp, and into the dirty reality of the world we all have to live in once our scholarships run out. Give it a try. And when you push out this way, I mean to have a better bed than I showed you in Big Sur—no meat hanging over it, and no blood dripping on the face. Right now I am living in an Okie shack, but there are several possibilities, and by the time you get back we should be settled.

I'll send a Dylan record within a week or so. When are you coming back? And what for? Joan Baez is so far ahead of you that you'll be 40 before you catch up, and even then you'll have to learn to sing like a nightingale. And I think poor ignorant Hudson has better sense than both of us together—but then that's conjectural prejudice, eh? And I've made a real effort to be reasonable. In all, your belated comments are so far removed from what is happening that I can't find a context for them, and have no choice but to lay them aside as flotsam. You seem to know as much about what is happening here as I know about what is happening there.

Why don't you subscribe to *Time*?

Yours for a focus—HST

TO ELEANOR RAWSON:

After reading Thompson's article about the Aspen Mountain Strike in the National Observer, *Rawson, a New York book editor, wrote to him, wondering whether he would be interested in authoring or co-authoring a book on Colorado ski bums.*

March 17, 1964
Gen. Delivery
Glen Ellen
California

Eleanor Rawson
David McKay Co.
750 Third Ave.
NYC 17

Dear Mrs. Rawson:

I received your letter on the ski bum book and forwarded it to Ralph Jackson, "the king of the ski bums," in Aspen. If he comes through with a bulky text, and if it shows real promise, I will attempt to whip it into presentable shape in no more than three weeks' time. Otherwise, I have no interest in that business. But I will advise you if anything pops.

As for other subjects, I'm afraid I've been a rotten correspondent. That ski bum thing was a sidelight, at best, and hardly worth a letter except that I told Jackson to do it. At the moment I am whirling in the black eye of chaos. I have been evicted for the third time in six months, my wife is ready to have god knows how many children (at any moment), and I have no home. At the same time I am supposed to be doing "political profiles of politically significant U.S. cities" for *The Reporter,* and I am also the West Coast correspondent for the *National Observer.* I am also trying to rewrite my world-beating novel, The Rum Diary. I maintain an office at *The Wall Street Journal* and my neighbors call me a Communist. A woman is writing from Bolivia, threatening to finish me off,[19] and Marlon Brando has hired thugs to teach me a lesson. My brother is getting married and wants me to be the best man; my other brother is getting ready to quit me because I haven't sent his Christmas present. Shall I go on . . . ? I think not.

Anyway, you asked at one time about "book-length projects." Well it happens that I am a seasoned Latin America hand, formerly the *Observer's* LatAm correspondent, and for the past year I have been under severe pressure to resume my previous duties. Which I may indeed resume, in light of the fact that my mother-in-law is scheduled to arrive at any moment. The moment of birth, as it were. I have told the *Observer* I will go to Mexico and do a handful of articles for them—probably some for *The Reporter* as well—and it dawned on me that perhaps a swing further south might be beneficial all around. Charley Kuralt, formerly CBS correspondent in South America, tells me I should write a book on the plane, basing it on my articles, which he likes. He says publishers are hungry for such efforts and will pay at once. To that end, I enclose some of my stuff from the last swing, and toss up the idea that we will need another swing to get it all up to date. Considering the glut of Latin America books now on the market— the *Observer* sends them to me for reviews—I can't see any future in doing another heavy-handed, "sound-the-alarms" sort of thing like the ones I've been reading. Most of them are swill, badly written swill at that, and closer to fiction than fact.

My idea when I was working down there was to keep as far from what other people were doing as possible. Or as far as possible from what other people were doing. So maybe a 200-pg. book of the same sort might be

19. Thompson had made the mistake of inviting a Bolivian woman to America, promising her a green card. Once stateside, Thompson reneged on the offer.

worth thinking about. Not so much an analytical tome, but a series of word photographs that will take Latin America out of the realm of economic graphs and political countries, populated by real people who defy the clichés that are constantly wrapped around them by visiting "journalists."

I enclose a bundle of old clips to illustrate my aim. The bundle represents about ten percent of what I have on hand, although most of it needs updating. If it grabs you at all, let me know ASAP. I plan to move out for Mexico the minute my mother-in-law arrives, and that would be a logical first step in the long haul around SA. In looking back on this letter, I see that I haven't been real clear. What I have in mind is a small book, a series of vignettes—perhaps with explanatory material to bridge the gaps—on life and politics in various Latin countries. The idea would be to focus on a dimension that most politically-oriented writers never get to. It's a hard thing to explain, but maybe this will help: Most LatAm journalists will leave from New York or Miami and arrive in Rio, Lima, or Buenos Aires within a handful of hours. But it took me six months, on horses, boats, jeeps and bush planes, to get from New York to Rio. And believe me, there is a difference. (See my Letters piece.)[20]

Don't confuse this idea with the ski bum thing. That was in essence a favor to a friend, who may or may not come through with something, now that the onus is on him. At any rate, I appreciate your long letter on that score. But what I am pondering here is a serious effort, which may or may not make money, but that is your end and I see no sense in worrying about it. I absolutely believe I can write the best book any American has done yet on Latin America, if only because I can drink with the worst of the drinkers and intimidate the sleaziest of the whores. This is not quite what the Alliance for Progress had in mind, but it is reality in South America, and somebody may as well face it.

As for my novel, I have not sent it because I have not yet had time to even read it again, to see if it should be sent to a lady editor. Frankly, I see no hope in that area, although I suppose the Book Clubs deal mainly with women. I need more time to ponder it. Meanwhile, give me your thoughts on the South America thing, and if necessary you can reach me by phone at *The Wall Street Journal* newsroom in San Francisco. It's on Market Street, but I don't know the number.

Sincerely,
Hunter S. Thompson

20. The *National Observer* had published Thompson's correspondence as "Chatty Letters During a Journey from Aruba to Rio" on December 31, 1962.

TO WILLIAM J. KENNEDY:

Thompson couldn't resist teasing Kennedy about his admiration for the fiction of Eudora Welty.

March 22, 1964
Glen Ellen, California

Dear Eudora:

I don't recall getting any letters from you recently, but this is an answer anyway. I mean to tell you about myself; I am fucked up. The lad who agreed to rent me his house backed out when I arrived. Two other people backed out since then. Am I a nigger? What is it? Denne P. has turned out to conform very strictly to the somewhat harsh standards you set when you discussed him at our last meeting. It is another victory for your instincts. He is a good lad, and means well up to a point—but it is about the same point most people in Hollywood mean well up to. I am not so sure about this coast, but I mean to give it a try. It is so damn big and varied that something must grow here. But if I find it barren I mean to move on—probably the next spot is Mexico City.

Beyond that, I am in the same condition here as I was in Woody Creek, only in less colorful and pleasant surroundings. I have no conversations except on chance meetings in San Francisco. Once a month, at best. My only hope is to make enough money to get to New York at once and run out my mouth to the detriment of the populace. I have just finished another masterpiece for *The Reporter*. They have treated me gingerly and I have given them the mad dog treatment. I believe it a decent outfit. Maybe. The *Observer* is decent, but I often wonder about their motives. Or maybe it is just my queries, but I detect a trend in the acceptance of frothy pieces and disinterest in meaty ones. With luck, I will be driven back to fiction.

It is all a lost cause; the victory is to avoid bitterness. Maybe New York is the answer. Good conversation if nothing else. You know Rust Hills quit *Esquire* and went to the *Saturday Evening Post*. You might try *Esquire* now with some stories. Me too. Given a christian break here, I might find a place to set up my typewriter and level out. There is no question that I have honed my skills to the point of unbelievable sharpness. The thing I just sent *The Reporter* is razored from beginning to end—18 pages of perfect calumny.

I understand you met Lee Berry.[21] He was overwhelmed by you. I barely know him, but he seemed like a righto when I heard a bit of his talk. Like

---

21. Lee Berry was a free-lance reporter from Albany Thompson had met through William Kennedy.

Brendan Behan said about Oscar Wilde: "Good man yourself, Oscar, you had it every way." By the time I cash in I hope I will have hidden enough of my rottenness so that somebody can say that about me.

Aside from my random comments, I have nothing else to say. I have no home. I have an office at *The Wall Street Journal* in San Francisco, but it is likely to be taken away at any moment. I have a fat wife and a bad penchant for listening to bullshitters. What about you?

HST

TO JOHN MACAULEY SMITH:

Thompson had become a father on March 24, 1964.

April 2, 1964
Glen Ellen, California

JonMac:

Your letter is old, but maybe you are still there. I just got back from a week in Big Sur, celebrating the birth of my issue, name of Juan. Healthy, male and noisy.

We should sit down soon for a talk on areas. This California move was a disaster and I already miss Woody Creek more than I want to admit. This is a shitty place and I mean to move on at once; the ideal house we had went by the boards on the mindless whim of some Okie contractor, a friend of a friend of a friend. You got that?

Anyway, I believe it is imperative to find out where the decent living might be had. I refuse to have my son grow up with a jukebox on one hand and a status register on the other. If I cannot find a decent place in this country I will go to Mexico. Anyway, I am bending my efforts in the direction of New York at the moment and hope to stop in on you for a talk. More on this when travel plans jell.[. . .]

Yours for a break, HST

TO PAUL SEMONIN:

April 7, 1964
Glen Ellen, California

Dear Blowhole:

Your foggy tome arrived yesterday and, despite grave circumstances here, I will now attempt to deal quickly with it. The concept (of the article) seemed real enough, but I can't imagine anyone actually reading it through. Except for your mention of Harold Cruse,[22] the whole thing is foam from your own brain, unsupported by any facts, pointers, possibilities or recent happenings to justify what you say. You may be right, but what reason do I as reader have to think so? You cannot write like that—and get paid for it—until your name rings bells; then you can foam to your heart's content. I have the same continuing problem, and am constantly hung on it. Whether you are a journalist or not, the only way to attempt journalism is to assume you know nothing at the start, and then only write what you find evidence to support—along with the evidence, so neither the editor nor the reader is forced to take your word for it. So much for that; I said much earlier that I was keeping hands off your professional efforts, so pardon this release and do what you will.

Anyway, I will take the piece, plus the letter, and see if I can stir up any comment in the murky world of San Francisco negro politics. I won't use your name, but it should be interesting to toss your ideas around in the San Francisco Freedom Movement and see what happens. I am not too worried about being rejected for my whiteness, although I do in all truth think the idea of a Negro Nationalist party in the country is madness, because there are too many people in this country just waiting for an excuse to act like the racists they are. Hell, I have a strain of it myself, and the only thing that has brought me around this far is the fact that every time I've seen a black-white confrontation I've had to admit the negroes were Right. Once it turns into power-politics the negro loses his leverage on my conscience. Malcolm X amuses me and I bear him no malice at this time, but when he starts carrying a gun and talking about blowing my head off, there the dialogue ends. If this is what you see in the making, I think we are all in for a bad time. Malcolm X is a black Goldwater, and apparently just as dense.

Anyway, now I have a son named Juan. Ten days old. Not a cent in the house and no cents coming in. I am seriously considering work as a laborer. They don't give scholarships to my type. Beyond that, I am deep in the grip of a professional collapse that worries me to the extent that I cannot do any work to cure it. A failure of concentration, as it were, and a consequent plunge into debt and desperation. It has been going on ever since I got back from SA, and the cure is nowhere to be seen. That is the dullness on my knife, and not any lack of Marxist theory books. Frankly, I would welcome a race war, just to put a bit of zip in things. I am seriously considering a move to L.A. (Los Angeles). What are your plans? You never

22. Cruse was an African-American critic and playwright who emerged on the civil rights scene in 1964. In 1967 he would author *The Crisis of the Negro*, one of the most important black nationalist texts of the era.

say anything specific. Your Dylan records will come when my cheques arrive. Yeah. I am immobile, incoherent and not without a sense of the waters closing over my head. In short, I am down and out.

HST

TO EUGENE W. MCGARR:

Considering himself a practitioner of "impressionistic journalism," Thompson informed McGarr about his new reportage assignment: writing a series of articles for the National Observer *on the American West.*

April 9, 1964
Glen Ellen, California

Well, McGarr, it's twenty minutes of one here and I'm just starting to work, which means, of course, just about what it would seem to mean. With luck, I will rattle off an answer to yours of today before I pass out. I read it in the Rustic Inn, which is the subject of a piece I am now doing for *The Reporter,* and which they may refuse to buy even though they've okayed it. I have discovered the secret of writing fiction, calling it impressionistic journalism, and selling it to people who want "something fresh." I just sold the *Observer* one on the Beat Generation; it required one hour's work, has a vague base in historical rumor, and they loved it. I am doing more of these things.

I talked with the *Observer* yesterday and asked them what I should do, now that they've vetoed all my serious story suggestions. "Well," said Ridley, "we bin wonderin what's goin on up in Montana and the Dakotas. Why don't you take a run up there and check it out? Figure two weeks and maybe three stories, like say 'Saturday night in Butte, Montana.' Just give us your impressions, Thompson." So next week I'm off, all expenses paid, to wander around in the badlands and dig the scene. What it boils down to is a thing I've suspected all along: that people would rather read my letters than my work. And so be it. At $175, plus expenses, per letter, a man could do worse. My guess is that I will get to Bismarck, North Dakota and capitalize on the fact that it is 55 miles closer to New York than to San Francisco. A shorter trip, as it were. But that depends on whether I can interest *The Reporter* in this swing; they have become leery of me recently, and I have not done much to allay their fears. Next I will move to the *Saturday Evening Post,* which pays $2000 to start.

When I get to New York I expect you to have some lucrative contracts for me in the Creative field. If they think they got a fearless type with you, they need an hour or two of me and some Tulamore Dew. I believe I could scare up some rich contracts for us all, with very little effort beyond normal conversation. You appear to have stumbled into that parlor where people have more money than brains. I need a contact of that sort. I am one of the most reliable tax deductions a man could find in this land. I will, of course, count on camping in your quarters, but from the way you talk it will be sort of like visiting [John] Clancy, who looks, when he walks, sort of like a belly-dancer in reverse. He makes $250 a week, or some such, and he keeps a little box beside his telephone, for dimes. It is said to be the principle of the thing. Soon he will have permanent folds in his rump, deep ridges in which a man can place dimes with no fear of their falling out.

Your orgasm film sounds nice. How about one on "The Myth of Semen"? I'll write the script. My son is here with me; he can't sleep at night except by the typewriter. He is not well coordinated; he can yank the false tit out of his mouth, but he can't get it back in. He groans and thrashes about constantly, as if in close combat with the dark forces of re-action. He has a dangerous amount of energy and a huge set of balls, a sure formula for trouble.

My best to the other hot shits.

HST

TO PAUL SEMONIN:

April 28, 1964
Glen Ellen, California

Paul:

Well bastard, it is now a year since I got back from South America with my head full of wisdom, my wallet full of money and my future full of fat leads. But the year has been a bust; for some reason I can't speak the language here. I am not with it. For the past two months I have been in a black bog of depression, fathering a son, living among people more vicious and venal than I ever thought existed, and bouncing from one midnight to the next in a blaze of stupid drunkenness. Now—tomorrow—I am shoving off for Butte, Montana, Jackson Hole, Bismarck, ND and that area. The *Observer* wants me to go up there and see what's happening. They're pay-ing. So I'm going. Maybe three weeks. Actually, I don't particularly care what's going on up there, but I see it as a prepaid chance to get off and think—and also ponder a book called the Badlands Journal that I am al-ready wheeling and dealing with. It will consist of everything I should delete from my novel in order to make it a work of fiction. Sort of like your Vagrant Thinker thing. Or like *The Fire Next Time*. Personal Journalism is the Wave of the Future. Art is passé, and so is *The New York Times*. Now we mix it all up and come on strong.

You have avoided all mention of your plans except to say that in maybe two years you're going to stomp over us all with the Big Secret. But I doubt it; my reluctant conclusion is that Marxists are the Beatniks of world politics. In twenty years you and your boys over there will be like the veterans of the Lincoln Brigade. The Syndicate has taken over here with a vengeance. My view of Johnson has scared both the *Observer* and *The Reporter*. It's a massive bandwagon: [James] Reston, Drew Pearson, [Walter] Lippmann, the TV Boys, Max Ascoli[23]; there is no dissent. None. (I just heard on the radio that Johnson is running well ahead of Robert Kennedy in the Massachusetts primary.) This sheep mentality has given me the fear; it is a very German thing and the negroes in this country are up against more than they know. The brute conservativism of the U.S. is the number one fact of our politics. Despite my royalist tendencies I am put down everywhere by a dirty leftist radical; you would be locked up.

I am considering a drift into the Underground, New York or LA—or Mexico City as a last resort. I have had no action in so long that it's a wonder I can still write. You will have to wait for the *Journal* to know it all; that is the only way I can salvage this worthless, wandering year. It starts tomorrow and will be a loose and speedy job; I don't want to let any torment seep in. Yeah.

Hudson went out to Hawaii to pick up his boat. His woman went back to Trinidad and he has a new New York nymphet who is nice but not real hot stuff. Mac [Macauley Smith] is coming west in a trailer and Cooke is hustling in New York after his Booth marriage.[24] I'm glad that clicked. I'm supposed to go back to Louisville in June for Davison's wedding, but I hate it like the plague and will duck out if at all possible. The only hope is The Road. A clear head in a bad hour. Things are not breaking like they should. I think the boys in Zanzibar read the signals pretty well; it won't be long before we have Castro on *Meet the Press* again . . . We are coming to another Eisenhower age, and everybody digs it. Even Nixon, who is back in style after a short winter. Johnson has eight years unless he croaks. We will all be old men by then. What do you have on tap?

Hunter

23. Max Ascoli was the publisher and owner of *The Reporter*.
24. Don Cooke had married Judy Booth, Thompson's old girlfriend.

TO PAUL SEMONIN:

Marooned in Butte, Thompson pondered the spectacle of American politics.

May 23, 1964
Finlen Hotel and Motor Inn
Butte, Montana

Dear Bobo:

You have failed in every way to combat my wisdom. I therefore urge you to forswear politics. It is a tub of dirty water. The more I write about it the more I piss on it. The fatbellies are well entrenched, long-rooted and much tougher in the clinches than I thought. What we knew in Louisville were the drone bees of the system; the big boys all carry Magnums. Their strength is not in their action, but their staying power and godawful resilience. I am coming to have a lot of sympathy for Mao, but less and less belief as time goes by.

By dealing in politics you accept their terms. Politics is economics, and when you deal in that league you are on the fatbellies' home court. All political revolutions start out to create a frame of reference, and end by accepting one. Marxism is over the hump for the time being; we will both be old men before the world power structure rests on another three-cornered sense of humor like Khrushchev, Kennedy and Pope John.

I was wrong when I said the negro had already won his fight in this country. In the flux of the Kennedy structure he was on his way, but the Johnson gang is sewing up the holes on us all. That is the climate. Political fatigue is on us all, even Castro. The tides have shifted considerably since you left last summer. Look at Brazil. If you can refute this with any conviction I'd like to get the word. Out here in Butte it is not easy to be sure about anything, but I get the scent and I have to trust it or lay myself open to bullshit from every angle.[25]

I am on a swing and it is a fucking nightmare. Nevada, Idaho, Montana, the Dakotas, Wyoming and back to San Francisco. The language barrier is immense. If you thought you were in the "West" down in Aspen you better think again. That is a suburb of Manhattan with Western trappings. What it will come to I can't say, but I am seriously considering Mexico — but not for the politics.

Send word c/o Glen Ellen. I am half mad for communication. The finality of the choice has just come into focus for me, and it makes me nervous.

HST

---

25. Thompson published his thoughts on Butte's future as "Whither the Old Copper Capital of the West? To Boom or Bust?" in the *National Observer*, June 1, 1964.

TO LYNDON JOHNSON:

Drunk and in good humor at the Holiday Inn in Pierre, South Dakota,
Thompson appealed to President Lyndon Johnson for a job.

> June 3, 1964
> Holiday Inn of Pierre
> Pierre, South Dakota

Lyndon Johnson
The White House
Washington, D.C.

Dear Lyndon:

It is with great pleasure and a sense of impending achievement that I
make myself available at this time for the governorship of American
Samoa. Given a certain knowledge of the character of one Joe Benetiz,
who previously occupied that position—and having no knowledge outside
a good instinct concerning that person who holds it at present—I feel that
my offer can only be rejected at our collective peril. In this I refer mainly
to the American Samoans, but certain tangential effects necessitate the inclusion of the rest of us, as well.

My position at this time is in flux enough to allow my serious consideration of such a move. I am a roving correspondent for the *National
Observer*, a sporadic contributor to *The Reporter*, and a fiction writer of
no mean merit. All this, plus a general humanity and a good instinct for
the openings, would seem to guarantee my candidacy beyond much
doubt.

Beyond this, I have a need for an orderly existence in a pacific place, in
order to complete a novel of overwhelming importance to the sanity of this
era. This need alone should snap your mind into the proper orbit for the
required action.

For the next ten days I will be in Pierre, Jackson Hole and Sun Valley.
After that I can be reached at my home near San Francisco. In the meantime, I remain,

> most sincerely,
> Hunter S. Thompson

FROM LARRY O'BRIEN, SPECIAL ASSISTANT TO THE PRESIDENT:

> June 17, 1964
> The White House
> Washington

Mr. Hunter S. Thompson
Owl House
9400 Bennett Valley Road
Glen Ellen, California

Dear Mr. Thompson:

The President has received your recent letter and asked me to thank you for it.

He has noted your desire for an appointment to the Governorship of American Samoa and you may be sure you will be given every consideration.

> Sincerely,
> Larry O'Brien
> Special Assistant to the
> President

TO WILLIAM J. KENNEDY:

> June 24, 1964
> Glen Ellen, California

Dear Willie:

Here's ten for that silly phone call. I was hardly worth talking to and you should have refused it. I wouldn't have called collect except that my bill was already so high with the hotel that I feared my ability to pay if I loaded up a long call on it.

Your acceptance was christian, none the less. I've been putting off writing because I thought I had a New York trip coming up and I've been waiting for it to break, but I think it's out now. My friend McGarr, whom you may or may not have met, thought he had me a $6000 film-writing assignment for National Educational Television, whatever in hell that is. But the honcho is scared of me, although he dug my clips. Now there is only one chance in a thousand he'll relent and hire me instead of some hack. We've talked several times on the phone, but he's too nervous.

I just sent the *Observer* a $1654 bill for my expenses on the Montana trip.[26] God knows what they'll do with it. They were figuring on about

---

26. Thompson had written "Living in the Time of Alger, Greeley, Debs" for the *National Observer* (July 13, 1964) while in Montana and South Dakota.

$400, but the good-will aspect of the tour was more than they'd counted on. But not me. I knew what it was going to be. Unlimited free booze for six weeks for me and quite a few others. In six states. It was a whore of a trip and almost killed me. The Hemingway piece was the only one I still feel like claiming.[27] That front-page monstrosity (upper left) sent me off in a rage. I called Candida Donadio at four in the morning and finished myself there; I was seeking a grant to go back into fiction, but she snapped and snarled like a bull-dyke dealing with a subway masher. Ugly.

Your comment about "regressing" stuck in my ears. I think part of the reason you feel that way is because you regressed geographically. I'd probably commit suicide if I found myself working back in Louisville. Even so, there is more to it than that. A journalistic retrogression can be a big step forward if you can get another prong going for you. That's what I'd like to do now, but my mind is blank for ideas. I couldn't possibly quit journalism, put in six penniless months on the novel, then start again on the old round of "Dear Sir, here is my novel, I hope you, etc. . . ." Those rat-bastards would drown me in no time. I am coming to view the free enterprise system as the greatest single evil in the history of human savagery. I am also beginning to believe Goldwater could win in '64. At heart, this is a sick and vicious country, hiding from itself behind a veil of romantic sentimentality. In order to see this you have to know the West, where the myth is still extant.[28]

Every Republican in the land should be horsewhipped—and every Democrat, too, for that matter. It is a horrible circus and I think LA must be the center ring. For that reason I believe I will move there and try to last a year. Then off again to the periphery, maybe then for good. We need a two-week session to loosen us up. Semonin will be back in New York in July and that will quicken my incentive for a trip. But the money problem remains. The *Observer* wants me out here and *The Reporter* don't dig me at all no more. Martin wrote and explained the score. Nobody likes me now except Max Ascoli, and I can't get to him. Like Philip Graham was my only contact in that other outfit. It's the old Air Force story: the sergeants are still fucking me. I just tried an end run and wrote Lyndon for a job as governor of American Samoa; Larry O'Brien wrote back saying I

27. Thompson's article "What Lured Hemingway to Ketchum?" appeared in the *National Observer* on May 25, 1964.
28. While in Missoula Thompson wrote two pieces for the *National Observer*: "The Atmosphere Has Never Been Quite the Same" (June 15), about student unrest at the University of Montana, and "Why Montana's 'Shanty Irishman' Corrals Votes Year After Year" (June 22), about Senator Mike Mansfield's consistent ability to get reelected.

would be given "every consideration." I am going to press for it. If they'll consider Joe Benetiz, I should be a shoo-in.

Anyway, hold this check at least ten days. It won't be any good until they send my expense check. But don't hold it too long after that. I am going to have to buy another car to replace my dead Rambler, so get your ten before I wipe it all out again. And send a line. Right now I am stone broke and just sitting here, waiting for the check. If they reject my claim, I'm dead. I owe every human being I know, and quite a few I don't know. In all, I may be ready for a giant retrogression myself, but we'll have to talk first. Zingo—HST

TO LARRY O'BRIEN, SPECIAL ASSISTANT TO THE PRESIDENT:

> June 25, 1964
> Owl House
> 9400 Bennett Valley Rd.
> Glen Ellen, California

Larry O'Brien
The White House
Washington, D.C.

Dear Mr. O'Brien:

Many thanks for your letter of June 17. Immediately upon receipt of same, I went to Brooks Brothers and purchased several white linen suits and other equipment befitting the Governor of American Samoa.

When can we get with it? Does Lyndon realize the importance of timing in this thing? It would augur ill for a new governor to be appointed in the fall. I know the thinking of tropical peoples. They set much store by the season. A new governor should arrive when the feazlewood trees bloom, when the fish spawn, and when the sun goes orange on a flat line towards China in the evening sky. No other time would be suitable.

I am eager to be off. My wife is more eager than I, and my Doberman senses a big move in the offing. Haste will benefit us all, and especially the American Samoans. My arrival will have the greatest meaning for them; it will be the dawn of a new and more humane era.

Send word at once. Given the present situation in the Far East, a sane appointment in the Pacific might have all the force of a blockbuster in our foreign relations. A massive switch, as it were.

In expectation of an action-packed reply, I remain,

> quite sincerely,
> Hunter S. Thompson

TO MR. SUNDELL, *PAGEANT*:

Searching for a new outlet for his work, Thompson pitched a list of possible articles to Pageant *magazine, a serious competitor to the* Reader's Digest— *and they paid well.*

> June 25, 1964
> Owl House
> 9400 Bennett Valley Rd.
> Glen Ellen, California

Dear Mr. Sundell:

Thanks for your comments on my Hemingway piece in the *National Observer*. I just got back from six weeks up in that country, and did seven or eight more, but the one you saw had the odd luck to come through unedited, and thus is the only one of the lot I have any feeling for.

At any rate, I'd be happy to write a thing or two for you. Do you have anything in mind? My steady market is the *Observer*, with an occasional sale to *The Reporter*; that should give you an idea, although the *Observer* is just about as general as your book seems to be. In the main, I like the off-beat stuff, the "negro problem," Latin America (I was the *Observer*'s man in Rio for a year or so), and anything dealing with writers, writing and contemporary fiction. I do a lot of book reviews for the *Observer*, but people keep writing from places like St. Petersburg, saying I gave them a bum steer on books like J. P. Donleavy's *Singular Man*, to mention the worst offender to date. The senior citizens didn't dig that one at all.

This is what I have cooking at the moment:

1) A piece on the horrors of a Tijuana abortion. In California, it's either that or some dirty table in a midnight suburban kitchen. So far I have four first-hand accounts. The idea of the piece is to shock people into thinking about making abortion legal, but I somehow doubt the *Observer* will go for it.

2) A piece on race relations in "the Paris of the West," as Gene Burdick calls it. I haven't decided how to slant this one yet; I have two queries out on it, but yell if it interests you, and how.

3) Some sort of profile on Los Angeles, in light of the new apportionment decision. What is L.A.? I'm curious.

4) A piece on "the untenable position of the white liberal if negro militants continue to gain power in 'the movement.'" This began as an idea for a seminar at Hot Springs Lodge in Big Sur, where topics like this are bandied about on summer weekends by big names. Mike Murphy, who runs the place, is an old friend (I used to live there), and he thinks we'll need some guaranteed prestige publicity in order to attract the people who would make such a seminar newsworthy. Maybe so. I'm thinking in

terms of Dick Gregory, Norman Mailer, Hodding Carter, Paul Jacobs, Ralph Gleason, Charles Mingus, and one or two of California's young black socialists. This would take weeks to organize and would cost you a hell of a lot more than that $300 "average fee" you mention in the *Writer's Digest*.

5) I'm also thinking of a trip to Mississippi this summer, but as yet I haven't talked to the *Observer* about it. By the time you get this I'll know their thinking, so let me know if it interests you.

6) I'm also trying to find an excuse for a trip to New York in July. If you can think of a piece I might apply my touch to, I'm agreeable to almost anything. As a matter of fact that's the way I usually work with the *Observer*. I pick a place, make a few suggestions, then zoom in with an open mind and a good eye. One that has always interested me on New York is "The Girl Who Didn't Make It." I used to live there and I know a few. They come for the glamorous job, the hotshot husband, the light fantastic and all that sort of thing—and only a few of them make it. Where do the others go? I have a head start on that one, but it would take a week or two of research to get it done. Let me know on this.

That should do for now. Your letter was a bit of a surprise, by the way. I've never paid much attention to *Pageant*, mainly because of the name and the housewifey covers, I guess, but the inside sort of surprised me. Especially the publetter calling for a new look at Red China. Anyway, give me a ring if you think we should talk. Thanks.

Hunter S. Thompson

TO MIKE MURPHY:

Novelist Murphy and Thompson were considering holding a seminar at Big Sur's Esalen Institute on "White Liberalism and Black Militarism." Race relations was the subject of the day: on July 2 President Johnson had signed the most sweeping civil rights legislation in the history of the nation.

July 8, 1964
9400 Bennett Valley Rd.
Glen Ellen, California

Dear Mike:

Seems the only way I can say anything sane and sober to you is by mail, and so be it; that's par for my course. I'll be down again when I regain my health, and midweek next time, so maybe we can talk. In the meanwhile, consider what we talked about last time.

To wit: A seminar on the position of the White Liberal in the event
that negro "militants" gain a dominant voice in the "civil rights" movement. (The reason for my quote marks is too complex to explain right
now.) The subtitles would be full of meat: 1) Are negro militants really
racists? Or, what is the difference between Malcolm X and Dick Gregory? 2) What is a white "liberal"? (Clare Boothe Luce said yesterday:
"I'm still a Liberal, but I agree with Senator Goldwater on everything except civil rights." Yeah.) 3) In the event of the various "conflicts" predicted by civil rights leaders if Goldwater is nominated and the civil
rights bill proves toothless in their eyes, whose side is the "white liberal"
on? Or, as Charley Mingus said to Ralph Gleason, "Man, you gotta know
where you stand when the fighting starts in the streets." Or Louis
Lomax[29] when he talks about the coming "night of the long knives."
Which way do I point my .44 Magnum if both sides think I'm against
them? (For others, that question might have to be paraphrased to some
extent, but the meaning is the same.)

I've given it a lot of thought, but I haven't got moving due to a great
backlog of *Observer* stuff and these godawful binges in Big Sur. I wouldn't
want to do it for the *Observer* because I think it deserves more space than
they could give it and I'm not sure that audience is exactly what we'd
need to attract the sort of talent that would give the seminar real meaning.
But selling the article is my problem; setting up the seminar would be
your end.

How about telling me:

1) If it still interests you—in this rough form or some other, but at least
the general idea.

2) When (dates) we could think about getting some people together, so
I'd have something to say when I call.

3) What you pay participants in this sort of thing—if anything—and
again, just so I'd know what to say.

Obviously, I'm not going to start calling around and setting up a seminar in your lodge, but these are things we should talk about if the idea
interests you at all—mainly because these are things any potential partici-
pant would ask at once. I could do it as a series of interviews, but I think it
would go better as an article if it tied in with Big Sur and a seminar with
photos—sort of like the piece I did on the Aspen Institute.

H

29. Louis Lomax was a prominent African-American musicologist and activist.

TO LOREN JENKINS:

Jenkins, an aspiring journalist, had written to Thompson for some tips on how to become a big-time reporter; a warm friendship soon developed between them. Jenkins went on to win the 1983 Pulitzer Prize for his coverage of the Middle East for The Washington Post.

July 21, 1964
Glen Ellen, California

Loren:

I thought the Peace Corps took care of your sort, guaranteed jobs upon discharge and all that, no? Well, this writing is a bad racket to fool around with unless you can't do anything else, which is my case, and if I were you I'd take potluck with the PC placement thing and have done with it.

I don't know how good you are so I can only speak in broad generalities. With a Ph.D. in government you should go to work for Lyndon; after last week's convention I think he is going to need all the help he can get around October and maybe sooner.

Anyway, New York is by far the toughest nut to crack and I guess San Francisco is next, for different reasons. If you hang around New York until you run out of cash you'll probably end up working on some trade paper like *Baker's Weekly*. The dailies in general won't touch a man without several years' experience in the trade; that's the way the Guild has it set up and exceptions are rare—like editors' sons, and that. If you are really serious about journalism I'd say the first thing to overcome is the idea that you're going to stay in New York (or any other decent place) and come up with an "interesting" job. I suppose it can be done, but everybody I know has had to go to the provinces first.

The idea is to get clippings and parlay them into bigger and better things. With enough good clippings you can virtually buy a job; I've come to think of mine as currency. A few good clips and a good idea will generally get you an assignment or at least an interested editor. So the gimmick is to get somebody to print your stuff; a good manuscript won't do the trick.

I went to the Headline agency, which came up with five or six offers within ten days, and finally found myself working for the *Middletown Daily Record* until I was fired almost instantly and then went on unemployment with plenty of time to free-lance. Headline is a good bet for a small paper gig, and they can generally come up with one close enough to New York so you can get in now and then. You might call a friend of mine named Bob Bone, who lives on Cornelia St. in the Village, and ask him about this. He's closer to the job market; I haven't held a job in five years and probably never will again, so it may be that I'm out of touch. Or Don Cooke, 58 W. 25th; he managed to get on at McGraw-Hill with no experience and he may have some wisdom. Gene McGarr might know something about the TV end; he is at 245 W. 104th. They're all in the phone book.

If you're pretty good at putting an article together you might query my editor at the *National Observer* (Cliff Ridley) and see if you can sell him something. Address: 11501 Columbia Pike, Silver Spring, Md. Look at the *Observer* before trying it; they carry almost anything.

I got some good clips by writing for the New York *Herald Trib* travel section; also the *Chicago Tribune*. They don't pay much, but it helps to have clips from name papers.

I'm dealing strictly with the mechanics of this thing because I assume you realize nobody starts out writing editorials for *The New York Times* or lead articles for *The Reporter*. Some people might be good enough to start out that way, but Mr. Charley won't believe it. There is an amazing amount of resentment, among aging hacks, toward a young hotshot trying to bypass the bullshit jobs that none of them could avoid.

In all, the first thing to do is get some sort of writing slot; I'd say a general reporting beat on some small paper, because that would give you the most leeway to pile up the clips that would interest New York editors. It would also give you a base from which to free-lance for things like *The Nation* or *The New Republic*, which don't pay in money so much as prestige. It would also get you into the writing habit, which is harder than most people think, and put you onto little spacing and countless other habits that make a man's copy look like he knows what he's doing. Most editors fear for their jobs and would always prefer to publish a mediocre pro than a talented amateur who might get him in trouble. Editors, by nature, are the sort of people who use condoms.

This is about all I can say for now; all I have is your name, a brief handshake in the Aspen book store, and second-hand info from Peggy [Clifford] that you're "looking for a writing job." I could probably do you more good if I knew more about your situation, experience, interests and that business. Send word if you think I can do you some good. In the meantime, and in sum, all I can say is 1) don't limit yourself to New York unless you have a good in, 2) avoid San Francisco at all costs; this is a dead end place and if you doubt it, read the San Francisco papers, 3) consider a year or even six months on a small paper that will give you enough freedom to get some good clips, 4) check with Headline and the names I mentioned, register at some of the agencies that handle writing jobs, and generally cast a wide net.

Like I said, it's a shitty business, in all, and unless you think you can put up with it I'd consider just about anything else. Anyway, let me know.

Sincerely,
Hunter S. Thompson
Owl House
9400 Bennett Valley Rd.
Glen Ellen, California

TO DON COOKE:

Thompson had just attended the Republican National Convention at the Cow Palace in San Francisco, at which Arizona senator Barry Goldwater was nominated for president.

August 19, 1964
Owl House
Glen Ellen, California

Dear Daddio:

The report from this end is ugly. Mister Charley is leaning on me for real. The wolves have broken down the door and found me too broke to buy ammunition. I was long gone in funk until finding your old March 7 letter tonight; its leaping tone brought me up short. I most definitely need a jaunt to New York for the purpose of reviewing reality with you and others who've been dealing with other tentacles. I think I must have come to grips with the main muscle. The brute is sitting on my chest and smacking my eyes whenever I try to roll him off.

I went to the Republican convention and put on a bulldrunk that scared the shit out of the *Observer* honchos sent out to put me to work. They got the honest fear and did me in with their reports back to D.C. (Our man in the West is a foaming anarchist, a naked boozer who never sleeps and won't work and thinks Goldwater is a nazi.) So they wrote and told me to straighten up or fuck off—and I still haven't decided which way to swing. On top of that my man at *The Reporter* [Dwight Martin] split with Max Ascoli and his successor is determined to do away with all traces of the old regime, including me. Thus, my income is nil at a time when my expenses are running high and my debts are fantastic. The car is dead, I am two months behind on the rent, they are coming for my phone on Monday, and I have about ten more days before they chop the electricity.

So much for that. I can flee, of course, but that would portend a shift back to that other league. I would have to learn to play the guitar, and bum cigarette butts. At the moment I have slim hopes of obtaining a loan in Big

Sur and making a move to somewhere, but I have no idea where. San Francisco, Montana, Alberta, Mexico, Los Angeles, New York—all possibilities, at least in theory. I don't want to stay here and I can't think of anyplace else; that is the nut of the thing. I was hoping Semonin would have some wisdom in this area, but his one call from Louisville had to do with black nationalism or some such swill and right now I don't feel up to joining a movement. If the idea is to bring down the government, I'm all for it. But you don't do that on a grant from the Ford Foundation.

Hudson has sailed to Tahiti. McGarr is due on the coast in a few days. I am off to LA next week to do a piece for *Pageant* magazine (yeah) on why people are moving to S. California. They wrote and asked for the privilege of publishing me. But at the moment I don't even have gas money to get to San Francisco, much less LA, and before I go I'll have to lay hands on another car. There is a possibility of a truck in Carmel, a real hotrod that will handle the Big Sur road at night doing 100 on the straightaways and 80 on the curves. I've put it to the test, but every time I take somebody along with me they get hysterical. I'll know about that in a few days; take over payments. Yeah. Take over the car and move out like a big hyena.

My shack has been full of people for two months, even including my mother and little brother. Steady visitors for two goddamn months. Two just left, a folksinger from Boston and a doomed young bride from Florida. Another singer due tomorrow, and then McGarr. At times like these I think seriously of British Columbia. I got a $71 phone bill last month, and another $50.24 today. Fantastic. Everybody makes calls and gives me fifty cents, which I promptly spend. Then comes the ticket, the sharp jab, and then severance. My landlady plays the organ. My guns are in pawn. My sanity hangs by a thread.

I think perhaps the only answer is an instant rewrite of The Rum Diary and a quick sale to the movies. My gimmick is an interracial orgy that should stand hair on end from London to Long Beach. The KKK will send goons after me if the thing ever appears. My birth certificate will be removed from the files in Louisville, and burned. Semonin, Dylan and Baez will chip in to have me croaked. And if they send me cash on the barrelhead I will buy a gross of .44 Magnum slugs and do a fine dogdance on Jack London's tomb.

Otherwise, I have nothing to report. Your last card was vague, saying things about "seeking employment" and "going up the Hudson." What does that mean? Are you on the dole? What action is up the Hudson? If it's real I might check that area myself. My man Kennedy is in Albany; see him before making any rash moves in that direction. Bill Kennedy—*Albany Times-Union*. A fine man with the rum and a christian to boot. I've been sending people to see you but can't say if any showed up. Mostly in the job-advice area. Now you say you were fired up the Hudson. I trust you dispensed good advice to any who called for it. ("Fuck off up the Hudson, boy, that's where things are happening!")

I may even seek employment myself, but I doubt it. It would be like lopping off my balls. After five years on the fringe, I couldn't handle anything steady.

Thanks for the good words on the *Reporter* piece. There won't be any others. Probably not many more in the *Observer*, either. This is the end of an era and god knows what the next one will bring. I will try, as always, to get to New York at once. The truck would make the run in two days, but that's still unsettled.

Hello to Judy[30] and keep me posted on any movements or shifts. Did Semonin leave any address? Do I have an address? What's in an address, anyway? "Up the Hudson" sounds good. Or simply "West." Send wisdom at once.

                              HST

TO WILLIAM KILPATRICK, *PAGEANT:*

The Thompsons had left Glen Ellen and moved into an apartment in San Francisco. Eager for cash, Thompson pitched another Big Sur story to an editor at Pageant.

                              October 23, 1964
                              318 Parnassus
                              San Francisco

Willie K.:
    Yours of 10/21 got here today and put a bit of egg on my face. Re: my comments on the lunacy of a "Big Sur Service piece." But the most impressive thing about your package was your correx on my San Francisco to Big Sur distance. I said 150, a lazy generality taken from Telegraph Hill to somewhere around Anderson Canyon, the more or less center of what's supposed to be Big Sur. Your figure of 125 was only two miles off the map distance from the San Francisco city limits to the Big Sur highway sign just north of the village store. The exact figure is 127. And I say that from reinvigorated memory.

    Which means nothing at all to our ultimate purpose, but we can't deny that you racked a few good points on it. I'll watch you from now on. You must have a custom-built World Almanac.

---

30. Cooke's wife, née Judy Booth.

(Before I forget, I sent Sundell about a month or six weeks ago a piece on "The Rustic Inn & Jack London & The Valley of the Moon." It was a pure color job, but a good one, and I'm beginning to think it never got there. *The Reporter* assigned it, then lost my original manuscript, and the ensuing fracas pretty well blasted our relationship. That and the demise of my editor. Anyway, let me know if you ever saw or heard of it. I don't really want to think it's your meat, but it's damn sure somebody's and I want to get it out on the market again.)

Now, as for Big Sur: I liked the preciseness of your comments, but I'm afraid you've swallowed the Big Sur myth. I lived there for a year and I still get down every few weeks and the people I drink with are now in the process of buying up the place, so I've seen both sides of the argument. I've also heard a lot of fascinating "Big Sur stories" that were pure balderdash. I hear stories about myself that put Henry Miller's stuff in deep shade. You say, "Big Sur, in its heyday, had more talent per square inch than Paris in the '20s." Well, Willie, I don't want to seem churlish, but I'll have a lot of knowledgeable people on my side when I say that simply ain't true. The best to come out of Big Sur is none too good. Miller wrote only one book there. Dennis Murphy wrote most of *The Sergeant* in his grandmother's house, where I lived for a year. I guess Bennie Bufano is the only guy who really produced anything consistently in Big Sur, and even he was a short termer.

Too many people, including me, have pampered this myth of Big Sur as a boiling vat of creativity, but it's not so. The most interesting aspect of the Big Sur syndrome, in truth, concerns the "artist" who goes there to "create" and winds up a local windbag. Or else he quits real quick. The fine distinction is that the myth of Big Sur attracts talent, but the reality of Big Sur erodes talent. This is a complicated subject and much too hairy for us to deal with here. All I mean to say is that the stories you mentioned ring several bells that bring a handful of stories to mind, but as a former resident and a man who's done a hell of a lot of both formal and informal research on the place, I'm not about to open that Pandora's box of fuzzy Big Sur legends and sign my name to any one of them.

I enclose, purely FYI, a piece I did in 1961 when I lived there. It got me evicted within 24 hours of the time it appeared on the Monterey news-stands, and my name is still anathema to a lot of people down there. Until Bill Trombly did his blitz in the *Saturday Evening Post* last year, mine was generally deemed the most rotten thing ever written about Big Sur. Trombly is barred forever, and I'd be in the same fix if I didn't have an underground going for me, and unlimited bar tabs with "the syndicate." (That's a local joke, son.)

The red-marked photos are the ones I mentioned. They're mine. I have the negs. *Rogue* botched the layout on the big shots, and over-inked the small ones. The two I marked are the ones I mean to send.

So I'll re-do this one over the weekend and ship it off by Monday. If it suits you, I'd appreciate payment ASAP. This hyper-social summer put me way down in the debt-hole and I'm sore pressed for funds. Instant funds. If your instincts are christian, you will keep that in mind.

On Thursday or Friday I'll skip out to Idaho for a bit of hunting and a boondock election-day piece for the *Observer*. That should take a week or 10 days, during which time my address will be c/o Leadville, Box 201, Ketchum, Idaho. If you think of anything I can get for you up there, send a wire. But it would have to be something quick and short. I have to get back here by the middle of the month, rap out five or six more pieces, then flip out again for New York. I'll be there around Christmas and will give a ring. Chances are I won't get to the LA piece until after the Idaho trip. Your questions were more involved than they seemed at a glance, and I've already far exceeded the $50 "expenses" tab. With unlimited expenses I could answer all your questions and clear up all the fuzziness in three days. But my phone bill won't stand that kind of abuse, so I'm having to rely on mail queries and personal leg-men to clear up such conundrums as "Neeny's Hot Dog Stand" or "Neeney's Roadside Rest"?

OK for now. Check on "Rustic" piece and let me know. Your suggestions on Big Sur seem as clear as I need. The LA thing will take a bit longer, but you can count on it. If I had more time and less madness in my life I could handle these things quickly and efficiently. But if that were the case I'd probably have a job somewhere, and not be writing at all.

Say hello for me to The Troops.

Bingo,
Hunter S. Thompson

TO PAUL SEMONIN:

November 15, 1964
318 Parnassus
San Francisco

Dear Tail-Chaser:

I read your eight-page autobiography some 48 hours ago and am now ready to undertake it again. Since I always read my mail at breakfast I can never afford to take it very seriously—like the newspapers—until I am fully awake later in the day or even later in the week. The main thing I remember about yours is a flavor of hysteria, a sort of high-pitched chattering whine that led me to believe you will soon join some of our more vulnerable brethren in the luxury wards of the Norton Infirmary.[31]

But since I'd hate to see that, I am now prepared to read your tome again—in hopes of finding some thread of muscle or continuity to make me change my mind. Something of value, as it were. Mr. Roark[32] said that. Or merely something to indicate you have not been flipped by a rising wave of spleen. I said that.

Yeah, I know. Plagiarism. Like [James] Baldwin using your phony Marx quote and not crediting Marx. As I recall, he used it to describe Scott Fitzgerald. The idea is pure bullshit, in any case, because it makes suicide the only logical human act. Or, shooting from another angle: who decides when a "situation" requires illusions? Who originates the demand to renounce them? And what, for that matter, is an illusion? I know you feel qualified on all these counts, but you might have trouble mounting a true consensus without the help of a loaded pistol.

And now to read your letter again.

I note right off the bat that you appear ignorant of the true-certain historical fact that all of Bolivia's large tin mines were nationalized in 1952 by the government that was just deposed. A government agency titled COMIBOL has been running them since then—and running them deep in the red, I might add, to the general misfortune of nearly every Bolivian citizen except a few in the government and some 8 to 10,000 strongly unionized miners under the leadership of a man named Lechin. [. . .] The morning I spoke with Juan Lechin he caused a delegation of some 50 peasants to wait outside his office while he had himself shaved and barbered. He then emerged, looking and smelling somewhat like Ronald Reagan, and mingled with the mob like an oily Lyndon Johnson. After waiting with the other peasants for an hour and a half, I felt a sense of real gratitude when the prick finally deigned to speak with us. This man makes Nixon seem on a par with Pope John.

As for your implication that I didn't feel at home with the anarchists in South America, I can only deny it. I am at home with anarchists anywhere. A true anarchist is the only man who can afford to relax in this world; his vision is clear and true, his aims are simple, and his appetites are tiny compared to the various packs of jackals who make up the opposition. His only problem is that he can't afford to be right, so most anarchists end up lying in the name of some necessary evil. The most important political breakthrough of the past five centuries will come when some desperate half-

31. The Louisville hospital where both Thompson and Semonin were born.
32. Howard Roark was the architect in Ayn Rand's *The Fountainhead.*

mad truth seeker learns how to justify his instinct to anarchy. It has to come, because it's the only possible reconciliation between a man's best instincts and his worst realities.

I saw something about Frei's intentions re: China and Cuba, but I was up in Idaho for 10 days over the election and I didn't see much of anything in the way of political bombast. But it does interest me to see how quick you switched your taste from Allende to Frei.[33] He had the Pope on his side, you know. And Kennecott Copper, too. Are you selling out? When I was grilled by "this Covian guy" last year you were both telling me how Allende was going to mop up in Chile. Maybe I couldn't learn much from Covian after all, eh?

Aside from that, I don't think it would make much difference in this country if Frei turned out to be Raul Castro in disguise. Latin America is out of the news. Nada. A free-lancer down there now would pay hell making a living. The press has tuned itself to Johnson's interests—pocketbook issues, as it were. Things like excise taxes on lipstick and Medicare. Johnson doesn't know Chile from chili, and doesn't give a damn, either. I think we are in for the final slide; eight years of it, unless he dies.

That "brain of your manhood" is a good line; where did you steal it?

I am reading now, seeing your comment on my meeting with you & Covian and his wife. In my mind it was a mercifully quick running of the gauntlet, but I see now how I "rejected" the fellow. Out of simple viciousness, no doubt. Or a hatred of the strangeness in him. Indeed.

Your massive sentence on page three is about the "heaviest" I've ever read—as you noted. Your phrase "fugitive logic" defines it pretty well. I look forward to talking to you on whatever distant day you finally realize you were put down in this muck for a very short time, and only once, and that nobody—despite the advertisements—has whipped up the dish you know you want to taste. I don't imagine you're far from the time when you'll begin to get the fear that you'll die hungry, but perhaps right now between Mr. Marx and Mr. Ford[34] they are still teasing your taste buds, and you don't know it yet. You are the Gatsby of the Marxist Left, old sport; he had his silk shirts and you have Tomorrow's Gospel, and I hope we're still able to talk like human beings when you find out that his Green Light was a hell of a lot more than a slack rich girl from Louisville.

Your idea that maybe next year I'll be wise enough to absorb the wisdom of your friends is so petulant and patronizing that I don't see any sense in

33. Eduardo Frei Montalva became president of Chile in 1964, instituting social programs and gradually nationalizing foreign-owned mining companies. Salvador Allende Gossens, a Marxist, succeeded Frei in 1970 with a third of the national vote.
34. Semonin had recieved a Ford Foundation grant to study African politics.

talking about it. I'd enclose Mailer's piece on the GOP convention—primarily for his comments on Baldwin—but the postage would be too much and you'd probably forget who sent it anyway. In some small way Mailer has come back from the dead. The depth and decency of his despair make Baldwin sound like a crotchety fag reading somebody else's poetry.

For a man who has given up literature and art, for politics, you talk very heavily of literary influences. But, just for your own information, I get my irony and two-fistedness from a general shortness of cash, my apocalyptic vision from booze and desperate naiveté, and my sense of tragedy from Nancy Fitzhugh.[35] And my money—like yours—comes from people who don't take me seriously.

You still seem to have an ear for Faulkner's rhetoric, but your quote about "that which is highest in us" (which I don't recall) but which, if he said it, was stolen from a little fellow named José Martí, who described Simón Bolívar as a man, or perhaps a legend, who "appeals to that which is best and manliest in us." Martí wrote that before Faulkner was born.[36]

You ask me what I mean when I say all systems are against me. I mean exactly that. Any organization is necessarily a pyramid—the few controlling the many—and every system requires an organization, much as you might hate to admit it. You only had six months in the Corps. It took me longer than that to get over the shock of the AF, and I'd been in at least a year before I calmed down enough to see it for what it was. You call yourself an "optimist," but everything you say is masochistic pessimism. My feeling is that a man is born with decent instincts (and fuck this idea of original sin) which are steadily pressured and perverted every day of his life until he is either driven mad or turns into a vicious insensitive monster. The trick is to keep your feet in the shitrain, and any man who can do that deserves whatever ego he has left. I agree with you entirely that the U.S. is a root-rotten structure, menaced from without by justified resentment and buttressed from within by moneyed fear—but your alternatives strike me as being about as feasible as Bob Butler's.

Your bullshit about "who is the enemy in San Francisco" makes me wonder. Your bloated rhetoric makes mine seem like cold hard logic. "The enemy," the fucking silly enemy, is the same right here as he is over there. The enemy is any man who is willing to take the necessary steps to protect his own short-term interests—now or later, often never admitting it even to

---

35. Nancy Fitzhugh was a close Louisville friend of Judy Booth's who attended Smith College. Thompson had dated Fitzhugh when he lived in New York. He considered her another one of his "doomed lovers."
36. Martí led Cuba's revolution against Spain in 1895.

himself, rarely understanding his own implications, and always a little too human for any moral censure except in the name of fate and expediency. Hitler was a hero until he fucked up. So was Khrushchev. And good old Ike was such a hero, for two terms, that he was finally permitted to lay a golden egg, named Nixon, who came very near being king.

(I see I am beginning to chatter and whine a bit, myself, so I'll cash in and cool off till the next session. Selah.)

Hunter

TO PAUL SEMONIN:

November 25, 1964
318 Parnassus
San Francisco

I feel pretty snappy and eloquent tonight, and that just about sinks any possibility of thinking seriously on your letter. I suppose you're foaming and pissing after what you've already read, but this is 10 days later—a wild and active ten days, I might add, but not explain, in deference to your new humorlessness—and the air around here is highly charged. I have spent the evening watching television: the news from Stanleyville, a film on Mussolini's conquest of Ethiopia, and finally a film dealing with army turncoats. Also the commercials, which I avoided by reading five or six book reviews on the subject of Kennedy.

The result of all this, in my mind, is an overwhelming desire to get out of the country. I've been shouting for so many hours that right now it seems silly to put it all on paper because I know you'll nit-pick it to death with borrowed clichés and hashish wisdom that will not make much contact by the time it arrives here cold and stale 2 weeks after you write it. This is not to say I don't look forward to your letters, because you're about the only contributor to my mailbox who talks like a blood-filled human. (That's "filled," in deference to your defensiveness.) It was not meant as an attack on you. Honest.

As for facts, Butler has not shown up here since I wrote the last letter, but there are still a few hours left in this night and it would not surprise me at all for him to arrive ten minutes from now in the company of H. Boone,[37] whom I haven't seen or heard from since our visit. In 1960. Noonan shaved off his beard and seems generally confounded. San Francisco remains essentially a hiding place. Sandy is going to New York

37. Hannah Boone Kirby was a Louisville debutante who had dated Butler and Thompson.

for Xmas but I think I'll stay here—unless I get a spate of money, and that's not likely as long as I take time to write these goddamn long letters. Seven or eight of my checks bounced this week. I have just about decided not to write any more journalism except for my memoirs. The only problem now is to figure out how to live on fiction. Maybe you can get me a grant, eh? Tell 'em I'm secretly OK, but willing to rave a bit if the pay is right.

I am writing nothing. I have no interest in it. The hump is not far off. When I get really desperate I'll undoubtedly plunge into political action of some kind, knowing all the while that the more feverishly I involve myself with ludicrous movements, the happier it will make the fatbellies. I never had a course in political science but somebody told me in a bar once about how most visible politics are efforts to divert somebody's attention away from the real fight. The Kennedy-Nixon thing was an exception and a rare one. But this last farce was . . . well, hell, you know all about that.

I was ready to hoot at you for apparently believing that your news from *La Monde* gave you an inside track on U.S. politics. But maybe you don't carry your delusions quite that far. Sorry. Anyway, your comments on what happened here are essentially correct, and hardly novel. Mailer is miles ahead of you, saying that in some secret, half-perverted way he hoped Goldwater might win—if only to bring about another confrontation. Peggy Clifford reports a shade of this from Aspen, and before Mailer's piece appeared. I don't know whom she overheard, or where, but when she said it I remember thinking, "Yeah, why not set the bastards up for a *real* fall?"

But there was an element of that in my thinking all the way from beginning to end. I recall standing on the floor of the convention when GW made his acceptance speech and actually feeling afraid because I was the only person not clapping and shouting. And I was thinking, God damn you nazi bastards I really hope you win it, because letting your kind of human garbage flood the system is about the only way to really clean it out. Another four years of Ike would have brought on a national collapse, but one year of Goldwater would have produced a revolution.

That's my anarchist talking. But as a good, god-fearing, one hundred percent liberal American with nice common sense and a normal share of cowardice I would have voted for Johnson if I'd been eligible to vote. Which I wasn't and that makes me happy. But I honestly think now that I wish GW had won. Maybe if we ever talk on this thing I can give you some ideas on your "violence in America" piece. Or maybe I already have. But I see your boys in the Congo are learning quick. And I had to laugh at your idea that the Algerians are shocked by "brutality photos" out of Vietnam. Just like I'd be shocked by a photo of a dead dog. What kind of stuff are you smoking, boy? Do you know what fucking country you're in? Did you see any photos out of Algeria in those eight years? What in hell are you talking about? You seem to imply they are all gentle children with no eye for reality at all. I wonder how many people you deal with over there know Mr. Ford is giving you $6,000 a year to study them and write about their problems.

I suppose I should explain here that none of what I say implies a loss of faith in your brain or balls, but I can't help but get excited when you throw that kind of hash at me. And when I talk with an ugly tongue I am talking to your political ear, hoping you can differentiate between a personal attack and a rhetorical judo match.

And that, I guess, is the problem. You seem at times to have lost that split-level vision you used to have, that thing that Hemingway called a "built-in, fool-proof shit detector," which he claimed was the most important thing any artist could have. But what is art, really, but a good instinct for staying alive in your own alley? And maybe that's not important. Maybe I'd be better off writing tracts for some Marxist-oriented union, or free-booze movement. At least I'd have drifted off to some kind of frustrated sell-out like a university cubicle, to pass their useless bitterness on to younger, less frightened souls.

Right now I suppose I am as pessimistic about your future as you seem to be about mine. I think we both know they are beating the bush for us in this country—subtly right now, but soon there won't be any need for subtlety. "The System," "They," "The Establishment," "The Power Structure," call it what you will. It is all these fucks who smile on the TV screen, and when you talk about "the enemy" and say you're going to get them, jesus, I wonder. Who's going to get whom?

Well, I've got to get off this thing or I won't be able to afford the postage to mail it. I appreciate more of what you say than I let on here, but you seem more interested in an argument than anything else and I just can't see much sense in wracking my mind all this time just to knock you off balance for the next round. We are talking about different worlds. I envy your situation in that you seem to be comfortably lock-stepped with a consistent viewpoint, and for that very same reason I can't take your talk as seriously as I could if I knew you were forging it yourself. You keep saying you have "found" something, and maybe you have, but if you're really that hip I wonder why it doesn't come across in what you say and write. Frankly, I take a lot of what you say on a faith that comes from knowing you, and not because of what actually comes across. I'm sure you're honest, and god knows, your facts are right most of the time (or maybe it's just your negative opinions that I agree with), but I wish you could tell me something more than to subscribe to the *Liberator* and get across the Bay and join the Free Speech Movement. I am snatching around for tools and you offer me cookies. This is a tougher world than that, and the biggest enemy of all is the face on the clock.

Yeah, I guess that's more rhetoric. But I'll have to wrap up now if I want to get this to you before December 15. I felt a hell of a lot better when I started this than I do now. We are not accomplishing much in this correspondence because our current frames of reference are so different. Yet I hope you keep sending your bullshit, if only because it smacks my brain. I just wish to hell you could convince me you are on to something real, instead of just another theoretical escape hatch from the Big Business, which is all too mean and private for your kind of public panaceas.

There is, in all, too much talk about this sort of thing. We are not going to solve the mad riddle by mounting long attacks on each other. Your comments on my pose have about as much effect as if I talked about your pose, and neither of them matters a rat's ass. The main effect your attacks have on me is a quick, verbal anger that is obviously dead end. If you could just mix in a few specifics—that photo of you with the Ghana geisha was worth five pages of your political foam—we could handle this thing a lot better. I see no hope but to deal with you in person. I believe that's what you're hiding over there. My wisdom is too mean for you. Come back and pop a kid or two, then tell the world what it needs. Or wants. You are living right now in real luxury—and consequently, not with it. You are no more in tune with realities in America than in Algeria. You are a privileged specimen. Which is not at all bad while it lasts, but don't kid yourself into thinking you're a representative creature.

Nor am I, certainly, but then I know it. And when you tell me to get off to Berkeley for the sit-ins I say no thanks I think I'll go out to the beach and run in the fog and try to stay human in the smell of my own sweat. In a world like this I want to stay as tough as possible and I've never derived much strength from sitting in a mob and chanting in unison. Which is not to say the Berkeley mobs aren't right. They are. Joan Baez is over there telling them so. And if I thought they were as serious as they are noisy, I might even pitch in. And so much for that. Send word and your new address. I am on the verge of a boom-out. Dakar sounds good. Maybe Rio too.

As usual—HST

TO CAREY MCWILLIAMS, *THE NATION:*

McWilliams, editor of The Nation, *had written to Thompson praising his articles in the* National Observer. *Thompson's response marked the beginning of a fruitful relationship.*

December 18, 1964
318 Parnassus
San Francisco

Dear Mr. McWilliams:

Thanks for your note; I think you are the only person in New York who reads the *Observer*—or maybe just the only one who admits it.

At any rate, I've been meaning to write you for several weeks, ever since Gene McGarr at NETV [National Educational Television] made the suggestion. Ever since the GOP convention the *Observer* has taken great pains to keep me doing harmless, nonpolitical stories and I am now casting around for other founts of cash. So your note was timely, as well as encouraging.

It is also a fact that I am leaving for the East on Monday. One of the stories I'll do en route is a sort of "Saturday night in the Kentucky mountains" thing, which might also be a chance to get an Appalachia piece for you. By the time I've spent 65 hours on the train to Louisville I should be full of wild ideas, so if a Kentucky mountain piece of any kind interests you, send word at once: 2437 Ransdell Ave., Louisville. I'll be there until just before January 1, then on to New York to stay with McGarr at 245 W. 104th. If I don't hear from you in Kentucky I'll give a ring in New York; maybe you'll have time for a beer and some talk. Whatever comes of it, I like the idea of doing a thing or two for you. San Francisco is my base at the moment, but I'm not sure how long that's going to be the case. New York always puts the itch in me and I'm just as likely to keep on going towards Dakar as I am to come back here and stagnate in this goddamn fog.

The Berkeley Free Speech Movement is another good possibility, but not until after the holidays. Then I think we'll get more action. *The New Republic*'s piece this week was pretty thin.

Anyway, we'll come up with something.

Sincerely,
Hunter S. Thompson

*Thompson took this photo when he spent a day with
Marlon Brando in Oregon discussing
Native American rights.*
(PHOTO BY HUNTER S. THOMPSON; COURTESY OF HST COLLECTION)

Spider *magazine was the newsletter of the
Berkeley Free Speech Movement.*
(COURTESY OF HST COLLECTION)

Carey McWilliams of The Nation.
(COURTESY OF HST COLLECTION)

1965

SAN FRANCISCO IN THE WEIRD YEARS . . . PLUNGED INTO POVERTY, RAMMED THROUGH THE LOOKING GLASS . . . FROM *THE WALL STREET JOURNAL* TO DRUG RIOTS, HELL'S ANGELS, FREE SPEECH, KEN KESEY, TOTAL VIOLENCE, TOM WOLFE, LSD 25, AND THE ELEGANT MADNESS OF ALLEN GINSBERG . . .

California, Labor Day weekend . . . early, with ocean fog still in the streets, outlaw motorcyclists wearing chains, shades and greasy Levis roll out from damp garages, all-night diners and cast-off one-night pads in Frisco, Hollywood, Berdoo and East Oakland, heading for the Monterey peninsula, north of Big Sur . . . The Menace is loose again, the Hell's Angels, the hundred-carat headline, running fast and loud on the early morning freeway, low in the saddle, nobody smiles, jamming crazy through traffic and ninety miles an hour down the cen-ter stripe, missing by inches . . . like Genghis Khan on an iron horse, a monster steed with a fiery anus, flat out through the eye of a beer can and up your daughter's leg with no quarter asked and none given; show the squares some class, give em a whiff of those kicks they'll never know . . . Ah, these righteous dudes, they love to screw it on . . .

--Hunter S. Thompson, <u>Hell's Angels</u>
  (written at 318 Parnassus,
  San Francisco, September 1965)

TO MOON FAY NG:

*Just returned to San Francisco from a holiday train trek east, Thompson
lodged a polite request with his landlord, who would now also be his new
neighbor.*

January 11, 1965
318 Parnassus
San Francisco

Dear Mr. Moon Fay Ng—
　　I understand from Mr. Westbrook in 320 that you are planning to move
into 318A. If this is true, could I respectfully urge you to consider the possibility of laying down rugs in that apartment? The simple noise of a person walking comes through the floor like the pounding of a hammer
and—by reverse conduction—the noise of my electric typewriter is likely
to be extremely unsettling to anyone trying to sleep in the back two rooms
at night. We have had this problem before. It is a lack of insulation against
noise. Given the construction of the building there is no real cure for it,
but rugs between apartments are a big help.
　　My difficulty at the moment is that I am working desperately to finish
a book that was due before Christmas. It will take several more weeks but
will be finished before February 1. Due to my schedule I work all night,
every night at the typewriter—and I normally sleep during the day. My
young son also sleeps each afternoon, but last week when there was activity in 318A neither one of us could sleep. I'm sure you don't mean to be
noisy and I apologize for mentioning this subject, but from past experience I can say for sure that neither I nor anyone else could live in peace
in 318 unless something is done about the noise transmission problem.
For instance, it is now 10:00 a.m. on Tuesday and I have been up all night,
writing the book. This happens to be an unusual day and I won't try to
sleep until later, but if I tried to sleep now—as I normally do—it would
be impossible due to the noise upstairs. There is nothing unusual about
the noise. I am sure it is only normal—just as my typewriter is normal—

but in this building normal noise seems to travel a long way. It has all the makings of a very nervous situation that I would like to avoid, if possible. Since I moved here there have been two different families in 318A and I assure you the noise from upstairs was very severe in both cases. Just as it is now, in connection with your preparation for moving in. It is not so much a problem for Mr. Westbrook, because he works a normal 8-hour day and goes to bed early at night. But I recall when the Spanish-speaking family was in 318A Mr. Westbrook said he could not get any sleep on weekends.

Again let me say how sorry I am to have to mention this, but I think it is better for you to know. Even if I were to move out of the lower apartment you would have the same problem with the next tenant. The only unusual thing at the moment is my work schedule, which requires me to type all night for the next several weeks and try to sleep during the day. If I can be of any help in working out any solution, please let me know. Sincerely—

Hunter S. Thompson

TO EDITOR, *TRANSATLANTIC REVIEW:*

January 28, 1965
318 Parnassus
San Francisco

Editor
Transatlantic Review
33 Ennismore Garden
London SW7, England

Dear Sir:
I have been informed that you are holding a short story contest for writers under thirty. My entry, "Hit Him Again, Jack," is enclosed. I fully expect to win this contest and receive funds from you in the future. I am 27 years old and have published only one story, although I earn my living as a roving correspondent for the *National Observer* and am, as it were, a journalist of the first rank. I'm not sure just what you publish, besides stories, but if you think we can get together for any further business, by all means let me know. I am actively seeking new markets for both journalism and fiction. At present my situation is desperate; I urge you to be quick with the funds.

Sincerely,
Hunter S. Thompson

TO CAREY MCWILLIAMS, *THE NATION:*

Tired of writing for the National Observer *and* The Reporter, *Thompson began cultivating a working relationship with* The Nation.

January 29, 1965
318 Parnassus
San Francisco

Dear Mr. McWilliams:

After a long and rambling illness I am back in the tomb. Kentucky was a Wolfean nightmare and New York was a goatdance. I got there after you left for California, and left just before you got back. Which is probably just as well; after ten days in fifth gear I was not in any shape to seek assignments. Rather than hang around and see you, I fled, sparing you what surely would have been a shock. The only way I can handle New York is to live there; it is a disastrous place to visit.

And so much for that. I have a few ideas out here, none of which strike the sort of sparks I need right now, but I'm not sure whether that's the fault of the ideas or my money situation. I am long past the point of simple poverty, and well into a state of hysterical destitution. The wolves have eaten my door.

On the basis of my recent journey, the most obvious piece I see right now is a thing I'd call "Go East, Young Man, Go East." The final collapse of the myth of San Francisco. I've been toying with this for a few months, but this week's uproar over the threatened collapse of the Actor's Workshop has put the thing in a quick little package that I think would make a good piece. I'm sure you know about Irving and Blau going to the Lincoln Center. This would have been shocking enough by itself, but a lad named Jeremy Ets-Hokin (the old man of the San Francisco Arts Commission) has seized the occasion to mount another attack on the city's stagnant cultural scene, his second blast in as many months. None of what he's saying is new, but the odd thing about the affair is that even people like Herb Caen are finally admitting that San Francisco is losing its cultural guts.

My contention is that it never had any—not since 1945 at any rate, or maybe 1950, when New York finally established itself as the capital of the world. Since then, San Francisco's personality has gone from neurotic to paranoid to what now looks like the first stages of a catatonic fit. The simple fact of New York has brought San Francisco to its knees. There was also the shock of LA's new music center, which, coupled with the Lincoln Center raid, had the effect of lowering the boom on even the local myth-mongers. They had learned to live with the fact of New York, but the idea of a cultural challenge from LA was beyond the pale. Now Ets-Hokin says San Francisco is "on par with Salinas," which is not so bad a joke as it seems at a glance.

Anyway, all that merely gives me a peg to roll off on my own feelings about New York: the fact that it is no longer just the axis of American culture, but is rapidly becoming a refuge and even a culture of its own. The only consistent line of advice I got in New York concerned the necessity of my moving there at once. "No free-lance writer can make a living outside of New York," they said, and in some perverse way I was glad to hear it, because it seemed to explain the condition of poverty that I've cultivated for a year and a half in the boondocks, first in Colorado and then here.

The bulk of the piece would have to be based on my own experiences both here and in New York, with perhaps a slice of LA tossed in on the side. The finished product would promote a lively dialogue. I'm thinking it out as I go along, so the idea might seem a bit ragged in embryo, but I imagine the subject has crossed your mind more than once during your travels out here. Dick Elman[1] tells me you're an old California hand anyway, so I think you know pretty well what I'm after here. In a nut, I plan to finish a novel in San Francisco, then move back to New York, and I think my reasons might be interesting—not so much because they're mine, but for all the general wisdom they might contain.

I think, in fact, that I'll query to *Playboy*—for the money that might be in it—and see if they might want a piece along these lines. If so, I could do one for you, then use it as a guide for a longer, hairier piece for the college market. Just thinking here; bear with me.

Another possibility right now is [Governor] Pat Brown's new budget proposals, entailing stiff increases in just about every kind of state tax. Another tax plan, proposed by an Assemblyman named Petris, would bring about such vast reductions in property taxes—while boosting sales and other regressive-type levies—that it might be construed as another sign of California's drift toward the Right. But, as usual, there are enough inconsistencies in the thing to make any quick generalities impossible. For the moment, at least; the Petris plan was just announced this morning. Lumping them both together, however, the one generality that does emerge concerns the apparently widespread realization that California is coming to a new era, that the Boom is nearly over, and now the bills are coming in. The American Nightmare, as it were, the after-effects of free enterprise.

1. Richard Elman was a liberal writer who would later review Thompson's *Hell's Angels* for *The New Republic*.

But that's a pretty damn big piece and I'd rather wait a while on it, at least until the lines are drawn on some tangible issues. If it interests you in the future, let me know.

Another idea, less than ten minutes old; my wife just got back from her first night as a telephone solicitor for a famous dance studio. Her job is to find prospects for the lessons, but not negroes. She has her sales pitch, word for word on the wall in front of her, but the moment she suspects she's contacted a negro she has to back off, squelch the pitch and ad lib out of the contact. There are 12 women calling, four hours a night, and they each start with 100 names & phone numbers, but no idea of who's on the other end. No different from any other phone pitch, but here we have this racial thing to queer the routine and inject high social drama. Sally Snodgrass, fired from Kelly Girls for not wearing proper deodorant, drifts into part-time work as a dance studio solicitor. She has her instructions: SELL, but not to coons. She makes her first 30 calls, and no dice. By the 55th call she is desperate, fearing a night of failure, perhaps dismissal. Then, on the 61st call, a voice responds: "Yeah baby, tell me more. . . ." Her eyes light up, and she rambles into the spiel; her job is saved, she can sell. The man agrees to come down to the studio for an interview, but just then Sally tenses. A nigger in the woodpile, this man is a coon . . . or is he? How does a young girl know, how can she be sure? Will Sally make the sale and chance the ultimate disaster—a coon showing up at the studio—or will she somehow ascertain the pigment, then do her duty and queer her only sale?

Indeed. Tomorrow night my wife will find out exactly how she's supposed to know when a coon is on the line. Maybe they have some foolproof test, like GI sentries during the war (Nazis can't say W, coons can't say G, or is it R?). A good solicitor can ferret out the pigment in 10 seconds, they say, but the trouble is that any good solicitor won't be doing part-time work for that dance studio. What happens when a coon shows up? How do they handle him? Has it ever happened? Why not, for that matter, set it up? I could have my wife set up interviews for me and a negro together, then we'd get the action first-hand. How much would you pay for a thing like this? I like the idea. But you'll have to be quick because my wife won't last very long in this slot, probably not more than a week or so—let's say February 5. So be quick with the word if you think we should deal with this thing.

That's about it for now. This is a hell of a long letter. I started off to do a few paragraphs, but this is the first time in a while that I've done any queries for anyone but the *Observer* and I'm not used to being interested. Anyway, send word, and, again, sorry to have missed you in New York.

Sincerely,
Hunter S. Thompson

TO BILL GILES, *NATIONAL OBSERVER:*

This is the last letter-article Thompson wrote for the National Observer. *It was not published.*

> February 4, 1965
> 318 Parnassus
> San Francisco

Bill:

Here's the train job. See what you think and let me know. I'm not sure I understand why the other was "thin," or what could have been done to make it fat, but at any rate thanks for the quick reply.

Oh yeah, I have a nice scenic-type photo of the *City of San Francisco.* Let me know if you want it. Since my last letter I've found that it's possible for me to take incoming calls; the problem is that I can't make any. It's an interesting set-up, but I'd be happier if it were the other way around.

> HST

"Dr. Slow: Or, How I Learned to Save Money, Lose Weight, and Love the Airplane . . ."
Chicago, Ill.

This is as good a place as any to start the story, because this is where it started in my mind. Or maybe it was Scott Fitzgerald's mind. Or maybe Thomas Wolfe's. At any rate I arrived in Chicago on the verge of collapse, a victim of the railroad myth. I had seen America the hard way: 51 sleepless hours on the San Francisco Chief, pride of the Santa Fe Railroad. Two days and two nights in a speeding iron box, all for $67.39, plus another $30 or so for meals, drinks, magazines, tips, and pillow rental. By air, the price would have been $110.72, including a free meal. And a saving of 47 hours.

The longest flight I've ever endured was 12 hours, from Lima, Peru to New York City. But 12 hours on a train is nothing at all. I boarded in San Francisco at noon, and at midnight we were just getting out of California--with Arizona, New Mexico, Texas, Oklahoma, Missouri, and Illinois still to cross.

Only then did it dawn on me: Two days . . . and two nights . . . on this train. I adjusted the reclining seat, then realized I was nearly in the lap of the woman behind me. She whispered something to her husband and I quickly straightened up.

By midnight I had read an entire novel and two magazines, spent half the afternoon in the club car, sat in the crowded vistas dome and tried to write, lingered over a $3.50 fish dinner that would have cost $1.10 in any roadside hash house, and now, as the barren desert flashed past outside my dark window, there was nothing to do but stare and pray for sleep.

We left California at a little town called Needles, an arid outpost in the Mojave Desert that enjoys a certain fame each summer for consistently being the hottest place in the continental United States. But Needles is reasonably cool in the winter, and from a train window it looks half pleasant. Behind the white adobe railroad station is a garish city hall that looks like leftover scenery from a Tennessee Williams play. I would not have been surprised to hear the few people on the platform speaking Spanish, instead of English.

Beyond Needles the night was more empty and the train seemed to pick up speed. The lights were turned off in the coach cars and some people slept. In the seat to my left a very old man kept sliding over until his head touched my shoulder, then he would come awake with a jerk and slide the other way. Perhaps a midget could sleep comfortably in a railroad seat, but for anyone over six feet it is sheer misery. By two in the morning most people had dropped off from exhaustion, but all round me in the heated darkness of the car I could hear the shifting and grumbling of the reluctant nightwatch.

Now and then would come the rasp of a match, a sudden glow on the metal roof, then darkness again and the long hiss of smoke being exhaled by some cramped traveler who'd simply given up and decided to get through the night on cigarettes. The club car had

long since closed, and anyone who might have dozed
off with the help of a nightcap was out of luck.

Somewhere around 3 a.m. a torrent of coughing cries
erupted from a baby near the front of the car, shat-
tering the silence like breaking glass. First came
the crying, then the mother's angry hissing. You
could almost hear the tension as more and more people
came awake.

It was dawn when the train rolled into Flagstaff
and I must have slept, because the next sound I heard
was the howl of the "news agent," an all-purpose merchant who hawks his wares in every corner of the
train, 18 hours a day. He is a human vending machine:
selling coffee and donuts for breakfast, canned
"Cokes" and candy bars for lunch, and dry ham or
bologna sandwiches for dinner. When I woke up he was
pushing "special, high-quality Santa Fe playing
cards," which he held aloft as he moved down the aisle.

"Souvenirs for you and your family too," he shouted.
I fled to the dining car for breakfast, wondering if
my nerves would hold up until we got to Chicago--33
more hours.

Before leaving San Francisco I had re-read <u>The
Great Gatsby,</u> so I knew what to expect at the other
end of the line. Fitzgerald had his narrator, Nick
Carraway, describe it like this:

"One of my most vivid memories is coming back from
the West from prep school and later from college at
Christmas time. Those who went further than Chicago
would gather in the old dim Union Station at six
o'clock on a cold December evening, with a few Chicago
friends, already caught up in their own holiday gai-
eties, to bid them a hasty goodbye. I remember the fur
coats of the girls returning from Miss This-or-That
and the chatter of frozen breath and the hands waving overhead as we caught sight of old acquaintances, and the matching of invitations: 'Are you
going to the Ordways? or Schultzes?' and the long
green tickets clasped tight in our gloved hands. At
last, the murky yellow cars of the Chicago, Milwaukee
& St. Paul railroad, looking cheerful as Christmas
itself on the tracks beside the gate."

Well, gentlemen, it's not like that anymore. Fitzgerald's people are all at the airport these days, and the bulk of the crowd at any railroad station will be made up of senior citizens, children, ne- groes, and servicemen. Not many jet set types; not much expensive luggage, either.

Yet the difference is not all monetary. A one-way coach ticket between San Francisco and Chicago is rel- atively cheap, but a bedroom in a Pullman car for the same trip costs $131.46 on the Santa Fe, and roughly the same on any line. Meals and other extras will bring that up to $150, minimum, which is quite a bit more than air fare. And, not surprisingly, most of the people who can afford the time and money it takes to travel by Pullman are well along in years. Train travel, in the main, is the province of the aged and the indigent, but there are a handful of exceptions. One of these is the City of San Francisco, which runs between Chicago and the Coast across the Continental Divide by way of Denver. The City, as it's called in the Rockies, is one of the few trains that occasionally lives up to Wolfe's and Fitzgerald's romantic but long out-dated railroad myth. This is especially true in the winter, when the train is full of young skiers, bound for resorts like Vail and Aspen in Colorado, Alta in Utah, and Sun Valley in Idaho, which are hard to reach by air. The City is my favorite train, and some of the evenings I've spent on it would have pleased Jay Gatsby himself.

But the City is a rare exception in the run-down, worn-out world of space age railroading, and despite its various advantages it's still a train. No doubt there are several good reasons for crossing the coun- try by rail, instead of by plane, but once you've done it a few times, that's it, you've done it, and the next step is to admit that airplanes have as many basic ad- vantages over trains as television has over radio. For good or ill, the space age is very much with us, and if Wolfe and Fitzgerald were alive today they'd surely be traveling by jet.

The America you see from a train window is an older, greyer, junkier land than the one you see from planes or superhighways. There was a time when land beside the railroad tracks was very valuable; railroad depots were centers of travel and many a town grew up around them. But the automobile changed that pattern; since World War II most towns have done their growing around major highways and intersections, while areas around railroad depots filled up with slums, warehouses, heavy industry, honky-tonk bars, and sleazy hotels. The cumulative effect of all this, after 51 hours at a train window, is a feeling of age and depression.

The man who flies sees new airports, sleek jets, fashionably dressed passengers and late-model "rent-a-cars" or taxi cabs. The man who drives turnpikes and freeways sees a bright, colorful and prosperous-looking America; a land of glass, leather, Formica, and pre-stressed concrete, where even hamburger stands are chic and modern.

The man who rides trains sees a part of America that has out-lived its usefulness: abandoned homes, automobile junkyards, and quonset huts housing marginal "industries" like Frank's Welding Shop, somewhere beside the tracks near Fresno in California's green Central Valley. America seen from a train window might be fascinating to a sociologist, but to the normal run of passengers it is not real inspiring.

To Wolfe a train meant excitement, distance and escape. To Fitzgerald it was more a melancholy thing, a glamour tinged with sadness--like Jay Gatsby, standing on the platform of a train leaving Louisville and the shattered hopes of his love for Daisy: "He stretched out his hand desperately, as if to snatch only a wisp of air, to save a fragment of the spot that she had made lovely for him."

You could do that sort of thing in 1925, but if Gatsby left Louisville by train today, and went out to "snatch a wisp of air," he'd be jolted out of his reverie by the snarl of a porter or a prowling conductor: "Hey you! Get back inside! That's against the rules."

Once you get on a train today you are not only on it but _in_ it. The windows don't open, there are no outside platforms to stand on, and anybody brazen enough to open the top half of the Dutch doors between cars is likely to be put off at the next stop.

Train crews are not to be trifled with, especially conductors. I recall an evening in Texas on this last trip when a gentleman of quick temper took exception--and rightfully so, I thought--to the way he'd been snapped at by a crotchety conductor. It was somewhere around midnight when he moved to demand an apology, and not long afterward I looked out the window and saw him standing on the platform as the train pulled out of a dark little hamlet called White Deer. I still have his sunglasses, which he left on the club car table.

Despite the hazards of time, tedium and the benevolent tyranny of railroad crews, train travel still has a devoted following. When I finally got to Louisville an old and well-traveled cousin congratulated me on having the wisdom to travel by rail, instead of air.

"I took a plane once," she told me. "It was from Sydney, Australia to San Francisco. I wanted to see Sydney Harbor from the air because I heard it was one of the three most beautiful harbors in the world. But when we got up in the air the plane banked the wrong way and I couldn't see anything but sky," she chuckled sadly. "I never did see Sydney Harbor, and after that I never took another plane. I like to _see_ when I travel; I want to know where I've been."

Well, maybe so. But once you've ridden trains for five years over the same routes you begin to lose that sensitivity. A small-town railroad crossing in Mansfield, Pennsylvania looks very much like one in Shattuck, Oklahoma--especially when the train windows are covered with a thin layer of dust and soot. You can appreciate just so many late-night depot platforms, with steam in the air and baggage carts rolling back and forth while men in grey jackets move silently along the tracks with their cigarettes

glowing in the darkness. The depots are ancient and
the schedules are chalked on old blackboards lit by
yellow bulbs.

Perhaps there's a touch of glamour in it all, but
there's also a sense of something dead or dying. One
of the most obvious realities of train travel is the
advanced age of conductors, porters and even ticket
agents. Some of the long-haul Western lines have new
cars and equipment, but compared with planes even
this seems sorely out of date. And most of the branch
lines--such as the rail link between Chicago and
Louisville--are using cars that would have seemed
old and moldy even to Thomas Wolfe. In all, it is hard
to avoid the impression that the railroads have given
up on passenger service--or at least given up in any
sense of competing with the airlines--and are now
merely hanging on, doing their duties with a shrug
instead of a smile, until the inevitable progress in
other forms of transportation renders them totally
obsolete.

Not long ago, in San Francisco, I talked to a man
who had just come back from Los Angeles. "I wasn't
pressed for time," he said, "so I thought I'd take a
train and see what it was like." He shook his head
sadly. "I wasn't surprised when the agent said it
would take 12 hours, but when she told me the ticket
cost $33 I nearly flipped. Hell, I paid $12 for a plane
ticket and got here in 45 minutes."

Comparisons like that are hard to argue with. It's
not so bad that trains should be slow; people expect
that. But when they are also dull, uncomfortable,
and expensive, with bad food and worse service, to
boot--then it is pretty hard to find reason to keep
riding on them, except perhaps as a novelty or a nostalgic gesture to a myth that out-lived its creators.

TO PAUL SEMONIN:

*Thompson filled Semonin in on his trip to Louisville and New York while is-
suing pointed barbs about his commitment to the struggle for racial equality.
Semonin had gone to Paris on a Ford Foundation grant to research Fanon.*

February 5, 1965
318 Parnassus
San Francisco

Well, Bobo, your last letter had some music in it and I've been meaning to bounce some back for about 10 days, but so far—and even now—the desperate rush for money has kept me away from anything personal. (There is wisdom in that line.) The first thing you should learn in Paris is to discount any propaganda you get from Marin County. That is like somebody from Greenwich telling you New York is "great, man, just great." You ask me for the word on San Francisco and I can only give you mine, which is "*nada.*" This is what I meant in an earlier letter when I said we should have paid more attention to the things we sensed earlier, and less to what we've learned since we got wise. (Yeah, I know—you have the handle now, but the most truthful and human of your letters are the ones in which you sound like you did a few years ago; I think all you've found in your travels is historical justification for your instincts.)

Anyway, I just got back from New York about a week ago and found your latest along with one from Hudson ("Southwind," Royal Suva Yacht Club, Suva, Fiji). He's money-whipped but still trying to get around the world on his boat. It was me that called from New York, but not from McGarr's office. I was abandoned in a strange apartment and found a phone; I'd have kept after you but a maid came in and I felt a bit awkward giving the operator such obviously expensive instructions. It was a pretty strange situation anyway, so I finally gave up. Sorry. They said you came in only now and then, but that Lee [Berry] would be back in an hour and would I like them to call me when he arrived? I said no.

McGarr got pretty jittery about me using his phone; pretty jittery period, for that matter, but I can't say that I blamed him. I'm a bad enough guest on my own, but with Juan and Sandy in tow it was a bit like the Snopes family who came to dinner. Eleanor got a bit edgy, but McGarr bore up heroically under the strain—and since Eleanor gave birth (a girl) 10 days after we left I suppose her edginess was heroic in its containment. I was there about 10 days, but Sandy stayed nearly 3 weeks. Luckily McGarr's affluence was a cushion of sorts: he is, you know, living high on the hawg.

I'm now rereading your account of nights in Paris and I'm struck again by your apparent assumption that you have somehow crossed the color line. Have you done something to yourself? Why are you the only white man that all your negro friends will tolerate? You say, "They (the whites) mix with the negroes about like oil and water." I'm not trying to pull any white jingo stuff on you here, but I'm curious. I wonder if you're really as hip as you seem to think you are, or just deluded. In other words, are you

just another one of these nigger-loving liberals, or have you found that secret bridge that Mailer keeps looking for?

Your comments on "the whore cock of life" (eh?) are interesting too. I
believe that's what I talked about several letters ago, advising you to wait
until you've taken a few long thrusts before you lay down laws for the general populace. And since we're down on this Freudian kick, it's also interesting that you'd identify the cock with pain and evil. Mailer called it "the
avenger of my crotch." Is there something in this?

Your talk on Paris strikes a chord of some kind; in Louisville I listened
to Minnish[2] tell me why I should go to Spain and/or Mallorca, but for
some reason it didn't interest me. Now, with your comments, I understand
more of what I half-understood then, and vaguely suspected three years
ago: that Europe is no longer a valid haven from the malady.

As for the action-centers, my last spurt in New York convinced me that
nothing else compares with Manhattan right now. California is just beginning a period of honest ferment, but I don't believe I can stand to sit here
five years and wait for something to happen. In a lot of ways this is the most
reactionary state in the union. This is the dead end of America and the
next five years will prove it. But I'd say the tories have the muscle right now
and will have for at least 2 more years, then the balance will begin to shift
and we'll see a series of head-on collisions. Prop. 14[3] was just the beginning. Ronald Reagan is the prototype of the new mythological American,
a grinning whore who will probably someday be President. Once California fills up with people like the rest of our country, it will have the same
tragic and paradoxical dilemmas. Right now it is heaven for the negro and
the Bircher alike, but only because there is still some space out here. Colorado is the next California, and after that I suppose it will be Montana
and then Canada. If you mistake the current action for a simple racial conflict you are missing the biggest point: we are simply running out of room.

But I don't want to get into that area right now. There isn't enough time
and these big-talk long-distance debates are pretty futile anyway. [. . .] I
have come to grips with the main question in this country: "How holy is
the system?" And I say not holy enough. This kept popping up in New
York, especially with the humanist conservatives that most people call liberals. They have too much reverence for the social structure; it is like a
civil rights rally at an Athenaeum meeting. I realize I don't sound exactly
like I did this time last year and I suppose your letters have something to
do with it. The very incoherence of your convictions made me curious as

2. Tad Minnish was a Louisville friend Thompson kept in touch with.
3. California's Proposition 14, passed in November 1964, overturned the Rumford Fair Housing
Act, which had prohibited discrimination on the basis of race or national origin by property owners. Proposition 14 was declared unconstitutional two years after its passage.

to what you were dealing with. Now I find it's not necessary for me to read Marx because I already agree with him (re: your Prometheus quote). What interests me about him is not what he thought but how he managed to get so many people to agree with him. Maybe he just talked a little closer to man's best instincts. I don't know, but that would be the basis on which I'd compare him to Jefferson. The truth is really pretty simple; it's the mechanics of making it work that breaks men down (that's copyrighted).

Now I am going down to the integrated donut shop for some late coffee and furtive scribbling. It is raining here. I'd like to go into the "New York vs. the Coast" business a little further, but there ain't enough time right now. When are you coming back? Your idea of starting a paper sounds good if you have enough CASH to carry it for a while. Maybe a long while. Everybody and his bedbuddy are starting papers and little magazines these days and most of them are rotten. I saw [Porter] Bibb in New York; he could handle the business end for you. He's back for the duration. Cooke is marking time. McGarr is up to something that I can't quite figure out. I stopped in Aspen & saw Harcourt[4] & he asked me how to join SNCC.[5] I told him to write you.

Hunter

TO CHARLES KURALT:

Charles Kuralt of CBS News had been one of Thompson's drinking buddies in Rio when they both lived there in 1962 and '63.

March 1, 1965
San Francisco

Dear Charley:

If you ever get the feeling that you've lost touch with everyday John Doe reality, go out and do what I did today. Look for a job. Not a TV slot or anything where you already have leverage, but just any job that several thousand people in the immediate vicinity can do just as well as you can. It is a truly humbling experience. I haven't done it in five years, and then only for a few months in New York, which is different. But jesus! I didn't realize until today why so many people re-enlist in the army. I also used to think "dehumanizing" was a New York liberal cliché. My treatment at the hands of various clerks and receptionists reminded me of the old Nazi theory about giving little people just enough power to let them feel big. [. . .]

---

4. Harcourt Kemp, a Louisville friend.
5. The Student Nonviolent Coordinating Committee, formed in 1960 to battle segregation through direct action.

My situation today was like that of a man whose job has been croaked forever by automation. Assuming that was his only real skill, he can't compete in any other job market—so he gets in line for whatever comes up for grabs. Down in the ditch, scrambling for the high ground, elbows churning. This may be a white cousin of the Harlem syndrome: degradation leading to frustration leading to violence. If so, rape and mugging will soon be passé. The new thing will be senseless violence, an outburst of supposedly normal people running amok in the streets with tire irons and butcher knives. At the end of the afternoon I came home and kicked the dog. And that was only one day.

I see that my unnerved state has prevented me from fully explaining what I undertook today. Not much, really. Very simple: I offered myself on the labor market, claiming experience in just about everything but journalism. And I suppose that 20 or so days of the same brutal seeking might lead to employment of some kind, but at the end of 20 days I'd be reduced to jelly. You ought to try it sometime, especially if you ever hear yourself deploring the public's taste for escapist entertainment. If what I got today was a valid taste of the workaday world I can easily understand why the poor bastards who never get out of it don't want documentaries on Vietnam or "problem dramas" when they get home at night.

Anyway, I gave up. Or maybe not, but if I try again it will have to be something physical. Right now I'm hustling on a short story that should sell, interrupting the novel I've been wrestling with ever since you left. I'm writing somewhat desperately of late, but fiction doesn't depress me like journalism. It's harder, but much more human work.

Needless to say, your loan was a godsend. After you mentioned it the first time I gave it some thought and decided to ask you for fifty to get the landlord off my back. The one-ten sounded like a fortune—for about 12 hours. But it did in fact get the landlord and PR&E [electric company] off my back. At times I think I've drifted all the way past communism, to a stance of violent anarchy. I have a definite suspicion that most minds in this country's power structure view the poor as Mistah Kurtz, in "Heart of Darkness," viewed the Congo natives: "Exterminate the brutes!" Which would not bother me so much were it not that I'm one of the poor. In this light I can see [Lee Harvey] Oswald's act as a massive achievement, a sort of ultimate retaliation. Warped reasoning, no doubt, but in Oswald's mind it must have seemed beautiful. You don't just belt a fat-face clerk at some employment agency or write letters to the editor or march on some violent picket line, but flip completely out of the framework of conventional protest and go for the holy jugular. Aside from being a fantastic shot, the man had a hell of an imagination. What will they do with the money he accumulated in his social security account?

Another story I want to work on ASAP concerns the reaction of the press corps to the president's decision to grow a beard. First a rumor, then a planned leak by desperate staffers, and finally a nightmarish appearance before a joint session of Congress. But no mention of the beard, no explanation, no official comment. How does it strike you? Could I sell it to Friendly?[6] Would Eric Sevareid buy it?

This is the sort of thing that doomed me with the *Observer*. Anyway, let me know if you think a TV version has possibilities. We could do it like the Orson Welles Martian thing—pull it off as a newscast, follow it day by day, interviews with Cabinet men and pundits. The meaning of it, sir? Is the president quite mad? How to prepare the public for it?

Well, I see I sound a bit drunk here, but I'm not. I think it's the shock of coming in contact with the job market after a long absence. God help us when this Beatle generation begins to feel the screws tightening on them; that will be the time to move to Montana for real. Anyway, a definite hello to Petey[7] and thanks again for the night on the town. As I said, it was particularly good for Sandy because she rarely gets out and she misses the action. Send a line when you have time, and a card ahead when you get out this way again. *Ate Logo*—

Hunter

TO LYNDON JOHNSON:

Morally outraged at President Johnson's policy on escalation in Vietnam, Thompson withdrew his offer to serve his administration as governor of American Samoa. The condemnation would prove prophetic.

March 11, 1965
318 Parnassus
San Francisco

Lyndon Johnson
White House
Washington, D.C.

Dear Mr. Johnson:

This is to inform you that I have reconsidered my application for the governorship of American Samoa and wish to void it at once. After watching your foreign policy develop over the course of the past few months I've decided I could not, in good conscience, serve your administration in

6. Fred Friendly, then executive producer of CBS News.
7. Kuralt's wife.

any way. Nor would I feel physically safe representing this nation outside our own borders.

I refer specifically to your hysterical Vietnam policy, which has put the United States in a position very much resembling Nazi Germany's in the Spanish Civil War. I am neither a pacifist nor an advocate of non-violence, but my sensibilities are grossly offended by the spectacle of a small group of old men whose mania for blood and bombing will inevitably cause thousands of young men to be killed for no good reason.

As a white Anglo-Saxon Air Force veteran and shooting enthusiast I can't be shrugged off as a politically impotent East Coast minority-group liberal beatnik draft-dodger. Nor am I totally ignorant of foreign affairs. In 1962–63 I was South American correspondent for the *National Observer* and spent more time defending this country in arguments than I did earning a living. God knows, I would hate to be down there now, trying to explain and/or justify our Vietnam policy.

It is also a fact that I actively supported John Kennedy in 1960 and you in 1964—but in your case I've been badly disappointed. The specific actions of the U.S. in Vietnam are not nearly so ugly as their implications. Where do you mean to bomb next? Will you send Marines to the Congo if that flares up again? Do you mean to police the entire world? Are you getting your foreign policy advice from Goldwater and Nixon? Is it true, as I've read and heard, that your real intention is to provoke Red China into action over Vietnam and then bomb the Chinese nuclear sites?

If so, count me out. If you get this country into a war I have no intention of being pressed into military service, regardless of the consequences. Beyond that, I can only wish you the worst of luck in 1968.

In closing, I suppose I should offer a solution—if only so I can't be labeled a frustrated nay-sayer with no alternative to what I oppose. OK. We should get the hell out of Vietnam and not apologize for it to anybody. We have no business there in the first place and certainly no business spending several million dollars a day in order to stay there. We cannot possibly prevail in Asia, any more than Hitler could prevail in Europe. And that money could be damn well spent here in the U.S., as I'm sure you know.

So, let's simply quit. Call a spade a spade and admit that we overextended ourselves. And stop trying to peddle this balderdash about the menace of Red China. They're not going to bomb or invade us. Russia hasn't, and they've had nuclear weapons for nearly twenty years. And I don't think I need to explain why.

Anyway, those are my ideas. You didn't ask for them, but then I didn't ask for yours either in 1960. If Kennedy had lived I believe he would have us on the way out of Vietnam by now, while you have us sunk to the eyeballs. So it's your war and I leave you to handle it without my help. You can't win it without eventually killing us all, and—unless you start acting like a thinking human instead of a senile political beast—you are going to end up the goat, with a belly-full of blame for your own mistakes as well as other people's.

Sincerely,
Hunter S. Thompson

TO CAREY MCWILLIAMS, *THE NATION:*

The turning point in Thompson's career came when McWilliams gave him the idea to write about the Hell's Angels for The Nation.

March 18, 1965
318 Parnassus
San Francisco

Dear Mr. McWilliams:

Your cycle idea came this morning & was a pleasant surprise. I'd just as soon not explain why. No reflection on you or *The Nation*, but on the press in general. I'm surprised anybody in an editorial slot would be interested in a long look at this action.

I got the report this afternoon and talked a bit with the boys in the Attorney General's office. None of them has ever made contact with the cycle boys: the report is a compilation of query-answers from various California police chiefs. I could give you—or the *Observer*—a synopsis of the report, I guess, but I'd rather not fool around with that kind of journalism: "247 police chiefs condemn motorcycle gangs, etc." So what? Police chiefs will condemn anything that makes noise. Which is not to say these cycle boys aren't mean and dangerous beyond anything that ever got paroled in the name of high spirits.

Anyway, I like the idea and will do the piece for you or somebody else. It's one I've been following, but with no idea of getting an article out of it. You may or may not know that the Hell's Angels honchos have appealed to the ACLU [American Civil Liberties Union] for support. Tomorrow or the next day I'll try to see some of the cycle people; I can't imagine doing a story without their point of view. *Newsweek* is ahead of us on this one and I hope they don't queer it for any other journalist. I'd hate to be drinking with those boys when one of them showed up with a vicious & double-crossing article by the *Newsweek* man. [...] To my mind, the Hell's Angels are a very natural product of our society. Just like SNCC or the Peace Corps or the permanent unemployed. But different people. That's what I'd like to find out: who are they? What kind of man becomes a Hell's Angel? And why? And how? The mechanics.

I figure on a week's work on this and certainly some expenses, which I'm not sure you'd be willing to meet. Since I've already decided to do the piece, I'd like to know roughly what you might pay for it and what kind of expenses you'd bear. I'm not bargaining, just asking for figures. Given a break or two in the way of contacts this one is right up my alley. As of now it looks good.

The new Berkeley story is not so much a peg as a confirmation. How do you read it? I wouldn't mind getting into that one now. On Saturday I'm going up to the CDC [California Democratic Council] bash in Sacramento, for good or ill. And FYI. OK for now, & thanks for the idea.

Sincerely,
Hunter S. Thompson

TO CHARLES KURALT:

Researching the Hell's Angels had inherent dangers.

March 26, 1965
318 Parnassus
San Francisco

Dear Charley:

It's been a wild day here. At 6:30 this morning I finally rooted the last Hell's Angel out of my living room and went to bed, just as Sandy was getting up to do her four-hour stint at the real estate office. I'm doing a piece on motorcycle gangs for *The Nation*—no money but plenty of kicks. Before I let them into the house last night I explained that I didn't go much for fist-fighting, but preferred to settle my beefs with a double-barreled 12-gauge shotgun. They seemed to grasp this concept and we got along fine; Sandy's hysteria abated, I was a gallon of wine and a case of beer poorer, but in the end I think I got the makings of about five fine stories.

That's what prompts me to write you tonight. I've done many more hours of research on this than any *Nation* article (at $100) deserves and right now I'm wondering what to do with the rest of it. As you know, I guess, both *Time* & *Newsweek* did pieces on it this week, but mainly arms-length bullshit, despite the *Newsweek* claim that their man submerged himself in the action. About half those quotes came out of *Chronicle* clips: a very funny and colorful series done by my old friend George Draper and my new friend Birney Jarvis.[8] He just left. It's midnight here and we're going

---

8. Draper and Jarvis both worked for the *San Francisco Chronicle*. Jarvis—who appears as "Preetam Bobo" in *Hell's Angels*—introduced Thompson to the biker gang.

sailing with him tomorrow. He's a *Chronicle* police reporter, who lives in Sausalito on a 40-foot sloop and is quitting soon to head for the Caribbean. He's also an ex–vice president and lifetime member of the Hell's Angels. A golden contact, as it were: he put me in touch with the Angels and last night I boomed in on one of their meetings at the DePau Hotel bar, near Hunter's Point. Very tense. Who is this big cat? A fucking reporter! Beat his ass! etc. I made a beautiful speech, awash in five hours of beer, to the effect that I was there to do them the ultimate favor of telling the American people the truth about them; I had come out at midnight to this filthy neighborhood, unarmed, and busted into their meeting in my Montana sheepherder's jacket, for no other reason than to bring their own weird truth to the attention of an American public so long conned by *Time* & *Newsweek*—whose articles I presented as horrifying evidence of what happens when a lazy, ignorant, cliché-laden reporter does an article on rough and ready types like "you guys."

I was dead serious, and after a bad half-hour they came around. Their normal action, of course, is to steer way clear of any news media, or else confront any news type with their drunk-nazi, enemy-of-the-people act. The simple fact that I brought them back to the apartment—five, out of some thirty at the meeting—should be enough to tell you they're human and, in fact, peculiarly decent when they're off guard and relaxed. Even so, I'd like to know what my neighbors thought when they looked out their windows and saw those Hell's Angels jackets filing into my apartment.

Anyway, why don't you do a special on it? I can guarantee you a cut-off-from-everybody-else contact situation, plus all my research and prior knowledge. As far as I know I'm the only person in the world right now who could assemble Frenchy, Filthy Phil, Puff, Okie Ray, Crazy Rock, and some twenty others for a filming situation. Believe me, that meeting last night would have knocked your eyes and ears off. It made that Indian thing[9] seem like a Rotary meeting; this is great stuff for film and my words can't touch what it really looks and feels like to be in the midst of it.

Two guys I know on *The Wall Street Journal* are trying to do a piece for *True* on this thing, but they can't get anywhere near the action. Twice in the past week I was inside situations that they tried to crash and got turned away from. Until yesterday Jarvis was the only guy who could talk to the Hell's Angels on anything like human & realistic terms. Today, it's me, too. When my article comes out I may be stomped—I promised to send them a few copies—so if you want to do a film story on this action it will have to be fast. Contacts like these last only until you say the wrong thing. As it

9. The Native American equal rights rally in Oregon Thompson had covered for the *National Observer*.

happens, my speech last night created a situation wherein I'm the hero-translator. Anybody with a camera would be more difficult to put across because a lot of these guys are running from the cops, but of the five mentioned above, only Okie Ray is currently wanted. He's a burglar; a wild-looking guy, with long blond hair, a fine Edwardian mustache and a gold earring in one ear. Filthy Phil weighs 300 pounds and could not be allowed near a sound camera. The odd thing is that these guys are like wild children, extremely volatile, genuinely dangerous in a wrong situation, but very open, curious and even moral when they figure they're talking to a straight person. You should have heard Frenchy last night when I played a Bob Dylan record for him. That's the angle I'm working for *The Nation* and it could also be a good film thing. [. . .]

I happen to know these guys are busted (the club treasury) because the current sec-treasurer has blown all the funds, so they'd be tremendously amenable to any small but not too small (say, $200, more or less) contribution to the treasury; they're in deep hock to their bondsman and none of them has much money. It would take two days of talk & argument to convince them to cooperate on a film bit, but the natural ham in them would inevitably prevail over their eminently justifiable fear of press and publicity. They've been stung every time they've cooperated. I've assured them my *Nation* piece will be an exception; I haven't written it yet and can only hope it will be. If not, I might find myself dealing with them *en masse* some night—but as long as I have the 12-gauge here I don't worry. With that long hallway, I'm just about invulnerable.

Enclosed is the *Newsweek* clip, FYI. Also, for no particular reason, is a copy of something I just finished writing in an odd, off moment. Send it back whenever you can.

In all this I wouldn't want to give you the impression that Hell's Angels in general aren't a badass ugly bunch to deal with. The gimmick here is that they can be reached, but probably not for long. It could be a damn good TV special—half-hour or even an hour if we could go with them on a run. I'm an old cycle hand myself, so you could ride with me if it came to that. We could rent a cycle. A big one, and run the bastards into the ground. Burn 'em out. Dazzle 'em with the Rio spinout.

OK, do me the quick favor of saying how this looks to you. I wouldn't be writing this many pages if I wasn't sure it was a good thing for us all. I figure the least [Fred] Friendly can do is hire me as a consultant at $300 a day, which seems a fair price for the risks I took last night. If I had lost control of that thing for an instant the result might have been Sandy raped, me badly beaten and the apartment destroyed. Because of all this I was in an extremely high, hypersensitive condition all afternoon—which I spent with them at a garage—and all night, at the DePau bar, which they commandeered for their meeting, and then here at the apartment. When it was all over I had a wild, exhilarated feeling that still prevails. I feel like a badass. With a shotgun, and that's a big factor. They can't top my act. (One of these days I'll speak with Gene Burdick about this; he drives an XKE and says guns are a sick sublimation.)

Oh yeah, *Pageant* finally wrote to say that they were buying that L.A. piece you read, for $350, and the editor is said to be overwhelmed by my "research" zeal. I could easily sell them a cycle gang piece, but for the moment I want to try it on other, fatter markets. This is too good a story to shrug off on *Pageant* for $350 or $400. *Esquire* is a possibility, I think, and maybe the [*Saturday Evening*] *Post*.

And that's that. I have to get out on the Bay in three hours and right now it's raining like hell. Hello to Petey and send word when I can watch for your Conservation thing. It wasn't listed here on either the 22nd or 23rd. I guess this *Gemini* bullshit pushed everything else out of the way. The worst thing about TV news is that it tends to be narrow-minded, stampeded to the obvious, the Big Story, while the meat of reality goes ignored. I've lost interest in the evening TV news because it's so goddamn dull and narrow, like reading *Pravda* must be, all three networks saying the same predictable things about the same few stories. I know you have a penchant for the other stuff and that's why I thought of you on this Hell's Angels thing. This could be a hell of a weird documentary. Let me know how it strikes you. Christ, I haven't written a five-page letter in years. I must be boiling over. Send word.

Sincerely,
Hunter S. Thompson

Thompson revealed his journalistic technique for striking a "balance of terror" with the Hell's Angels.

March 27, 1965
San Francisco

Cliff:

Assume you've seen current *Time & Newsweek*, re: Hell's Angels, Calif. outlaw motorcycle club; rape, violence, etc. Carey McWilliams at *The Nation* asked me to do a behind-the-scenes kind of piece on that action and I consequently went out of my head and invested six—no, seven days' worth of research in it. Last night I busted into a H.A. meeting at the

DePau Hotel bar near the waterfront and survived the ejection sentiment by dint of my size, reckless half-drunk attitude and a beautifully wasted speech on the function of the outlaw press. Me. I showed them the *Time & Newsweek* articles, then told them I was there to get the real picture. I also said I was going to write the story anyway, so they might as well co-operate. A concept they finally grasped, but not until we had some bad and hairy moments.

Whatever I write for *The Nation* will consume a small part of my "research"—like, I had five Hell's Angels here in the apartment until 6:30 this morning—and it strikes me you might want a first-person bit on the same subject. You know, "Me and the Hell's Angels," or "A Tough Night at the DePau Hotel." Yeah, that sort of thing. I'm doing a sociology-type piece for *The Nation*. I know you don't dig my sociology, but it occurred to me you might like some of the other, color-action humor sort of thing. I dare say I'm the only reporter in the history of the world who ever got wound up in a story to the point of going to a Hell's Angels meeting and then taking five of them home for a drinking bout. After all this rape/beating publicity, you can imagine how Sandy felt when we showed up; she was quietly hysterical for five hours. Before I let them in, I explained that I wasn't in the habit of settling my beefs with my fists, but with a double-barreled 12-gauge shotgun. Which was obvious to them upon entry. This seemed to strike a balance of terror that eventually dissolved into a very pleasant evening. These guys are the ultimate rejects from our half-born Great Society; they aren't half as mean and rough as they seem to be. They can be vicious as hell at times, but last night they struck me—after we leveled out—as a fairly straight bunch with very primitive concepts and honestly puzzled about whatever it is that makes them a source of trouble wherever they go. Like Goldwater, as it were, with all that energy and no socially acceptable place to put it.

Don't take this as an apologia because for the past week I've spent enough time with these guys to know how bad and ugly they can be, and have been. In addition, my original contact on the story is a former Hell's Angel who is now a *Chronicle* police reporter. In about three hours we are going sailing with him on the bay; he lives on a boat in Sausalito. I say this only to show you the scope, depth, and irregularity of my sources on this thing. Without this guy I would never have come close to actually talking with these people.

Anyway, I'm doing a piece for *The Nation*. I don't know if you figure them to be competition in the realm of circulation, but I thought it would be worth a query—especially since I've been working on this stuff in lieu of the Wino piece for the past week. If any angle on this story interests you, send a quick line before I lose interest and re-focus to something else. It's a good story, with three or four possible pegs and approaches. No photos, however; my camera is hocked.

Send word, ASAP.

Sincerely,
HST

TO CAREY MCWILLIAMS, *THE NATION:*

The article Thompson sent with this note would become the centerpiece of his first book, Hell's Angels.

April 9, 1965
318 Parnassus
San Francisco

Dear Mr. McWilliams:

Your gram arrived this afternoon and spared me the awful toil of another rewrite. This thing is pretty well out of control as it is, and doing more work would probably have caused me to destroy the manuscript altogether and cease communicating with you.

As it stands, I can only hope it makes sense. It is probably too long, but my main feeling is that too much has been left out. A one hundred page piece would have been much easier. This one is pocked with a number of footnotes, FYI as much as for publication.

As for sources for my seemingly authoritative but frequently unsupported remarks, I depended almost entirely for general (true) background on one Birney Jarvis, a charter member of the Frisco Hell's Angels and now a police reporter on the *Chronicle.* It was his briefing that enabled me to fend off bullshit from the Angels on one hand, and the police on the other. As far as I know, I am the only journalist besides Jarvis whom the Angels have ever dealt with on a friendly social basis. Jarvis wasn't with me when I went to the meeting and subsequently had five of the wildest ones over to the apartment for a drink-out. He did, in fact, advise me against putting myself in such vulnerable positions with people he knew to be mean drinkers, sunday-punchers and chain-whippers.

I say all this only to emphasize my efforts to find out what this thing really is, and to support any statements of mine that might seem wild or presumptuous. I trust, of course, that what I've written is as clear to you as it is to me after several weeks of hashing and re-hashing. If nothing else, I enjoyed dealing with it.

Let me know ASAP how this strikes you.

Thanks,
Hunter S. Thompson

TO PAUL SEMONIN:

After a long sojourn overseas, Semonin was planning to return to New York to study Marxist theory at Columbia University.

April 18, 1965
318 Parnassus
San Francisco

Dear Ph.D.:

I think you'd better stick with the foundation boys and take that Columbia offer; the other action is getting real ugly. Get a degree of some respectable kind and dip into teaching somewhere; that is what everybody else is doing—that, or writing Hip & Camp books for fun and profit. Or pop art.

I envy your illusions but not what you face when you come back here and start dealing with the machine. Along these lines I've been watching the slow, day by day action over at Berkeley. About all I can see finally coming off it is the drafting of Mario Savio[10]; he missed court the other day to take his physical, and supposedly passed with flying colors. The reason the whole thing came to a publicity head in the first place was a giant Establishment fuckup by a Chancellor named Strong, who has since resigned under pressure—not for doing what he did, but for doing it so blatantly . . . like the difference between Goldwater and Johnson. But the end result has been the same: constant pressure, penalties & restrictions. If you get arrested once, for instance, a sympathetic friend or liberal benefactor might be happy to make bail. The second time, maybe—depending on what kind of publicity is involved. But then on the third try when the reporters are tired of the story & besides it has since been brought out that you have two convictions for lice-carrying, then bail is a hell of a lot harder to make and you wind up paying a bondsman, which is non-refundable. And then it starts hurting, especially if you don't have the money or have to piss people off to get it. That's what's happening now—not just the bail business, but other small & ugly harassments, like being drafted. You think Savio's name popped out of a hat?

On the whole, the main reason I've been silent for so long is that I'm going into a kind of mad-dog funk after too many days with the *Chronicle* and the *Examiner*. And television, and radio—and random conversations. I have gone into a kind of karate tenseness; the super contraction of all muscles so it won't hurt when you're hit. One technique I haven't mastered as yet is the puffing up of the jaws to create an air pocket around the

---

10. Mario Savio was the spokesman for the Berkeley Free Speech Movement.

teeth. Which is a thing I think we all need. The trouble with writing you about what my mind is up to is that this goddamn machine—and the other one too—is too damn slow. We need a sort of give and take, instead of this rotten formal presentation. By the time I've finished a sentence I usually see three or four ways to refute it or at least improve on it—but by that time I'm already thinking about something else.

What I'll do right now is skim over your letter and lash at the main points, then, if possible, go back and try to clarify.

I'm not sure how well you know the value of the word you used ("infrastructure") in relation to the projected difficulties of publishing that magazine. But that is a word you want to keep in mind. It covers a lot of ground and too many situations to name. You are fortunate enough now to be dealing outside the infrastructure—but not really, I almost forgot about Mr. Ford. Even so, I think you're mentally outside it, and apparently most of the people you deal with are out there too.

A few weeks ago when the "nausea gas" story broke I happened to have the TV set on for all the network dinnertime newscasts. I got into NBC a bit late and only got a snatch of the story because it was right up front. Then, on CBS, it was the lead story and I was with it for all details, Capitol Hill reaction, etc. Then came ABC, and like the others their man [Peter Jennings] comes on with a quick capsule for the day's news in headline form, then they switch off for a commercial. The headline technique is called a "teaser." Anyway, the gas bit was number one for the day, then came a commercial. Then—for about five seconds—Jennings came back on for about ten words' worth of the gas story: "Capitol Hill was buzzing tonight after official etc. . . ." and then another commercial, obviously spliced in, and ending some 30 seconds before the story itself came to an end, so a viewer also got the tail end of the gas action, but nobody who hadn't heard it before could have known what Jennings was talking about. I did, but since I have no phone I had to walk three blocks to call the station and ask why the gas story had been censored. I was told there was nobody in the newsroom qualified to answer my question. I then wrote Carey McWilliams, editor of *The Nation*—for whom I just did a piece on outlaw motorcyclists—and told him about it, asking if he thought it was worth pursuing. The next day I went down to the station, introducing myself to the news director as a correspondent for the *National Observer*, and asked him why the gas item had been deleted from his newscast. His nervous answer—and he was obviously stunned by my query—was that the network shows are edited in L.A. and he was "just as surprised" as I was to see such a thing. He then gave me two ABC vice-presidents to query in L.A.—and McWilliams wrote back to say that they might use the item in a "paragraph" form, which form also pays $25 at most and sometimes $10. Which left me with a big, ugly story possibility on my hands and no money to pay the rent, the same situation I'm in now.

In other words, "who can afford to give a fuck?" I'm all right Jack, etc. (I just had to get Sandy up to change the margin on this rotten bastard and now the house is full of hell—this marriage thing is not a killer in itself but in the small routines and trivial obligations that come with it.) Besides that, I seem to be doing everything humanly possible to finish myself with booze and general physical abuse, pills, no sleep, etc.

The truth of it all is that I'm in a nearly perpetual rotten mood and rubbed raw each day by new lashings of bullshit. This Vietnam thing has driven me to the point of a continuing froth. I wrote Johnson, telling him to fuck himself and count me out under any circumstances—and although I already have one letter on file (to the AF) saying I would never again put on a uniform, that I wanted to reiterate this feeling and especially to withdraw my application for the governorship of American Samoa since I felt I could under no circumstances serve this administration either at home or abroad. It was a serious letter, in all, bearing down heavily on my prior Dow-Jones affiliation so they couldn't write me off as a cloistered kook, and saying all any citizen would have to say in these times to get on all the wrong lists. When I go to vote, they'll probably X me out, and the next time Johnson comes to San Francisco I expect to be interred for the duration of the visit. What I want to do in the meantime is a story of some kind on the FBI.

Well, we are not getting real far in this letter, eh? I now have freedom to run to the right edge of the paper and I feel better for it, but not much. Sandy says this is a worthless electric typewriter, an ancient and discredited model. So much for the natural integrity of my friendly typewriter merchant. This is a royal example of the shit that is driving me wild, of the horrible predatory rot that pervades the whole system. Once you become conscious of it, actually formulate it in your mind, then all manner of once-innocent and natural-seeming things begin falling into a pattern of imperialist savagery. But nowhere like on the TV screen. There is the furthest expression of the American dream.

Anyway, I've come all the way around, to agreeing with most of what you say—not because you've convinced me, but out of total despair of finding anything here to refute your arguments. Nor, however, do I see much on your side of the fence to give me any hope that even the most far-reaching Marxist takeover would get the stench off the decks. I read all these magazines out of New York, Harlem, etc., but one of the basic things about them is that their writers are worthless in the sense that they can't put words together to mean what they're trying to say. Something like this letter; I'm so pissed off in general and so out of tune with this rotten machine that I can't say what I mean to say, and therefore waste all manner of time and paper nagging at something I should be able to outline and explain in a page and a half.

One interesting item for the future may be this anti-OAS [Organization of American States] proposal that the Chilean boys are preparing for the Rio Conference in May, or June. It is supposedly a bombshell, aiming at booting the U.S. out of Latin planning, and replacing us with Cuba. If this gets a majority vote it will be interesting. But it probably won't and even if it does I can't see much coming of it in the long run. Like the Selma march, a TV spectacular—next summer we'll have the Harlem Riots, presented by Monsanto Chemicals. I may be sick and a bit daffy, but something in me rebels at the idea of 500 or 5000 negroes kneeling on the streets of Selma, singing "I Love State Troopers in My Heart." I think this whole non-violent thing was planned from the start by Cardinal Spellman. There is apparently a big underground split between SNCC and CORE [Congress of Racial Equality] but since SNCC can't buy any exposure I think they're out in the cold.

John Macauley's idea of "talking to key people" in those various fields you mentioned is wholly preposterous and even depressing. Again, the infrastructure. The other end of the problem is, of course, how do you publish, pay for and distribute a readable magazine without it? You could put out a mimeographed newsletter, but before you go that route you'd better talk to some of the other people who've tried it and quit. If you are really serious about this magazine thing I think you'd be better off setting up in England or Spain or Chile or anywhere except this capital of high costs, hard-nose risk capital and 100 million fatbellies. There is plenty of money in this country, but only for the "right" things. The more I learn about how the machinery works the more depressed I become. The *Observer* and I have long since parted company on any but an occasional, off-beat story or book review basis, and I'm waiting now to see how *The Nation* handles the piece I just finished. *The Reporter* is another pass, since they bounced my editor. All their articles these days are by retired Generals.

I see here on the last page of your tome you say the "humanist conservatives will have to be separated from the swingers." Well, good luck—but when you finish this separation you're likely to find yourself in camp with some very funny people. Like Hubert Humphrey, Joan Baez and [steel tycoon] Henry Kaiser. What you can't seem to get through your head is the fact that the Establishment over here is swinging like mad and they pay well to be cleverly harassed. This is part of the game. Your mean judgments on the *National Observer* LatAm newsbook and the *Herald Tribune* stuff is wholly wasted. None of the hipsters read that shit, not even me. But they don't read Fanon either. (Actually I'm probably wrong here; what I should say is that none of the hipsters will *admit* to reading that shit, which is a different thing, eh?) And don't tell me you meant Swingers instead of hipsters, because here it's all the same. In a nut, it is hip to be a swinger and Camp is in. And I'm out—further so, I suspect, than you because you still seem to think you can talk reason to a man with profits on the line. Even after all this time and all these mental gymnastics I have to go back to Mailer for a good nut: "The shits are killing us" and god help you if you still think you can take them for $5000 a year without coming up with anything in return. They are slow at times, but they can afford the machinery to be very thorough in the long run. And a lot of well-intentioned people, like Clark Kerr,[11] are sitting in that machinery, making it go, because the people who own it still don't wholly understand how it works or what it really means. I think Sartre does, and his answer recently was simply to refuse to come to this country and talk about it. I admire that kind of brazen honesty, but I think it bodes ill for your apparent hopes of a dialogue and a reformation of some kind.

But what the hell am I getting at except another night of unprofitable work and a big postage bill with this heavy stationery? We both have several years to look forward to and I'm damned if I want to spend them hashing around with this sort of bullshit that we both know and knew a long time ago. As for realities, your best bet if you come back to this country is to stay in New York—that is the capital of HIP and I read tonight that Westport, Conn. is now the "communications capital" of the U.S. because all the media people live there and I damn well don't doubt it from what I see and hear in the media. You'll at least find sympathetic spirits there and probably enough money to keep on being a genteel loser in a long-lost cause that has finally become fashionable because it no longer seems to be real threatening. (I say "seems" because I think you're right in saying some real action is afoot in Africa & other non-American soil but unless De Gaulle manages to bust the Dollar sometime soon I think we are many moons away from seeing any real power shifts. On the other hand, this Vietnam thing could boil over any moment if Johnson really means to prod China into enough involvement to justify bombing their nuclear sites. That's the word from [Oregon senator] Wayne Morse. He says the Pentagon has decided we're bound to have a war with China eventually so we might as well hit them before they get a Bomb arsenal. What do you think?)

11. Clark Kerr was the president of the University of California at Berkeley.

As for me, I half-heartedly mean to move to New York next fall, if only because that's where the money lives and at least I'll have some congenial company on the way down the tube. Out here is like Tulsa with a view. You ask for my monkey wrench and all I can swing on you at this stage of the game is a new version of an old meanness, and a much surer knowledge of what we face in the way of possibilities. I think this is what they mean by Maturity and all I can do is reject it. I suppose your suggestion would be that I paint a big sign and join some non-violent picket line; but no thanks again. That is for people who feel guilty and I don't. I feel like I've been leaned on for a long time by people who don't even have to know my name and should probably have their fucking heads blown off on general principle. I have in recent months come to have a certain feeling for Joe Hill and that Wobbly crowd who, if nothing else, had the right idea. But not the mechanics. I believe the IWW was probably the last human concept in American politics.

I spent this afternoon watching a karate class in action. In the past year it has suddenly dawned on me that people are goddamn dangerous. My good time badass fuckaround is going out of style; the general threat pressure of life in the country seems to be spawning its inevitable results — several "secret armies" in Calif., a tremendous upswing all over the country in crimes of pillage, robbery, and violence, cops with shotguns riding every subway in New York between 8 pm and 4 am — that's the truth — and an estimated 6 or 7 thousand working karate busters in the Bay Area alone. This last is a frightening thing when you consider they are a vengeful lot to begin with and that they leave each lesson with a secret yearning for somebody to say something pushy to them. I know because I went to a bar with two of them afterwards and had to keep one little guy from chopping up an old man who had no idea in hell what he was dealing with; another guy, on leaving my apartment tonight, kicked a chunk out of a telephone pole. So, when you get back to New York be careful who you snarl at in taverns — I think that's why coffee houses are so popular these days; they're generally safer. New York seems to be a peatbog of slow-heating violence, physical and otherwise. If and when I go back there I definitely mean to carry a small pistol and take my chances with the Sullivan Act. I think there is a terrible angst on the land, a sense that something ugly is about to happen, an hour-to-hour feeling of nervous anticipation. Whether it's the Bomb or a simple beating, you never know — but, in your terminology, there is a feeling of push coming to shove and what the hell of it? [. . .]

Ah, this fucking rotten machine. One more strike against those pigfuckers. In closing I remain, increasingly savage and unreasonable — HST

TO CAREY MCWILLIAMS, *THE NATION*:

Thompson reflected back to the late 1950s, when he saw Jack Kerouac at a tavern near Columbia University, and looked forward to writing about Ken Kesey's LSD-inspired antics in the Bay Area.

April 28, 1965
318 Parnassus
San Francisco

Dear Mr. McWilliams:
a axgghs;;;;llf ;mbvcbh   n   njwqk/   fB   Q
M   QAW   bmfddxxsxfr   zx s bdfxse3rv
fx   zczsqw   ZAnmmm   ,

Well, that was a message from my year-old son, Juan, who just woke up and can't be kept away from this electric typewriter. I guess it shoots to hell Thurber's old theory that a bunch of apes set loose on typewriters will eventually turn out wisdom. Or maybe not, maybe there's something in the above declaration that neither of us can grip. He stares very carefully at the keys before making his choice, and who are we to call him incoherent? (That is, of course, the generic "we"; you and I are the exceptions, eh?)

And now to your letter of April 23. I am, of course, quite familiar with the "non-student" phenomenon, and have been since I was playing that role around Columbia in '58–'59. At that stage of the game I believe we were called "bums," although "beatnik" quickly became popular. I recall one night in the West End Tavern, when hundreds of people gathered to watch Kerouac's first appearance on TV. It was the John Wingate show, and when Kerouac came slinking out of the wings a great cheer went up in the West End. He was, I suppose, the Bob Dylan of his day—and saying that makes me feel damned old.

Anyway, it sounds like a good idea for a piece and also for me, but I don't want to commit myself to it until I get hold of some people who can give me the real score. I've made a few calls and have a few names, but for the past few days I've been dealing with a different story, which may interest you.

Ken Kesey and 13 of his friends, including Neal Cassady (the Dean Moriarty of *On the Road*), were busted last week on a general charge of possessing marijuana. Kesey wants to make a real case out of it—a confrontation with the law, as it were—but his attorneys are inclined to fight it on an "illegal search and seizure" basis. I just got back from talking to Kesey and his attorneys and of course I'm all for the head-on confrontation. Probably I should warn you that I represented myself as "a writer for *The Nation*," which is a hell of a lot more comfortable on a story like this than being from the *National Observer*, which is what my business cards say.

At any rate, I mean to follow the story, for good or ill, and regardless of whether I get any assignments on it or not. Kesey seems like a very decent guy and certainly nobody's hophead. If the attorneys lose control of the defendants, which I deem likely, some of them are capable of making a real case of this thing. The argument, which I presume you know, is that marijuana is not a narcotic but a psychedelic—a consciousness-expanding drug, rather than an addictive opiate, and in no way harmful except to the prejudices and opinions of the bourgeoisie. If it comes to this it will make a fine story, but if the lawyers have their way, it won't. Actually there is a story merely in Kesey's problems in explaining his position to a lawyer. One of the big arguments tonight concerned what manner of garb the defendants should wear at the arraignment May 10. Kesey and his people resent the suggestion that they should wear coats, ties and stockings.

This is not a "typical beatnik" case, in that Kesey and the others are constructive, creative and articulate, by any comparison to the stereotype—and certainly by comparison to the "typical middle-class American." Of course all this must sound pretty hazy to you now, but if the idea interests you, let's keep it in mind. As far as I can see, there is no real time factor involved unless we want to make one. What concerns me in this thing are the questions of attitude and structural anachronisms that will be brought to bear on the case. Sooner or later the Law is going to have to face some of these "dangerous drug" questions, and this case may turn out to be a big step in that direction.

Ok for all that. Keep in mind that I'm already with this one and will stay with it for the duration. As for the non-student thing,[12] I'd like to do it and I think I could do it well, but I can't guarantee the performance until I see who I get in the way of informants and examples. Unless you have somebody else in mind, why not send the material along. By the time I get it I'll have found—or not found—the people I need for the story, and a look at your material should give me a good idea what you have in mind. I would only work on a story like this if I were sure we're both talking about the same thing. Otherwise, it would only be frustrating, and if I'm going to be frustrated I may as well work for *Life* or *Look* and get paid for it.

Once again, I'm not haggling over prices. If I thought you could pay $500 for an article I'd damn well demand it, but unless I'm totally misinformed, that's not the case. On the other hand, when I work a week or two for $100 I think I should have the luxury of being pleased with what appears in print. I liked the galley version of the Hell's Angels piece and I look forward to seeing it in the book. But until your last letter I had no real

---

12. McWilliams wanted Thompson to write on the Berkeley Free Speech Movement. As a result, Thompson wrote "The Non-Student Left" (*The Nation*, September 27, 1965).

idea whether I'd written the sort of thing you wanted, or not. On that front, I think we're both thinking along the same lines on this non-student thing. Either way, let me know. I'm inclined to do it, so unless you have another writer in mind, let's give it a whirl.

Sincerely,
Hunter S. Thompson

TO DON COOKE:

Covering Kesey for The Nation, *Thompson offered his first impression of La Honda and the Merry Pranksters.*

May 2, 1965
318 Parnassus
San Francisco

Cooke—

Whether it's gratuitous or not I have to insist you read *One Flew Over the Cuckoo's Nest.* Reading it gives a man faith that the Combine is still buying madmen's work, and if so, what do you think?

Along these lines I was down at Kesey's house in La Honda last night, bearing witness to one of the strangest scenes in all Christendom—a wild clanging on tin instruments on a redwood hillside, loons playing flutes in the darkness, mikes and speakers planted all over, mad flashing films on a giant trampoline screen; in all it was pretty depressing—that a man with such a high white sound should be so hung up in this strange campy kind of showbiz. He MC'd the whole bit, testing mikes and tuning flutes here and there as if one slip in any direction might send us all over the cliff in darkness. Like a kid's home circus, a Peter Pan kind of thing, but with sad music somewhere up in the trees above the kiddie carols. I drank twenty beers and left sadly sober, remembering Mailer going off that diving board in Las Vegas and all those guys in the press room laughing at the fat boy with the ping-pong snorkel and the fat hips that he tried to roll like Brando, but couldn't. Then halfway back to the city with Sandy asleep on my lap I suddenly went blind drunk and came twenty miles along cliffs in what they call the Devil's Slide area not knowing from one minute to the next when we might go off and down like a rock to the surf.

It's bad on the nerves to see a toughass in quicksand, and if you read the *Cuckoo* book you'll know what I mean. Here he was last night, the Kooky King of the Woodsy Beatniks, orange jacket and headphones and bossing it all while I kept waiting for him to grin and look sane for a minute but he never did. It reminded me of me in some of my worst hours, and the only excuse I could make for him is the one I make for myself—why bother to make it right when nobody knows the difference anyway? But there's always some shithead around who does, like me last night, and you now and then when I get sloppy, and sometimes Sandy when she's wearing her glasses. Ah, if I could tell you about the girl I saw tonight, and she went off with a commercial artist from LA, a guy with a white rolled collar and a line like say baby, let's me and you etc..... christ I need a long hill and a cold morning sun to get myself tuned again. I wonder if this writing to get famous isn't probably like working to get rich, or all the other shit they tell you at Bauer's (Louisville) and P. J. Clarke's (New York) and the Buena Vista (San Francisco).[13] Maybe the only human way is to go off and chop your own score and just leave it somewhere and let whoever finds it figure it out. But that's a pretty tough way to go out, to win by a nose with nobody watching and no press around to tell the world by god here's a man who beat it and let's give him a hand and maybe a prize or two. I think that might take a third ball.

Yeah, and I weakened at the last moment yesterday and went roaring off to a good horse bar and watched the fucking Derby with all the other hard losers and, like I predicted, one of them even bought me a drink, and without me even having to tell him I was from there. A guy I talked to tonight said he'd lived in twenty-one towns for the first twenty years of his life and now when he got homesick he didn't know where to call home. I told him he didn't know how well off he was but he didn't know what I meant.

Ah, that girl, that fine beautiful little human package—from Warwick, New York, of all places, up by Semonin's old cabin where I nearly died one night when that scooter went down on a wet road. I still see those sparks when I think about it; all the while it was going over I kept telling myself no daddy this ain't happening to you just lean a little bit and pull it back up again, but we kept going over and the metal was grinding off with all those sparks and then zango, all black and no hurt at all. I think that's the way to go out, running the Big Sur highway on a big cycle with no lights and keep turning it over until the engine goes off in a wild scream and on one of the curves you keep going straight over, then turn on the headlight for the surf, and hold tight.

Well, I just wanted to send this note because it seems in my mind that I sent a shitty card or letter the other night and I thought I'd get this to you before it had to look like a reply or a comeback of some kind for anything you might already be sending. Your guns, as it were. I don't claim to be invulnerable, but the one thing I insist on is that I can't be croaked except when I give the word.

13. Bars Thompson used to frequent.

OK for now, and sorry if my letter sounded ugly but I couldn't figure out which of my earlier things you were calling gratuitous because that's one of those words you could call almost anything and for all manner of reasons. Anyway, send one of your drafts and let's see what you're up to, for good or ill.

HST

TO DAVE HACKER:

Thompson's friend Hacker, editor of the National Observer, *was in the hospital, recuperating from a heart attack.*

May 3, 1965
San Francisco

Dear Dave:
[. . .] Things here proceed worthlessly. My total income for the year thus far is $500. Needless to say, that virtually cuts booze out of my budget. It's my private suspicion, by the way, that you wouldn't have had any troubles if you hadn't given up booze. It tends to flush out the system, including the arteries—no matter what the quacks try to tell you.

I sent Tom Wolfe one of my drunken, night-life postcards the other night, offering him the use of my private army in his fight against the fags, but he will doubtlessly toss it off as the work of a loon, so I'll count on a look at your material whenever you can send it. Needless to say I'm all on his side but I don't want to come out publicly, as it were, until I've read the piece(s). He writes so close to the edge at times that it wouldn't surprise me if he strayed into bad excuses now and then, but so far I've never seen any evidence of that. I've already asked Cliff [Ridley] for a shot at his book, coming out soon, and definitely look forward to it.

My recent work here has dealt with topless dancers, garbage in the bay, marijuana, karate and a generally non-publishable hellbroth of vagrant interests made possible by the part-time work of my faithful wife. Last night, in the course of my research, I smoked off a large reefer and went groggy for something like 12 hours. It was like drinking a gallon of stale beer, the same effect. I've never had much use for the stuff, mainly because it's never done anything to or for me—even in pipeloads—but last night's action was my last. I am lazy and unproductive enough on my own hook, without the help of a weed.

Anyway, I'm sorry as hell to hear about your heart thing, but like you say, it doesn't sound real dire. It seems to me that they could just lift out that fatted-up section of the artery and replace it with something synthetic.

I think the quacks have a vested interest in keeping us all scared half to death. My advice to you is get out of the hospital and whack off a bottle of John Powers Irish; that should get the life-juices flowing again, and knock out all the stops. For the moment, you sound pretty lively, although I can't say much for your handwriting. I knew something was wrong with you the minute I tried to read the first paragraph; it looked like the work of a man far gone with *delirium tremens*.

In closing, all I can say is don't let the bastards scare you. We are tougher than they want us to think.

HST

TO RICHARD SCOWCROFT, STANFORD UNIVERSITY:

Ken Kesey and Dick Elman had told Thompson that Scowcroft gave grants to aspiring writers.

May 13, 1965
318 Parnassus
San Francisco

Dick Scowcroft
English Dept.
Stanford Univ.
Palo Alto

Dear Mr. Scowcroft:

I've been putting off writing you because my letters have wrought more ill than good, recently, but after a bit of a layoff I figure it's time to take a chance again.

Dick Elman suggested I contact you regarding the possibility of gaining funds to keep The Man off my back while I rewrite a novel called The Rum Diary. All he said was that you "help give out money for creative writing grants."

I would certainly like some and could put it to good use. At the moment I'm free-lancing as little as possible while trying to turn out as much fiction as possible after a long layoff—nearly three years. For a year and a half of that time I was the *National Observer*'s accredited correspondent in Rio de Janeiro. Then back to Colorado, mainly for the *Observer*. I just sold a piece on the Hell's Angels to *The Nation* and I guess it will run soon. And I've sold articles and fiction to *Rogue*, although that was a long time ago when I was living in Big Sur and doing the first draft of The Rum Diary. I'm 27, married, one child, broke, holder of many pawn tickets, fighting eviction, etc. I guess you've heard that story before.

I've never given much thought to grants but now that LeRoi Jones has a Guggenheim I have to consider the possibility of a new era, for good or ill. So if you're sitting down there on a bundle of loose cash I'd appreciate any and all advice as to how I might lay hands on some of it.

Thanks,

Hunter S. Thompson

TO SARA BLACKBURN, PANTHEON BOOKS:

Blackburn, an editor at Pantheon (a division of Random House, Inc.), had expressed interest in publishing "The Rum Diary." The "fringe book" she suggested Thompson write eventually developed into Hell's Angels.

May 17, 1965
318 Parnassus
San Francisco

Dear Mrs. Blackburn:

Thanks for your letter of the 12th. I was beginning to think the FBI had put a seizure-type mail watch on me. After my last letter to Lyndon I see no reason to believe I am not under constant surveillance; the next time he comes to California I expect to be locked up for a few days.

And be all that as it may. I was pleased and somewhat puzzled at your "fringe book" suggestion. I'm not sure what you mean. The idea interests me but I'm leery of actually saying "yes" because I have no idea how you people work in the area of expenses. In the past I've agreed to do articles that simply cost too much. Nearly all of them, in fact. So if I seem a little uneasy here it's not because I don't like the idea but that I'm not sure what grounds we're dealing on.

I could, for instance, do an outline for a book on Hard-Rock Diggers, Carny Hustlers, *Braceros* [migrant workers], Hell's Angels, Aspen Philosophers, free-lance foreign correspondents, ski bums and Kentucky Mountain disc jockeys—but that would cost a hell of a lot of money and require a bit of travel. I know because I've been there, as it were, and I know who pays for the drinks when a writer shows up and starts buttonholing "fringe types" for information. The other way is to play it like John Howard Griffin when he wrote *Black Like Me*. But that wouldn't be possible in a book dealing with entirely different types—and besides, as I said, I've already been there. And it's no fun. (As a matter of fact I'm still there; on Saturday I was evicted, tomorrow I'll sell a pint of blood for $10, and on

Wednesday I'll shape up at 5:00 a.m. to deliver circulars with a gang of winos for $.60 an hour.)

All I'm really getting at here is the question of who foots the bill. I see no sense in doing an outline for a book I couldn't deliver. But if you're willing to pay my expenses for a while, that's a different thing—and it would also be a giant factor in determining what kind of book I could do.

The nut of it is that I'd very much like to do the sort of book I think you have in mind, but I can't possibly do it on my own hook.

As for the novel, I completed it three years ago and now find it generally embarrassing. What I've been trying to do for the past few months is rewrite it, but every time I get settled down to the job I have to zip off on some wholly unrelated article, just to pay the rent. So again, the problem is funds. My angst is permanent, I think, and I've learned to live with it.

The novel, however, will be finished sooner or later. There is no real question on that score—although now and then I have my doubts and that's when the angst really bothers me.

There's a possibility that I could send all or part of it to you for a quick look, but I'd have to go over it again to make sure I want it read at all. Parts of it are fine and require little work, but other parts are worthless—such as the first 100 pages. I am also starting up a new one, a very different thing, which began from a phrase in a letter: ". . . a telegram to the right people, explaining my position." I could send a few pages of that too, but they'd probably frighten you.

In all, I think the best bet right now is The Rum Diary, although I can't really tell about the "fringe" thing until I know how you operate on expenses. It might be that a "fringe" book would buy me enough time to finish the novel. Or perhaps someone will simply send me a barrel of cash; I have a secret faith that this will happen—like Gatsby and his goddamn green light. And you know what happened to him.

So . . . send a line and say how it is on your end. Keep in mind that I'm interested and even eager to get dealing on something, but my position right now is like that of a man being carried off by wolves and shouting to his poker companions: "Go right ahead boys, deal me in, I'll be right back."

Or, like Bobby Cleary[14] was telling me that night in Missoula: "That's the way it goes, first your money, then your clothes."

And that's my wisdom for tonight. What's yours?

Sincerely,
Hunter S. Thompson

---

14. The hobo Thompson wrote about for the *National Observer* on his Western trek.

TO CLIFFORD RIDLEY, *NATIONAL OBSERVER:*

On May 2, President Johnson had raised the number of U.S. troops in the Dominican Republic to fourteen thousand to "prevent another Communist state" from arising in the hemisphere.

May 18, 1965
San Francisco

Dammit Clifford, I've been sitting here for three hours working on a piece pegged generally to the Dominican situation, but no matter how good it looks I'm faced with a near certainty that you wouldn't run it anyway, so I finally had to give up. Politically, it's a pretty apolitical thing, based on my feelings that there should be no question as to whether this "revolution" is Communist-controlled or not. If we had competent ambassadors and political attachés in these countries, plus adequate press coverage, we would know the score without any doubt and avoid this general angst concerning the wisdom of our actions down there. I've read everything I can get my hands on from the D.R.—including Chew's Embassy copy—and I'm damned if I know even now. My instinct, of course, is to assume that the 58 Communists are no more than a red herring, but on sober reflection I know there's a possibility that the revolution is in fact a front for a Castro takeover.

My argument is that we could avoid these quandaries by not waiting until the crisis breaks to figure them out. It's on the day-to-day level that the Reds are beating us in LatAm. Hell, by the time they light the fuse they know how it's going to burn, while we apparently don't. So, as usual, we're on the defensive, leaping from one massive reaction to the other— while the whole ugly business could have been headed off a year ago if we'd had a decently staffed embassy down there. Hell, when I was in Brazil I knew the names of any Communists likely to be part of a rebel command—and if I didn't recognize a name I could find somebody who would. But not through the embassy, and there's the rub. Now that I've started paying taxes I'm personally offended at the idea that some worthless clerk is being paid good money to sit down there in a plush office and do nothing at all. Of course the situation varies with the different personnel from one embassy to the next, and that's what I was writing about before I gave up.

Well, what the hell. Is there any sense in my continuing to submit stuff? What happened to the A. B. Guthrie review? The Kurt Vonnegut thing? How do we stand on the money front? There are several things I could do for you but I can't work up much enthusiasm for writing stuff I figure is going to bounce anyway. Have I been put in the "Crazy Red" file? I can't find anyone who agrees with what I write or think these days, so I guess I must be getting closer to the truth. [. . .] I'm beginning to understand why Castro went Red, and the fact that I feel saner than ever probably means I'm losing my mind. Send word of some kind. Any kind. And also say if my (above) thesis interests you in the form of a piece.

Sincerely,
Hunter

TO CHARLES KURALT:

Thompson was impressed by a CBS News special Kuralt hosted on U.S. intervention in the Dominican Republic.

May 31, 1965
318 Parnassus
San Francisco

Charles Kuralt
34 Bank Street
NYC

Dear Charley:

In keeping with the *déjà vu* consistency of my life in this city of stale realities I was wondering today what had happened to you—and then Sandy noticed your name in a blurb for the CBS Dominican special. I had planned to watch it anyway, after seeing the NBC job the other day, but it was comforting to flip on the box and see your face for a change. I thought you had gone up to Maine and bought a trout farm, or something equally sane.

Anyway, it was a damn good job. Somehow, you have developed a sort of [Edward R.] Murrow image, a gaunt and baleful presence that implies authority, credibility, a tone of reluctant judgment on the actions and affairs of less candid men. Sevareid, by contrast, came off as just another failed icon, gone soft in the gut from too much dealing with "unimpeachable sources." [. . .] Quint[15] seemed sharp and sensible, but entirely too young for anyone who remembers Eisenhower to take seriously. I think you have to be at least 35 in this country before anyone will believe a word you say, no matter what it is.

All in all, I think the film was a more valuable thing than NBC's, although their on-the-scene footage was incredible. Yours had a perspective, a point of view, that theirs lacked. Scenes like the lawyers marching and

---

15. Burt Quint was a CBS correspondent in Latin America.

the talk with the Marine privates at the checkpoint were worth ten minutes of filmed combat. And of course Imbert[16] on film is his own prosecutor. [. . .] In a nut, I was damned impressed by the thing. So much so, in fact, that I'm beginning to feel the old action mania, the compulsion to get where things are happening. I wish to hell I could have been in Santo Domingo, but of course the *Observer* would not have printed my stuff. They sent their society reporter down there and he sent back transcripts from the Embassy. I wrote and told them as much, but they didn't answer. I believe our divorce is final.

Plans now are to hustle this novel, then come to New York in the fall and seek action. I'll probably send feelers to the *Times* and the *Trib*, and perhaps even CBS, although my total lack of experience in that line is not much of a lever. If I decide to try it, however, I'll surely be bugging you for possibilities. Meanwhile, the situation here continues to deteriorate in every way. We had to give the dog away to avoid eviction, but the threat is ever-present. I'm trying to finish another piece for *The Nation* to pay last month's rent. I think I had them send you my motorcycle piece. If you got it, send a comment when you have time. I liked it, but in saving so much of the "chemistry" for another (still unwritten) piece, I think it came off a bit stuffy. My idea was to do another first-person job, for more money, but thus far I haven't managed to sell anyone on the idea.

The last weekend was spent in a fog of drunken violence, as befitting my position in society. I am beginning to feel "poor" instead of just "broke," and that's a bad sign. I suppose the only hope now is a job, and that means New York. San Francisco is worthless for moneymaking. I have found that out the hard way. The weekend before last I passed out at the wheel and ran into what they call a "bridge abutment" at 70 mph, but somehow managed to pull out of the spin without hitting anyone. The right side of the car is wiped out but the beast still moves and I have to think I was lucky beyond anything I deserve. It scared me so badly that I am still afraid to drive. [. . .]

Sandy shouts from the kitchen to be sure to tell you hello. Juan is asleep and the dog, I am told, has a good home with a game warden in the north of Sonoma County. He may have found his action; what remains is for me to find mine. Time is getting short; every midnight I feel 48 hours older. And twice as useless.

OK for now. Send a line when you get time. Hello to Petey and tell Sevareid he should go to St. Petersburg.

Hunter

16. Antonio Imbert Barreras, Dominican junta leader.

TO CAREY MCWILLIAMS, *THE NATION:*

Thompson had spent a week hanging around Berkeley to write "The Non-Student Left," which appeared in The Nation *on September 27, 1965.*

June 8, 1965
318 Parnassus
San Francisco

Dear Mr. McWilliams:

Well, here is the final non-student piece. There is no use in telling you what I think I've made of this piece because I'm sure you don't need pointers. I didn't really expect it to turn out this way, but somewhere along the way my own rationale loomed up and kept a hand in. Despite all that I think it is a good piece and maybe closer to the truth than something "objective" might be. In talking to these hustlers I had a weird feeling of *déjà vu,* intensely personal. These people have I.Q. numbers, though, and a genuine respectability that all of us has-beens lacked. I think it would be a mistake to write this off as just another bolt of sophomore idealism. There is too much continuity now. The other day when I listened to I. F. Stone at the Teach-In I wrote on my pad that he had "finally found his audience." They cheered him like Jesus. This continuity is crucial and if it holds it can't help but be a breakthrough of some kind.

I trust I have made the point that the difference between an activist student and an activist non-student is purely non-academic. The "non" term is really a misnomer and I had some trouble explaining what I was after. And that thing about it all being a "moral, rather than political" rebellion was quickly exposed as a hopeless non sequitur. I don't know if I happened to find an unusually bright bunch or not, but that *Spider*[17] crew really put me over the jumps. They're a tough lot. Dealing with them was mentally exhausting. I came back home each time and had to watch TV until my mind got a rest.

OK for now. I trust I have stressed the urgency of quick payment—based on the assumption, of course, that you are going to buy this one. If not, well . . . christ. But I have to allow for the possibility, so what the hell. All us non-students learn to bounce; it's one of the first tricks in the book.

HST

17. *Spider,* a Berkeley-based magazine, was the voice of the Free Speech Movement.

TO PAUL SEMONIN:

Upbeat about the positive response to his Hell's Angels piece in The Nation, *Thompson felt encouraged to continue writing about the revolutionary attitude in the Bay Area.*

June 9, 1965
318 Parnassus
San Francisco

Dear Seekoff:

I have tried and failed to find your last letter, but I think you owe me one anyway. Things here are chaotic, but not all bad. I have just finished the most biased, violent and wholly political piece I've ever written. For *The Nation.* If they run it I will be clamped for all time in the black (or Red) mold of the dirty outlaw. It is a far cry from my *Observer* stuff. Enclosed is my cycle piece, which I hate to send for several reasons: 1) because it will cost so fucking much, and 2) because your comments are bound to be cheap. But in deference to your ignorance and informational deprivation, I'm sending it.

It has, by the way, drawn four letters from publishers. I am hysterical at the prospect of money and book publication, and will surely blow the whole thing, but right now it looks good. I am trying to play them off against each other, angling for immediate funds to solve my present rent crisis. Luckily, Sandy is still working and brings in the food and beer money. The big apple at the moment seems to be The Rum Diary, which I have to rewrite at least in part before any of these bastards will send me a cheque. But it is a wild feeling to have fatbellies actually seeking me out, calling McWilliams at *The Nation* who has been inundated with swine asking how to get hold of me. If I had the novel in shape right now I could knock off a $1500 advance tomorrow. But, sadly, it is not good enough to send out. The next few weeks will be a hell of long hours and steady work. I have to punch while they're digging me. [. . .]

I have spent the past two weeks doing a piece on the non-student at Berkeley. It took me into the world you recommended last year, the hardnose radicals, etc. I found them sympathetic but not impressive. My piece is not as mean as it should be, however, and for a bunch of 22- and 23-year-old punks they are raising a good amount of hell over there. Some of them may last. I am coming around to a revised notion of this action on the Coast. It is amateurish, but hellishly persistent and not without guts. The Legislature is now organizing a full-scale investigation of Cal, to begin next year, and that should bring the roof down. I may have to stay out here until Xmas or so, just to cover the action.

As for what I said earlier about the Coast, I think it was right in that context, but I didn't realize the number of hard-nosed busters who are lurking in this area. Beyond that, the Establishment here is incredibly disorganized and bumbling. So far, the battles have all been lost, not won. But things are more open here and it is easier to get a grip. My advice now is to keep an open mind until we can talk it out. You might fare better out here but I can't say for sure. If you can work it I think you should probably check in for a few weeks in late September and get the feel of it. I can put you in touch with the people you'll feel like contacting. At least I think I can. I'm not real sure just which group you'll want to compare notes with.

I am also hooked up with *The New Republic* for a piece or two from here. I could do some stuff for the wild boys but unfortunately I have to pay my rent. As I said, the radicals can't write a fucking line. All the pros have been hired by the other side. When I read that radical stuff I suffer for them. If the fuckers could say what they really mean, without resorting to old clichés, they might be able to shake some people. As it is, the best thing to date on the "New American Left" was in the *Saturday Evening Post.* Even the Berkeley boys agree. There is no money on the Left. That is one of the basic problems. At the Berkeley "Vietnam Teach-In" the other day I finally had to leave because too many cups had been rattled under my nose. It gives the whole thing a Losers' smell.

Even so, I think we are getting some action here. Press coverage of Santo Domingo borders on anarchy and Vietnam is nearly the same. They are smoothing Johnson, hip and thigh. His hired liars are being grilled mercilessly. Mavericks are popping up in strange places. *The New York Times* for all practical purposes queered the administration's stance in the Dominican. The consensus is falling to pieces. I think you will find a different atmosphere than the one you left here. Dr. [Benjamin] Spock, for instance, is traveling around the country berating our Vietnam policy. Mailer, at Berkeley, told a crowd of 10,000 that Johnson is insane, and they cheered wildly. Strange pollen is in the air. NYU is where most of the talk is, but the action is busting out everywhere: Michigan, Yale, Mississippi, Chicago and even L.A. Things are happening, for good or ill. [. . .]

HST

TO ANGUS CAMERON, ALFRED E. KNOPF:

The renowned editor had written Thompson to inquire whether he would be interested in writing a book on "American Loser-Outsider types."

June 10, 1965
318 Parnassus
San Francisco

Dear Mr. Cameron:

Thanks for your good letter of June 7. There was a tone of decency about it. Besides that, getting letters from publishers is good for my morale. It makes me feel like a writer—the public kind.

As for your Loser-Outsider thing, I have plenty of ideas along that line. Some people will tell you I have an obsession. My original opening graph on the Hell's Angels piece went like this: "In a prosperous democracy that is also a society of winners and losers, any man without an equalizer or at least the illusion of one is by definition underprivileged." My title was: "A Question of Equalizers, and Some Notes on the Anatomy of Outrage." For some reason I haven't understood, the whole concept of "equalizers" was chopped from the piece. Unfortunately, it was my central thesis, although it seemed to get through anyway, but without my fine rhetoric.

Another publisher wrote and asked if I could do a book on "fringe types," which sounds very much like your own idea. I replied that I could, but would need a bit of expense money to deal with it. So they asked to see my novel.

At any rate, there are more people "out of the ballgame" than anyone in New York could possibly understand. Or maybe that's unfair, but as a generality it holds up. I enclose a piece I did for the *National Observer* last year when I was a roving correspondent for them out here. Before that I was their South American correspondent for a year and a half; I am enclosing one from that era, too. Please return them. If nothing else, they should give you a sense of my drift or bent.

For six months or so I tried—with a friend at NETV in New York—to hustle up $100,000 for a film on these Boomers, Drifters, and Hard Travelers. They are wandering echoes of the Wobbly era, a weird breed to fall among. I have a working knowledge of Boomer bars all over the West, but mainly in places like Ely and Elko, Nevada; Butte, Montana; Moab, Utah; Wallace, Idaho and Auburn, California. There are plenty of other stops on the circuit. Denver is a big one; Casper, Wyoming is another, an oil town.

San Francisco is going to be big in a year or so when they start on this rapid-transit project, driving tunnels under the Bay. Gay Talese did a good piece in *Esquire* on one aspect of this thing, the Indian high-steel workers who follow the payroll from job to job.

Hell, I see where I'm headed for a six-page letter if I don't get a grip on myself real quick. I look forward to seeing Christopher Lasch's book on "the intellectual as loser."[18] That would follow, although it might depend on his idea of an intellectual. I have recently developed an outrageous theory about the American Dream being essentially an Irish vision, challenged now by a view of reality that is basically Jewish. It has to do with Jay Gatsby and John Kennedy, the I.W.W. and the Hell's Angels, the New York syndrome, the "bogeyman factor" that dominates the press, and god only knows what else. Mike Murphy, who runs the mystic establishment down in Big Sur, tells me someone has been putting LSD in my gin.

The temptation here is to carry on, but it's late and I have to go over my novel for a few hours, then get up tomorrow and write something about abortions. I have just finished another piece for *The Nation*; it concerns the "non-student" at Berkeley. There is another Outsider for you, but this one is a new breed. The reason that Losers are so important these days is that there are so many of them, and some are only Losers by other people's definitions. The truth is that real Losers don't interest me; the thing I enjoy is the irony of an unnatural pecking order, and that sense of something about to break, for good or ill. On the other hand, I have a pretty esoteric definition of Losers. Ten years ago it was only a grudging suspicion, but now, incredibly, it is proving out. I leave you to ponder it, and to send whatever word seems fitting.

Sincerely,
Hunter S. Thompson

TO EDITOR, *THE NATION:*

A letter to the editor had appeared in The Nation *challenging Thompson's statement, in the article "Motorcycle Gangs: Losers and Outsiders," that wild boar are aggressive.*

18. Christopher Lasch, *The New Radicalism in America* (New York, 1965).

June 14, 1965
318 Parnassus
San Francisco

Editor, *The Nation*
New York

Dear Sir:

I am always pleased to see someone defending wild boar, and especially Kay Boyle, for she has a certain eloquence. But I would rather not be pegged, even eloquently, as a man who knows nothing of these animals simply because I haven't romped with them in the forests of France and Germany.

I assume Miss Boyle is aware that Monterey County, California, where I used to live and still hunt, has either the largest or second-largest concentration of "European" or "Russian" boar in the country. The other boar community exists in the Cherokee National Forest between Tennessee and North Carolina. At a rough guess I'd say I've spent between 200 and 300 days hunting boar, and the first one I ever saw came at me so fast and suddenly that I couldn't even aim my rifle. I have also seen them tear up dogs. Monterey County is full of hunters who know how dangerous the wild boar can be.

I say "can be," just as I said in my article that they are "tough, mean and *potentially* dangerous." Miss Boyle says that they are "violent and dangerous only in despair, when cornered, or in defense of their young." And obviously, no animal being hunted with rifles is going to be friendly. They seem to know, long before being shot at, although deer and elk—with their placid temperaments—don't have the wild pig's penchant for explosive rage when he feels he's being tampered with. A deer will always run away from you, while a boar will very often run at you.

And this was precisely the point of my comparison of wild boar and Hell's Angels. Both animals are very easily threatened, and their reaction is generally violent, rather than evasive. The problem is that so few outside the breed know where the line is drawn. And I thought I had made it pretty clear that a sense of despair is one of the most pervasive realities of a Hell's Angel's existence.

I appreciate Miss Boyle's concern, and when she comes back to the coast I'll be happy to take her boar-hunting in Big Sur. If we are lucky enough to encounter pigs at close quarters I want her to have a good bullhorn, so she can explain to them that they are not mean animals.

Sincerely,
Hunter S. Thompson

TO CHARLES KURALT:

Thompson had just signed a contract with Ballantine Books (a paperback division of Random House) to write Hell's Angels.

> June 23, 1965
> 318 Parnassus
> San Francisco

Dear Charley:

If you'd been here last weekend you wouldn't have had to buy all the booze. I went on an Irish whiskey whoop, having just nicked Ballantine for a $6000 guarantee to do a book on Motorcycle Gangs. $1500 to sign. Indeed. I paid my rent two months in advance. Got my guns and camera gear out of hock. I was even drunk enough to think about paying you that $110. But I figure I'll save that for when I get the final money lump. Unless you need it—and say so whenever you do.

Anyway, Ballantine thinks this is going to go. My guarantee is just for the paperback; hardcover, movie and TV rights are yet to be negotiated. I think you should get hustling at once on the TV rights. Did you get a copy of my piece from *The Nation*? I put you on the list, but if you didn't get one, say so and I'll send a copy. (Or it's the May 17 issue if you have one on hand.) For the next few months I'll be booming around California on a cycle, talking to as many vicious thugs as I can find. I trust you noticed where my men got blamed for that New Hampshire riot last weekend. They trained in Mexico, under Red cadres. Sho nuff. The Guvnah said so. This could make a hell of a feature film, as I think I explained in a long-ago letter.

That *Nation* piece drew all sorts of action from publishers, but none so lucrative as this one. I would rather have got a fat advance on my novel, but this broke first and I couldn't let it slide. If nothing else, it should give me good leverage for the novel. I have a feeling of general leverage right now. My agent [Theron Raines], who dumped on me two months ago, just sent me $400 to get my phone turned on. I don't know what kind of phone he expects me to get, but I paid the deposit today and it will be listed under the name of Sebastian Owl—FYI.

Send word, or come out and take a cycle spin with me. I'd hate to think you were getting too old for this kind of a story. There is plenty of zing in it. And these guys aren't half as dangerous as they sound—you know how the mass media does these things, eh? OK for now; come out of your ivory tower and write.

> Sincerely,
> Hunter

TO THE NATIONAL RIFLE ASSOCIATION:

Thompson took pride in the eclecticism of writing for The Nation *while belonging to the NRA.*

> June 26, 1965
> 318 Parnassus
> San Francisco

National Rifle Association
1600 Rhode Island Ave., NW
Washington 6, D.C.

Gentlemen:

I let my NRA membership lapse when I went to South America two years or so ago, and now I'd like to renew it. Enclosed is my check for $5, which I assume is still the initiation fee. If not, please bill me for anything above $5.

Since I have no application form at hand, I'm not sure what benefits I'll get from this, but I assume I'll be put on a subscription list for the *American Rifleman,* and, beyond that, receive all other benefits of a regular member.

I would like to go on record here—since we seem to be coming to very peculiar times in this country—that my application for membership is in no way indicative of any political views on my part. Nobody has ever called me a Conservative and as a matter of fact I am a writer for the Liberal press, but I'm concerned about the possible passage of illogical firearms laws and I'm glad to hear you people have taken what strikes me as a reasonable position on this question.

That's why I'd like to re-activate my membership. I assure you that if the NRA's overall viewpoint ever seems unreasonable to me, I'll terminate my membership at once. In the meantime, count on me for any help you feel I can give.

> Sincerely,
> Hunter S. Thompson

TO ANGUS CAMERON, ALFRED E. KNOPF:

> June 28, 1965
> 318 Parnassus
> San Francisco

Ah, Mr. Cameron . . . here I am with a dead letter and a mad poem and then a letter and a book from you and some weird inclination to wrap it all well and make the whole thing dance. What I am really doing is sitting here at 4:18 a.m., awash in good Napa Valley burgundy, and pondering the meaning of it all. For good or ill—the cats are screaming outside my high window, the coons must be in the garbage and the cats have the fear. Believe it or not these coons that raise such hell below my window can lift up a big garbage can and dash it against a wall to break the seal. A terrific racket. Now and then I crack off a 12-gauge blast at them, but nothing ever comes of it.

And so much for all that. This man Christopher Lasch. I see you published his book so I dare not knock it from an ignorant stance; it just came the day before yesterday and I've been trying for two days to buy a good portable tape recorder. Since your last letter, and mine (which I include, FYI), I signed a contract with Ballantine to do a cycle gang book, which I trust will make my fortune. A man in my fringe condition can't turn down that kind of money, especially for a book that could be a big roller. This cycle stuff is not just a part of the fringe, it is the furthest extension of something comparable to whatever the Beat Generation might have been in 1952. This is the stupid vanguard of the Fourth Reich, and all I can say is that it's nice and colorful and I admire the foresight of a man who is willing to pay for a book on it.

Of course I can say a lot more than that, and certainly intend to. But that is another story.

As for your ideas on "Losers and Outsiders." I see it occurred to you at the end of your letter that we were talking in terms of the Ultimate Book. Non-Fiction won't handle a subject that big. Honest journalism is enough to addle the sanest man, and if I've learned nothing else in five years of writing articles I think I've learned that. And that's why I want to get this cycle book out of the way and get back on my novel—or novels, because The Rum Diary is becoming two books. Fiction is a bridge to the truth that journalism can't reach. Facts are lies when they're added up, and the only kind of journalism I can pay much attention to is something like *Down and Out in Paris and London*. The title story in Tom Wolfe's new book[19] is a hell of a fine thing, I think, and so is the one on Junior Johnson ["The Last American Hero"]. But in order to write that kind of punch-out stuff you have to add up the facts in your own fuzzy way, and to hell with the hired swine who use adding machines.

Well, I see I'm running on here, and I suppose it's a bad thing. A man should not run on. But I'm looking at the cover of Lasch's book about two feet behind my typewriter and I wonder what in the hell was in his mind when he undertook such a thing. I haven't opened it yet so I can't possibly

19. *The Kandy-Kolored Tangerine-Flake Streamline Baby* (New York, 1965).

know, but I look at the title and the time-span and I wonder. You para-phrased the title as "The Intellectual as a Loser," and from the reviews I've read I'm sure that's pretty apt. But what could be more obvious? People who write books like these strike me as profit-oriented sado-masochists, and needless to say, compulsive losers. Think of the time and mental effort he spent on such a vast subject, and what a waste! I do, of course, have pe-culiar opinions on these subjects, and the last thing I can do is cite good reasons for them—it is all instinct, and you'll have to take it like that. Per-haps the book is a soaring wonder of pungent truth, but I doubt it. I suspect it is just another bundle of facts that would be as hard to argue with as they would be to accept in any way that's meaningful.

I wonder what you think of *The Great Gatsby*. If you have a moment I'd like to know. To my mind it's the great american novel, and in some im-mensely strange way Lee Oswald wrote the ending. If History professors in this country had any sense they would tout the book as a capsule cram course in the American Dream. I think it is the most American novel ever written. I remember coming across it in a bookstore in Rio de Janeiro; the title in Portuguese was *O Grande Gatsby*, and it was a fantastic thing to read it in that weird language and know that futility of the translation. If Fitzgerald had been a Brazilian he'd have had that country dancing to words instead of music; the Brazilian personality is that same double-faced, two-hearted thing that makes *Gatsby* a classic. If he had lived in Rio they'd have made him an emperor. Dom Scott I, the man with that strange horn that played everything off-key except the high white note.

And that's a bundle of stolen words and phrases for you, eh? And why not? For all I know you're one of these people who think the great ameri-can novel will be written by John Updike or even Terry Southern. Well, where were we? I was talking about your idea for a book, which you wisely despaired of in your P.S. You say it's "too much for one book," but I flatly disagree with you unless you insist that a "book" also means a Novel. I don't think so, and if this goddamn grey sky weren't coming up on me here I'd have time to tell you why. The dawn is killing me off, the fog is on the windows, the coons have robbed the cans, and down in Rio it is 8 a.m. and the whores who missed last night are already out on the beach in their fine little bikinis and if I could get my hands on just one of them I would be God's happiest man. But that's not likely tonight, so I'll get some sleep and wake up tomorrow with a fix on the Hell's Angels.

Sometime soon I will send you a report on Lasch's book. I appreciate your sending it and if you come across one with a high, white sound, by all means send that along too.

Sincerely—
Hunter S. Thompson

TO JIM RIDGEWAY, *THE NEW REPUBLIC:*

After his "motorcycle gang" piece had appeared in The Nation, *Thompson pitched an article to Ridgeway, an editor at* The New Republic. *Ridgeway wrote back asking Thompson to write on teenage fruit-pickers in California.*

June 28, 1965
318 Parnassus
San Francisco

Dear Jim:

Finally got back on the teen-*bracero* thing today and here's what it looks like, according to Jack Rucker, who handles the program (for the California Employment Office) for the northern part of the state.

818 teen-types came in from out of state two weeks before the California high schools got out for summer. 52 of those are still here. The others left for a variety of reasons, low pay being paramount. The growers contend (and Rucker seems to agree) that the promised wage of $1.40 an hour proved wholly uneconomical in most cases because the lads were simply too slow. A crate of strawberries that would sell for no more than $2.25 was costing $2.80 to get off the vines. So the strawberry pay rate was adjusted somewhat drastically to $1.00 a crate, and this brought on a labor mutiny when it became apparent that many of the lads could earn no more than $2 or $3 a day. The situation now is mixed. Strawberry picking is over the hump and the next big stoop crop in the Salinas area is lettuce, which is heavier and tougher than strawberries. If the (market) price of lettuce drops, as Rucker implied it would, the pro pickers are expected to move north to Santa Clara and Alameda for apricots, a tree-crop which is easier to pick. That will leave lettuce for the teen-*braceros*, and there will be a lot of hernias.

As of now the "teeners" are guaranteed pay (at varying rates) for 64 hours in a two-week period. That's $89.60 for each two weeks, and the minute that looks uneconomical the growers will do something about it. And even that $89.60 is the top estimate. What happens is that they hire on in a sort of blanket agreement, with different pay rates for different crops. Pay rates also vary from grower to grower. A kid might be picking strawberries in the morning at $1.00 a crate, and carrots in the afternoon at $1.40 an hour. A professional picker in the same field as a kid might earn twice or three times as much, depending on how they're paid.

What it boils down to is that for any kind of real story I'd have to go down to the Salinas valley, clamp onto Ben Lopez (the growers' labor honcho) and zero in on one specific situation. The kids are obviously being exploited to the hilt, but in order to explore the growers' point of view I'd have to go down there and get a real handle. There are two sides to the story but that doesn't mean it's evenly balanced. Tom Pitts from the AFL-CIO takes a harder line than the State Employment people, but the truth is that this labor is so ill-paid that the union fatbellies can only see it in terms of principle, not people. Have you ever heard Woody Guthrie's song about "Deportees"? It fits here.

The nut of it is the situation is too in flux for any quick piece from the desk. And needless to say I can't go to Salinas for a weekend and then sell a short piece for $30. For that you need a dilettante of some kind, and I ain't he. Maybe Paul Jacobs is loose enough right now for that stuff, but I doubt it.

The reason I've been tardy in replying is that I've been dealing hard and fast for the past two weeks on a book contract, which I finally signed Saturday. For the next few months I'll be doing a book on Motorcycle Gangs, but in the process I'll be moving around the state quite a bit and might be able to get some stuff for you that I couldn't reach otherwise. (Hell, I see here where I've sold you badly short at "$30 for a short piece." At eight cents a word, 750 comes out to $60, which is slightly better. Now if you wanted 2000 words . . . yeah, the old story, eh?)

The view right now from my end is that I'd like to do a piece or two for you and I'll do what I can, but since I have a deadline on the book I can't afford to spend much time on anything extra unless I get decently paid for it. I can't guarantee you that three days in Salinas will produce a good Fuck the Growers story, but I suspect something like that would come out of it. As a matter of fact I happen to know a lettuce grower in Salinas and he's a Fascist lunatic, but we'd need a few details before I'd be willing to sign my name to any such testimony. At a rough guess I'd say the story I have in mind would be worth a minimum of 1500 words, which comes to $120 by your count, since I figure it would cost me no less than $25 a day for three days and that's scrimping. On the other hand I've always prided myself on being christian, so I'll do it for $175—of which $75 will go toward expenses.

This is really pretty cheap dialogue, eh? I don't mind haggling about $7500, but going to the mat for $75 is pure ugly. I leave you to ponder the meaning of it, and—in looking back over this note—I see upstairs that I appear to be calling Paul Jacobs a "dilettante." Not so; that was a jab that didn't come off, but what the hell.

Anyway, send word. And what became of my "Grounds for Eviction" poem? I expected to see it on this week's cover.

Sincerely,
Hunter S. Thompson

TO TOM WOLFE:

When the National Observer *refused to run Thompson's review of* The Kandy-Kolored Tangerine-Flake Streamline Baby, *he forever severed his ties with the magazine. He did, however, send Wolfe the carbon of his review along with this letter.*

July 6, 1965
318 Parnassus
San Francisco

Dear Mr. Wolfe:

I owe the *National Observer* in Washington a bit of money for stories paid and never written while I was working for them out here, and the way we decided I'd work it off was book reviews, of my own choosing. Yours was one; they sent it to me and I wrote this review, which they won't print. I called the editor (the kulture editor) the other day from the middle of a Hell's Angels rally at Bass Lake and he said he was sorry and he agreed with me etc. but that there was a "feeling" around the office about giving you a good review. I doubt this failure will do you much harm, but it pisses me off in addition to costing me $75, so I figured the least I could do would be to send the carbon along to you, for good or ill. Unfortunately, I wrote it with the *Observer* format in mind and my normal comments would be a bit louder in all directions. But I understand you used to work for the *Post* so I figure you know that score.

Anyway, here's the review, and if it does you any good in the head to know that it caused the final severance of relations between myself and the *Observer*, then at least it will do somebody some good. As for myself I am joining the Hell's Angels and figure I should have done it six years ago.

Sincerely,
Hunter S. Thompson

TO TOM WOLFE:

At Wolfe's request Thompson sent him a copy of his Hell's Angels article.

July 14, 1965
318 Parnassus
San Francisco

Dear Tom—

Here's the *Nation* piece. A guy named Whitworth did something on them for the *Trib* a few Sundays back; that's probably where you heard about mine. If and when you have no use for this copy, please ship it back. I'm writing a book on the Hell's Angels & other cycle gangs for Ballantine, and copies of this piece are in big demand among the troopers. It is my big In.

In the same mail with yours today came a wild fang job from the *Observer,* calling me every kind of sneaky shithead for sending you that carbon. They seem to fear some kind of action from you. I suspect their revenge will be to cut me out of the upcoming *Observer* anthology. The guy who compiled it told me I had seven pieces in it, more than any staffer. And that—after this episode—will never do. Hopefully, my cheque is already vouchered; I will cash it at once with the Dow-Jones office out here, thereby coming back at them like a scorpion.

Definitely look forward to seeing you out here and will lay in some John Powers Irish for the drink-out. When do you plan to be in San Francisco? At some point in August I'll be down in LA, check on that end of the cycle action. But my schedule is loose, so give me an idea of yours and I'll plan to be here. You're welcome to the extra bed in my writing room if you feel up to the drinking that would inevitably ensue. My number here is 664-xxxx, listed under "Owl," not Thompson. OK for now, and thanks for the good letter.

HST

TO CAREY MCWILLIAMS, *THE NATION:*

Thompson prepared to head to Los Angeles to write on the motorcycle clubs there.

July 20, 1965
318 Parnassus
San Francisco

Dear Carey:

In my letter of April 25 I made an error which I would now like to correct. I said that "by June, all the FSM [Free Speech Movement] leaders will be either in jail or the army, and Don Silverthorne will be Chancellor [of the University of California at Berkeley]." I should have set a September deadline on both predictions. Sentencing began this week for the Sproul Hall sit-ins and I suppose you saw the results. Steve DeCanio, who figures in my non-student story, drew 60 days, not suspended. He was over here at the apartment Sunday night and didn't seem worried at all. I tried to reach Silverthorne today, hoping for a comment on rumors of his pending appointment, but he can't be reached. [. . .]

I had a very off feeling today when I realized that most of the people I've done stories on recently are headed for jail—and I haven't been writing crime stories. On my list to call when I woke up this morning were De-Canio, Ken Kesey, and Sonny Barger, president of the Oakland Hell's Angels. DeCanio was sentenced yesterday,[20] Kesey is out on some sort of complicated appeal, and Barger goes on trial August 18 for attempted murder.[21] I think there has to be some sort of a story in this—perhaps a reflective, opinionated creed of some kind, or a nervous warning that the front lines are getting closer every day. For instance, I counted myself lucky that some FBI types didn't check by my place prior to Johnson's visit and ask how I'd like to take a ride up to a swimming camp on the Russian River for a few days, congenial company guaranteed and all meals free. I say this because about a month ago I wrote Johnson a pretty wild-eyed letter, canceling my application for the governorship of American Samoa, a post I've coveted for some time. Larry O'Brien was carrying the ball for me until he quit. Then I figured Johnson wouldn't have the imagination to appoint me on his own, so I bowed out with a great skirting of anti-administration rhetoric.

Well, my point in writing this letter has nothing to do with the above. I merely wanted to know how I might get hold of Laslo Benedek.[22] I'm going down to L.A. sometime soon to check that end of the cycle action and I thought it might be nice to check with Benedek, Brando and Lee Marvin for some motorcycle gangs. For they had quite a bit to do with publicizing the cult and I think their ideas might make interesting reading. But I have no idea how to reach any of them and I recall you saying you knew Benedek. Send me an address if you can.

I'll also check on the hot-rod action in L.A. That is the capital. As for Non-Student, I am holding the galleys as long as possible because I know I'm going to have to do some rewriting and I don't want to do it too far prior to publication. Send a line when you can.

Thanks—HST

TO MURRAY FISHER, *PLAYBOY:*

Thompson had been commissioned by Playboy *to write on Ken Kesey and the Hell's Angels.*

20. Steve DeCanio was a twenty-two-year-old Berkeley radical and editor of *Spider*.
21. The trial ended with a hung jury and eventual reduction of the charge to assault with a deadly weapon, to which Barger pleaded guilty and served six months in jail.
22. Director of *The Wild One*.

August 9, 1965
318 Parnassus
San Francisco

Dear Mr. Fisher:

Here are a few notes, questions, etc. on the Hell's Angels action:

How about fotos? The Angels themselves keep a vast scrapbook and they'd be more than willing to submit a selection, but the *Post* is ahead of us on this (unfortunately I gave the *Post* man a hell of a lot of help— but not realizing I'd soon be competing with him) and we'd have to wait until we see which ones they use, if any. I know a lad in L.A. who has some pretty good stuff, but some of that went to the *Post*, too. The papers here have some decent crime-type photos; the *Chronicle*, in particular, has one very good set, and I know the police reporter who helped them get it. I might even try some myself. I'm good, but spotty. Anyway, let me know.

Also, I'd like to have an official-looking letter from you, saying I'm doing the story for *Playboy*. Last night I was grabbed by the gendarmes at Ken Kesey's loony bin in La Honda. (I introduced him to the San Francisco Angels last week and he decided to have a party for them; the locals flipped and the road in front of Kesey's house was swarming with cop cars.) They stopped everybody either coming or going and went over the cars for possible violations. My tail-light lenses were cracked, so they cited me, and would have taken both me and Allen Ginsberg to jail, I think, if I hadn't been sporting a tape recorder. Ginsberg was so enraged by the harassment that he might want to write an ode about it. If it interests you, I'll ask him. Anyway, neither my woodsy garb nor Ginsberg's foot-long beard made the right sort of impression, and a letter from you might have saved me $25 — which I think in all fairness should go down as an expense item, since the incident will go into the article.

On the subject of expenses, how much would you people be willing to go for towards rental of a big bike? I think I should ride with these boys for a few weeks, to get the feel of it, but as it stands now I won't be able to afford it until I get my second hunk of money from Ballantine, which won't be for several months. So far I haven't found a place that rents big stuff, so I might have to buy one—a junker of some kind, but good enough to hold up for a month or so. If it comes to that, would you be willing to contribute, in the form of expenses, toward the purchase? And how much? Let me know on all this stuff ASAP. Thanks,

Hunter S. Thompson

TO WILLIAM J. KENNEDY:

August 10, 1965
318 Parnassus
San Francisco

Dear Willie:

It's raining like hell here and I'm seized with one of those 3:00 a.m. desires to get back to my roots, etc. My desk is a mountain of shit and I just found the letter you sent from Puerto Rico, pinned to my wall, blank side out, with the address of a wrecking yard on the back. I have no idea why.

Anyway, it seems like a hell of a while since I've heard from you. The last I heard, you were sitting in the Cafe Riviera, waiting for some loony to rush in and hurl a sack of lime in the place. I'd like to have been there. What the hell are you doing? I see your name in the *Observer* even less frequently than mine, which is to say, nada. I had a bad wrangle with them on a Tom Wolfe review, and we said a mutual fuck you, with me about $500 ahead. I should have got off that dead man's train two years ago, but I was too lazy.

As I think I told you, this Hell's Angels thing has just exploded for real on me. In addition to the book contract, I just got an assignment from *Playboy*—turning down a *Cavalier* offer in the meantime—and now even the *Stanford Literary Review* wants a Hell's Angels piece. Yesterday a producer from the Merv Griffin show called me, asking if they could do a half-hour on the Angels. I said probably not, and turned him over to some crazed monster with a full beard and shoulder-length hair who was at that time sitting in my living room, jabbering into a tape recorder. After a few minutes the man hung up, but I'm sure he'll call again. My luck on this is that the Angels dug my *Nation* piece, and now consider me the only straight press type they know. So I'm in a position to deal with other people more or less savagely. The one exception was a guy from the *Saturday Evening Post*, here last week for a cycle story, whom I helped way too much for my own good. But in any case, he's a very decent guy and if you ever get to Princeton, look up a man named Bill Murray. You'd get along.

Also, before I forget, *Pageant* finally ran my Big Sur piece in the current (September) issue. Pick it up and comment. I may be approaching the point where I think everything I write is great, just because it's published.

My action here consists now of dealing exclusively with motorcycle thugs—almost to the point of becoming one myself. As a matter of fact I am now pressing *Playboy* to pay for a bike, so I can ride with these guys and get the feel of it. Ballantine, as far as I can tell, expects me to take the expenses out of the $6000. All I've done for them so far is sign a contract and cash their check for the advance, which leaves me at the moment with $22. I haven't even sent them an outline.

As things stand now, I have a (to be revised) piece due at *The Nation* by September 1, also a book review for them on the same date. Also a 5000-word piece to *Playboy* by then, and a short but pithy thing for *Stanford Literary Review.* The first half of the book is due September 15, and so far I haven't written a word. This is in fact a kind of showdown for me; the *Playboy* piece, for instance, carries a $300 guarantee, and they're not the sort to overlook a failure on that level. Nor would Ballantine be happy to write off $1500. In short, if I blow the action, I'm done. And I never even asked for it. All I wanted was a $1500 advance on the novel, with no guarantee at all. The moral here, I think, is never knock *The Nation* just because they pay $100. All that stuff I wrote for the *Observer* apparently died on the vine, but this one job for *The Nation* paid off in real gold. If you get any kind of socio-political story out of Albany, call Carey McWilliams and say I sent you. He's a hell of a decent editor; for $100 each, he has to be.

In all, my life has gone into a very strange groove. The other night I was arrested with Allen Ginsberg, as we left Ken Kesey's party for the Hell's Angels. My rent is paid two months in advance, which is perhaps the most unusual thing I can say at this time. And my home is full, night and day, of heinous thugs. On Friday one of them is bringing over some cubes of LSD and we are going to lock ourselves in. Sandy is terrified of it all, and Juan cries at the sight of these monsters, but the phone keeps ringing and people keep talking about money. I hope to be finished for good with this thing by Christmas, then go to either Brazil, Mexico or Chile. By then I should be able to get an advance on either The Rum Diary or some other novel, so I'm feeling pretty tough on that score.

Otherwise, life here continues along the same lines. What about yours? What general plans? I would again suspect a try at *Cavalier*; they apparently start at $750, at least that's what they offered me, which is half the *Playboy* figure, but a much easier and more human bunch to deal with. I plan to pursue that one later. Hell, I plan to pursue a lot of things later, but it's still raining here and I'm a long way from whatever I wanted to say when I began. You'll have to pardon the manic tone of this letter; this recent action has jangled my concepts. All this money-talk, plus living with the Hell's Angels, is changing my brain. Send a word to clear the air, and say what's happening there. I think there's a good chance we'll see you around Christmas, en route to somewhere. Hello to Dana; Sandy and Juan are both asleep, but I'm sure they'd say something decent if they knew I was writing you right now. Juan has become a dangerous bomb. Shit, I'm tired. It's 4:17. For christ's sake, write.

Precipitously,
HST

TO EDITOR, *SAN FRANCISCO CHRONICLE:*

*Thompson, not wanting his friends at the newspaper to know he was the let-
ter writer, used the pseudonym Dawn Thompson. (Dawn was Sandy's middle name.)*

September 17, 1965
318 Parnassus
San Francisco

Sir:

From the wilds of Colorado I followed your campaign against the de-
humanization of phone numbers. Some of San Francisco's "best minds"
were in the vanguard, I'm told, yet it all came to naught. Out there in the
frozen Rockies I toasted the lost cause, and sympathized. There go the
foundations, I said to myself; from now on it's just a matter of time.

Now, many months later, I find myself living in San Francisco. Today
the phone company sent a man to hook up my phone—and, sure as hell,
I had a seven-number digit that neither man nor beast could ever get
straight in his head. The prefix was 891, followed by four others. A monster, and a senseless one, for sure, when you consider that New York City,
with some 10 million residents, still manages to find word prefixes for all
the phone exchanges.

I stared at my number, 891. Six letters to play with, and quite a few possible words. In the end I created my own exchange, "Otter 1." Why not?
There's no forgetting it, and the system allows for a much higher degree of
personalization than the old standards. Consider the possibilities—a virtual riot of individuality.

The only sad thing about it is that nobody thought—while the phone
company was being so ugly and arbitrary—of beating them at their own
game. The inevitable defeat of the anti-digit-dialing boys was just another
example of the San Francisco syndrome at work—digging in the heels,
looking desperately backward, and finally being whipped into line by corporate entities with neither the wit nor the will to understand what the
diehards were talking about in the first place.

Why not try the "Otter 1" approach for a change? Try a little offense, instead of defensive heel-dragging all the time. The Opposition ain't that
tough. Sincerely,

Dawn Thompson

September 18, 1965
San Francisco

Dear Willie—

I was just about to ship off another postcard, but I figured it would piss you off, so I'll try a short letter.

I've just sent a postcard to Cooke, trying to straighten him out on what I at least meant to say—and think I said, for that matter—when I called him on whatever night it was. The idea that "nobody cares" has never occurred to me, especially since I feel a long way from "making it." What I tried to do was convey to Cooke the wisdom that "nobody knows." In other words, I had just realized the hopelessness of seeking or even tolerating advice on what or how to write, and since Cooke was at the time trying to put things on paper, I thought he might benefit from my wisdom.

Behind that feeling was the realization, which came in a rush, that if I hadn't got fucked up with the *Observer* I might still be turning out one or two pieces a month for them, and fighting to scrape up enough here and there for a bottle of booze. The seemingly incredible reaction to that *Nation* piece made me realize how sadly I've been wasting my time for two years. I've written better pieces for the *Observer,* but nobody read them. For that matter, I've even clipped them and sent samples around, but due to the ingrown timidity and insecurity of the Establishment, it seems you need certain stamps and endorsements before you can be real. And *The Nation* is apparently one of those stamps. Anyway, it pissed me off to think we are dealing with a gang of punks who don't have the vaguest idea what's good or bad until somebody puts the stamp on it. Like the novel. I think it's awful, you think it's awful, and Random House just bought hardcover rights on the unwritten cycle book in order to get an option on the novel.[23] The woman at Pantheon loves it; she's afraid my rewrite will fuck it up. Christ, what am I to think? I don't have the crazy balls to say, "No, I'll refuse to let you publish it." And besides, I'm broke.

Anyway, I don't give a flying fuck who cares or doesn't care about my status situation, and primarily because it ain't even real enough to make me halfway comfortable. The whole thing is based on a book I haven't even started; two publishers have bought it without seeing more than the

23. Jim Silberman, who was senior editor at "little" Random House (the eponymous flagship division of the corporation that owned Pantheon and Ballantine), had seen early chapters of *Hell's Angels* and insisted that his division should bring it out in hardcover before Ballantine published the paperback. The contract Silberman and Thompson signed effectively took "The Rum Diary" away from Pantheon, though Random House never published it.

Nation piece and an outline I did wild drunk in less than an hour. At the moment I'm taking time out from a long-overdue *Playboy* piece, which is giving me rottenass trouble, and which could make the difference between solvency and sadness for the next two months, while I wrestle with the cycle book. A bounce will put me in a terrible hole. The trouble is I know so much I can't begin to fit the whole thing into 5000 words—which was easy for *The Nation*, because I didn't know anything at all. My research on that was one afternoon at the *Chronicle*, going through clips, and one night at the apartment with five drunken Angels. But now I have six months of massive research to distill, and it's going to be a hell of a lot easier for the book than it is for an article. In a nut, this whole thing gives me the fear. If all I had to do was work a few months on the novel, with guaranteed publication, I'd be a happy man, but the way it stands now is a fucking nightmare. Besides that I've already been nailed to the floor on the contract and the money for it all is shamefully small. That sluggish motherfucking Raines[24] really set me up for a raping. I am now trying to get rid of him, but it's not easy.

Your comments on the *Pageant* thing were apt, but what the hell? I bought only one copy of the magazine and couldn't care less. There's another one coming out in December; don't bother to comment. I should also have one in the September 27 issue of *The Nation*, which might be decent. It was written last spring, though, and I've forgotten what I said.

As for LSD, I highly recommend it. We had a fine, wild weekend and no trouble at all. The feeling it produces is hard to describe. "Intensity" is a fair word for it. Try half a cube at first, just sit in the living room and turn on the music—after the kids have gone to bed. But never take it in uncomfortable or socially tense situations. And don't have anybody around whom you don't like. [. . .]

You sound happier with your "insolvency" that I am in my panic. I feel like I've been hoisted toward the sun on the end of a very sharp sword, and the first wrong move will do me in for real. In the meantime, don't rejoice at my "success." I'm a long way from home, and I'm scared. Why don't you just write me a long happy letter about how great I am. As it is, my status in the neighborhood derives entirely from the basketball court, and that's not much help on these long nights.

At the moment, Sandy and Juan are down in Monterey for the Jazz Festival, and I'm supposed to be here whipping the *Playboy* thing. Yeah.

HST

---

24. Theron Raines was Thompson's agent for *Hell's Angels*. Thompson dismissed him shortly after this letter.

TO JIM THOMPSON:

After hearing the Jefferson Airplane play, Thompson was so impressed that he telephoned Ralph Gleason, cultural critic for the San Francisco Chronicle, *and brought him down to the club. Thompson also hurried to tell his brother Jim, then fifteen, about his discovery.*

September 25, 1965
318 Parnassus
San Francisco

Dear Jim—

As it happens, your letter came the morning after I saw Lightnin' Hopkins at a club here called The Matrix.[25] I know one of the owners and go there pretty often. If you're looking around for some action on the folk-rock scene, get set for a group called the Jefferson Airplane, which also works out of The Matrix. They will lift the top of your head right off. A really wild sound. It won't be out for a while; they just went to L.A. to record last week, but when it comes out it's going to go like Zaannnggg!!! They make those silly goddamn Beatles sound like choirboys.

In the meantime, be careful what you tell your friends about my fame and fortune. We could both end up looking pretty silly. At the moment I've sold two books—one of which is lousy, and the other isn't even written. So take it easy. It looks like things are happening, but these things happen real slow as far as fame and fortune are concerned. And a lot of damn good people aren't making a dime.

Speaking of that, I have another article in this week's *Nation* (September 27), and I guess the December *Pageant* will have another one. They're both old things and I barely remember what I wrote, but if you see them send a line and say what you think. I'd really like to know how my style strikes you on various pieces. Also tell Mom that Dow-Jones is putting out something called *The Observer's World* in November, and they tell me I have a few pieces in it. I think it's a good book. Anyway, look for it.

As far as whatever stage you're in, and whatever you think about your destiny, I sure as hell wouldn't worry about it. When I was your age my future was nothing less then grim—and I suppose it still is, to some god-fearing people—but since then I've managed to get around a bit and do just about what I intended to do in the first place. All you need to do is figure out what your action is and hang on, no matter what they tell you. And even if you never make it, you'll feel better trying instead of giving up and going along with the noise crowd. But right now you don't have to worry

25. The Matrix was the seminal nightclub for the Jefferson Airplane, Big Brother and the Holding Company, and other "acid rock" bands.

about what you're going to *do*. The important thing is to follow your instincts about what you *aren't* going to do. Most people wind up going against their instincts, and it makes them miserable for the rest of their lives. It'll be five more years before you really begin to get the drift of what you should be doing. So, in the meantime, keep loose and listen to Dylan. And write me again. You write damn good letters. I was 20 before I could write a decent postcard.

Love, Hunter

TO CAREY MCWILLIAMS, *THE NATION:*

Thompson thought the following sidebar should accompany his article on the nonstudent left in The Nation.

September 30, 1965
San Francisco

Dear Carey:

You may or may not want to run this as a box. I think it's the nut of the issue, perhaps even deserving of another article, which I can't possibly do right now. Anyway, here is a short commentary.

HST

This article was written last spring, but it missed a June deadline and consequently had to be updated. Since then, more than time has passed. The political climate has changed. In June it appeared from the student (and non-student) viewpoint, that the University administration—and hence, the "Establishment"—was actively seeking a new view, a meeting of the minds, a thaw in the guerrilla warfare between two massively disparate generations.

But the long lull of summer gave the Governor, the Regents, the University administration and other hired technicians a chance to re-group, and now they are no longer on the defensive. In June, for instance, the new and legal definition of a "student" was liberal enough to include such recent drop-outs—and prospective re-entries—as Mario Savio and the bulk of the FSM leadership. But the new directives, issued by Pres. Clark Kerr on July 1, drew a very heavy line between the official definitions of a "student" and a "non-student." Previously, it had been realistically vague. The reason for the re-definition is the new law on "outsiders," which makes it a misdemeanor for any non-student to enter the campus for the purpose of disturbing whatever peace may or may not exist, according to the University authorities. As the law stands now, Mario Savio could be arrested on sight, anywhere on the campus, on the assumption that he was there to stir up trouble.

Such was not the case at the end of last semester, when there was much ado in the press about the "new look" at Berkeley. The impression given then was that a new clique of "progressive" Regents had seized control from the "Old Guard." The facts of the matter were so finely suppressed that I—living in San Francisco and daily clipping all three papers for my files—had no idea of the change in this critical weight distribution until I made a routine phone check with the University's General Counsel in the course of updating this article.

The moral of this story, I suppose, is "Never Lose Your Momentum." But it is more specific than that. If this increasingly "illegal" tumult in Berkeley and the rest of the Bay Area proves nothing else, it should at least explode the myth of California as a "progressive, enlightened state." The truth is that there is a new and very resilient Conservatism booming here. The news value of a radical minority crowds political reality out of the headlines, and gives a false impression that dies all the harder on election day. The only reason Richard Nixon is not Governor of this state today is that he never learned the new Establishment vocabulary. But the saddest truth of all is that even if Nixon were Governor, hardly anyone would know the difference.

—Hunter S. Thompson

"COLLECT TELEGRAM FROM A MAD DOG"

Spider magazine,
October 13, 1965

Not being a poet, and drunk as well,
leaning into the diner and dawn
and hearing a juke box mockery of some better
human sound
I wanted rhetoric
but could only howl the rotten truth
Norman Luboff
should have his nuts ripped off with a plastic fork.
Then howled around like a man with the
final angst,
not knowing what I wanted there
Probably the waitress, bend her double
like a safety pin,
Deposit the mad seed before they
tie off my tubes

or run me down with Dingo dogs
for not voting
at all.

Suddenly a man with wild eyes rushed
out from the wooden toilet

Specifically Luboff and the big mongers,
the slumfeeders, the perverts
and the pious.

The legal man agreed
We had a case and indeed a duty to
Right these Wrongs, as it were
The Price would be four thousand in front and
ten for the nut.
I wrote him a check on the Sawtooth
National Bank,
but he hooted at it
While rubbing a special oil on
his palms
To keep the chancres from itching
beyond endurance
On this Sabbath.
McConn broke his face with a running
Cambodian chop, then we
drank his gin, ate his blintzes
But failed to find anyone
to rape
and went back to the Mariners' Tavern
to drink in the sun.
Later, from jail
I sent a brace of telegrams
to the right people,
explaining my position.

TO SARA BLACKBURN, PANTHEON BOOKS:

Working around the clock on Hell's Angels, *Thompson touched base with Blackburn about "The Rum Diary." With the $1,500 he'd received on signing the contract for the Ballantine paperback edition of* Hell's Angels, *he purchased a red BSA 650 Lightning—the fastest bike available—so he could ride with the Hell's Angels.*

October 22, 1965

Dear Sara—

The bike has not actually blown up, but three mechanics say it's going to any minute—for three different reasons—so I took it back with a minor tuneup and am now driving the hell out of it, and damn the consequences. If I was done out of a grand I'm going to get some kicks, if nothing else.

For the time being you should do whatever you want with The Rum Diary manuscript. Everybody except my lawyer says Ballantine owns it, so I guess they do. I have now retired on pills and cheap whiskey, not to emerge again until this godrotten Hell's Angels thing is whipped, which might be quite a while. Until then there is no possibility of my writing a cheerful letter to you or anyone else. The only time I feel human is when I'm booming out on the motorcycle, which I think I'll do now, a quick run on the Coast Highway to clear my brain.

Sincerely,
Curt Testy

TO NORMAN MAILER:

Curious as to what Mailer thought about the Hell's Angels, Thompson sought a quote from him to use in his book.

November 4, 1965
318 Parnassus
San Francisco

Norman Mailer
c/o G.P. Putnam's Sons
200 Madison Ave.
NYC 16

Dear Norman:

Somewhere in late 1961 or so I sent you a grey, paperbound copy of Henry Miller's *The World of Sex*, one of 1000 copies printed "for friends of Henry Miller," in 1941. You never acknowledged it, which didn't show much in the way of what California people call "class," but which was understandable in that I recall issuing some physical threats along with the presentation of what they now tell me is a collector's item. I had no intention of "flogging you into a coma," of course, but if memory serves your sense of humor at that stage of the game was not what it might have been and I can see where there was not much point in your visiting a potential flip-out, in Big Sur or anywhere else.

And so be it. I hope you have the book and are guarding it closely. In your old age you can sell it for whatever currency is in use at the time.

In the meantime, I think you owe me a favor—and if you don't come through with it I'll have to put you down as a paunchy cocktail punk or maybe a noisy ape still trying to imitate his betters. Which reminds me of something I read somewhere, in the old days.

Anyway, by December 1, 1965 I'm supposed to have 80,000 words on the Hell's Angels to Ballantine—which they, in turn, have sold to Random House for April publication, and so far I have spent $4500 on booze, LSD and one giant bike for myself in the course of six months' research, while turning out a total of 34 first-draft pages. So I now have 25 days to come up with a massive jolt of words and wisdom—if for no other reason than that the fate of my already-written novel seems to ride on the commercial fortunes of this pre-sold, unwritten jumble of rape and violence.

The favor I'm asking is that you send me whatever bundle of words you can muster on the subject of the Hell's Angels. I'm assuming you know what I'm talking about here. If not, well . . . I guess it was bound to happen. (I maybe should add here that for the past eight months I've spent nearly all of my time with the Angels and I have plenty of stuff—but it occurred to me that you might have some original ideas on the thing, an odd comment or two that could add some zang to my text.)

Or maybe I should just say that I'm interested in your views on the thing, and leave it at that. I wouldn't want you to think that the book depends on you in any way, for I know you're a busy man and of course I understand. But if you have any comments on the Angels I'd be happy to include them in my text if they seem at all interesting. The book is a grab-bag of word-photos, libel, straight narrative, and occasional wisdom. Anything you might send would fit in the format I'm using—whether it actually has to do with the Hell's Angels, the psychic roots of the motorcycle syndrome, sex as a long-haired vision on two wheels, or anything else with even a slim pertinence. Needless to say, I would use your stuff however you wanted it used, or not at all. My own idea would be to come on with something like: "Norman Mailer, a would-be Hell's Angel for many years, put it all in a big plastic bag, to wit . . . etc."

Anyway, send what you can, but only if you feel up to it. I tend to assume an interest you might not have—or maybe you got over it. But even the reasons for that would be worth a look, and probably worth printing. My gimmick on this book is that I'm already so far into them on the money score that they can't quarrel much with what I send. Especially since they want a book on the Angels and I'm the only one who knows anything real about them. I say this to assure you that whatever you might send would definitely be for print.

So do what you will, and thanks for anything that helps.

Sincerely,

Hunter S. Thompson

TO R. A. ABERNATHY, PRESIDENT, AMERICAN MOTORS CORP.:

Thompson was fed up with his 1959 Rambler Custom, which kept breaking down.

December 1, 1965
318 Parnassus
San Francisco

R. A. Abernathy, Pres.
American Motors Corp.
14250 Plymouth Rd.
Detroit 32, Mich.

Dear Mr. Abernathy:

I see in a recent Standard & Poor notation that your Ramblers are not selling as well as they might, and it occurred to me that I might be able to give you at least one small reason why. On the same very minor scale I can also suggest a remedy, to wit:

It happens that I own and drive a 1959 Rambler Custom that is literally falling to pieces. Today some sort of crucial seal blew out in the transmission, spewing fluid all over the engine. I solved this by jamming a large cork in the filler pipe, but I suspect the transmission is on its last legs anyway. On the other hand I have felt the whole car was on its last leg for at least six months, and for that reason I long since abandoned any idea of paying for repairs.

To release the emergency brake (in place of the handle, which broke off) I use a tack hammer. To counter the absence of a parking gear (which broke off in my hand one foggy afternoon) I use a large wooden chock under a front or a back wheel, depending on which way I'm facing on these steep San Francisco hills. The prospect of the car breaking loose from its feeble moorings is not a pleasant one. The car, on its own, is easily capable of causing severe damage or even death. I have insurance against this sort of thing, but no amount of insurance could prevent the ugly scene that would certainly transpire if the car ran amok in downtown San Francisco.

These are the only serious safety hazards in the car's make-up right now . . . unless we could include a teeth-rattling front-end shimmy that I have paid to have corrected twice in three years and am not about to pay for again. At 55, the car shakes like it has just been broadsided by a bazooka shell, and anywhere between 40 and 70 it is a real effort to keep the thing in a lane. Crossing the Golden Gate Bridge, for instance, is such a nightmare that I only make that trip when absolutely necessary. Another safety hazard, now that I think on it, has to do with the fact that all four door latches have apparently frozen in the open position. The two back doors are tied shut by a large rope across the back seat, making it impossible for them to be opened under any circumstances. I did this to make the back seat safe for my young son. But the front doors are a different matter: anyone getting in on either side has to pull the door closed and then reach out with a sort of putty knife—which I keep on the dashboard—and pry the outside latch in such a way that it will engage and thus keep the door from swinging open on turns.

Other, less serious safety problems include inoperative turn signals, broken tail-light lenses (due to the lights being in a position to be broken by any car maneuvering into a parking space behind me), unreliable windshield wipers and dead shock absorbers which allow the car to lean dangerously on curves. I don't want to write a monster letter so I'll merely sketch the rest of the problems:

1.) A loud rod knock, despite a new crankshaft 3 years ago and a complete lower-end overhaul less than two years later. 2.) An almost entirely rebuilt—piece by piece—electrical system, including both a new starter and generator. 3.) New brake cylinders and shoes on both rear wheels—installed after I lost my brakes entirely one day in the middle of Glenwood Springs, Colorado. 4.) The defroster has jammed and the windshield washer has failed. 5.) The heater fills the car with such a stench that I can no longer use it. 6.) The driver's seat has deteriorated completely, making the car extremely uncomfortable to drive.

I could carry on with this wretched indictment, but there would be no point in it. The fact is that I am driving one of the worst advertisements on the road, and until very recently I was driving the car all over the Western United States. In 1963 I was a West Coast correspondent for the *National Observer*, driving all over California and making trips now and then as far as Butte, Montana, Denver and Las Vegas. In 1963 I put about 35,000 miles on the car; in 1964 it was about 20,000 and this year I have spent most of my time working on a book, which cut my travel to less than 10,000 miles in all. I mention my travels because I have lost count of the times I have had to stop in service stations for minor repairs, and sometimes for major repairs—which can be damned expensive when some out-back mechanic has you entirely at his mercy. In the course of these tribulations I have cursed the car savagely in service stations all over the West—not with any intention of queering the Rambler image, but usually in a fit of anger that finally became a ritual as the car failed me more and more often.

The obvious solution to my problem would of course be to get rid of the car by trading it in on some newer and more dependable model . . . and there is the catch, and the reason I'm writing this letter. Since leaving my position as correspondent for the *Observer* I have been making a living as a free-lance writer, and in that capacity I can't get a dime's worth of credit. The irony of the thing is that I'm making more money now than I did on a regular income: just last month, for instance, I paid cash for a brand new $1375 motorcycle, which has taken the burden of driving this rotten car off my own shoulders and placed it on those of my wife, who is scared to death of it.

Perhaps I might have been wiser to put that motorcycle money into a car, thus getting rid of this junker. But I thought I'd be better off with a new, warrantied motorcycle than I would with another second-hand, four-wheeled liability . . . and I still think so, even though my wife is still cursing me.

In any case—referring back to my opening paragraph—I'm certain that this horrible failure of a car that I'm forced to drive and display is a more effective advertisement for Rambler than any half-dozen TV spots or magazine ads you are laying out quite a bit of money for. When you consider the impression that this wreck—along with my raving about it—has made on probably 150 service station attendants in the course of two years, there can be no doubt in your mind that this thing is a serious liability and a threat to the Rambler image.

My suggestion, therefore, is that you supply me with a new and dependable Rambler that I won't have to curse about and apologize for at least once a day. I don't mean to suggest in any way that you *owe* me a new car, but I think it would be mutually beneficial for you to supply me with one. I have, after all, supported this erratic offspring of yours for nearly three years, with considerable mental anguish for both myself and my wife. But then we both understand that ours is a free market economy and the devil takes the hindmost. Mr. Barnum described it pretty well with his classic line about a sucker being born every minute.

But I also suggest that American Motors is in no position these days to follow Barnum's lead. I don't need a Standard & Poor sheet to tell me your share of the market is slipping. All I have to do is look around. And if your public relations people have any kind of imagination they can get a lot of press mileage by using this letter as a reason for putting me behind the wheel of a new Rambler. As a gimmick it would cost you less than nothing in terms of your advertising budget, but if your people handled it with any élan it could easily be turned into an original and effective advertisement.

Obviously, I'm not taking all this time and space with the idea of doing you a favor. The nut of my argument is that I'm driving around in something that I—in your position—would go to great lengths to hide from the general public. If my fiscal position were such that I could obtain a loan to buy a newer and better car I would certainly take advantage of it and not bother you with this kind of correspondence. Honesty compels me, however, to say that if I had the funds to finance a new car I would not buy a Rambler. And I don't believe you would, either, if you had the kind of experiences that I've had with this one.

So that's about it, from here. I look forward to hearing from you in one way or another. I won't be holding my breath until somebody presents me with a gift certificate for a new Rambler, but as I said earlier I think you can do more with this letter than brush it aside as the ravings of a crank . . . which I may be, but I make my living writing for national magazines, so I leave you to ponder the meaning of it.

Sincerely,
Hunter S. Thompson

TO R. A. ABERNATHY, PRESIDENT, AMERICAN MOTORS CORP.:

Thompson had received a bland, form-letter response from American Motors Corp.

December 10, 1965
318 Parnassus
San Francisco

Dear Mr. Abernathy:

I received the letter from your flunky and consider it a challenge to my imagination. With the help of several friends I am going to turn my car into an exhibit. It will move around the Bay Area, covered with various signs and slogans taken from Rambler advertisements. I am very proud to be aware of my pride. Today I arranged for a sign-painter to reproduce selected portions of our correspondence. It will take a week or two before the exhibit is complete. At that time I shall send you a few color photographs.

In closing, I remain, yours for more creative advertising.

Sincerely,
Hunter S. Thompson

*Hell's Angels Terry the Tramp (left),
Mountain Girl, and Sonny Barger at Ken
Kesey's La Honda retreat.*
(PHOTO BY HUNTER S. THOMPSON;
COURTESY OF HST COLLECTION)

Thompson after his stomping by Hell's Angels.
(COURTESY OF HST COLLECTION)

1966

----

318 PARNASSUS . . . ABANDON ALL HOPE YE WHO ENTER HERE . . . SAVED BY CHARLES KURALT . . . FALLING IN LOVE WITH A 650 LIGHTNING . . . ARMED AND DRUNK ON HIGHWAY 101 . . . STOMPED BY GREEDY ANGELS . . . FAMOUS WRITER FLEES RONALD REAGAN . . . FROM THE SHIT HOUSE TO RANDOM HOUSE . . .

Far from being freaks, the Hell's Angels are a logical product of the culture that now claims to be shocked by their existence. The generation represented by the editors of Time has lived so long in a world full of celluloid outlaws hustling toothpaste and hair oil that it is no longer capable of confronting the real thing. For twenty years they have sat with their children and watched yesterday's outlaws raise hell with yesterday's world . . . and now they are bringing up children who think Jesse James is a television character. This is a generation that went to war for Mom, God and Apple Butter, the American Way of Life. When they came back, they crowned Eisenhower and then retired to the giddy comfort of their TV parlors, to cultivate the subtleties of American history as seen by Hollywood.

--Hunter S. Thompson,
  Hell's Angels (published 1966)

TO JOAN BAEZ:

Thompson had met Baez in 1960 while living in Big Sur. The folk singer was starting a "school for nonviolence" in the Carmel Valley.

January 19, 1966
318 Parnassus
San Francisco

Dear Joanie—

After nearly a year writing a book about the Hell's Angels I am tired of violence and am seriously considering a try at your school. Could you send me a bulletin, brochure, etc.? On the matter of tuition I think we can probably work something out: in exchange for some peace at your place I'll put you onto the Angels. They represent a massive potential for many things. Ginsberg has softened them up a bit, but I think you'd fare a lot better. In the meantime, please send me all pertinent information and a valid application blank. Sandy is asleep, but if she were awake she'd say hello, so consider it said.

Sincerely,
Hunter S. Thompson

TO LYNDON JOHNSON:

January 26, 1966
318 Parnassus
San Francisco

Lyndon Johnson
White House
Washington, D.C.

Dear Mr. Johnson:

Now that somebody outside the Administration has finally come up with a workable "middle-way" solution to the Vietnam disaster, I feel it is only reasonable for me to withdraw my former advocacy of total withdrawal and urge you to go along with the "holding strategy" proposals by Gen. Gavin[1] and Walter Lippmann. This would at least give us a chance to pull in our horns and get the feel of things.

If, however, you are still goaded by your advisors to an all-or-nothing choice, I would have to stick with total withdrawal. I say this to emphasize that I have not in any way come around to your own point of view; but as a reasonably intelligent human being I think I have the sense to see that a controlled compromise is better than a total loss. I am not at all confident that you feel the same way, but the least I can do is write a five-cent letter and hope it will have some effect.

You can probably disregard all these letters—including any from Gavin, Ridgway[2] and Lippman—without endangering your position for 1968. But you will have hell on your hands keeping the door open for Humphrey in 1972, and by then every one of today's draftees will be voting.

I suppose this comes under the heading of a "dissenting letter," and I understand you turn all of these over to the FBI. But if wanting to avoid an Asian war makes me a subversive, then you have my address and you can put me in the file with Eisenhower and MacArthur.

> Sincerely,
> Hunter S. Thompson

TO PAUL SEMONIN:

Semonin was now a regular contributor to The Nation.

> February 9, 1966
> 318 Parnassus
> San Francisco

Paul—

Midnight again. No time to think about human contacts. Thanks immensely for the draft on Chase Manhattan Bank. How does it feel to be a running dog of capitalism? I refuse to believe you have any grip on reality until you stop chasing nymphets from Louisville. [. . .] Get yourself a sturdy wench who is dedicated to class struggle.

Save the high boy for me. I plan to make the swing before April unless they deliberately prevent it. My ambition now is to ride the bike to the NCAA basketball finals and then load up on LSD for all four games. I'm

---

1. General James Gavin was chief of staff to Supreme Allied Commander Dwight Eisenhower during World War II. He retired from the military in 1958 and became a critic of LBJ's Vietnam policy.
2. General Matthew Ridgway was U.S. supreme allied commander for the Korean War. After thirty-eight years of military service, he retired in June 1955, and later became another critic of LBJ's handling of Vietnam.

looking for a Kentucky-Duke final, which should generate real hysteria even without acid.

Sorry about the note to Sara [Blackburn], but these bastards won't answer my nice letters so I have to snap now and then. Significantly, I have no idea what sort of action you're referring to about Sara doing "everything she could." What happened? What couldn't she prevent? I can only assume that Pantheon was forced to reject The Rum Diary. But what's this about "hardback rights . . . turning her flank"?

Pantheon is a hardcover house. It's precisely this kind of splintered wisdom that's driving me wild. The last I heard, Pantheon was set to publish The Rum Diary. As far as I know they have both manuscripts. I have none. If the fuckers won't tell me anything I have no choice but to write vicious letters. From this distance there is literally nothing else I can do. Somebody wrote the other day and said they saw an article of mine in some magazine that I've never even heard of. Meanwhile I have to borrow money to pay the rent. It's maddening.

Today I got word that the bike engine is shot—in addition to $200–$300 worth of chassis damage. Apparently the accelerator jammed on full throttle while I was unconscious and burned out a main bearing. Another $200, minimum.

If it looks from your end like I won't make it by April, don't be polite about bugging me for the $200. I tend to put debts out of mind unless goaded. By the way it looks now I'll have to get there, just to find out what's happening on the money front. [. . .] I've never turned down $100 a day for anything, and never would. Tell Cooke to read Going Away before he starts any labor reporting ([it's by] Clancy Sigal). OK for now. I'll save the grant queries until I can get there and zero in. I'm still certain that something terrible is going to happen and this Hell's Angels book will go down the tube somehow.

Hunter S. Thompson

TO NELSON ALGREN:

Thompson greatly admired Nelson Algren, the Chicago-based novelist.

February 10, 1966
318 Parnassus
San Francisco

Dear Mr. Algren—
I am about finished with a book that is supposedly about the Hell's Angels. The motorcycle gentlemen. And for some reason I find that I've injected a large part of the opening to A *Walk on the Wild Side* into my own manuscript. This kind of snuck up on me. I'd intended to take off on your

Linkhorn bit, relating it to the wave of bastard types who settled in California after the war.

These people are Linkhorns, no doubt about it. But a Linkhorn on a big Harley is a new kind of animal. Anyway, I figured I'd better warn you and maybe even ask your permission to quote you to the extent that I have. It looks like about a thousand words, all wrapped up in quotes and prominently attributed to both you and your book. (No, it looks more like 500 words, which I could probably steal legally anyway, but I figure it's better to write and ask.) The stuff is too good to paraphrase, especially now that Linkhorns are making news all over, even running the country.

If you have any objections let me know quick, because the book is already three months overdue and the final deadline is March 1. Random is handling the hardcover. It was scheduled for April, but christ knows when it will come out now. If you don't get vicious about the quotes I'll tell them to send you a reviewer's copy.

I've reviewed two of yours for the *National Observer*—or rather one of yours and Shag Donohue's tome.[3] Donohue seemed to like his, but they wouldn't print the one I did on [*Notes from a*] *Sea Diary*.[4] You have got to get over the idea that you have a sense of humor. No, that's not it. It's this gag-line stuff. You're not a comedy writer. Neither was Conrad, but he wrote some very funny stuff. At any rate, I've given up book reviewing and the *National Observer* too.

Let me know if you have any objections to using your Linkhorn description. If I don't hear from you by March 1 I'll figure it's all clear.

Thanks—

Hunter S. Thompson

FROM NELSON ALGREN:

February 16, 1966
Iowa City, Iowa

Mr. Hunter S. Thompson
318 Parnassus
San Francisco, California

Dear Hunter Thompson,

Thanks for asking my advice. It is that using 500 words of *anything*, without permission, would lay you wide open to the legal department of the copyright owners of that book: i.e.: Farrar Straus & Giroux.

3. H.E.F. "Shag" Donohue edited a book of Algren interviews titled *Conversations with Nelson Algren* (New York, 1964).
4. *Notes from a Sea Diary: Hemingway All the Way* (New York, 1965) was one of Algren's least successful books.

Nor can I say that I find the idea of someone using a part of a book of mine as his own highly appealing. I don't have the time—nor the loot—to engage in some coast-to-coast legal pursuit. All I'd do would be to advise the publisher of your book that I'd written part of it, that's all.

Frankly, I can't see what good stuffing somebody else's material into your own work could do anybody. It's always a good idea for a writer to do the best he can with what he has.

Best wishes,
Algren

TO NELSON ALGREN:

Stunned by Algren's rejection of his request, Thompson fired back, unable to contain his disappointment.

February 19, 1966
318 Parnassus
San Francisco

Dear Mr. Algren:

Your letter arrived this morning and gave me pause. I don't want to argue with you about this Linkhorn business, regardless of what I end up doing about it, but even if I change the whole bit I don't want to leave you with the impression that I ever considered "stuffing" your material into my own work and calling it mine. And as for a writer doing "the best he can with what he has," maybe you should take another look at the *Sea Diary*. It seems to me you quoted a few people here and there: Villon, Hemingway, several critics, etc. What kind of special copyright law do you operate under? It must be a real hellbuster if it makes you legally immune to being quoted. It sounds like one of Nixon's laws.

I normally go out of my way to quote people who threaten to sue me for doing it, and so far I haven't been nicked for a penny. But I'll grant that maybe you misunderstood my letter. The tone was pretty sharp and boozy, but if you'll check line 13 and 14 you'll see where I said everything I intended to use is "all wrapped up in quotes and prominently attributed to both you and your book."

Which makes me wonder why you'd threaten to "advise" my publisher that you'd written the stuff. Do you think the fucker is blind? Why would he need letters from you to tell him what is already a part of the manuscript? I've quoted dozens of people in the book and most of them will have good reason to want to sue me, but not for plagiarism. When you file your legal papers you'll be in good company: *Time*, *Newsweek*, Nixon, Sen. George Murphy, the Attorney Gen. of Calif., the mayor of Laconia,

N.H., the Kiwanis Club and about 200 cops. Hell, I welcome lawsuits. The more the merrier. But I want them to be for the right reasons.

So let's leave it like this: I'm enclosing (hell, I'll make it part of the letter) a copy of that section of my manuscript that leads into the Linkhorn bit. It never occurred to me, frankly, that you'd be anything but pleased, or of course I wouldn't have written. I'm not even sure why I wrote, but I suppose it was because I found myself using more of your Linkhorn description than I planned to when I started. Regardless of what you think, I know damn well that no law prevents me from quoting you. If you want to call it "stealing," that's cool, but don't exclude yourself. I'm also using that "In my own country I am in a far off land . . ." thing that you stole from Villon. So I guess I'll see you both in court.

In the meantime, here's the context in which your Linkhorn description appears, as the text stands now. It begins on page 304 of the typewritten material, so you see I've developed a few leads before getting down to the Linkhorn angle. It is not a pillar of my narrative. Anyway, after devoting 300 pages to telling about the Hell's Angels, I decided to trace them back a ways—to develop their family trees, as it were. On pg. 303 I have a verse of a song that I stole from Woody Guthrie. This theft is clearly noted in the text, the words of the song are in italics (32 words in all) and the title is "Do-Re-Mi." Immediately following Guthrie's chorus, the text continues like this: "The song expressed three frustrated sentiments of more than a million Okies, Arkies, and Hillbillies who made the long trek to the Golden State and found it was just another hard dollar.

"By the time these gentlemen arrived, the Westward Movement was already beginning to solidify. The 'California way of life' proved to be the same old game of musical chairs—but it took a long time for this news to filter back east, and meanwhile the Gold Rush continued. Once here, the newcomers hung on for a few years, breeding prolifically, until the war started. Then they either joined up or had their pick of jobs on a booming labor market. Either way, they were 'Californians' when the war ended. The old way of life was scattered back along Route 66, and their children grew up in a new world. The Linkhorns had finally found a home.

"Nelson Algren wrote about them in *A Walk on the Wild Side*, but that story was told before they crossed the Rockies. Dove Linkhorn, son of crazy Fitz, went to hustle for his fortune in New Orleans. Ten years later he would have gone to Los Angeles. Algren had worked with Linkhorns, and got drunk with them in the midnight roadhouses of Texas and Oklahoma. When the time came to describe them, he did it about as well as it has ever been done . . ."

It is at this point that I interjected about six paragraphs of your stuff on the Linkhorn ancestry, beginning with, "Six-foot-one of slack muscled shambler, etc. . . ." and ending with the thing about Fitz and the White Trash convention, using only those paragraphs that seemed to apply to the Hell's Angels. After your stuff, my own text (or "stuff") picks up again, to wit: "Anyone who drives the western highways knows the Linkhorns didn't stay in Texas either. They kept moving until one day in the late 1930's they stood on the spine of a scrub-oak California hill and looked down on the Pacific Ocean. They had come to the end of the road. . . ." After this point I was forced to fall back on my own resources for another 200 pages, although toward the end I was tempted to compare an Angel who was killed on his 29th birthday (no, his 30th birthday, or several hours before it) to Bruno Lefty Bicek. The reason I didn't was that I figured I'd already given you enough credit, and if I mentioned you again some motherfucker like Fiedler[5] would call me an Algren fag and put me down the tube as a "naturalist." I had the same problem with Thomas Jefferson; he said too many good things.

So that's how it is. I'm not sure what I'm going to do about the Linkhorn angle, but I won't do anything until I find out from the Random House lawyers just what kind of a law you and Nixon have brewed up to keep me from quoting you. It would be easy enough for me to call the bastards "Buckhorns," or "Scroggins," and just paraphrase your stuff about their background. You aren't the only person who ever wrote about white trash going west, but for one reason or another you just said it better. My whole point is that the Hell's Angels didn't jump out of some Hollywood garbage can, and I thought your Linkhorn angle would help to put them in context. I still think so. They are the 1st generation of Anglo-Saxon boomers, and they have a lot of names besides Linkhorn.

I'm sorry if my letter of February 10 led you to believe I was going to steal a portion of your book. Maybe the letter wasn't very clear. But I should think this letter is about as clear as it has to be, and although it's not necessary that you reply I wanted to get it down in writing to make sure you don't sue me for the wrong reasons. If you are addled enough to think you can't be quoted or even mentioned in the public prints, it makes me feel kind of sad and the best advice I can offer is that you change your lawyers. I find this incredible, but of course you have a right to your own ideas and opinions. In any case, I don't want you roaming up and down Muscatine Street, brooding and bitching about some punk on the Coast who's stealing all your stuff. I happen to think you've written some very good stuff, and not even the most swinish letter from you will change my opinion or my tastes.

5. Leslie Fiedler was an extremely influential literary critic best known for *Love and Death in the American Novel* (New York, 1959).

Beyond that, let me emphasize that this letter is in no way a request for either permission or advice. Unless I hear from you to the contrary I'll assume that you intend to sue me for one reason or another, and naturally I'll advise Random House to get braced for it. If you think it will help things, I'll urge you to write them too.

My inclination is to close on a decent note, but I don't want to lay myself open to another weird blast. Things like that ruin my breakfast. You can rest assured that whatever I decide to do about Linkhorn will be judgment-proof. Changing a name and rewriting a few paragraphs will have no effect on the book. If I have to do it, naturally I'll be pissed off—mainly because I felt I was paying you a compliment of sorts in deferring to your description of White Trash. It was well done, no doubt about it, and if I still insist on stealing it—or trying to—I hope you'll feel properly proud.

I also admired that line at the end of your letter: "It's always a good idea for a writer to do the best he can do with what he has." You have cultivated some tough ideas since you talked to Donohue. Or were you referring to *other* writers? Everybody except Algren. You are the only one around with a good right hand, and you haven't used it for years. I'm curious. Do you ever hear any high white sounds out there in Iowa? I'll close on that stolen note and get back to work.

Sincerely,
Hunter S. Thompson

TO CAREY MCWILLIAMS, *THE NATION:*

At last Hell's Angels *was completed and Thompson was free to blow off some steam.*

March 17, 1966
318 Parnassus
San Francisco

Dear Carey—

I'm now trying to get a grip on myself after three weeks of running totally out of control. Got the book off by March 1, as planned, and then went into a wild spiral up and down the coast, stuffing myself with every kind of drug and booze imaginable. Now my head feels a bit clearer and of course I'm dead broke again. Something has to be done on the article front.

I've talked to Shir-Cliff[6] at Ballantine and [Jim] Silberman at Random, both of whom insist I start on another non-fiction book at once.

---

6. Bernard Shir-Cliff was the executive editor of Ballantine Books.

Their first suggestion was an exposé of the "Minutemen,"[7] which I quickly rejected. My own idea was to go back to Mexico for 6 to 8 months and do a sort of sketch-book of American expatriates. This didn't seem to groove them, and when I said I thought I'd write a novel or two they suggested I find gainful employment while doing so. Not really that harsh, but almost. It was as if I'd said I wanted my next project to be a book of LSD poems.

They then asked me what interested me, but I couldn't explain it on the phone and probably can't in a letter either. The closest we could come was a sort of tentative idea for a book on the drug-hippie action, which I'm now mulling over. I told Silberman that since the Hell's Angels idea had been yours in the first place, that I'd consult with you again to see if you had any more ideas for articles that might evolve into a salable book. (Unless they're putting me on, they seem to think the Hell's Angels book is going to reap some cash.) But not for a while, and in the meantime my rent is overdue again and the Chinese landlady is getting ugly.

Do you have any ideas? (I think that hotrod thing is too close to what I've been living with for too long.) How about getting a Guggenheim? How could I get some information on the mechanics of this? How can it be done . . . or had? Send word.

Thanks—
Hunter

TO NELSON ALGREN:

March 23, 1966
318 Parnassus
San Francisco

Dear Mr. Algren:

In the course of tying up loose ends of the Hell's Angels action I came across your letter of February 16 and remembered that I've since heard from Candida Donadio.[8] I forwarded her letter to Random House and requested that they deal with the situation in whatever manner they saw fit. As I said, the loss of your six paragraphs is not going to cripple the book. You can now rest assured that you've fought off another savage attempt to steal your stuff.

---

7. The Minutemen were a right-wing militia group operating in the West. They were the military arm of the John Birch Society.
8. Donadio was serving as Thompson's agent.

Maybe you have good reasons for acting this way, and for the sake of politeness I'll assume that you do. But in fact it strikes me as either lunacy or senility or both, and goddamn if I can make sense of it. I suppose I'll see you somewhere in the public prints, but I ain't real worried. Good luck on Muscatine St.

Sincerely,
Hunter S. Thompson

TO MR. JED STRODTBECK:

Strodtbeck, an independent scholar, had written his own study of the Hell's Angels.

March 23, 1966
318 Parnassus
San Francisco

Dear Mr. Strodtbeck:

After finishing the Hell's Angels book I started going over various mail, loose ends, etc., and came on your letters of last fall. Your questions of August 4 seem more critical, now that it's all over, than they did at the time. I'm not sure I answered all of them in the book, but I think you'll find it interesting in one or two ways. I'm not sure how to describe the book, but it's not at all what I had in mind when I started. I gave the "adults and authorities" a pretty rough time, and my only regret along that line is that I didn't have another six months to really dynamite them. I don't really see any "solutions" except to document the madness (and the mad humor) of a society that breeds Hell's Angels just as surely as it breeds Nixons and LeMays[9] and Negro gangs on darktown streetcorners. But maybe we differ here, too. In any case, thanks for the book and the letters. I don't recall stealing anything from you, but the book gave me a basis of comparison, for good or ill. Mine should be out "this summer," according to Random, and I've told them to send you a free copy.

Sincerely,
Hunter S. Thompson

TO DON MCKINNEY, *SATURDAY EVENING POST*:

At this point the Saturday Evening Post *was one of America's most popular weekly magazines.*

9. Major General Curtis LeMay ran the U.S. Strategic Air Command 1948–1957. Following his retirement from the Air Force in 1965 he became a bellicose advocate of bombing Vietnam.

April 12, 1966
318 Parnassus
San Francisco

Don McKinney
Saturday Evening Post
641 Lexington Ave.
New York City 22

Dear Mr. McKinney:

I've been meaning to get off a note to you for the past few weeks, but as always I'm running behind schedule. In my letter of October 6, 1965 I said I'd contact you when I got loose and finished the Hell's Angels book, which is more or less the case now. I still have some revisions to do, but as far as I know the thing will be out this summer.

In the meantime I'm haggling about the subject of my next book and looking around for some article work to fill the money gap and keep me on my rails. I have several ideas, but none that would call for any quick action except the enclosed clip on the Russian fishing fleet. I'm not sure how long they'll be there, but I imagine it will be a matter of one to three weeks. Last spring a much smaller Russian "fleet" hovered off the coast near San Francisco for about ten days, but with 200 vessels I'd figure this one to be around a bit longer.

I think it would make a good piece, but I couldn't tell you much more about it without going up to Oregon for a look. My idea would be to go up to Newport [Oregon] and go out with one of the U.S. boats—and then, by any means available, to get aboard one of the Russian boats and get their side of the story. I have a talent for getting into strange places, and my only worry would be finding a Russian who spoke English. There is no Russian consul in San Francisco, but I could probably get some help from the Yugoslav Consul-General. Once I've seen the Oregon situation, then I could come back here and talk to consuls from Chile, Peru, Japan, etc., to get a worldwide perspective on the thing. Chile and Peru, for instance, have arbitrarily extended their offshore boundaries as far as 200 miles, and enforced the restrictions with gunboats. This, at least, was the word on tonight's ABC network newscast. About two years ago in Lima I talked to some U.S. tuna fishermen about their problems, but I never got around to doing the story. It's an interesting problem with some weird ramifications and I'm sure it will keep cropping up.

Anyway, let me know ASAP if it interests you. I'm loose right now but I can't say for certain that I'll be loose next week unless I hear from you pretty quick. Nor can I guarantee the continued presence of the Russian fleet.

As for money, I'd need some expense cash ahead and a guarantee of some kind, but I'd prefer that you work this kind of thing out with my agent, Scott Meredith.

I think photos would be a necessity for a piece like this and I'd be more than willing to shoot as many rolls as you'd want, but I'd want you to know in advance that I'm not a Magnum-type photographer. Josh Eppinger has seen some of my stuff from the era when I was trying to sell you a Hell's Angels cover photo, so you might ask him if he thinks it's worth the risk. If I could get on one of the Russian boats I don't think it would matter what kind of photographer I was, as long as I had a light meter and dry film. To this end I'd be willing to charter a private boat and go right out to one of the Russian trawlers, willfully ignorant of all protocol and that sort of thing. I doubt that I'd be in any danger except maybe from the U.S. Coast Guard, who would probably be nervous about private boarding parties. Perhaps the Yugoslav consul could make some kind of arrangement to get me around this problem, but if not I'd be willing to try it anyway.

So that's about it for now. There's not much more I can tell you without going up to Oregon for a closer look. As for the pitch and yaw of the piece, I'm thinking of something focused down on the people involved, rather than international law and industry drum-beating. That would of course be a factor, but more as background than meat. I'd like to let the fisherman tell the story, instead of getting it from a congressman.

Enclosed are some old clips that might give you a vague idea as to how I'd approach a thing like this. Please send them back when you can. My style is not quite the same as it was when I labored for the *Observer;* I think the *Nation* stuff would give you a better idea what to expect. Anyway, let me know. I have some other ideas that I'll send as soon as I can.

Sincerely,
Hunter S. Thompson

TO NORMAN MAILER:

Although Mailer never did share with Thompson his views on the Hell's Angels, he did send a friendly letter commenting on how much he had liked Thompson's articles in The Nation.

April 26, 1966
318 Parnassus
San Francisco

Dear Norman—
No harm done with the mislaid letter. I barely remember it but I know it was one of those late/drunk ones. Anyway, I was just casting around. At

one point I quoted Algren on white trash and got myself in a hell of an argument with him and his agent. He threatened to sue me. I thought I was paying the man a compliment, but he came at me like Nixon. So it's probably best that you stayed clear.

Anyway, Random House has postponed the Hell's Angels book until fall and I'll tell Silberman to make sure you get a copy ahead of time. You might like it. It's a frontal assault on everybody involved or even implicated. Mainly the press. And the cops. I'm looking for some action when it comes out.

I haven't seen anything of yours recently, but assume you're working on something with a bit of thrust. I probably owe you a conditional apology for some of that wild bullshit I sent you from Big Sur a few years back. But it was all in a human spirit, so what the hell? Incidentally, the novel I was working on then (The Rum Diary) has finally been bought by Random. I'll need the next few months for a rewrite, but it's nice to know all that work wasn't wasted.

That's about it from here. Good luck with whatever you're working on.

Sincerely,

Hunter S. Thompson

TO MARGUERITE GIFFORD:

Gifford, a Louisville portrait artist, was Thompson's favorite cousin.

April 27, 1966
318 Parnassus
San Francisco

Dear Cousin Marguerite—

Thanks very much for the letter and I'm sorry to be so long getting back to you. Things have been very hectic here and the summer looks about the same way. I finished the book on the Hell's Angels motorcycle gang (to be published in the fall) and just signed another contract for a novel and a second non-fiction book. This is not a particularly lucrative situation, but it gives me a guaranteed minimum income to write books for the next year or two. If one of them happens to sell, that will be a different story, but of course I have no control over that. To me it is a matter of getting by from day to day and getting the writing done. I work entirely at night and sleep until noon every day. In the afternoon I deal with the normal problems of life and play basketball with the local hoodlums to keep in shape. Sometimes I take Juan out to the beach around sundown. We just got another Doberman pup and he needs daily exercise, so I guess I'll be getting to the beach more often. Sandy works two hours a day at a local real estate agency. We lead a pretty quiet life and hardly the sort of thing most people associate with "wild writers." Writing is very hard work and at times I wish I didn't have to depend on it, but of course it's the only kind of work I can do and enjoy. As an artist, you probably know what I mean.

Speaking of art, we have your painting of the boy at Angkor Wat, Cambodia on a wall in the hallway where everybody who comes in the door is face to face with it. I have bought four large paintings since we moved into this place, but yours is the only one I feel any blood relationship with. Our family is not laden with artistic instinct, so I'm happy to have some painted evidence that my own talent didn't spring out of nowhere.

As for travel, we plan to go to Mexico soon, but I think I'll have to finish this second book before we move anywhere. In the meantime it will be the same old grind. Wake up late, work late, and hope for the best.

Thanks again for writing. I always enjoy hearing from you and knowing you're still full of energy down there on St. James Court. I feel a long way from there now. From the window of my studio I can see the Golden Gate Bridge and hear the boats coming through. Foghorns always make me feel like going somewhere . . . like train whistles. This is a pleasant place to live, at least for a while. It's late now and I have to get to bed. Write again when you have time. Sandy says hello and sends her love.

Yours,
Hunter

TO WILLIAM J. KENNEDY:

May 24, 1966
318 Parnassus
San Francisco

Dear Slumlord—

My flu-deadened brain won't organize all the things to be said, but I'll make a typical 3:00 a.m. effort. First, here is a copy of my poem; I'd appreciate a comment, as usual, with no holds barred. I like the thing, whether it's a poem or not. If I had outlets I'd write a lot of these, but *Spider* folded and the editor is now in jail for "trespassing" (sit-in).

News from here is a fraud. The Rum Diary is sold to Random and Ballantine on the condition that I rewrite it. No suggestions. Dealing with these people is maddening. It seems incredible to me that somebody like Max Perkins[10] ever existed. I honestly don't believe it; I think he was the cre-

---

10. The legendary Scribner's editor of Fitzgerald, Wolfe, and Hemingway.

ation of critics who didn't like Hem, Fitz, Wolfe, etc. After pushing me desperately for months, the BalRandom combine required three months to read the finished manuscript (*Hell's Angels*) and make a few penciled comments in the margin. At a glance it seems like the very opposite of magazine editing, but the trouble is I can't believe it. They made fewer changes in my 480-pg. manuscript than Ridley normally made in a 10-page article. Now I have three days to make my final revisions and corrections. Pub. is scheduled for Sept., with the paperback 6 months later. Even if it makes money I won't see any before 1970. The contracts are a horror, but of course I have no choice but to sign them. The last one I signed is for two: The Rum Diary and an un-named, un-specified non-fiction book. At a glance it looks like a $10,000 advance for two books, but what it really amounts to is ill-paid bondage for an indefinite period of time. I am very discouraged with the book business. The money is illusory and the cheap realities are all the more shocking because they are hidden, like rocks in the surf, by decades of paternalistic myth. At the moment I am living on a $100 a week dole from my agent, who has sold me into slavery. It is like the company store.

As for getting to New York, I have given up doing it before September, when the combine will pay my expenses. They will probably house me in the Y and schedule four sessions a day with Women's Clubs. In effect, writing a first book for a publisher is like being a cub reporter on a paper; I am without proven value and am treated like an ill-tempered leech. Random, after all, has Truman Capote, and Ballantine operates like a pawn shop. My only hope is to get a lump sum and invest in AT&T.

Anyway, that's my situation. They've nailed me down. I am seriously considering a newspaper job of some kind. In the meantime I have to rewrite The Rum Diary and would appreciate any overall suggestions you could make. I recall your feeling that it should be junked, but now that it has to be published do you have any ideas? I'll probably tear it up completely. They don't seem to give a damn how I do it, since they've put it in a "joint account" with the other books—which means that any losses it might incur will be taken out of my other earnings. In other words, I might end up paying to have it published. Everybody's covered but me.

My reaction is naturally to make it a good novel, and not just a wasted gesture. Any suggestions from your end will be appreciated. The work will take all summer, and that means I'll be here until September. At that point I mean to move—but who knows where. Something will have to happen then. I am fed up with this mole's existence out here, but right now I can't say what direction I'll be moving in the fall. But by that time I'll be in your area and we can talk. You may be right about me and the east. I can't imagine living there; it's too mean and crowded. The whole country is that way.

The great experiment has failed. The Vietnam thing is the beginning of our end. I want to get out of the country before I get locked up. The problem is I don't know where to go.

Your own action was not well covered in your last letter. The most cogent note was the mention of the Ink Truck Log[11] becoming a novel. I don't know how you mean to do this, but I think you should try. At this point I think we should all write at least one book about how it looks, or maybe even how it is. There is no way to do this with journalism. I've already had to drop two true accounts in my book because of possible (or very probable) libel suits. The contract stipulates that I will defend all legal claims and pay all judgments. Fiction is the only way to get around this roadblock. Objectivity is impossible in journalism.

Well, I'm getting wasted here and my head is wavering. Rest assured that nothing is happening. I sleep until 2 or 3 every day and go to sleep at dawn. Not much else. Except that my motorcycle is being repaired (now that I've put $200 in escrow), and soon I'll be wailing around at good speed.

                                               Hunter S. Thompson

TO SONNY BARGER:

Oakland Hell's Angels leader Barger was in jail at this point.

                                               June 2, 1966
                                               318 Parnassus
                                               San Francisco

Dear Sonny—

Steve DeCanio came by last night and told me how much you are enjoying your health cure. He also mentioned a prediction you made to one of the keepers . . . but I guess I shouldn't mention this sort of thing, because I'm sure all the mail is censored. Anyway, it's good to know your head's in good shape and that not much time is left.

You should get out about the time the book is published. It was postponed from July to September and I'm still working on final corrections, etc. Since this is my first book, I don't know how they work on advance copies, but I'll make sure you get one of the first batch available. According to my contract I only get ten free copies. After that I get a discount, but not enough to let me go around handing out free books. I told Terry and some of the others that I'd give the Angels 15 free copies, mainly to the guys who helped me most—which would naturally include you, Terry, Tiny, Frenchy from Frisco, Pete, Ronnie and about ten others that I can think of.

11. *The Ink Truck Log*—about a strike at a newspaper—became William Kennedy's first published novel.

I'm saving one free copy for Mr. Lynch,[12] because I know how much he'll dig it.

As far as action, the whole scene has been pretty quiet—except for the Petaluma rape—for about the last four months. Kesey is still out of sight, Ginsberg is in Australia and Mountain Girl[13] got married to a guy in Santa Cruz. I've been mainly at the desk, working on this book and a novel I've sold. Sandy says hello; she's still working, so if anybody thinks I've made any money on this book they can think again. There's a chance I might make some when the paperback version comes out in early 1967, but until then I'm still kiting checks.

I did, however, get together the $200 necessary to get my bike rebuilt and I think it will be ready this weekend. If so, I should be mobile for the next big run, which probably won't happen until you get out. I think you realize this, but in case you don't, you should know that the Angels aren't the same without you. The style is still there, but the focus is missing. I'm not the only one who's looking forward to having you back on the street. Write if you have time. If not, I'll see you then.

Sincerely—Hunter

TO MOON FAY NG:

Thompson was not swayed by an eviction notice from his landlord.

June 14, 1966
318 Parnassus
San Francisco

Moon Fay Ng
730 Washington St. #101
San Francisco

Dear Sir:

I received your letter of eviction today (June 14) and immediately consulted my attorney. His advice was to ignore your letter entirely, but since we have generally maintained a good relationship during the twenty-one (21) months of my tenancy I thought I would send a note. I would prefer to avoid any argument or unpleasantness.

Nevertheless, on advice from my attorney, I have to reject your demand that I evacuate these premises within 16 days, or as of June 30. Such short notice is not in keeping with any legal or ethical standard. I am naturally sym-

---

12. Thomas G. Lynch was the attorney general of California who had written the original report identifying the Hell's Angels as a menace.
13. Mountain Girl was one of Kesey's Merry Pranksters. She later married Grateful Dead guitarist Jerry Garcia.

pathetic to your desire to place the elderly members of your family in a decent apartment, but after living here for nearly two years I find two weeks' notice insufficient. I am further advised to inform you that neither you nor your family nor any agents of same shall be allowed to enter these premises for purposes of harassment, renovation or other forms of temporary occupation until we have arrived at some mutually acceptable date regarding termination of my tenancy. My own feeling—in accordance with the law and the standards of most humane-thinking people—is that thirty (30) days is the very least amount of time I should be allowed to make other arrangements. This would set July 13 as the deadline for my abandoning the premises.

I understand, of course, that you might be able to advance this date by several days by means of court order or other extreme means, based on a plea of hardship regarding yourself or other members of your family. If you find yourself in the grip of a real emergency I would naturally be inclined to help as much as possible. Otherwise—considering my own situation—I shall make plans to vacate this apartment on or before July 13, on which date you may begin your various renovations.

Regarding my rent payment—due on the 15th—I will naturally postpone any further payment on my account until we come to some agreement regarding termination and my own freedom to live and work in peace, free of any threats on your part to invade, inspect and/or renovate my apartment at any time you see fit. I regard this as a fitting arrangement between civilized people and expect you feel the same way. Until I hear from you, then, I remain,

Sincerely,
Hunter S. Thompson

TO CAREY MCWILLIAMS, *THE NATION:*

Considering an offer to write a book on the extreme right in California, Thompson digressed into a lament on the death of the American Dream.

June 18, 1966
318 Parnassus
San Francisco

Dear Carey—

Enclosed is some stuff from the latest *Newsweek* and a copy of the two pages I sent you last fall for a possible box in the Non-Student piece. When I came on the *Newsweek* thing I had a feeling it sounded familiar, so I thought I'd match them up.

My own two pages were a bit vague, but there didn't seem to be any reason, at the time, to stretch them out. My comments were sort of an afterthought to the article, which didn't need any windy predictions about the future California elections. You'll notice, however, that it struck me as a possible article—the rising tide, etc.

Anyway, both Ballantine and Random are pushing me toward some kind of non-fiction book on the Right Wing. I've been resisting it for several months, but now that the nutcracker has started to close I'm getting more interested. I'm beginning to think that there might be a good book in the Right Wing vis-à-vis the fate of California. It is really a microcosm of American history. The destruction of California is a logical climax to the Westward Movement. The redwoods, the freeways, the dope laws, race riots, water pollution, smog, the FSM, and now Governor Reagan—the whole thing is as logical as mathematics. California is the end, in every way, of Lincoln's idea that America was "the last best hope of man." Here is where the sins of the fathers and forefathers are being visited on the sons, who in turn visit them on the land and each other. For 100 years the bunglers and rapists had an escape valve; they could always move west, to something new. But now they have come to the end, and they have to live with whatever they can make of it. The story has all the elements of a tragic parable. California is the ultimate flower of the American Dream, a nightmare of failed possibilities.

Well, that's my paragraph for tonight. Sorry to seem sluggish on the article ideas, but for the past month I've been wrestling with revisions on the *Hell's Angels* manuscript. I want to take a break in this book action and go to Africa or South America. Books are too slow. Only old men should write them. But since I already have a contract for another non-fiction book I think it should be on the most pertinent subject I can find. Right now the above paragraph strikes me as a possibility, both for a book and an article—and possibly a grant of some kind. If you have any ideas along these lines, send word.

Thanks,

Hunter S. Thompson

TO BOB DEVANEY:

Devaney was the latest in Thompson's string of literary agents. He worked for the Scott Meredith Literary Agency in New York.

June 26, 1966
318 Parnassus
San Francisco

Dear Bob—

Silberman was here and seemed pleased with the *Hell's Angels* revisions, which are almost done. It has been a goddamn nightmare, complete with soaking sweats, pill stupors and my Chinese landlord whipping on the door. I won't let them in under any circumstances and the only reason they haven't put me out on three days' notice is that they think I'll pay my back rent if they wait long enough. This bubble will burst pretty soon, but at least I've made time for night work. I am counting on some form of money from sales of other rights on the *Hell's Angels* book. Silberman and I agreed that *The New Yorker* should have first shot at magazine rights, since they've already asked, and that anything beyond that would be up to you and/or Scott [Meredith]. In any case, I should have the manuscript back to Ballantine by the end of this week.

Work on The Rum Diary is going to be chaotic for a while, until I find a place to live and work. I am trying to sell the bike, but the only way to sell it quick is to take a brutal loss. I am also pawning my guns and trying to borrow from my friends in the professions. Probably I'll have to use my Teamsters connection to pick up a paycheck or two by some kind of labor. It pays more than writing and I need something like that to get back in shape.

Silberman shrugged when I said The Rum Diary couldn't possibly be finished by August 1. God only knows when I'll finally finish it, but by the time I do the vultures will have already claimed the final $1000.

Nor did we come to any decision on the non-fiction thing, although it seems to be narrowing down again to their original suggestion for something on the Extreme Right. I don't look forward to working another year for $7000, including expenses. Of the $6000 I got for the Hell's Angels book, about half went for valid expenses. The bike alone was $1300. I'm not telling you this out of pique, but to point out that my choice of subjects is severely limited by the expense factor. I am not about to undertake a project that will eat up every penny I get for writing it, especially since I won't get the $4000 lump until the whole thing is finished and I'm tied down again by a legion of creditors.

Well, there's no sense carrying on with this. I have to get back to work. The Hell's Angels rape trial finally begins tomorrow—after nine days of picking the jury (one male and eleven [11] women, plus one woman alternate). There may be an article in it, but I'm not sure what to tell you in terms of sales potential. There is going to be a dramatic clash of stories; the girl claims she was gang-raped by nine Angels, but the four defendants say it was voluntary. No doubt she was done several times, but it wasn't rape— at least not the first few times. In most counties the case would never have come to court, but Sonoma County has never dealt with the Angels and various town councils are up in arms. The prosecutor, one John Hawkes, seems to feel that the sanctity of every crotch in the county depends on his getting a conviction. Only one of the Angels has managed to hire a lawyer;

the other three are going with public defenders whom I'll talk with tomorrow or the next day, depending on how long I can stay awake. What it all amounts to is a sort of modern-day witchcraft trial. The Sonoma County power structure is made up of new rich Okies and chicken farmers (Petaluma, where the rape is said to have occurred, is known as the Egg Capital of America).

I used to live in Sonoma County, about ten miles out of Santa Rosa, where the trial is being held, and I've spent many a night in Petaluma taverns. I also know the Angels; three of the four defendants have been among my best contacts—Tiny, Mouldy Marvin, and Terry the Tramp. Tiny is the beast who attacked the Vietnam protest march in Berkeley last year and supposedly broke a cop's leg; he was featured in wire service photos from coast to coast—*Daily News* in New York, also Boston (his original home), Louisville, Denver and the whole west coast. (Last week he was finally acquitted, when films showed him falling on the cop's leg after being clubbed in the head by another cop.) Terry is a middle-class refugee with one brother in the Peace Corps and another in a monastery. He is the featured Angel in the book and still comes by the apartment about once a week. We are pretty good friends; at the moment I'm trying to sell his bike so he can pay a decent lawyer.

The point of the above is that I know enough about the trial to write a multi-dimensional piece on it. I know what happened that night in Petaluma, I know the alleged rapists and I know Sonoma County and its "people," as represented by the county prosecutor. I have all the book research as background, plus the confidence of the defendants and a friend who's covering the trial for the local paper (the S.R. *Press-Democrat*).

It seems we could sell this somewhere and especially now, in this time of critical need. Expenses wouldn't run much—$200 tops, but I could get away with much less. An article would also have the effect of promoting the book, which could mean a few dollars for all of us. The only problem would be in the risk of killing the sale for some part of the book, but if we could get a decent price for an article right now I'd be willing to take the chance.

Anyway, let me know ASAP. I'll be following the trial—in person as much as possible—and I'm considering a possible appearance as a witness, but this is unlikely. I may contribute some data and background information, but I want to avoid doing anything, such as taking the stand, that might queer the chance of an article sale. There is also the fact that my own car has a ruptured brake cylinder, so my only transportation right now is the bike—and round-trip to Santa Rosa is 140 miles in a bad wind on a very dangerous freeway.

That's about it for now. Let me know quick if there's an article sale in this trial. And don't forget the Jack London–Rustic piece.[14] If you can dig up even rumor of good news, send it along. I feel myself going down the tube.

Sincerely,
Hunter

TO ALLEN GINSBERG:

Ginsberg granted Thompson permission to use his poem "To the Angels" in his motorcycle book.

June 28, 1966
318 Parnassus
San Francisco

Dear Allen—

It looks like my Hell's Angels book will finally be published this fall and I've tentatively included your poem, "To the Angels," which I got from that copy of the *Berkeley Barb* you gave me one night last winter when I boomed into your Fell St. apartment in a jabbering pill frenzy.

Jim Silberman, my editor at Random House, was out here last week and I told him that, although I've laced your poem into the manuscript, I still felt we needed more formal permission from you than a 5 a.m. gift of the *Berkeley Barb*. I very much want the poem in the book: it gives another dimension to that whole Kesey-VDC[Vietnam Day Committee]-Angels scene that we were both a part of. I can't possibly pay you for the poem unless you want an IOU that will only be good if the book sells. Right now I'm trying to sell my bike for money to move into a new apt. The Chinese evicted me from this one last week, mainly because the neighbors reported it as a Hell's Angels hideout.

Anyway, I'm stone broke and desperate, which means I can't pay you anything for use of the poem. I think, however, that Random House can and will. Silberman seems like a decent sort, and he speaks well of you. But when I told him we should ask you before using the poem he copped out and said I should write the letter.

So this is the letter. And the message is to contact Silberman and tell him what you want for using the poem. I think you should get something and if I had any money I'd give it to you, but I honestly don't. If you want

14. Thompson had written a scathing article about the Rustic Inn in Glen Ellen, California, the famous watering-hole of Jack London. The owner, Chester Womack, threatened to sue *Cavalier* magazine for slander.

an IOU, let me know and I'll sign a document promising you any reasonable amount, to come out of my royalties on the book, if any. But if I were you I'd nail Silberman for something definite. He seems malleable and I think he'd be a bit awed if you called up and said, "This is The Man and I want cash."

Try to let me know something—or contact Silberman—as soon as possible. Until I hear something I'll keep the entire poem (the *Barb* version) in the manuscript, pending some word from you. The final revisions are done and a lot of the original zap is gone from the book, but there are parts of it I think you might like. I'll have them send you a copy. It's dawn here and in a few hours I'll ride up to Santa Rosa for the rape trial. Terry, Tiny, Marvin and Little Magoo are going through what amounts to a witchcraft trial. If you have any rich friends who might hire a lawyer for them, let me know quick.

> Thanks—
> Hunter S. Thompson

TO MAX SCHERR, EDITOR, *BERKELEY BARB:*

Thompson had read an article in Scherr's magazine that said the best thing to do if pulled over while driving was to hand the police officer your driver's license through a slit in your car window. Thompson tried it on a California Highway Patrolman with near-disastrous results.

> July 20, 1966
> 318 Parnassus
> San Francisco

Max Scherr
Editor, *Berkeley Barb*

Dear Mr. Scherr:

The recent *Barb* article on Western Union prompts me to write a letter I've been meaning to send for many weeks—or ever since I got arrested while trying to follow some rules of behavior laid down by a contributor (several months ago), who spoke knowingly of what police could and could not do when dealing with a suspected traffic violator.

First, the Western Union thing, which reminded me of my own very similar experience: One dawn several months ago—after a long night at the typewriter—I received the *Chronicle* from the delivery boy and went into a rage upon reading some front-page statement by [Secretary of Defense Robert] McNamara. (I forget which one it was, but that hardly matters.) In my strung-out condition I grabbed up the phone and told the

Western Union operator I wanted to send a "public service message" to the president, a service they advertise at 85 cents per fifteen-word message. I gave the operator the following message:

FIRE MCNAMARA AT ONCE
HE IS A LYING BLOODTHIRSTY BEAST.

This did not pass, and my call was quickly transferred to a supervisor, who also refused to have the message sent. I persisted, and was passed up the line to the Mojo Jefe, who tried to be reasonable and said he would pass everything except the words "lying," "bloodthirsty" and "beast." He seemed to feel I could find adequate synonyms, but I insisted on the original wording and the message was killed.

I managed to send it later that day, however, by calling it in to an operator I'd come to know pretty well in the course of sending frequent and lengthy press messages. At the time I was patronizing Western Union two or three times a week, frequently to the tune of 1500 and 200 words a crack. So my operator sent the message without comment—but when I got the bill it was slightly more than $3.00, and not the 85 cents as advertised. I have, of course, refused to pay for it.

The moral of that story, I guess, is "Always exploit your contacts instead of making a frontal assault." Which is not much of a moral, in any league.

The second incident, having to do with the California Highway Patrol, is less instructive. I had read the piece by your contributor—who cited some press credentials and experience, as I recall—and one of the points that stuck in my mind had to do with the (victim's) legal right to remain in his car and roll down his window only far enough to pass his driver's license out to the "investigating officer." This struck me as a hell of an improvement over my usual technique of leaping out of the car and getting as far away from it as possible, hoping to keep the cops away from anything that might be incriminating. I had my first chance to try your contributor's method last spring, on the northern outskirts of Gilroy about 2:00 a.m. on a weekday night.

About a week earlier I had finished a book (on the Hell's Angels, scheduled this fall by Random House) and I felt that I needed about a week of total degeneration to cool out my system. To this end I went down to Big Sur and Monterey and filled my body with every variety of booze and drug available to modern man. For six or seven days I ran happily amok—spending money, sitting in baths, and futilely hunting wild boar with a .44 Magnum revolver. At one point I gave my car away to a man who paid $25 for the privilege of pushing it off a 400-foot cliff.

So it was, at the end of my visit among old friends and haunts, that I had to buy another car to return to San Francisco. One Friday afternoon I bought a Saab and started back to the city just before midnight. The debris of my cooling out was heaped on both seats of the new car.

At Gilroy, on 101, I noticed a CHP car behind me and very carefully stashed a tall metal cup of bourbon and ice I was drinking, easing it between the seats and onto the floor in back. The CHP car followed me for about a minute, then dropped back to trail me again. I knew something ugly was happening and drove with extreme caution and five miles under the speed limit. Despite this, the CHP car finally pulled me over with the traditional flashing light.

But I knew my rights and I was relatively straight. Instead of getting out of the car I sat tight and reached into my pocket for my license, which I intended to pass out through the small opening next to my head. I watched the officer approach and reached up to hand him my license.

At that instant the right hand door flew open and I was faced with a cop, a flashlight and the black hole of a .38 Special. At almost the same time the left door came open and I was pulled out of the car. Both officers got into it: one sat in the driver's seat and the other made a methodical search of everything from the glove compartment to my shaving kit. I watched from outside and finally said, "You can't do this—it's illegal search and seizure."

The cop in the driver's seat looked up and gave me a nice, two-years-of-college CHP smile and replied: "Yeah, but we're doing it, aren't we?" And they kept on rooting through the car while I stood on the highway and cursed the bastard who wrote that bullshit about staying in your car and passing your license out through a slit.

They found two bottles of bourbon, one which I'd brought down from San Francisco a week earlier and had completely forgotten about. The other was a quart I'd bought earlier that night for $6.80 and which was only an inch away from being entirely full. They found the booze almost by accident, in the course of pushing clothes and baggage around to get at small crannies.

After ten minutes of searching they gave up on the Dope angle and came out to talk to me. The press cards in my driver's license holder changed their attitude considerably. It was the friendly old CHP again, reluctantly doing their duty and tagging me for having "unsealed containers" in my car. One of the two, who had earlier referred to the Saab as a "pile of shit," showed new interest in its handling characteristics. When I asked why they'd searched it so viciously they explained that more and more people, these days, are coming out of innocent-looking cars with guns blazing. They were worried that I might be armed and drunk.

Which I was, but they never noticed. The .44 Magnum was fully loaded in a leather bag on the back seat and my tall tin cup of straight booze and ice was sitting on the floor behind my seat. But they missed them both. They were so intent on going through my shaving kit that they overlooked a huge, loaded revolver with an eight-and-three-quarter-inch barrel, sitting in plain view in a holster on the back seat. And this dangerous possibility, they said, was precisely what made the search necessary. If I'd had the inclination I could have easily shot them both as they walked back to their car, seized their citation book, and gone quietly on my way. We were stopped on a pretty empty stretch of highway and anything that happened out there would have been a very private thing.

This is certainly one of the keys to their action. They had a victim with no witnesses in a strange-looking beatnik car that was probably full of Dope. When I asked why they pulled me over in the first place they said it was because I had "amber tail-lights," instead of the mandatory red. The incident cost me a $29 fine, a nearly full quart of bourbon, and the cancellation of my liability insurance. I ignored the ticket for "amber tail-lights" and never heard anything about it.

The moral of that story is hazy. Since then, however, I have kept my car doors locked when traveling on any highway and the next time I get stopped I'll get out of the car as fast as I can. Regardless of what the law says, to sit there and defy two meat-hungry cops is a form of masochism. It's like the man said: "Yeah, but we're doing it, aren't we?"

They were, and they did, and unless I'd had the instincts of a cop-killer there was damn little I could do about it. When I told my attorney I wanted to go to court and protest the $29 fine he advised me to pay it and keep quiet. "Don't go near that goddamn court," he said. "Those cow-town judges can put you away for six months for having an open (unsealed) container (of booze) in your car—you'll go to jail for sure if you start raising hell in a courtroom."

And that's about the way it is. The only lesson to be learned from it is one that people who've dealt with cops should have learned a long time ago: your legal rights are contingent on a whole bag of factors that vary from one situation to another. But that's too broad a thing to face right now; the point of this screed is the difference between legal rights and actual rights. A cop with a gun on a midnight highway is his own law, and he knows it. If he violates any "individual rights" he can be turned around, but only with the help of a very expensive or very dedicated attorney. There are also time and nuisance factors to consider, along with the baleful necessity of avoiding the offended cop's turf for the rest of your natural born life.

Well, that's about it. This letter has been sitting in the typewriter for several days and I want to get it out of the way. Feel free to use it any way you want—or to not use it at all—but if I get arrested for anything that appears in the *Barb* over my signature I may be forced to claim the whole thing was a typo. My original intent was to make available the doubtless benefits of my experience on two fronts you've already opened. But I'm not sure the letter is as clear as it might be. I could wrap it all up in a cogent little nut of advice, but I have to live in this state a while longer so I'll keep that for later.

Sincerely,
Hunter S. Thompson

P.S. I am writing a piece now for *The Nation*, tentatively titled "California, The Progressive Penal Colony," and I'm looking around for examples and/or indications of creeping police-statism. If you have one or two you'd like to recount, maybe we can get together for a beer some afternoon and exchange atrocity stories. Give a ring if you ever get over this way. I'll do the same.

TO BANK OF ASPEN:

August 16, 1966
318 Parnassus
San Francisco

Gentlemen:

I cannot tolerate the horrifying color combination of the checks and check-holder you sent me. Nor can I countenance the flagrant disregard of my proper address, which is simply "Owl House." No more, no less. Those people in Kansas City had the gall to add "San Francisco, California," as you can see.

As for colors, these (this sick red and yellow) would only be displayed by a fag with mononucleosis. I think I'll have to have a black check-holder, since there aren't many shades of that, and I can't easily go wrong in ordering it. As for the checks, these people obviously have decent colors: witness the bright red on the box that contains the checks, or both the red and the blue on the mailing labels. Hell, if worst comes to worst, I'd prefer those weird-looking blue checks that you give away. As a matter of fact that's what I'll be using until these Kansas City pastel-people send me something decent. Nor will I have any zip codes on my checks. What kind of swinish outfit are you dealing with? If all they have is this sick, pastel, zip-code garbage, to hell with them, and send me some of those regular Bank of Aspen checks.

Thanks,
Hunter S. Thompson

TO CAREY MCWILLIAMS, *THE NATION:*

Thompson's landlord, Moon Fay Ng, had finally forced him to vacate 318 Parnassus after a series of damaging Hell's Angels parties. He then prepared to move back to Aspen, Colorado, despite a wave of articles characterizing the resort town as a playground for the rich.

> August 20, 1966
> 230 Grattan
> San Francisco

Dear Carey—

I am finally working on that article about California: The Progressive Penal Colony that I mentioned weeks and/or months ago. "Minor revisions" on the Hell's Angels book turned into a nightmare of long haggling and desperate work, which kept me from working on anything else and dropped me so far into the financial pits that I was evicted from my other apartment. I have not yet begun to recover and plan to flee the state on September 15, but before I go I want to do this article.

If you no longer want it or if you have something similar on order, let me know so I can aim it elsewhere. My subscription to *The Nation* was canceled a few weeks ago, along with all my other subscriptions and all my local credit, so for all I know you've already published something similar.

From here I am going to Aspen, and then—if the book comes out on time—to New York. I took considerable issue, by the way, with your recent piece on Aspen. *The New Republic* ran a similar attack about two years ago and I disagreed with that, too. When I lived in Woody Creek my neighbors were too goddamn poor to build gingerbread gables on their houses or brass handles on their doors. They were worried about the collapsing beef-cattle market and the fact that speculators from "the east" (and Los Angeles) were buying up all the grazing land. They were not real concerned about dressing up their homes to suit the notions of city planners working for foundations and architecture critics traveling on expense accounts. The rotten tavern that your man mentioned is the only place in Aspen where the second-generation locals can afford to eat . . . and when I lived there it was one of the two places where I could afford to drink. (The other is now gone, converted to an expensive steak house where no writer's foot will ever tread unless he has come to town by invitation of the incredibly (almost viciously) pompous Aspen Institute or the Writer's Workshop.) If all the houses in Aspen were "refinished" to suit the taste of visiting New Yorkers I couldn't possibly live there. I couldn't even afford the weekly painting, much less the rent. Hopefully you haven't been in New York so long that you think of the rest of the country as a potential resort (well worth the expense) for people who spend most of their lives in concrete cubicles. Well, this is a rambling letter and not entirely coherent, but at least it raises a point. I'll try to expand on it later. Sincerely—

Hunter S. Thompson

TO CAREY MCWILLIAMS, *THE NATION:*

Going through some old papers, Thompson came across what he had written November 22, 1963, upon hearing the news of JFK's assassination. As the National Observer *had not published any of it, he sent it now for McWilliams's consideration.*

August 21, 1966
230 Grattan
San Francisco

Dear Carey:

In re: Aspen, here's a thing I filed for the *Observer* (*National*) on the evening of Kennedy's death. They didn't use it, so if you can make any use of it there will be no problem about "rights," etc.

I was just going through my old articles and I find, to my general despair, that most of the best things I wrote were never published. This is one of them . . . although I'm not sure the writing is so good that it's held up over the years, like Wendell Berry's stuff.[15] But in coming on it by accident in my heap of old articles I felt a new and more painful sense of perspective than I did on the day it happened. Then, it was only speculation . . . but now, after three years of Johnson, I have a better, deeper idea of that "sense of loss" that Berry mentioned in his poem. The thing that interests me about this little piece, though, is that it was written within hours after Kennedy's death . . . but the few quoted comments contain the seeds of that doomed and busted sensation that has only become coherent in the wake of Johnson's evil, truthless croaking above the rubble of our dead possibilities.

There was not a lot of truth in Kennedy, but it was hard to doubt—after listening to him talk—that he at least knew what the word meant. He had a capacity for backing off and watching himself perform, and later commenting on what he'd seen and heard with a quick, half-sublimated sense of humor that often made him seem like a pillar of sanity in the thieving,

---

15. Wendell Berry is an agrarian poet-essayist-novelist from Kentucky.

swinish chaos of American politics. He seemed like the only man who knew what was happening, and although there was rarely any way to guess what he might decide to do about it, there was always the chance that he might find an opening to do something right.

Johnson conveys only the impression of a man whose sole interest is in closing every door, crack and window that might let in fresh air. And the thing that interests me about this Aspen piece is that even people in the drugstores and beerhalls of a Rocky Mountain town seemed to know, within hours of Kennedy's death, that it was the end of an era. The sense of loss was almost as clear then as it is now . . . the only difference is that now it's been documented.

Anyway, I thought I'd send this along, with the vague idea that you might want to use it. If not, please send it back (to this address) as soon as possible. It's my only copy and I want to keep it.

Thanks—
Hunter

TO VIRGINIA THOMPSON:

August 26, 1966
230 Grattan
San Francisco

Dear Mom:

Right now I am in the middle of one of the biggest writing jags of my life. On the basis of a ten-page outline I submitted, Ballantine is now try-ing to sell hardcover rights to Random House, which could mean quite a bit if it goes. I also have a *Playboy* assignment on the same subject, which is sort of chancy right now, but a good possibility. I also have the novel [The Rum Diary] at Pantheon; an editor from there was here last week, and insisted on reading it. It's awful, but under these new circumstances I'm pretty sure I can make somebody take an option, which would give me time and perhaps money to rewrite it. The whole situation here is chaotic and under terrible pressure. I am up until dawn every night, beating these rotten keys. And no rest in sight until at least the first of the year, if then. This is a nerve-wracking period. There is real money just around the cor-ner, but turning that corner is going to be hard as hell. It is going to take an incredible amount of good pages in an incredibly short space of time. Sandy is getting depressed with the constant urgency of things. There is not a moment to relax. I couldn't handle this pace if I thought it was any-thing but a temporary thing. But if the book goes big, in hardback as well as paper, I'll be able to relax for a while.

How about there? What's happening? What is Jim up to? Send a line, a newsy sort of letter. I haven't heard anything in a long time.

Love—

Hunter

TO SONNY BARGER:

On Labor Day weekend a group of Hell's Angels had "stomped" Thompson near Cloverdale, California, smashing his face and nearly killing him. Thompson was bleeding profusely when he arrived at the hospital in Santa Rosa. The brutal act ended his involvement with the motorcycle gang—and afforded his book the perfect postscript. Barger was not around when the beating occurred.

September 25, 1966
230 Grattan
San Francisco

Dear Sonny—

Thought I'd send you a note on the way east. I'd hoped we could have a beer and get straight after that bad show at Cloverdale, but Terry didn't come by like he said he would and I didn't figure it was my action to be making any diplomatic phone calls.

Anyway, I assume you heard about the stomping up there and I'm sorry you weren't around to cut it off any quicker. As it was, I figure Tiny did me a hell of a favor by getting me on my feet before I got kicked to death—so when you see him tell him I said "thanks" and if he needs a good favor some day, tell him to get hold of me.

There's not much sense in talking about it except to say it was a completely "no class" piece of action and I'm glad none of the guys I liked and trusted were part of it.

I'm not sure how or why the thing started and I never even saw the first thump that got me, but I assume it was a sort of drunken spontaneous outburst that I had the bad luck to get in the middle of. Earlier that day I'd noticed some resentment about my taking pictures, but I didn't worry about it because I figured you were straight enough to tell me to my face if we had any problems. We've never bullshitted each other and I'd grown sort of accustomed to taking you at face value.

In all, I had no reason to expect that sort of action—as I'm sure you realize—and in general it disappointed me about the Angels. Not everybody, but at least a few. Obviously, I wouldn't be writing this letter if I was down on the whole club. Like I said, if Tiny hadn't been there to help me I'd probably be in a graveyard right now.

Anyway, I'm off on another book now, and if you people want to sue me for any money regarding the Hell's Angels book I think you should get as much as you can. I can't go into detail—especially in a letter—but if we had sat down and talked I think we could have worked something out. I'm still willing to talk, but it will have to be on my turf next time. I don't ever intend to be that much outnumbered again.

Before you do anything, though, I think you should read the book, which is now scheduled for January. I think you'll like it, but maybe not. If nothing else it should be interesting.

Hunter

TO PAUL SEMONIN:

Thompson was back in Colorado with the book's finished first draft and his face recovering from the Hell's Angels stomping.

October 4, 1966
Box 783
Aspen, Colorado

Dear Bobo—

Trust you got Sandy's phone message that we got here alright. No break-down until Aspen, and that was your man's left front wheel brake, which I think is more the province of your friend at the crossroads, rather than the downtown alignment man. It now grabs so violently that it will throw the car into a circular spin if we drive it in snow—which fell to the tune of seven inches yesterday. What it is, I'm sure, is the left front brake cylinder leaking fluid on the brake linings, but of course that's what you pay people to tell you—rather than figuring it out yourself while adding up a bunch of canceled checks from various garages.

So much for all that. Noonan "forgot" to tell me that he was finally get-ting married last week and that I was to be the best man. It was a frighten-ing experience, with a priest and all the Catholic action, and needless to say it brought on a wave of drink that has yet to subside. The priest learned to hate me, and I was naturally terrified of him. It was a gruesome show, with the bride's parents hurling condemnation on me throughout. All Catholics should be garroted. At the Rustic Inn, on a slow Thursday night.

In all, this looks like a good scene for a month or so. Sandy is working behind my back to dig up a house for the winter, but my own plans still focus on a drift to New York around Christmas, then back to California to do another nonfiction book. Objectively. I think we'll light on your doorstep sometime in January.

In the meantime, could you send another Rx for 100 Dexedrines, 5 mg, and, if possible, another Rx for the nose-spray, the name of which I can't recall.[16] Unfortunately, I can't seem to breathe without the spray, and in this altitude breathing is important. I'm afraid I'll have to use my Blue Cross hospitalization to cut a channel through my nasal passage. Is that your province? Let me know what you think.

The scene here is good—a big house with a one-room cottage for writing . . . in the best of neighborhoods. A far cry from any action with the Angels. Juan has turned into a whining monster and I try to stay away from him. Sandy is not much better. Noonan says hello and we both think you should run out here in the truck for a day of shooting. It's about thirty hours on the road, which is only half your weekend. And besides that, Aspen is a goldmine for orthopods, and you should by all means check it out. Let me know on this too.

Bruno

TO CHARLES KURALT:

Kuralt had mailed Thompson a new essay book: The Best of the National Observer, *which included more articles by Thompson than by any other journalist.*

October 19, 1966
Aspen, Colorado

Dear Charley—

Thanks for the book. I appreciate the idea of making permanent print, as it were, and in spite of my grumbling I also appreciated the check—which kept the phone company from putting me in isolation again.

As for the choice(s) of my stuff, I figure you're not to blame so I can tell you I'm appalled. I suppose that "timelessness" factor might explain some of it, but even taking that into consideration I can point to at least ten better pieces I did in those years. But what the hell? I don't see any sense in bitching to Bill Giles—who can't be blamed either and who's already torn enough hair on my account—so I thought I'd aim this at you and consider the matter ended.

Or almost ended, and on this other count I think you ain't blameless. That is the matter of bylines in sniper-vision type, which I think reflect poorly on the value the *Observer* places on the people who write these articles. I may be unique on this score, but not one of those seven pieces in

16. Thompson needed the medication and nose spray in the wake of his beating.

588 / Hunter S. Thompson

the book originated in anybody's mind but my own; nor were any written with the help of expense money. What I mean is I figure some of that was my world, too, and my ego doesn't fit real well into footnotes. So those are my bitches and I figure you owe me some drinks on the latter score, at least. When I get East I'll try to collect. [. . .] OK for now.

—Hunter

TO CHUCK ALVERSON:

Alverson was a friend of Thompson's who worked at The Wall Street Journal. *He provided Thompson with police documents regarding the Hell's Angels.*

November 28, 1966
Owl Farm
Woody Creek, Colorado

Chuck—

Sorry to be so late with an answer to your last. You sounded pretty down, but I hope things got straight with Jane—or at least straighter. What the fuck made you divorce her in the first place? I don't know any secret formulas or potions—not even my own—but if it's any comfort to you, rest assured that I'll keep your action in mind the next time I consider leaving Sandy.

And now to better news: Money. I've been trying to figure out ways to send you $150, but since my bank account is $67 overdrawn and steadily rising, it's been hard. Finally, in a flash of insight, I sent Random House a bill for your services (to be taken out of my royalties) and to my astonishment they agreed to pay. If you don't get a check from them within two weeks, let me know at this address and I'll bug them again. They insisted on paying Sonny [Barger] $25 for his telegram to Lyndon (I wanted to make it $1000 until I learned it was coming out of my alleged royalties) so I think they'll send you $150 without much argument. The book is due on January 27, barring further delays. I no longer give a fuck. There must be an easier and less painful way to make a living. You asked about the Angels stomping me. Indeed. It came as a total surprise, with no warning, but it put me in the emergency ward of the Santa Rosa hospital and caused me to look with new affection on my .44 Magnum. Sonny wasn't around and I didn't talk to him about it afterwards, so all I know is what little I can piece together from the day that led up to the outburst. . . . Labor Day run, I wanted a book cover photo to counter Random's idea of using some phony design work, vaguely uneasy reception at the gathering point, Fat

Freddy trying to run me down with his bike about noon, then 5 or 6 hours of loose and easy talk with people like Zorro, Jimmy & Magoo (& Tiny, who cashed a check for me), but all the while a mean undertone from a lot of new Angels I didn't know. . . . I guess my mistake was in thinking Sonny, Tiny, Terry & Co. would keep the uglies from giving me a hard time. I forgot bylaw No. 10: "When an Angel punches a non-Angel . . ." So when somebody teed off on me, whamo!

Everybody else joined in. Not a hint of warning. Tiny got me on my feet after a while and probably saved my life. (See the book for details.) It was a cheap, chickenshit show—like the Big Nigger incident in Oakland[17]— but when I went over the book galleys afterward the only change I made was the adding of a postscript. Validation by fire, as it were. If you talk to Sonny and he offers an explanation, I'd be curious to hear it. But I'm not about to ask for one myself. As far as I'm concerned I've already written it. OK—write.

Hunter

TO CAREY MCWILLIAMS, *THE NATION:*

Thompson had failed to send The Nation *his promised article on the extreme right in California.*

December 8, 1966
Owl Farm
Woody Creek, Colorado

Dear Carey—

I feel guiltier every time I hear your name, which for some reason is quite often. You came up in a conversation with Bob Craig (ex–Aspen Inst.) the other night, and again when I talked to Shir-Cliff at Ballantine . . . and also about two weeks ago when I was talking with a copy editor at Random House.

Anyway, I want you to know I haven't forgotten the California piece, nor have I put it aside. I've made about four false starts and the focus keeps changing so radically that I'm no longer sure what I'm writing. The only line I want to keep out of what I have is this one, from a draft done more than two weeks ago: "It seemed like a good time to be leaving California." What started out as a detailed, political prediction sort of piece was ruined by Reagan's election, which took all the foresight-wisdom out of my ap-

---

17. A group of Hell's Angels had beaten up a large African-American man at a bar, nearly killing him.

proach and made me sound like just another headline-sifter. (Another example: two weeks or so ago I predicted sarcastically in a letter to Random that John Wayne would unseat Kuchel[18] in 1968—and this morning I read (in the *Denver Post*) an interview with Wayne, somewhere in Mexico, in which he denied any intention of running for the Senate. Probably if I joked tonight about Walt Disney running in 1968, I'd read Drew Pearson's column tomorrow and find that the Disney PR firm had decided to make the big move in 1970, on the assumption that George Murphy[19] will have moved up to the presidency in 1968.) The dark fog of madness is moving in on California politics so fast that it's no longer possible to joke about it. When I wrote the non-student piece, for instance, I could mock the Nazi camp and even Clark Kerr . . . but with a vague, bottom of mind sort of instinct that Reason would prevail and that I'd eventually sound like a seer. Now I feel like anything I write could send me to jail when I go back to the coast . . . or, if not that, I don't know what manner of vicious absurdity I can write about without having my thesis cut out from under me by tomorrow's headlines. I kept telling my Liberal compatriots that Reagan would win by a million votes and put them all behind bars, but I didn't really believe things were that bad until about two weeks ago—when Reagan announced that he'd take the oath at 12:10 a.m. There was no doubt, at that point, that Dr. Strangelove was real.

Anyway, the only nut I have right now is that one sentence. I took it out of a 5–6 page start I made on a piece that was actually a midnight highway reflection that I worked up on napkin notes while driving from San Francisco toward Aspen on Election night. By the time I got to Reno the polls had closed on the coast, and by the time I got to Elko [Governor Pat] Brown had conceded and the Republican landslide was on. I drove all night across Nevada, so I had plenty of time to think . . . and although I had several good non-political reasons for fleeing to Colorado, probably my big reasons were indirectly political. The original title I had for the piece, "California, the Progressive Penal Colony," now seems as apt as it does dated. Kesey went to jail, [the cops] busted the strike at Berkeley, and Reagan is making noises that should cause Eastern Liberals to forget about Germany and ponder their own Promised Land. I no longer see any point in making dire predictions about California; they'll all come true by the time the article is printed. The state scares me. The whole country scares me. And I don't say that in any abstract sense because I have a bad tendency to argue with strangers in strange places, and on several recent oc-

18. Thomas Kuchel, a Democrat, was a U.S. senator from California.
19. George Murphy was a right-wing Hollywood actor who ran for the U.S. Senate in California and won.

casions I've been given to understand that I'm not one of the boys. If my neighbors in Woody Creek could read my mail they'd have me locked up . . . although I get along fine with them when all we talk about is snow, horses and credit at the WC store.

Probably by now you have the drift of my thinking, which is largely out of focus. The only thing I can write with any sense of certainty that won't be dated by tomorrow's headlines is a sort of personal reminiscence about how it was in California Last Year, and How It Is Now. The vast alter- ations . . . the failure, as it were, of the Revolution of Expectations. (That's Adlai's phrase, by the way, and he originally said it in reference to South America about 1960 . . . and since then South America has been traveling the same route as California, only faster. . . . Brazil continues to interest me immensely, and especially since it's done a 180-degree political turn since I left in 1963, so if you know anybody who'd pay me to go back to Rio and write something profound, by all means let me know.)

I am, in fact, at loose ends for ideas. I have a contract with Random for two books in addition to *Hell's Angels*, but one is a novel that needs a total rewrite and the other is a non-fiction book with no subject or title.[20] The novel was due last August 1, and the other is due August 1, 1967. So I'm in a definite bind. I finally got page proofs from Random and I'll send them to the Guggenheim people as soon as I can figure out what sort of project I want their money for. I've suggested to Random a book on Los Angeles as the Full and Final Flower of the American Dream, but they say it won't sell. Shir-Cliff wants something on Cops, but ap- parently somebody else is about to publish one like that. The Minute- men don't interest me and the only other thing I can think of is a mean exposé of pro football—which I'd like to do and could probably do pretty well. Not a [George] Plimpton-style job, but a real root-grabber. That's about all my ideas right now. About ten sentences from here I cut out for 30 minutes to shovel a cut in the snow so I can get out tomorrow. We had the heaviest storm since 1934 yesterday and today, and it's still coming. I can't let it build up on me, or I'll never get out. I'm the only dude in this far bend of the Woody Creek canyon; the other two are way down below—and this ranch has a history of breaking dudes' spirits . . . last winter both tenants fled, and it was a pretty mild winter. But I lived out here before (down the road a piece) when it got down to 40 below for 4–5 days at a stretch, and the sale of British rights on the Hell's Angels book (to Penguin) gives me enough to buy snow tires, chains and a big shovel. I also board 21 horses, one of which got loose when I was out shoveling a

20. Thompson would fulfill this obligation in 1971 when he gave Silberman his classic *Fear and Loathing in Las Vegas* to publish.

while ago, and I had to chase him up the creek with a two-cell flash-light—in knee-deep snow. Horses regard strangers with the same amount of snorting, devious hostility that I learned to live with among the Hell's Angels . . . so I get along pretty well with them. So far. The Angels, as I think I told you, put me in the Santa Rosa emergency ward on Labor Day, and just as I was getting over that I slid down a shale cliff during an elk hunt and almost turned into a basket case. It's been a rough year. My only hope for salvation is that Random will promote the book in such a way as to make me a fortune.

That's about the story from here. I wish I could tell you I had four or five articles ready to send, but I don't—to you or anyone else. The last ar-ticle I wrote, in fact, was the non-student piece. (No, I wrote one for *Playboy* on the Angels, which they first bought, then rejected when the *Saturday Evening Post* beat them to the stands . . . and I got a partial re-prieve recently when *Esquire* bought part of the book for the upcoming January issue. . . . I have no idea what they plan to use. . . .

In all, I feel a need to write about what's happening—here, or anywhere else. If you think the California personal reflection piece sounds interest-ing, let me know and I'll do it. One of the best items I'd plan to include is a letter from Steve DeCanio (ex-editor of *Spider*), who is now a grad stu-dent at MIT [Massachusetts Institute of Technology] after spending all last summer in various jails, serving terms for the FSM and Auto Row convic-tions. It's a good commentary on the whole Berkeley scene.

Beyond that, I'll be happy to hear any ideas you have . . . for anything. But keep in mind I'm looking for a non-fiction book subject and would much prefer any article ideas to have book-length potential. Thanks for everything you can send. I meant to write a short note to cure you of any no-tion that I wasn't sending you articles because I'd become rich. That ain't the case. It's just that I had my original idea shot out from under me, and since then I've been groping. As a matter of fact I haven't written anything new since I finished the Hell's Angels book . . . and that makes me nervous.

Sincerely,
Hunter S. Thompson

TO ART KUNKIN, *LOS ANGELES FREE PRESS:*

Thompson had learned about the death of his friend Lionel Olay from an obituary in the Free Press. *Kunkin was the magazine's editor.*

December 14, 1966
Owl Farm
Woody Creek, Colo.

Dear Mr. Kunkin—

I was jolted to see your death notice on Lionel Olay in the December 9 issue, which got here today. I talked to Beverly on the phone right after Lionel had the second, bad stroke in the hospital and everything she said sounded bad . . . but then ever since I first met him in Big Sur Lionel always seemed on the brink of some new disaster, yet he always managed to prevail or at least endure. I wrote him at the hospital, expecting to get a hard-witted little note in return, but I guess I won't.

Anyway, I wonder if you could root me up a copy of that piece he did for the *Free Press* on Lenny Bruce. I think it was sometime last spring . . . a long while before Lenny died. It was one of the best things Lionel ever did and, as I recall, it was as much an obit for himself as it was for Bruce . . . although they were both very much alive when he wrote it. He sent me a copy, but I left it with my letter file in San Francisco and I won't get back there until February.

I'd like to write something about Lionel and I think his Bruce article would be a big help to me. He always struck me as the crown-prince of free-lancers, a congenital anarchist like his father, running out his string in a world that had less and less use for him. I've owed *The Nation* a piece for a long time and I think they'd like the one I have in mind on Lionel and where he lived. (I don't mean Topanga, but where his head was.) OK, and thanks for any effort it might take to locate the article.

Sincerely,
Hunter S. Thompson

"THE HYPE OF THE CENTURY" (ARTICLE PROPOSAL SENT TO VARIOUS EDITORS):

A die-hard San Francisco 49ers fan, Thompson floated to various editors this proposal for an exposé on the politics of professional football.

December 25, 1966
Woody Creek, Colorado

THE HYPE OF THE CENTURY

A THESIS—TO BE WRITTEN BY A RABID FAN—IN WHICH IT IS ARGUED, RESEARCHED, PROVEN AND OPENLY DISPLAYED THAT PROFESSIONAL FOOTBALL IS A VICIOUS UN-SPORTING HOAX—A VIOLENT SICK JOKE, BEING PERPETRATED ON A SICK SOCIETY—WITH THE FEELING FOR ULTIMATE GALL—

IN THE PERSON OF PETE ROZELLE—THAT CAN ONLY BE
MAINTAINED ON A LEVEL BEYOND THE WILDEST DREAMS
OF HISTORY'S GREATEST HYPE-SELLERS.... AND A SEC-
ONDARY THEORY THAT SUCKERS IN THIS COUNTRY ARE
MADE, NOT BORN.... A MERCILESS EXPOSÉ ON THE ROLE
OF SPORTSWRITERS IN THE GREAT INDUSTRY OF SPORTS-
PROMOTING....

I don't have any solid ideas about who might print this article, but it's a
fine bundle of possibilities and I can't think of anybody better suited to
write it than your friendly veteran sportswriter, HST. For one, I have paid
first $40 and then $50 for season tickets to the San Francisco 49er games
during the past two years.... I sit in my regular seat with all the other animals, drunk and shouting, and even though I know I'm being taken, I get
a boot out of it . . . and when either the 49ers or I (am/are) out of town, I
seek out the nearest TV set and squat religiously in front of it, whether the
game comes on at 10:00 in Baltimore, or 7:00 in Los Angeles. Even after
moving to Aspen in mid-autumn, I've managed to see all but one of the
49ers' Sunday crusades, either via television from Grand Junction, or by
driving back to San Francisco for various professional reasons that allow
me, by coincidence, to occupy my seat at Kezar [Stadium] on Sunday afternoons.

[. . .] My second fine credential has to do with the fact that the first
words I published for pay or otherwise were as a sportswriter, a wretched
profession that I pursued for at least two years, or until I learned better. I
began my writing career as sports editor of the Eglin AFB (Florida) *Eagle*,
and the main part of my duties lay in detailing the weekly glories of such
as Zeke Bratowski (who quarterbacked the fabulous Eagles to the Air
Force championship), who hurled passes to Max McGee . . . for many
yards gained, and many touchdowns, primarily because the bohunk defensive backs on other Air Force teams couldn't understand why nice,
quiet-talkin' fellas from the Green Bay Packers had to always grab people's belts when they ran out for a pass.... It didn't seem quite fair, and
of course it wasn't . . . McGee would run about 20 yards with his hand
resting easily on the defensive back's hip, and then when the ball started
dropping on them he would suddenly root his antagonist to the ground
with a violent downward shove, and step off all alone to catch the pass. I
was sports editor of the *Eagle* for two years: for the first of these I merely
sat in the press box and did my job, but after the coach (a flight colonel)
realized what a champ he had going for him, he ushered me into the hi-
erarchy. At the end of the '56 season I forged enough ballots to elect four
of the Eglin Eagles to the All-AF eleven (or maybe it was All-Service, I
forget).

Anyway, the next season, due to circumstances beyond my control, I was purged as sports editor and threatened with reassignment to Iceland because of things I had written. The football coach, sensing a loss more crucial even than the retirement of Bratowski to civilian life, pulled enough strings to have me reassigned to an entirely new military slot—football statistician and official biographer of the wondrous Eglin Eagles. [. . .]

All this is a sort of weird background for the piece I want to write . . . a sort of sidelight, as it were, to the underground side of professional football. The rest I would have to do in the guise of a fan, one who has sat through many wretched, drunken afternoons with the 49ers . . . and then haggled with the hired punks and sportswriters on long spring afternoons on the subject of the 49ers' chances in the coming year, and always being lied to, cheerfully, by people who knew better.

The fact is that the 49er management (the club is owned by two old ladies) didn't care about winning or losing in 1966 because they had sold enough season tickets (like Otto Graham[21] said in his classic "fuck the public" quote) to make the season a profit whether they won or lost. The main factor was an $800,000 settlement (one each to the 49ers and the New York Giants) from the AFL, in exchange for rights to place a competing team in NFL territory—according to terms of the merger (the Oakland Raiders and New York Jets). There was also the strange episode of [49ers quarterback] John Brodie's $900,000 contract, a settlement made necessary by the fact that failure to settle might result in a lawsuit that could upset the NFL-AFL merger. (A big part of Brodie's money was paid by the AFL and Bud Adams, the loud and witless owner of the Houston Oilers, who stupidly nailed himself down to a verbal contract regarding Brodie's maybe jump to the AFL.) Another, similar story had to do with *Al Davis*, who went from coach of the Oakland Raiders to "commissioner" of the AFL at the same time the two leagues were in the making. Davis got enough out of the settlement (which entailed his demotion and discharge) to come back and buy the team, and one of the two or three major stockholders.

Another key to the story is Emmanuel Cuellar, the representative from Brooklyn, who did all he could to stymie the merger in Congress . . . on the grounds that pro football is a business, not a sport, and should therefore be subject to antitrust laws. But other congressmen got the word from other pressure-sources, and since there is not a pro football team in Brooklyn (unless the Jets might qualify on the basis of performance and subway distance), Cuellar got whipped by means of one of

21. Quarterback Otto Graham led the Cleveland Browns to six straight NFL championship games from 1950 through 1955.

the most peculiar and devious moves in recent congressional history. A congressional rider was tacked onto something like the foreign aid bill (I think it was Senator [Everett] Dirksen who did it) and Cuellar was dodged. Needless to say, the bill passed, and the merger of the two leagues became a reality at least until 1967, when Cuellar will have another shot at it. So now we have the "Super Bowl," from which each member of the winning team will glean $15,000 . . . and the losers, something around $7500. (A sport, not a business.) One game, played before 100,000 of the faithful in the L.A. Coliseum (at an average of $8–$12 a head), and for which a combination of TV networks will pay $125,000 a minute for their commercial advertising (or maybe it's the sponsors who'll have to pay that sum . . . this is something I can find out in the course of my research. . . .), in any case, $125,000 a minute is the cost of advertising on TV for the Super Bowl.

As for the mechanics of the article, I see it as something to appear either during the (late) 1967 season, or shortly afterward. I'd want to spend some time in the summer pro training camps and also in the dressing room and on the field during the first few games of 1967. But mainly I'd want to contact some of the most articulate players during the off-season and get them talking over a bit of the Old Crow . . . which brings to mind John David Crow, of the 49ers, who has a construction business in Arkansas when he ain't on the field whacking people . . . and Bernie Casey (also of the 49ers), who's a good enough artist to be exhibited in San Francisco and also to teach art at (I think) Bowling Green State College (Ohio) or maybe it's Miami U. (Ohio) in the off season.

My interest—at least for this piece—is the view of pro football from an insider's off-season perspective. Not the boom-boom bullshit of the [Washington Redskins quarterback] Sam Huff films, but a sort of investor's view . . . since it's obviously a business, not a sport . . . and what kind of a business it really is.

There are oddities in the same . . . such as Frank Ryan's Ph.D. in math, and Lance Rentzel's conviction for child molesting.[22] And what caused the Bears to fold in 1966, when all the in-money had them as champs? I don't know, but I think some good legwork—which the sportswriters either won't do or can't write—might pay off with a mean fat article, which none of the league's PR men (Rozelle's included) will want any part of when it's published.

But of course there's always the objection that pro football is an "American Institution," like the hollow husk of baseball, and that only an Un-

---

22. Frank Ryan was a quarterback for the Cleveland Browns, and Lance Rentzel a wide receiver for the Dallas Cowboys.

American Freak would write ugly words on the subject as long as everybody in the game or in any way connected with it is making good money. That's not my concern. I'd like to write something real about the "game," and I already know enough about it to guarantee that anything I write won't be a PR puff. Anyone interested is urged to contact:

Hunter S. Thompson
Owl Farm
Woody Creek, Colorado

Hell's Angels.
(Photo by Hunter S. Thompson; courtesy of HST Collection)

Terry the Tramp and friend.
(Photo by Hunter S. Thompson; courtesy
of HST Collection)

1967

TRIUMPH OF THE WILL . . . WHOOPING IT UP IN THE PLAZA FOUNTAIN . . . NAKED AND ALONE ON THE CELEBRITY CIRCUIT . . . HERO OF *THE NEW YORK TIMES* . . . SAVED BY STUDS TERKEL . . . SWARMED OVER BY PARASITES . . . FUCK YOU, YOU'RE FIRED . . . THE FIRST VICTORY LAP . . .

There is no shortage of documentation for the thesis that the current Haight-Ashbury scene is only the orgiastic tip of a great psychedelic iceberg that is already drifting in the sea lanes of the Great Society. Submerged and uncountable is the mass of intelligent, capable heads who want nothing so much as peaceful anonymity. In a nervous society where a man's image is frequently more important than his reality, the only people who can afford to advertise their drug menus are those with nothing to lose.

--Hunter S. Thompson,
  "The 'Hashbury' Is the
  Capital of the Hippies,"
  The New York Times Magazine,
  May 14, 1967

TO JOHN WILCOCK, *LOS ANGELES FREE PRESS:*

Thompson paid tribute to Lionel Olay, "the ultimate free-lancer."

January 5, 1967
Woody Creek, Colorado

Dear John:

You asked me for an article on whatever I wanted to write about and since you don't pay I figured that gives me *carte blanche.* I started out tonight on an incoherent bitch about the record business . . . I was looking at the jacket copy on the Blues Project album and I noticed that none of the musicians' names were mentioned anywhere on the album . . . but the "producer's" name was in huge script on the back, and underneath it were four or five other names . . . punks and narcs and other ten-percenters who apparently had more leverage than the musicians who made the album, and who managed to get their names on the record jacket.

I was brooding about this—which I'll write about sometime later—when I picked up the latest *Free Press* and read an obituary for a three-year-old kid named "Godot" . . . which is nice, but as I read it I was reminded again of Lionel Olay and how the *Free Press* commemorated his death with a small block of unsold advertising space that had to be used anyway, so why not for Lionel? I am also reminded that I've asked you twice for a copy of his article on Lenny Bruce (in which Lionel wrote his own obituary), and that you've disregarded both queries. Maybe there's no connection between this and the fact that the Blues Project people were fucked out of any mention on their own album, but I think there is. I see it as two more good examples of the cheap, mean, grinning-hippie capitalism that pervades the whole New Scene . . . a scene which provides the Underground Press Syndicate with most of its copy and income. Frank Zappa's comments on rock joints and light shows (*Free Press* 12/30/66) was a welcome piece of heresy in an atmosphere that is already rigid with pre-pubic senility. The concept of the UPS is too right to argue with, but the reality is something else. As Frank Zappa indicated, if only in a roundabout way, there are a lot of people trying to stay alive and working WITHIN the UPS spectrum, and not on the ten-percent fringes. That's where *Time* magazine lives . . . way out there on the puzzled, masturbating edge, peering through the keyhole and selling what they see to the big wide world of Chamber of Commerce voyeurs who support the public prints.

Which brings us back to Lionel, who lived and died as walking proof that all heads exist alone and at their own risk. Maybe I'm wrong; maybe his funeral procession on the Sunset Strip was enough to bring even cops to their knees . . . but since I didn't hear anything about that action, I have to doubt it. I suspect Lionel died pretty much as he lived: as a freelance writer, promoter, grass-runner and general free spirit. I'm sure a lot of people knew him better than I did, but I think I knew him pretty well. I first met him in Big Sur in 1960, when we were both pretty broke and grubbing for rent money. After that we did a lot of writing back and forth, but we'd only met (usually at the Hot Springs in Big Sur) after long months of different action in very different worlds. He was broke somewhere in New England when I was in Peru, and later in Rio I got a letter from him with a Chicago postmark . . . when I got back to New York he wrote from L.A., saying he'd decided to settle there because it was the "only home we had."

I've never been sure if he included me in the definition, but I know he was talking about a lot of people beyond himself and his wife, Beverly. Lionel saw the west coast of the 1960's as Malcom Cowley saw New York after World War One—as the "homeland of the uprooted." He saw his own orbit as something that included Topanga, Big Sur, Tijuana, the Strip and occasional runs up north to the Bay Area. He wrote for *Cavalier*, the *Free Press*, and anyone who would send him a check. When the checks didn't come he ran grass to New York and paid his bills with LSD. And when he had something that needed a long run of writing time he would take off in his Porsche or his Plymouth or any one of a dozen other cars that came his way, and cadge a room from Mike Murphy at the Hot Springs, or in his brother Dennis's house across the canyon. Lionel and Dennis were old friends, but Lionel knew too much—and insisted on saying it—to use that friendly leverage as a wedge to the screen-writing business, where Dennis Murphy was making it big. Lionel had already published two novels and he was a far better plot-maker than most of the Hollywood hacks, but every time he got a shot at the big cop-out money he blew it with a vengeance. Now and then one of the New York editors would give him enough leeway to write what he wanted, and a few of his articles are gems. He did one for *Cavalier* on the soul of San Francisco that is probably the best thing ever written on that lovely gutless town. Later he wrote a profile on Lenny

Bruce (for the *Free Press*) that if I ran a newspaper I'd reprint every year in boldface type, as an epitaph for free-lance writers everywhere.

Lionel was the ultimate free-lancer. In the nearly ten years I knew him, the only steady work he did was as a columnist for the Monterey *Herald* . . . and even then he wrote on his own terms, on his own subjects, and was inevitably fired. Less than a year before he died his willful ignorance of literary politics led him to blow a very rich assignment from *Life* magazine, which asked him for a profile on Marty Ransohoff, a big-name Hollywood producer then fresh from a gold-plated bomb called *The Sandpiper*. Lionel went to London with Ransohoff ("first-cabin all the way," as he wrote me from the S.S. *United States*) and after two months in the great man's company he went back to Topanga and wrote a piece that resembled nothing so much as Mencken's brutal obituary on William Jennings Bryan. Ransohoff was described as a "pompous toad"—which was not exactly what *Life* was looking for. The article naturally bombed, and Lionel was back on the bricks where he'd spent the last half of his forty-odd years. I'm not sure how old he was when he died, but it wasn't much over forty . . . according to Beverly he suffered a mild stroke that sent him to the hospital, and then a serious stroke that finished him.

Word of his death was a shock to me, but not particularly surprising since I'd called him a week or so before and heard from Beverly that he was right on the edge. More than anything else, it came as a harsh confirmation of the ethic that Lionel had always lived with but never talked about . . . the dead-end loneliness of a man who makes his own rules. Like his anarchist father in Chicago, he died without making much of a dent. I don't even know where he's buried, but what the hell? The important thing is where he lived.

And there's the chill of it. Lionel was one of the original anarchist-head-beatnik-free-lancers of the 1950's . . . a bruised forerunner of [Timothy] Leary's would-be "drop-out generation" of the 1960's. The Head Generation . . . a loud, cannibalistic gig where the best are fucked for the worst reasons, and the worst make a pile by feeding off the best. Promoters, narcs, con men—all selling the New Scene to *Time* magazine and the Elks Club. The handlers get rich while the animals either get busted or screwed to the floor with bad contracts. Who's making money off the Blues Project? Is it Verve (a division of MGM), or the five ignorant bastards who thought they were getting a break when Verve said they'd make them a record? And who the fuck is "Tom Wilson," the "producer" whose name rides so high on the record jacket? By any other name he's a vicious ten-percenter who sold "Army Surplus commodities" in the late 1940's, "Special-Guaranteed Used Cars" in the 1950's and 29-cent thumb-prints of John Kennedy in the 1960's . . . until he figured out that the really big money was in the drop-out revolution. Ride the big wave: Folk-rock, pot symbols, long hair, and $2.50 minimum at the gate. Light shows! Tim Leary! Warhol! NOW!

Now what? While the new wave flowered, Lenny Bruce was hounded to death by cops. For obscenity. Thirty thousand people (according to Paul Krassner[1]) are serving time in the jails of this vast democracy on marijuana charges, and the world we have to live in is controlled by a stupid thug from Texas. A vicious liar, with the ugliest family in Christendom . . . mean Okies feeling honored by the cheap indulgence of a George Hamilton, a stinking animal ridiculed even in Hollywood. And California, "the most progressive state," elects a governor straight out of a George Grosz painting, a political freak in every sense of the word except California politics . . . Ronnie Reagan, the White Hope of the West.

Jesus, no wonder Lionel had a stroke. What a nightmare it must have been for him to see the honest rebellion that came out of World War Two taken over by a witless phony like Warhol . . . the Exploding Plastic Inevitable, Lights, Noise, Love the Bomb! And then to see a bedrock madman like Ginsberg copping out with tolerance poems and the same sort of witless swill that normally comes from the Vatican. Kerouac hiding out with his "*mère*" on Long Island or maybe St. Petersburg . . . Kennedy with his head blown off and Nixon back from the dead, running wild in the power vacuum of Lyndon's hopeless bullshit . . . and of course Reagan, the new dean of Berkeley. Progress Marches On, courtesy, as always, of General Electric . . . with sporadic assists from Ford, GM, AT&T, Lockheed and Hoover's FBI.

Hunter S. Thompson

TO SONNY BARGER:

Thompson had learned of the death of a Hell's Angel.

February 8, 1967
Woody Creek, Colorado

Sonny—

I was surprised and saddened to hear about Elsie.[2] I didn't get any details, just a late-night collect call from San Francisco, so I don't know how it happened. But it doesn't really matter now. She was good people in every sense of the word.

---

1. Paul Krassner was the editor of *The Realist*, a Los Angeles–based counterculture magazine.
2. Elsie was Barger's "old lady" at the time. She died in a motorcycle crash, leaving behind a young son.

One thing I can't really understand about the Angels is that the ones who get killed, snuffed, or whatever you want to call it, always seem to be among the best of the breed. You might give this some thought, because it puts you right up there at the head of the class.

Anyway, I was sorry as hell to get the news about Elsie. I hope you'll do whatever you can for the kid; he always struck me as being pretty bright and decent.

Take care of yourself.

Sincerely,
Hunter

TO SELMA SHAPIRO, RANDOM HOUSE:

Random House had assigned Shapiro to do the publicity for Hell's Angels.

March 21, 1967
Woody Creek, Colorado

Dear Selma. . . .

Sorry for the outburst today. But another piece of evidence that the CBC was fucking around with me was more than I could handle without shouting. They've lied to me about every aspect of this thing, so why should I assume they're being straight about the $500???[3] And since I took your word that I'd be paid for that fiasco I figure you're responsible for getting the $500.

The outburst was also triggered by the fact that I got no sleep last night . . . just lying there, sweating, from midnight until 5:30, when I got up and smoked some grass. And for all those 5½ hours I thought about RH, the contract and the future. So when I woke up at 2:30 to find the CBC hassling me again, I flipped out.

Unfortunately, you just happened to be the one on the other end. But against the background of my absolute conviction that Silberman and Shir-Cliff have deliberately screwed me, I doubt that today will be the last time you'll have to take that kind of bullshit. If I thought it would do any good, I'd scream the same way at Silberman, but I don't think he has any blood in his veins. Every time I start yelling at him he just laughs sort of hopelessly and defensively, as if he were talking to an idiot child. Every time he says, "Don't look back," I focus more intensely to the rear, the past, and the indefensible fucking I got on the *Hell's Angels* contract. And I'd rather not hear the same kind of corporate, pawnshop bullshit from you.

3. CBC was supposed to pay Thompson for appearing on their television talk show.

Silberman is very candid about admitting that he screwed me, so it hardly becomes you to go reaching for those awkward misinterpretations that you've been trying to pass off on me. You may as well live with the fact that I see our whole thing on two very distinct and separate levels, and when you try to mix them up I begin to distrust you. I suggest you recall what you told me about your benefactor and mine (no corporate names, of course) long before this dirty argument came out in the open. So don't try to whitewash him now. And don't assume, either, that I'm basing what I say and think on what *you* told me. I'm a better reporter than that . . . and if my bitching seems too loud and crazy to you, keep in mind that I've given the whole thing enough quiet consideration to think that I know what I'm doing.

In a nut, I don't see that I have anything to lose by pushing Random House far enough to break the contract for the next two books. I couldn't possibly do any worse with another publisher—not at this stage of the game, anyway. If the book stopped selling tomorrow I'd be in a good bargaining position, simply on the basis of reviews. And since Silberman doesn't want to bargain, fuck him. He may think Random House is the only publisher in New York, but a look at the *Publisher's Weekly* bestseller list you sent me the other day would indicate that there are at least a few others. Aside from *Hell's Angels*, I didn't see any Random House book either listed or noted as "comers." So if this is his first "success" in two years, as far as I'm concerned it's going to be his last—at least at my expense.

And so much for that. Let's keep ourselves straight by not arguing any more about the contract situation. I don't blame you for it, and I don't like you putting yourself in a position where you have to defend it. It makes it harder on both of us. Let's keep the human side of publishing separate from the knife-in-the-back side. (Incidentally, I re-read—before writing this—your letters of March 10 and the one from the Boston plane. And I felt like a bit of a monster for yelling at you this afternoon . . . but then I am a bit of a monster, so what the hell?) Anyway, do us both a favor and keep in mind that we'll get along a lot better if you don't try and mix up your roles on me. I relate to Selma, not Random House . . . and if you come back at me with company bullshit, then expect that kind of reply. OK for now. . . .

                                        Hunter

TO TERRY THE TRAMP:

Thompson was conspiring to get his Hell's Angel friend Terry the Tramp free copies of his book.

March 21, 1967
Owl Farm
Woody Creek, Colorado

Tramp, you worthless beast! Random House finally forwarded your letter through to me. What the fuck is the Angel's Inn?? What are you doing? Whatever it is . . . beware. Anyway, here's how to get some books: call (collect, during the day, New York time) Selma Shapiro, publicity manager of Random House, and tell her I said to send you five (5) books and put them on my account. Two of these should go to Skip[4] . . . the crazy bastard came up to Toronto and screamed bullshit at me for an hour on national TV. But I told him I'd send five books, so two of the five are his (they cost me $3 each). Also tell Skip to send me his address and I'll send a check for that mystery keg of beer that everybody seems to think I owe the club. I don't remember agreeing to any specific keg, but the fact is that I intended to have a mind-bending publication-day party that would have made beer a minor consideration. As for free books, I wrote Sonny and told him exactly why I was going back on that agreement.[5] I was pretty pissed off about getting stomped and I was disappointed, frankly, that you didn't come around afterward and at least get the story straight. Skip told some kind of incredible tale that made me sound like a combination of Marshal Dillon, Superman, and a Lunatic. He admitted afterward that it didn't make sense, and I was on a radio show—by remote control—with Pete Knell[6] and some others last weekend, and we got the story more or less straight.

Anyway, when you call Selma you'll have to convince her that your request is legit—in other words, that I've sanctioned it—so you'll have to tell her that you know the password: "Chicago." And if that doesn't work, we're both out of luck. My relations with Random House are sinking in shit, due to the fact that they've screwed me so badly on my book contract that not even a best-seller will pay my expenses for two years of work. I get 22½ cents for every book sold; you figure it out.

Anyway, I'm evicted from here as of May 1, and I should be back in San Francisco for the summer freak-out by sometime in June. Send me a line c/o Selma Shapiro at Random House, 457 Madison Ave., New York 22, and tell me how to get hold of you quietly, without violence. But if we're dealing with people holding grudges, forget it. This is a big, wide world, and I have all the action I need without stupid feuds. OK for now. . . .

Hunter

---

4. Skip Werkman, a Hell's Angel, was a surprise guest on the Toronto (CBC) talk show.
5. Thompson had agreed to give the Hell's Angels all free books, an offer he reneged on after the stomping.
6. A San Francisco Hell's Angel.

TO HUGH DOWNS, *TODAY:*

Downs hosted NBC's Today *show, on which Thompson had been interviewed.*

April 1, 1967
Woody Creek, Colorado

Dear Hugh. . . .

In the midst of working on an article for *The Realist* on that whole, rotten publicity stunt for the *Hell's Angels* book, I remember how much I appreciated your help—first on the "Kup" show[7] and then again on *Today.* The Kup thing was the first time I'd ever been on TV, and when he said, "Tell me, Hunter, what do you *think* about the Hell's Angels?" I figured the best thing I could do was walk off the set. So it was a hell of a relief to have you re-phrase the question in manageable terms. I didn't miss that.

As for *Today*, I still can't understand how anybody can function at that inhuman hour and I'm sorry I wasn't more lively, but if you and Paul Cunningham[8] hadn't carried me as well as you did it might have been a total disaster. (Oddly enough, I got a lot of comments saying that my wretchedness made the thing seem more "real.") But everybody agreed that I looked wretched, for good or ill.

Which is a pretty good definition. I could have used some of your help in L.A., where I had 36 appearances in five days. Anyway, I want you to know that I realize you went out of your way to keep me afloat in a bad time . . . and if I can do you a favor sometime, let me know.

Sincerely,
Hunter S. Thompson

TO LEWIS NICHOLS, *THE NEW YORK TIMES BOOK REVIEW:*

Although Thompson loathed the publicity tour for Hell's Angels, *he had a great time at his lunchtime interview with journalist Lewis Nichols, who wrote about the experience in his "In and Out of Books," a regular feature in* The New York Times Book Review.

April 5, 1967
Woody Creek, Colorado

Dear Mr. Nichols. . . .

I was just reading over your tale of our lunch in the *Book Review* of March 5 and I enjoy it as much now as I did when I first saw it. My main

---

7. Thompson had appeared on Irv Kup's eponymous TV show.
8. Paul Cunningham was a news reporter on the *Today* show.

pleasure in it is that Selma was sure, from beginning to end, that I was living, walking proof of everything you might find offensive. She was still worried after we parted with you, but I told her she was crazy. I enjoyed talking to you and I had to assume it was at least tolerably mutual, because otherwise we couldn't have talked at all. There were some really wretched scenes on that tour—strange plastic freaks babbling at me, asking stupid questions, no hope of human communication. You were a sort of oasis; I had a good time and even a good lunch. Scallops. I am now an authority on the quality of scallops in New York restaurants.

Another thing: thanks (to you or whoever did the deed) for carrying the *Hell's Angels* book so long on the "New and Recommended" list. After my somewhat qualified comments on the *Times* in the book, I was overwhelmed to the point of being addled at the decency of your reaction.

At first I thought it was a sort of massive retaliation in the way of turning the other cheek, but the other day I got a call from Harvey Shapiro (on the [*New York Times* Sunday] magazine), asking if I wanted to do a piece on the history and meaning of almost everything—with anecdotes, personality sketches, geography and wisdom—in 4000 words or less. . . . I immediately saw the pattern: Benevolent Crucifixion. But I think I might surprise the bastard . . . and then where will we be? I might have to retire.

OK for now, and thanks again for a good lunch, a good talk and your good ear.

Sincerely,
Hunter S. Thompson

TO KEN LAMOTT, *LOS ANGELES TIMES:*

April 20, 1967
Woody Creek, Colorado

Dear Mr. Lamott. . . .

I was just reading your piece in *West*[9] on the Golden Gate Be-In and remembered that I've been meaning to write you for a month or so to say thanks for your *Book Week* review of my Hell's Angels saga. I haven't had time to sit down and read all the reviews with a hard critic's eye, but I read them all at least once on the run, and—at the risk of sounding like a fraud and a flatterer—I recall yours as being the best and most perceptive of the lot. As a matter of fact it surprised me; I've read some of your other reviews and I remember that some of them read like they'd been written with a hatchet. So if anyone had told me that you were going to review my book

9. *West* was a progressive magazine in Los Angeles.

for *BW,* I would not have looked forward to reading it. Needless to say, it came as a very happy surprise.

And so much for that. I'm reading your *West* piece in connection with a desperate rush job on the Haight-Ashbury for *The New York Times Magazine . . .* and I was struck by the weird similarity of your comments on Dr. Tim [Leary] and my own rude judgments in an already written first draft. It makes me uneasy to find myself in agreement with a self-confessed old fogey, but what the hell? I'll be 30 this summer. Here's the deal: I'll trade you a pound of my fallen hair for one knit tie and a pair of *Playboy* cufflinks. That seems fair.

OK for now. I was in San Francisco last week, but I got mixed up with a rotten crowd. Next time I get over I'll give you a ring and maybe we can have a drink—if booze is still legal. Again, thanks for reading my book without a pre-cocked hatchet . . . and also for hearing the music, for good or ill.

> Sincerely,
> Hunter S. Thompson

TO JIM SILBERMAN, RANDOM HOUSE:

Thompson moved into an abandoned, dilapidated ranch house fifteen miles outside of Aspen. He dubbed it Owl Farm and began massive renovations.

> May 13, 1967
> Woody Creek, Colorado

Dear Jim. . . .

This is my first letter in the new house, new desk, new writing room, etc. . . . painted red, white and blue by a dope freak that I hired from the trailer court. But the old music prevails . . . right now it's Dylan's "Desolation Row," wailing out of an alcove full of paint cans and dirty brushes. And Sandy's still in bed with her half-happened miscarriage. [. . .]I've had to hire a girl to wash dishes and take care of Juan.

I'm doing the hiring these days . . . which brings me to the point: Rather than get hung up in a long series of letters you never answer anyway I think I'll call and ask you some questions about money. You're aware, I think, that I've so far received a total of $1,000 on *Hell's Angels.* This does not seem equitable in light of even a 20,000 sale. I'm not happy with the apparent death of sales, but then I can't really know figures or even the business, so what the hell? Anytime you want to talk about altering the money situation on that second contract, just let me know. Right now I'm just coasting along on article sales, waiting for [Scott] Meredith's contract to run out. Selma is the best agent I've ever had . . . she's the only one who's ever put me in touch with money people. I just sold a second-rate piece to the *Times*, which should be out tomorrow, and a weird, unclassifiable thing to *Pageant*, which is due in July. Both Selma's work. And now I'm working on a piece for *Harper's*, which allegedly sold through Meredith. It's already a month late, but I'm not hurrying because I don't believe anything that comes from Meredith anyway. I think he's blown his mind; he's now signing himself "Sydney." Other people keep writing me, talking of lucrative sales in strange lands, but I never see any checks so I just put the letters in my big box. Devaney quit and wrote me a letter confirming most of what I suspected all along . . . jesus, how do you stand that business?

Now . . . here's a thing I wish you wouldn't ignore or shunt off to your file-clerk in the basement: I'd like an assignment from somebody to do a piece on the great "Grand Canyon Be-In" later this month, or maybe in June if the current rumor proves out. Anyway, the plan is for a half-million hippies to convene in the bottom of the Grand Canyon and I think it would make a hell of a color piece . . . sort of like the Angels' funeral. I can get down there from here in my car and mix non-violently with the crowd, for good or ill. So if you run across anybody who'd like me to write them a few words on the action, let me know. I won't count on hearing from you, but if you feel up to pushing this, give me a ring so I don't get crossed up with my sales pitches. The only other person I'm thinking of contacting at the moment is Tom Wolfe, who called me the other day and said he and some other people were going to launch *New York* as an independent magazine—which perhaps I might write for. So that sounds like a logical outlet for the Grand Canyon thing. Anyway, let me know if you have any ideas. I took my phone number with me, so the old Woody Creek number is still reliable. We're all reliable out here in Woody Creek.

OK for now. I'd still like those "ten free books" if you can get around to handling it. Meanwhile, I'll be working on The Rum Diary. The other non-fiction book is rapidly fading into the distance . . . although I do have a quick possibility which I'll tell you about pretty soon. In light of Wolfe's evaluation of my contract, the thing I have in mind just about fits the bill. Bingo. . . .

Hubert

P.S. . . . if you see Lynn Nesbit,[10] tell her I'm still alive and wondering if she is . . . although, given a choice right now, I think Selma has the action & I'll let her handle things until somebody better shows up.

10. Another literary agent, who would represent Thompson in later years.

TO SCOTT MEREDITH:

Meredith was just one in a long line of literary agents who Thompson felt had bilked him.

May 19, 1967
Woody Creek, Colorado

Scott Meredith
580 Fifth Ave.
New York City 36

Dear Scott:

This is to formalize a decision that I made quite a while ago, to wit: that I'd like to terminate our relationship as soon as possible. I know the contract says you can hold me until December 15 of this year—and I have enough money to hold out until then, if necessary (by that I mean I can go without writing anything more)—but in the interest of common sense and decency you can do us both a favor by cutting the cord amicably and at once.

I've given this thing a lot of thought and if you're curious about reasons I think you can find most of them in various letters I've sent you. The main one, of course, is that I don't believe you exist. I've said that pretty often before and maybe you thought I was kidding, but I wasn't. I've never seen you or heard your voice even on the phone, and the only time I came to New York you were too busy to see me. As far as I'm concerned my "agents" in New York are a tribe of people, totally unknown to me, who for some reason are allowed to use your name. Every letter I get from your agency is signed by a different person . . . and the last one somehow cut me out of $1000 from the *Ladies' Home Journal*, telling me I wouldn't have enough time to do it when I'd all but finished the piece. Beyond that, I'd agreed to write the goddamn thing three days before your man got around to telling me about the offer.

Don't bother to send me another letter like that last one . . . telling me what a stupid, naive, ungrateful prick I am, because none of that has any real bearing on our relationship as writer and agent. I am probably worse than you think, as a person, but what the hell? When I get hungry for personal judgment on myself I'll call for a priest.

As for the two-book contract Devaney arranged before quitting your agency, I have yet to run across anyone who doesn't consider it a rotten contract. It is, in fact, a wretched, predatory document, and the fact that you seem to be the only person in New York who thinks it's a good deal for me (according to your letter) is a main point in my decision to end our relationship.

Further, I have no intention of being bound by that contract and I've told Random House that I don't want any more of their advances. This was something I was very anxious to deal with when I came to New York, but Devaney didn't want any part of the argument and you weren't available. I managed, on my own, to negotiate a better deal on the *Hell's Angels* contract, despite the fact that you told me it couldn't be done.

My only project for this summer and fall is The Rum Diary. I made this decision two weeks ago and noted it in the enclosed letter that I didn't mail in the chaos of moving, sickness, deadlines, etc. All I want right now is a bit of peace and quiet: some days to write at night and bang around on my bike during the day. The Rum Diary will be finished sometime in the fall and I suppose, considering the terms of the contract, that you'll want some kind of percentage on it. If you want anything beyond a token fee, however (for getting me into a contract that I have to break), I suggest you weigh the advantages of a small financial return against absolute certainty of a lifetime (mine) of bad advertisements.

Anyway, the point I mean to make about The Rum Diary is that it's the only book that's going to be delivered on that stinking contract . . . and if it weren't already written, needing only a quick rewrite and a lot of cutting, I wouldn't even deliver that. Maybe you're right . . . that I really am a lucky low-life bastard to even be allowed to stand in line for the literary dole . . . and in that case you'd look a bit foolish hanging onto my coat-tails for ten percent. But do whatever you want, and by all means let me know . . . along with sending those checks (less your fee, of course, for the French and Brazilian rights). As for the *Harper's* piece, I'm still working on it. That's about it from this end. Fire at will. Sincerely. . . .

Hunter S. Thompson

TO TOM WOLFE:

May 24, 1967
Woody Creek, Colorado

Dear Tom. . . .

I'm back here in one of those square-shaped states, digging in for the duration of the crisis with an invalid, pregnant wife, a new bike and so many bouncing checks that not even a best-seller can pull me out. *Hell's Angels* sales are tailing off at about 25,000, of which I got 10%. Not a hell of a lot of money for two years of my life, but I can think of worse ways to make a living. It beats the hell out of writing for the *National Ob-*

server . . . we parted company over the Goldwater convention and the Berkeley FSM demonstrations. I don't miss that gig at all.

It's 4:00 here and I want to get this off before you move out for Da Nang or someplace like that. For christ's sake take it easy over there; the whole war isn't worth a rat's ass, much less yours. I'm going to register next year, for the sole purpose of voting against Johnson, regardless of who runs against him. I won't go into any life details until I'm sure I have the right address. Is this it?

Mine (the Owl Farm) is more or less permanent, but the Random House address is OK too. I have a novel to finish by the end of the summer and another non-fiction book that we haven't figured out a subject for yet. If you have any solid ideas about these anti-social types you mentioned—like any good contacts in some specific area—let me know and I'll ponder. Life in the Rockies is good, but I don't want to go stale. Maybe I'll see you in Vietnam; I'm trying to get *Esquire* to let me do a profile on [General William] Westmoreland. Send word on your movements, dates, etc.

Ciao,
Hunter

TO MR. SHENCK, EDITOR, *RAMPARTS:*

May 27, 1967
Woody Creek, Colorado

Dear Mr. Shecnk [sic]:

Or however you spell your name—my apologies, of course, for not getting it right. Anyway, I wasn't particularly bothered by the cheap, pompous and self-serving tone of your review of my book in *Ramparts*—but when you did it again on McBird I figured you were really looking for an argument with the people that you might, in some better world, have agreed with—so allow me to introduce myself as the man who's going to take your head off at the first good opportunity. It will probably be a while and—oddly enough—I don't feel any sense of personal animosity about it—but you strike me as a bellowing, greedy phony—in the same discount league with Tim Leary and Alan Watts—and that automatically makes you fair game.

Again—nothing personal. But since you persist in your old-womanish view of almost everything—and especially because of your obvious lack of decency, graciousness and humanity—which translates as a common form of cheap meanness—I can't avoid the obligation to deal with you . . . the Dean Rusk of the underground. I look forward to reviewing your next book.

> Sincerely. . . .
> Hunter S. Thompson

FROM CHARLES KURALT:

> June 1, 1967
> New York

Dear Hunter,

The $110 I'd rather just let hang there. Of course it was my money, but I don't need it. I need a hell of a lot more than that because the IRS just counted up all the days I *was* in the country in 1960–1963 when I told them I wasn't in the country at all. As for this specific $110 I would rather drink it up all at once with you some night, or at least carry in the back of my mind the promise of same.

The book is good, really good. I read it at a sitting, and read the best parts again. You write damned well, which I guess I knew all along but of course I've never had a chance to read extended Thompson before, and it really pleased me. The notices I've seen were all great, the ads were big and imposing, and withal, a *succès d'estime*, and I hope as big a success financially.

I am so late in replying because I have been covering an expedition to the North Pole, 40 below, frozen beard, muskox stew, the whole thing. Two months of it and I just got back. Came back through San Francisco and thought to call you, only to realize I couldn't remember the street or your phone number, and on thinking about it decided in your literary success you'd probably forsaken that Chinaman anyway. Owl Farm, very well. I may come see you . . . there or in California. As soon as we finish editing The White Hell or whatever we end up calling it, I'm going to do a tour around the country doing rural stories for Cronkite in a kind of *Travels with Charley* vein, only Charley, come to think of it, was a dog. Anyway, I should like very much to have an evening together. I have thought of a lot of things to tell you over the months, and I want to hear about your confrontation with the Publishing World. I had occasion to say Hunter Thompson, *Hell's Angels* on the radio before I left for the Arctic, by the way, so consider Selma Shapiro repaid for her two copies, East Coast and West Coast editions.

I think it is nice that Sandy is pregnant. Petie, who has always been one of your champions (against the *Los Angeles Times* cabal as I recall) and who also liked the book, says hello.

> As ever,
> Charles

TO DON ERIKSON, *ESQUIRE:*

June 5, 1967
Woody Creek, Colorado

Don Erikson
Esquire
488 Madison Ave.
NYC 22

Dear Don:

Here's another quick idea, and if somebody else has already done it I plead ignorance. I was thinking of a piece on the Reagan-Kuchel split in California, but I just read a *Chicago Daily News* piece saying Reagan is going to call his dogs off Kuchel in 1968 so he can face the GOP convention as the "man who restored unity to California Republicanism." This would preclude a vicious primary fight for Kuchel's Senate seat.

So I sort of lost interest in that one . . . until, way down in the story, I saw where Kuchel's 1968 campaign is being handled by Spencer-Roberts—the same L.A. public relations firm that handled Reagan in 1966 and Rocky [Nelson Rockefeller] in the crucial 1964 primary. And it occurred to me that maybe Spencer-Roberts might make an interesting article, for you or somebody else. Think about that.

This is obviously a high-powered outfit; its operations influence national politics on the highest level—and the only time they get any press is a few weeks out of every election year. Who are they? What are they up to? And why? And what are the implications of a super-successful Public (political) Relations firm?

Anyway, it looks like a good seed. What do you think? I'm not offering it to you, just casting around for interest, bids, rejections, etc. I see it as a piece for about January 1968, so there's no hurry in getting on it. But if you like the idea, let me know and we can talk seriously about it. I haven't mentioned it to anyone else (editors), and I probably won't for ten days or so, because I'm scrambling desperately to finish a long-overdue *Harper's* piece. I sprained my wrist about two days ago and today I nearly tore my leg off trying to ski down a mountain on a motorcycle. Beyond that my wife has become an invalid and my lawyer flipped his wig on the coast and came out here to avoid being committed, causing me no end of trouble.

So I won't be ready for any new travel for a few weeks, at best. Send a line when you have time. Thanks. . . .

Hunter S. Thompson

TO PAUL KRASSNER, *THE REALIST:*

June 6, 1967
Woody Creek, Colorado

Dear Godspeed. . . .

Your note came today. Good. I've blown every deadline I've had for the past two months and it's good to find somebody with a schedule as fucked up as mine. The action here for the past two months has been unbelievable. All at once I got evicted, my wife went into a lingering two-month miscarriage and my lawyer came out from San Francisco and flipped out so badly that two sheriff's deputies took him one Saturday night 200 miles across mountains to the state loony bin. I'm still dealing with that; he was picked up with a pound of grass and then tore up the jail. This is the black-suit tax lawyer. Those people are going under. Beware—they're going to take us down with them. You too. I've heard their plans.

As for [Art] Kunkin, I sent him a dirty screed and fuck him if he doesn't publish it. Larry Lack[11] wrote and said they would; he also said the review was "gratuitous character assassination," which hardly matters. But I guess I don't understand that kind of journalism. Anyway, I got that out of my spleen so don't worry about it polluting anything I write for you. Or maybe not much . . . I still want to talk a bit about old beatniks. We'll see. As for acid, thanks but I'm suddenly OK. There's so much dope in the air that I'm beginning to wonder if maybe Owsley[12] hasn't struck a bargain with Pat Nugent.[13] People keep showing up at the house with all kinds of drugs. They bring light-boxes and guns. And motorcycle parts . . . all of it for sale. And now Ralph Ginzburg[14] is sending a Kerista[15] team out for my impression. And my lawyer is in the loony bin. I came out here to hide from all that. All these people are hippies, very hairy people, full of flower power . . . they want to sell me things like surplus army carbines and stolen machinery, along with the acid. Where have all the holy men gone? [Charles] Starkweather was right, and [Charles] Whitman too.

Anyway, for a good many reasons I can't explain, I've been writing a completely different piece for you (sort of an extra), but for the same kind of reasons I'm writing it under a phony name. Jefferson Rank. The local vigilantes would croak me if they knew. And the hippies might do worse. They're mov-

11. H. Lawrence Lack, publisher of the *Los Angeles Free Press.*
12. Stanley Owsley, the legendary LSD chemist.
13. A well-known dealer of psychedelics.
14. Ginzburg had been an editor at *Esquire* and *Eros* and was now an editor at *Fact* magazine.
15. Kerista was a loosely formed cult-like tribe at the time. It evolved into a well-known commune several years later.

ing in, huge tribes, bent on taking over the county. Death stalks the back roads: people are being torn apart and jammed in unmarked graves. It's a secret civil war. And Jefferson Rank is on the scene, absorbing the whole story—wild shrieks in the night, dog packs, flutes screaming in unison, ugly behavior. There may be a story in it. I'll get the other first, but keep this one in mind. It will scare the shit out of any hippie who plans on a trip back to the land. The siege of Woody Creek will go down in history as the Watershed of Dope. Take my word for it . . . or rather the word of . . . Jefferson Rank.

TO CHARLES KURALT:

> June 6, 1967
> Woody Creek, Colorado

Charley. . . .

[. . .]Thanks for the good letter and whatever you said on the radio. I'll tell Selma. One of the most frightening questions on the Random House publicity questionnaire was: "Who are your powerful and influential friends in the world of communications?" or something like that. I started to list Julian Hart's wife,[16] but on second thought I figured you might be more fitting. Sorry, again, that I missed you in New York. Do me a favor and tell Jim Jensen[17] that I only failed to get by for a screening of that motorcycle film because I was screwed up beyond reason or understanding. The story of that tour will appear, god willing, in the next issue of *The Realist* . . . and, again, god's mercy on us all.

I seem pretty god-oriented these days . . . maybe it's because Sandy has been bed-ridden for 6 weeks with a pending miscarriage and the total ignorance of the local medical cabal has forced me to fall back on the deity—whom I regard with all the pious faith of a death-row lifer confronting his favorite screw.

Anyway, thanks to Him, I am now fairly permanently sunk into this Woody Creek fortress that I call Owl Farm. We have a governess and other servant-types, but my checks are still bouncing. The difference now is that the bank pays them and sends me a polite notice to that effect. Everybody in Aspen thinks I'm rich and you'd be amazed how that kind of myth can change a man's life. I no longer deal in cash.

By all means stop by. Bring Walter [Cronkite] and I'll give him a colorful discourse (punctuated by volleys from my .44 Magnum) on how it is

---

16. Julian Hart was the press officer at the embassy in Rio. His wife helped the U.S. press corps get access to officials.
17. Jim Jensen, a CBS reporter, was working on a story about motorcycle gangs.

out here in the badlands of dead-end America. This Jew-Arab business has caused me to order more bullets and gunpowder. You understand, of course, that my invitation is void in case of nuclear attack. In the event, I have 2 bullet molds and 5000 marijuana seeds to carry me through. All visitors will be blown apart.

Your gig at the North Pole sounds like the sort of thing I need to break my image as a hippie-thug writer. All kinds of people want me to write things; today I got an offer from an encyclopedia . . . the *Record*, as it were. The trouble is right now that I can't leave because of Sandy's ever-present emergency. The other reason is that I'm running way behind on two articles that are already paid for—one for *Harper's* (on Aspen), and the other for *The Realist*. Beyond that, *The New York Times Magazine* calls about every four days with some new idea . . . and in my spare time I'm trying to fire not only my agent but my publisher. It's a very tricky business but I'm getting to like it. I think I missed my calling: I should have been an agent, or—worse yet—an editor. In lieu of all that I'm considering a high-powered campaign for a county commissioner's post—and after that the Senate. In the hideous power vacuum of these times, I might even be president. And if you want to contribute some funds at the outset, I'll give you every consideration for the appointment as my press secretary. $110 will do for a start, but once I get my power base as a county commissioner, we'll have to up the ante. Give it some thought.

In the meantime, I have a new motorcycle and a half-new Volvo wagon . . . and also a large house with plenty of room for visitors. In all seriousness, I have two half-furnished guest rooms and a fireplace in the basement, so if you can arrange to stop through Aspen on your western trek, you can count on lodging here. As a minor local deity in my own right, I have a certain influence on the prevailing winds. So in case of attack, give a ring: (303) 925-XXXX.

Bring Petie if you can. I have until recently refused to make any public statements about the *LA Times* cabal and all others of that ilk (those without faith, as it were), but now—since the *LA Times* is after me for articles—I no longer feel any need to make statements, crush detractors, even old scores, etc. The deed is done . . . and, as long as we're on that subject, thanks for the good words on the book. You're right: it *is* good . . . but I get a fine boot (about 10–1 ratio) out of compliments from somebody whose taste and judgment I respect. Thanks again, and let me know when your North Pole thing will be on. Hello to Petie (and Walter, of course), but if you have to make a choice between which one of them to bring with you for a visit, I think I prefer Petie. Tell Walter I'll see him in Gaza—at $100 an hour. OK for now, and send word. Ciao. . . .

Hunter

June 14, 1967
Woody Creek, Colorado

Dear Paul. . . .

Can I get any leeway on the July 1 delivery date in re: that article you've paid for? If not, I'll get it there by then . . . but I'd like to have another week or two so I can fully and properly arrange for the burial of some people connected with the *Free Press.* Some pigfucker from the Hashbury, aided and abetted by L. Lipton, has attacked me with about nine salvos of outright lies. I wrote [Art] Kunkin asking for equal space, and if he doesn't give it to me I told him I'd write a forced obituary for all the Old Beatniks into the article I'm brewing up for *The Realist.* If Kunkin has any sense of fairness at all he'll give me the space, but I still want to put some fang-marks on Lipton & his ilk. So let me know about the time-pressure and also if a mad rap at the Lipton syndrome would bother you personally or politically. If all else fails, I'm going out there to pull out his teeth with a pair of wire-cutters. That cartoon in your last issue ("Love Me, You Bastard") was a fine comment on these venomous old swine, but I think they need more. I've never claimed to be anybody's Flower Child, so I can go for their teeth without any worries about bogging down in hypocrisy. Some flower-power creep was out here a few days ago and told me what "beautiful ferns" I have growing behind my house. I should have told him to go ahead and eat as much as he wanted. The shit is hemlock . . . or Lipton, by any other name. Lipton's Tea, as it were.

I don't mind getting pissed on for not "loving" the Hell's Angels, but that stupid bag of pus who wrote the review actually accused me of giving away Kesey's address in Paraguay "at a time when that was fairly private knowledge." Yeah . . . it was so fucking private that the only people who knew about it were Lipton and that freak who wrote the review. Kesey was *never* in Paraguay . . . and for Lipton to print bullshit like that puts him down in the hole with *Time.* The whole review is the work of liars and fools, and I think they need something to fill the vacuum where their sense of humor might have been.

Well . . . shit, I see I'm already rapping off on the article. I'm not losing sight of what you originally asked for, but I've decided to update it a bit. In the meantime, you can send me some acid to help me level out. And I'll send you a dozen just-born marijuana weeds. You can plant them in Central Park. OK. . . .

Hunter S. Thompson

FROM DALE (FOURTEEN-YEAR-OLD BOY):

June 25, 1967

Dear Mr. Thompson,

I just got done reading your book on the Hell's Angels, and it's really great. That book is really *great*, I don't know what to say it's so great.

I'll tell you the Honest to God truth, I never read a book and finished it in full and this goes for school books, too. As for this book I didn't miss a word in it.

You know when I get my driver's license in two years I'm buying me a big Harley and going to Cal. Believe what I say.

If possible I would like some pictures of any of the Angels, especially Sonny Barger, I dig him. I will be more than glad to pay for them, I'll pay anything for some pictures of them. I would like to receive a letter for framing. The letter from you of course. Please write and I will be very thankful, really. Thank you.

P.S. Man I think you're really *great*.

Sincerely yours,
Dale
A follower of the Angels
They're *great*, too

TO SALES MANAGER, BSA MOTORCYCLES—WESTERN:

June 26, 1967
Woody Creek, Colorado

Sales Mgr.
BSA
Motorcycles—Western
2745 E. Huntington Dr.
Duarte, California 91010

Dear Sir. . . .

Please send me, by return mail, all information pertinent to establishing a BSA dealership. I'm in the process of putting together a bike agency here in Aspen and I'd like to have BSA, Greeves and at least one smaller Jap bike. The market here is booming beyond belief: when I lived here three years ago there wasn't a motorcycle in the county . . . now, in a permanent population of 2500, there are 218 *licensed* bikes and more than 100 unlicensed. And all those belong to residents; the summer population is not only wealthy, but tremendously bike-oriented.

At the moment there are only two dealers in town. One is Bultaco, a part-time operation; the other is Alpine Triumph, which also handles Montesa and Yamaha. Both of these operate in a lazy, left-handed way that would end in immediate bankruptcy if this weren't such a sellers' market. Both sales and services are so worthless here that many people drive 250 miles across the Continental Divide to Boulder, and buy their bikes there. I've had first-hand experience with the Bultaco dealer and it's nearly turned my hair white. At the moment I'm trying to buy a Greeves . . . and proof of the situation here is that I'm having it shipped out from New York. The only bike mechanic in town works for the Triumph dealer and spends most of his time racing in California. The Bultaco dealer doesn't even stock carburetor jets, but he managed to sell sixteen (16) new Bultacos in the past three months. I spent more than a month looking for a used 441 Victor anywhere within 200 miles of here, and finally gave up. Maybe there's a BSA dealer in Denver, but I never get over there. It's easier to drive 1200 flat miles to San Francisco than to cross the mountains of Denver.

The point is that Aspen is here in a strangely isolated situation . . . with a lot of people who could easily afford bikes if they had any access to them. The surrounding terrain is ideal for Victors; as a matter of fact there were nine Victors in town last summer, but the agonies of trucking over to Denver for even warranty repairs was too much. As a result, there isn't a single BSA on the street this summer — or in the hills, either. Bultaco and Montesa have the whole market, with a handful of Greeves and Triumphs on the periphery. The problem is that nobody can repair all the bikes that are sold here. The Bultaco dealer, for instance, has no mechanic at all.

I have a good friend who's been the chief mechanic at a BSA/Greeves shop in the Bay Area for the past five or so years. He wants to leave California and I've told him about the prospect of setting up a serious professional bike agency here. He'd like to come out and I have to let him know something pretty soon. So if you could give me all pertinent details by return mail, I can assess where I stand vis-à-vis a BSA dealership. I don't want to run the agency; I'd leave that to my friend, the mechanic. But it looks like such a good economic possibility that I can't pass it up — at least as an investment. I've written the Greeves and Kawasaki people, and I have four or five other letters to write. But the BSA seems like such a natural that I thought I'd sound you out on the first round. Let me know how it looks from your end.

Thanks,
Hunter S. Thompson

P.S.—I gave BSA some nice plugs in my recent book on the "Hell's Angels." You should probably send me a Victor on the basis of that. At the moment I'm riding a Bultaco. Let me know if you're in the mood for a trade. I'll even pay the freight charges. You can have my Matador and four elk feet, in exchange for a 441. You can't beat that. HST

TO LARRY O'BRIEN, POSTMASTER GENERAL:

Having served as President Johnson's campaign director in 1964, political strategist O'Brien had been named postmaster general early in 1965.

June 26, 1967
Woody Creek, Colorado

Larry O'Brien
Postmaster General
Washington, D.C.

Dear Larry. . . .

You can imagine my shock and despair when I picked up the *Denver Post* last week and read that some mossback senator's son had been appointed governor of American Samoa. I thought we understood each other on that score . . . it never occurred to me that you'd knuckle under to political expediency. How can I explain this to my aged mother? She was ready to move to Samoa and live out her days in peace.

I hate to say this, but I suspect that rotten inner-tube ain't strong enough to keep both you and Hubert afloat. A few years ago you seemed like a man with his balls intact and with maybe even a small sense of humor. But I guess it was just a reflection.

And just for the record—in case you've really gone thick—the above paragraph has nothing to do with the governorship of American Samoa. The implications of your whole act are too depressing for any discussion here. Maybe, with a bit of luck, I'll bump Dominick[18] out of the Senate next year and then we can talk seriously about these things. In the meantime, I'll keep my eyes open, along Interstate 70, for the "Larry O'Brien Memorial Drinking Fountain."

Sincerely,
Hunter S. Thompson
Spiritual Governor of
American Samoa

18. Peter Dominick was a Republican senator from Colorado.

TO H. LAWRENCE LACK, *LOS ANGELES FREE PRESS:*

June 28, 1967
Woody Creek, Colorado

Dear H. Lawrence Lack. . . .

Thanks for the note and the straight comment on Anderson's review of my book: "*Hell's Angels: The Strange and Terrible Saga of the Outlaw Motorcycle Gang,* by Hunter S. Thompson. Random House, 278 pp. (no pix) $4.95 plus tax outrage."

That's the way the *Free Press* presented it in the issue of June 2–9. It wasn't part of the review; what I've just quoted is that little box telling what book is being reviewed. I've run across a lot of pigfuckers in my time, but I never expected to encounter anybody so thick that he'd blame a writer for the tax imposed on a book. And, for that matter, I never expected to find an editor who'd publish that kind of cheap, amateurish sniping. It's a mockery of every decent idea and instinct that might exist in journalism. Larry Lipton is listed as "editor" of that "Living Arts" section, so I'm not particularly surprised at the sloppy, vicious, ignorant style of the review. But I *am* surprised that people like you and Kunkin would let it be published in the *Free Press.* I've been reading the paper for about three years and I've always considered it basically fair and straight. But after reading that review of my book I'll never be able to take anything I read in the *Free Press* at face value . . . because if you let one vicious punk fill a page with lies and stupid rambling, how can I or any other reader be sure that the rest of the articles are as straight as they claim to be?

That review was more rotten than anything ever conceived of by *Time* magazine. The whole concept of an "underground press" is based on a sense of trust between the papers and the people who support them . . . and you betray that trust by publishing outright lies. The "underground press" has only one basic advantage over the "establishment press" . . . that's the freedom to publish whatever the editors consider true and important, and fuck the consequences.

The basic function of the underground is to croak the establishment's bullshit. But when the "underground" starts publishing slanted venom so obvious that it would embarrass a cub reporter in Omaha . . . what then? Probably I could give you a long-winded answer, but I don't feel up to it right now and, beyond that, the question pretty well answers itself.

I said, at one point, that I'd written you an article on the poison problem that comes with mixing old beatniks with young hippies. This would focus on Lipton and his creature Chester Anderson, that witless jackal who signed the book review. Maybe I'll write that one a little later. Right now it doesn't seem important enough to spend a lot of time on . . . especially since I have no assurance that Lipton won't be given a chance to "edit" it. (I don't really think you'd do that, but then I didn't think you'd publish a bundle of vicious garbage in the guise of a book review either, so I'll wait and see what you do with this thing I'm writing now before I send anything else.)

In the meantime—since I've accused you of publishing "lies and bull-shit"—I'll try and be more specific. I appreciate your admission that the review was "gratuitous character assassination," which it was. But that aspect of it never occurred to me until I got your letter. The possibility that Chester Anderson might not like me doesn't really stand my hair out on end. But now that I look back over the review I see where he says it's "a lucky thing for him (Thompson, the tax man) that he didn't try and write a book about hippies." The obvious implication is that my head would have been brutally twisted if I'd ever had the gall to sneak into Anderson's fief in the Haight-Ashbury, for the purpose of gathering gossip.

Jesus! I can see those words right here on the desk in front of me, but I can't quite believe them. Some weird, mentally-stunted creep named Chester is warning me to keep away from the "hippies" and, in effect, to stay out of the neighborhood where I lived for two years until people like him made a commercial sideshow out of it. As a matter of fact I spent two weeks on Haight-Ashbury Street just recently, in mid-April—writing an article on the hippies for *The New York Times Magazine*—and if I'd known Chester was gunning for me I'd have stopped by to say hello. As it was, I didn't think he was important enough to include in any article on "hippies," so I didn't bother checking with him. Next time I won't be so negligent.

Anyway . . . back to the "lies and bullshit." Anderson's review was typical of most screeds turned out by cheap hacks, in that he used a lot of words and bilious raving to say almost nothing specific. It's hard to deal with bullshit like that except on its own level, which is down around zip guns and switch-blades.

He accuses me, for instance, of betraying Ken Kesey's secret hideout in South America after Kesey had jumped bail and disappeared. Here's how Anderson tells it: "(Thompson) gave away (page 233) Ken Kesey's Paraguay address at a time when that was fairly private knowledge."

Yeah, I did it. I blew Kesey's cover because I thought he belonged in jail. He was a degenerate, pure and simple, and I wanted him locked up. That's the reason I wrote what I did: this is the way it appears on page 233 of my book: "On January 31, 1966, Kesey jumped bail and disappeared. A suicide note was found in his abandoned bus on the Northern California coast, but not even the police believed he was dead. Results of my own investigation are very hazy, although I managed—after many months of digging—to locate his forwarding address: c/o Agricultural Attaché—U.S. Embassy—Asunción, Paraguay."

How about that, Chester? *You* fucking waterhead. How dense does a person have to be to actually believe that Kesey jumped bail on a felony charge in the U.S. and sought out asylum at the American Embassy in Paraguay?

Chester believes it. And if he ever gets busted and decides to jump bail he'll make tracks for Paraguay and apply for a fugitive/marijuana scholarship. It's common knowledge that they're available at any embassy; all you need to qualify is a negative IQ.

I wish Chester had cited more examples like that. I could have a lot of mean fun with them. But that's the only one he wanted to mention—the terrible betrayal of poor Kesey in Paraguay.

And so much for all that bad noise—except maybe to note that at the time I wrote that joke about Paraguay it was common knowledge, not only among local heads but even to *San Francisco Chronicle* reporters, that Kesey was in Mexico. Everybody knew—except Chester, and he didn't even catch on when Kesey came back and held a press conference to tell where he'd been. Huge articles appeared in the *Chronicle* about "Kesey's adventures in Mexico." Even the *New York World-Journal-Tribune* published a story. But Chester still thinks Kesey went to Paraguay and holed up at the U.S. Embassy . . . or at least he still thought so when he wrote his book review, which was nearly a year after Kesey returned.

The only other specific charge Anderson makes in his review goes like this: "(Thompson) spied on the Angels. He violated their privacy for money. He wormed his way into their company, even their friendship & confidence, & learned more facts about them than they knew themselves—solely in order to sell them out, sell all his gooey information to the highest bidder."

Well, that's such evil bullshit that it's not even worth arguing with. It's just as ignorant as the Paraguay thing. The whole history of my gig with the Angels appears in considerable detail, in the book itself. They knew from the very beginning that I was writing a book on them, and they liked the idea. They spent hours in my apartment reading the slowly-building manuscript aloud to each other. They went out of their way to explain things to my always-visible tape recorder . . . and to pose for photos that weren't used because their inclusion would have made the book too expensive. A higher price would have also increased the tax, and everybody at Random House knew this would bug Chester Anderson. His opinion of the book was probably our chief concern; it was important that he not only like it, but LOVE it.

That's about all I feel like saying right now. All further inquiries will be referred, by me, to either Sonny Barger, president of the Hell's Angels Oakland chapter, or to Chester Anderson at his summer home in Paraguay.

As a sort of closing note, let me remind you again that—although I appreciate your accurate comments on the review—I have to keep in mind that the *Free Press* gave a fat block of space to a venomous, lying hatchet-job on a book that deserved at least a truthful appraisal. If it had been no more than a "gratuitous character assassination" I wouldn't have bothered to write this kind of reply. But the fact that the *Free Press* published a bag of vicious lies carries ugly implications. And there's also the dirty little fact that Chester Anderson considers himself a "spokesman" for the hippie community. Those poor bastards deserve something better than a mouth-piece like Anderson, and for that matter they deserve better than lies in a newspaper they support.

If I were an editor of an "underground paper" I'd think a long time before I published a bag of lies, by accident or any other reason. Because when you do that you're giving up the only real weapon you have. A stupid lie, regardless of who writes it or tries to justify it, is still a stupid lie . . . even when it's wrapped up in flowers.

Sincerely,
Hunter S. Thompson

TO DALE:

Thompson responded promptly to the fourteen-year-old who'd written to say how great Hell's Angels *was.*

July 6, 1967
Woody Creek, Colorado

Dear Dale. . . .

Thanks for your good letter. I got it this morning. And thought I should send a line before you get too caught up in the Hell's Angels gig. I appreciate the good things you said about the book, but I never in hell intended it to be a propaganda job for the Angels or any other cult. You could do a lot better than getting lost in that kind of action. Not necessarily because it's *bad,* or ugly, or any other word like that . . . but because you sound bright enough to make something happen on your own, instead of looking around for something to join. You say it'll be two years before you get your driver's license, so I guess that makes you about 14.

When I was 14 I was a wild, half-wit punk who caused a lot of trouble and wanted to tear the world in half if for no other reason than it didn't seem to fit me too well. Now, looking back on it, I don't think I'd change much of what I did in those days . . . but I've also learned at least one crucially important thing since then. And that's the idea of making your own pattern, not falling into grooves that other people made. Remember that if you can do *one thing* better than anybody it'll make life a hell of a lot easier for you in this world—which is a pretty mean world, when you get to know it, and a lot of people in it can ride big Harleys . . . especially in California. The best of the Angels—the guys you might want to sit down and talk to—have almost all played that game for a while and then quit for something better. The ones who are left are almost all the kind who can't do anything else, and they're not much fun to talk to. They're not smart, or funny, or brave, or even original. They're just Old Punks, and that's a lot worse than being a Young Punk. They're not even happy; most of them hate the lives they lead, but they can't afford to admit it because they don't know where else to go, or what else to do. That's what makes them mean . . . and it also makes them useless, because there's already a big oversupply of mean bastards in this world. And I don't see any sense in you wanting to go out to California and get in on a game that's a dead end. If you're bright enough to write me a good letter at your age, you're also bright enough to avoid putting yourself down the tube.

I'm sure you didn't expect this kind of letter and I don't mean to sound like some kind of water-headed "guidance counselor," or anybody else like the kind of people I've had trouble with all my life. That includes teachers in school, sergeants in the Air Force, and cops on the highways. But people like that can screw you up pretty badly if you argue with them on their own turf, and that's the mistake most Angels have made. They're not bright enough to create their own scene . . . which is pretty easy once you know what you're doing.

Like right now I'm a *writer*, not a motorcycle freak, so I can do a lot of things I couldn't get away with if all I knew how to do was ride bikes. As a matter of fact I just bought a new bike shop with the money from the book. My rent gets paid with no hassle and I have a lot of time to hunt, get drunk, and raise as much hell as I want to. But I couldn't do any of this if all I did was boom around on a bike and get in arguments with cops. It's amazing how much you can get away with if you don't go out of your way to cause trouble . . . which the Angels do, for their own reasons, but their reasons don't make much sense for anybody who isn't stuck with them. And you aren't.

So remember this letter when you think about going out to California to ride with the Angels. And even that might be a kick if you can do it without getting caught in it. But the secret of not getting caught in it is to have something of your own . . . some kind of skill or talent or action that other people have to respect. That way, you can ride when you want, and back off when you want. Believe me, it's a hell of a lot better way to go. It's the difference between being your own man, and a sheep in the herd. Maybe you don't consider that real important now, but I can say from experience that it is.

OK for all that noise. I just don't want you blaming *me*, 10 years from now, for giving you a bad lead. All I'm really saying is, right, be an outlaw . . . but do it your own way, for your own reasons, and for christ's sake don't blow it as badly as the Angels have. Sincerely,

Hunter S. Thompson

TO RALPH GINZBURG, *FACT:*

After reading Hell's Angels, *Ginzburg thought Thompson should write a story about the explosion of religious fringe groups in America.*

July 7, 1967
Woody Creek, Colorado

Ralph. . . .

What the fuck are you trying to do to me? Yesterday I got a letter from some fuck-freak who told me he was screwing about five different people with a new typewriter and pretty soon they'd be out here to visit with me. One of them, in fact, was already en route.

I'm deadly serious when I say I have all the goddamn problems I need out here. The town is overrun with refugees from the Haight-Ashbury: they're all heads, they're all weird looking, and they all claim connection with me. The sheriff has already taken one of my friends to the state loony bin (after booking him for possession), and right now I'm probably the hottest man on the western slope. I came out here to get away from all that shit and the last thing I want on my hands right now is a religious nut with a portable harem.[19] If part of this religion is bugging people who want no part of it, I'm the last person in the world he should come to for publicity. I hate preachers. All of them. Anyway, the only way I'll touch that article is on my own terms — and they don't include bread and board for a sex freak. If I see the bastard at all it'll be on his turf, not mine. I'm capable of writing some pretty rude shit, but I can't think of anything that would bug me more than some breast-beater rolling in here to foul my air with a lot of noise about his sex action. He should talk to a priest; that's what they're for.

OK for now. I'll finish off the things I have going and see what happens on the Kerista thing. One of the big "ifs" is whether I get some kind of assignment on the coast . . . something I could do in conjunction with

19. Pope Dau, a charismatic cult leader, wanted Thompson to write about his messianic powers.

Kerista. I'll let you know. But meanwhile, advise those people that I'm serious about not offering any hospitality here. Beware. . . .

Hunter

TO WILLIAM J. KENNEDY:

July 12, 1967
Woody Creek, Colorado

William—

I have just captured a young skunk . . . and have paid the price. It's 12:45 a.m. here and the smell is ungodly. Everything—me, the dog, the car, the house—a hideous odor. The thing looked so small that I figured he wouldn't have much of a blast. But he did. I now have him locked outside in the horse trailer. Tomorrow, the scalpel . . . and then the whip. I shall prevail. This skunk will write the Great American Novel.

Along those lines, yes, I'm writing a few letters tonight. Severing all connections. Agents, editors, publishers—all the scum. Even the innocent. I just wrote *Harper's*, saying I couldn't write the article they bought because I don't want my agent to get 10%. And I wrote Random House, demanding all my money, at once. There will be no Rum Diary as long as that contract exists. Nor will there be any "non-fiction project." I feel experimental these days. Something new is wanted. A new novel, perhaps. Something the ten-percenters don't have their hooks into yet. Those soul-fuckers should all be killed.

Anyway . . . what are you up to? The last time I talked to you it was off the job and into the marketplace. Beware. You mentioned a loan, and right now I have 197 dollars to my name. My only concern is getting my royalties from RH. They won't even send me a statement. So far, I've made $1500 off the book. If and when I get some royalty money I'll send you some. Beware of agents. Get a good lawyer instead. That's what I'm looking for now. Send word on your movements. And hello to Dana.

Hunter S. Thompson

TO DON ERIKSON, *ESQUIRE:*

July 13, 1967
Woody Creek, Colorado

Don. . . .

Here are two more ideas you might ponder: 1) a profile on Joan Baez, and 2) a curious look at the Joint Chiefs of Staff.

1) I know Joanie in a weird sort of way that might or might not make for a good piece. We lived next door to each other in Big Sur in 1960, before she crashed through, and we had a bit of a hassle then about violence and non-violence. I've seen her off and on since then, but not in a personal way, as it were, until we were both on the same CBC show in Toronto last March (a few weeks after I saw you in New York). We had a sort of reconciliation, and I got a new sense of the real roots of non-violence (put that in quotes). Anyway, she interests me considerably, both as a person and as a totem figure in a cult that can't afford to understand itself. Joanie, for instance, has some fairly violent instincts. But that's a fuzzy thing to say. It would take me a while to distill that contradiction down to an article. I think she'd talk to me, but I might be wrong. She's home in Carmel now and I could zap over there pretty soon, if the idea interests you. Let me know if it does—and also how much you could pay. I don't want to call her until I have something definite. Thanks.

2) See enclosed *San Francisco Chronicle* clip. This is something I've been thinking about for several months. Who in the hell *are* these people? This "small group" around Lyndon? Every time I read something about the "Joint Chiefs of Staff" I wonder if they really exist, as human beings, or whether they might be werewolves or maybe a clique of White Russians. They're hardly ever mentioned by name or context, but apparently they're the people who call the national shots these days. I'm personally curious about who and why they are. A recent bill fixed their terms at four years, rather than having them at the mercy of the executive temper . . . so they're going to become a hell of a lot more powerful than they were.

It might be interesting to take a long look at them—collectively and individually. It has the shape of an *Esquire*-type piece: a gallery of full-page photos, along with a vaguely menacing title and a lot of earthy background material on each man . . . plus a bag of commentary on their influence. I think it would raise a nice bit of hell in that Boston-to-Washington strip city you call home.

Let me know about both of these things. Frankly, I'd rather do the thing on Joanie right now, because the other would require a hell of a lot of time and effort that might not be worth my while. And it would obviously cost you more. But they're both good seeds, either for *Esquire* or somebody else.

My own situation is pretty rabid right now. I'm engaged on all fronts and barely holding my own. It's the same old story: contracts, shysters, liars, thieves, etc. The net result, unfortunately, is that I'm somehow prevented, legally and financially, from writing another book. It's a weird situation—the dirty underbelly of the writing industry. The foul crotch of literature. How's that for a title? Or this: "Royalties or Dingleberries?" Hot damn! But that's what Krassner wants, and since he's already paid for it, I think it's his.

OK for now. And if Scott Meredith or any of his henchmen ever mention my name to you again, tell them you've never heard of me. I was arrested last week in San Diego, for unspeakable crimes. Selah.

Hunter S. Thompson

**check the current (Aug) *Pageant* (yeah, *Pageant*) for my article on hair-fairies. I daresay it will make some weird reading in all our dentists' offices. The dry-rot runs deeper than we know.

TO RALPH GINZBURG, *FACT:*

KERISTA   Pope DAU the Pied Piper   Philosopher at Large   Avant
Garde Therapy, Nirvana Sessions for Donations   Revivals at Tompkins
Square Park   982-xxxx   7th Street & Avenue B   or 4-xxxx

July 25, 1967
Woody Creek, Colorado

Dear Ralph. . . .

Pope Dau of Kerista finally got the message and sent a crotch-thumping apology for menacing my peace of mind in Woody Creek. Thanks for getting through to him . . . but even so, I think I'll back off that article. Pope Dau strikes me as a bad combination of Billy Graham and an oregano dealer.[. . .] His first letter turned me off completely and his second convinced me that he should be croaked for the greater good.

Anyway, I suspect there might be some decent people hung up in Kerista and I'd just as soon spare them the kind of mean bias I'd bring to any article concerning Pope Dau. If you'd put me on to one or two of the love goddesses I might have stayed interested . . . but the last thing I need right now is a lot of bullshit from a phony priest. It couldn't work at all, and you probably wouldn't want the article.

So let's scratch it. If you get any more ripe ideas, let me know. I'm usually game for almost anything weird, but Pope Dau struck me as a depressingly familiar sort of con man. You can tell him whatever you want about my reason for copping out on the article: tell him I'm a secret fag and his charisma was so fucking powerful, even on paper, that I knew I'd go all to pieces if I ever encountered him in person. I'm sure he'd buy that.

OK for now. Let me know if you want a piece on The Love Slaves of Kiwanis, or something like that. Gross libel and madness. I'm getting bored with straight writing. Ciao. . . .

Hunter

TO ART KUNKIN, *LOS ANGELES FREE PRESS:*

August 14, 1967
Woody Creek, Colorado

Dear Kunkin. . . .

I was standing in a bar in New York about three days ago when one of my lawyers who was supposed to be in San Francisco rushed out of the beery darkness and announced that I was being sued (along with *Cavalier*) for $5.5 million and also that I was suing the *Free Press*. And the reason I was standing in the bar in the first place was to talk with my New York lawyer who's defending a lawsuit against my lawyer. I have many lawyers; one just went to the loony bin.

Anyway . . . well, no, I probably shouldn't put anything like that in print because I no longer trust you people. I don't think you're dishonest; just incompetent. Your man H. Lawrence Lack wrote me to ask for my reply to that piece of vicious libelous bullshit that you published about my book . . . so I sent it to him . . . and you didn't print it. In other words, you took advantage of your position as a publisher to libel me in terms you couldn't possibly defend in court . . . and then, while eulogizing yourself as a hard-pressed, honorable champion of the "free press," you won't even acknowledge receipt of my reply to the abovementioned libel — much less print it.

That's all I asked, and I can't see how it's anything but fair. So what the fuck am I supposed to think when you ignore my efforts to at least correct the obvious, indefensible lies that you printed about me? What kind of "free press" are you running?

But that's your problem for now, and next time you read about it . . . it won't be in a letter. Beyond that, I'm going to let my mad-dog torts lawyer push his case for whatever he thinks he can get. I don't have much stomach for the suit, but I don't have much stomach for being stabbed in the back, either . . . and, given a choice like that, I'll spend everything I have to on a mad-dog lawsuit if you want it that way.

Frankly, I can't understand what the fuck you're thinking about, but, again, that's your problem. I just wanted you to know that I haven't forgotten that thing . . . and now that I know I'm suing you, I'm not going to forget that either. If you want to talk about printing that piece I sent, I'm open . . . if not, well, I guess I've said all that, so to hell with it.

Sincerely,
Hunter S. Thompson

TO *ASPEN DAILY NEWS:*

A public debate erupted in Aspen because Secretary of Defense Robert McNamara had decided to purchase a home in the valley. Thompson was infuriated that the local newspapers were asking citizens to embrace the U.S. overseer of the Vietnam War when he arrived because it would be "good for the tourist business." Thompson took part in a vigilante march to try and burn McNamara's house down.

August 15, 1967
Woody Creek, Colorado

Dear Sir. . . .

Please pass this message along to the good people of Aspen. It is, after all, for their own good.

My friend, Martin Bormann, will be visiting here next week, and I think we all agree that he needs a rest. His wife, moreover, is recovering from a recent hoof operation and his doctor insists on total calm. She wants a separate peace.

So I urge the population to keep their own best interests in mind and refrain from bothering the Bormanns during their short vacation here. Demonstrations and howling will not be tolerated; we have ways of dealing with such things.

Fortunately, at least half the local press has already gripped this question in a responsible manner. Indeed (and here I quote from the *News* of 8/10), "Aspen's total dependence on tourism dictates that we play host to people seeking rest and relaxation. In our own self-interest we should make sure that they leave here rested and refreshed. If we don't supply the privacy and relaxation they seek, people will soon go to some other place that will."

This is true. It was only my considerable influence that prevented Herr Bormann from taking his rest at Vail. The same editorial in the August 10 *News* explained my thinking with an eloquence that I could never hope to achieve. To wit: "Our top public officials are already burdened with tremendous responsibilities, endless criticism and pressures from dissenting groups and the tensions of mountainous work loads. Too much criticism voiced against these officials is irresponsible, negative and hate-inspired. Many capable people retire from public office, discouraged by the endless barrage of criticism, misunderstandings and lack of public appreciation of their efforts. They must be able, periodically, to renew their energy, enthusiasm and perspective if they are to continue functioning efficiently."

Well said! And shades of Dink Stover.[20] Thank god not all the press has gone to pot. In any case, my purpose in writing this message is not to debate Herr Bormann's policy or behavior. He's only doing his duty, implementing directives from his superiors. Surely this is understandable.

We must also keep in mind that Herr Bormann is both tougher and smarter than the rest of us. He never backs down. In our conversations by wireless, he assured me that any half-mad *schwein* who disagrees with him will be given a fair hearing at the proper time, *mano a manos*. (Note: the first *mano* is singular, the second is plural—delete this note from the published version.)

In closing, perhaps I should add that Martin has agreed to keep off the public playgrounds and out of the meat markets. Certainly we can ask no more—except perhaps that he takes all his meals at Guido's Restaurant. For his own peace of mind.

So let us rally now, around our long tradition as a hospitable community. Martin Bormann wants to get away from it all, if only briefly. We can make him feel welcome in Aspen. Our hippies can give him flowers, our liberals can take him to lunch, and our conservative gentry can seek his advice on the international gold and currency exchange. Despite various foul rumors, Martin doesn't care what Aspen can do for him, but only what he can do for Aspen.

Let's take advantage of his visit. He won't be with us for long, and, as the responsible press has noted, let us not forget that "Aspen lives entirely on tourist satisfaction and approval." We have a responsibility to ourselves, our heritage and our children, to make Martin Bormann feel at home here.

Sincerely,
Hunter S. Thompson

---

20. Dink Stover was the hero in a series of upbeat stories for teenagers.

TO HERB CAEN, *SAN FRANCISCO CHRONICLE:*

Caen was the Chronicle's *most popular local columnist.*

August 28, 1967
Woody Creek, Colorado

Dear Mr. Caen. . . .

Perhaps you can put me in touch with a maker of bumper stickers. I want a thousand copies of one saying: HUBERT HUMPHREY IS MARTIN BORMANN IN DRAG. Actually, I'll pay for 50,000 of these, if we can find a reputable distributor. I have just placed that phrase as a classified ad in the *Aspen Times* for the next four weeks. My "Bormann Letter" (see enclosed) ran in both the (liberal) *Times* and the (nazi) *Illustrated News* last week . . . and the *News* actually ran it on the editorial page, although it's a patent mockery of their editorial, one week earlier, which said [Secretary of Defense Robert] McNamara shouldn't have been harassed here by the likes of Bishop Pike and his hippie followers—which he was—because Aspen should be nice to its tourists. The *News,* owned and published by Harold Pabst of the brewing Pabsts, claimed that old Bob should have been left in peace, if only to lick his wounds. (McNamara is buying a house here; maybe he knows something about fallout drift.) But his recent visit was not peaceful; Pike led a march of the local heads on his house, and the *News* was incensed.

Thus, my letter—which puts the words of Pabst's editorial in a somewhat different context. The only trouble was that only a handful of people in the town knew who Martin Bormann was. They thought he was just another one of my flipped-out lawyer friends from San Francisco—like the one who came out earlier this summer and terrified half the town by smoking grass in public for three weeks before they finally busted him for chasing a girl with a chain . . . when the sheriff arrived, he (the San Francisco lawyer) was smoking his inevitable pipe and when the sheriff asked, "Do you have any more of that?" he replied with fine dignity: "Not with me, but if you want to run over to the Alps, there's a plastic bag on the bar." And there was. The sheriff picked it up . . . but the lawyer was never charged with possession because his prior behavior had been so weird that he was adjudged "temporarily insane." You might pass this on, for whatever it's worth. Although maybe the insanity statutes are different in California.

In any case, I can tell you this because I'm leaving the country in about ten days . . . for a variety of reasons: foremost among them being Lyndon's bloodlust and a $5,500,000 lawsuit filed against me and *Cavalier* magazine by the greedy lunatic Chester Womack, who runs the Rustic Inn in Glen Ellen. I remember that right after I wrote the article he kept saying,

"When's it coming out, Hunter? When can I read it?" And when *Cavalier* finally ran the goddamn thing, Chester sued for $5.5 million. Never trust a bartender.

Anyway, I'm getting over the border and leaving all you poor sheep to your respective and ill-deserved fates. Whatever that means. But I've retained a high-powered New York lawyer to watch over my various lawsuits. The Rustic Inn action is of course the main jewel in my tiara—but the other one I mean to pursue is a libel action against the *Los Angeles Free Press,* based on a vicious and fraudulent review of my Hell's Angels book. I was accused, among other things, of betraying Ken Kesey's address in Paraguay, after he jumped bail and left the country. The address I gave in a footnote was c/o Agricultural Attaché, U.S. Embassy, Asunción, Paraguay. Down there with Martin Bormann. But this freak who wrote the *Free Press* review took it seriously, and claimed that I blew poor Kesey's cover. Which I guess I did, except that everybody including *Chronicle* reporters knew Kesey was never within 5,000 miles of . . . well, what the hell? The point of all this is to say that Henry Luce has no monopoly on malicious bullshit and careless editing. Time Inc. has always had a good appetite for rebels, and the word right now is that this current crop from the Underground Press is the best in a long while. Anyway, I'm suing the *Free Press* for 400 motorcycle tires, to be given at *FP* distribution points on the Sunset Strip. I plan to distribute them myself, in drag.

Anyway, it's been a fairly active summer here in the Rockies. The town has been swamped by refugees from the Haight-Ashbury, and this caused a general freak-out among local merchants who fear for the tourist trade. "Hippies ain't good for business," they say, and maybe they're right. But Martin Bormann is presumably OK. Tonight, taking off on my letter, an ex-KJAZ staffer named Les Hansen ran a half-hour interview on the local radio station (KSNO) with a middle-aged German just recently arrived from Argentina and dismayed with the "flabby attitude" of local youth. Christ, I guess I'm getting old. I was just interviewed on that station about six months ago.

And all I meant to do, when I started this letter, was to send a short note, to explain my "Martin Bormann letter" and ask about possible printers for the Humphrey/Bormann bumper sticker . . . yeah, maybe that's the way it should read: Just—HUMPHREY/BORMANN IN 1969. Why not?

Why not, indeed? And be sure to check with me if you ever have to run the border in haste. I can, of course, be reached c/o Random House. And if you have any religious preferences, write me c/o Cardinal Spellman . . . he's just across the courtyard. [. . .] That should do it.

Sincerely,
Hunter S. Thompson

TO JOHN GRABREE, *PLAYBOY:*

Grabree was the feature editor at Playboy. *After reading* Hell's Angels, *he wanted to commission stories from Thompson.*

> September 4, 1967
> Woody Creek, Colorado

Dear John. . . .

I'm off to the coast in about two days and, now, in the midst of all this chaotic action prior to takeoff, I've just had a decent idea. This had nothing to do with your "Werewolves, Vampires and Ghouls" action, which I can't even evaluate until I get the fruits of your research. I have, however, discovered a book titled *Man into Wolf,* which purports to be a case study (or two separate studies) of men who actually turned into "wolves." The only copy now extant (unless you have one) is in Ketchum, Idaho . . . although it will shortly be in Woody Creek. Anyway, I'll be working sort of loosely on that until I get your research package; then I'll see what we have.

This other idea has to do with about two hours of a taped interview that I've been sitting on for 3 or 4 months. I got the stuff in the course of my research for that *New York Times Magazine* article on the Haight-Ashbury, but after listening to what I had on tape, I decided to keep it for a separate article. It's a very long talk with Ed Denson, manager of Country Joe and the Fish. We started off talking about hippies, but the focus got pretty fuzzy and we drifted into everything from the Beat Generation to Dope to Goldwater and the difference between East and West Coast rock music, Flower Power, civil rights, the FSM . . . the whole thing. So what occurs to me now is a chance of turning this interview with Denson into the nexus of a piece titled something like, "A profile of a rock band that *made it.*" That's not a title, just a working idea. Denson is an immensely articulate guy; he can explain, in 3 or 4 dimensions, why the rock bands and the hippies suddenly emerged as a cultural force in 1966, instead of, say, 1961. He understands the *context,* as it were, of his own action. And as far as I'm concerned, it's a goddamn interesting subject.

Anyway, I just got a letter from Denson (in reply to one of mine, regarding the tapes), saying he'll be in San Francisco when I get over there around September 20. I mentioned the tapes as a vague article possibility—perhaps for *The Nation,* since I've owed them a piece for over a year—but tonight, with greed creeping in, I decided to look for a framework worth more than $100. And naturally, you came to mind.

The idea, in a nut, is a detailed background piece on a big-name rock band. There was a time when I could have done one, from the very beginning, on the Jefferson Airplane, but my friend who began as their manager got sacked when his wife—the lead singer on their first album—was replaced with Grace Slick, who was part of a worthless group called the Great Society in that year when all the West Coast rock bands were premiering at The Matrix, a cheap club in San Francisco's Marina district. I recall the Airplane's debut at The Matrix, and afterwards calling Ralph Gleason to give him the word.

Maybe we could weave the Airplane's rise to fame into the cerebral stuff I have on tape. Denson and Country Joe (McDonald) are flaming intellectuals, compared to Marty Balin, who heads the Airplane, and Jerry Garcia of the Grateful Dead. But the contrast is interesting and I see a good article in a detailed look at the past, present & future of the acid rock bands. Like, "What made it happen?" and "What now?" And "Why?"

But this is all talk off the top of my head. If the idea sparks in your area, let me know quick. I'll be in Lake Tahoe, California from September 8 to 17 (you can reach me c/o Judge Laurence Hyde at the Univ. of Nevada . . . (702) 784-xxxx. Ask for Señor Thompson of *The New York Times*; that's my employer for the week.[21] After the 17th, and until the 22nd, you can reach me via Peter Collier at *Ramparts*, in San Francisco. I'll probably be talking to Denson during that week, so if you like the idea for the piece, I'd just as soon talk about it while I'm loose in San Francisco, and sitting on top of the subject, as I would on some grey afternoon here in Woody Creek. So do whatever's right. . . .

Ciao,
Hunter

TO WARREN HINCKLE, *RAMPARTS:*

Thompson had met Hinckle, executive editor and associate publisher of Ramparts, *in early 1967. They became fast friends, and Hinckle, who went on to found* Scanlan's Monthly *in 1969, would play a pivotal role in the development of Thompson's gonzo journalism.*

October 2, 1967
Woody Creek, Colorado

Dear Warren. . . .

A good visit but totally disruptive. That fucking monkey[22] should be killed—or at least arrested—on general principles. Anyway, I came by Monday—or maybe Tuesday—and found you in some kind of drunken

---

21. Thompson was writing a Nevada-based story for *The New York Times.*
22. Hinckle had a spider monkey in his office, which Thompson despised.

limbo, Stermer in Kansas, and Collier gone off with a priest. I finally got to Berkeley on Tuesday, after pointing off in that direction on Friday night.

Big Sur was a terrifying experience. I think we have a good article idea in something like "The New Quackery: Or, The Transmogrification of Big Sur." Probably I'll run that down in the first handful of columns. So far, I've run up a list of 30 or 40 instant-necessary subjects. Collier agreed to pay me $1500 a month for the column; I think that's about right—fair and equitable, etc.

We did, by the way, manage to get together with Pierce, the mayor of Richmond.[23] He tried to cop out, fearing a treacherous belly-shot from *Ramparts*, but it worked out pretty well. There's a hell of a wretched, fucking story there, but you have to keep in mind that Pierce is worried—and not without reason—about what you might do with whatever he tells you. Collier will have to catch him about three in the morning with a head full of gin to hear the real gospel. That's when he forgets who he's supposed to be protecting.

As for me, I'm trying to wrap up the *New York Times* (Tahoe judges' conference) piece and that other thing for Krassner before zapping off to deal with the Texas Rangers. I'll get it to you on or about November 15 . . . but keep in mind that I have a funny sense of time. Anyway, I'm focused on the TexRanger thing, so make some kind of room for it.

I have a head full of other possibilities, but right now I don't have any time to work on them. That *National Observer* thing—which you asked about very quickly—makes me a little bit uncomfortable. They treated me pretty decently, for a freak, and I'd rather not comment on them—at least until they publish something that seizes me . . . but when that happens, it's every man for himself. (Our final split, for instance, came when they refused to publish my favorable review of Tom Wolfe's book . . . so I sent a copy of the review to Wolfe, along with a letter, and a copy of the (Wolfe) letter to the *Observer*. The problem was that somebody on the *Observer*—in a reject position—had worked with Wolfe on *The Washington Post* and hated the air he breathed. One of the editors explained this to me as part of his "yes, but" rejection of my review and then flipped out when I passed the word to Wolfe.) But that's pretty personal shit, and not worth much without a bigger handle. I was pissed off because it was the first thing of mine they'd bounced in more than two years—they even published my letters, begging for money in Quito, Rio, La Paz, etc.—so I can't work up much of an appetite for zapping them.

Or maybe—it just occurs to me—you didn't really intend to zap them. In that case, we might make a good piece of it. They try, but they have certain structural defects . . . and they don't hire people who can't ignore them. Hell, it might be a good piece . . . but not as a fang job, at least not

---

23. Dave Pierce was the mayor of Richmond, California.

for me. They published some of the best things I've done—and they still do some first-rate things (see current piece on Western Union, for example), so we might whip up something decent about the possibilities of journalism in a nation of hoodlums. But to hell with all that, right now. It's getting light outside and I need sleep. *The Times* is hassling me for that Tahoe piece, so that's the project for the next few days.

Again . . . it was a good show over there, and my advice to you is to give up all forms of booze and book-keepers for the duration of the crisis. Moderation in all things. When you turn up a freak on the staff, don't just fire him/her—pursue him into the very bowels of the economy and queer his act for all time. And get that nigger off the premises. You've got to get a grip on yourself. Otherwise . . . they'll cut your throat.

Beware. . . . -245*@
(Hunter)

TO JOAN BAEZ:

October 3, 1967
Woody Creek, Colorado

Dear Joanie. . . .

Here's another weird pitch. I sort of backed into it with a jangled grin . . . but what the hell.

Anyway, Gerry Walker, an editor of *The New York Times Magazine*, was telling me on the phone today how he needed $7800 to pay for this full-page ad (the tax protests, etc.) in *The New York Times*. Weird, eh? So I said, "Why not ask Joan Baez? She's kind of invested in this game." And he said, "Why don't you ask her?" And I said, "Why the fuck should I?"

But I finally agreed, under considerable duress, to at least call this thing to your attention. Frankly, I don't think you should whack out $7800 to pay for the ad. So far the list includes about 350 names, at $10 each, so that's half the nut right there. But it might be nice in case Walker ends up owing his employer $3500 or something like that, if he felt he could call on you in case of some terrible emergency. Probably he'll be fired, anyway—like I'll be dunned for six years of back taxes—but by then we'll be at war with China and it won't make much difference. Selah.

I was over there last weekend, bumping around in that piggish shopping center at the mouth of Carmel Valley, buying booze and ice for a 2-day run to Big Sur . . . which didn't work too well, due to my own state of mind & Fulton's[24] madness, so I wound up sleeping in the back of my

24. Thompson's lawyer. His name has been changed here.

Volvo world-cruiser somewhere above Santa Cruz on the beach highway. The Volvo has become my womb: I have a bed, a freezer, food, drink and a fine reading light in the back lounge—with music. But I was hounded by the notion of stopping by your fort and saying something like Hello . . . and it ruined my night. I thought it would be a good thing to stop by, but I was afraid I might run into Harry Belafonte, Marlon Brando, Peter Wingo and all those people. And you know how I am with public appearances. So I settled for the beach.

Tragic. But again, what the hell.

Fulton said he'd seen you, but I got the impression he did all the talking and I offer my condolences. He's pretty well flipped. Seriously. He came out to Aspen and wound up in some straightjacket en route to the Colorado loony bin. Sometimes he makes good sense for a while, then he jumps to his own private limbo. On balance, he's nuts . . . so consider this if you have to deal with him again.

That's about it for now. I'm still not certain you're getting—or reading—the mails, and I don't feel like communing with any of your public secretaries. So if you feel like doing something in re: this tax protest, that's fine. And if not, that's fine too. I'll tell Walker that your receptionist is taking it under consideration.

> Ciao. . . .
> Hunter

TO KEN KESEY:

> October 5, 1967
> Woody Creek, Colorado

Dear Ken . . .

I fucked up. First, I was three days late getting to San Francisco, and when I got there it turned out the people I was staying with were getting a divorce and I had to cope with it. Second, when I finally got to *Ramparts* on Friday afternoon I was instantly plunged into a drinking bout of mind-scrambling proportions and didn't escape until eleven that night—and then only to drive like hell to Big Sur, where I found my tax lawyer still out of his mind and everybody else reading about themselves in *Time*. So I fled from there, too, and wound up sleeping in the back of my Volvo somewhere on the beach above Santa Cruz. By the time I got back to San Francisco I was long overdue in Aspen and the people who were keeping my dogs—and living in my house—were ready to leave for Europe. So I loaded the car with as much furniture and other garbage as it would hold, and boomed off for the hills.

Anyway, I'm sorry I missed you . . . but it looks like I'll get over there again pretty soon. . . . I have hazy memories of agreeing to write a lot of things for *Ramparts* . . . and besides that I think I've fallen in love with a transvestite in Watsonville.

What the hell? Gerald Walker at *The New York Times* tells me you refused to sign the tax protest, or maybe you didn't. He couldn't seem to tell, from whatever reply you sent. If I were you I'd try to clear that up, or you're likely to wind up in jail without knowing why. I signed the bastard and I'm not particularly worried about it, but whatever you do is your own business.

OK for now. I'll check with you again on my next westward run. Ciao. . . .

Hunter

TO CAREY MCWILLIAMS, *THE NATION:*

October 7, 1967
Woody Creek, Colorado

Dear Carey. . . .

I'm just back from a month on the coast and found your note. I can't blame you for grumbling about my lack of action—at least for *The Nation*—but I could use five pages telling you why. [. . .]

I missed Ed Denson, manager of Country Joe and the Fish, in San Francisco; that was the article I mentioned to you a few months ago. But the awful reality of that one is that even getting the tapes transcribed is going to cost me $40 to $50, and then I have to talk to Denson again. So it involves a lot of time and effort, just to break even. I'm not excusing myself, just pleading guilty to the obvious counts—greed, necessity, disorganization and lack of time. Despite what everyone seems to think, I haven't made much money on the Hell's Angels book—and I've had to hire a New York lawyer to get rid of Scott Meredith and try to break all my publishing contracts. I spend about half my time writing legal letters and making long distance calls in re: Meredith's thieving behavior. And I've just been named a co-defendant in a $5.5 million lawsuit in California, which requires more legal action. And I'm also in tax trouble; my lawyer flipped out and I still haven't filed for 1966.

So those are just a few reasons why I haven't been deluging you with articles, or even ideas. I have, in fact, written only two articles since the Hell's Angels book came out—for a total net of $1400. This recent outburst is more desperation than anything else. I feel madness coming on if I don't write something . . . but writing gets harder and harder. Next week I have to go to Texas to profile the Texas Rangers for *Ramparts*; and after that, Billy Graham.

I've told everybody else—including Ballantine and Random House, who keep after me for a second non-fiction book—that I've given up on the idea that I can sell my own article ideas. I haven't pursued one of these since I split with the *National Observer.* Even the two for you were both based on your ideas. And as far as I'm concerned, they are two of the best things I've ever done. Everybody else wants me to write things on hippies, hoodlums and various cults . . . but I refuse to do any more of that stuff; I think it's called "spin-off" in the trade, and I'm not that hungry.

Bernard Shir-Cliff and I have more or less settled on a book on the Joint Chiefs or the Military Establishment—but so far we don't really have a focus. I'm still under contract to Random House, but I have no communication with them and I don't see much hope for establishing any. The big problem now is my failure to deliver the Rum Diary . . . but since I can't afford to deliver it under the present contract, we're completely bogged down.

If you have any good ideas in re: the Joint Chiefs and/or the Military Establishment, why don't you send them along? I still think your idea about those towns like Huntsville, Ala. and other defense industry cultures is one of the best. You might give Shir-Cliff a ring at Ballantine; he has a very vocal respect for your idea bank and you might be able to come up with something I could get started on. It's all a matter of focus . . . and if you come up with a peg, I promise you a full-length piece, for *The Nation,* on whatever it leads to. My own interest, right now, is in the Joint Chiefs. I want to know *who* they are; not by name, but in every other sense. Does that strike any sparks? Send Word.

Hunter

TO PETER COLLIER, *RAMPARTS:*

October 11, 1967
Woody Creek, Colorado

Dear Peter. . . .

[Mayor Dave] Pierce got here a few days ago [. . .] so with that, and three days of vicious stomach flu, I'm running about a week behind schedule. But it looks pretty definite that I'll be taking off for Texas on October 16, which still leaves me a month to get the article in, and I have to assume that'll be enough. So until I send word on the next time-fouling disaster— you can count on the piece by mid-November.

As for the "column," I have about five rough drafts, all on different subjects, and one that went completely amok and wound up 16 hand-written pages—on New Journalism. Which I contend is simply an updated version of the best Old Journalism. But, if this sort of excess keeps up, we might have to adjust our schedule to make room for an occasional "extra" full-length piece . . . because I sometimes get caught in the Leon Uris syndrome of trying to see the world in a grain of sand . . . and once in a while I need more than 1200 words to do that.

Anyway, the simple *idea* of a short-yardage outlet has my brain zapping along in a new way. Now I can consider writing things I used to only talk about . . . and so much for that and everything else, for right now. I have to get this goddamn piece written.

Also enclosed is a phony expense sheet for my visit over there. It seemed easier to bill you on a straight mileage basis, and to hell with all the daily food, room and miscellaneous expense details. Obviously, I could adjust the mileage to fit in with the *Times* expenses on the Tahoe story—but then I'd have to sit down and think about how to bill you for roughly the same amount, but in a very complicated fashion. I'll do it that way, if you want— but it seems to me that this is a lot quicker route to the same end, and to hell with the tax man. Let me know how this fits with your financial practices. And if it does, feel free to send a cashier's check at once. Selah. [. . .]

OK for now. I enjoyed my quick, high-powered visit over there and look forward to a dead-game replay when I'm in better condition. Tell Hinckle he'd better take some liver exercises . . . and also to get braced for my wild cards, which don't always mix real well with grapefruit juice and bourbon.

Until Texas, I remain. . . .

distractedly. . . .
Hunter

TO PAUL KRASSNER, *THE REALIST:*

Thompson had bungled his Hell's Angels *book tour by appearing on TV and radio shows either drunk or tongue-tied.*

October 22, 1967
Woody Creek, Colorado

Dear Paul. . . .

There's no avoiding the fact that I blew this one completely. And I still can't understand why. The horror of the TV tour has dimmed a bit, but my subsequent dealings with Random House, Ballantine and Scott Meredith still have the glow of rottenness. I no longer believe, for instance—as I think I did when I talked to you in New York—that the Random House handling of the book was a compendium of sloth and incompetence. Now I think it was a matter of deliberate, slothful, incompetent policy . . . done strictly by rote, with all the human factotums constantly apologizing for the heinous decisions sent down by somebody who was never named. I have never been able to get a line on the person—or people—actually responsible for the hopelessly bungled handling of a book that might have made us all a bit of money. As it is, I'm sending you $200 of the $1900 I now show as book-profit on the hardcover edition. So now I have $1700.

Meanwhile, both Random House and Ballantine are advertising the book as a "best seller." (See special banner on the paperback edition that comes out this week.) I'm hoarse from screaming at the bastards—not only in re: the old contract but also on the new one, which I've repudiated in every possible way, but which still exists—so I'm effectively taken off the book market. None of this would have happened without the fine aid of that motherfucking black-minded pig-whipping cocksucker Scott Meredith. As a matter of fact, if you want to make the following announcement in *The Realist*, surrounded by a big fat black border, you have my consent:

"The Scott Meredith Literary Agency is a stinking, shit-spined monument to everything that sinks to the bottom in the sediment pool of human responsibility. Scott Meredith is a fascist soul-fucker whose reputation as an agent rests on the sawdust remains of all young, no-leverage writers who've been conned into signing with his agency. Any writer considering a contract with Meredith should contact me for the same bill of particulars that I'll give to that bastard's lawyers when they sue me for this statement. I further attest, at this time and in my right mind, etc., that I have every honest and serious intention of wreaking a thoroughly personal and honest vengeance on Scott Meredith himself, in the form of cracking his teeth with a knotty stick and rupturing every other bone and organ I can make contact with in the short time I expect will be allotted to me. I might further note—for Meredith's own interest—that I recently flew to New York with a heavy club, for no other reason than to crash into his office and whip on him. I was persuaded against this action by the attorney I eventually had to hire to keep Meredith from stealing all my funds. This theft has continued, with no hint of apology or remorse, to the point where I now feel compelled to deal with Meredith on his own terms and lawsuit be damned. The very existence of his agency is a testimony to everything foul and corrupt. Even the people who work there are compelled, by reason of conscience, to write letters at night to people they've abused and misled during the day. Eichmann, of course, was only obeying orders. Like Hubert Humphrey. The present political climate precludes any threat to Humphrey's teeth, for the same obvious reasons that make it advisable for me to join in Hubert's whimpering prayer for Lyndon's dental health. But Scott Meredith is both stupid and arrogant enough to use Johnson's methods in an area not usually protected by the FBI."

... jesus, I seem to be out of my head, but my brain has really been jangled by dealing with this pig. I didn't believe this kind of shit existed—but it does, and legally. Anyway, if you want to shift the focus of the piece away from Random House and toward Meredith ... but what the fuck? Who gives a hoot in hell about that? I guess I could still write a funny piece about TV promotion shows, but that's not what I'm pissed off about right now. Maybe I'll do it when I get rid of these articles I'm supposed to be working on ... but the whole satire/protest gig seems more and more a waste of time. Not even your hideous Johnson/Ladybird jokes are funny anymore, because the bastard is worse than anything you can say about him. He probably laughed when he read about him fucking JFK's corpse in the neck.

With Johnson as president, I can't even work up an honest rage against Meredith, who's constantly stealing from me. I feel on the verge of a serious freak-out ... but if I get over that hump I'll write a good article for you. In the meantime, we're at least even on the money. This check is good. I've sworn off money articles a/o December, so maybe I'll level it out then. If not, I might run for the Senate ... or send off for a Carcano.[25]

Savagely,
Hunter S. Thompson

TO TOM SLOTSKY:

Slotsky was an Aspen ski bum who did carpentry work for the Thompsons at Owl Farm.

October 31, 1967
Woody Creek, Colorado

Dear Tom. . . .

I got your letter about two hours ago and was naturally depressed to hear about your spider nightmare. I was going to write you on Nevada State Prison stationery, but I figured that might cause trouble on your end. In any case, I know some good people at NSP, due to that National College of Trial Judges Conference at Lake Tahoe that I covered for *The New York Times*.

From what you say, however, you won't have any problem if you were the victim of an invalid and illegal search, which of course it would have to be if you were stopped on a phony stolen car complaint. Any good lawyer should be able to handle that. I don't know any attorneys in Las Vegas, but if things get critical, I know some good ones in California. This is a rotten, stupid situation and very difficult to deal with in a letter, and it

25. The brand of rifle purportedly used to kill JFK.

goes without saying that I don't have much sympathy for you, considering that I warned you many months ago about the kind of people you were getting mixed up with. That dope crowd is pure trouble, especially for people who are too young to know better. I didn't want to argue with you then, but I guess I should have. I knew, from talking to the sheriff, that a lot of the people you thought were just "happy-go-lucky" types were actually under suspicion for using narcotics. Now, in retrospect, I see that I should have been more frank with you. But since I didn't know you that well, and since you were doing first-rate work on the house, I didn't see any sense in creating problems by presuming to butt into your business.

Frankly—and I say that in all seriousness here—I don't know what the hell to say about the 20-pound charge as you state it. It's an ugly situation, and especially so, to me, after spending the day in Nevada State Prison as the guest of Warden Hocker. To add to the horrible irony of the situation, I just talked to the editor of *Playboy* today about writing an article comparing marijuana in the Sixties to booze in the Twenties. The article they want me to write is based on their educated assumption that marijuana will be legal by 1970—or at least that's what they said. (I just interrupted this to call one of my lawyer friends in California and he said you should try, if you're not firm with a lawyer right now, to get a guy named Robert Foley, who went to law school with a friend of mine named David Pierce, the ex-mayor of Richmond. Foley is an ex-D.A., and Pierce says he's as knowledgeable as anybody you could get down there.)

This whole thing seems insane—to have you arrested for a "crime" that will shortly be made legal. Like getting a letter from somebody who got arrested in Reno for having a case of Old Crow. It's hard to know what to make of it. Anyway, let me know if there's anything specific I can do to help. [...]

Hunter

TO PETER COLLIER, *RAMPARTS:*

November 14, 1967
Woody Creek, Colorado

Dear Peter. . . .

Yesterday's telegram was inevitable. I sent four, all nearly identical, disclaiming all responsibility for articles long overdue. Today I went to my friendly local doctor and got shots in both arms—and I felt pretty good until I saw the Sevareid–Eric Hoffer[26] chat on TV tonight. I hope you did that

26. Eric Hoffer was a popular Bay Area socialist writer.

article right. Hoffer is pathetic; the whole thing was a nightmare ... it, along with my penicillin and Vitamin B overloads, jolted me out of the month-long sloth I've been in.

The failure with Texas was the lack of hard charges against the Rangers. The bundle of material that I put off reading for way too long was woefully inadequate, in terms of hand-holds. I'm sure the Rangers are vicious bastards, but everything I know about the Oakland cops makes the Rangers seem tame. I mention this disparity only in the context of entrenched positions. I felt a bit naked, in terms of the required moral outrage, after going through your Texas file, one clip at a time. But, even then, I decided to do an article simply on Texas, using the Rangers as a leitmotif ... and then I went down the tube with my second case of flu in two months, and with even a normal Aspen winter coming on, I was obviously setting myself up as a non-resistant disease magnet—and I don't really feel like I want that invalid scene right now.

But that's only half of it. I've been blowing fat assignments almost as punctually as they've come up for the past six months ... and now that I've "evened" all the old, symbolic scores that I could dredge up in the meaningless, overtime vengeance of these Woody Creek nights, I feel sort of burned out. [...] Anyway, I've been agreeing—with my left hand—to write a fantastic variety of articles, while my right hand has been refusing, for reasons I'm just beginning to understand, to do anything at all. Sort of "which side are you on?" That gig. And that's the world's longest story for everybody, so why fuck around with trying to explain it here? There was also the massive fuck-up of my car by the local Volvo dealer, which would have left me in possible need of a rent-a-car gig in Texas ... and that would have come to several hundred bills, which I have a card for, so that wouldn't have crippled me ... except that I got a bit nervous about the lack of response (from *Ramparts*) to that expense bill I sent after the San Francisco trip. I only billed *The New York Times* for half the transportation on that thing, due to the fact that I'd sent you an over-simplified ticket ... so I put myself in shape to lose about $200 on the thing, if anything went wrong, and when it looked like something might go wrong I had powerful second thoughts about running up big transportation bills in Texas, to be reimbursed by *Ramparts*. No doubt this is a petty consideration, and in some months it wouldn't matter, but this is one of those months when I'm running pretty tight on the dollar count, and on top of everything else about the last thing I need is a money crash due to uncovered outlays.

So my only physical efforts for the past few weeks have been in the direction of becoming a Volvo mechanic by default (the dealer's default) and stealing about nine cords of winter firewood from the American Cement Corp. That last card I sent you about leaving for Texas was sent on Friday night, very late, prior to my total collapse from flu Saturday night and Sunday, just about the time I was scheduled to take off . . . which, obviously, I might have done anyway, but given all the factors: illness and probable car problems running into money, plus a relatively weak case against the Rangers, and the dread possibility of getting financially sucked into an article that might eventually cost me in terms of my own expense, etc. . . . so it came to me, in a terrible flash one night, that if I was going to get sick and broke all at once, I'd be better off doing it here, where at least I have credit. My image is very fat in Aspen . . . my hope is to get through the winter without spending a nickel, running up huge bills and mumbling something about "Random House" if anybody ever mentions payment . . . and then coming to grips with it all in the spring.

In the meantime, I'm preparing a 1200-word "column" shot for you, to be dispatched momentarily . . . and I've put the Texas job in a sort of instant limbo where it can be tapped or maybe unleashed on a moment's notice. Or a week's or a month's. Texas will always be there, and it won't change much. That's one of the few things we can count on in this world, for good or for ill.

OK, send word if you got out from under Hoffer without injuries. Is there room for anything I might send as a "column"? Is there real money involved? Are you there?

Constructively,
Hunter S. Thompson

FROM TOM WOLFE:

Although Thompson had never met Wolfe, he enjoyed his "new journalism" essays.

November 23, 1967

Dear Hunter,

As you may have seen in the famed truth stash TIME MAGAZINE, the erstwhile *Herald Tribune Magazine NEW YORK* has, in fact, been revived, on its own, coming out weekly, starting in March. I trust it will be a maniacally rich source of NEW JOURNALISM, the face of which we may all discover, and I hope you will contribute. The magazine will be about NEW YORK mostly, but we will stretch a point for all good stuff, from wherever. I see by the columns, Herb Caen's particularly, that you may split because of the libel ogres—but I don't truly believe it. Don't let the bastids squash you. Honkytonk owners are unlibelable, their very limbs are inflammable scandals to the penetrating gaze of Dr. Strange. I am in Virginia finishing a book about Kesey and the Pranksters at last; will deliver the manuscript, 900 typeriddled pages, this weekend. I'll spend a couple of weeks cutting if I have the stamina, but the mother is finally off my back anyway. Well, you knew the feeling first. I see *HELL'S ANGELS* on every paperback rack everywhere, here in Virginia included. I think you may be a rich devil, except that the paperback people are so slow settling up. Anyway—

Many salutes,
Tom

TO TOM WOLFE:

November 28, 1967
Woody Creek, Colorado

Dear Tom. . . .

Your letter came as a fine shot in the liver, or wherever I've been needing a shot recently. Oddly enough, somebody the previous night had mentioned Kesey in connection with Jackson Hole and I suddenly thought about the tapes I said I'd send[27] . . . so it was a bit of shock to wake up and find your letter. Especially from Richmond. It was like falling back in time, since another one of my haggles these days is a mandatory trip to Kentucky for Christmas. The idea that anybody still goes back to Richmond to finish a book rings a brain-bell that I'm not sure I want to hear anymore.

Anyway, I've spent half of this Saturday (or sattidy) nite listening to my bag of tapes and all they tell me is that I should never have told you I'd send them in the first place. But I'm winging two or maybe four in your special envelope and you will see for yourself. Like I said, they weren't what you were looking for . . . so now that you've finished the book you won't have to apologize to me for not using them. Just be sure to send them back sometime, so I won't have any holes in my family album. You'll need a small, cassette-type recorder to hear them at all, and most of what you'll get is my own drunk-talk. I use the machine primarily to make notes, not to gather slices of life for the market. I've never enjoyed sticking mikes or cameras in front of people. As a matter of fact I'm getting to the point where I don't even enjoy writing.

27. Thompson had recorded the La Honda party/meeting between the Hell's Angels and Merry Pranksters on cassettes and had promised to send them to Wolfe, who would later use them in *The Electric Kool-Aid Acid Test* (New York, 1968).

You guessed right about my not splitting, at least for the moment, but my legal/contractual dealings have become so heinous of late that I might as well be in a Mexican jail. I've been quoting your $20,000 figure for the past few months and everybody says, "Yeah, we'd give it to you except we're afraid of being sued by Scott Meredith." Well. . . . Balls. . . . It's 5:10 on a very cold and snowy Sunday morning here, and I have to be up by noon to watch the Bears rap the Packers (remember, you read it here first) and then a nightmare struggle between the Colts and 49ers. I've been supporting myself recently by whipping locals around on the weekly point spreads. Nobody will bet with me tomorrow, and these are two fat-city games I've been waiting for. People spook easily in these mountains.

On other fronts. . . . It was good to hear about *NEW YORK*. I gave up reading *Time*, along with most other things, a few months ago. But I'm still curious about the New Journalism, although I doubt Manhattan Island is going to yield a hell of a lot of it, at least in terms of source material. Your best stuff in *Tangerine*, etc. was all geographically strange. Some punk named Fitzgerald explained it in terms of a "sense of wonder." New Yorkers shouldn't write about New York, like I shouldn't write about Aspen . . . although I probably will. I've blown enough assignments recently to support five writers for five years. I just kept putting them all off until they were all impossibly overdue and then I sent off a bunch of ugly telegrams, saying I was overcome by a fit of bad angst and had canceled obligations. So now I'm stone broke and deep in my Wood Period. Working constantly with wood. Many walls, shelves, tables, firewood . . . tonight I put up a huge wall of cork in my living room. So I guess we're getting toward the Cork Period. And shotguns. Many clay pigeons off the porch, and a touch of the strange grass while the barrels cool off. I have also become a Volvo mechanic and a sound freak. Everything but writing. I have a tentative agreement to write a book on the Joint Chiefs, but all this legal bullshit has caused me to pull my brain in like a turtle every time I talk to somebody from New York. I'll be there again sometime after my bluegrass xmas, mainly to settle things one way or another, so if you're going to be in town, let's have a peaceful drink . . . and right now I'm going to cut this off and finish it tomorrow, after the olympian struggles on TV. . . .

. . . now, 24 hours later, hurting from all those unmade bets. Yeah, the Packers won (so I blew that), but not by enough to hurt any sound-minded investor. The Bears copped out on two huge occasions; the Packers keep winning on the same principle that Mailer keeps writing . . . but I guess I'll save that for some other time. Anyway, I hurt because I'm poorer than I should be right now . . . these swine won't even watch the games with me any more, much less bet in advance. . . . I think they fear the half-time wagers, which can be treacherous. And so much for all that. I'm about to dump another article and devote the rest of this wrong year to straightening out my personal papers.

I wish to hell you were right about my being a "rich devil," but the truth of the matter is that I'm down to $200 or so and *Ramparts* sent my last check to Austin, Texas. God only knows why. I'm now trying to pry it out of the postmaster down there, but I figure he has instructions to burn anything in a *Ramparts* envelope. I agreed to write a "column" for them, but I have no idea how to start. . . . I just hung an antelope's head over my fireplace. Things are happening. And I have credit, so I've given up worrying about cash except that I have to settle this contract thing somehow. If you see Lynn Nesbit . . . no, fuck her. I think she has the fear. But I'm really at my wit's end in these dealings. I've developed such a loathing for the typewriter that I rarely even enter this room. In all truth, this is the first half-human letter I've written in nearly two months. I've instructed Sandy to tell anyone who calls to say I'm not at home and probably won't be. The only people I'll talk to are those who want to place hard-rapping bets. Wagers on olympian spectacles. The Woody Creek line would appear to be very generous, but with massive discrepancies and lunatic deviations from the Reno judgments. And so much for that . . . again. You see why my mind is in trouble.

As for Kesey, I'm uncommonly curious about your book [*The Electric Kool-Aid Acid Test*] and I'm not sure why. Kesey doesn't need any gratuitous canonization at this point. (Is canonization a word?) Did you see that *Chronicle* headline the day after he got out of jail? I thought of writing and offering anonymous limbo here, but our general relationship was always so goddamn drugged that I'm not even sure I know what he's like when he's straight. And I don't know how many people he'd want to bring in. A scene like he had at La Honda would have me on Death Row in two months.

. . . but on that score, and on the subject of hospitality, etc., consider this as a standing invitation—room, board, etc.—if you feel like coming out for a shot at the mountains. One of my projects this winter is to master this ski business. I've done it a few times, but not enough to come to grips . . . but now I'm going to deal with it. So if you have any loose time, come on out. I have all the extras.

Yeah, and it's getting late again. Eight above zero & very crisp outside. If you know any good, human agents, send me a name or so. All I really need right now is somebody to keep my act in line . . . like I just alienated *Playboy* permanently, due to my angst. What I really need is a personal manager. Send word if you know of any. Or send word anyway. I'm sending the tapes in a different package, with a different stamp and a different drummer. Beware. . . .

Hunter

TO LEE BERRY:

> December 7, 1967
> Woody Creek, Colorado

Lee—

[. . .] Your goddamn cop's badge[28] has caused me nothing but trouble. Everybody in Aspen thinks I'm a cop . . . so I bought a "police" badge for my hat and the other day on the radio I said I was the Woody Creek Narcotics Magistrate. A lot of the IQ-70 types tremble at the sight of me. You sound like you're stoned all the time; what's happening to those articles you wrote? Try the *National Observer*. [. . .] You're right about free-lancing, but it's fun when you hit.

The hippie thing is over; now they're all desperate refugees and beggars. Or serious dope freaks. They're a drag to be around, but in fact they always were. People who were fucking the Sun and calling me uptight six months ago now show up at the house driving cars with New York and California plates, trying to borrow money or sell me everything they have—including the clap-ridden teeny-boppers who own the cars. Depressing. Grass is down to $50 a kilo in San Francisco; the market is glutted, the whole scene is glutted—bad news and losers. Hostility and paranoia. Fuck it.

Christ, it's five in the morning here. I just realized it. I'm sore as hell after tumbling down Ajax [Mountain] yesterday on a pair of borrowed White Stars. This time I'm going to make a real run at it—lessons, etc.— to get good so I'll know if I like it or not. But starting out at the top of Ajax is ugly. I gave up hunting for a while; I got tired of dragging the bodies. Now I shoot clay pigeons off the porch. And I do a lot of wood-work— shelves, walls, etc. Somehow, I forgot how to write. Blew $6,500 worth of assignments in two weeks, just threw up my hands and said to hell with it. Yeah, that goddamn agent is suing me. I have to get around him somehow. The paperback is selling better than I expected, but I can't get the money. Somewhere in New York I have a half-million nickels, but so far I haven't seen one. I don't know how it's going to turn out, but right now it looks bad. That's why I'm going to New York again.

Actually, I don't think it makes much difference. Johnson looks ready to take us all over the brink in a fit of stupid rage and frustration. He fucks up every time he turns around, but he still has the main clout. I wrote Eugene McCarthy and said I'd help if he thought he needed any, but that looks pretty bleak, too. Right now I should be writing my new "column" in *Ramparts*, but I can't get up the zap for it. We're into a very evil bag. I want to get my new passport arranged and get a fat advance for some non-existent

---

28. Berry had presented Thompson with an official police badge to use if he found himself in a legal jam.

book, so I can leave the country on 24 hours' notice. The bastard is looking for a reason to declare war officially, and all hell will break loose when that happens. I see a Nixon-Johnson election coming up, and that's too much for my head. Maybe the dope freaks are right.

No word from Kennedy in months. I don't know what it means. McGarr has turned devious and fuck crazy, jumping from one bad scene to another, hanging me up with friends, etc. I don't even know what to make of it, but I guess he'll eventually calm down. [. . .]

Off to bed now, almost dawn here. 4–5–6 inches of snow on the ground, cold as hell, probably as good a place as any to hide right now. The last address I had for Noonan was AmExpress, Paris. If you're heading south try that, but I think he's in Spain by now. I gave him your Amsterdam address. Sandy is pregnant again. Sow and ye shall reap. . . .

Hunter

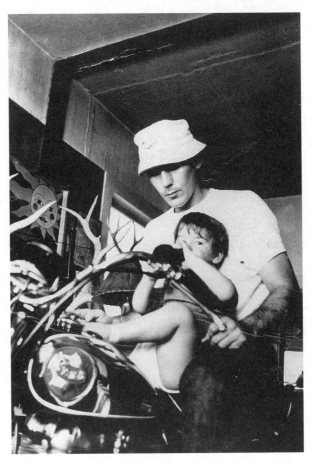

Hunter and Juan Thompson.
(Photo by David Pierce; courtesy of HST Collection)

EPILOGUE

"MIDNIGHT ON THE COAST HIGHWAY"

San Francisco, 1965

All my life my heart has sought a thing I
cannot name.
--Remembered line from a
long-forgotten poem

Months later, when I rarely saw the Angels, I still
had the legacy of the big machine--four hundred
pounds of chrome and deep red noise to take out on
the Coast Highway and cut loose at three in the morning, when all the cops were lurking over on 101. My
first crash had wrecked the bike completely and it
took several months to have it rebuilt. After that I
decided to ride it differently: I would stop pushing
my luck on curves, always wear a helmet, and try to
keep within range of the nearest speed limit . . . my
insurance had already been canceled and my driver's
license was hanging by a thread.
    So it was always at night, like a werewolf, that I
would take the thing out for an honest run down the
coast. I would start in Golden Gate Park, thinking
only to run a few long curves to clear my head, but in
a matter of minutes I'd be out at the beach with the
sound of the engine in my ears, the surf booming up
on the sea wall and a fine empty road stretching all
the way down to Santa Cruz . . . not even a gas station
in the whole seventy miles; the only public light
along the way is an all-night diner down around
Rockaway Beach.

There was no helmet on those nights, no speed limit, and no cooling it down on the curves. The momentary freedom of the park was like the one unlucky drink that shoves a wavering alcoholic off the wagon. I would come out of the park near the soccer field and pause for a moment at the stop sign, wondering if I knew anyone parked out there on the midnight humping strip.

Then into first gear, forgetting the cars and letting the beast wind out . . . thirty-five, forty-five . . . then into second and wailing through the light at Lincoln Way, not worried about green or red signals but only some other werewolf loony who might be pulling out too slowly, to start his own run. Not many of these--and with three lanes on a wide curve, a bike coming hard has plenty of room to get around almost anything--then into third, the boomer gear, pushing seventy-five and the beginning of a windscream in the ears, a pressure on the eyeballs like diving into water off a high board.

Bent forward, far back on the seat, and a rigid grip on the handlebars as the bike starts jumping and wavering in the wind. Taillights far up ahead coming closer, faster, and suddenly--zaapppp--going past and leaning down for a curve near the zoo, where the road swings out to sea.

The dunes are flatter here, and on windy days sand blows across the highway, piling up in thick drifts as deadly as any oil slick . . . instant loss of control, a crashing, cartwheeling slide and maybe one of those two-inch notices in the paper the next day: "An unidentified motorcyclist was killed last night when he failed to negotiate a turn on Highway 1."

Indeed . . . but no sand this time, so the lever goes up into fourth, and now there's no sound except wind. Screw it all the way over, reach through the handlebars to raise the headlight beam, the needle leans down on a hundred, and wind-burned eyeballs strain to see down the centerline, trying to provide a margin for the reflexes.

But with the throttle screwed on there is only the barest margin, and no room at all for mistakes. It has to be done right ... and that's when the strange music starts, when you stretch your luck so far that fear becomes exhilaration and vibrates along your arms. You can barely see at a hundred; the tears blow back so fast that they vaporize before they get back to your ears. The only sounds are wind and a dull roar floating back from the mufflers. You watch the white line and try to lean with it ... howling through a turn to the right, then to the left and down the long hill to Pacifica ... letting off now, watching for cops, but only until the next dark stretch and another few seconds on the edge ... The Edge. ... There is no honest way to explain it because the only people who really know where it is are the ones who have gone over. The others--the living-- are those who pushed their control as far as they felt they could handle it, and then pulled back, or slowed down, or did whatever they had to when it came time to choose between Now and Later.

But the edge is still Out There. Or maybe it's In. The association of motorcycles with LSD is no accident of publicity. They are both a means to an end, to the place of definition.

THE *PROUD HIGHWAY* HONOR ROLL

David Amram
Joan Baez
Bob Braudis
Douglas Brinkley
William Burroughs
Johnny Depp
Donna Dowling
Wayne Ewing
Stacey Hadash
Hal Haddon
Laura Heymann
Abe Hutt
Don Johnson
William Kennedy
Lee Levert
Annie McClanahan
P. J. O'Rourke
Julie Oppenheimer

Beth Pearson
Curtis Robinson
David Rosenthal
Shelby Sadler
Madeline Sloan
Juan Thompson
Virginia Thompson
George Tobia, Jr.
Oliver Treibeck
Gerald "Ching" Tyrell
Townes Van Zandt
Jennifer Webb
Jane Wenner
Jann Wenner
Lawson Wills
Jennifer Winkel
Molly Wright
Warren Zevon

CHRONOLOGICAL LIST OF LETTERS

INDEX

ABOUT THE AUTHOR

Born in Kentucky in 1937, Hunter S. Thompson attended Louisville Male High School and was inducted into that city's prestigious Athenaeum Literary Association. He enlisted in the United States Air Force, where he wrote for and edited his base's newspaper. Receiving an honorable discharge after two years of service, Thompson began free-lance writing. He became the Caribbean correspondent for the New York *Herald Tribune*, and in 1962 he started reporting from South America for the *National Observer*. Soon, Thompson became a national correspondent for *The Reporter*, *The Nation*, and *Spider*, the voice of the Berkeley Free Speech Movement.

Thompson's first book, *Hell's Angels*, was published in December 1966. This account of a year spent with the notorious biker gang caused a critical sensation and became a bestseller. His next full-length work, *Fear and Loathing in Las Vegas*, began life as a two-part article in *Rolling Stone* magazine in 1971, as did his subsequent book, *Fear and Loathing on the Campaign Trail*, about the Nixon-McGovern presidential race.

The first volume of Thompson's "Gonzo Papers" appeared in 1979 as *The Great Shark Hunt*, and was followed by 1983's *The Curse of Lono*, a South Seas odyssey in the tradition of his Vegas book. *Generation of Swine* (the second Gonzo Papers volume), which drew heavily upon Thompson's regular columns for the *San Francisco Examiner*, was published five years later. In 1990 a third Gonzo volume was published, *Songs of the Doomed*, which detailed the much publicized police action against Thompson the previous year.

Thompson returned to national political coverage in 1994 with *Better Than Sex*, his observations on the Bill Clinton presidential campaign and the death of Richard Nixon. And in 1996, on the twenty-fifth anniversary of its first appearance, the Modern Library issued a special edition of *Fear and Loathing in Las Vegas*.

Thompson lives in a fortified compound near Aspen, Colorado, where he ran for sheriff on the Freak Power ticket in 1970 and has been feuding with the local authorities ever since. He is currently at work on a novel, *Polo Is My Life*.